D0722831

Studies in Textile History

HAROLD B. BURNHAM

Studies in Textile History
In Memory of Harold B. Burnham

Edited by Veronika Gervers

RÓM

Royal Ontario Museum
Toronto, Canada

©Royal Ontario Museum, 1977
100 Queen's Park, Toronto, Ontario, Canada M5S 2C6

ISBN 0-88854-192-9
Printed and bound in Canada by THE ALGER PRESS

This book has been published with the help of a grant from the Humanities Research Council of Canada, using funds provided by the Canada Council.

Contents

A Tribute

NO one would have appreciated the present volume more than Harold Burnham himself, for the varied nature of its content reflects his own wide range of interests and professional commitments. Some of the articles were inspired by his own suggestions and enthusiastic encouragement; others would have broadened his horizons and opened new vistas for his incredible expanse of knowledge and diversity of research projects. Self-educated in the realm of art historical, archaeological, and textile studies, he was one of an all too rare school of generalists ready to tackle a wide range of problems and capable of steering his efforts to a successful conclusion.

Harold Burnham's forebears were of many races: English, Irish, Scottish, Dutch, German, and North American Indian. Most of them came to Upper Canada in the late eighteenth century as part of the Loyalist exodus from the American Colonies at the time of the Revolution. He was born the son of an electrical engineer in Edmonton, Alberta on 17 January 1912. At the end of the Great War the family returned to Ontario where he received most of his education, graduating from Oakwood Collegiate in 1928. Although he wanted to enter university the means were not available and on account of his strength in mathematics, he anticipated becoming a chartered accountant. The stock market crash of 1929 cancelled that plan and he remained with the Bank of Toronto, where he had been gaining business experience since leaving school.

This banking "interlude" lasted for twenty-four years. But even though this career was going well, other more intellectually stimulating interests were beckoning. He had been enthusiastic about museums since, at the early age of eight, he met and was greatly encouraged by Dr. C.T. Currelly, founder of the Royal Ontario Museum. His marriage in 1944 to Dorothy MacDonald, then Curator of Textiles in the ROM, was shortly to lead to the beginnings of a new career. Through her he became interested in weaving and especially in weaving technology. In 1947, when the Textile Department of the Museum initiated a programme for the study and collection of early Canadian textiles, he supported the project and, by devoting free time to field trips and research, helped to ensure its success.

In 1954, at the height of his banking career, he decided to resign and become a professional weaver. The Burnhams moved to the village of Jordan in the heart of Ontario's vineyards and there they set up looms and went to work. At a time when the Canadian handicraft movement was in its infancy he wove his way, if not to prosperity, to the position of a nationally recognized craftsman. The experience and knowledge that he gained of looms, techniques, fabrics, threads, and dyes were later to become invaluable.

In 1955 the French-based International Centre for the Study of Ancient Textiles (CIETA) set out to prepare a multilingual vocabulary of weaving terms; his collaboration in the project was solicited soon thereafter by Dorothy Shepherd of the Cleveland Museum of Art. He became a mainstay and guiding force for the English version, travelling to Europe for the first time in the autumn of 1957 to attend the CIETA meetings and participate in the planning and development of the vocabulary. On the same occasion he initiated research into what was to become one of his major preoccupations: European and Oriental velvets. His work on the Chinese material was followed with great interest by the Royal Ontario Museum and in 1958 he was invited to join the staff of the Textile Department. His third career had begun.

The publication that same year of his monograph on Chinese velvets was an eye-opener for textile historians. Forever wary of conclusions built on art historical and stylistic evidence alone, he emphasized the importance of technical analysis in determining origins, provenance, and chronology. His technical know-how and practical mind converged to produce a clear thesis of fact which remains undisputed. Subsequently, his research continued on the European and Persian velvets, particularly the latter, on which his unpublished notes are virtually complete for all existing early examples.

Once he had become a member of the Textile Department, there was no stopping Harold Burnham from pursuing projects he had begun or envisioned at a time when other demands on his time frustrated his progress. From 1957 on he made biannual trips to Europe to attend CIETA meetings, to travel widely in search of comparative materials, and to study methods of textile conservation. Nineteen sixty-three found him in Ankara analyzing the textile remains from Çatal Hüyük, a follow-up of work he had previously done on archaeological material from Hasanlu. The same summer, at the Musée de l'Homme in Paris, he catalogued the early Canadian Indian skin garments and their techniques in the Dauphin Collection, and traced other examples of North American Indian costume to museums in Copenhagen, Helsinki, and Oxford. In 1965 he travelled to Switzerland and England to further the Indian research and begin work on the sources of early Canadian handweaving; in 1967 he went to Leningrad to record Captain Cook's West Coast Canadian Indian blankets in the Hermitage, and then back to Germany and the British Isles to make a comprehensive study of the origins of Canadian woven textiles.

At home he worked constantly on enlarging the Canadian collection and during a quarter of a century travelled many thousands of miles across the country in search of early Canadian weaving. His efforts resulted in the Museum's acquisition of an unparalleled number of coverlets, which he and his wife published jointly in a monumental volume entitled "*Keep me warm one night*". The book, whose title is borrowed from the suggestive and inviting name of a particularly favoured coverlet pattern, is more than a comprehensive study of early handweaving in Canada; it is an exceptional example of how carefully and laboriously conceived utilitarian objects, which might otherwise have gone unnoticed and eventually been discarded, can be preserved for posterity.

Harold Burnham was Curator of Textiles in the ROM for nearly four and a half years. The fourteen that he had spent in the department saw the development, through his efforts and those of his predecessor and successor, Katharine B. Brett, of one of the finest and most broadly based textile collections in the world. Together, they enriched the Museum's present holdings in Spanish velvets, European silks, Japanese cottons, Coptic and Islamic archaeological textiles, and every kind of Canadiana from Indian garments made of salmon skins to straight-cut baby clothes. In recent years he encouraged the expansion of an already splendid collection of European and Middle Eastern ethnographical textiles and costumes, soliciting, as so well he could, support and donations of objects from Canada's many ethnic communities. One of his last interests led to the department's nascent collection of West Asian felt.

Harold Burnham's interest in preserving Canadiana and promoting the manufacture of high-quality handicrafts was far from restricted to textiles. He was extremely knowledgeable about early Canadian pottery and was responsible in 1969 for organizing "Craft Dimensions Canada", a major exhibition of contemporary craft work. He was at one time president of the Ontario Guild of Crafts and later of the National Canadian Guild. He was otherwise a Fellow of the Royal Anthropological Society and of the International Institute of Conservation, was elected to the Conseil de Direction of CIETA in 1957, and held a cross-appointment in Fine Art at the University of Toronto.

Harold Burnham always had many threads to his loom. When he died, prematurely, on 12 May 1973, he left copious notes about his various projects. They contain vast quantities of information on looms, Persian and European silks, Chinese rugs, skin costumes of the North American Indians, and Selish blankets of the West Coast Indians. These notes, together with his irreplaceable library on textiles, are presently in the Royal Ontario Museum, where they will remain available to interested scholars wishing to continue his work.

All those who knew him personally, or who had occasion to correspond with him, know how willing Harold Burnham was to share his seemingly infinite repertoire of knowledge. He collaborated actively wherever he could, offered constructive advice if it were sought, and gave generously of his time to assist younger scholars and craftsmen in their work. Our indebtedness to him may be expressed in many ways, but the most enduring tribute to his unselfish career is to be found in the pages that follow.

MICHAEL GERVERS
Toronto, 22 August 1975

Bibliography of Harold B. Burnham

Books and Articles

1958

The Ming dragon robe velvet.
Royal Ontario Museum, Art and Archaeology Division Bulletin 27: 14-16. 3 figs.

1959

Une armure gaze complexe chinoise.
Bulletin de liaison du Centre International d'Etude des Textiles Anciens 9: 29-35. 2 figs.

Chinese velvets – a technical study.
Toronto: Royal Ontario Museum, Art and Archaeology Division, Occasional Paper 2. 64 p. 15 pls. 14 figs.

An exhibition of modern ceramics from abroad.
Toronto: Royal Ontario Museum, Art and Archaeology Division. 19 p.

Fabrics: a vocabulary of technical terms (with D.C. Shepherd and D. King).
Lyon: Centre International d'Etude des Textiles Anciens. 39 p.

A Spanish velvet weave.
Bulletin of the Needle and Bobbin Club 43(1-2): 22-36. 5 pls. 2 figs.

Suggestion d'un prolongement au vocabulaire.
Bulletin de liaison du Centre International d'Etude des Textiles Anciens 9: 9-13 (technical terms in English and French).

Un velours impérial chinois d'époque Ming.
Bulletin de liaison du Centre International d'Etude des Textiles Anciens 9: 53-60. 1 pl. 1 fig.

What is a professional craftsman?
Canadian Art 16(4): 248-249.

1960

Some European silks.
Royal Ontario Museum, Art and Archaeology Division Annual: 60-63. 3 pls.

1961

The conservation of Ontario textiles.
Toronto: Ontario Historical Society, Museums Section. 7 p.

1962

Four looms.
Royal Ontario Museum, Art and Archaeology Division Annual: 77-84. 3 pls. 3 figs.

Konserveringsproblem under debatt (with A. Geijer).
Fornvännen 57: 243-246.

1964

Vocabulary of technical terms: fabrics. English – French – Italian – Spanish (in consultation with D.G. Shepherd and D. King), 2d ed.

Lyon: Centre International d'Etude des Textiles Anciens. 62 p.

The world's oldest textiles.
Meeting Place 1(1): 105-108.

1965

Canadian textiles 1750 – 1900: An exhibition.
Toronto: Royal Ontario Museum, University of Toronto. 30 p.

Çatal Hüyük – the textiles and twined fabrics.
Anatolian Studies 15: 169-174. 3 pls. 3 figs.

Catalogue of the exhibition of Japanese country textiles (with K.B. Brett).
Toronto: Royal Ontario Museum, University of Toronto. 40 p. 18 pls.

Technical aspects of the warp-faced compound tabbies of the Han Dynasty.
Bulletin de liaison du Centre International d'Etude des Textiles Anciens 22: 25-45. 2 pls. 3 figs. (with French summary).

Textiles, terms and tempers.
Meeting Place 1(3): 92-96.

1966

Canadian textiles and their problems.
Bulletin de liaison du Centre International d'Etude des Textiles Anciens 23: 31-35 (with French translation).

In search of the Maritimes.
Meeting Place 1(8): 107-108.

Niagara coverlets.
Canadian Collector 1(3): 10-11. 4 figs.

1967

Han polychrome silks — technical notes.
Oriental Art 13(4): 245-249. 3 figs.

A quest for coverlets.
Scotland's Magazine 63(5): 16. 1 pl.

Tapestries.
In *Man and His World: International Fine Arts Exhibition,*

Expo 67, Montreal, Canada, pp. 66, 132, 232. Ottawa: National Gallery of Canada.

Tshmishian and Tlingit.
Canadian Antiques Collector 2(7): 16-18. 3 pls.

1968

Early Ontario floor coverings.
Canadian Antiques Collector 3(2): 22-23. 3 figs.

The preparation of silk yarns in ancient China.
Bulletin de liaison du Centre International d'Etude des Textiles Anciens 27: 49-58 (with French translation).

1969

Craft dimensions Canada; an exhibition sponsored by the Canadian Guild of Crafts (Ontario) and the Royal Ontario Museum.
Toronto: Royal Ontario Museum. 78 p. 58 pls.

A Naskapi painted skin shirt. (Text by F.H. Douglas — 1939. Revised by H.B. Burnham — 1968.)
Denver Art Museum, Material Culture Notes 10: 53-59. 1 pl. 2 figs.

1970

Canadian crafts — old and new.
Canadian Antiques Collector 5(1): 23–25.

The Royal Ontario Museum and the Department of Textiles.
Bulletin de liaison du Centre International d'Etude des Textiles Anciens 31: 13–20 (with French summary).

1971

Bolton "quilts" or "caddows": a nineteenth century cottage industry.
Bulletin de liaison du Centre International d'Etude des Textiles Anciens 34: 22–29. 3 figs. (with French summary).

Keep me warm one night — an exhibition of early Canadian handwoven textiles.
Toronto: Royal Ontario Museum. 19 p. 10 pls. (Re-

printed as *Handweaving in Pioneer Canada,* Royal Ontario Museum, 1976.)

"Keep me warm one night" — an overshot pattern from Cape Breton.
Guild of Canadian Weavers Bulletin 14(1): 1–7. 1 pl. 2 figs.

Ontario — the textile arts.
Canadian Antiques Collector 6(5): 65–67. 3 pls.

Some additional notes on the warp-faced compound tabby silks of the Han Dynasty.
Bulletin de liaison du Centre International d'Etude des Textiles Anciens 34: 16–21. 3 figs. (with French summary).

1972

Introduction to *Oriental rugs from the collection of Mr. John Schorscher,* by L. Cselényi.
Toronto: Royal Ontario Museum. 6 p. 3 figs.

"Keep me warm one night" — early handweaving in eastern Canada (with D.K. Burnham).
Toronto: University of Toronto Press. 387 p. 491 pls. 40 figs.

Links with the homeland — Latvian knitting and weaving preserved in the ROM.
Rotunda 5(2): 12–17. 4 pls.

The textile arts.
Canadian Antiques Collector 7(1): 51–53. 4 figs.

1973

Prehistory of textiles in the Old World (with M. Hoffmann).
Viking 4: 49–76. 9 figs.

1974

Handweaving and textiles (with D.K. Burnham).
In *The book of Canadian antiques,* edited by D.B. Webster, pp. 282–295. Toronto: McGraw-Hill Ryerson. 18 pls.

Book Reviews

1970

(Review of) *From the Bosphorus to Samarkand, flat-woven rugs,* by A. Landreau and W.R. Pickering. Washington: The Textile Museum, 1969.
Oriental Art 16(4): 401.

1972

(Review of) *Coptic textiles in the Brooklyn Museum,* by D. Thompson. New York: Wilbour Monographs, 1971.
Oriental Art 18(3): 281.

Weaving the *Pinatikan,* a Warp-Patterned *Kain Bentenan* from North Celebes

Rita Bolland

AT the close of the nineteenth and beginning of the twentieth centuries, European museum curators and ethnographers began to take an interest in woven products from tropical countries. Fabrics and occasionally looms were acquired for museum collections. Design and decorative techniques received intensive study; the process of weaving itself also attracted attention. Since that time decorative techniques such as *batik, ikat,* and *plangi* have remained a focus of interest. Studies have also been made regarding the function of textiles within the social structure of given societies. Concern for the process of weaving, however, diminished after the 1920s.

Interest all but ceased in the so-called *kain bentenan* produced in the Minahassa, a region in the north of the large Indonesian island, Celebes (figs.1,2).

Three kinds of fabric can be designated by the name *kain bentenan*:[1] the *tonilana,* a cotton tabby with warp-faced rib and coloured stripes running longitudinally; the *kaiwu,* a cotton tabby with warp-faced rib, decorated with warp *ikat*; and the *pinatikan,* a cotton tabby adorned with zigzag lines, lozenges, and honeycombs produced by a particular manner of floating the warp ends (fig.3).

This article will discuss the *pinatikan,* with emphasis on the way in which the cloth is woven. Whenever in the following pages the term *kain bentenan* appears, it is intended to signify the *pinatikan* unless specified otherwise.

Before examining the loom, it may prove instructive to look at the textile itself. The cotton threads of both warp and weft are hand-spun with a Z-twist.

On the face of the cloth the weft is barely visible; on the reverse side it is easily seen in places where the pattern appears. The warp ends which are white, red-brown, and light and dark blue constitute longitudinal stripes. These stripes are alternately woven in warp-faced rib and in the special warp-pattern weave which is characteristic of the *pinatikan.* Sometimes the entire fabric is woven in this warp-pattern technique. All three kinds of *kain bentenan* are woven on a loom with a continuous circular warp. If the fabric is intended for a woman's skirt then the whole warp is woven to yield a seamless tubular cloth. Two or three of these tubes are sewn together along their selvages into a skirt. In the making of a shawl, which consists of one or two woven panels, the warp ends which are not woven form a short fringe.

While the three varieties of *kain bentenan* seldom appear in textile collections, the looms upon which they are woven are even more rare. Comment in the literature about technical aspects of making the *pinatikan* is limited to postulation, since writers have had only pieces of cloth at their disposal and not actual looms. For this reason I am particularly indebted to the Museum voor Land- en Volkenkunde in Rotterdam for permitting me to study the five *pinatikan* looms in their collections, most of which seem to have come from North Celebes.

These looms have marked similarities. The weaving of the *pinatikan* will be described with reference to the loom in the best condition, and then the other four looms will be briefly discussed.

Acc. no. 24704 A

Acc. no. 24704 A was acquired in 1920 (reported or-

1

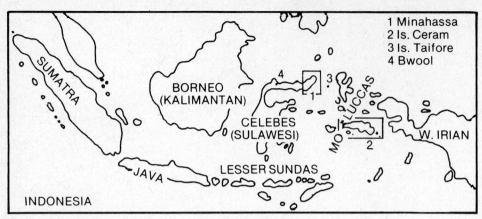

1 Minahassa
2 Is. Ceram
3 Is. Taifore
4 Bwool

Figure 1.   Indonesia.

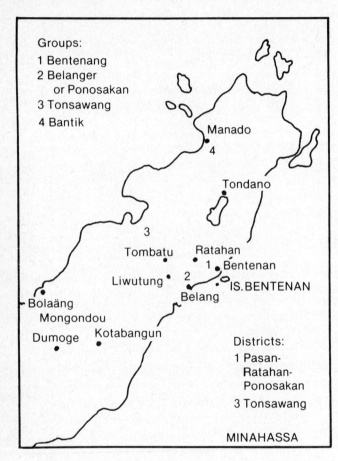

Groups:
1 Bentenang
2 Belanger
  or Ponosakan
3 Tonsawang
4 Bantik

Districts:
1 Pasan-
  Ratahan-
  Ponosakan
3 Tonsawang

MINAHASSA

Figure 2.   Minahassa, North Celebes (North Sulawesi).

igin: Tombatu, North Celebes). It is a loom with a continuous circular warp (circumference ca.132 cm, w. 24 cm) which the weaver keeps taut with a wooden backstrap (missing from this particular loom). In place of the cloth beam there is a stick of black wood pointed at one end (l. 80 cm, dia. 1.2 cm), which may not be the original cloth

beam. About 9 cm of fabric have already been woven and the weave reveals longitudinal stripes with lozenges and hexagons in *pinatikan* technique alternating with stripes in warp-faced rib; the warp is white, red-brown, and light and dark blue (Z-singles, hand-spun) (fig.4). The red-brown weft (Z-singles, hand-spun) is wound about a bamboo stick-shuttle (l. 65 cm). The first pick is a slender bamboo stick. Next to the first and last picks, on the reverse side of the cloth, a temple is stuck in the fabric. This temple is a sharpened rod of bamboo 0.5 cm wide.

The warp ends are bound in six different ways. Warp ends numbered 1 to 4 float in a definite rhythm over three picks; warp ends numbered 5 and 6 bind in plain tabby. Picks A to F also move in six different ways through the cloth (fig.5).[2]

The many components which we find in the warp can be divided into two groups: parts which constantly remain in the warp (the tabby heddle rod, the shed stick, pattern heddle rods 1 and 2, pattern sticks g, h and i); and parts which during the weaving process are pushed in and out of the warp (the sword and six laze rods a-f).

To weave a single repeat the laze rods are used one by one and removed from the warp after each carries out its function in forming a shed; they would be in the way during the weaving of the next pick. When a repeat has been woven the six laze rods are once again inserted in the warp with the aid of the pattern heddle rods and the pattern sticks which remain permanently in the warp.

The weaver left this loom with all parts in place in the warp. While enumerating these parts beginning from the woven bit of cloth, I will mention which ends are lifted by each part (figs.4,5).

2

 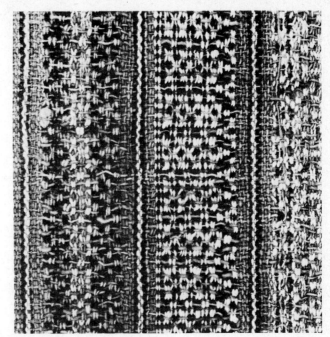

Figure 3. Woman's tubular skirt in *pinatikan* weave, detail.
Left: face; *right*: reverse. Ratahan, North Celebes.
Tropenmuseum, Amsterdam, acc. no. 48-19.

Sword: a flat stick of black wood pointed at both ends (l. 71 cm, w. 2 cm). The sword is now inserted in the warp to make the shed for the last woven pick (D).

Tabby heddle rod: a stick of white wood pointed at both ends (l. 28 cm, dia. 0.4 cm) with pendant string heddle loops. Through every heddle loop runs a single warp end. With the tabby heddle rod the even ends of the warp are lifted.

Laze rod a: a flat bamboo stick (l. 65 cm, w. 1 cm). Every end numbered 3 runs over laze rod a.

Laze rod b: a flat bamboo stick (l. 62 cm, w. 2 cm). Every end numbered 1 runs over laze rod b.

Laze rod c: a flat bamboo stick (l. 62 cm, w. 1.2 cm). Every end numbered 3 runs over laze rod c.

Shed stick: a round bamboo stick (l. 66 cm, dia. 1.8 cm). The odd ends of the warp run over the shed stick.

Laze rod d: a flat bamboo stick, pointed at the left end (l. 56 cm, w. 1.5 cm). Ends numbered 1, 2, 3, and 5 run over laze rod d.

Laze rod e: a flat bamboo stick (l. 64 cm, w. 1 cm). Ends numbered 1, 3, 4, and 5 run over laze rod e.

Laze rod f: a flat bamboo stick, pointed at the left end (l. 54 cm, w. 1.4 cm). Ends numbered 1, 2, 3, and 5 run over laze rod f.

Pattern heddle rod 1: a bamboo stick with heddle loops (l. 69.5 cm, dia. 0.7 cm). Warp ends numbered 1 pass in pairs through each heddle loop.

Pattern stick g: a flat bamboo stick (l. 64 cm, w. 1.2 cm). Every end numbered 3 runs over pattern stick g.

Pattern heddle rod 2: a bamboo stick with heddle loops (l. 78.5 cm, dia. 0.8 cm). Through every loop pass a number of ends which may vary from two to eight. Ends numbered 1, 3, 4, and 5 run through heddles on pattern heddle rod 2.

Pattern stick h: a flat bamboo stick (l. 65 cm, w. 2 cm). Ends numbered 1, 3, and 5 run over pattern stick h.

Pattern stick i: a flat bamboo stick (l. 64 cm, w. 1.3 cm). Ends numbered 1, 2, 3, and 5 run over pattern stick i.

Warp beam: a bamboo stick (l. 77 cm, dia. 3.5 cm).

The threads used for the heddle loops are of white cotton spun in Z-direction. The loops of the tabby heddle rod consist of a single continuous thread;

3

those of pattern heddle rods 1 and 2 consist of a double continuous thread.

The majority of looms in museum collections have been prepared by their previous owners for the weaving of a successive repeat or of an integral part of a pattern. This is also true of this loom, as is apparent from trial weaving performed upon a replica. The repeat or weave unit of this *pinatikan* is made up of the ten picks A-B-C-B-A-D-E-F-E-D which are woven with the following aids:

pick A: tabby heddle rod plus laze rod a lift ends numbered 2, 3, 4, 6, then removed.
pick B: the shed stick lifts all odd warp ends.
pick C: tabby heddle rod plus laze rod b lift ends numbered 1, 2, 4, 6, then removed.
pick B: the shed stick lifts all odd warp ends.
pick A: tabby heddle rod plus laze rod c lift ends numbered 2, 3, 4, 6, then removed.
pick D: laze rod d lifts ends numbered 1, 2, 3, 5, then removed.
pick E: tabby heddle rod lifts all even warp ends.
pick F: laze rod e lifts ends numbered 1, 3, 4, 5, then removed.
pick E: tabby heddle rod lifts all even warp ends.
pick D: laze rod f lifts ends numbered 1, 2, 3, 5, then removed.

These ten picks make up one repeat. During the weaving of a repeat the six laze rods are taken from the warp after they are used in turn. In order to weave the following repeat they must again be inserted in the warp. This is accomplished as follows:

laze rod a — with help from pattern stick g.
laze rod b — with help from pattern heddle rod 1.
laze rod c — with help from pattern stick g.
laze rod d — with help from pattern stick i.
laze rod e — with help from pattern heddle rod 2.
laze rod f — with help from pattern stick i.

Afterwards the weaver starts with pick A to weave a new unit.

One wonders whether it is not a cumbersome manner of working to thread six laze rods through the warp and then pull them out again. Indeed, it is also possible to create the sheds for picks A to F with the assistance of those parts which remain permanently in the warp. Both ways of proceeding require the same actions. Weaving with the six laze rods, however, is much more restful since the making of a single repeat takes place in two stages. In the first stage the laze rods are put in place, in the second stage the repeat is woven. This combines actions

Figure 4. *Pinatikan* loom. Tombatu, North Celebes. Museum voor Land- en Volkenkunde, Rotterdam, acc. no. 24707 A.

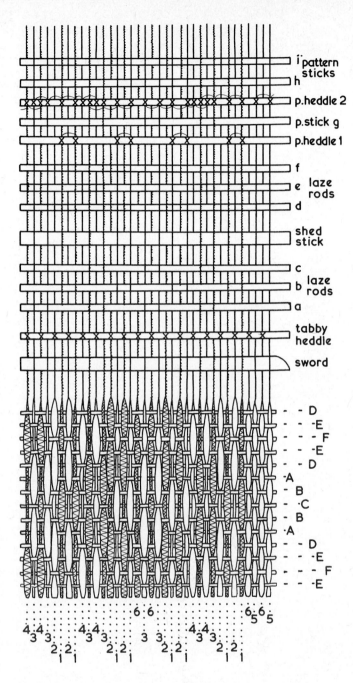

i pattern
sticks

h

p.heddle 2

p.stick g

p.heddle 1

f

e laze
rods

d

shed
stick

c

b laze
rods

a

tabby
heddle

sword

- - D
- - -E
- - - F
- - -E
- - D
-A
- B
- ·C
- B
-A
- - D
- - -E
- - - F
- - -E

Figure 5. Diagram of fabric including the warp with all components, woven on *pinatikan* loom acc. no. 24707 A, Museum voor Land- en Volkenkunde, Rotterdam. Numbers 1 – 6 denote warp ends; letters A – F indicate picks. Warp ends are marked with an x along a heddle leash. When two or more ends pass through a particular leash, the crosses designating these ends are bracketed together.

into two groups, each of which has a consistent internal logic. A kind of rhythm comes into being and the weaver will be much less likely to make a mistake.

In studying Indonesian looms, I constantly rediscover that every mechanical aid has its own function which cannot be replaced by another without seriously disrupting the weaving process. We can therefore presume with great certainty that weavers who sixty and more years ago wove the *pinatikan* came to use this loom with its thirteen components[3] as the result of extensive experience.

The other four looms in the collections of the Museum voor Land- en Volkenkunde in Rotterdam closely resemble the one just described in detail. The continuous circular warp is held taut by the weaver with the help of her own body. The cotton threads are hand-spun in a Z direction. The weft is wound about a long wooden stick shuttle. In the warp, in addition to the tabby heddle rod and the shed stick, are pattern heddle rods, pattern sticks, and laze rods. The temples are inserted in the reverse side of the cloth. The fabric has longitudinal stripes in warp-faced rib alternating with stripes in the *pinatikan* technique.

We recognize in the weave the warp ends 1 to 6 and the picks A to F. The sequence in which these picks are woven appears from the various looms to be often identical or nearly so. In contrast, the sequence of the warp ends, in combination with variations of colour, produces a diversity of motifs such as zigzag, lozenge, cross stripes, or hexagons.

Acc. no. 5118

Acc. no. 5118 was acquired in 1887 (reported origin: Celebes). The continuous circular warp has a width of 37 cm and a length of 232 cm, 142 cm of which have been woven. The cloth beam and the warp beam are round bamboo sticks. The wooden backstrap is missing. Of the two stick shuttles present, one is wound with white and the other with blue cotton weft.[4] The cloth has white stripes which run lengthwise in warp-faced rib alternating with blue-white stripes in *pinatikan* technique with ornamentation of lozenges and cross stripes. The sword sits in the shed opening for pick D, the last pick of the completed repeat. This final weave unit displays an irregularity in its second half on account of which the blue stripe has become broader and the lozenge deformed (fig.6). This appears to have been caused by a "mistake" in the sequence of the wefts shown in figure 7 with a dotted line.

In the warp all laze rods are present to enable the weaving of the next repeat.[5] It seems that there are twice five laze rods in the warp instead of twice three. After laze rods a,b, and c come b_1 and c_1, and after laze rods d, e, and f come e_1 and f_1. If we were to proceed to weave further with these ten laze rods, the sequence of wefts would be A-B-C-B-A-B-C-B-A-D-E-F-E-D-E-F-E-D. In one weave unit, then, the "mistake" appears twice. It is possibly not an error at all but the intention of the weaver. In the piece of fabric already woven this irregularity does not occur.

Pattern heddle rod 1 has a broken loop in three places. Through the heddles a bamboo stick has been inserted, over which the ends, which should go through the broken loops, pass. The stick probably serves to replace the broken loops. Behind pattern heddle rod 1 is a square stick of dark brown wood that is 1.5×2 cm thick and pointed at one end. All odd warp ends run over this stick; they also pass over the shed stick. The function of this dark brown stick is not evident to me. Pattern sticks h and i as well as the dark brown stick do not sit properly in their entirety between the ends. Apparently they have slipped and have not been put back into place in a wholly correct manner. Unfortunately this is a recurrent phenomenon among looms in collections.

A spindle of dark brown wood also belongs with this loom (l. ca. 34 cm). There is white cotton Z-spun thread on it. It is apparent from the ring notched at the top end of the spindle-stick that it was used hanging free. The weight is a dried fruit, probably from some variety of *Quercus*.[6]

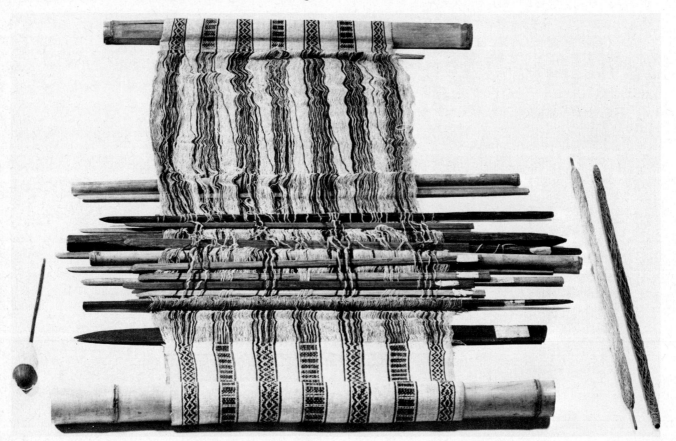

Figure 6. *Pinatikan* loom (the laze rods and pattern sticks partially overlap). North Celebes.
Museum voor Land- en Volkenkunde, Rotterdam, acc. no. 5118.

6

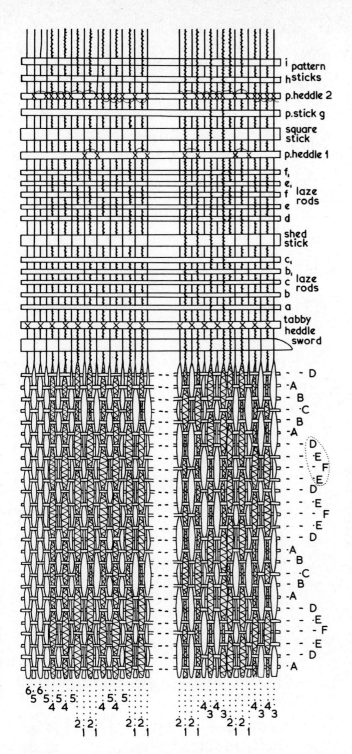

i pattern
h sticks
p.heddle 2
p.stick g
square stick
p.heddle 1
f,
e,
f   laze
e   rods
d
shed stick
c,
b,
c   laze
b   rods
a
tabby heddle
sword

- - D
- A
  B
- ·C
  B
- A
  D
  E
    F
  E
  D
- - ·E
  - F
  ·E
- A
  B
- ·C
  B
- A
  D
- ·E
  - F
  ·E
  D
- A

Figure 7. Diagram of fabric including the warp with all components, woven on *pinatikan* loom acc. no. 5118, Museum voor Land- en Volkenkunde, Rotterdam. Numbers 1–6 denote warp ends; letters A – F indicate picks. Letters E-F-E-D printed in a dotted line point out a possibly erroneous repetition.

Acc. no. 20136

Acc. no. 20136 was acquired from Mr. Wittich in January 1913 (reported origin: Celebes). The loom is in poor condition. Many warp ends are broken; the cloth beam and shed stick are both missing. Many of the tabby heddle loops are destroyed. The sticks from pattern heddle rods 1 and 2 are also missing, but fortunately the loops are still in the warp. Nonetheless it is worth the trouble to pay attention to what still remains of this loom because it will appear that this conforms with our observations of the other *pinatikan* looms. The continuous circular warp is 19 cm wide and has a circumference of 114 cm, 41 cm of which have been woven. A temple is next to the last weft. The brick-red weft thread is criss-crossed lengthwise about the stick shuttle (l. 64 cm). The brick-red, white, and light and dark blue warp ends form lozenges, crosses, and zigzag lines across the entire width of the cloth. There is a stripe in warp-faced rib (w. 0.4 cm) only along the selvages.

The ornamentation is not especially distinct, because the ends do not float in pairs over three wefts in that special fashion which we noticed on other looms (fig.8). Here we have an exception to the rule that the weaver leaves her loom with a weave unit completed and with all in order for weaving the next repeat. The last pick is F. To finish the repeat, which here too consists of the picks A-B-C-B-A-E-D-F-E-D, E and D must still be woven. Pick E is done with the assistance of the tabby heddle rod, and pick D with the assistance of laze rod f which is still stuck in the warp. When the weave unit is completed in this manner, the parts with which we are familiar remain fixed in the warp, with the exception of the shed stick which is missing. The three bamboo sticks and the bamboo slat, which accompany the loom, are probably laze rods.

Acc. no. 24726

Acc. no. 24726 was acquired from Mr. G. P. Rouffaer in June 1920 (reported origin: North Celebes). Various parts of this loom are only half-secure in the warp, while others have fallen out. On every part a piece of paper is fastened on which a number is written in ink. In the remarks that follow these numbers will be reported in brackets. The continuous circular warp is approximately 10 cm wide and

7

has a circumference of 116 cm; it encircles the warp beam [8], a round wooden stick, together with the cloth beam [2a/b]. The cloth beam is comprised of two semicircular wooden sticks pointed at one end, between which the woven material is held tight (fig.9).

The already woven cloth, 9.5 cm long, has the typical *pinatikan* ornamentation of lozenges, hexagons, and crosses across its entire width in white, brown, and light and dark blue. Along the selvages runs a brown stripe in warp-faced rib (w. 0.5 cm). On the reverse side of the last woven stripe is a temple.

The weave unit consists of wefts A-B-C-B-A-D-E-F-E-D. The sword [7] is in the warp shed of pick D, the last weft of the completed repeat. The leashes of the tabby heddle rod [3a] are of machine-spun and plyed cotton thread. Pattern heddle rods 1 and 2 [3b and 3c] have loops of cotton thread spun and plyed by hand.

Also in the warp are three pointed bamboo sticks [6a, 6c, and 6d] which are respectively inserted as laze rods a, c, and b. The three loose pointed bamboo sticks [6b, 6e, and 6f] are presumably the remaining three laze rods. Also present, unattached, are a round wooden stick [4] which is probably the shed stick; three bamboo sticks, two pointed [11 and 13] and one not [12], in all likelihood pattern sticks g, h, and i; a stick shuttle [10] with brown weft thread criss-crossed lengthwise; a semicircular stick [9] sharpened at one end which looks very much like half a cloth beam but whose function is unknown; and a model of a wooden warping frame [1] that will be discussed in detail below. No part numbered 5 was come across (could this have been a wooden backstrap?). All these parts appear new and have a length of approximately 35 cm.

There is a round bamboo stick (l. 48 cm, dia. 2.7 cm) with this loom, which looks as if it had received intensive use. A handful of pebbles have been poured into the stick and both ends closed, one with a knot of *ikat* yellow-brown cotton thread and the other with a wadded cotton rag. A piece of paper is attached on which the work *boengboengan* is written in ink along with no. 9. All these identifying marks are most probably by the same hand. I hesitate, nevertheless, to accept that this jingling bamboo stick belongs to the *pinatikan* loom. In East Java, and

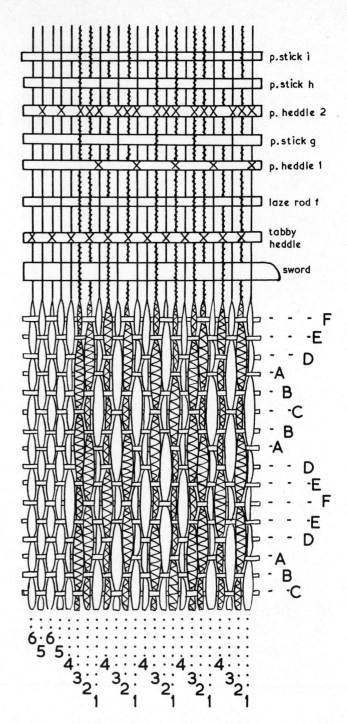

Figure 8. Diagram of fabic including the warp with all components, woven on *pinatikan* loom acc. no. 20136, Museum voor Land- en Volkenkunde, Rotterdam. Numbers 1 – 6 denote warp ends; letters A – F indicate picks.

8

among the Sasaks on the island of Lombok, east of Java, *boengboengan* is the indigenous name for the shed stick. *Soelang*[7] is the name of the shed stick which belongs to the loom on which the *kaiwu*, the *kain bentenan* adorned with *ikat*, is woven (the only *bentenan* loom for the parts of which we know the indigenous names). It may also be added that on the Talaud Islands to the north of Minahassa, weavers sometimes fill the bamboo warp beam with fruit pits. One can then hear that diligent weaving is being done. This warp beam containing pits is called *bahgebah*, while without pits, it is known as *dedale*.[8]

The manner in which the parts of this loom are numbered supports our theory about the function

that each part fulfils during the weaving of a single repeat. The six laze rods constitute the group 6a to f; the three heddle rods form the group 3a to c. The shed stick and the pattern sticks are numbered separately.

The model of a warping frame [1][9] also confirms our empirically established weaving procedure. It is a wooden beam (l. 36 cm, w. 6 cm, thickness 4 cm) with two square and six round shallow holes on its upper plane (fig.9). In the two square depressions [2a and 2b], the two half cloth beams are set, presumably with their flat surfaces facing each other (see the warping frame which is part of loom acc. no. 34754, figure 10). The six small round holes are

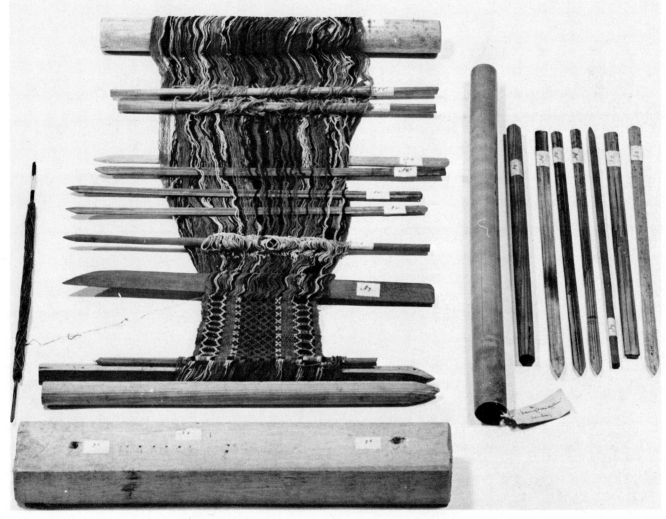

Figure 9. *Pinatikan* loom with model of a warping frame.
North Celebes.
Museum voor Land- en Volkenkunde, Rotterdam, acc. no. 24726.

not numbered. In the two holes which are situated opposite each other the shed stick and the tabby heddle rod are set. Pattern heddle rods 1 and 2 and pattern sticks g and i are placed in the four holes which are in a row. As pattern stick h is threaded through the warp in an identical way to the shed stick, so that it can be put in position later, we are able to conclude that all fixed parts which are necessary for weaving a *pinatikan* are present and in place with a warp stretched out upon this mounting apparatus.

Acc. no. 34754

Acc. no. 34754 is a complete *pinatikan* loom about which, lamentably, we know neither the year of acquisition nor the origin. It turned up unnumbered in the Celebes collection in 1953. It looks so new that we may assume that it was made upon request for the collector. Everything looks authentic and all parts of a *pinatikan* loom are present. The cotton threads are hand-spun. Labels bearing a letter written in ink are fastened on some of the components.

A loose piece of paper with a D leads to the supposition that originally all parts were marked. Throughout the following commentary the identifying letters are given in brackets.

The continuous circular warp with a circumference of about 120 cm and a width of 23 cm is stretched between a cloth beam consisting of two semicircular wooden sticks [B and C], pointed at one end, and a warp beam in the form of a round wooden stick [0] (fig.10). In the 5.5 cm long piece of woven cloth on the loom white stripes in warp-faced rib alternate with stripes of white and blue lozenges and crosses in *pinatikan* technique. On the reverse side of the beginning and the end of the fabric there is a temple. The white weft is wound criss-crossing around a narrow stick shuttle. This loom has a 61 cm long wooden backstrap [A]. The sword [F] is placed through the warp before the last pick D of the repeat, which here also consists of ten picks A-B-C-B-A-D-E-F-E-D. All parts necessary to weave the next weave unit are present in the warp (fig.11). Those which are marked include the tabby heddle

Figure 10. *Pinatikan* loom. North Celebes.
Museum voor Land- en Volkenkunde, Rotterdam, acc. no. 34754.

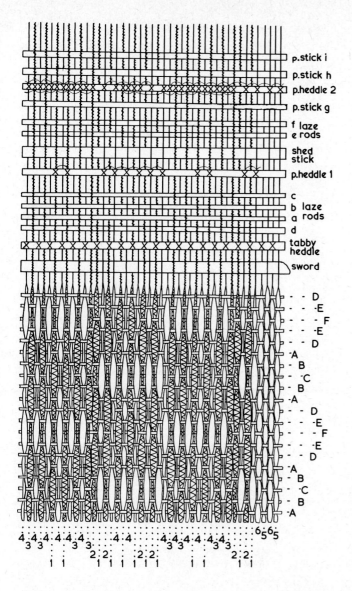

Figure 11.   Diagram of fabric including the warp with all components, woven on *pinatikan* loom acc. no. 34754, Museum voor Land- en Volkenkunde, Rotterdam. Numbers 1–6 denote warp ends; letters A–F indicate picks.

rod [G], the shed stick [H], four of the six laze rods [I], pattern heddle rod 1 [K], pattern heddle rod 2 [M] and pattern stick h [N]. Several parts occur in the warp in a sequence slightly different from that of acc. no. 24707 A, the loom upon which we reconstructed the weaving of the *pinatikan*. Laze rod d sits directly behind the tabby heddle rod and the shed stick is behind pattern heddle rod 1. It appears, however, that this poses no obstacle for the making of the shed openings for the weaving of the next repeat.

A wooden spindle (l. 28 cm) also belongs with this loom. It is apparent from the small knob at the end of the shaft that it was used hanging. Z-twisted, white cotton thread is wound on the spindle, and a piece of paper is caught between the strands of thread bearing the word *wawilingan* in ink. According to Jasper and Pirngadie, the indigenous name for the spindle in Ratahan is *wawilingen*.[10]

In addition the loom also includes a pointed bamboo slat, the function of which is unknown, and a model of a warping frame (l. 70 cm, w. 6 cm, thickness 4 cm) (fig.10), on which a paper is pasted with the word *tatanoeman*. Alongside the four holes, the indigenous name of the stick which should be inserted there is written on the white wood: *loebang tempat haepes* C [hole for *haepes* C] next to the left hole; *loebang tempat haepes* B next to the right hole; *loebang tempat* Ca–*wawiwawian* next to the two middle holes; and *loebang tempat* Cb–*wawaloekan* below and above. Furthermore the instruction *lihat gambaran tatanoeman* [see writing about mounting apparatus] is also written on the wood, which has not been found. From the semicircular form of the two extreme holes in the warping frame it is apparent that they are meant for the upright inserting of the two halves [B] and [C] of the cloth beam. In this model, however, the holes are not deep enough for this to be possible. In the two middle holes come the cross sticks which afterwards will be replaced by the shed stick and the tabby heddle rod. It is also possible that already during the stretching of the warp the leashes are made.

Jasper and Pirngadie describe a warping frame of the Minahassa[11] called *tatanoemen*. In the block there stand four sticks: on both extremities the *halèpes*; in the middle, opposite each other, the *wawaloeken* which will be replaced by the shed stick; and the

11

wiwi which will be replaced by the heddle rod. This demonstrates a thorough similarity with our warping frame.

On a warp which is stretched in this fashion cloth can be woven only in tabby or in warp-faced rib, and not in the *pinatikan* technique. According to Jasper and Pirngadie, a weaver who wants to weave a *pinatikan* begins with a warp in which only the shed stick and the tabby heddle rod are present. For pattern formation she lifts the proper warp ends from memory and inserts rods.[12] While setting up a small trial loom for a *pinatikan* I discovered that this manner of working is quite possible. But from memory — no, that is a feat of which I am not capable!

There is one component in the warp whose function has not yet been remarked upon. That is pattern stick h at the rear of the warp. The odd-numbered warp ends pass over it. It is not entirely clear to me what role it plays. It is one of the fixed components, and is placed through the warp between the ends just as the shed stick is. During the formation of the sheds, as described previously, it takes no part. Yet, this stick cannot be placed there without a purpose. Experience teaches that every part of the Indonesian loom has its own function and is indispensable for smooth weaving. It is not very plausible that this stick is a cross stick. The ends form no cross here. In the short warp of the *pinatikan* loom, moreover, the cross sticks can be easily done without.

During my experiments on a small *pinatikan* trial loom, the shed stick did not obstruct the weaving of picks D-E-F-E-D. It is possible, however, that on a wider loom the heavy shed stick could be a hindrance during the weaving of the second part of the repeat. After completion of picks A-B-C-B-A the shed stick should be able to be removed from the warp. Once the whole weave unit has been woven and the six laze rods again put into place, the shed stick can also be brought back into position with the aid of pattern stick h. On loom acc. no. 20136 (fig. 8), where the last two picks of the repeat remained to be woven, no shed stick is found in the warp. This could be a piece of evidence in support of the validity of the above-described manner of working. The fact that the shed stick of loom acc. no. 34754 is not at hand loose, in turn weakens this argument.

Although at the end of the nineteenth and beginning of the twentieth centuries numerous authors wrote about the *kain bentenan* as well as about the people who made and used them, the origin of the name *bentenan* has not been established, and we are not even certain where exactly these cloths were woven. The missionary teacher N. Graafland made a journey through his working area in the Minahassa, North Celebes (fig. 2), in May 1859 and again in January 1860. In his diary[13] he commented that the rather rough cotton textiles of *bentenan* make, as he identified them, had a pattern reminiscent of the skin of a patola snake. They were a symbol of wealth and served to bedeck the thrones of leaders and priests; sometimes they were also used for sarongs. Previously (i.e., long before 1859), he wrote, a person could only commence weaving if an expensive *fosso* (a series of ceremonies conducted by a priest) intended to promote weaving had been held. Even in 1859 some people still considered a *fosso* a prerequisite, which meant that weaving was not undertaken lightly.

Graafland postulated that the population of the Minahassa was of diverse origin, and had arrived in successive groups at different points of time from beyond the sea. To the early groups possibly belonged the *Bentenang*, the *Bantik*, and the *Tonsawang*, who mingled extremely little with the groups that arrived later. According to old folk tales, the name *Bentenang* originally belonged to a small island off the east coast of North Celebes, close to Belang, where the migrating group touched the coast for the first time. They assumed the name of the island for themselves and subsequently gave it also to the region where they settled permanently in the Minahassa. Graafland reported that because of conflicts over inheritance the region of Bentenang split to become the districts Passan and Ratahan.

The missionary teacher J.M. Wiersma called the population of the Minahassa *Alfoeren*. In 1876 he described the two tribes among whom he worked as the *Benthener*, living in the district Passan-Ratahan, and the *Tonsawanger*.[14] He cited still a third, smaller tribe, the *Belanger* or *Ponosaker*, who for the most part are Muslims. About weaving Wiersma had nothing to say.

Josephus Nerdon, government teacher at Liwutung, however, provides us with copious detail about the weaving of the *pinatikan*. Upon the request of the former associate district commissioner C.J.W. Wijnaendts, Nerdon took the trouble to acquire considerable relevant information.[15] Nerdon reported that people had formerly used the rough but strong textiles for jackets, trousers, and sarongs. Because the weaving took much time and trouble, and more beautiful and less expensive *kain*s were for sale at the market, young girls no longer wanted to learn how to weave. In former times all women from Ratahan District wove fabrics called *kain bentenan*, named after the place where they were first made, the small island of Bentenang.

After an extensive search, Nerdon found one seventy-year-old woman who still wove the *kain bentenan* and who still owned several of them. She, however, did not let him see the loom. It was the harvest season when no one had time to weave and all weaving implements had been put away. It was believed, moreover, that to bring the loom out into the daylight without planning to do some weaving would bring misfortune. Nevertheless, she told Nerdon everything about the preparation of the cotton, the spinning, the dyeing, and the weaving. He noted that it was not easy to describe the weaving itself, "especially the weaving of floral *kain*s, because for this various implements are used in alternation. The work progresses very slowly which is why it takes months until such a *kain* is ready."

Nerdon included in a note the report of C.J.C. Wijnaendts about the region Ratahan which consists of three small districts: Pasan and Rathan, where the population is Christianized, and Ponosakan, which is inhabited by Muslims. Wijnaendts, while district officer in the Minahassa, sent a *kain bentenan* as a gift to his alma mater, De Instelling voor Onderwijs in de Taal, Land- en Volkenkunde at Delft. It was at this institute that future administrative officials for the Dutch Indies received their training. In the catalogue of 1888 describing the collection of the Instelling,[16] the woman's dress from the Minahassa was designated as a *kain bentenan*. This is the first time that the expression *kain bentenan* appeared in the literature. When the Instelling at Delft closed down in 1901, its entire ethnographical collection was transferred to what is now the Indonesisch Ethnografisch Museum in Delft, and the *kain bentenan* was accessioned as no. S 222/1. It is a woman's dress woven in *pinatikan* technique consisting of three continuously woven lengths of cloth.

It was almost a century ago that J.A. van der Chijs catalogued the ethnological collection of the Bataviaasch Genootschap van Kunsten en Wetenschappen,[17] now housed in the Museum Pusat (Central Museum) at Djakarta. The catalogue from 1885 lists under acc. no. 2758 "a piece of linen from an indigenous fabric, previously produced widely in the Minahassa". Questions in Djakarta elicited the information that this cloth is a woman's cotton skirt which consists of three continuously woven lengths of cloth ornamented in warp *ikat*. It is therefore a textile of the *kaiwu* type. The catalogue of 1895 includes two cloths (acc. nos. 6308 and 6320) under the name *kain bentenan*, about which the museum at Djakarta was kind enough to send more detailed data and photographs. Both are women's cotton skirts consisting of three continuously woven lengths of cloth. Acc. no. 6308 is clearly a *pinatikan*. Its separate lengths are in warp-patterned weaving with lozenges, zigzag lines, and honeycomb decoration. The garment came from Bwool.[18]

The catalogue reports that acc. no. 6320 was a so-called *poesaka* object, a sacred heirloom of the Manapo family, that once, about 1800, belonged to the Sultan of Bolang-Mongondo. The edges along the bottom of this tubular skirt are woven in a simple warp-patterned technique. The warp ends which float over and under three picks form small rectangles. One wonders whether this is perhaps a predecessor of the *pinatikan* weave. Van der Chijs only calls the dress with warp-patterned ornaments a *kain bentenan*, and does not designate with the same name the woman's skirt with *ikat* coming from the same area. In 1903 A.B. Meyer and O. Richter studied the *pinatikan* intensively, which they too called *kain bentenan*. In their description of the collection which the brothers Paul and Fritz Sarasin compiled between 1893 and 1896 in Celebes,[19] Meyer and Richter discussed two tubular skirts. No. 67 came from Kotabungun and no. 68 was a gift of the harbor master of Bolaäng. The authors said that the dresses were very rare. They were the first to provide a detailed account of the way in which the floating warp ends generate the pattern, and the first to report that the pieces of the dresses are continuously woven.[20]

In a second publication, also in 1903, Meyer and Richter pursued further these textiles and their origin.[21] They described at length the four *pinatikan*s, which are the property of the Ethnographical Museum in Dresden. All four are continuously woven tubular skirts. Acc. no. 12668 has a top panel of cornflower blue European cotton. The attached bottom panel is woven in the *pinatikan* technique with machine-spun cotton threads. The other three (acc. nos. 12667, 12669, and 12670) were reported to have originated among the Bantiks of Manado. In addition, the Dutch collector commented of acc. no. 12667 that it was "garb that was spread upon the floor by priests and priestesses during their ministrations; earlier produced upon Bentenang near Belang, have now no longer any looms". From available data in the literature and from museum collections, the authors arrived at the cautious conclusion that the *kain bentenan* was woven, or had once been woven, on the island of Bentenan and the facing mainland coast of the Minahassa; it was their opinion that the neighbouring areas of Bolaäng Mongondou were also perhaps the scene of *kain bentenan* manufacture.

As a conclusion, they reproduced a letter dated 13 June 1903, from A.C. Veenhuizen, district officer at Kottobaroe (Bolaäng Mongondou), which they received when their article had been completed. The most significant points of this communication are the following: The *kain bentenan* was in former days specially woven in the Minahassa, on the island of Bentenan opposite Belang on the south coast of the Minahassa; the *kain bentenan* is no longer woven and after the passage of some time it will no longer be possible to acquire them here (i.e., at Bolaäng Mongondou); the *kain bentenan* appears more frequently in Bolaäng Mongondou than in the Minahassa and is the most highly prized of all cloths; and finally, the *kain bentenan* belongs to the most valuable of the goods with which people by preference pay dowries, fines, etc.

In the literature discussed up to this point, the name *kain bentenan* was employed exclusively for fabrics in warp-patterned weaving. In 1909 J.E. Jasper[22] made *kain bentenan* into a collective name for three kinds of fabric from the Minahassa: the *pinatikan* in warp-patterned weaving, the *kaiwu* in warp *ikat*, and the striped *tonilana*. According to Jas-

per none of the three was any longer woven. They were to be seen, however, at the Fourth Industrial Fair at Soerabaja in 1909, and at the General and International Exhibition of Brussels in 1910.[23] At these exhibitions, Ratahan was constantly cited as the origin of the *pinatikan*s.

In their standard work on weaving in Indonesia,[24] published in 1912, Jasper and Pirngadie went into considerable detail about the origin of the *kain bentenan*, relying for their arguments on findings from literature and on information which they personally gathered. They concluded that the *pinatikan* was known in the Minahassa at an earlier date than the *ikat kain bentenan*. They reported that several people said that a girl from Doemoge in Bolaäng Mongondou brought weaving to Bentenan. As far as the *pinatikan* is concerned, Jasper and Pirngadie did not rule out such a possibility. They asserted, however, with certainty that the art of *ikat* weaving in the Minahassa was brought from islands farther to the east, including Taifore among others.

Concerning the origin of *pinatikan*s the following have been noted in museum collections: four cloths from Minahassa and Ratahan in the Tropenmuseum in Amsterdam; seven pieces of fabric from Minahassa, North Celebes, Ratahan, and Tombatu in the district of Tonsawang in the Museum voor Land- en Volkenkunde in Rotterdam; and two *pinatikan*s from the island of Bentenan in the Museum für Völkerkunde in Frankfurt-am-Main.

I would not exclude the possibility that a connection existed between weaving in the *pinatikan* technique in the Minahassa and on the islands to the east of Celebes. There are textiles from the island of Ceram which have stripes woven in this technique. The Tropenmuseum in Amsterdam owns three such cloths. Acc no. 1772-1202 is a woman's tubular skirt of cotton (l. 119 cm, w. 110 cm). To make this garment a length of cloth, approximately 220 cm long and 60 cm wide, was cut into two equal parts, and these halves were joined to each other horizontally along the selvages. Then this rectangular cloth was sewn into a tubular skirt in which the warp runs horizontally. The cotton fabric in warp-faced rib is fine and tightly woven (count: 29-33 ends by 15 picks per cm). The machine-spun threads were in all probability purchased by the weaver already dyed. The weft is blue, the warp is predominantly purple with fine stripes in white, yellow, orange, light red, light blue, dark blue, and green. The *pinatikan* weave which is evident in multicoloured stripes of 0.3 and 1.1 cm width accords totally with the structure which we discovered in the *pinatikan*s from Bentenan (fig.12). The order of the warp ends conforms to the simplest method: 1,2,1,2,3,4,3,4, and the sequence of the picks is A-B-C-B-A-D-E-F-E-D.

Acc. nos. H 3186 and 0-403 in the Tropenmuseum are woven of palm-leaf fibres knotted to one another. They are 148 and 163 cm long respectively, with 9 cm long fringes of loose warp threads at both ends; their widths from selvage to selvage are 68 and 74 cm. Both cloths are in warp-faced rib (count: 8-13 ends by 4 picks per cm). They have a red-brown weft; the warp is for the most part red-brown with narrow stripes in yellow-brown and dark brown. In stripes approximately 5.5 cm wide there appear details in *pinatikan* weave alternating with sections in warp-faced rib (fig. 13). For the lozenge pattern the order of the warp ends is 1,2,1,2,3, 4,3,4, and the sequence of the picks A-B-C-B-A-D-E-F-E-D.

Cotton cloth, acc. no. 1772-1202 in the Tropenmuseum, was acquired on Goram, an island east of Ceram (fig. 14). Such a textile also appears in several other collections, including the Museum für Völkerkunde, Frankfurt-am-Main (acc. no. NS 31601, from Gah, East Ceram), and the Museum für Völkerkunde, Basel (acc. no. IIC 6959, from southeast Ceram).[25]

All we know about the two leaf-fibre textiles in the Tropenmuseum is that they come from Ceram. In the Indonesisch Ethnografisch Museum at Delft, there is another leaf-fibre textile from Amahai, South Ceram, which has stripes in *pinatikan* technique,[26] and a similar specimen should be part of the collection of the Musée de l'Homme in Paris, as a gift of the Commission des Indes Néerlandaises from the Exposition of 1889.

On Ceram, only women from the Alune tribe in the west (fig. 14) weave with leaf fibres. Their looms have a continuous warp which the weaver

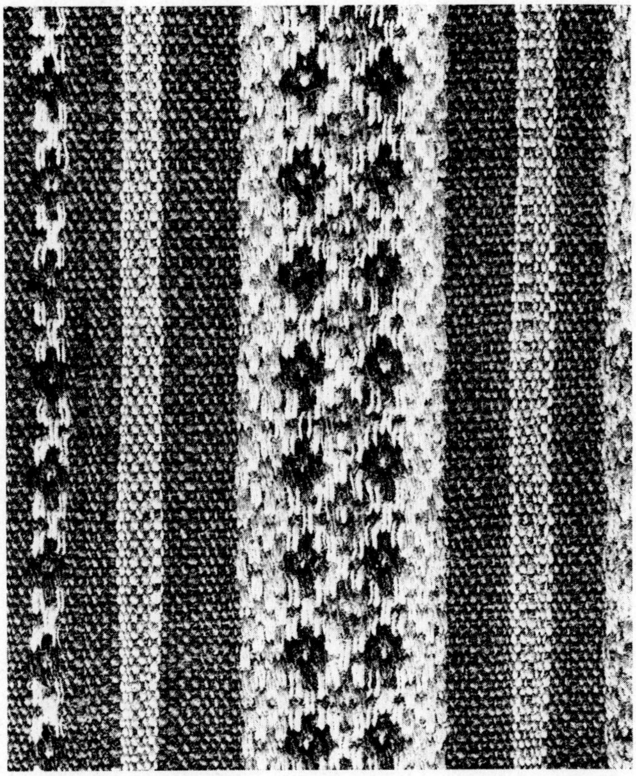

Figure 12. Cotton skirt with stripes in *pinatikan* weave, detail. Island of Goram.
Tropenmuseum, Amsterdam, acc. no. 1772-1202.

Figure 13. Detail of a leaf-fibre textile with stripes in *pinatikan* weave. Island of Ceram.
Tropenmuseum, Amsterdam, acc. no. H 3186.

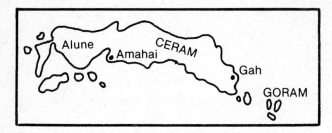

Figure 14.   Island of Ceram.

maintains taut with her body. A simple design of crosses composed of ends floating over three picks is formed with the assistance of a single pattern stick (Tropenmuseum, acc. no. 296-2) or a pair of pattern sticks (Tropenmuseum, acc. no. 171-49). On a loom (acc. no. 556-92) in the Tropenmuseum there is a similar cloth with a pattern formed by warp ends of white cotton. They can be lifted by a pattern heddle rod. Without knowing of other looms from

Ceram with a number of parts remaining constantly in the warp, which are helpful for pattern formation, I do not dare to venture the opinion that we are dealing with predecessors of the *pinatikan* loom.

In the scope of this article it was not feasible to conduct a more thorough investigation of the origin of the *kain bentenan*. Such a study would need to encompass not only the *pinatikan* but the other two sorts of *kain bentenan* as well, the *ikat kaiwu* and the striped *tonilana*. Many similarities characterize these three textiles. The very same coloured threads are made use of for both the *pinatikan* and the *tonilana*. Furthermore, it is known that the *pinatikan* and *kaiwu* have a continuous circular warp which is sometimes completely woven into a tubular panel. It is worthwhile to keep in mind the very distinctive *pinatikan* weave while examining textiles and looms which came from the Minahassa and from islands further to the east.

Notes

1. J.E. Jasper, *Verslag van de Vierde Jaarmarkt Tentoonstelling te Soerabaja* [Account of the exhibition at the fourth Annual Fair at Soerabaja], 1909, p. 35 f.

2. All drawings by the author.

3. The function of pattern stick h will be discussed later.

4. It is questionable whether the stick shuttle with the blue thread belongs to the loom, for in the already woven part of the cloth the weft is consistently white. Furthermore the two shuttles differ in form. The white is of light brown wood and is pointed at both ends. The blue is of dark brown wood and has a knob at both extremities.

5. A bit of paper is pasted to many parts of the loom. The paper itself is quite damaged and words in ink have been bleached into illegibility so that it is no longer possible to discern what was once written.

6. It was impossible to ascertain with certainty the precise name of this fruit. Varieties of *Quercus*, fam. Fagaceae, do, however, grow on the island of Celebes.

7. J.E. Jasper and Mas Pirngadie, *De Weefkunst, De Inlandsche Kunstnijverheid in Nederlandsch Indië* [The art of weaving. The native applied arts in the Dutch East Indies], vol. 2, Den Haag, Mouton, 1912, pp. 121,144,149.

8. Jasper and Pirngadie, *De Weefkunst* (1912), p. 146.

9. For mounting a continuous circular warp a mounting apparatus can be used that consists of a square wooden beam which is slightly longer than half the circumference of the warp. Sticks are inserted vertically in holes on the upper surface of the beam, and the warp thread is wound around them in a prescribed manner. See also Jasper and Pirngadie, *De Weefkunst* (1912), pp. 103-104, fig. 84. In figure 9 it can be seen that the row of four small holes has been supplemented with two lightly drawn in dots. Whoever sketched these two points with a pencil was probably preoccupied with the problem of how to weave a *pinatikan*. He reached faulty conclusions and "improved" the work of the person who made the model in North Celebes.

10. Jasper and Pirngadie, *De Weefkunst* (1912), p. 37.

11. Jasper and Pirngadie, *De Weefkunst* (1912), pp. 103–104, fig. 84.

12. Jasper and Pirngadie, *De Weefkunst* (1912), p. 144.

13. N. Graafland, *De Minahassa*, Rotterdam, M. Wyt, vol. 1 (1867), pp. 9, 85, 225; vol. 2 (1869), pp. 55, 60 f., 153.

14. J.N. Wiersma, *Ervaringen gedurende mijn twaalfjarig zendingsleven* [Experiences during my twelve years as a missionary], Rotterdam, 1876, pp. 10, 70, 110, 157.

15. J. Nerdon, "Kain Bentenan", *Het Koloniaal Weekblad, orgaan der Vereeniging Oost en West* [The Colonial Weekly, newspaper of the Society East and West], vol. 3, no. 37 (Den Haag, 26 Nov. 1903).

16. *Catalogus van de Ethnologische verzameling der Instelling voor onderwijs in de taal-, land- en volkenkunde van Nederlandsch Indië te Delft* [Catalogue of the ethnological collection from the College for language, geography and anthropology of the Dutch East Indies], Delft, 1888, p. 23, no. 281.

17. J.A. van der Chijs, *Catalogus der Ethnologische verzameling van het Bataviaasch Genootschap van Kunsten en Wetenschappen* [Catalogue of the ethnological collection from the Batavian Society of Art and Science], Batavia, 1885 and 1894.

18. The name Bwool appears twice on Celebes, both as a village in the northwest (fig. 1) and as a district in the Minahassa. Which Bwool is designated here is difficult to say.

19. A.B. Meyer and O.Richter, "Celebes I. Sammlung der Herren Dr. Paul und Dr. Fritz Sarasin aus den Jahren 1893 – 1896", *Publikationen aus dem Königlichen Ethnografischen Museum zu Dresden*, vol. 14 (1903), p. 27 f.

20. When Rouffaer described the *pinatikan* from Delft (acc. no. S 222-1) he called the undecorated band where the textile was closed "a sort of *kepala*". In Indonesia the special decorated front part of the *sarong* (skirt) is often called *kepala* (head). G.P. Rouffear, *Catalogus der Oost-Indische Weefsels, Javaanse Batiks en Oud-Indische Meubelen van de Tentoontelling van Nederlandsch Oost-Indische Kunstnijverheid, derde groep* [Catalogue of the Indonesian textiles, Javanese batiks and Old-Indonesian furniture at the exhibition of applied arts from the Dutch East Indies, third group], Den Haag, 24 July – 1 Oct. 1901.

21. A.B. Meyer and O. Richter, "Die Kains Bentenan", *Ethnographische Miszellen II. Abh. u. Ber. d.K. Zool. u. Anthr. – Ethn. Museum zu Dresden*, vol. 10/6 (1903), pp. 68-71. Dress no. 68 is in the Museum für Völkerkunde in Basel (acc. no. 11C 341); see A. and K. Bühler-Oppenheim, "Die Textiliensammlung Fritz Iklé-Huber in Museum für Völkerkunde and Schweizerischen Museum für Völkskunde Basel", *Denkschriften der Schweizerischen Naturforschenden Gesellschaft*, vol. 77/2, Zürich (1948), p. 192, fig. 102.

22. J.E. Jasper, *Verslag vierde Jaarmarkt Tentoonstelling* (1909), p. 35 f.

23. *Catalogus der Nederlandsche Afdeeling van de Algemeene en Internationale Tentoonstelling van Brussel* [Catalogue of the Dutch Pavilion of the World Fair in Brussels], Amsterdam, 1910.

24. Jasper and Pirngadie, *De Weefkunst* (1912), pp. 270, 272.

25. H. Niggemeyer, "Baumwollweberei auf Ceram", *Ciba Rundschau*, no. 106, Basel (1952), p. 3884.

26. *Catalogus v.d. Ethn. verz. Delft* (1888), p. 23, no. 285. (Today the acc. no. is 167 – 3.)

Some Eighteenth-Century French Woodblock Printed Cottons in the Royal Ontario Museum

Katharine B. Brett

THERE are several important collections of French eighteenth-century printed cottons in North America; one of them is in the Royal Ontario Museum. These collections are not eighteenth-century trade importations, as is the case with many of the English printed cottons in American collections, but are the fruit of wise and careful acquisition by collectors and museums. The collection in the Royal Ontario Museum was amassed by an Englishman, Harry Wearne, who was a designer, first of wallpapers in France, and later of textiles while living in New York from World War I until his death in 1929. In 1934 his widow presented the collection to the Royal Ontario Museum. It is typically a designer's collection; it was neither the provenance, the documentation, nor the condition, but the patterns which were of primary importance to Harry Wearne. He used many of them as inspiration for his own work and it is therefore not surprising that the eighteenth-century French woodblock printed cottons, numbering about two hundred pieces, are extremely varied technically.

With a few exceptions, the collection dates from the last quarter of the eighteenth century, the most productive period of the great French textile printing industry following the lifting of the ban in 1759 on the manufacture of printed cottons in France. Many of the leading factories are represented in the collection, particularly the Oberkampf factory at Jouy en Josas and the products of the Nantes factories. The sources of some pieces are well known from paper impressions or well-documented pieces. The original gouache drawings survive for others. These are of primary importance because in an era when copyrights did not exist and copying was an accepted practice, it is all too often impossible to say which of several variants was the original design, or which factory first produced it.

The fabrics employed in woodblock printing were cotton tabby and a tabby with linen warp and cotton weft, both having the fairly even balance of warp and weft so desirable for printing. In the Wearne collection, the quality of these fabrics varies enormously from coarse, loosely woven cottons, which might almost be called sleazy, to fine Indian cottons such as are found in the best Indian painted and dyed cottons of the same period. Those of mixed fibres, in many cases probably of French manufacture, vary in weight but are always firm. Oberkampf seems to have been fond of the characteristic broken effect in the colour masses on these fabrics where the dye took well on the cotton fibres but not on the linen ones.

Blocks of various woods, pear, oak, or holly, to mention only a few, were cut with great care and precision and were themselves masterpieces of craftsmanship, especially those in which fine metal studs were inserted to give a dotted or picot ground or filling and which used metal strips to give fine lines, though surprisingly fine lines were also cut from the wood. Some designs with a single colour required only one block, while others with large repeat patterns for house furnishings required as many as six sets of blocks, a total sometimes of as many as thirty-six blocks for a single unit of a design. They were usually cut with a hand grip at the back and were a manageable size. The carefully prepared cotton was stretched on a padded table,

18

and after an application of mordant or dye to the surface, the block was laid on the cotton and pounded with a heavy wooden mallet to make a strong and even impression.

The woodblock printing technique displayed in eighteenth-century woodblock printed cottons was an intricate and exacting one. It derived from the methods of mordant dyeing used by the chintz painters and block printers of India, techniques not understood in Europe until the last quarter of the seventeenth century, but fully mastered in France by the time the ban was lifted in 1759, in spite of all that had been done to enforce the law year after year during the first half of the century.

First the outline, or key, blocks were cut. Some designs have black outlines only and would require only one block. Others have black and red outlines as so many Indian chintzes do, the latter mostly for red flowers, and so would require two key blocks. Besides these, every colour and shade of colour required a separate block. Reds, violets, browns, and black were printed with the aid of mordants. Alum mordant, in varying strengths, was printed for reds and iron mordants, each with the proper other ingredients, were printed for violets, brown, and black. When this lengthy process was completed, the cotton was dipped in a vat of madder dye and laid in surrounding fields to bleach. Where no mordant had been applied, the madder faded out completely, leaving the required colours fast in the printed areas. Blue (indigo) was frequently painted on, a method which rendered the dye fugitive. There are, however, only a few examples in the ROM's collection which appear to have blue printed on. Yellow (weld or quercitron) was printed or painted either directly or with the aid of mordants. Green, orange, and some other colours were obtained by printing or painting over blue and the madder colours.

The designs discussed below date from the last quarter of the eighteenth century and are a selection of those in the ROM's collection for which, in most instances, the original gouache drawings exist in the library of the Musée des Arts Décoratifs in Paris. The descriptions below give the volume number for each design. Four of them are Jouy designs, the others Nantes. In most instances the colours of the printed cottons follow those of the drawing, with

the same number of reds, violets, etc., but curiously enough the sky blue in some of the drawings is quite different from the indigo blue of the printed cottons. In some instances the woodblock print is the same size as the drawing; in others there is a difference of some centimetres. All the woodblock printed cottons with an accession number beginning with 934.4 are from the Harry Wearne collection, and are the gift of Mrs. Harry Wearne.

1. Piece from a chair seat or stool cover (fig. 4).
   Jouy, 1780s.
   Acc. no. 934.4.190. Neg. no. ROMA 3057.
   Design of two repeating Chinese still life groups.
   Repeat: l. 40 cm, w. 47 cm. Two sets of blocks.

The gouache drawings of the two motifs in this design occur in volume AA24 entitled *Modeles de toiles imprimie pour l'ameublement, Manufacture de Jouy, XVIII siècle*, on pages 109 and 110 (figs. 2,3). That with the square-sided vase is inscribed in pencil "G Champs" and the number 6240.[1] A number of designs in the AA volumes are inscribed with names, many of which appear to be written by the same hand. Henri Clouzot states that, according to the records, these were "engravers". The designer of this repeat pattern took his motifs directly from a Chinese source. The Boston Museum of Fine Arts owns a Chinese woodcut depicting the still life group with the square-sided vase (fig.1).[2] Differences between the Chinese print and the gouache drawing lie only in details. The colour scheme of the drawing is three reds, two violets, sky blue, yellow, and black. The outlines are black and red and there are also green and orange, which would be produced in the printed version by over-printing. The group with a narrow-necked vase has the same colour scheme but only one shade of violet.

The woodblock design is printed in reverse to the gouache drawing and the motifs in both are the same size in every detail.[3] The design is printed on a fine cotton tabby (warps 25 per cm; wefts 24 per cm) with three reds, dull yellow, and black, and only one violet. The outlines are black and red, and blue has been painted on. There is over-printing for green and a dull orange.

19

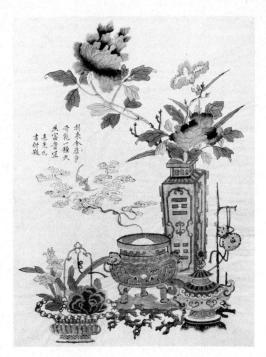

Figure 1. Woodblock print, Chinese, seventeenth century. Source of no. 1. Otis Norcross Fund 33.601. Courtesy of the Museum of Fine Arts, Boston.

Figure 2. Gouache drawing for no. 1. Courtesy of the Bibliothèque, Musée des Arts Décoratifs, Paris.

Figure 3. Gouache drawing for no. 1. Courtesy of the Bibliothèque, Musée des Arts Décoratifs, Paris.

Figure 4. Woodblock printed cotton (no. 1). The Harry Wearne Collection, Royal Ontario Museum.

2. Border (fig. 6).
   Jouy, 1770s-1780s.
   Acc. no. 968.158.24. Neg. no. 70 TEX 134.
   Design of radiating vases of flowers.
   Repeat: l. 66 cm, w. 21.5 cm.

There are gouache drawings of a wide and a narrow border of this design in volume AA26[3] entitled *Modeles de toiles imprimée pour la Manufacture de Jouy, XVIII siècle, Bordures et rayures*, pages 1 and 2 (fig. 5). The narrow one is a modified version of the design in the wide border and both are painted in three reds, blue, yellow, and black; there are also green and orange but no violet. Four different guard borders are depicted on the wide design, two on each side, and it is inscribed 5581. In volume AA24[1], page 5, there is a gouache drawing of the matching allover repeat design. It is on a much larger scale, measuring 46.5 cm × 59.5 cm, but has the same colour range as the borders. This drawing is of interest here because there is in the Royal Ontario Museum a painted and dyed Indian chintz (acc. no. 961.7.3) with this design drawn to the same size, less a centimetre and a half in each direction. The colour scheme is the same except that there are two violets. Only one unit of the design appears in both the drawing and the chintz. The alternating reverse, which appears in the borders, is not included.

The woodblock printed border matches the wide border in AA26[3], page 2 and is the same size. The guard border is the same as one of those in the drawing. It is printed on cotton tabby (warps 24 per cm, wefts 20 per cm) in two reds, brown, yellow, and black. The outlines are black and red, and blue is painted. Brown appears to have been substituted for one of the reds in the drawing.

Figure 5. Gouache drawing for no. 2.
Courtesy of the Bibliothèque, Musée des Arts Décoratifs, Paris.

Figure 6. Woodblock printed cotton border (no. 2).
Royal Ontario Museum.

Figure 7. Gouache drawing of upper part of allover pattern
matching no. 3.
Courtesy of the Bibliothèque, Musée des Arts Décoratifs, Paris.

Figure 8. Gouache drawing of lower part of allover pattern
matching no. 3.
Courtesy of the Bibliothèque, Musée des Arts Décoratifs, Paris.

Figure 9.   Woodblock printed cotton border (no. 3).
The Harry Wearne Collection, Royal Ontario Museum.

3. Border (fig. 9).
   Jouy, 1770s-1780s.
   Acc. no. 934.4.175. Neg. no. 74 TEX 353.
   Design of stylized pears, cornucopia, flowers, and
   foliage.
   Repeat: l. 47 cm, w. 22 cm.

There are two gouache drawings of narrow versions of this border design in the Jouy volumes. One is in volume AA26[3], page 2, the other in AA28[5], page 124. The former, which is the wider, is painted in three reds, yellow, blue, and black. The outlines are black and red and there are green and orange but no violet. It is inscribed 5463.

Again, as with number 2, gouache drawings of the allover design survive. In volume AA24[1], pages 1 and 2 (figs. 7,8), there are two parts which match and form the complete unit of the design. Together the design would measure 67 cm × 93 cm, an unmanageable size for a woodblock. The two parts no doubt indicate where the break in the design was intended to come for the two sets of blocks. The colours are three reds, two blues, yellow, and black. The outlines are in black and red. A curious feature is that the drawing on page 1 depicting the lower part of the design is inscribed "Le By" in pencil and the upper part on page 2 "Chevally", both well-known engravers at the Jouy factory.[4] The hand is the same as on many other drawings in the Jouy volumes. That on page 1 is also inscribed 5153.

The woodblock border is printed with three reds, dull yellow, and black. The outlines are black and red, and blue is painted in. Though wider than either of the gouache borders the colour scheme is the same. There were sometimes as many as three or four widths of border drawn for the design.

4. Border (fig. 11).
   Jouy, 1770s-1780s.
   Acc. no. 934.4.183. Neg. no. 74 TEX 36.
   Design of flowers and fruit clustered on rocky hillock.
   Repeat: l. 49.5 cm, w. 18.5 cm.

The allover repeating pattern and two matching borders are to be found in the Jouy volumes, the former in volume AA24[1], page 3, and the latter in volume AA26[3], pages 3 (fig. 10) and 17. The repeat design, measuring 40 cm × 46 cm, is not, in this instance, a larger version of the border design as in numbers 2 and 3 but is more elaborate. Two colour schemes are shown and paper has been pasted on part of one with further colour changes. Both the borders are painted in three reds, two violets, blue, yellow, and black, a colour scheme which differs slightly from the allover pattern. Only one unit of the design is shown, not the reverse, and measures l. 33 cm, w. 16 cm; and l. 16 cm, w. 8.5 cm respectively.

The woodblock printed border is closest in measurements to the wide border, and the design includes both the unit as shown in the drawing and the reverse. It is printed on a cotton tabby (warps 24 per cm; wefts 12 per cm) with three reds, two violets, yellow, and black. The outlines are black and red, and blue is painted in.

Figure 10.   Gouache drawing for no. 4.
Courtesy of the Bibliothèque, Musée des Arts Décoratifs, Paris.

Figure 11.   Woodblock printed cotton border (no.4).
The Harry Wearne Collection, Royal Ontario Museum.

5. Panel with two matching borders (fig. 13).
  Jouy, probably 1780s.
  Acc. no. 934.417.2a. Neg. no. ROMA 3001.
  Repeat: allover pattern l. 125 cm, w. 49 cm.
    Wide border: l. 33 cm, w. 22.5 cm. Narrow
    border: l. 15.5 cm, w. 9.5 cm.

The drawings of motifs incorporated into this design
are contained in volume AA22 entitled *Dessins copies
d'après de anciennes toiles peintes de la Perse et d'Inde,
Provenant d'Oberkampf, Fabriqué de Jouy 1760-1790*.
One, on page 26, is signed Oberkampf. They are
drawn to size from an Indian painted and dyed
cotton[5] and obviously derive from as yet unknown
botanical drawings. On pages 25 and 27 in volume
AA26, there are gouache drawings, four border patterns from this source in three different widths,
numbered 6701 (fig. 12), 6702, and 6703 respectively. The fourth is without a number, and all are

painted in three reds, one violet, yellow, blue, and
black. The outlines are black and red, and there are
also green, red-violet, and orange. All have different
guard border patterns on each side.

The woodblock printed panel, with a large repeat
pattern requiring three sets of blocks, has two
matching borders stitched to the right side. The inner one is the same width as the widest of the drawings, no. 6701, and the narrow one is approximately
the same width as no. 6702. The colours are three
reds, one violet, brown, yellow, and black. The outlines are black and red, and blue is very carefully
painted in. There is over-printing for green and red-
violet. All are printed on cotton tabby (repeat design: warps 29 per cm, wefts 25 per cm; wide border: warps 23 per cm, wefts 24 per cm; narrow border: warps 27 per cm, wefts 23-30 per cm; uneven
beating).

Figure 12. Gouache drawing for no. 5.
Courtesy of the Bibliothèque, Musée des Arts Décoratifs, Paris.

Figure 13. Woodblock printed cotton (no. 5).
The Harry Wearne Collection, Royal Ontario Museum.

Figure 14.   Gouache drawing of large figure group in no. 6.
Courtesy of the Bibliothèque, Musée des Arts Décoratifs, Paris.

6. Homage of America (fig. 15).
   Nantes, 1780s.
   Acc. no. 934.4.82. Neg. no. c88.51.
   Group of standing figures before the seated figure of France.
   Repeat: l. 47 cm, w. 98 cm. Two sets of blocks.

This design appears to derive from a Jean-Baptist Huet design for a copperplate printed cotton brought out by the Oberkampf factory between 1785 and 1789. The gouache drawing of an adaptation of part of it for woodblock printing in three shades of red may be seen on page 10 of volume FF3², entitled *Empriente et dessins pour toiles imprimées ameublement* (fig. 14), and a paper impression in brown of the deepest red on page 11. The latter is inscribed "N2410 L'Independence Enluminie". There is an ink drawing of another part of woodblock design, two figures under a palm tree, in volume FF³ on page 10.

The woodblock design, printed on a cotton tabby (warps 21 per cm, wefts 20-25 per cm, beating uneven) in three shades of red, is identical to the gouache drawing in volume FF3² and to the same scale, but it also includes the two figures under a palm tree. The ships and rocky hills which are part of the copperplate design do not appear. The copperplate design is the same scale as the woodblock print.

Figure 15.   Woodblock printed cotton (no. 6).
The Harry Wearne Collection, Royal Ontario Museum.

7. Peonies on a picot ground (fig. 17).
   Nantes, 1780s.
   Acc. no. 934.4.111. Neg. no. ROMA 3007.
   Branch meander with peony heads.
   Repeat: l. 29.5 cm, w. 41.5 cm.

A paper impression of this design in black and red with picot ground, appears in volume FF3^2 on page 64 (fig. 16) and opposite it drawings with suggested white, red, and picot grounds. In the same volume, on page 54, there is a paper impression of a variation in red with a red ground and in volume FF3^3, page 49, a pencil drawing of the black areas only. The volume is inscribed *Collection de modèles de la Maison Favre de Nantes 1770-1840*.

The design of the woodblock printed cotton is identical to the paper impression in volume FF33^2 on page 64, and is printed in the same colours. It has a black picot ground. The cotton is tabby and the spinning uneven (warps 17 per cm, wefts 14 per cm).

Figure 17. Woodblock printed cotton (no. 7).
The Harry Wearne Collection, Royal Ontario Museum.

Figure 16.   Paper impression and drawings for no. 7.
Courtesy of the Bibliothèque, Musée des Arts Décoratifs, Paris.

28

8. Large panel (fig. 19).
   Nantes?, 1780s.
   Acc. no. 934.4.218. Neg. no. ROMA 3054.
   Flowering branch with large birds.
   Repeat: l. 103 cm, w. 41 cm. Two sets of blocks.

A sepia paper impression of half the design, showing the two birds of pheasant type, has a painted sepia ground (fig. 18) in volume FF3[3], page 21, entitled *Collection de modèles de la Maison Favre de Nantes 1770-1870*. It illustrates well the irregular shape which some blocks have as they follow the outline of the motifs.

The woodblock printed cotton shows the entire design printed in three reds, one violet, yellow, and black. The outlines are black and red, and blue is painted in. It is the same size as the paper impression but in reverse, and there are differences in the markings on the birds and small leaf and flower sprays. It must therefore be considered a variant of the original design produced either by La Maison Favre or another factory.

Figure 18.   Paper impression related to no. 8.
Courtesy of the Bibliothèque, Musée des Arts Décoratifs, Paris.

Figure 19.   Woodblock printed cotton (no. 8).
The Harry Wearne Collection, Royal Ontario Museum.

29

KATHARINE B. BRETT

Notes

1. Guillaume Vincent Champs, born at Bièvre in 1756, is first recorded as an engraver in the Oberkampf factory in 1780. He was a foreman of the engravers from 1796 until his retirement in 1815. I am grateful to M. Sergé Chassagne for this information.

2. I am grateful to Miss Gertrude Townsend, former curator of the Textile Department, Boston Museum of Fine Arts, for drawing my attention to this source. Both this woodcut and the one which is the source of the second motif are prints from a set of twenty-five presumed to have been brought back from Japan by Kaemper in 1692-1693. See *British Museum Catalogue of Chinese and Japanese woodcuts*, 1916, p. 582, nos. 23 and 24.

3. There are other pieces in the Metropolitan Museum and the Victoria and Albert Museum, and there is a variation with a blue ground in the Museum of Fine Arts, Boston. There is also a more crowded version in the Circulation Department of the Victoria and Albert Museum.

4. George Le By was an engraver at the Oberkampf factory from 1774 to 1781. Chevally is probably intended for Hilaire Chevalier who was an engraver at the Oberkampf factory from 1774 until 1813, the year of his death. At least two of his daughters worked at the factory as *picoteuses*. I am grateful to M. Sergé Chassagne for this information.

5. A valance of this Indian cotton is privately owned in New York and there is another piece in the Josephine Howell scrapbook, now in the Cooper Hewitt Museum of Decorative Arts, Smithsonian Institution.

30

Constructions Used by Jacquard Coverlet Weavers in Ontario

Dorothy K. Burnham

WHEN research on a subject is carried on over an extended period of time there comes a moment of cold truth when the worker knows that the excitement of the chase must be interrupted. A line must be drawn beyond which no new work is undertaken while the results of the research are committed to paper. After years spent in joyful pursuit of information on early Canadian handweaving, Harold Burnham and I drew our line this side of a technical analysis of the weave constructions used by hand jacquard weavers in Ontario. Since the publication of our book "*Keep me warm one night*",[1] the omission of this information has been

regretted. It seems suitable in this volume to provide the diagrams and descriptions to fill in one more aspect of our shared research.

It is hoped that this information will clarify matters for those of us working locally in Ontario and will also provide a basis for the researchers who are wrestling with the far greater problems of provenance presented by the huge volume of material in the United States. As this is a postscript to our book, illustrations in that book will be given by number after the analysis of each construction and in captions, and the reader is referred to it for further information.

Background

Decorative coverlets with semi-realistic floral and other non-geometric patterns were a much desired item of household furnishing during the middle and latter part of the nineteenth century in rural Ontario (figs. 1, 2). From the earliest days of settlement there had been a steady demand for warm bed coverings. Many trained weavers, displaced by the progress of the Industrial Revolution in Europe, came to Canada intending to farm but found a way of making a living more suited to their abilities by supplying their neighbours' needs for woven materials. At first, coverlets were woven on shaft looms of varying complexity; then weavers started arriving with knowledge of loom improvements that had been made in France. In 1806, Joseph-Marie Jacquard perfected a mechanism using perforated

cards to control the lifting of the warp threads, thus replacing the cumbersome arrangements previously used to produce non-geometric designs. Although the term "jacquard loom" has come into general use, Jacquard's invention was an attachment that could be mounted on any substantial loom, and after its introduction to North America by William Horstmann of Philadelphia in 1823, its use spread comparatively rapidly. With training and the purchase of some essential parts the early professional weaver could make much of his own monture and set up in the specialized production of "fancy" coverlets.

In the northern United States jacquard weaving became an important local craft and many professional weavers in small centres took to the work. In

Figure 1.   Coverlet, free doublecloth (proportion 1:1, warp and weft decoupure 2). Woven in 1842 by Wilhelm Armbrust, Lincoln County, for the marriage of the donor's great-grand-parents, William and Ann Miller of Niagara-on-the-Lake. White cotton and indigo blue wool.
ROM acc. no. 965.190.3, no. 426. Gift of Miss Adelaide Lash Miller.

Figure 2.   Coverlet, weft-patterned tabby. Woven between 1885 and 1895 by the Noll brothers, Waterloo County. White cotton and bright red wool.
ROM acc. no. 950.190, no. 464. Gift of Miss G. Robinson.

Canada this special production was carried on only in a limited part of the province of Ontario, where the earliest recorded date for a jacquard coverlet is 1834 and the last 1902. During that period there were probably not more than thirty jacquard weavers in the province. Each weaver, however, was fairly prolific and the volume was large even though it was usually only a sideline to an even larger production of standard utilitarian goods produced on simpler looms.

Although the individual weavers often worked out the patterns and punched the cards, the patterns have strong connections with those produced south of the border. In general, there was a consid-

erable time lag as the designs moved north. There was a curious mixture of originality and copying among the earlier weavers, but in the later period many bought their cards ready-made in the United States and there was no attempt at originality. Designs could be changed easily by inserting a different set of cards, but the capacity of the loom was constant and the tie-up which resulted in a certain technical weave construction could not be readily changed. The early weavers, possibly owning more than one loom with jacquard attachment, often produced work in two different constructions, but the later weavers' work is characterized by one construction only.

Construction Analyses

The following nine figures show the main constructions used by jacquard coverlet weavers in Ontario. In the diagrams warp and weft have been spread so that they not only show on the face, where they are shaded, but also can be followed in line where they are actually hidden from sight on the reverse of the fabric. Beside each diagram a photograph of the weave in actual size shows the real appearance of the construction.

Where two functions are performed by the warp threads they have been differentiated by shading. Sometimes these warps are of differing weight and colour but often they are identical white cotton yarns. The woollen weft yarns have been shown in solid black while the cotton weft matches its warp, except in figure 3, where both wefts match the warps that they interlace with.

Two technical terms require definition: proportion is used where there are two sets of warp threads and refers to the proportion of one set to the other (proportions of 1:1, 1:2, and 1:4 are illustrated); decoupure is the smallest gradation (warp decoupure or weft decoupure) that forms one step in the outlines of a design. (Decoupures of 1, 2, and 4 are illustrated.)

A1   Free doublecloth

Proportion 1:1, warp and weft decoupure 2
Fig. 3
This is the most common construction used for early jacquard coverlets. Two separate and balanced tabby weaves, one wool and the other usually white cotton, change places on the face and reverse of the textile as required to form a design. The weave is closely related to geometrically patterned doublecloth produced on complex shaft looms. This construction was suitable for small orders involving the weaving of one or two coverlets at a time, when the customers provided the weaver with the yarns spun, plyed, and dyed at home. Construction used by:

Wilhelm Armbrust, Lincoln County. 1834–1848. Nos. 425–428

Moses Grobb, Lincoln County. 1853–1873. Nos. 444, 445

Unknown, Welland County. 1835–about 1856. Nos. 431–433, 436–438

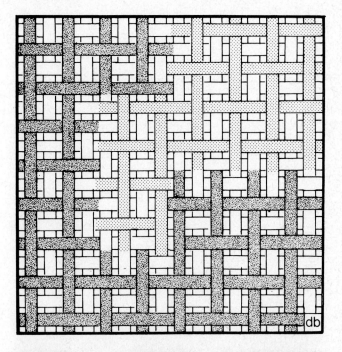

Figure 3.   Free doublecloth (proportion 1:1, warp and weft decoupure 2).
Diagram and detail of coverlet woven by Armbrust, Lincoln County, dated 1847.
ROM acc. no. 968.117.1, no. 428.

A2   *Free doublecloth*

Proportion 1:1, decoupure 1

Not illustrated

This is similar to the previous construction but the pattern moves over one thread at a time instead of two, making the drawing of the design more precise and less angular. Construction used by:

"Four Hands" weaver, Peel or York County. 1840–1860. Nos. 453–455

William J. Hunter, Ontario County. About 1865– 1910. Nos. 479, 480

The "Four Hands" weaver was in the early tradition combining warps of the customer's wool and cotton yarns. Hunter's warps were all cotton and he, undoubtedly, cut his production time by setting up standard warps of considerable length.

A3   *Free doublecloth*

Proportion 4:1,[2] warp and weft decoupure 2

Fig. 4

This also has two separate layers of tabby changing place to form the pattern but while one is a balanced weave in white cotton the other has a heavy wool weft working with a widely spaced cotton warp which is quite unobtrusive. Construction used by:

John Campbell, Middlesex County. About 1860–1885. Nos. 481, 482

A4   *Free doublecloth*

Proportion 2:1, warp decoupure 2, weft decoupure 1

Not illustrated

This construction has been found with standard all-cotton warps, and cotton and wool wefts. Construction used by:

Unknown weaver, Elgin County. Late nineteenth– early twentieth century. No. 491

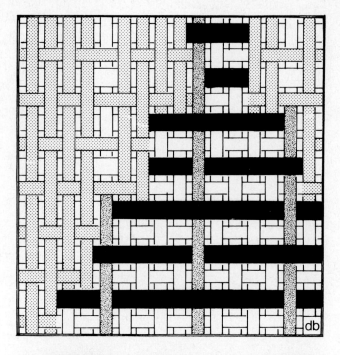

Figure 4.   Free doublecloth (proportion 4:1, warp and weft decoupure 2).

Diagram and detail of coverlet woven by Campbell, Middlesex County, 1884.

ROM acc. no. 962.75, no. 481.

B1 *Weft-patterned tabby[3]*
Every third warp used to tie pattern weft
Fig. 5

Although very similar in appearance to the tied doublecloth constructions (C and D), this is not a doublecloth but has a cotton tabby ground and an extra wool pattern weft. Every third warp thread is used to tie the pattern wefts but the ties alternate in successive rows so the basic pattern skip is of five threads. The weave is reversible with a pattern which is dark on a light ground on one face, and light on a dark ground on the other. Construction used by:

Aaron Zelner, Haldimand and Waterloo counties.
About 1845–1868. Nos. 456, 457

Noll Brothers, Waterloo County. 1868–1905. Nos. 458–464

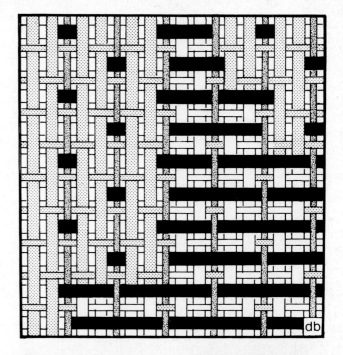

Figure 5. Weft-patterned tabby.
Diagram and detail of coverlet woven by Noll, Waterloo County, dated 1872.
ROM acc. no. 965.224.1, no. 460.

B2   *Weft-patterned tabby*

Every fifth warp used to tie pattern weft
Fig. 6

Like the previous construction, this is not a double-cloth. Every fifth warp thread is used to tie the pattern wefts and these warps combine with the other warp threads to form a perfect tabby ground. In figure 5 the warp threads are of two weights; here they are identical. The weave is reversible, light on dark and dark on light. Construction used by:

Wilhelm Armbrust, Lincoln County. 1834–1848.
   Nos. 429, 430

Unknown weavers, Welland County. About 1835–1850. Nos. 434, 435, 441

B3   *Weft-patterned tabby*

Every fifth warp used to tie pattern weft
Not illustrated

This construction is the same as shown in figure 6 but a decoupure of 1 produces more rounded contours in the design. Construction used by:

Unknown weaver, Welland County. About 1850–1855. Nos. 439, 440

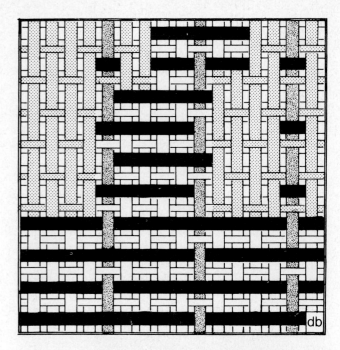

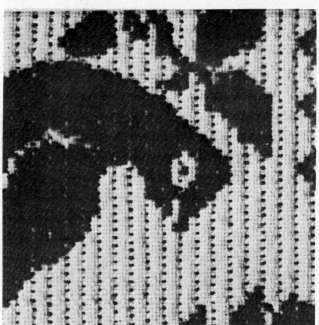

Figure 6.   Weft-patterned tabby.
Diagram and detail of coverlet woven by an unknown weaver, Welland County, dated 1838.
ROM acc. no. 968.96, no. 435.

C1   *Free doublecloth with tied areas*
Proportion 2:1, warp and weft decoupure 2
Fig. 7

As in the totally free doublecloth constructions, two layers of tabby exchange places to form the pattern, but here the two faces of the textile are different in appearance. The warps are both cotton, often identical white yarns but sometimes differing in weight, and the one that ties the wool weft may be coloured to make it less obtrusive. In the lower right of the diagram in figure 7 the layers are completely free with the woollen weft unobtrusively tied by a light cotton warp on the face and a balanced cotton tabby on the reverse. In the upper left the layers are held firmly together by the way the dark wool weft interlaces with its warp, holding the ground warp and weft firmly between them. On the face of this section the white cotton warp is in ridges composed of two threads with spots of woollen weft showing between them, while on the reverse the woollen weft covers the ground entirely. This gives the same appearance as the face of the free doublecloth section but it is actually firmly attached to the other layer of cloth. For the appearance of the reverse side of this construction compare figure 8. Construction used by:

Moses Grobb, Lincoln County. 1853–1873. No. 446

William Withers, York County. About 1850–1870. No. 476

Johan Lippert, Waterloo County. 1870–1890. Nos. 465–467

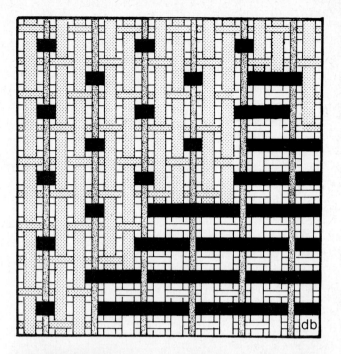

Figure 7. Free doublecloth with tied areas (proportion 2:1, warp and weft decoupure 2).
Diagram and detail of coverlet woven by Grobb, Lincoln County, dated 1873.
ROM acc. no. 969.220.1, no. 446.

C2 *Free doublecloth with tied areas*
Proportion 2:1, warp and weft decoupure 1
Fig. 8
Similar to the previous construction but with the softer contours of a decoupure of 1, this is shown from the other face. The clear-cut tied area showing the heavy woollen weft in the upper left of the diagram contrasts with an area of free doublecloth in the lower right. For the reverse side of this construction compare figure 7. Construction used by:
Edward Graf, Welland County (in all his later work). 1870–1890. Nos. 447–452

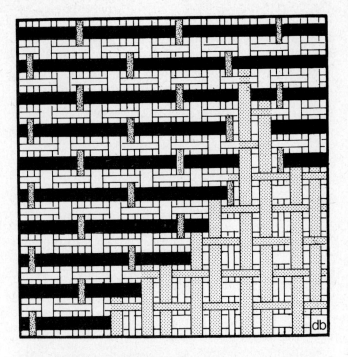

Figure 8. Free doublecloth with tied areas (proportion 2:1, warp and weft decoupure 1).
Diagram and detail of coverlet woven by Graf, Welland County, about 1875.
ROM acc. no. 950.93.3, no. 450.

C3 *Free doublecloth with tied areas*
Proportion 4:1, warp decoupure 4, weft decoupure 2
Fig. 9

This construction is basically the same as the two previously illustrated, but with a warp proportion of 4:1 the vertical ridging of the warp is stronger, and with a warp decoupure of 4 the drawing of the designs is necessarily coarser. Construction used by:

Wilhelm Magnus Werlich, Waterloo County. About 1865–1912. Nos. 469, 470

August Ploethner, Waterloo County. About 1865–1890. Nos. 471, 472

Daniel Knechtel, Waterloo County. About 1870–1900. Nos. 473, 474

This specific construction is the one used for the classic old German *Beiderwand*. This term has recently been used, very loosely, to describe jacquard coverlets if not of completely free doublecloth.[4] Although it is tempting to consider the tied doublecloth construction a heritage that trained weavers from Germany brought with them to North America, it is unwise to use the term for a wide group of weaves which may well turn out to stem from different origins. It may be significant that this construction occurs in Ontario only in the work of the group of weavers who are thought to have purchased their pattern cards ready-punched from the United States.

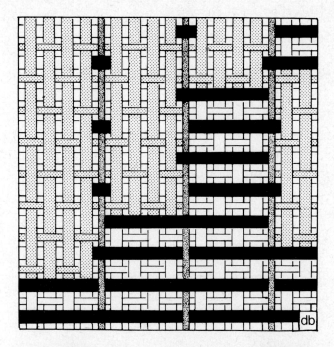

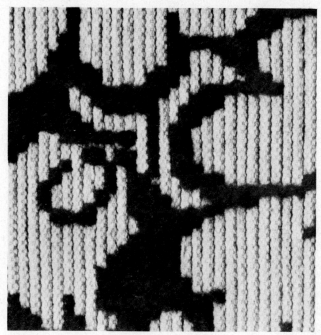

Figure 9. Free doublecloth with tied areas (proportion 4:1, warp decoupure 4, weft decoupure 2).
Diagram and detail of coverlet woven by Ploethner, Waterloo County, 1870-1890.
ROM acc. no. 968.66.1, no. 471.

D1 *Fully tied doublecloth*

Proportion 2:1,[5] warp and weft decoupure 2

Fig. 10

This is a unique construction which has been observed in the work of only one man, Christopher Armstrong, who took over the loom of William Withers when that man died (compare Withers' construction: C1, fig. 7). A white cotton warp and weft form one layer of the doublecloth in a tabby weave. Between each pair of these warps a lighter weight warp ties a woollen weft in tabby. Threads of this secondary warp lie alternately on the face and the reverse of the textile which has the effect of bunching the main warp into ridges consisting of four threads and gives the appearance of a warp of 4:1 proportion. This construction gives a reversible fabric with light and dark areas alternating on the two faces. Construction used by:

Christopher Armstrong, York County. About 1870–1910. Nos. 477, 478

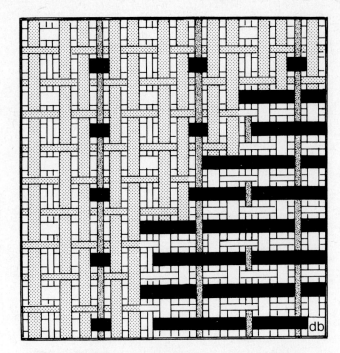

Figure 10. Fully tied doublecloth (proportion 2:1, warp and weft decoupure 2).
Diagram and detail of coverlet woven by Armstrong, York County, 1880-1890.
ROM acc. no. 963.1.2, no. 477.

E1   *Satin damask*

Warp and weft decoupure 2

Fig. 11

This construction has been recorded in the work of only one weaver in Ontario. It is a simple form of satin damask (5–end) with a dark woollen weft contrasting strongly with a white cotton warp.

Construction used by:

"Weaver Joe", Ontario County. 1850–1880. Nos. 484–489

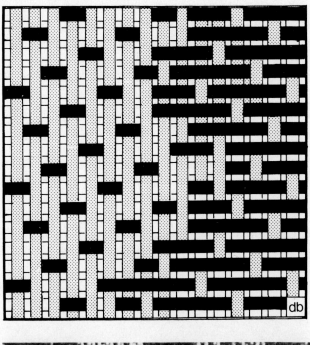

Figure 11.   Damask (5-end satin, decoupure 2). Diagram and detail of coverlet woven by "Weaver Joe", Ontario County, 1865-1875. ROM acc. no. 967.281, no. 487.

Conclusion

In "*Keep me warm one night*" the constructions of the Ontario jacquard coverlets are separated into four basic types: free doublecloth, tied doublecloth, tied doublecloth with free areas, and damask. With the closer examination required to prepare the diagrams for this paper it now appears necessary to alter the terminology of one category. In spite of similar appearance to tied doublecloths with free areas, constructions previously called tied doublecloth have only one set of warp threads and should be called tabby with weft patterning. One exception is Armstrong's construction (D1, fig. 10), a fully tied doublecloth, which probably results from a slight change of tie-up from the construction of the former user of the loom (C1, fig. 7).

Twelve variations of construction have been re-corded above. In these there are two rare types (D and E), and three main categories: free doublecloth (A), weft-patterned tabby (B), and doublecloth with tied areas (C). The constructions used undoubtedly owe much to the training weavers received before coming to this country. Many weavers were of German origin. Many others came from southwest Scotland and we must look to the carpet weaving of that country for parallels of pattern and construction. Figure 11 definitely suggests a man who was fully trained as a linen weaver, probably in the north of Ireland. Many influences were at work, and there is much research yet to be done on all aspects of this colourful part of the nineteenth-century scene in North America.

Notes

1. H.B. and D.K. Burnham, "*Keep me warm one night*": *Early handweaving in eastern Canada*, Toronto, University of Toronto Press, 1972.

2. In "*Keep me warm one night*", 1st and 2d printing, Campbell's construction was wrongly stated to have a proportion of 2:1.

3. In "*Keep me warm one night*", 1st and 2d printing, constructions of the B type were listed as tied doublecloth. It is prefera-ble to consider them as weft-patterned tabby.

4. Mildred Davison and Christa C. Mayer-Thurman, *Coverlets: A handbook of the collection of woven coverlets in the Art Institute of Chicago*, 1973.

5. In "*Keep me warm one night*", 1st and 2d printing, Armstrong's construction was wrongly stated to have a proportion of 4:1.

The Clothing of a
Fourteenth-Century Nubian Bishop

Elisabeth Grace Crowfoot

THE fortress city of Qasr Ibrîm — the Roman Primis and Christian Phrim — stands high above the Nile, and throughout the whole period of the Christian Nubian kingdom was a place of considerable importance, the seat of a bishop, and probably the site of the civil administration of northern Nubia. Though essentially a fortified position, designed as a place of refuge for the local population in times of danger, it contained within its walls a great cathedral. This church, with its five aisles, red granite columns, and carved grey capitals, the finest ecclesiastic building in the whole of Nubia, was naturally one of the first areas to be cleared during recent excavations by the Egypt Exploration Society, led by Professor J. Martin Plumley of Cambridge. [1]

On 6 January 1964, while the well of the stairway leading down to the North Crypt was being cleared, an undisturbed burial was discovered. Owing to the dry conditions inside the fortress and its abandonment since 1812, the preservation of organic remains has been exceptionally good, some areas yielding layers of domestic textile and fragments of manuscripts. The body, which had been laid on a thick deposit of soft earth inside the entrance to the crypt, was still fully clothed and wrapped in a shroud. Underneath it, upon the lower half of the shroud, were two paper scrolls, which when unrolled proved to be the Letters Commissary from the Patriarch of the Coptic Church for the enthronement of Bishop Timotheos of Ibrîm, with the date of his consecration, A.D. 1372. [2]

From his skeleton, it appears that the bishop was a short man (172 cm/ca. 5'7") and probably of early middle age. His slightly contracted position with knees bent to the south and feet to the east may have been due to the limited space available, but the fingers of his hands were curled and one foot was missing. At first it seemed possible that he had died a violent death, though his burial inside his own cathedral and the inclusion of his consecration deeds show that there was no attempt to conceal his identity, and that he must have been buried by friends. Professor Plumley has suggested that the cause of death may have been snakebite, and that amputation of his foot was undertaken in a bid to save his life. However he died, his clothing suggests that burial had to be carried out hastily, perhaps on his arrival at Ibrîm, since his everyday garments were not changed for the vestments normally used for the interment of a bishop.

The body (fig. 1) had been wrapped in a fine cotton shroud, doubled over at the feet, with the ends tied around the neck; across the middle it was again secured by cords passing around two buttons. Around the bishop's waist was a narrow cotton body belt, and over this were full coarse trousers with a drawstring. A long white tunic, suggesting an alb but with wide sleeves, had been gathered at the waist by a leather belt. A fine iron benedictional cross was suspended from his neck by a blue plaited cord and lay on his left breast. His uppermost garment, a bell-shaped cloak, had lost its outer layer, since this was of wool and had been attacked by insects; the red-brown lining of cloak and cowl, parts of a blue edging, and a panel of silk tapestry which had decorated the back and shoulders were all that remained. A pale blue cotton veil was wrapped

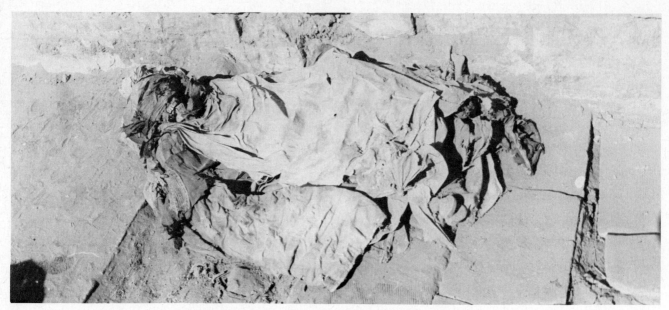

Figure 1.   The body of Bishop Timotheos (*in situ*), Qasr Ibrîm, Nubia.

around the head and placed over the face. A hand-kerchief of fine white linen, ornamented with blue silk, had been tucked into the line of the neck.

The shroud was a rectangular piece of cloth, torn at the end that wrapped the feet; the complete woven width is 66 cm, and the length preserved is 164 cm. The warp and weft, of undyed cotton, were Z-spun and rather uneven; the weave is a regular tabby with counts from 14/16 to 17/18 threads per cm owing to variations in the yarn; the selvage had two paired warps. At a distance of 1.5 cm from the end were two bands, 3.5 cm apart, each of three rows of untidy decorative running stitches, one in single blue cotton thread, the other in similar yarn used double (fig. 2). At the end where the shroud had been tied around the bishop's neck, the two corners have been knotted round bunches of seven to eight S-spun, Z-ply threads, whose ends were then twisted into S cords. Further down (90 cm on one edge and 98 on the other) are two "buttons", each formed by a small bunch of the cloth filled with earth and tied round by similar threads. Fifty cm of the cord, which fastened them together under the body, still dangle from one button. The rough improvisation of the arrangement suggests haste in the burial, though the mourners selected a cloth of good quality, perhaps belonging to Timotheos himself.

The body belt (fig. 3) is now in two separate strips

joined in circles, but it is clear that originally the bands fitted one inside the other. Both are of the same undyed cotton, Z-spun, a regular tabby weave with a close thread count of 20–21/18 per cm and simple selvage. The woven width of the cloth is 68 cm, and to each 9 cm wide strip cut from the full width of the material a small piece has been added to bring the circle to 75 cm on the inner strip, 76 cm on the outer. The seams are stem-stitched in fine, S-ply, linen thread, cut edge to selvage; when the bands are placed together naturally the rough side of the seams is hidden. The edges are turned under singly, and broken stitches on both strips show that two were held together with a line of white silk stem stitch; the other two edges have been hemmed or oversewn with silk, but in parts this is unbroken, and perhaps this edge of the band was left open. The whole belt seems narrow to have passed over the hips of a grown man, but its position was clear, and obviously Timotheos must have been slender.

The trousers (fig. 3) again are of undyed cotton, Z-spun in tabby weave (count: 10–11/11–12 per cm), both spinning and weaving loose and variable; the selvage has six paired warps, and the whole width of the cloth is 66–68 cm. The trousers were made in four pieces. A full width of fabric was used for each leg, and two large triangular gussets were joined under the legs, cut on the bias from a finer Z-

Figure 2.   Left: decoration on the shroud of Bishop Timotheos.
Right: interlinked sprang.

spun tabby with a count of 13/14 per cm. The selvage to selvage seams, i.e., the leg seams and the
short seams centre back and front above the gusset,
are oversewn with Z-ply thread; the gusset seams
are run and fell. The ends of the trouser legs are
neatly hemmed from left to right with Z-ply thread.
The wider hem at the waist, turned over onto the
front to act as a waistband, has an opening back
and front, with the corners neatly turned back and
stitched under.

A few fragments of the drawstring remain, the
best 9 cm long and ca. 5 cm wide, made with fifty-
four interlinked coarse S-spun, Z-ply wool threads
in the simplest form of sprang (fig. 2) — a well-
known technique used in Egypt since early Coptic
times for bags and belts.[3] The likeness in texture to a
modern interlocked pyjama cord is obvious and the
function the same: a soft drawstring that gives comfortably and yet holds the trousers up firmly.

The tunic or alb is a long garment with wide
sleeves (fig. 4), woven of fairly fine, undyed linen
(Z-spun) in a close, even tabby with a count of
15/13–15 threads per cm, and one paired warp at
the selvage. The width of the cloth is ca. 66 cm. The
tunic is lined throughout with undyed cotton tabby,
again Z-spun, but coarser and softer (count: 10/9
per cm, two paired selvage warps). The two layers
were made separately, with single run seams on

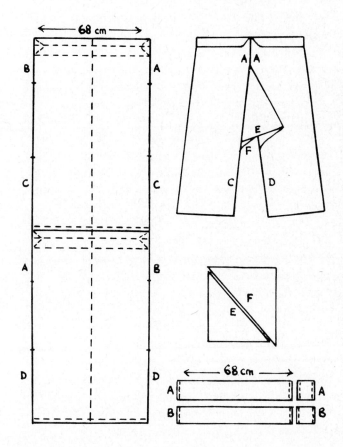

Figure 3. The trousers (above) and body belt (below) of
Bishop Timotheos.

both tunic and lining, alike for cut edges and selvages. The linen garment was made of nine pieces: a full width of the fabric for each sleeve; a continuous piece folded on the shoulders for the centre panel of both back and front; two pieced side panels, tapering towards the underarm; and two small underarm gussets. The main seams of the lining follow the same pattern as in the tunic, though there is some extra piecing in the side panels. The lining is held to the tunic by rows of surface running stitches alongside the main seams and also in the centres of the wider side panels. Without the gussets, which like those in the trousers are from a finer tabby weave (count: 19/22 per cm), the tunic would have needed a length of 710 cm of cloth.

The hem and sleeves are finished with a facing of linen similar to that of the tunic, cut on the bias, 4 cm wide on the back, hemmed to the lining as in a modern facing, but worked from left to right in S-ply thread. A line of running stitches at a distance of 1 cm from the edge gives a decorative finish and keeps the edge firm. The neck, a simple slip-over slit with no fastening, is finished with a very narrow coloured neckband, a 1.8 cm wide strip cut on the bias from a fine striped tabby of Z-spun cotton, in which one system is blue (count: 56 threads per cm), while the other has narrow stripes of yellow or white and two shades of blue (count: 24 threads per cm). Only 4 mm of the coloured fabric show on the front, the rest being turned under and hemmed to the lining with S-ply white cotton, with the corners neatly mitred. The whole tunic is a very efficient piece of tailoring.

The voluminous cloak of Timotheos was bell-shaped, and had an attached hood (fig. 5). Just enough of the wool of which the outer layer was made remains to show that it was of excellent quality, of fine unpigmented fibre, dyed with indigo in a dark blue which, except in bright sunshine, now looks black; the weave is a fine Z-spun tabby with 30/21–22 threads per cm. The comparatively well-preserved lining is of cotton, again Z-spun, woven in tabby with a count of 13/14 threads per cm and selvage with two paired warps. Since it was dyed with madder, it may originally have been a rich cherry colour, much redder than its present brownish shade. The garment was made from ca. 840 cm of material, 65 cm wide from selvage to selvage. One

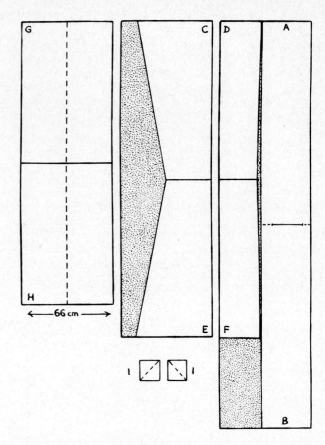

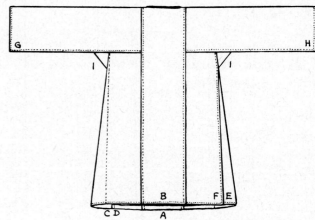

Figure 4.   The tunic of Bishop Timotheos.

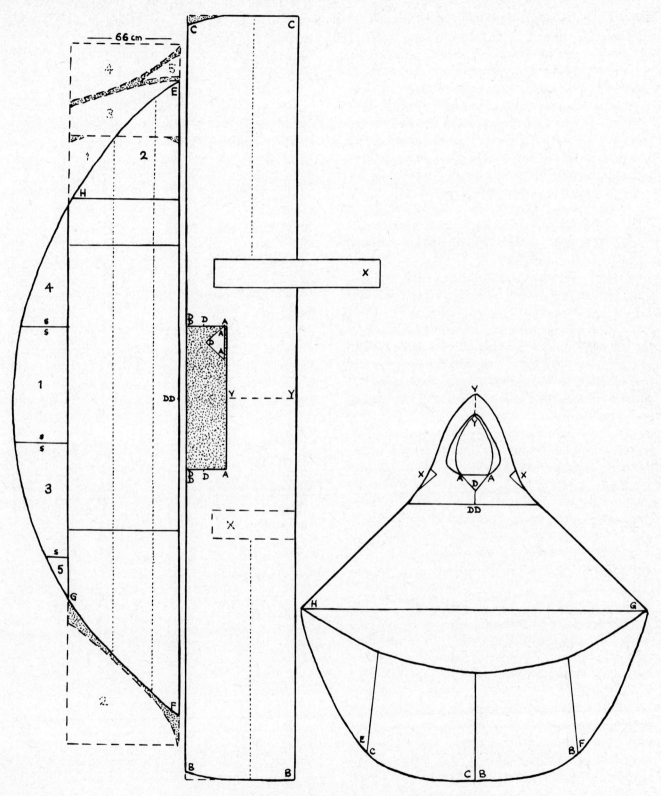

Figure 5. The cloak of Bishop Timotheos. *X*: tapestry woven panel; *Y – Y*: fold line at top of hood; . . .: blue silk tacking threads; *S*: selvages in pieced sections of lining.

47

length of ca. 440 cm of the full width was folded in two at the top of the hood, while another full width and a smaller curved section were added in front, with a gusset at the throat. In the lining the two front sections are a patchwork of nine pieces which can be reconstructed by their selvages into a second length of ca. 400 cm, though no doubt, as in the case of the tunic, the blue wool was cut with more regard for appearance and less for economy than the lining. The seams joining the panels of the lining are rather roughly run, with an occasional back-stitch, in Z-ply blue linen thread.

Inside the hood and all around the hem of the cloak was a turquoise blue silk facing, 6 cm deep, cut on the bias. The silk tabby weave has a fine, very slightly Z-spun warp, and a rather darker and coarser weft with a count of 39/24 threads per cm and selvage of ca. 14 paired warps. As in the tunic, the lining has been held to the fabric of the cloak by lines of running stitches in a deep blue silk, which proved very helpful during the reconstruction of the garment by Dr. G.H.S. Bushnell and Mr. C. Lilley at the University Museum of Archaeology and Ethnology, Cambridge.

Across the back and shoulders the cloak was decorated with a panel of silk tapestry (fig. 6), 27 by 101 cm in size, with cut edges top and bottom and both selvages turned under and hemmed to the cloak with Z-ply thread. The tapestry, discoloured, but originally probably in white, gold, black, and pale blue silk, is woven on Z-spun white silk warps used in fours, 18 (i.e. 72 warps) per cm; the weft count in the narrow bands of leaves and the step and scroll patterns varies from 28-30 to 56 threads per cm.

A detached fragment of the blue wool, which may have come from below this panel (fig. 7), shows a narrow band in purple wool and gold silk over three warps (extended tabby) with smaller bands with a stem-stitch edge on either side of it showing rather geometric floral patterns embroidered in gold silk thread in stem and running stitches. Above and below these bands are preserved a few letters from an inscription, worked in stem and satin stitches. This type of band obviously derives from earlier examples with Coptic inscriptions on either side of decorative tapestry bands dating from the ninth to tenth centuries A.D.[4] Though very incomplete, enough remains of the letters on Timotheos' cloak to suggest that the inscription is probably, as in other cases, meaningless. The Coptic weavers, being perhaps unable to read, used the letters simply as patterns, a process already beginning in the eighth century.[5]

The veil, which was wrapped around the head, had slipped forward or been pulled down to cover the face. It was of very soft, Z-spun, turquoise blue cotton, the warp uneven, the weft finer, woven in open tabby with a slightly crepe surface (count: 23/20 threads per cm; selvage of seven paired warps). Three ragged fragments survive (measurements: ca. 50 by 48 cm, 35 by 11 cm, and 12 by 20 cm), from which it is impossible to establish the original width of the fabric. This cloth must have formed a sort of turban under the hood, the equivalent of the stiff, round turban-like hat worn by Coptic bishops today.

The handkerchief (mappa) is a beautiful piece of weaving, measuring 71 by 82 cm, with both selvages and cut warps above and below. Warp and weft are of fine but variable Z-spun, undyed linen. The weave is an open tabby with counts varying from 24–25/29–32 threads per cm; the 4.3–4.4 cm wide strips along the selvages are in pairs of practically unspun white silk (66–68 per cm). At top and bottom, a narrow band of five throws of blue silk is followed by a few centimetres of plain linen and then an almost 4 cm wide patterned band (fig. 8). This is formed of a narrow band of 2/2 twill with white silk weft, three narrow bands in dark blue Z-spun silk over paired warps (extended tabby), a band of 2/2 diagonal twill in flax, and five wider blue silk bands in which a few throws of white silk make different small chequered patterns. The order of the bands is slightly different in the two borders, and in one the larger twill area has the flax weft thrown four threads together. The elaboration of the selvage seems designed to carry the pattern of twill and coloured stripes right to the edge of the weave. Together with those required for the centre, a total of sixteen shafts would be necessary. Dr. Peter Collingwood has made the interesting suggestion that in the professional weaving shop from which the mappa came, perhaps some specialist handkerchief weaver had a warp set up like this so that he could produce any sort of elaborate border which might be required; in which case, sixteen shafts would be used

Figure 6.   Tapestry woven panel from the cloak of Bishop Timotheos. Detail.

Figure 7.   Fragment with inscription from the cloak of Bishop
Timotheos.

49

for the selvage and a further four for the centre.

Apart from the handkerchief, the weaves and materials from the bishop's burial are of the simplest types. But everyday mediaeval clothes in ordinary materials have not been preserved to the same extent as regal and ecclesiastical robes and vestments, and the particular interest of this collection lies in the completeness of the garments, with their useful evidence of cutting and tailoring methods, firmly tied to the date A.D. 1372. In most pieces the complete width of the woven cloth is present. All the plain tabby weaves, cotton and linen, are between 64 and 68 cm wide, very narrow compared with contemporary European professional standards. The decorated pieces, the handkerchief (w. 82 cm) and the tapestry panel (w. 101 cm) are wider, and are obviously very skilled professional work.

The high proportion of cotton may indicate that it was already more commonly used in Egypt than linen. Even the flax thread in this burial is Z-spun instead of S, unthinkable in pre-mediaeval Egypt, a habit caught from people used to other fibres without a natural spinning direction, such as wool and cotton. Nubia, and particularly Meroë, had long been famous as a cotton growing area. In A.D. 1173, when Shams ed-Doulah raided Ibrîm, he carried off a quantity of cotton found in the town and sold it for a handsome sum.[6] But physical characteristics suggest that Timotheos was of Nubian origin, and would have understood the useful properties of cotton in the difficult climate to which he was returning.

These garments, though not necessarily episcopal robes, have an ecclesiastical flavour. The tunic is of a traditional Egyptian style.[7] An earlier tunic from a burial at Ibrîm, possibly of the eleventh or twelfth century A.D., is of identical cut, apart from the piecing of the side panels, though unlined and of very inferior tailoring. In spite of an Arabic inscription (*tiraz*) on one sleeve, this and other inscribed pieces used for shrouds of the same date certainly come from Christian monastic burials. The beauty of the fine *mappa* suggests that this may have been part of the bishop's priestly equipment, the napkin used to wipe his hands during celebration, rather than a personal handkerchief.

Figure 8. Decorated band from the handkerchief of Bishop Timotheos. Detail; scale ca. 2:1.

The deep blue cloak, falling on the ground behind, would have had to be looped over the bishop's arms when he walked, showing the blue-edged red lining and the white tunic beneath. The soft blue cotton of his turban toned with the facing and the blue, white, and gold of the tapestry decoration on his shoulders. Simple as the garments are, they are well designed for comfort and protection from heat and cold when travelling, and they are of the high quality suited to Timotheos' rank.

Acknowledgments

The author would like to acknowledge gratefully Professor J.M. Plumley's permission to use personal communications and unpublished material in the preparation of this paper, and for the photograph in figure 1; Dr. Peter Collingwood's suggestion on the weaving of the handkerchief; the assistance of Dr. M.L. Ryder, Animal Breeding Research Breeding Organisation, Roslin, Scotland, and Dr. D.F. Cutler, Jodrell Laboratory, Royal Botanic Gardens, Kew, for fibre determinations; the assistance of Professor M.C. Whiting and Mr. Takeo Sugiura for identification of dyes; and the help of Mr. Cyril Lilley and Mr. Patrick Smith at the University Museum of Archaeology and Ethnology, Cambridge.

The photographs in figures 6, 7, and 8 are reproduced by kind permission of the University Museum of Archaeology and Ethnology, Cambridge (6,7), and the British Museum, Department of Mediaeval and Later Antiquities (8).

Notes

1. J.M. Plumley, "Some examples of Christian Nubian art from the excavations at Qasr Ibrîm", *Kunst und Geschichte Nubiens in Christlicher Zeit*, Recklinghausen, Aurel Bongers, 1970, p. 129.

2. J.M. Plumley, "Qasr Ibrîm, 1963-1964", *Journal of Egyptian Archaeology*, vol. 50 (1964), pp. 3, 4.

3. P. Collingwood, *The techniques of sprang*, London, Faber, 1974, pp. 35–44.

4. N.P. Britton, *A study of some early Islamic textiles*, Boston, Museum of Fine Arts, 1938, acc. no. 11.1398, p. 42, fig. 18.

5. S. Gaselee, "Lettered Egyptian textiles in the Victoria and Albert Museum", *Archaeologia*, vol. 23 (1924), p. 82, figs. 6, 7.

6. R.J. Forbes, *Studies in ancient technology*, vol. 4, Leiden, E.J. Brill, 1956, pp. 47, 48.

7. Britton, *Islamic textiles* (1938), pp. 16–17, figs. 95, 97–100.

The Loom Representation
on the Chiusi Vase

Agnes Geijer

PROBABLY no loom representation has been reproduced so frequently in printed works as that which adorns one side of a fifth-century B.C. Greek *skyphos* discovered near the little Italian town of Chiusi, where it is now in the custody of the local museum (fig. 1). The representation first became known as the result of a line drawing (fig. 2) published in 1872 by the Archaeological Institute in Rome.[1] It is above all this version which has been reproduced so often in the literature, both in learned treatises on the technology of weaving and, in various languages, in popular handbooks on textiles. The last volume of the *Griechische Vasenmalerei*,[2] which appeared in 1932, contained a new version of the Chiusi loom. This gave an illusory depiction of the red-figured style in which the vase is painted (fig. 3). The first photographic reproduction appeared only in 1968.[3] On this occasion, the representation of the Chiusi vase served to illustrate an article based on a number of literary sources on textile manufacture in the ancient world. The author, primarily a classical philologist, was unfamiliar with textile technology. Consequently she did not react to the differences between the photographic reproduction and the two drawings.

The photograph came as a shock to those who were familiar with the earlier reproductions and who had to a greater or lesser extent followed the highly controversial discussion on the subject of "Penelope's loom", for the photographic reproduction lacks both the perpendicular warp ends and their weights, on account of which the loom in question had originally been characterized as a warp-weighted loom. How is this to be explained?

Could the first drawing have been a figment of somebody's imagination, inspired among other things by the warp-weighted looms known from Iceland and the Faeroes, and published by Olaus Olavius in 1780 and 1787 (the latter in German), and by J. A. A. Worsaae in 1848?[4] This in turn would imply that the draftsman who made the Furtwängler illustration might have made an addition under the influence of the first drawing from 1872. There might be, however, a more innocent explanation. It is possible, as has been stated concerning another red-figured vase,[5] that the warp threads were executed as fine relief lines which are not visible in the photographic reproduction. To decide this, of course, the original in the Chiusi Museum has to be studied.

While not having settled this matter, I would still venture to offer some observations which may help to dispel the mystery surrounding the Chiusi loom.

Instead of going into a general discussion of ancient looms, I will refer the reader to the great work by Marta Hoffmann entitled *The warp-weighted loom*.[6] In her survey of the looms of classical antiquity, particularly those depicted on Greek vases, Hoffmann mentions that more than one type of loom might have occurred in the ancient world, and that it is absurd in this context to speak in terms of the primitiveness and relative ages of the different types. Various loom types may have been in use simultaneously, though for different purposes.

One must assume that there were at least three types of looms. First is the warp-weighted loom, in which work proceeds from the top downwards and the weft is beaten upwards with a sword beater

Figure 1.   Penelope and Telemachos before the web depicted on a Greek vase, fifth century B.C.
Museum of Chiusi. Photo: German Archaeological Institute, Rome, neg. no. 63,564.

Figure 2.   The loom of the Chiusi vase, after Conze (1872).

Figure 3.   The loom of the Chiusi vase after Furtwängler et al. (1932).

53

within the shed. Above all it was used for plain and everyday fabrics, mostly woollens. Judging from figural vase painting, tapestry woven textiles for clothing also occurred in classical Greece, but the loom employed for this kind of work seems not to have been depicted, presumably because the implement as such was not very spectacular in appearance. However, various other sources give an idea of what this loom looked like. As a rule it may have consisted of two vertical uprights supporting two beams, the upper one for rolling the warp, and the other for the woven textile. The essential purpose of the construction was to get the warp firmly stretched. Apart from these two types, which were employed for completely different purposes, the ancient world also knew a third, the tubular warp loom. The widespread existence of tubular weaving has been established by Margrethe Hald, who analyzed several Danish textiles from the early Iron Age, dating between the fourth and first centuries B.C. She found parallels not only in ethnographic material, but also on some Graeco-Roman representations of costume showing tubular woven *peplos*.[7]

Returning to the Chiusi vase, I decided to consult Homer, an authority who appears to have been somewhat neglected by textile scholars. Archaeologists agree that the pictures of the Chiusi vase refer to the homecoming of Odysseus: on one side he meets his wife (he is still unknown to her; his name is written close by); and on the other side we see what Penelope is talking about, their son Telemachos, and the weave with which she deceived her suitors. Homer writes:

The wise Penelope comes down from her apartment, looking as lovely as Artemis or golden Aphrodite. She takes her usual place by the fire. She invites the Stranger, the noble and stalwart Odysseus, to sit down. Penelope opened their talk. I am left to my misery: the powers above have heaped so many troubles on my head. For of all the island chieftains that rule in Dulichium, in Same, and in wooded Zacynthus, or that live here in our own sunny Ithaca, there is not one that is not forcing his unwelcome suit upon me and plundering my house. I simply wear my heart out in longing for Odysseus. Meanwhile they are pressing me to name my wedding-day. I have to think out tricks to fool them with. The first was a real inspiration. I set up a great web on my loom here and started weaving a large and delicate robe, saying to my suitors: "I should be grateful to you young lords who are courting me now that King Odysseus is dead, if you could restrain your ardour for my hand till I have done this work, so that the threads I have spun may not be alto-

gether wasted. It is a winding-sheet for Lord Laertes. When he succumbs to the dread hand of Death that stretches all men out at last, I must not risk the scandal that would be among my country women here if one who had amassed such wealth were laid to rest without shroud." They had the grace to consent. So by day I used to weave at the great web, but every night I had torches set beside it and undid the work. For three years they were taken in by this stratagem of mine. A fourth began and the seasons were already slipping by, when they were given the chance by my maids of catching me unaware at my task. They loaded me with reproaches, and I was forced reluctantly to finish the work. Penelope has been working at her weave for several years and the work is now complete.[8]

Homer's description alone is enough to show that Penelope was not weaving a plain fabric on an ordinary warp-weighted loom. As a rule, a loom piece woven on such a loom, common as it was in ancient Greece, should not have taken many days to complete. Tapestry weaving, on the other hand, was a slow job, and the finer the yarn and the more complex the pattern, the slower the work was bound to proceed. If, moreover, the weft yarn was partly undone — which is quite easily accomplished using this technique, but in the long run impossible with a plain weave — it is not unlikely that one could work on a single piece for years on end, especially in the case of a large textile. Furthermore, a shroud for Penelope's revered father-in-law, Laertes, could hardly have been anything but a costly fabric, a richly patterned tapestry.

No doubt the painter of the Chiusi vase was perfectly familiar with the ordinary loom, whose characteristic features are depicted on so many vases in a great variety of ways.[9] On the other hand, the total form of the tapestry loom must have been fairly indifferent to him, unless he wanted to reproduce the design of the woven textile, but this would have disrupted his picture. He therefore produced a compromise, a hybrid of the two implements. Whether the warp threads and weights were included or not, he achieved a calm background for the main scene. The expensive tapestry weave was represented by the border of fabulous beasts and probably too, as has been suggested, by the row of upright pins and balls adorning the uppermost crosspiece, which may well depict an authentic device for keeping the differently coloured weft yarns in order. We have to realize that Penelope's web was a divine web, hence the artist may never have intended to depict an ordinary loom.

Notes

1. A. Conze, "Il ritorno di Ulisse", *Annali dell' Istituto di Corrispondenza Archaeologica*, Rome, 1872; and *Monumenti dell' Istituto*, vol. 8, pl. 42.

2. A. Furtwängler et al., *Griechische Vasenmalerei*, vol. 3, Munich, 1932, pl. 142, p. 124.

3. Helle Salskov Roberts, "Hon sad i sit hus og spandt uld" [She was spinning wool at home], *Nationalmuseets Arbejdsmark* [Yearbook of the Danish National Museum], Copenhagen, 1968, pp. 45–58.

4. O. Olavius, *Oeconomische Reise durch Island*, Dresden and Leipzig, 1787; J. A. A. Worsaae, *Afbildninger fra det Kgl. Museum for nordiske Oldsager i København* [Pictures from the museums of northern antiquities], Copenhagen, 1848.

5. M. Hoffmann, *The warp-weighted loom: Studies in the history and technology of an ancient implement*, Oslo, Universitetsforlaget, 1964, in the series Studia Norvegica, no. 14, p. 315, fig. 133.

6. Hoffmann, *The warp-weighted loom* (1964), "The looms of classical antiquity", pp. 297–336.

7. M. Hald, *Olddanske textiler* [Old Danish textiles], with English summary, Copenhagen, Nordisk Forlag, 1950; M. Hald, "An unfinished tubular fabric from the Chiriguano Indians, Bolivia", The Ethnographical Museum of Sweden, monograph series, Stockholm, 1962; *Jernalderens Dragt*, Copenhagen, Nationalmuseet, 1962; A Geijer, *Ur textilkonstens historia*, Lund, CWK Gleerup, 1972.

8. Homer, *The Odyssey*, a new translation by E. V. Rieu, Penguin Books, 1953, p. 289 f.

9. See Hoffmann, *The warp-weighted loom* (1964), pp. 125-127, 130.

An Early Christian Curtain in the Royal Ontario Museum

Veronika Gervers

THE Royal Ontario Museum possesses a large, light-weight, linen curtain, said to have been found at Akhmim, the ancient Panopolis (fig. 1).[1] Fragments of curtains or hangings have not been uncommon finds in the various Egyptian burial grounds dating from late Roman to Islamic times, but the Toronto piece is certainly one of the largest and best-preserved examples (l. 351–355.5 cm, w. 231–232 cm). The selvages at the sides show that the loom width is complete. The framed decorative frieze at the top, the openwork band (ht. 6.5–7 cm) across the bottom, and the short warp fringes are ample indication that the curtain has retained its original length. A vertical seam along the centre and several patches are signs of ancient repairs.[2]

An 82 cm long fragment of linen tabby is sewn along the upper left selvage. Small fragments of tapestry woven trefoil ornaments can be seen on it opposite the top frieze. In all probability, these belonged to the leaf-meander frame of a similar frieze, suggesting that the upper part of our hanging was joined to an identical curtain to form a pair.[3]

The decoration of the curtain is worked in tapestry weave, principally with black and some faded red, orange, yellow, green, and blue wool[4] against an uneven bleached linen tabby ground.[5] Within the dark figures, many details are freely outlined with an extra weft of bleached linen thread.

Divided into twenty-one cassettes and framed by a simple meander of trefoils around all four sides, a 21–22.3 cm wide frieze runs across the width 31 cm below the top (figs. 9, 10). With the exception of a single bird at the right end, these cassettes are filled with confronting pairs of birds alternating with confronting pairs of animals (lions, lionesses, dogs, leopards). While this type of composition may have originated in drawloom fabrics brought to Egypt from West Asia, the realistic representation of the animals shows that the artist was familiar with his subject.

Underneath this frieze, in eleven registers, an elaborate hunt is represented with numerous horsemen regularly interspersed amongst such somewhat stylized animals as lions and lionesses, leopards, hares, wild goats (*capra ibex* and *capra aegagrus*), and a deer (fig. 2). Only one fabulous animal appears: a griffon in the second register from the top. Foreign to the fauna of North Africa, the deer in the bottom register is treated quite unrealistically. In each row, a galloping horseman is depicted either raising his right hand in a gesture of triumph (fig. 5) or holding in it an unidentified object, not necessarily a weapon. Presumably because his mount might tire or be injured during the hunt, a riderless bridled horse accompanies him as a replacement. Four dogs also participate, in each case following these horses. The figures are separated from one another by a conventionalized tree. Not only do these trees suggest that the hunt is taking place in a wooded landscape, they also project a sense of spatial illusion. There is no attempt, however, to create perspective or indicate distance. Everything is placed in the foreground and the trees simply alternate with the hunters and the animals. In this somewhat monotonous repetition showing neither crowding nor ten-

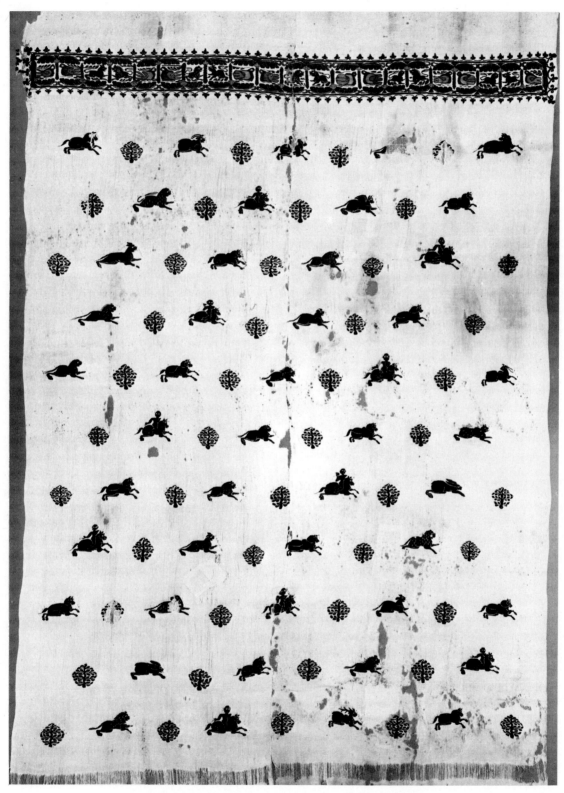

Figure 1. Linen curtain with tapestry woven decoration in
wool. Egypt, sixth century.
ROM acc. no. 910.125.32.

sion, the viewer tends to consider each figure separately, and is thus not disturbed to find a hare as large as a deer or a lion.

Principles of decoration, symmetry, and stylization rather than reality control the separate compositional elements. Although a hunt is represented, the emphasis is not on the scene as a whole but on the supremely rational organization and distribution of its separate elements. Besides their horizontal repetition, the figures and trees of the superimposed registers are arranged vertically into diagonals where lines of trees alternate with lines of animals and lines formed by the repetition of horsemen and horses. These both divide and unite the composition. No motif is placed arbitrarily. Instead, each element falls into its predestined place according to a planned geometrical order. Despite the rigid lines of composition, care was taken to balance everything in consideration of the hunt as a whole. The head of the last animal at the end of some registers turns backwards, drawing the eyes of the viewer towards the left and thus back into the continuation of the scene.

It is certain that collections of patterns existed for weavers as for artists using many different mediums.[6] In addition to the evidence provided by other art forms, the similarity of so many motifs from extant textiles suggests that various compositions of the same subject and such single elements as huntsmen, animals, or floral ornaments were gathered together in these collections. They appear to have been used over considerably long periods, during which time succeeding generations of artists and weavers could refer to them again and again. The craftsmen seldom copied straight from these collections but, according to their needs, skills, mythological knowledge, and the wishes of those who commissioned their works, often created new compositions by borrowing from different designs. Through these copyings and recopyings, the models were transformed and themselves became sources for new creations. As time progressed, these copied versions often resulted in distorted and misunderstood designs.

There can be little doubt that the individual motifs for the ROM curtain were taken from pattern books. The figures of horsemen, bridled horses, various different animals, and trees are all known individually or as part of quite different scenes appear-

ing on the innumerable archaeological textiles found in Egypt. It must be emphasized, however, that the arrangement of these separate elements into a large-scale hunting scene is rare amongst surviving examples. Their composition must have been worked out by an artist before the weaving process began. The size of the cloth on which this composition is set is also most unusual. Though hunting scenes were frequently produced by weavers, most are composed of no more than one or two huntsmen enclosed within the borders of circular or square-shaped medallions. Normally the number of game animals is also limited, and they seldom appear in confrontation with hunters. More frequently they are placed around the horseman in repeating compartments or within the foliage of highly conventionalized scrolls. In this manner they can be connected to the hunt only through the imagination of those who are familiar with their significance. In those few cases where numerous huntsmen are represented, as for example in the *clavus*-bands of some tunics, the hunt is generally inactive, the figures are confined by the geometric narrowness of their borders, and the scale of the design is limited.

Narrative subjects other than hunting scenes are unusual on textiles. If existing textile fragments from curtains or hangings can be considered typical, we may conclude that the most characteristic patterns consisted of repeated conventionalized flowers, rosettes, leaves, stylized birds, or geometric motifs. Such monumental hunts as that depicted on the Toronto curtain are few and far between, yet all similar examples can be associated closely with one another. They will be described and discussed here individually.

Berlin curtain

The Early Christian and Byzantine Collection of the Staatliche Museen in East Berlin (formerly the Kaiser-Friedrich Museum) once housed a curtain very similar to the Toronto example (fig. 3). Of unknown provenance, it came to the museum in 1906, but was totally destroyed by fire during the Second World War.[7]

Made of bleached linen tabby and decorated with tapestry woven ornaments of purple wool, this curtain was 230 cm wide, nearly identical to the width of the ROM piece, and had selvages at either

Figure 2a,b.   Details of figure 1.

Figure 2c.   Detail of figure 1.

side. The pre-war length was 270 cm but it must originally have been a good deal longer. Surviving photographs show that the curtain was sewn together horizontally from three larger sections, possibly the result of an ancient repair.

Particularly striking is the fact that the Berlin curtain depicted a hunting scene almost identical to that on the Toronto specimen. Only eight registers of the hunt were extant, but a reconstruction makes it clear that there were once eleven. With the exception of the two upper rows, in which two bridled horses alternate with wild animals, there is a galloping horseman (fig. 6) in each of the registers accompanied by one or two bridled, riderless horses and two animals. These figural elements alternate with conventionalized trees. Aside from slight differences, the horsemen, horses, animals, and trees are more or less the same as those on the ROM curtain. The reconstruction further demonstrates that the major plan of the design was also similar: diagonals formed by trees alternating with diagonals of horsemen and bridled horses, and of game animals, support the framework of the entire composition. Un-

like the Toronto curtain, however, the finishing openwork band went across the top, and the twenty-one-compartment frieze, framed with a meander of trefoils, ran across the bottom. The compartments of the frieze were nevertheless filled with confronting pairs of similar stylized birds and animals (fig. 11).

Although comparisons of a technical nature can no longer be made, the design, composition, and original size of the Berlin curtain so resemble those of the ROM curtain that one can conclude that they were not only contemporary products of the same workshop but also that they were very likely part of the same set of curtains. Numerous early repairs suggest that they were used during a considerable length of time. When buried, probably as grave goods, they were undoubtedly considered unsuitable and too old for hanging in a building.

Chicago curtain
The Field Museum of Natural History in Chicago possesses a significant portion of another related curtain, also of unknown provenance (fig. 4).[8] Rep-

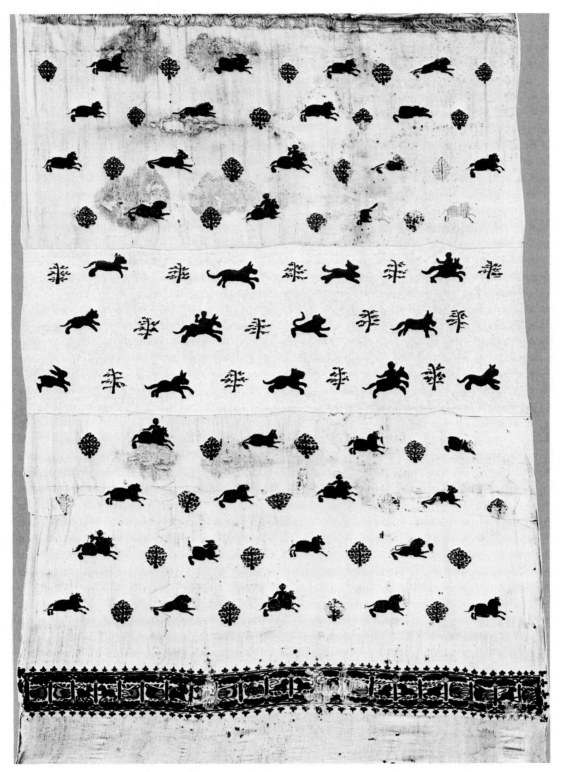

Figure 3.   Linen curtain with tapestry woven decoration in
wool (reconstruction by author). Egypt, sixth century.
Formerly in the Early Christian and Byzantine Collection of
the Staatliche Museen, Berlin, acc. no. 6233. Courtesy of the
Staatliche Museen.

resenting a similar hunting scene in tapestry weave and composed mainly of dark blue with some yellow and red wool against a bleached linen tabby ground, seven horizontal registers of a hunt could be reconstructed from the numerous fragments. In each row, at least one horseman (fig. 7) was depicted amongst wild and fabulous beasts alternating with conventionalized trees. Since this curtain is so incomplete, it is impossible to ascertain either its original length or width.

It has been suggested that a tapestry woven fragment, also in the Field Museum, of blue wool and bleached linen with three compartments depicting a hare within triple-leaved branches, might have belonged to the closing frieze of this curtain (fig. 12).[9] This small surviving detail depicts a design totally different from the friezes of the Toronto or Berlin curtains, but the possibility that it belonged to the other fragments cannot be overlooked.

Although the individual figures of the Chicago hunt are generally similar to those on the Toronto and Berlin curtains, and the conception of the scene together with the compositional order is basically the same, there are some notable differences. All the motifs are drawn in a more rigid and stylized manner. Such details as a lion's mane or the ribbons tied around an animal's neck are totally different. The proportion of fabulous animals appears to have been greater: two griffons are depicted on the relatively small section of the curtain which remains. Even more important is the absence of the riderless bridled horses. As a result, the diagonal construction of the composition consists of lines of mounted horsemen alternating with lines of trees and animals; there is no repetition of order within the diagonals themselves. Also of note is the more prominent use of coloured details. Most colour in the Toronto curtain is concentrated in the closing frieze, and only highlights of blue and red are present on the figures of the horsemen and the horses. On the Chicago fragments, coloured touches are even added to the uppermost leaves of the trees. The small inner details executed freely with an extra weft of bleached linen, so characteristic of both the Toronto and Berlin curtains, are hardly used here.

Depicting a horseman with a tree, two small fragments of unknown provenance in the collection of the Staatliche Museen in Berlin[10] are so similar to the details of the Chicago curtain that they may even have been part of it (fig. 8). Judging from the style, the workshop which produced them could hardly have been the one that executed the Toronto and Berlin hangings. Regardless of similarities in design, the greater stylization of the Chicago piece and the small Berlin fragments might have resulted from the general artistic development of a slightly later period.

With only a limited number of related textiles[11] and without any evidence of provenance, only tenuous conclusions can be drawn from the preceding discussion of similarities and differences based on stylistic comparisons alone. Although these three curtains were probably not the products of a single workshop, the possibility still remains that they may have belonged to a single set. As such sets often included twenty curtains or more, several workshops would undoubtedly have been commissioned to fill an order. Presented with certain iconographical and compositional requirements, each workshop was very likely free to add its own characteristic details. If for economic or other reasons a large set of curtains was produced over a relatively long period of time, style and workmanship could have differed considerably even within a single workshop.

Whether or not they belong to one or two sets, or were manufactured at somewhat different periods, these linen curtains form a definite group from which not only small fragments but complete or almost complete pieces have survived. In this regard they are unique examples of a little-known and rather obscure period in the art of textiles. In order to throw some light on the time when they were woven, and in particular on the subject of their representations, we shall go on to consider the interrelated questions of the iconographic significance of hunting scenes in late Roman and Early Christian times; the changes in the compositional principles of hunting scenes; the dating of the Toronto, Berlin, and Chicago curtains; and finally the function and historical development of curtains in general.

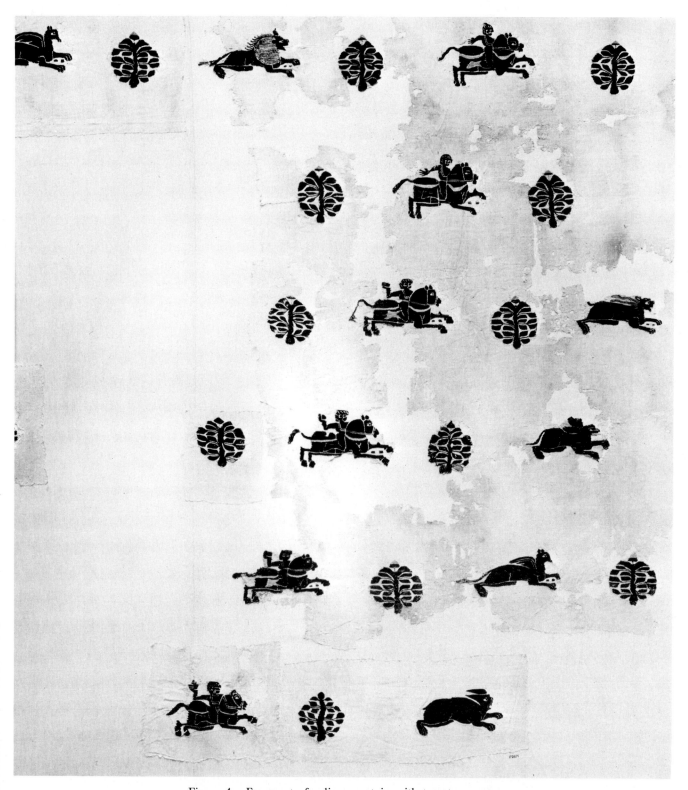

Figure 4. Fragment of a linen curtain with tapestry woven
decoration in wool. Egypt, sixth century.
Field Museum of Natural History, Chicago, acc. no. 173671.
Courtesy of the Field Museum.

Figure 5. Detail of figure 1.

Figure 6. Detail of figure 3.

Hunting Scenes

Iconography

Although it has often been emphasized that the origins of hunting scenes, particularly those carried out on horseback, are to be found in the East, the motif became an integral part of the repertory of Graeco-Roman culture at an early stage. With the exception of such obviously oriental figures as horsemen with bows and arrows, it is unquestionably the classical interpretation of the hunt which remains dominant in the late Roman and Early Christian periods. We need not, therefore, be over-concerned with the possibility of oriental influence when seeking the iconographic background of the hunt as it is represented on our curtains, but must look instead for explanations and analogous material in late classical art and its derivatives.[12]

At a time when narrative scenes became increasingly rare in the art of the Empire as a whole, not only did hunting scenes remain in favour, but their popularity increased. Evidence provided by some of the magnificent floor mosaics is especially important in this regard. Most mosaics were covered not with figural compositions but with single ornamental devices, or with small units of simple patterns repeated over the pavement to give a carpet-like impression. A large group of pavements, however, have survived which form an exception: those with hunting scenes and animals.[13]

At a time when artistic tendencies turned towards conventionalized stylization and preferred ornamental to monumental subjects, only a strong tradition could preserve such iconographical schemes as the hunt. Explanations for this exception can be found through an examination of the hunt's meaning.

In the older formulations, these scenes appeared as part of such great mythological themes as the Calydonian boar-hunt, or the hunt of the divine and heroic Alexander the Great.[14] By the beginning of the Christian era, these specific meanings became less prominent. The huntsman became less and less associated with a specific historical or mythological character, and developed instead into a victorious prince that had little to do with reality. Sitting on horseback and conquering wild animals, he was frequently depicted unarmed, raising his right hand in the gesture of triumph.

There are numerous literary passages, from as early as the first or second century A.D., which help to clarify the meaning of this particular symbolism.[15] In these references, passion, evil, and death are referred to as wild animals; their conquest is frequently interpreted as a victory over wild beasts and as an allegory of human life. The victory of Good over Evil was as much a part of the classical way of thinking as of Christian symbolism, and in the latter case remained an element of iconographic convention for many centuries to come. It may be added that the picturesque subject of the victorious hunt also belonged to the elaborate official cycle of imperial themes in Constantinople, where — in a symbolic sense — such scenes represented the bravery and triumphant strength of the Emperor.[16]

In a period which otherwise avoided narrative subjects, this important, many-faceted symbolic content perpetuated the representation of hunting scenes. There can be little doubt that it is this symbolism which stands behind the elaborate hunts on the Toronto, Berlin, and Chicago curtains. The depiction of triumphant horsemen without weapons underlines the philosophical idea which they import, and removes us one step further from a realistic scene. Suggesting perhaps different vices, the many animals depicted might have been meaningful individually.

The symbolic overtones make it impossible to determine whether this set of curtains was originally intended for the interior of a religious or a secular building. The scene could have been equally meaningful in either case.

Dating

The dating of textiles unearthed in Egypt is a most difficult problem indeed, particularly since their provenance is rarely known and archaeological evidence is usually nonexistent. Owing to the often clandestine excavation which brought them to light for the antique market, or the insufficient documentation of their more professional excavators, none of

Figure 7.   Detail of figure 4.

the some 100,000 textile fragments — housed in both public and private collections — can be properly dated. In this unfortunate situation, scholars who have attempted to determine a chronological sequence could only work on the often insufficient ground of stylistic analysis. After much confusion and uncertainty, two major schools of thought developed. One attempts to associate the pieces as closely as possible with the end of antiquity, while the other favours a wider chronological spread and extends the period up to the twelfth and even thirteenth centuries. Both schools have their strengths and weaknesses, but as far as dating is concerned uncertainty will prevail until scholarly archaeological work is renewed in Egypt on a large scale. The problems are further confused by the contemporaneous existence of important workshops in such centres as Alexandria, and of more provincial centres which produced textiles with different degrees of artistic sensitivity, stylization, and execution. Such differences cannot be properly distinguished without corroborative archaeological data.

In the case of well-designed, iconographically understood representations, one may nevertheless make stylistic comparisons with better-documented art forms which can provide a fruitful point of departure for the dating of textiles. The best analogies to the large-scale hunting scenes of the curtains oc-

cur on mosaic pavements. Although mosaics are rarely dated with inscriptions and while other archaeological evidence is often scarce, their chronological sequence is comparatively well worked out and agreed upon. Thus, since a study of the changes in their compositional development can greatly facilitate our dating of the textiles, we shall examine the characteristics of mosaic composition at the end of classical antiquity and the early Middle Ages, the period during which our curtains must have been made.

From the fourth century there are a number of outstanding examples of mosaic pavement, the most important of which are the Great and Small Hunts of the Piazza Armerina in Sicily, very likely dating from the early part of the century.[17] There is also the Triclinium Pavement of the Constantinian Villa at Antioch, which can be dated to A.D. 325,[18] not to mention some smaller monuments in Rome.[19] Finally, there are the hunting scenes of the Triclinium from Apamea, believed to have been made at the end of the century, but judging from the quality perhaps earlier.[20] Composed for viewing from multiple directions, all these mosaics bear certain common characteristics. Since the entire floor space is treated as a single unit, they generally have no subdivisions. Each detail is carefully drawn. Signs of Hellenistic illusionism may be traced in the shad-

Figure 8. Fragment of a linen curtain with tapestry woven decoration in wool. Egypt, sixth century.
Staatliche Museen, Berlin, acc. no. 6237. Courtesy of the Staatliche Museen.

ows, in the depiction of the figures in profile, three-quarter view, or facing outwards, and in the realistic landscapes. While details can be looked at as separate units, they seldom stand alone. An organic and dynamic strength in the composition leads the viewer from one figure to another with a movement which is almost artificially arrested by the borders of the mosaics.

In the fifth century, changes occurred which affected not only the execution of details but the compositional principles as well. Some of the Antioch floor mosaics, as for example the Megalopsychia Hunt of the Yakto villa (ca. 450)[21] or the Worcester[22] and Dumbarton Oaks hunts[23] of ca. 500, show clearly that while the pavement is still considered as a whole, the design has become more rigid and repetitive. There is a good deal less realism in the depiction of men and animals. Nature is present only in the form of conventionalized stage scenery. Shades and shadows are rare. No longer dynamic, the composition becomes geometric, a tendency emphasized by trees placed diagonally or straight in the corners of the mosaic or the centre of its sides. Practically any detail could be lifted out from the surface and replaced by another element without changing the basic scene.

By the sixth century the realism of the past had been almost completely abandoned, with the result that tendencies towards stylization and repetition were further emphasized. The new principles of mediaeval art were about to be born. Two major mosaics from this period must be mentioned here. One, the Hunt of the Amazons from Apamea, may date from the first half of the century.[24] Shown in a schematic frontal view, almost identical Amazons are here represented on horseback, alternating with stylized trees and separated by them. There is no coherence in this composition; each figure is perfectly independent. The very same elements could be repeated vertically as well as horizontally without creating a major change in the overall impression.

The other mosaic is from the Great Palace of the Byzantine emperors in Constantinople.[25] Recent research places it towards the end of the century, and the suggestion has been made that it may have formed part of the building programme of Tiberius II (578–582). Classical principles based on old standards can still be seen in the sensitive depiction of details, but even more striking is the totally innovative composition of the pavement as a whole. Without subdivisions, the figures are placed in three superimposed longitudinal registers against the dominant whiteness of a plain background. The individual elements are completely unassociated with one another. Though trees and other landscape ele-

67

ments appear here and there, they do not suggest a coherent background in which the many separate activities take place. Instead, they underline the general importance of a measured balance which must have been the major interest of the artist.

While there are many differences between these two sixth-century mosaic pavements, they nevertheless have definite affinities in their principles of composition, the degrees of stylization, and the love for repetition. Whether as a result of careful attention to detail and lack of concern for connecting the separate elements of the design into a "story", or of the unimaginative repetition of similar motifs forming the overall effect, there is a sense of rigid abstractness in both pieces. Within these lines of endless, unbordered repetitions, where the narrative aspect is not only lost but considered unimportant, a strange geometric order is created. The landscape elements are uniquely used as compositional divisions.

The principles that inspired the decoration of our curtains are similar to those of these sixth-century mosaics. Totally different from the ideals of previous centuries, they all show a new artistic preference for the geometric arrangement of figural elements, and break away from the old traditions of Hellenistic illusionism and reality. Neither curtains nor mosaics could have been produced before A.D. 500, yet based as they are on strong classical antecedents, they do not fit into the more mediaeval and "western" concept of style which belongs to the period after 600.

According to style, composition, classical ties, and iconographical programme, the Toronto, Berlin, and Chicago curtains fit into the art of the sixth century. The artistic excellence of their design and the abstract nature of their monumental composition are representative of first-quality examples from the period. Thus they must have been the products of outstanding workshops in an important centre of Egypt, where the craftsmen were aware of and open to new tendencies and changes in international style. They did not simply copy, but were able to apply innovative ideas to the general compositional trends of the new styles.

Function and Historical Development of Curtains

Although it is presumed that light-weight curtains with woven or applied decoration must have been used in religious and secular architecture during the entire period of classical antiquity, they were not depicted in artistic representations or referred to in written sources before late Roman times. It was then, particularly in the Early Christian period, that their popularity seems to have greatly increased even though they were not used solely by Christians.

It is clear from artistic representations as well as from archaeological evidence that in the synagogues curtains were placed in front of the Torah shrine from at least the third century A.D. These curtains replaced the carved screen which was formerly used to separate the world of man from heaven. Formerly, with the screen, the sacred symbols and the shrine itself were brought out to the worshipper, while in the later period both would be revealed when the curtains were opened.[26] The earliest evidence for such curtains is from the synagogue of Dura Europos in Syria (A.D. 245), where the supports for the curtain rods were found.[27] Similar remains have been discovered in Beth Alpha[28] and the island of Aegina.[29]

The curtains are frequently depicted on wall paintings, mosaics, and amongst the minor arts. Symbolizing heaven, a third-century A.D. wall painting of a Jewish catacomb in Rome (Villa Torlonia) exhibits an open Torah shrine flanked by two menorahs underneath the two sides of a looped curtain.[30] Fringed, patterned curtains, presumably made of linen with tapestry woven ornaments, are represented hanging in the arch of the shrine on the mosaic floors of two Palestinian synagogues, one at Beth Alpha,[31] and another at Beth Shean.[32] The ornaments and general appearance of these curtains are reminiscent of actual textile fragments unearthed in Egypt, and of curtains depicted in Christian art.[33]

As Richard Krautheimer has clearly explained, the liturgy required a number of distinctly separate

Figure 9. Detail of figure 1.

Figure 10. Detail of figure 1.

Figure 11. Detail of figure 3.

Figure 12. Fragment of a linen curtain with tapestry woven
decoration in wool. Egypt, sixth century.
Field Museum of Natural History, Chicago, acc. no. 173942.
Courtesy of the Field Museum.

sections within the churches or the Christian meeting rooms. During the early centuries, part of the
building was usually accessible even to non-believ-
ers and postulants. Other provisions were made for
the numerous *catechumens* who, though under instruction and not yet baptized, could attend part of
the service, but had to withdraw during the mass.
The faithful themselves were often divided into
groups, men and women occupying different places.
Usually raised above the congregation, the clergy
had its specific area around the altar. These divisions were most frequently created by the use of
screens or the even more manageable curtains.[34] If
nowhere else, textile hangings separated the clergy
from the congregation, that is to say the sanctuary
from the nave.[35] Draped curtains concealed the altar tables from the eyes of the believers. That these
elements were common at least as early as the
fourth century is clear from two independent
sources which describe the donation by Emperor
Valens (364 – 378) of precious gifts to the church of
Caeserea (Kayseri) in Cappadocia. Gregory of Na-
zyance relates that Valens "passed through the curtain, thus coming within Basil's sight and hearing".
Théodoret describes the same episode: "And Basil
invited him to enter inside the divine curtains where
he was seated."[36] We also know that around A.D. 400
the baldachin above the shrine of Saint Peter in the
church of San Pietro in Rome was linked by archi-
traved columns to the corners of the apse, whose
opening was closed by pairs of curtains.[37]

The custom of separating sections of religious

buildings with curtains continued into the later centuries. When the Hagia Sophia in Constantinople
was built (532 – 537), such curtains received an
even more elaborate symbolic role. In this most
monumental church of all, the aisles and galleries
were half-hidden behind screens and curtains, and
the large crowds of the faithful who gathered there
could catch only glimpses of the building's magnificence and the religious ceremonies. Only those who
were allowed to enter the nave and the chancel,
that is, the Patriarch with the clergy and the Emperor with his court, were permitted to see the entire spatial design of the church. Members of the
clergy nevertheless remained inside the chancel
most of the time, where they were completely hidden by curtains and columns. Except during proces-
sions and ceremonials in which they participated
with the clergy, the Emperor and his court also
stayed within the curtained imperial enclosure. Already at the time of Justinian (527–565), the Eu-
charist was celebrated behind the drawn curtains of
the ciborium which enclosed the altar.[38]

Numerous artistic depictions in various mediums
from as early as the third and fourth centuries show
how the curtains were hung from rings attached to
rods in doorways as well as between interior pillars
and columns. In the latter cases, light-weight examples — particularly those made of linen — were often twisted around or fastened in some other way to
the pillars, or were tied in a large knot hanging
down in the centre of the arch. In many early
churches the emplacement for these curtain rods

70

may still be seen above the entrance doorways and the capitals. In others, the actual metal rods have survived.[39]

The best curtain representations appear on mosaics, where they are frequently depicted in nearly life-size proportions with every detail of their decoration. On the apse mosaics from San Vitale in Ravenna (consecrated in 547), which show the empress Theodora and her ladies-in-waiting being led into the church by an official, a knotted curtain pulled towards the left hangs in the doorway.[40] It is everywhere adorned with multicoloured rosettes, while the corners and borders are emphasized in gold. Elsewhere smaller, stylized, many-petalled flower heads, or stripes, squares, diamonds, and decorative bands, appear against the white ground of such curtains. Again in Ravenna, in the church of San Apollinare Nuovo (500-526), the Palace of Theoderic is represented by the arcades of its peristyle.[41] Originally Theoderic himself and his highest court dignitaries were depicted in these arches, but as a result of the restoration ordered by Justinian in the second half of the sixth century, the figures were replaced by the representation of a set of what one may presume to have been linen curtains adorned with tapestry woven ornaments. The pairs of curtains in the three central arches appear larger than the single flanking knotted ones at the sides. The central pair bears golden decoration with emphasized squares enclosing a medallion in the upper corners. Fringed and with golden borders, the other curtains are covered with red and green rosettes. This is an excellent representation of such curtain sets, and an important demonstration that secular as well as religious buildings were decorated with these magnificent textiles.

Religious figures and laymen alike seem to have received special honour by being represented in curtained arches. Just as the most distinguished archbishops of Ravenna are depicted below pairs of curtains on the mosaics of the Presbyterium in San Apollinare in Classe (533–549),[42] emperors, empresses, consuls, mythological figures, and saints appear in similar settings on many ivory carvings [43] as well as in early book illustrations.[44] This predeliction for representing honoured personages between open curtains in architectural settings remained in fashion for a considerable period of time. Until about the tenth century the four evangelists and certain favoured saints were depicted again and again on the pages of illuminated manuscripts sitting under curtained arches.[45] Even in this late period, the depiction of the curtains, the way they hang on rods placed above the capitals of the architectural frame and the manner in which they are pulled and fastened to the sides of columns or pillars, is astonishingly accurate. This realism, however, is seldom noticed by mediaeval art historians, who tend to emphasize the somewhat abstract nature of the whole picture and consider the curtains as conventionalized iconographical forms stemming more or less directly from a classical heritage.[46] Although these representations convey past traditions, we strongly believe that they denote more than the survival of an old convention. Even if coloured by formality and the rigid trends of Byzantine influences, they may be interpreted as idealized depictions of a contemporary reality, in which the major churches at least must have been draped with curtains, and when bishops, priests, and members of religious orders could be seen daily in that context. Had this not been the case, it is doubtful whether the artists could have understood so precisely how such curtains were hung: one would have expected instead to find some misrepresentations.

Indeed, during a considerable period of time, the abundance of curtains and hangings is obvious not only from their liturgical roles, from their frequent appearance in the major and minor arts, and from those thousands of textile fragments that were found in Egypt, but also from written documents.

Writing between 395 and 407, Saint Paulinus of Nola (b. ca. 353, d. 431) described those who brought precious gifts to his church at Nola (near Naples) on 14 January, the feast day of Saint Felix. Amongst these offerings were splendid curtains, some made of pure linen, and others adorned with figures presumably entered in tapestry weave:

> Cedo, alii pretiosa ferant donaria meque
> officii sumptu superent, qui pulchra tegendis
> *uela* ferant foribus, seu puro splendida lino
> siue coloratis textum fucata figuris.
> hi leues titulos lento poliant argento
> santaque praqfixis obducant limina lamnis.[47]

From the foundation charter dated 471 of a country church near Tivoli, we learn that in addition to the large number of silk curtains, this relatively small church had over forty others made from linen. They are described in detail: "*vela* linea auroclava clavatura quadras duo", "*vela* linea auroclava paragaudata clavaturas rotundas II", "*vela* linea paragaudata persica clavatura coccumellino prasinas duo", "*vela* linaea paragaudata persica clavatura subtile leucordina duo", "*vela* linea blactosima ortopluma II", "*vela* linea pura XIIII", "*vela* linea plumata maiora fissa numera tria", "*vela* linea rosulata VI", etc.[48]

In his famous mid-sixth-century description of the Hagia Sophia in Constantinople, Paulus Silentiarius described the presumably silk curtains commissioned by Justinian which hung between the four golden columns of the ciborium. According to this description, biblical figures were woven or embroidered onto the curtains in golden yarn and multicoloured Chinese silks. Richly embroidered in a similar manner, a mantle covered the silver altar table underneath the ciborium and unfurled veils were stretched over its four sides.[49]

Written testimony further illustrates that curtains of this type continued to serve the same purpose for many centuries to come. The *Liber Pontificalis* is an especially rich source of information for the churches of Rome, where sets of treasured curtains were so numerous they could be constantly alternated. Some churches owned hundreds, many of which were made of oriental or Byzantine silks. Since these showed the wealth of the famous basilicas, the descriptions emphasize the silk and those ornamented in gold or silver threads or precious stones. The more common linen curtains are mentioned less frequently. Inventories commonly list what appear to have been complementary sets of silk and linen curtains, usually consisting of twenty hangings each. Such double sets were systematically described during the time of Pope Hadrian (772–795):

Fecit et in basilica Apostolorum in via Lata *vela* de palleis siricis numero XX et linea XX . . . Nam et in ecclesia beate Dei genetricis ad martyres simili modo fecit *vela* de palleis siricis numero XX et linea XX. Item isdem santissimus pontifex fecit per diversa titula *vela* de stauracim seu tyrea, per unum que titulum numero XX et linea XX.[50]

Churches of the north were furnished along similar lines. According to the *Gesta Dagoberti*, written by a monk between 621 and 662, the entire nave of Saint-Denis near Paris was hung with gold-embroidered fabrics set with pearls.[51] At the beginning of the ninth century, there were more than eighty *pallia* and curtains at Saint Riquier, twenty at Saint Wandrille, forty at Flavigny, thirty-five at Marchienne, and twenty at Clermont. All were intended either for the walls, arches, and doors of these churches, or to decorate the altars and tombs of the saints.[52]

Written sources further indicate where in the churches these curtains were placed. The *Charta Cornutiana* lists curtains "ante consistorium", "in pronao", "intra basilica, pro portica", and "ante secretarium".[53] From the *Liber Pontificalis*, we may ascertain more precisely the functions of the curtains, their placement, and the relative importance of their material and decoration. From the time of Popes John VI (701-705)[54] and Zacharia (741-745)[55] we read of curtains hung in the churches "inter columnas" . Under Pope Hadrian (772-795)[56] curtains occur "per diversos arcos". Many other positions are listed during the time of Pope Leo III (795-816):[57] "pendent in arcora minores", "quae pendent in arcora X et alia X", "in circuito altaris", "*vela* modica quae pendent in regularem ante imagines", or "qui pendent ante regias maiores". Similar descriptions are known from the time of Pope Paschal (817-824),[58] when they are mentioned "per arcos presbiterii" or "in arcus presbiterii", "in circuito altaris", "in arcos maiores", and "ante imaginem". From the time of Pope Gregory IV (827-844)[59] we read of curtains "quae pendent per arcos ecclesiae", "ante portas maiores pendentia", "pendentem in regularem sub imaginem argentam", "quae pendent in circuito altaris", "quae pendent in presbiterium" or "per arcos presbiterii", and "quae pendent in arcos maiories".

These written references not only clarify our discussion of curtain representations, but also strengthen our conclusions concerning the realism of early and late artistic depictions alike. They present conclusive evidence for the survival of classical traditions and uses, and prove that we are not dealing here with an ancient iconographical scheme quite divorced from reality.[60]

When, in fact, does this tradition end? When did the curtains disappear from the churches, leaving a new environment for the development of architectural form? When did the curtains appearing in artistic representations become part of iconographic conventions instead of being stylized interpretations of contemporary church interiors?

From a study of many art forms, manuscript illumination in particular, it would seem that in the West the change probably took place some time during the tenth century, certainly before the year 1000. Although most representations from this period still tend to be realistic, a change may be noted in a French manuscript written and illustrated at Saint Bertin ca. 1000.[61] Profusely placed in the elaborate architectural frame of some of the miniatures, curtains are shown hanging directly from the curves of the arches instead of from a rod, a manner which would have rendered them quite unfunctional in life. They are often knotted, as though around a column, but the knots are simply decorative spirals which are seldom attached to the architecture. As far as we have been able to determine, this is the first instance in which the artist apparently had no first-hand knowledge of his subject. From this time on the hangings become purely decorative elements used to fill a background space. It can hardly be coincidental that descriptions of curtains also disappear from western documents at this time.

While at first these representations were no more than misunderstood interpretations of earlier works, from the eleventh century they became part of a new iconographic form in themselves. As a result the misrepresentations served as sources for new conventions. Their setting invariably formed according to the rules of ornamentation and line harmony, curtains were regularly hung illogically. In a Canterbury miniature of about 1070 representing Saint Jerome seated in an arch,[62] the background curtain is not only attached to the top of the arch-curve in a most haphazard way, but is twisted upon itself and hangs towards the right without being directed there by anything other than the forces of the composition. Depictions of these unrealistic, ornamental curtains continue well into the twelfth century, as is demonstrated on the whalebone Adoration of the Magi produced by a Channel workshop ca. 1100;[63] in the mid-twelfth-century illuminations of the Great Lambeth Bible,[64] an English manuscript showing strong Byzantine influence; or in the English Winchester Psalter [65] of ca. 1129 x 1171. All these examples follow the eleventh-century tradition. Together with the architectural settings, curtains represented here can be considered no more than abstract parts of a conventional stage scenery serving as a backdrop for the predetermined iconographical performance of the "actors". [66]

By the thirteenth century, when the historical origins of the curtains are further misunderstood, new elements appear which lead towards a new reality. Numerous plain curtains occur in the background of various scenes from an illustrated manuscript of the Old Testament begun in Paris ca. 1250, and possibly completed in Naples around 1300.[67] Though in most cases these curtains hang unnaturally, one element of their setting is particularly important: instead of flanking notable figures or important scenes, as was their major function in the art of the previous centuries, they are invariably above or in connection with a bed. Thus, although they may still relate iconographically to certain schemes of the past, these curtains are entirely dissociated from those which once served to decorate church interiors. Instead, they depict contemporary bed-curtains.

One may conclude from the foregoing that the classical custom of hanging light-weight curtains in the interior of religious and secular buildings alike disappeared with the rise of the Romanesque in countries dominated by the western Church. In the realm of the eastern Churches, however, the tradition of these curtains continued for a longer, as yet undetermined period. In such remote areas of Christianity as Ethiopia, fringed, often colourful curtains can still be seen in manuscripts of the seventeenth and eighteenth centuries. [68] That the stylized depictions in the miniatures are not merely the result of an ancient iconographical convention may be ascertained from the fact that large, light-weight curtains are frequently hung in Ethiopian churches up to the present day. In the rock-cut churches of Chergos Wugro, Abreha Atsbeha, Debra Ma'ar, or Tamba Mariam (Tigré Province), lengths of printed cotton hung between the pillars of the aisles, or were used to separate the sanctuary from the nave, in the 1960s.[69] Although made of cheap, individually unspectacular factory-woven materials, these curtains are important for our study since they are placed in exactly the same positions as the curtains seen on ancient representations and known from written sources. In Ethiopia, they are the late and somewhat decadent descendants of a tradition which goes back for more than a millennium, to the time when some of these churches were built.[70] This Ethiopian continuity is a local phenomenon, however, which—as far as we know— has parallels only from northern Mesopotamia.[71]

Curtains in the Greek Orthodox Church must have had a somewhat longer life than they did in the West. The pictured walls of the iconostases developed from those textile enclosures which hung between the colonettes of the choir and which were originally decorated with woven or embroidered ornaments.[72] Whether or not the doors of the iconostases are adorned with panelled wings, curtains are still placed in them as late descendants of this custom.

Probably owing to Byzantine tradition, curtains (generally referred to as *sutūr*) also played an important role in the culture of the Islamic world. They are mentioned in a secular context in innumerable mediaeval documents and are frequently depicted in the architectural framework of miniature painting.[73] In such representations, as in Christian art, they are pulled to the colonettes and are knotted or twisted around them. They are adorned with inscription or other decorative bands, and appear to have been made of plain fabrics or figured silks. The sources often refer to curtains of fine materials, such as ḳazz silk, adorned with inscriptions, and provide sufficient evidence for interpreting these depictions as reflections of contemporary reality rather than as copies of Byzantine models.

We learn from Khaṭib al-Baghdadi's (b. A.D. 1071) *History of Baghdad* that at the time of the Abbasids in the tenth century:

The number of curtains which hung in the palaces of the Caliph al-Muqtadir [A.D. 908-932] totalled 38,000. These consisted of gold brocade curtains embroidered with gold and magnificently adorned with representations of goblets, elephants, horses and camels, lions and birds. The curtains included large drapes of single and variegated colors from Baṣinnā, Armenia, Wasit, and Bahnasā, as well as embroidered drapes from Dabiq.[74]

It is also known that al-Muqtadir had Baṣinnā

curtains displayed for the visit of a Byzantine ambassador.[75]

Other documents describe the actual function of these curtains in special palace ceremonies. We read that when receiving visitors other than important foreign ambassadors in an Islamic court, "the prince usually sat at one end of the *majlis* [audience hall] on a large bench-like throne. . . . There was no organized ceremony of arrival and departure, although some Umayyad princes already liked initially to have a curtain drawn between themselves and their audience."[76] The custom was maintained through subsequent centuries.

Curtains were also used in the *majlis al-lahwah*, a place for entertainment and pleasure. It was this section of the palace that "the future al-Walid II [A.D. 743] had a curtain drawn across a pool filled with wine and jumped in after each song performed by a singer on the other side of the curtain."[77]

Curtains served as furnishings in the houses of the wealthy and the privileged. Al-Washshā' (d. ca. A.D. 936-937) mentions that in Fars, these were usually decorated with amatory verses, some of which he transcribed.[78]

While almost nothing is known about the use of curtains in religious buildings or in connection with religious services, the coverings used for the Kaaba in Mecca, many of which were manufactured in various Egyptian workshops, have been interpreted as curtains.[79]

Arab historians and geographers also mention the centres in which the best-known curtains were produced. In Egypt, Bahnasā of the Fayyum was especially famous for its curtains. Ibn Ḥawkal (wr. A.D. 977-978) remarked that these were adorned with figures of different animals, and "made with wool, linen, and dyes that do not fade". He also noted that "the length of a single one. . .was thirty dhirā. . .and the price of a pair. . .was about three hundred dinars".[80] Idrisī (work completed A.D. 1154) further commented that "no curtains. . .are made there without the names of the ṭirāz factories being placed upon them . . . a prescribed custom which the preceding age established", and added that "these curtains . . . are renowned throughout the earth".[81] We learn from Maḳrīzī (d. A.D. 1442) that in the neighbouring district of Kais, similar curtains were produced.[82]

Curtains and hangings were also manufactured in the eastern provinces of the Caliphate. In Khuzistan, Baṣinnā was the most celebrated of weaving centres. These stuffs always seem to be mentioned in connection with the courts of the rulers. Iṣṭak̲h̲rī (wr. A.D. 951-952) noted that "in Baṣinnā there are made the curtains which are taken to all regions with 'amal Baṣinnā' manufacture of Baṣinnā written upon them". He added that curtains are "sometimes made in Bird̲h̲awn and Kalīwān and other such towns. . . with 'Baṣinnā' written on them", which are "sold as Baṣinnā curtains".[83] Maḵdisī (wr. A.D. 958-959) goes on to note: "In the environs of Wāsiṭ, curtains are made on which there is written 'mimmā ꜥumila bī-Baṣinnā'; these are exported as coming from that place, but they are not like them".[84]

Amongst other places curtains were also woven in Fars (D̲jahram, Fasā),[85] Transoxonia (sold in the bazaar of Tīrmāh),[86] Iraq (Tigris district, Sawād, Maisān, Dast Maisān, Wāsiṭ),[87] and northern Mesopotamia (Mosul).[88]

Summary

Through a study of the large sixth-century linen curtain in the Royal Ontario Museum and the iconographic programme of the victorious hunt which adorns it, we have attempted to place this and related pieces in their historical perspective. They are interesting in themselves as the remnants of one or two major sets, and as possibly the largest surviving textiles of their kind from the period. The problems which they present are far-reaching and raise questions beyond those of origins, dating, manufacture, and geographic distribution. Although they were probably the works of Egyptian craftsmen, one would be quite misled to consider them solely under the generally accepted but far too broad category of Coptic art. They are outstanding examples of an international style born at the juncture of classical antiquity and the Middle Ages: a style which differed little between Alexandria, Rome, Ravenna, and Constantinople. It is, however, due to the favourable climatic conditions of Egypt, the dry heat and the sandy soil, that these textiles have survived, and it is in fact through the material unearthed in Egypt that we are able to interpret the contemporary textile art of a much wider geographic area.

We have seen that such textiles were important furnishings of religious and secular buildings alike at least from late Roman times until well into the Middle Ages. In such isolated places as Ethiopia and north Mesopotamia their descendants have remained in use to the present day.

A vast quantity of historical and iconographical material covering a millennium had to be considered in the preparation of this brief but broad examination. Choosing examples to illustrate the most important aspects of the subject was a difficult task, and we have been obliged by limitations of space to exclude numerous references to pertinent representations and written sources. This article is restricted therefore to a discussion of general trends. It will, we hope, serve as an impetus for further research on the historical background and development of textile hangings, without which few early churches, synagogues, and Byzantine or Islamic palaces can be imagined.

Acknowledgments

I wish to acknowledge my gratitude to those who in various ways contributed to the content of this study. I am particularly indebted to Mrs. Dorothy K. Burnham, ROM; Professor C.S. Churcher, University of Toronto; Professor Robert Deshman, University of Toronto; Dr. Lisa Golombek, ROM; Mrs. Rezan Gökçen, Toronto; Mrs. Neda Leipen, ROM; and Dr. Deborah Thompson, Dumbarton Oaks. I am especially thankful to Dr. Arne Effenberger of the Staatliche Museen, Berlin, and Miss Eva A. Ziemba of the Field Museum of Natural History, Chicago, who provided me with photographs and information concerning material related to the Toronto curtain. I am grateful to Mr. W. B. Robertson and Mr. B. Boyle, ROM, for photographing the Toronto curtain. I would also like to thank the Reverend Walter M. Hayes of the Pontifical Institute of Mediaeval Studies, Toronto, who kindly translated the relevant passages from Paulus Silentiarius' description of the Hagia Sophia.

Notes

1. Acc. no. 910.125.32, The Walter Massey Collection, acquired by Dr. Charles Trick Currelly in Egypt between 1905 and 1907. The following reference by Currelly may concern this curtain : "We have two fine Roman curtains and fragments of a number of others. These were found, with a few costumes, folded up in the tombs of a colony of weavers at Aachmim". (*I brought the ages home*, Toronto , Ryerson Press, 1956, reprinted by the Royal Ontario Museum, 1976, p. 286).

2. The patches all appear to be of the same linen tabby with triple bands of heavier wefts, and were undoubtedly applied at the same time.

3. Artistic representations provide additional evidence for the existence of such curtain pairs. See for example the three central curtain pairs on the mosaic depicting the Palace of Theoderic at S. Apollinare Nuovo, Ravenna (A. Grabar, *La peinture byzantine* , Geneva, Skira, 1953, p. 56).

4. S-twist, count : 6–8 warps in alternating groups of double and triple threads by 20–34 wefts per cm.

5. S-twist, count : 13–24 warps by 7–10 wefts per cm, near selvages 24–30 warps by 8–10 wefts per cm.

6. Concerning pattern books, see D. Levi, *Antioch mosaic pavements*, vol. 1, *Publications of the Committee for the Excavation of Antioch and its Vicinity*, no. 4, Princeton, N.J., Princeton University Press, 1947, pp. 8-10. A fifth-century A.D. design for the decoration of a tunic, painted on papyrus, is in the collection of the Victoria and Albert Museum, London (acc. no. T15-1946, gift of Prof. P. Newberry).

7. Acc. no. 6233, gift of the Freiherrn von Jenisch. Bibliography : O. Wulff and W. F. Volbach, *Spätantike und koptische Stoffe aus ägyptischen Grabfunden in den Staatlichen Museen, Kaiser-Friedrich-Museum, Ägyptisches Museum, Schliemann-Sammlung*, Berlin, Ernst Wasmuth, 1926, p. 45, pl. 71; W. F. Volbach and E. Kuehnel, *Late antique, Coptic and Islamic textiles of Egypt*, London, W. & G. Foyle, 1926, pl. 3; *Frühchristlich-byzantinische Sammlung*, Staatliche Museen in Berlin, Kaiser-Friedrich-Museum, Berlin, 1938, pp. 58-59, 78; K. Wessel, *Die Kultur von Byzanz*, in the series *Handbuch der Kulturgeschichte*, Frankfurt am Main, Athenaion, 1970, fig. 66; letter by Dr. Arne Effenberger, Director of the Frühchristlich-byzantinische Sammlung, Staatliche Museen zu Berlin (27.6.1974).

8. Acc. no. 173671, received 1 July 1925, as part of the André Bircher collection (selected by James Breasted, acc. 1596, specimen no. 568).

9. Acc. no. 173942, received 1 July 1925, as part of the André Bircher collection (selected by James Breasted).

10. Acc. nos. 6237 (bleached linen tabby with tapestry woven ornaments in purple, red, and yellow wool. Ht. 22 cm, w. 48 cm. Gift of the Freiherrn von Jenisch, 1906) and 9171 (bleached linen tabby with tapestry woven ornaments in purple, red, and yellow wool. Ht. 25 cm, w. 48 cm. Reinhardt Collection, 1900). Bibliography : Wulff and Volbach, *Spätantike und koptische Stoffe* (1926), p. 45, pl. 52; *Umetnost kopta*, Narodni Muzej, Belgrade, Drzavani Muzej, Berlin, Belgrade, 1970, pp. 47, 48, nos. 113, 114 (introduction by Günther Bröker, catalogue of the exhibition "Coptic Art" organized by the Berlin State Museum's Early Christian and Byzantine Department).

11. Three fragments in the Musée du Louvre, Paris, show similarities with the friezes of the Toronto and Berlin curtains. See Pierre du Bourguet, *Musée National du Louvre : Catalogue des étoffes coptes*, 1, Editions des Musées Nationaux, 1964, D140-141, pp. 172-3 (dated to the seventh century), and E121, p. 233 (dated to the eighth century).

12. That the horsemen represented on the Toronto, Berlin, and Chicago curtains are dressed not in tunics but in characteristic Persian riding coats and boots does not necessarily indicate the direct influence of Persian art. Such garments are known from Antinoë (Antinopolis) in Egypt; see A. Geijer, "An Iranian riding coat reconstructed", *Bulletin de liaison du Centre International d'Étude des Textiles Anciens*, no. 27 (1968), pp. 22-25; Wulff and Volbach, *Spätantike und koptische Stoffe* (1926), p. 137, pl. 126 (Berlin, Staatliche Museen, acc. no. 14231); M. Tilke, *Costume patterns and designs : A survey of costume patterns and designs of all periods and nations from antiquity to modern times*, New York, Praeger, 1956, pl. 4/5.

13. Levi, *Antioch mosaic pavements*, vol. 1 (1947), p. 613; E. Kitzinger, "Stylistic developments in pavement mosaics in the Greek East from the age of Constantine to the age of Justinian", *La mosaique gréco-romaine, Colloques Internationaux du Centre National de la Recherche Scientifique* (Paris, 29 Aug.–3 Sept. 1963), Paris, Centre National de la Recherche Scientifique, 1965, pp. 341-352.

14. Levi, *Antioch mosaic pavements*, vol. 1 (1947), pp. 237, 240, 340.

15. G. Downey, "The Pilgrim's Progress of the Byzantine Emperor", *Church History*, vol. 9 (1940), pp. 207 f; R. Eisler, *Orphisch-dionysische Mysteriengedanken in der christlichen Antike* (London, University, Warburg Inst., Vorträge der Bibliothek Warburg, 2, 1922-1923), reprografischer Nachdruck der Ausg. Leipzig & Berlin (1925), Hildesheim, G. Olms, 1966, pp. 71 f; E. Kitzinger, "Studies on late antique and early Byzantine floor mosaics, I, Mosaics at Nikopolis", *Dumbarton Oaks Papers*, no. 6 (1951), pp. 117-118 and notes 148-150; Levi, *Antioch mosaic pavements*, vol. 1 (1947), pp. 340-341. G. Downey pointed out that this type of interpretation of the hunting scene first appears in a passage of the *Pinax* by Cebes, a work from the first or early second century A.D. Here the struggle against intemperance, ig-

norance, error, and all vices as a whole is compared with the victorious hunt against every kind of wild animal.

16. A. Grabar, *L'empereur dans l'art byzantin, Recherches sur l'art officiel de l'Empire d'Orient*, in *Publications de la Faculté des Lettres de l'Université de Strasbourg*, fasc. 75, Paris, Les Belles Lettres, 1936, pp. 57-62, 133-144.

17. I. Lavin, "The hunting mosaics of Antioch and their sources — A study of compositional principles in the development of early mediaeval style", *Dumbarton Oaks Papers*, no. 17 (1963), pp. 244-251; G. V. Gentili, *La villa imperiale di Piazza Armerina*, in *Itinerari dei musei e monumenti d'Italia*, no. 87, Rome, 1954 (2d ed.); G. V. Gentili, *La Villa Erculia di Piazza Armerina, I mosaici figurati*, Rome, Mediterranee, 1959; G. V. Gentili, *Mosaics of the Piazza Armerina : The hunting scenes*, Milano, Arti Grafiche Ricordi, 1964; B. Pace, *I mosaici di Piazza Armerina*, Rome, 1955.

18. Levi, *Antioch mosaic pavements*, vol. 1 (1947), pp. 226 f., particularly pp. 236-244; Lavin, "The hunting mosaics of Antioch" (1963), pp. 190-193.

19. Lavin, "The hunting mosaics of Antioch" (1963), pp. 251-260.

20. Lavin, "The hunting mosaics of Antioch" (1963), pp. 270-271; J. Balty, *La grande mosaique de chasse du Triclinos*, Brussels, Centre Belge de Recherches Archéologiques à Apamée de Syrie, 1969.

21. Levi, *Antioch mosaic pavements*, vol. 1 (1947), pp. 326-345; Lavin, "The hunting mosaics of Antioch" (1963), pp. 189-190.

22. Levi, *Antioch mosaic pavements*, vol. 1 (1947), pp. 363-365; Lavin, "The hunting mosaics of Antioch" (1963), p. 190.

23. Levi, *Antioch mosaic pavements*, vol. 1 (1947), pp. 358-359; Lavin, "The hunting mosaics of Antioch" (1963), p. 190.

24. C. Dulière, *La mosaique des amazones*, Brussels, Centre Belge de Recherche Archéologique à Apamée de Syrie, 1968. Dulière concludes on stylistic grounds that the mosaic dates rather from the second half of the fifth century.

25. G. Brett, "The mosaics and small finds", reprint (1947) from *The Great Palace of the Byzantine Emperors*, a first report on the excavations carried out in Istanbul on behalf of the Walker Trust (The University of Saint Andrews), 1935-1938, pp. 64-97; D. T. Rice, ed., *The Great Palace of the Byzantine Emperors*, second report, Edinburgh, University Press, 1958; C. Mango and I. Lavin, "Review of *The Great Palace of the Byzantine Emperors*, Second Report", *The Art Bulletin*, vol. 42-43 (1960), pp. 67-73; Lavin, "The hunting mosaics of Antioch" (1963), pp. 266-269; K. Weitzmann, "The classical heritage in the art of Constantinople", in *Studies in classical and Byzantine manuscript illumination*, H. L. Kessler, ed., Chicago and London, The Uni-

versity of Chicago Press, 1971, chapter 6 (translated from the German article "Das klassische Erbe in der Kunst Konstantinopels", *Alte und Neue Kunst*, no. 3, 1954, pp. 41 f.).

26. Erwin R. Goodenough, *Jewish symbols in the Greco-Roman period, Bollingen Series* 37, New York, Pantheon Books, 1953-1965 (see index for references).

27. Goodenough, *Jewish symbols* (1953-1965), vol. 1, p. 231.

28. Goodenough; *Jewish symbols* (1953-1965), vol. 1, p. 242.

29. Goodenough, *Jewish symbols* (1953-1965), vol. 2, p. 76.

30. Goodenough, *Jewish symbols* (1953-1965), vol. 2, pp. 39 f., fig. 817; A. Grabar, *Early Christian art from the rise of Christianity to the death of Theodosius*, New York, Odyssey Press, 1968, fig. 108.

31. Goodenough, *Jewish symbols* (1953-1965), vol. 1, p. 242; vol. 3, fig. 639.

32. L. Yarden, *The tree of light : A study of the menorah, the seven-branched lamp-stand*, Ithaca, N.Y., Cornell University Press, 1971, fig. 95.

33. Curtains are also represented on some of the wall paintings of the synagogue at Dura Europos dating as early as the middle of the third century A.D. See C. H. Kraeling, *The excavations at Dura-Europos*, Preliminary report of the 6th season 1932-1933, New Haven, 1936; Comte du Mesnil du Buisson, *Les peintures de la synagogue de Doura-Europos*, Rome, 1939; C. H. Kraeling, *The synagogue*, with contributions by G.C. Torrey, C.B. Willis, and B. Geiger, in *The excavations at Dura Europos*, conducted by Yale University and the French Academy of Inscriptions and Letters, final report 8, part 1, New Haven, Princeton University Press, 1956.

34. R. Krautheimer, *Early Christian and Byzantine architecture*, in the series *The Pelican history of art*, Penguin Books, 1965, pp. 19, 24, 35.

35. H. Stern, "Nouvelles recherches sur les images des conciles dans l'église de la Nativité à Bethléem", *Cahiers Archéologiques*, vol. 3 (1948), pp. 82-105 with artistic representations of such curtains on pls. 1/2 (Bethlehem : Laodicée, eighth century), 1/4 (Bethlehem: Sardique, eighth century), 2/1 (Bethlehem : Antioch, eighth century), 6/1 (marble plaque, Lateran Museum), 6/2 (ivory plaque from Milan depicting Saint Menas). Jean Lassus mentions that the emplacement for the curtain rods can often be seen above the capitals of the pilasters which support the triumphal arch in the early churches of North Syria (*Santuaires chrétiens de Syrie : Essai sur la genèse, la forme et l'usage liturgique des édifices du culte chrétien, en Syrie, du IIIe siècle à la conquête musulmane*, in the series *Institut Français d'Archéologie de Beyrouth, Bibliothèque Archéologique et Historique*, vol. 42, Paris, Paul Geuthner, 1947, pp. 177-178, 205-207. See also "Corrigenda").

36. Lassus, *Sanctuaires chrétiens de Syrie* (1947), pp. 206-207.

37. Krautheimer, *Early Christian and Byzantine architecture* (1965), p. 35 and pl. 8a (representing an ivory casket from Pola. One side of this casket depicts the shrine and baldachin together with its curtains).

38. Krautheimer, *Early Christian and Byzantine architecture* (1965), pp. 158-160. For the curtains of the ciborium see the description by Paulus Silentiarius, note 49.

39. See for example Krautheimer, *Early Christian and Byzantine architecture* (1965), pls. 30, 32 (Salonika, H. Demetrios, late fifth century), 65a (Tigzirt, basilica, ca. 450), 72, 73a-b (Constantinople, Hagia Sophia, 532-537). In Syria, the placement of the curtain rods was found above the capitals of the triumphal arch in many churches (Lassus, *Sanctuaires chrétiens de Syrie*, 1947, p. 178, fig. 82 : reconstruction of the chapel of the martyrs, Qal'at Kalôta; pp. 206-207; "Corrigenda" on p. v).

40. Grabar, *La peinture byzantine* (1953), pp. 60, 63; W. F. Volbach, *Early Christian art*, New York, Abrams, n.d. (1961?), fig. 165.

41. Volbach, *Early Christian art* (1961?), fig. 152; M. Gough, *The origins of Christian art*, New York and Washington, Praeger, 1973, fig. 157, pp. 163, 165. See also note 3.

42. Volbach, *Early Christian art* (1961?), fig. 173.

43. See for example Volbach, *Early Christian art* (1961?), figs. 96 (ivory diptych with Consul Felix, Rome, 428; Paris, Cabinet des Médailles), 221 (ivory diptych with Muse and poet, ca. 500; Monza, Cathedral Treasury), 224-225 (ivory diptych with Christ between Saints Peter and Paul, and Mary with angels, mid-sixth century; Berlin, Staatliche Museen), 237 (ivory plaque with Saint Paul, originally part of an episcopal throne, sixth-seventh century; New York, Metropolitan Museum of Art); W. F. Volbach, *Elfenbeinarbeiten der Spätantike und des frühen Mittelalters*, Römisch-germanisches Zentral-museum zu Mainz, Katalog no. 7, Mainz, Römisch-germanischen Zentral-museums, 1952, pls. 13/51 (imperial diptych, ca. 500; Florence, Bargello), 13/52 (imperial diptych, Constantinople, ca. 500; Vienna, Kunsthistorisches Museum), 20/64 (a patrician?, Italian, first half of fifth century; Novara, Dom), 21/66 (two couples, Italian, fifth century; Brescia, Museo Cristiano), 50/153 (Saint Paul, sixth century; Tongern, Notre Dame Treasury), 50/154 (Saint Peter, sixth century; Brussels, Musée Royaux d'Art et d'Histoire), 55/177 (the women at the grave, sixth century; New York, Metropolitan Museum of Art); J. Beckwith, *Early Christian and Byzantine art*, in the series *The Pelican history of art*, Penguin Books, 1970, fig. 63 (imperial diptych with the empress Ariadne, Constantinople, early sixth century; Florence, Museo Nazionale); J. Beckwith, *Ivory carvings in early mediaeval England*, London, Harvey, Miller & Medcalf, 1972, fig. 15 (Visitation, the Genoels-Eldern Diptych, Northumbrian, last quarter of eighth century; Brussels, Musée Royaux d'Art et d'Histoire, acc. no. 1474).

44. K. Weitzmann, "Book illustration of the fourth century", in *Studies in classical and Byzantine manuscript illumination* (1971), p. 110, figs. 86-87 (Consul Constantinus II and Consul Gallus Caesar, 354; Vatican, Bibliotheca, Cod. Barb. lat. 2154, fols. 13r and 14r, copies of the seventeenth century).

45. For a few examples from this vast material see P. Dancona and E. Aeschlimann, *The art of illumination : An anthology of manuscripts from the sixth to the sixteenth century*, London, Phaidon, 1969, pl. 9 (St. Matthew, Lindisfarne Gospels, Hiberno-Saxon, ca. 700; London, British Museum, MS Cotton Nero D. IV. fol. 25v); A. Grabar and C. Nordenfalk, *Early medieval painting from the fourth to the eleventh century*, in the series *The great centuries of painting*, Geneva, Skira, 1957, p. 123 (St. Matthew, Codex Aureus of Canterbury, eighth century; Kungliga Biblioteket, Stockholm, A. 135, fol. 9v), p. 152 (Joshua, Moses, Aaron, and the Israelites, the Grandval Bible, Tours, ca. 840; London, British Museum, add. MS 10546, fol. 25v); *Karl der Grosse*, Die Ausstellung Karl der Grosse—Werk und Wirkung, Aachen, 1965, fig. 59 (Saint John, Codex from Lorsch, Palace School of Charlemagne, ca. 810; Vatican, Pal. Lat. 50, fol. 67v), p. 254, no. 418; J. Hubert, J. Porcher, and W. F. Volbach, *Europe of the invasions*, in the series *The arts of mankind*, New York, George Braziller, 1969, fig. 154 (St. Augustine dictating to a scribe, Verona, Codex Egino, late seventh century; Deutsche Staatsbibliothek, Berlin, MS Phill. 1676, fol. 18v); A. Boinet, *La miniature carolingienne, ses origines, son développement*, Planches, Paris, Alphonse Picard et Fils, 1933, pls. 48a (The first Bible of Charles le Chauve, mid-ninth century; Paris, Bibliothèque Nationale, lat. 1), 74a (Évangéliaire de Loisel, mid-ninth century; Paris, Bibl. Nat., lat. 17968), 83a (Évangéliaire de Saint-Frambourg de Senlis, second half of ninth century; Paris, Bibliothèque Sainte-Geneviève, 1190), 88 and 89c, d (Sacramentaire de Drogon, 826-855; Paris, Bibl. Nat., lat. 9428); H. J. Hermann, *Die frühmittelalterlichen Handschriften des Abendlandes*, in the series *Die illuminierten Handschriften und Inkunabeln der Nationalbibliothek in Wien*, vol. 1, Leipzig, Karl W. Hiersemann, pl. 4/1 and fig. 10 (Sammlung Medizinischer Schriften, no. 3, Cod. 93, fols. 2 and 2b, Italian, copy of a sixth-century MS from the first half of the thirteenth century).

46. Kurt Weitzmann believes that depictions of the Evangelists sitting in such architectural settings with parted curtains derive from the ancient theatres, where the statues of poets were placed in the niches of the *hyposcenium* wall. According to this theory, these *scenae frons* were introduced into miniature painting in the first half of the fourth century, when a strong parallel of the same architectural forms in secular and Christian book illumination may refer to an imperial scriptoria, which produced secular and religious luxury manuscripts side by side. He goes on to say that even such late examples as those tenth-century Macedonian Renaissance miniatures representing the Evangelists copy models from a very early period when these theatre

backgrounds were not yet ornamentalized ("Book illustration of the fourth century", 1971, particularly pp. 112-113). For the relation of the background of some Byzantine miniatures to ancient theatre architecture, see A. M. Friend, "The portraits of the Evangelists in Greek and Latin manuscripts, Part II", *Art Studies* (1929), pp. 4 f. Notwithstanding the possibility that certain links might exist between the theatres of antiquity and some of the later works representing architectural framework, the evidence of all other early depictions of architecture decorated with curtains suggests that theatrical scenes could only have been one of the sources for artistic inspiration. Curtains appeared everywhere in lay and religious life.

47. G. de Hartel, ed., *Sancti Pontii Meropii Paulini Nolani Carmina*, in the series *Corpus Scriptorum Ecclesiasticorum Latinorum*, vol. 30 (S. Pontii Meropii Paulini Nolani Opera, pars II), Prague, Vienna, and Leipzig, F. Tempsky, Bibliopola Academiae Litterarum Caesareae Vindobonensis, 1894, p. 98, poem 18, lines 29-35. English translation and commentary in R. C. Goldschmidt, *Paulinus' churches at Nola*, Amsterdam, 1940. For Paulinus' foundations above and near the grave of St. Felix see also Krautheimer, *Early Christian and Byzantine architecture* (1965), pp. 145-146.

48. *Charta Cornutiana*, MS published by L. Duchesne, ed., *Le Liber Pontificalis*, vol. 1, Paris, Ernest Thorin, 1886, p. CXLVII, lines 15-46.

49. P. Friedländer, ed., *Johannes von Gaza und Paulus Silentiarius: Kunstbeschreibungen justinianischer Zeit*, in the series *Sammlung Wissenschaftlicher Kommentare zu Griechischen und Römischen Schriftstellern*, Leipzig and Berlin, B. G. Teubner, 1912, photographic reprint : Hildesheim and New York, Georg Olms, 1969, pp. 248-250, lines 755-805, see also notes on pp. 290-291. For publications of works by Paulus Silentiarius, see C. Mango, *The art of the Byzantine Empire, 312-1453 : Sources and documents*, Englewood Cliffs, N. J., Prentice Hall, 1972. The poem about the Hagia Sophia was recited at the second dedication of the church in 562 in the episcopal hall of the patriarchate.

50. *Le Liber Pontificalis*, vol. 1 (1886), document 97, pp. 499-505.

51. *Monumenta Germaniae Historica, Scriptores Rerum Merovingicarum*, vol. 2 (*Fredegarii et aliorum chronica vitae sanctorum*), Hanover, Impensis Bibliopolii Hahniani, 1888, "Gesta Dagoberti I Regis Francorum", pp. 396-425, section 20, p. 407, lines 25-30 : "Nam et per totam ecclesiam auro textas vestes, margaritarum varietatibus multipliciter exornatas in parietibus et columnis atque arcubus suspendi devotissime iussit, quatinus aliarum ecclesiarum ornamentis praecellere videretur, et omnimodis incomparabili nitore vernans, omni terrena pulchritudine compta atque inestimabili decore inradiata splendesceret. Utque divina laus perpetuo ai Dei cultoribus ibidem agaretur, plurima et ingentia addidit".—Dagobert I : b. ca. 600–638, see U. Chevalier, *Répertoire des sources historiques du Moyen Age*, vol. 1,

Paris, Alphonse Picard, 1905. Gregory of Tour (ca. 540-594), in his *History of the Franks* (586-590), mentioned the curtains of the Catholic Queen Clotild, daughter of an Arian Burgundian and wife of Clovis, king of the Franks: ". . .the queen, true to her faith, presented her son for baptism; she ordered the church to be adorned with hangings and curtains, that the king, whom no preaching could influence might by this ceremony be persuaded to belief." (O.M. Dalton's translation, vol. 2, Oxford, Clarendon Press, 1927, p. 66 f.)

52. W. F. Volbach, *Early decorative textiles*, London, Paul Hamlyn, 1969, p. 73.

53. See note 48.

54. *Le Liber Pontificalis*, vol. 1 (1886), document 87, p. 383, line 15.

55. *Le Liber Pontificalis*, vol. 1 (1886), document 93, p. 432, lines 9-16.

56. *Le Liber Pontificalis*, vol. 1 (1886), document 97, p. 500, lines 6, 16.

57. *Le Liber Pontificalis*, vol. 2 (1892), document 98, p. 2 (lines 19-24), p. 3 (lines 10-11), p. 8 (lines 22-24), p. 10 (lines 3, 13 f.), p. 17 (lines 20-26).

58. *Le Liber Pontificalis*, vol. 2 (1892), document 100, pp. 54-62.

59. *Le Liber Pontiricalis*, vol. 2 (1892), document 103, p. 75 (lines 15-24), p. 79 (lines 9-13, 26-28), p. 82 (lines 18-19).

60. At the time when written references attested that curtains were hung in churches, curtains also appeared painted on the walls as a cheaper imitation of rich textile coverings. At the Santa Maria Antiqua in Rome, large sets of fringed curtains are painted on the lower sections of the walls, directly below the eighth-century figural representations (*tempore* Popes John VII, 705-707, and Paul I, 757-768), see W. de Grüneisen, *Sainte Marie Antique*, avec le concours de Huelsen Giorgis Frederici David, Rome, Max Bretschneider, 1911; J. Hubert et al., *Europe of the invasions* (1969), p. 116, figs. 131, 132, 137, 140. The custom of decorating the lower sections of church walls in particular with painted curtains continued well into the Romanesque period. Some frescoes date from as late as the twelfth and thirteenth centuries.

61. J. Porcher, *French miniatures from illuminated manuscripts*, London, Collins, 1960, pl. 6. See also Grabar and Nordenfalk, *Early medieval painting* (1957), p. 181 (St. John the Evangelist, the Grimbald Gospels, Winchester School, early eleventh century; British Museum, Add. MS 34890, fol. 114v). Interestingly enough, a predecessor of these misunderstood representations is already known from the ninth century from a Psalter of Charles

le Chauve (Boinet, *La miniature carolingienne*, 1933, pl. 94a, Paris, Bibl. Nat., lat. 1152, 846-869, where a sitting figure is represented underneath such a curtain pair).

62. Added to the tenth-century *Life of Paul the Hermit at St. Augustine's Monastery* (Cambridge, Corpus Christi College, MS 389, fol. L), illustrated in J. Beckwith, *The adoration of the Magi in whalebone*, Victoria and Albert Museum, London, Her Majesty's Stationary Office, 1966, p. 27, fig. 29.

63. Beckwith, *The adoration of the Magi in whalebone* (1966); Beckwith, *Ivory carvings* (1972), fig. 121, from the Webb collection, formerly in the Soltikoff Collection, Victoria and Albert Museum, acc. no. 142-1866.

64. C. R. Dodwell, *The Great Lambeth-Bible*, in the series *The library of illuminated manuscripts*, New York, Thomas Yoseloff, 1955.

65. F. Wormald, *The Winchester Psalter*, London, Harvey Miller & Medcalf, 1973 (British Museum, Cotton MS, Nero C.IV).

66. It should be noted, however, that in the last Spanish manuscript in Mozarabic style, the complete cross-section of a church is shown with curtains hanging in the arches of the nave as well as in the aisles (St. John and the Angel at the church of Thyatria, Commentary on the Apocalypse of Beatus of Liébana, executed ca. 1091 x 1109 at the monastery of Santo Domingo de Silos, near Burgos; British Museum, Add. MS 11695, fol. 64). This illumination obviously copies earlier models from the Beatus manuscripts.

67. New York, Pierpont Morgan Library, MS 638. Published in *Old Testament miniatures : A medieval picture book from the Creation to the Story of David*, introduction and legends by S. C. Cockerell, preface by J. Plummer, New York, George Braziller, n.d., fols. 5v (the Pharaoh's dreams), 6r (Benjamin sent to his brother Joseph), 7v (the hiding of the infant Joseph), 11v (the death of Joshua), 12v (Jael slays the sleeping Sisera), 19r (Ruth gives birth to Obed), 19v (Saume is born to Hannah), 20v (God calls Samuel), 31r (Michal's ruse for saving David's life), 33v (Nabal dies), 38r (the slaying of Ishbosheth), 41v (David commits adultery), 43r (Amnon and Tamar in bed). From that time on, nonfunctional curtain representations also appear in oriental Christian manuscript illumination. Usually set into three-lobed arches, these knotted curtains hang in the centre, their ends turned as if blown to the side by a wind. It is quite probable that their iconographical prototype was based on western models of the eleventh and twelfth centuries. See for example M. Cramer, *Koptische Buchmalerei : Illuminationen in Manuskripten des christlich-koptischen Ägypten vom 4. bis 19. Jahrhundert*, Recklinghausen, Aurel Bongers, 1964, figs. 90, 96, 103, 130 (bohairisch-arabisch, A.D. 1250; Paris, Inst. Cath., MS Copte Arabe no. 1, fols. 1v, 105v, 174v, 56v), 89, 94, 99, 104, 139, 141, 142 (bohairisch-arabisch, A.D. 1663; British Museum, Oriental MS 1316, fols. 2v, 67v, 111v, 182v, 110r, 15r, 18r), 93 (bohairisch-arabisch, A.D. 1812; British Museum, Oriental MS 1317, fol. 129v).

68. J. Leroy, *Ethiopian painting in the late Middle Ages and under the Gondar Dynasty*, London, Merlin Press, 1964, pls. 25 (the Annunciation of Zacharias, Four Gospels and Synodos, MS of the Octateuch, late seventeenth century; British Museum, Oriental MS 48, fol. 99r), 49 (Acts of St. John, eighteenth century; British Museum, Oriental MS 533). Representing the story of Solomon and the Queen of Sheba, numerous curtains are depicted on a probably eighteenth- or nineteenth-century painting which appear to have belonged to an Ethiopian church (oil on canvas; in the collection of Prof. A. Watson, Toronto).

69. D. R. Buxton, "The rock-hewn and other medieval churches of Tigré Province, Ethiopia", *Archaeologia* (Miscellaneous tracts relating to antiquity), second series, vol. 103 (1971), pp. 33-100, pls. 22b, 23b, 24a,b, 25b, 28a, 31d.

70. Curtains depicted in the early Christian tradition appear on the pages of the earliest Ethiopian illuminated manuscript, dating probably from the tenth century; see J. Leroy, "L'évangéliaire éthiopien du couvent d'Abba Garima et ses attaches avec l'ancien art chrétien de Syrie", *Cahiers Archéologiques*, vol. 2 (1960), pp. 131-143. For fifteenth-century representations see Leroy, *Ethiopian painting* (1964), pl. 2 (the Fountain of Life from a Gospel Book, the Canons of Eusebius; church of Jehjeh Giorgis, near Godar). According to Leroy, this is a theme inspired by a Hellenistic tradition as exemplified in the original Canon, the work of Eusebius of Caesarea (d. 339). This motif has disappeared from the Byzantine manuscripts which have come down to us but is preserved in the Ethiopian and Armenian tradition (L. A. Dournovo, *Armenian miniatures*, London, Thames and Hudson, 1961, pl. 31 from the Etchmiadzin Gospel, executed in the Monastery of Noravank', Siunik', 989) and in a number of Carolingian manuscripts. See also pl. 5 (Gospel Book, the Canons of Eusebius; monastery of Gunda Gundie).

71. Stern, "Nouvelles recherches" (1948), p. 96 and pl. 6/3 with reference to the churches of Mâr Cyriacus at Arnas, and Mâr Azizaël at Kefr Zéh in North Mesopotamia.

72. A. Grabar, *L'Age d'Or de Justinien de la mort de Théodose à l'Islam*, in the series *L'Universe des formes*, Paris, Gallimard, 1966, pp. 329, 334. See also the references in notes 35-37.

73. See for example R. Ettinghausen, *La peinture arabe*, in the series *Les trésors de l'Asie*, Geneva, Skira, 1962, p. 87 (De Materia Medica de Dioscoride: the Pharmacy, Baghdad, Iraq, 1244; New York, Metropolitan Museum of Art, acc. no. 57.51.21), pp. 106-107 (the Seances Maquâmât of al-Hariri, Abu Zayd before the Governor of Merv and the cadi of Sa'da in Yemen, Baghdad, Iraq, ca. 1225-1235; Leningrad, Oriental Institute of the Academy of Sciences, MS S.23, pp. 256, 250). For quite misunderstood representations in a manuscript of Jami 'al-Tawarikh, dated 1310, from the Mongolian School, see F. R. Martin, *The miniature painting and painters of Persia, India and Turkey from the 8th to the 18th century*, London, Holland Press, 1968 (reprint of the 1912 edition), pls. 27a (the nobles of Kashmir enthrone a fakir), 28a (Jacob with Leah and Rachel and three

of his sons), 30a ('Ala al-Din, Sultan of Dehli, receives the kneeling Firuz Shah).

74. J. Lassner, *The topography of Baghdad in the early Middle Ages: Text and studies*, Detroit, Wayne State University Press, 1970, pp. 88-89.

75. R. B. Serjeant, *Islamic textiles: Material for a history up to the Mongol conquest*, Beirut, Librairie du Liban, 1972 (originally published serially in *Ars Islamica*, vols. 9-14, 1942-1951), pp. 46-47.

76. O. Grabar, *The formation of Islamic art*, New Haven, Yale University Press, 1973, p. 149.

77. Grabar, *The formation of Islamic art* (1973), p. 156.

78. Serjeant, *Islamic textiles* (1972), p. 203.

79. Serjeant, *Islamic textiles* (1972), pp. 215-216 with further bibliography; see also index.

80. Serjeant, *Islamic textiles* (1972), p. 155.

81. Serjeant, *Islamic textiles* (1972), p. 155.

82. Serjeant, *Islamic textiles* (1972), p. 161.

83. Serjeant, *Islamic textiles* (1972), pp. 46-47.

84. Serjeant, *Islamic textiles* (1972), pp. 46-47.

85. Serjeant, *Islamic textiles* (1972), pp. 54-55.

86. Serjeant, *Islamic textiles* (1972), p. 100.

87. Serjeant, *Islamic textiles* (1972), pp. 35-36.

88. Serjeant, *Islamic textiles* (1972), pp. 38-39.

Tiraz Fabrics in the Royal Ontario Museum

Lisa Golombek and Veronika Gervers

AMONG its small collection of mediaeval Islamic textiles, the Royal Ontario Museum possesses a representative group of so-called *tiraz* (Arabic: *ṭirāz*) fabrics.[1] The majority of the pieces were manufactured in Egypt, and a few came from Iraq, Iran, and the Arabian peninsula. They date from the tenth to the early thirteenth centuries A.D.

The term *tiraz* is borrowed from the Persian word for embroidery, and originally designated any embroidered ornaments.[2] Inscriptions in praise of God were considered to be good augury, and textiles were often adorned with them. Mediaeval texts also speak of the custom of putting the ruler's name in the decorative bands of garments worn by him or by those upon whom such robes of honour were bestowed. Because of this custom, *tiraz* also referred to such inscription bands whether they were executed in embroidery or in some other technique. The word can refer to the band itself, or to the garment bearing the band, or to the workshop where the cloth was woven or ornamented.

The *tiraz* industry is well documented in the literature. Throughout the Islamic world from Spain to Afghanistan, the ruling authorities maintained textile factories, known as the *Dār al-Ṭirāz* or *Dār al-Kiswa*, until about the thirteenth century. All of these produced apparel and furnishings for the court, and some of them may also have sold to the public. In the latter case these factories represented a government monopoly on certain types of fabrics in addition to a royal convenience. These factories were supervised by appointed officials who controlled the use of materials and the quality of the finished product.

Thanks to the favourable climatic conditions of Egypt, many *tiraz* fabrics have been recovered from the various archaeological burial grounds. Because of the extensive trade within the Islamic world, especially in the Mediterranean, these Egyptian finds represent not only fabrics of local manufacture, but also export goods from both the eastern and western provinces of the Caliphate. In addition, a few important pieces are preserved in European church treasuries.[3] Numerous examples have been published. Some of their inscriptions contain the names of the ruling caliph, the vazir, and often the intendant at the workshop as well as the place and date of manufacture. Inscriptions specify whether the workshop was private, that is to say royal (*khāṣṣa*), or public (*ᶜāmma*). Textiles containing the full protocol of the caliph could be made in either type of shop. Over the past four decades scholars have identified this type of data on hundreds of inscribed fragments. The historical value of the inscriptions has indeed been underlined for, generally speaking, only those fragments that are dated or datable have been published. The interest in *tiraz* studies has paralleled that of numismatics, where the content of the inscription was initially the leading concern. The object itself, either coin or textile, was of secondary importance. More recently, numismatists have turned to the study of the intrinsic qualities of coins. With the publication of many texts shedding light on the social and economic history of the Middle East, particularly the Geniza testimony,[4] the time is also ripe for a reconsideration of the significance of the *tiraz* group of textiles. Leaving aside questions raised by the content of their inscriptions, which we feel should be left to the historians, we have chosen to preface our catalogue with a few remarks on three aspects of these fabrics that have received little attention: the technical characteristics, the sociological implications, and the epigraphical style.

Technical Characteristics[5]

With the exception of a few works, such as those by Pfister, Lamm, and Bellinger, the technical problems presented by the group have remained untouched.[6] In a number of catalogues, the ground fabric, together with the technique of the decoration, has been unrecorded or misrecorded.

The nature of the ground fabric is probably the most consistent feature of a given centre of production. As a rule, linen came from Egypt and cotton from India, Persia, Iraq, and Yaman. We know that there existed a linen–cotton dichotomy until about the twelfth century. According to the oft-quoted words of the Arab chronicler al-Thaʿālibī (d. A.D. 1037–1038): "People knew that cotton belongs to Khurasan and linen to Egypt."[7] Although threads were traded across the Islamic empire,[8] imported threads were used sparingly and for special purposes, usually in the decorative bands.

The undyed cotton fabrics of the east are finely woven in tabby weave with Z-spun yarn. They were often glazed, giving them the appearance of highly polished paper (ROM no. 1). Fabrics using cotton together with silk, called *mulham*, were also popular.[9] This "half-silk" (ROM nos. 2, 3) is a delicate, light fabric woven in tabby weave (usually weft-faced) with warps of fine, raw silk floss and wefts of heavier, Z-spun cotton. They are also sometimes glazed. Most *mulham*s were white. Al-Washsha (d. ca. A.D. 936–937) mentions, however, that some were dyed yellow with saffron for dresses worn by women, female singers, and slave girls. He also adds that "men may dress in such clothes in the time of venesection or medical treatment, during drinking and when they are alone. . . .Perhaps they use it for furnishing purposes and put it on while drinking or in order to appear elegant at entertainments. . . .as light clothing at home. To appear publicly in such apparel is not in good taste for ordinary people and

those who want to be elegant, but it is permitted to wealthy people and to sons of the Caliphs."[10] From other sources we learn that *mulham* was also used for women's veils[11] and wrappers,[12] and for festive garments worn by eunuchs in Constantinople.[13] *Mulham* fabrics are frequently mentioned by Arab geographers of the eighth to the fourteenth centuries as a product of Khwarizm in Western Turkestan, of Marv and Nishapur in northeastern Iran, and of Isfahan in central Iran.[14]

As decoration, the cotton and *mulham* fragments in museum collections bear relatively short inscription bands, most of which are embroidered in coloured silk floss (ROM nos. 1, 2). As a rule the main band is worked in chain stitch on the free-drawn lines of the lettering. The smaller band, which is not always decipherable, may be executed in variations of blanket and back stitches on a free-drawn inscription, or worked entirely on counted thread. Little technical difference can be noted amongst the embroideries of the different workshops.[15] Some of the cotton fragments bear inscriptions which are carefully but rather heavily painted, obviously a cheaper imitation of these embroideries. The style of the epigraphy is very similar if not identical to the embroidered examples (ROM 975.403.3). In Persia and Iraq another group of painted or printed, then gilded, inscriptions on either cotton or *mulham* fabrics are generally outlined in red ink, although the occasional black outline occurs (ROM no. 3).[16]

From the various cotton cloths manufactured in the Yaman, those with *ikat*-dyed patterning form a distinct group.[17] The rather thick, Z-spun, cotton warps of these fabrics were resist-dyed in shades of blue, brown, and white before weaving. In the finished cloth, this resulted in innumerable variants of splashed arrow patterns. The *ikat*-dyed yarn was usually set up on the loom in wide stripes alternating with narrower ones dyed in a single colour or a series of plain colours. They were bound with a light brown, Z-spun, thin and widely spaced cotton weft. Woven in tabby weave (often warp-faced), the fabric thus has pronounced stripes. While less frequently they bear tapestry woven (silk and cotton) or brocaded cotton ornaments, the most common decoration of these *ikat*s is an embroidered (ROM no. 4) or painted inscription band (ROM nos. 5, 6). Some of the inscriptions mention Ṣanᶜā'[18] as the place of manufacture, but it can be presumed that several other centres also produced similar textiles. The embroidery is worked in a limited number of coarse counted-thread stitches with two-plyed, undyed cotton thread (Z, 2S). Those with painted inscriptions are outlined in black ink, then gilded.[19]

From the ninth to the fourteenth centuries, Arab historians often mention these striped cloths of the Yaman.[20] They call them ᶜaṣb (pl. ᶜaṣā'ib), a word which refers to the act of binding the warp threads for resist-dyeing. Another name for them may be *washy*, meaning simply "decorated".[21] Both ᶜaṣb and *washy* were almost exclusively used for garments. Al-Masᶜūdī (d. A.D. 956–957) mentions that everybody had robes, gowns, trousers, turbans, and caps made of them. He recounts that the Ummayyad Caliph, Sulayman (A.D. 715–717) "was dressed in this stuff while riding in procession or sitting on the minbar. . . .He stipulated that his shroud should be of *washy*."[22] Others speak about the cloaks (*burd/burda*, pl. *burūd*) and gowns (*ridā'*, pl. *ardiya*) made of striped fabrics.

These Yamanite cottons were well known for their good wearing qualities and were favoured in many countries. In Egypt they were imitated in linen,[23] while in Spain and Persia similar textiles were produced probably in silk.[24] Al-Thaᶜālibī (d. A.D. 1037–1038) noted that "the striped cloaks of Rayy are just as famous as those from the Yaman; they are even called ᶜAdanī, so great is their similarity to those from Aden (ᶜAdan) in the Yaman."[25]

In Egypt linen tabby, woven with S-spun yarn, is the most characteristic ground material.[26] While together with S-spinning, Z-spun yarn appears in all Egyptian factories from the second half of the ninth century to the end of al-Rāḍī's reign (A.D. 934–940),[27] the Fatimid linens are Z-spun only in rare cases (ROM no. 18). Imitating the Asiatic

pieces, the early Egyptian *tiraz* were embroidered (ROM no. 9). From the second quarter of the tenth century, tapestry woven bands took the place of the embroidered ones, and remained popular under the Fatimids.[28] Embroidered stuffs with conventionalized decoration and cursive inscription friezes became popular again toward the end of the Fatimid period. A small group of these may be assigned to the thirteenth to fourteenth centuries, and to the early Mamluk period (ROM no. 24).[29]

Chain stitch, so characteristic of the eastern examples, was seldom used for the embroidered *tiraz* in Egypt where most inscriptions were executed in a considerable variety of counted thread stitches with coloured silk floss. In almost every case, a thread is drawn to mark the base line of the inscription, and embroidered lines often mark the placing for different parts of the lettering (ROM no. 9). The factories of Alexandria, Tinnīs, and Miṣr produced embroidered *tiraz* on a large scale. Each of these centres has its identifying characteristics, which can be readily distinguished.[30]

The tapestry woven inscription and decorative bands are worked with coloured silk wefts.[31] Occasionally gold filé on a yellow silk core is used (ROM 963.95.10,14, and 16).[32] Their complicated ornaments are often outlined with an extra weft of black silk floss. Bleached, or less frequently, dyed linen is used only for minor details. Some inscriptions are nevertheless executed in linen against the coloured background of the band (ROM no. 13); or the silk inscriptions are placed against a linen band (ROM nos. 14-17). While the inscriptions are almost always solidly tapestry woven, there is a tenth-century group with monumental inscriptions in which only the large letters are executed in this technique against the loose tabby weave of the cloth (ROM nos. 7, 8, 10). The silk tapestry is generally worked on single warps, although at Miṣr, Damietta, and Tūna paired warps also occur as a carry-over from the time when all tapestry woven ornaments were worked in coloured wool.[33] Instead of elaborate tapestry woven decoration, some fabrics are adorned with plain, solid bands of coloured wefts. Some of these bands are quite wide (ROM nos. 7-10, 13), while others are narrow. The latter are placed near fringed ends and seem to indicate only a start for more complicated ornaments (ROM 975.403.1).[34]

84

Sociological Implications

We have accepted the traditional definition of *tiraz* textiles for this catalogue of the Toronto collection and have included only those fabrics of linen, cotton, or *mulham* upon which the decoration is executed in a technique differing from that of the ground weave. We must, nevertheless, express reservations regarding the validity of this category, for while *tiraz* serves as a convenient designation for a group of fabrics, its boundaries are neither technically nor chronologically properly defined. The ambiguity of the term itself is the source of the problem. Although *tiraz* is frequently understood as the product of a *Dār al-Ṭirāz* or royal factory, these fabrics are not wholly representative of the output of such workshops. Similarly, so-called *tiraz* textiles may also have been manufactured outside a *Dār al-Ṭirāz*. On the other hand, if *tiraz* is defined as embroidery or simply ornament, one might include all those textiles bearing decorative bands which are not necessarily the product of royal workshops. The discrepancy of these two definitions has not heretofore been resolved, nor even recognized. A discussion of the group under consideration will show that both these classifications of *tiraz* are artificial, and that neither of them can be considered a real category.

The hierarchy of materials

The numerous literary texts referring to the vestments and furnishings of the court speak primarily of *silk,* not of linen or cotton. Robes of honour (*khilᶜa*) were traditionally of silk.[35] Garments for special occasions, even for the middle class, were ordered in silk.[36] The characters depicted in miniature painting and on ceramics of the twelfth and thirteenth centuries invariably wear robes of figured silks.[37] Consequently silk textiles, previously excluded from the study of *tiraz*, cannot be disregarded.

Although linens and other light-weight fabrics were produced for the court, they played a much more humble role. As an exception, texts do report a type of fine and costly linen called *qaṣab*, which seems to have been partially woven with gold filé (silk core wrapped with a gold wire).[38] From the written sources, however, it is difficult to know just

how the filé was integrated into the linen ground. Actual examples have rarely if ever been identified, although those linen fabrics ornamented in tapestry weave which incorporate gold filé might represent variants of *qaṣab*.[39] This type is clearly distinguished from the ordinary linens that make up the bulk of museum collections. Yet it is upon the latter that *tiraz* studies have focussed. Because of the fragmentary condition of most such textiles, the original function of the fabrics has been difficult to ascertain. Nevertheless, a careful inspection of examples in different collections suggests that we are dealing with a limited range of objects consisting mainly of summer outfits and undergarments, turbans, shawls, sashes, napkins, presentation towels, and probably such furnishing fabrics as curtains.

Only one complete garment with historical *tiraz* bands is known from this group, the so-called "veil of Saint Anne" in Apt Cathedral (Vauclose, France).[40] It bears the name of the Fatimid Caliph al-Mustaᶜli (A.D. 1094–1101) and was manufactured at Damietta in 1096–1097. Made of bleached linen tabby, the "veil" measures 310 cm by 150 cm (loom width), and is adorned with three parallel bands of tapestry woven ornaments in coloured silks and some gold filé. Across the centre are three medallions, joined by a wide band of interlacing circles. The largest medallion lies close to the selvage below the decorative neckline. All three medallions contain a pair of addorsed sphinxes and are encircled by historical kufic inscriptions. While the decorative bands found on the "veil" are quite common, the medallions, though not unique, appear to be less usual. Had they been more frequently associated with *tiraz* ornament, one would have expected them to have survived in greater numbers. They are highly reminiscent of roundels on Coptic tunics which were executed in wool or wool with linen, but those on the "veil" are worked in silk on linen warps.[41]

Marçais and Wiet convincingly suggested that the piece must originally have been an over-garment, similar to the ᶜabāya or ᶜabā', which is still worn in many countries of the Middle East.[42] Folded to form the fronts, the decorative bands of the ends adorned the centre front opening, while the band with the medallions fell at the centre of the back. At the sides, small slits were probably made for passing through the hands. Four late Fatimid fragments in the collection of the Metropolitan Museum of Art, New York, must have belonged to similar mantles. Instead of being woven in a single piece, these garments were constructed from two narrow widths of linen tabby (loom widths between 59 and 74 cm).[43] Related material also exists in the Victoria and Albert Museum, London.[44]

The ʿabāya is a huge, loose mantle. It is either made of a single width of fabric with selvages along the shoulder and hemlines, or is sewn together horizontally from two narrower widths. The variants of the mantle today are thus similar to those which are known from the Middle Ages. The common examples, made of heavy woollen fabric, are used for travelling and as protection against inclement weather in the desert. Others of finer material, some indeed of silk with tapestry woven decoration in metallic filé, belong to outfits worn for special occasions.[45]

In mediaeval times, such fine examples as those represented by the "veil of Saint Anne" and related material may have served as the summer mantles of the court. Simpler pieces with a minimal use of silk for their ornaments, as illustrated in two fragments from the Metropolitan Museum of Art (1974.113.14,a-b), probably reflect the fashion common amongst the less wealthy. Since these voluminous mantles could have been put over any kind of garment, their cut would have been suitable for robes of honour.

Amongst Fatimid fragments decorated with inscription bands, there are some which are quite long (over 80 cm; ROM nos. 14–17). Some of these could have belonged to ʿabāya-type garments, similar to that represented by the "veil of Saint Anne". Since some mantles, such as those in the collection of the Metropolitan Museum of Art, were constructed from two narrow widths, even narrower pieces might be considered as having once been part of an ʿabāya. The short length of most fragments may be the result of dealers or illicit excavators having cut off the inscriptions or decoration from the plain sections of the garments, particularly the sides.

The large size of the "veil" is unique among those textiles that have survived, and fragments can seldom be associated with any certainty to this type of garment. It is therefore difficult to determine how common these ʿabāya-type garments were. We do not know whether they appeared suddenly in the eleventh century, or whether they were already in fashion with the Abbasids. It is also unclear from the archaeological material whether the type was unique to Egypt or whether it was also worn in the eastern regions of the Islamic world.

It became apparent, while working through the Toronto tiraz materials, that here, too, many different types of products are in evidence. Besides information concerning the weave and any surface decoration, we have noted the exact format of each textile (size, selvages, signs of sewing, seams) in the catalogue in the hope that more information regarding the function of tiraz fabrics will emerge. While none of the Toronto pieces represents a whole garment or furnishing, or a significant portion thereof, certain types seem to recur. On a number of tenth-century Egyptian linens (ROM nos. 7, 10, 13) is a series of solid bands woven with wefts of coloured silk floss and occasionally of dyed linen above the tapestry woven or embroidered inscription (remaining width 33–56 cm). There are differences in the execution of the lettering. Some are formed by monumental characters (ROM nos. 7, 8, 10), while others are confined to a narrow tapestry woven band (ROM no. 13) or are embroidered (ROM no. 9). Yet the presence of the pronounced coloured bands and the lack of tapestry woven ornaments suggest that the whole group belongs to a single type of textile, perhaps a turban, or a presentation towel (mindīl). The length of the bands is too short to have decorated the centre front opening of an ʿabāya-type mantle.

No seams or signs of sewing were found on our Egyptian examples, while two of the three Perso-Iraqi fragments have the remains of stitching in a line exactly perpendicular to the end of the inscription (ROM nos. 1, 3). A related example in Cairo, dated H. 304/A.D. 916–917 and made at Bishapur, has a seam in an identical position.[46] Many others may bear evidence of such stitching but remain unrecorded in publications. One wonders whether they were once part of the sleeve of a specific light-coloured garment. Seams also frequently occur on Yamanite ikats (ROM nos. 4, 6).

These observations lead to the supposition that

86

during the reign of the Abbasid and Fatimid Caliphs, the garments of Egypt were still those simple tunics so well represented in the Coptic material, and mantles similar to what the "veil of Saint Anne" once might have been. As they were produced for the most part on simple vertical looms and required minimal sewing along the horizontally used selvages, it is quite natural that their fragments show little sign of stitching.[47] Typical products of the horizontal loom, the costumes of the eastern provinces, however, were constructed vertically from narrow widths of cloth. Although cut in straight, simple pieces, these garments must have required a considerable amount of sewing. Thus it is scarcely surprising that most seams on tiraz fragments are found on those originating in Persia, Iraq, or the Yaman. That seams also occur on such late Egyptian linens as those from Mamluk times (ROM no. 24) may indicate a change in fashion.[48]

Among the Toronto fragments, the most readily identifiable are the shawls, which seem to be typical of Yamanite ikats. Many of these, including ROM no. 4, have a wider plain stripe along the selvages, and a twisted warp fringe at the bottom. The inscription runs parallel to the fringe whether embroidered or painted, and a small word, usually inverted, is often placed near the fringe. An example with two selvages is in the collection of the University of Michigan.[49]

In addition to silk, another group of fabrics generally omitted from tiraz studies consists of woollen textiles ornamented in tapestry weave with wool, or a combination of wool and linen. Many of these are fragments of tunics adorned with two vertical stripes (clavi) both at front and back. Others might have belonged to garments similar to, though heavier than, those of linen with silk tiraz bands. Their decoration is formed mainly of repeating medallions filled with geometric motifs, or of stylized birds and animals, or consists of a series of highly conventionalized human figures. Stylistically many can be ascribed to the Abbasid and Fatimid periods even without specific historical data. However, they are often not considered to be Islamic, but are rather associated with Coptic textiles.[50] One exception is a tapestry woven Egyptian fragment from the first half of the ninth century bearing the following inscription in kufic script: "In the name of God, bless-

ing from God to its owner. What has been made in the tiraz. . ."[51] This example indicates that woollen fabrics were not only produced for Arabs, but were indeed manufactured in the tiraz factories.

If in terms of quantity the greatest production of the royal factories was linen or cotton fabrics, similar to those described earlier, these are not fully representative of the total output. It is clear from the foregoing that any discussion of the operation of the Dār al-Ṭirāz must include silk and woollen goods with the emphasis placed on the former. The best craftsmen were obviously engaged in the production of silk. It was in fact the garments and furnishings of this valuable fibre which constituted the most significant product of the workshops. It is probably to the remarkable figured silks produced in Persia[52] and Spain between the tenth and twelfth centuries that one must look for the haute couture of the mediaeval Islamic court.

Source of patronage

Even if on technical grounds we were to limit our scope to textiles with tapestry woven, embroidered, or painted and printed ornament, the boundaries of the tiraz category would still be ill-defined. Unless the textile bears a historical inscription, we cannot consider it to be the product of a royal factory. Yet there are many hundreds of fragmentary pieces in collections throughout the world that have never been published because they lack historical data. These are often technically identical to the more complete examples.

There are also textiles similar in execution to bona fide tiraz which bear purely decorative themes (ROM nos. 18–20), and generic or unintelligible inscriptions (ROM nos. 9, 11, 12, 23). Textiles with decoration of a generic nature could have been ordered by royalty from the very same workshops, where other pieces were produced with historical inscriptions. The two types might have served different purposes.

The question is further complicated by the fact that during the eleventh century non-historical inscriptions and kufesque (decorative script based on the angular Arabic kufic script) became fashionable. Parallel with this development, the decorative bands of animals in cartouches became more extensive and complex on a variety of fabrics (ROM nos.

18–21). We have no way of knowing the original destination of such textiles, whether for royal, aristocratic, or bourgeois purposes. The decline of historical inscriptions appears to be linked with a growing preference for figurative decoration, and is not necessarily an indication of the absence of royal patronage.

One group of questionable destination is associated with the Coptic community of Egypt. It consists of linen fabrics with tapestry woven, unusually large, summarily drawn animal and figural ornament, which is often accompanied by kufesque inscriptions. A characteristic example is ROM no. 18, which contains a debased representation of a winged, horned quadruped, perhaps a goat or a griffon, in a hexagonal cartouche.[53] The archaic style of the design, and particularly the dimension, have led scholars to attribute this group to the period of transition from Coptic to Islamic textiles, that is to say about the eighth and ninth centuries.[54]

Copts undoubtedly continued to form the backbone of the textile industry for an even longer period,[55] but by the tenth century their output reflected the taste of their Muslim patrons. While formerly they worked exclusively with wool and linen, the tapestry woven bands of late Abbasid and Fatimid times were executed in fine multicoloured silk floss. Technically speaking, this so-called Coptic group with large animal cartouches executed in tapestry weave belongs to this later rather than to the earlier period. Furthermore, the kufesque inscriptions compare with those on Fatimid textiles from the second half of the eleventh century, and cannot be earlier. We must, therefore, view the group not as representing a transitional style, but as a debased version of the finer tapestry woven examples depicting miniature cartouches filled with animals (ROM nos. 12, 19–22). This type of ornament, which makes a sudden appearance around the end of the tenth century, nevertheless recalls Coptic textiles.[56]

What remains to be explained is why, after an interval of several centuries, Coptic and classical themes reappear. Oleg Grabar has suggested that the arts of the eleventh century in general exhibit a taste for exotica and antique modes.[57] We are dealing, therefore, not with a continuation of Coptic techniques, but with a revival of interest in the Coptic and classical themes that inspired them. The

group with large medallions imitates a new fashion in aristocratic *tiraz* fabrics, featuring bands of animals in cartouches *à la copte*.

The same comments may apply to the so-called "Fayyūmī" textiles.[58] This group, whose association with the Coptic community can be documented,[59] is characterized by the reductive style of its animal and human representations and also by a peculiar script. The Arabic letters are transformed as much as possible into squares and topped by ornaments which look like fir trees. Some of these are an integral part of the letter; others are purely decorative. Most of the Fayyūmī inscriptions are illegible and probably ornamental. They are comparable to the kufesque inscriptions on ROM nos. 18 and 21. Two Fayyūmī inscriptions are historical, one giving the place of manufacture, that is to say the Fayyūm,[60] and the other the date H. 375 or 395 (A.D. 985–986 or 1004–1005).[61] Despite their links with the Coptic past, these textiles too could be seen as reflections of a late antique "revival".[62]

It is interesting to conclude from these two groups reflecting a "renaissance" that, while stylistically they can be associated with contemporary aristocratic textiles, they could not have been made for the court. The coarseness of their design, or the use of a heavier wool in the case of the entire Fayyūmī group, indicates that they were destined for a lower class. Indeed, if the inscription alone does not point clearly to the source of patronage, the range in quality represented by these textiles probably reflects its wide base.

The prince did not order exclusively from the royal factories, nor were their products reserved for him alone. There may in fact have been a great deal of mobility of personnel in these factories. In letters from the Cairo Geniza, a private master weaver complains of conscription into the *Dār al-Ṭirāz*.[63] The wide social base from which patrons of textiles were drawn is also clear from the documents. Textiles were needed by everyone, and what emerges from the sources is the preponderance of textiles in the trade of mediaeval Islam.[64] Grabar has pointed out that it was from textiles that people acquired their aesthetic judgment, citing Nāṣir-i Khusraw's comparison of lustre ceramics with *buqallamūn,* a textile which changed colours in the light.[65]

We can, therefore, expect that this extensive range of patronage is reflected in *tiraz* fabrics. Even within such a select group as the collection presented here, the pieces vary greatly in quality. If all of these examples were commissioned by the court, one would have expected greater consistency. We know from *Ḥisba* manuals and regulations that the royal factories were closely supervised.[66] Specifications were even given for the ratio of warp to weft in individual types of cloth.[67] Thus the technical poverty of ROM no. 3, or the "coarseness" of the design in no. 18, may well be indications of the absence of royal patronage. Conversely, one cannot be certain that the finer textiles always came from royal workshops.

Personalization

In studying mediaeval Islamic textiles, one attempts to distinguish those garments or furnishings that represent a unique and specific order from those made simply for the market. Those textiles which bear historical inscriptions clearly belong to the first category. We may say that they have been "personalized" through the introduction of an inscription.

If woven, such inscriptions had to be worked in at the same time as the cloth was woven. Thus, not only the ornamental band but also the fabric as a whole was made to order. But were such custom clothes the prerogative of the ruling class?

The Geniza letters show that highly personalized apparel was desired by the middle class as well. Special garments were ordered for weddings and religious holidays.[68] It is hard to imagine that such commissioned objects lacked any outward sign of personalization. No doubt, inscriptions must have appeared on some of them. There is in fact evidence that private individuals ordered their names inscribed on garments, although no examples have survived.[69] Custom-made textiles were therefore not the exclusive issue of a *Dār al-Ṭirāz*. In fact, contemporary sources demonstrate that the relationship between weaver and customer was often very close.[70] Especially in Egypt, where garments were often woven in a single piece, requiring minimal sewing, the finished look of the outfit was left to a great extent in the hands of the weaver. In the eastern provinces, where inscriptions were usually executed in the

form of surface decoration, such as embroidery or painting, personalization was not a difficulty either. Thus while the craftsman was producing a garment according to tradition and certain specifications, it was not much trouble for him to introduce personalized themes requested by private individuals, such as the name of the owner, Quranic verses, or even a love poem.[71]

Two other methods of personalizing fabrics should be considered side by side with tapestry woven, embroidered, or painted ornamentation. While it was complicated to set up a drawloom to include specific inscriptions within the evenly distributed patterns of silks, it was nevertheless possible to produce such inscriptions, even though the production must have been expensive. The ultimate in personalized textiles were those made for a specific occasion, such as the figured silk shrouds of Persia with their appropriate funerary inscriptions.[72]

The second method for personalizing a garment was to apply the ornamental band. This usage is well illustrated on Persian ceramics and in innumerable other mediums, where men sport kaftan-type coats of figured silk with inscription bands across the upper part of the sleeves.[73] The bands are also referred to in written sources. In Spain, the *Ḥisba* Treatise (eleventh to twelfth century) warns the weavers of *tiraz* against "changing the inscription (*rasm*) on a robe at the fuller's".[74] A similar usage is suggested for the Talmudic period in Iraq by Goitein.[75] How did these bands compare with those woven into the ground of the fabric? Were they applied simply because it would have been difficult to weave personalized inscriptions into textiles produced on the drawloom, or because woven, embroidered, or painted inscriptions would not have shown up against a multicoloured background? Were these alternatives to the usual *tiraz* or something entirely different?

At the other extreme, one would expect to find the equivalent of "yard goods" and cheap garments made in large quantities. Here much research remains to be done. While there is a considerable amount of documentary information on the needs of the prince and the mercantile class, we have little knowledge about those who clothed the working man and the peasant. Did they weave their own clothes? Or were there cheaper varieties of "mass-produced" textiles sold in the bazaar, available to poorer townsfolk and villagers alike? The Geniza letters speak of textiles for sale in the bazaar and of "bazaar-type" garments, but the significance of these terms is not clear.[76] They may even refer to *tiraz* textiles bearing generic inscriptions.

It is also uncertain from the published records whether cloth was sold in bulk or always in the form of a garment. The correspondence of merchants often speaks of raw goods or threads being sold on the open market, or of a particular type of outfit sold in the bazaar, but rarely if ever do they mention bolts of cloth.[77]

To conclude, we should emphasize that there are no characteristics which can be considered to belong exclusively to the *tiraz* category alone. *Tiraz* fabrics do not represent a cross-section of the output of the royal factories, nor do they stand apart in any significant way from textiles produced outside them. In every instance, whether regarding technique, destination, or quality, they appear to belong to broader classes of textiles.

It is hoped that the questions raised here will contribute toward the formulation of new categories into which both *tiraz* textiles and others may meaningfully be integrated. It is no longer possible to pursue *tiraz* studies in a vacuum. In order to understand the place and significance of archaeological material scattered through many collections, the mediaeval Islamic textile industry must be investigated as a whole in the context of socio-economic history. Indeed, the term "*tiraz* fabric" has become obsolete.

Epigraphical Style

Until the twelfth century the epigraphical styles occurring on textiles, as on other mediums, were based on the angular Arabic script known as kufic. The examples from the collection of the Royal Ontario Museum exhibit many variations of kufic script as well as one of *naskhi* or cursive script (no. 23). Some of the styles are peculiar to textiles because of the demands of the technique, particularly embroidery. The tendency to add floral ornaments to the letters or to bifurcate and foliate the terminals reflects the developments found particularly in architectural and lapidary inscriptions.

The most remarkable group from the point of view of epigraphical style are the Yamanite *ikat* cottons. The Toronto collection contains the two major types: those with embroidered decoration (ROM no. 4), and those with painted and gilded inscriptions (ROM nos. 5–6). A brief survey of published examples of both types suggests that the differences are significant. Dating between A.D. 883 and 923 (H. 270–310) and always made at Ṣanꜥāʾ when the place is specified, the first type, with embroidered decoration, is documented by several examples.[78] The epigraphy has the peculiarity that it contains an extraordinary number of "arcs" inserted for decorative purposes in the base line of the inscription and in vertical staffs. Studies of this detail elsewhere have shown that the arc as a decorative device first made its appearance in the lapidary inscriptions of Egypt in the early ninth century.[79]

The second type of *ikat* textiles has painted and gilded inscriptions. Their style of epigraphy is altogether different. The terminals of letters tend to develop foliate forms, some of which are quite elaborate. The tall necks of the *kāf*s sprout branches bearing half-palmette leaves. In addition to the foliation of terminals, the letters themselves are often plaited. The upper and lower bars of rectangular letters are interlaced, as are the vertical staffs of the article *alif-lām*. The arcs of the embroidered inscriptions of the first type of *ikat* are here transformed into complex interlaces (as in the word *Allāh*).

Outside of these examples of Yamanite *ikat*s, this elaborate form of plaited and foliate kufic is unknown in the contemporary West, but it did have a well-documented history in the East. In northeastern Persia it was used by the potters of Samarqand and Nishapur beginning in the early tenth century.[80] Close parallels to the *ikat* script can be found on a large group of these ceramics (figs. 1, 2). Plaited kufic did not spread beyond the confines of Khurasan until the eleventh century and reached

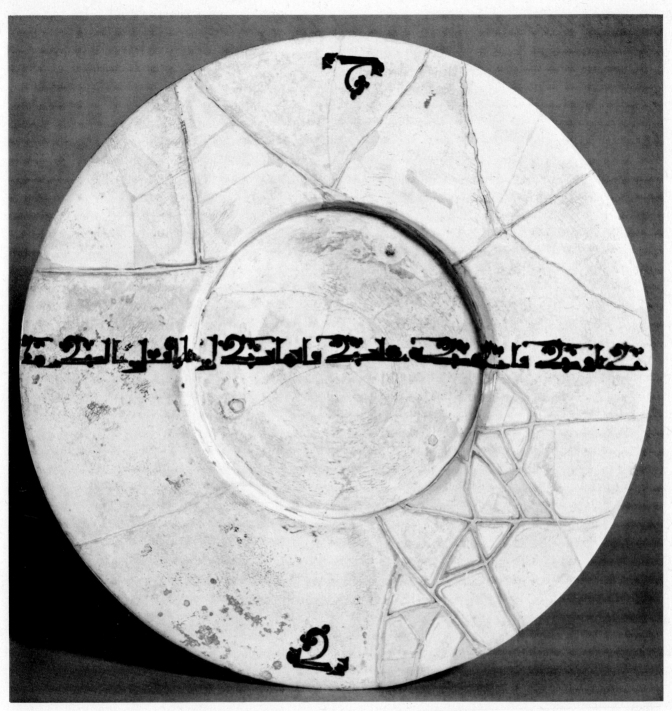

Figure 1.   Slip-painted plate, northeast Persia, tenth century.
Freer Gallery of Art, Washington, D.C., 54.16. Courtesy of the
Freer Gallery of Art.

Figure 2. Unglazed jug, northeast Persia, tenth – eleventh century.
Philadelphia Museum of Art, 19-632. Courtesy of the Philadelphia Museum of Art.

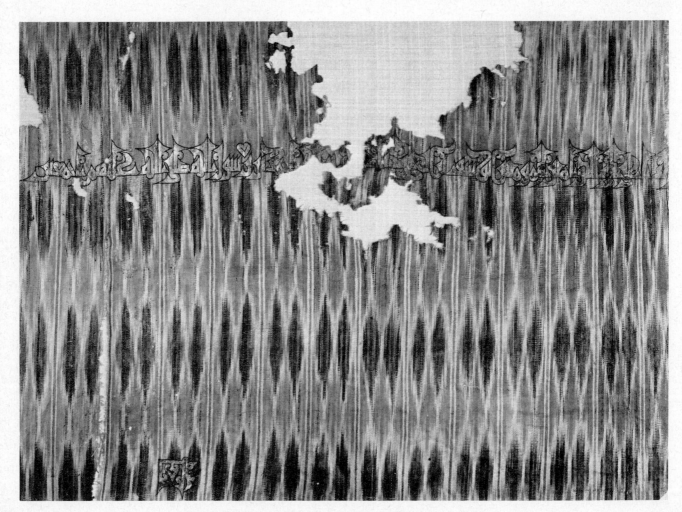

Figure 3. Cotton tabby (warp *ikat*) with painted inscription, Yaman, tenth century.
Cleveland Museum of Art, 50.353. Purchase from the John L. Severance Fund. Courtesy of the Cleveland Museum of Art.

the western Islamic world only in the latter half of the eleventh century.

When it did become popular in the West, its foliate character was reduced. For this reason, the plaited inscriptions on *ikat*s should probably be dated to the second half of the tenth century. The only datable *ikat* fabric with painted decoration, now in the Cleveland Museum (fig. 3), bears the name of the Imām of Yaman Yūsuf b. Yaḥyā, whose reign (A.D. 955–1003) corresponds precisely to this period.[81] The peculiarity of this piece is that, while its epigraphy is similar in feeling to the other known examples, it lacks the flamboyant interlaces which characterize them. Plaiting occurs only in the tall vertical staffs of the article *alif-lām*. The floriation is also more subdued. Perhaps the historical nature of the inscription ruled out a highly decorative treatment.

The question then arises as to how a style of epigraphy originating in northeastern Persia came to appear on textiles made in the Yaman. The simplest explanation is to suppose that one of the Khurasanian potters or a calligrapher familiar with their work brought the new style to Yaman and was put to work decorating Yamanite *ikat* fabrics. Perhaps he accompanied the Persian merchants who plied their wares across the Indian Ocean. The aphorisms which are inscribed on Khurasanian pottery do indeed display a bourgeois mentality fitting with the values of a mercantile class.

Of course there remains the possibility that *ikat* cottons with Khurasanian-type plaited script are Persian imitations of the Yamanite stuffs. Khurasan produced a kind of striped cloth which was sent to Baghdad as tribute.[82] Texts also mention Tus, Nishapur, Merv, and Herat as producers of a striped material (*ʿaṣb, abrād*).[83] An unidentified type of cloth known as *Saʿīdī* was made in both Yaman and Nishapur.[84]

While it should not be totally ruled out, this explanation makes it difficult to account for the Cleveland piece which was commissioned by the Imām of Yaman and is technically similar to the others. Further study of the epigraphy on the *ikat* group, and of the patterns and technical characteristics of *ikat* dyeing, may help to resolve this question.

While the twenty-four *tiraz* fragments presented below constitute but a very small contribution to the study of Islamic textiles, the questions which they have brought to our attention could be resolved through the study of richer collections elsewhere.

Catalogue

Abbreviations

Britton (1938) N.P. Britton, *A study of some early Islamic textiles in the Museum of Fine Arts Boston*, Boston, Museum of Fine Arts, 1938.

Kühnel, Bellinger (1952) E. Kühnel and L. Bellinger, *Catalogue of dated tiraz fabrics: Umayyad, Abbasid, Fatimid, The Textile Museum, Washington, D.C.*, Washington, D.C., The Textile Museum, 1952.

Volov (1966) L. Volov (Golombek), "Plaited kufic on Samanid epigraphic pottery", *Ars Orientalis*, vol. 6 (1966), pp. 107-133.

Ht. of letters refers to the distance between the lower extreme of the base line and the upper limit of the tallest letter.

Iraq and Persia

1. 963.95.7
Iraq or Persia
early 10th century A.D.

Fragment. Raw at all four sides. Near left edge, thick linen thread is drawn in indicating that the piece might have been part of a garment.
L. 35 cm
W. 55 cm

Technical analysis
Weave: tabby, glazed.
Warp and weft: white cotton; Z; count: 17 by 21 per cm.
Surface decoration: embroidered inscriptions in dark blue silk floss with chain and back stitches, in part worked on counted thread.

Inscription
Tall kufic with crescent-shaped tails. Many superfluous letters and strokes confuse the reading. End missing.* Above this a narrow band of kuf-esque (ht. 0.3 cm) ending in the word *Allāh.*

Text:

بسم الله الرحمن الرحيم وما توفيقى (؟)

الا (سد   ؟) بالله عليه توكلت و(اليه   ؟)

أنيب (؟) والعـز (؟) والغبطة والبر (؟)

صلى الله على محمد (؟) والرسول (؟)

الله وسلم (؟)

Ht. of letters 3.7 cm

Translation:
Bismillāh, the Merciful, the Compassionate. My support is in Allāh alone. In Him I put my trust (*Quran* 11:87). Power and beatitude and piety. May Allāh bless Muḥammad. . . . the Prophet. . . . Allāh and grant peace . . .

Acquired from Michel E. Abemayor, New York.

*Similar textile from Baghdad, A.D. 932, in the Museum of Fine Arts, Boston (32.109), illustrated by Britton (1938), fig. 4.

Number 1. ROM, 963.95.7.

2. **963.95.8**
Iraq or Persia
late 10th century A.D.

Fragment. Raw at all sides.
L. 8.9 cm
W. 20.2 cm

Technical analysis
Weave: tabby.
Warp: fine, pale yellow silk floss; count: 52 ends per
cm.
Weft: not fully bleached cotton; Z; count: 37 picks
per cm.
This type of fabric is called *mulham,* meaning half-
silk.
Surface decoration: embroidered inscription in dark
blue silk floss with chain stitches.

Inscription
An incomplete inscription band composed of tall
letters across the width and just above it a band of
minuscular letters. This example of the characteristic kufic of the period with tall vertical staffs and
crescent-shaped tails below the base line contains an
unusual amount of extraneous strokes.

Text:

(صلى الله على محمد النبى) خاتم

النبيين وعلى آله احمعين الطيبين الاخيا (ر)

بركة من الله ونعمة وسلامة وغبطة و ....

Ht. of letters 2.5 cm

Translation:
[May Allāh bless the Prophet Muḥammad]
Seal of the Prophets, and all the members of his
family, the good, the virtuous. Blessing from
Allāh, and grace, peace and happiness [to the
Caliph . . .]

A similar inscription, published by Pfister,* bears
the name of the Caliph al-Qādir billāh and is dated
either 382 H./A.D. 992 or 392 H./A.D. 1001-1002.

The small inscription (ht. of letters 0.3 cm) has not
been deciphered.

Acquired from Michel E. Abemayor, New York.

---

*"Toiles à inscriptions abbasides et fatimides", *Bulletin d'Etudes
Orientales,* vol. 9 (1945-1946), p. 54, no. 13.

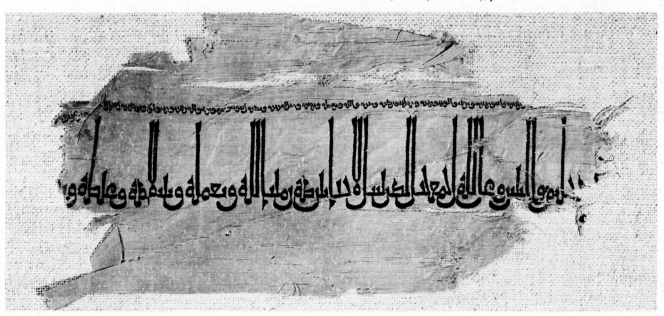

Number 2. ROM, 963.95.8.

3. **963.95.3**
Persia
10th century A.D. (?)

Fragment. Raw at all four sides. On left side, a brown linen (?, Z) thread is drawn in indicating that the piece might have been part of a garment.
L. 13.5 cm
W. 37 cm

Technical analysis
Weave: weft-faced tabby, glazed.
Warp: fine, pale yellow silk floss; count: ca. 50 ends per cm.
Weft: heavier, white cotton; Z; count: ca. 28 picks per cm.
This type of fabric is called *mulham*, meaning half-silk.
Surface decoration: gilded inscription outlined in black ink, printed with a single wood block. The block used for printing the inscription was not carefully aligned while the repetition was made.

Inscription
Text:

لا ا له الا الله

Ht. of letters 1.6 cm
L. of block 4.8 cm

Translation:
There is no God but Allāh (repeated five times).

Acquired from Michel E. Abemayor, New York.

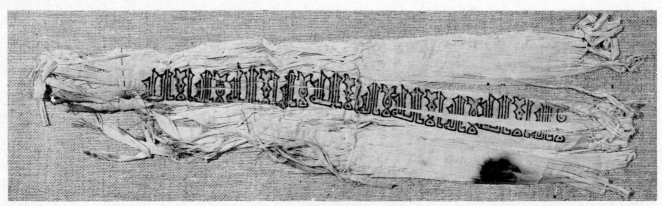

Number 3.   ROM, 963.95.3.

Yaman

4. **963.95.9**
Yaman
10th century A.D.

Fragment of a shawl (?). Top and sides raw, bottom with twisted warp fringes.
L. 39 cm and 11 cm fringes
W. 84.5 cm

Technical analysis
Weave: slightly warp-faced tabby with warp-*ikat* patterning of splashed arrows arranged in fifteen panels by white warp stripes. Plain brown panel along left side.
Warp: coloured cotton (white, brown; *ikat*-dyed in brown, blue, green, white); Z; count: 29 ends per cm.

Weft: brown cotton; Z; count: 14 picks per cm.
Surface decoration: embroidered inscriptions in white cotton (Z, 2S) with back and encroaching satin stitches, worked mostly on counted thread.

Description

A complete inscription runs across the width of the fabric. It is correctly positioned when the fringed end lies at the bottom. Near the fringe, at approximately the middle of the width of the fabric, in a script smaller than that of the main inscription and inverted, is a single word.

Main inscription

The salient feature of the kufic script is the insertion of arcs in the base lines. The trilobial arc in the word *Allāh* is particularly decorative. This device occurs as early as the ninth century A.D. in Egyptian tombstones.* The rhythmic quality of the inscription is enhanced through the pairing of addorsed wedge-shaped serifs at the end of tall vertical staffs.
Text:

بسم الله الملك لله

Ht. of letters 1.8 cm

Translation:
> Bismillāh, Dominion belongs to Allāh (repeated nine times).

Small inscription
Text:

السوى

Ht. of letters 1.2 cm

This word may be read in different ways, but none seems to have a recognizable meaning. It has been suggested** that the term is similar to the Hebrew הנשאי, meaning "the starcher" or person engaged in the trade of starching.

Acquired from Michel E. Abemayor, New York.

---

*G. Miles, "The development of ornament in 9th century Islamic tombstones in Egypt", unpublished MS. 1962. See example dated A.D. 805–806 in Volov (1966), p. 123, text fig. 3F, and discussion of this device (p. 121 f.).
**We are grateful to Professor S.D. Goitein, Institute for Advanced Study, Princeton, for this suggestion. He reports the occurrence of the term in the Geniza documents.

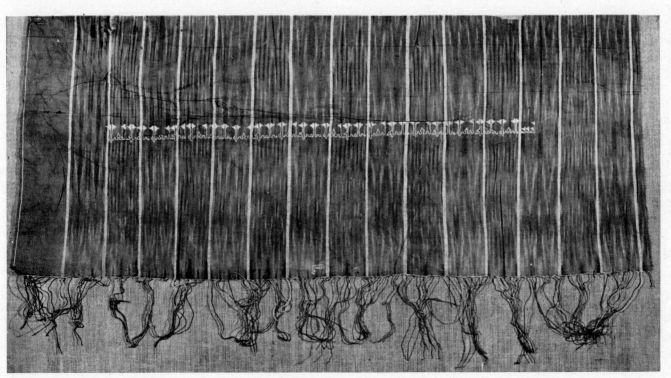

Number 4.   ROM, 963.95.9.

5. **970.364.19**
Yaman
10th century A.D.

Fragment. Raw at all four sides.
L. 28.8 cm
W. 72 cm

Technical analysis
Weave: slightly warp-faced tabby with warp-*ikat* patterning of splashed arrows arranged in fourteen panels by light blue warp stripes.
Warp: coloured cotton (light blue; *ikat*-dyed in white, brown, and blues); Z; count: ca. 30 ends per cm.
Weft: brown cotton; Z; count: ca. 13 picks per cm.
Surface decoration: gilded inscription outlined in black ink.

Inscription
The inscription, which runs across the width of the fabric, is complete at the beginning and at the end, but the middle section has been destroyed. To the right of the inscription lies a complex knot. The missing parts can be reconstructed by comparison with other *ikat* textiles.*
Text:

بسم ا لـ(ـلـــه و ص)ـلى الله

على محمــد

Ht. of letters 3 cm

Translation:
Bismillāh, and may Allāh bless Muḥammad.

The floriated and plaited kufic style of this inscription is more flamboyant than that of a similar painted *ikat* cotton in the ROM's collection (no. 6) and probably represents a local development based on the simpler styles which came out of Khurasan.**

Acquired from Michel E. Abemayor, New York.

———————————

*Britton (1938), 34.1115, fig. 92 (almost identical example).
**Volov (1966), passim.

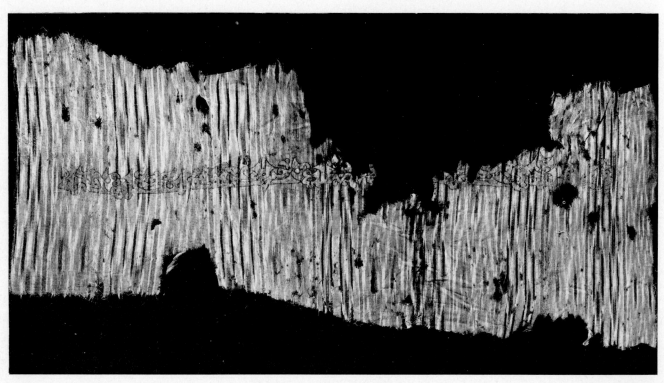

Number 5. ROM, 970.364.19.

6. **970.364.20**
Yaman
10th century A.D.

Fragment of a garment (?). Raw at all four sides; sewn together from two pieces of fabric.
L. 33.5 cm
W. 46 cm

Technical analysis
Weave: warp-faced tabby with warp-*ikat* patterning of splashed arrows, arranged in nine panels by triple stripes.
Warp: coloured cotton (blue, brown, and white; *ikat*-dyed in blues, brown, and white); Z; count: 27 ends per cm.
Weft: brown cotton; Z; count: ca. 8 picks per cm.
Surface decoration: gilded inscription and decoration outlined in black ink.

Inscription
The inscription starts some distance in from the edge of the fabric. It is preceded by a knot based on an eight-pointed star. The end is damaged. The first let-
ter is initiated by a complex cruciform knot. The rectangular letters are intricately plaited, as is the arc in the base line of *Allāh*. The rectangular letters sprout tree-like floriated terminals, similar to those found on the epigraphic pottery of Transoxania of the same date.*
Text:

الله   فسيكفيكهم

Ht. of letters 3 cm

Translation:
May Allāh be sufficient for you.

The longest single word in the *Quran*, hence magical. The inscription is underlined by a guilloche band, and above it is a single word in simple kufic,

العليم

meaning "The Omniscient", referring to Allāh (ht. of letters 1.5 cm).

Acquired from Michel E. Abemayor, New York.

---

*Volov (1966), Table, col. D-9.

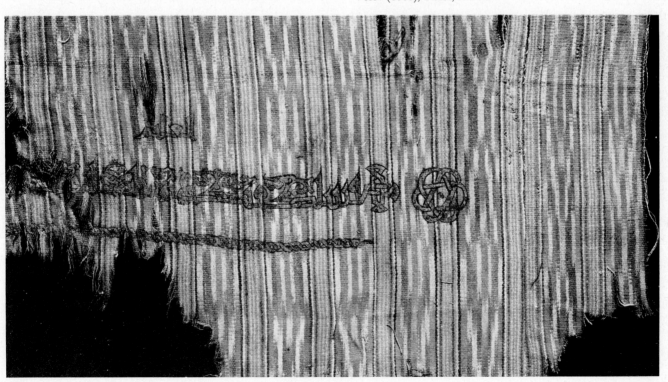

Number 6.   ROM, 970.364.20.

Egypt

7. 963.95.4
Egypt
Abbasid Caliph al-Muṭīʿ (A.D. 946–974)

Fragment. Raw at all four sides.
L. 26 cm
W. 33 cm

Technical analysis
Weave: slightly loosely woven tabby; decorated with broad, solid bands of coloured wefts across the top, and tapestry woven inscription.
Warp: bleached linen; S; count: ca. 20 ends per cm.
Weft: for plain ground, bleached linen; S; count: ca. 16 picks per cm. Blue (ht. 0.6 cm) and pale yellow (ht. 2.5 cm) silk floss for bands. Silk wefts of two other bands are worn out completely. Inscription in black silk floss.

Inscription
The bold, elegant inscription is characteristic of a large group of *tiraz* fabrics made during the reign of al-Muṭīʿ. The base lines are thick while the vertical staffs are attenuated. Terminals are foliated with the widest part of the leaf curled back to form an "eye". A tendril is extended from the point of the leaf forward, curling back again to form a smaller "eye". Final *nūn* has a curvilinear rising tail. The *ʿayn* is an inverted triangle.

Text:

بسم ا) للــه الملك لله الرحمن الرحيم (

لله (sic) الفضل (sic) لمطيع لله اطــ(ـال

الله بقاه)

Ht. of letters 4.8 cm

Translation:
Bismillāh, Dominion is Allāh's, the Merciful, the Compassionate. [ʿAbd] Allāh al-Faḍl [a]l-Muṭīʿ lillāh, [may Allāh] prolong [his existence].

This is an abbreviated form of the protocol but with omissions, such as "ʿAbd", the first part of the name ʿAbd Allāh, which make little sense.

Acquired from Michel E. Abemayor, New York.

Number 7. ROM, 963.95.4

8. **970.364.16**
Egypt
Abbasid Caliph al-Muṭīᶜ (A.D. 946-974)

Fragment. Raw at all four sides.
L. 43 cm
W. 44.5 cm

Technical analysis
Weave: loosely woven tabby; decorated with a
group of broad, solid bands of coloured wefts across
the top, and tapestry woven inscription.
Warp: bleached linen; S; count: 12 ends per cm.
Weft: for plain ground, bleached linen; S; count: 15
picks per cm. One of the decorative bands has
remains of marron-red silk floss, the silk of the
other bands is worn out. Inscription in dark
brown silk floss.

Inscription
Like ROM no. 7, this *tiraz*, executed in the same elegant monumental style, contains the abbreviated
protocol.
Text:

المطيع (الرحـ)يم الرحمن الله بسم)

(الله بقاء) اطا(ل الله لله

Ht. of letters 12 cm

Translation:
Bismillāh, the Merciful, the Compassionate
al-Muṭīᶜ lillāh, may Allāh prolong his existence.

Acquired from Michel E. Abemayor, New York.

Number 8. ROM, 970.364.16.

9. **972.428.4**
Egypt
10th century A.D.

Fragment. Raw at all four sides.
L. 49.5 cm
W. 56 cm

Technical analysis

Weave: tabby, decorated with six broad, solid bands of coloured wefts (ht. 13 cm) across the top.
Warp: bleached linen; Z; count: 14 ends per cm.
Weft: for plain ground, bleached linen; Z; count: 16 picks per cm. Blue linen (Z) and red silk floss for series of bands.
Surface decoration: embroidered inscription in crimson silk floss with various counted thread stitches. A number of horizontal rows of back-stitching give the guide lines for the inscription.

Inscription

The inscription is complete and does not extend the full width of the fabric. The letters are carefully proportioned; their terminals are wedge-shaped, some-times bifurcated. Round letters tend to be angular. The medial ʿayn rests on point between a pair of arc-ligatures and takes the form of a "horned" blossom with its centre in reserve. There are many extraneous letters and strokes, and some rising tails (*nūn*, *mīm*).

Text:

بسم الله الرحمن الرحيم (sic)

الله الملك الله (sic) العلى العظيم

الله توكل الله على محمد الله

Ht. of letters 0.8 cm

Translation:

Bismillāh, the Merciful, the Compassionate, Allāh, Dominion belongs to Allāh, the Exalted, the Mighty, Allāh, Trust in? (bless?) Muḥammad, Allāh.

Acquired from Dr. Halim Doss, Vienna.

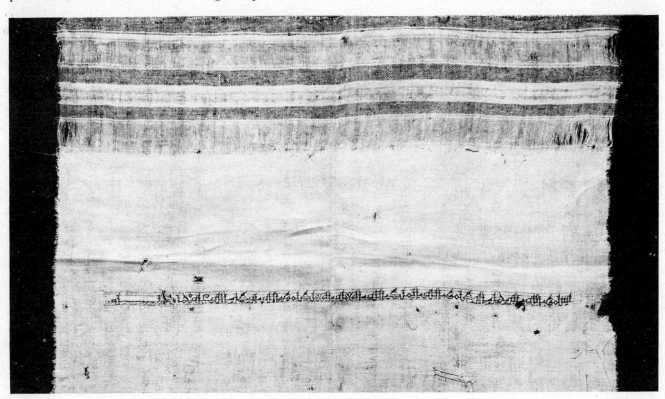

Number 9.   ROM, 972.428.4.

10. **963.95.5**
Egypt
Fatimid Caliph al-Muᶜizz (A.D. 969-975)

Fragment. Raw at all four sides.
L. 50 cm
W. 56.5 cm

Technical analysis
Weave: slightly loosely woven tabby, decorated
with tapestry woven inscriptions and four broad
solid weft bands across the top (ht. 14.6 cm).
Warp: bleached linen; S; count: 16 ends per cm.
Weft: for plain ground; bleached linen; S; count: 12
    picks per cm. Decorative bands in blue linen
    (S) and red silk floss, silk wefts of two other
    bands worn out completely. Inscription in red
    silk floss.

Inscription
It bears the name of the Fatimid Caliph al-Muᶜizz,
but the style harks back to the large monumental
inscriptions produced for the Abbasid Caliph
al-Muṭīᶜ.* The opening formula shows the same
tendency to abbreviate. Kühnel suggests that this
group was made at Tinnis.**
Text:

معد   الرحمن الرحيم   (sic)   (ــ)سم   (بـ)

...   تميم   ابى

Ht. of letters 5.7 cm

Translation:
    Bism[illāh], the Merciful, the Compassionate,
    Maᶜadd Abī Tamīm.

Acquired from Michel E. Abemayor, New York.

---

* Cf. ROM no. 7.
** Kühnel, Bellinger (1952), p. 57, acc. no. 73.509.

Number 10.   ROM, 963.95.5.

11. **963.95.11**
Egypt
10th century A.D.

Fragment. Top and bottom raw, selvages at sides.
L. 24.5 cm
W. 53.3 cm (loom width)

Technical analysis
Weave: slightly loosely woven tabby with tapestry woven decoration and inscription.
Warp: bleached linen; S; count: 33 ends per cm.
Weft: for plain ground, bleached linen; S; count: 22
   picks per cm. Decoration in coloured silk floss
   (crimson, golden yellow, green). Inscription in
   dark blue silk floss.

Description
Across the width, near the top, a narrow tapestry woven band (ht. 1 cm) is placed with repeating, framed, highly conventionalized floral ornaments.

Inscription
In very simple kufic, the same pair of words is repeated across the whole width of the fabric below the decorative band.
Text:

الملك لله

Ht. of band 0.5-0.7 cm

Translation:
Dominion belongs to Allāh.

Acquired from Michel E. Abemayor, New York.

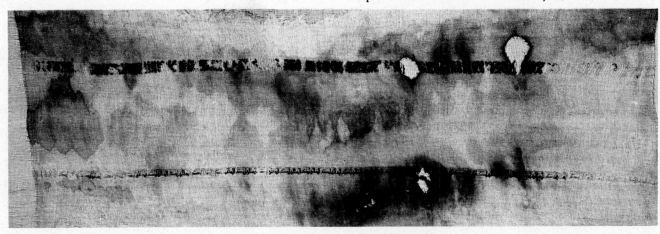

Number 11.   ROM, 963.95.11.

12. **970.364.8**
Egypt
Fatimid Caliph al-Ḥākim (A.D. 996-1020)

Fragment in small pieces, each of them raw at all sides.
L. 11.5 cm
Reconstructed W. ca. 35.5 cm

Technical analysis
Weave: very loosely woven tabby with tapestry woven decoration and inscription.

Warp: bleached linen; S; count: ca. 23 ends per cm.
Weft: for plain ground, bleached linen; S; count:
   ca. 17 picks per cm. Decoration in coloured silk
   floss (yellow with some green and black). Inscription in mustard yellow silk floss against
   crimson silk ground, small details in green silk.

Description
This very fragmentary *tiraz* was once a fine piece with a band of animals in medallions between two inscription bands (ht. of triple band 5.3 cm). The textile was unfortunately further damaged in wash-

104

ing. One of the better-preserved fragments is shown in figure 12.

Inscription

All that is preserved are sections of the usual Fatimid protocol for the Caliph al-Ḥākim. The kufic has a monumental quality with half-palmette terminals and an effective pairing of vertical staffs with addorsed terminals. This style appears to be derived from the grand scale inscriptions of the Caliph al-Muṭīᶜ, but with a scale now reduced (see ROM nos. 7-8).

Text (as reconstructed):

بسم الله (الرحمن الرحيم)   لا اله

الا الله محم—(ـد رسول الله (على

ولى الله) نصر من الله) لعبد الله

وليه المنصور ابى على (الامام الحاكم

بأمر الله صلوات الله عليـ—ه) ـه وعلى

آبائه الائمة الطاهرين وابنائه الا (كرمين) ...

Ht. of letters 1.2 cm

Translation:

Bismillāh, the Merciful, the Compassionate, there is no God but Allāh, Muḥammad is the Prophet of Allāh, [ᶜAlī is the Friend of Allāh], assistance from Allāh to the Servant of Allāh and His friend al-Manṣūr Abī ᶜAlī al-Imām al-Ḥākim bi-amr-illāh, Allāh's benedictions upon him and upon his ancestors, the pure Imāms, and his generous descendants...

Acquired from Michel E. Abemayor, New York.

Number 12.   ROM, 970.364.8.

13. **970.364.15**
Egypt
ca. A.D. 1000

Fragment in two pieces. Raw at all sides.
a   L.   ca. 32 cm   **b** L.   15 cm
     W. 40.5 cm   W.   16 cm

Technical analysis
Weave: tabby with tapestry woven inscription.
Warp: bleached linen; S; count: 21 ends per cm.
Weft: for plain ground, bleached linen; S; count:
    ca. 17 picks per cm. At the top, free warp
    threads indicate a broad and solid band woven
    across the width; the presumably coloured silk
    wefts are worn out completely. Inscription in
    bleached linen (S) against dark red silk floss
    ground (slightly S?).

Inscription
The *tiraz* forms a boat-shaped panel, with the inscription in reserve. The decorative effect of the pair of words repeated at least eight times is derived from the similar treatment of letters with rising tails (two *waws* and a *qāf*) and the use of curved ligatures. Vertical staffs are crossed by horizontal bars.*
Text:

والتوفيق   بالله

Ht. of band 1.8 cm
Reconstructed L. of inscription 47 cm

Translation:
    Success through Allāh.

Acquired from Michel E. Abemayor, New York.

---

*Almost identical: Kühnel, Bellinger (1952), acc. no. 73.44 (pl. 31), Fatimid Caliph al-Hākim.

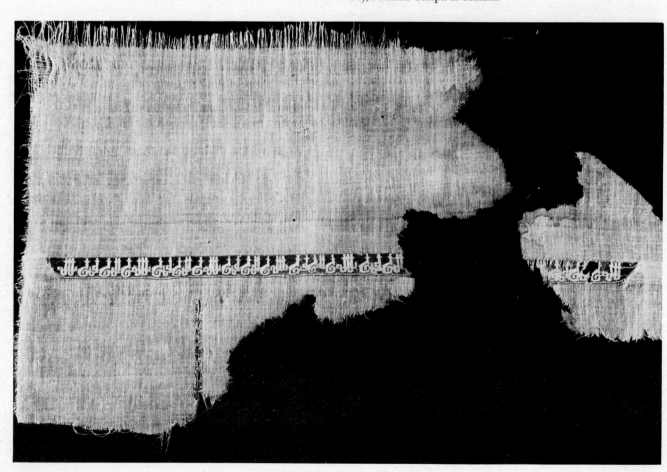

Number 13.   ROM, 970.364.15.

106

14. **970.364.2,a-b**
   Egypt
   Fatimid Caliph al-Ẓāhir (A.D. 1021-1036)
   Public factory, Damietta, 412 H./A.D. 1021-1022

Fragment in two pieces. Selvages at both sides, top
raw, bottom with warp fringes (?).
a L. ca. 22 cm **b** L. 19 cm
   W. 36.2 cm   W. 40 cm
Loom width ca. 82 cm

Technical analysis
Weave: loosely woven tabby with tapestry woven
decoration and inscription, some details freely outlined with an extra weft.
Warp: bleached linen; S; count: 26 ends per cm.
Weft: for plain ground, bleached linen; S; count: 17
   picks per cm. Decoration in dark blue silk floss
   and bleached linen (S). Inscription in dark
   blue silk floss against bleached linen ground
   (S).

Number 14.   ROM, 970.364.2, a-b.

107

Description

Two bands extend across the width (ht. 1.2 cm), decorated with linear meander based on repeating and reversing diamonds. The second band is flanked by inscriptions above and below.

Inscription

The two bands of epigraphy bear the same inscription, beginning from opposite sides of the fabric width. Although much of the fabric is lost, the complete inscription can be reconstructed. The kufic is in the "miniature" style typical of the eleventh century. The *ᶜayn* takes the form of a trefoil blossom. Delicate tendrils occur sparsely in the background and have but a tenuous connection to the script.*

Translation:

> Bismillāh, the Merciful, the Compassionate. There is no God but Allāh. Assistance from Allāh and speedy victory to the Servant of Allāh and his friend ᶜAlī Abī'l-Ḥasan, the Imām al-Ẓāhir li-iᶜzāz-dīn-illāh, Commander of the Faithful, son of the Imām al-Ḥākim bi-amr-illāh, Commander of the Faithful. Allāh's benedictions and His Mercy and His Blessings upon them both and their pure ancestors, the Imāms, the Guides, the Mahdīs. From what was ordered to be made in the public factory of Damietta, in the year 412 [A.D. 1021-1022].

This unusually complete form of the Fatimid formula appeared during the second year of the reign of al-Ẓāhir. The factory at Damietta had been active since the early tenth century A.D. This is the only published example from Damietta of the year 412 H., although others are known from 411 and 415.**

Acquired from Michel E. Abemayor, New York.

---

*Cf. Kühnel, Bellinger (1952), acc. no. 73.375, pl. 34 (A.D. 1050-1058).
**Répertoire chronologique d'epigraphie arabe*, vol. 6, nos. 2223 and 2338.

Text:

(بسم الله الرحمن الرحيم لا اله الا

الله نصــ)ـــر من الله وفتح قريب

لعبد الله ووليه على ابن الحسن الامام

الظاهر لاعزاز دين الله ...

(امير المومنيــن بن الامام الحا)كم

بامر الله

امير (المومنين صلوات الله ورحمته)

وبركاته عليهما وعلى ابائهـ(ـما الطا)هرين

الائمة الهادئين المهديين . مما امر

بعمله فى طراز العامة (بدمياط سنة

اثنتى عشرة واربع مائة)

Ht. of letters 0.8 cm

1. Missing from -b- lower band.
2. Missing from -b- upper band.
3. Missing from -a- and -b- lower band.
4. Missing from -b- upper band.
5. Missing from -b- upper band.

108

15. 973.424.8, a-b
Egypt
Fatimid Caliph al-Ẓāhir (A.D. 1021–1036)

Fragment in two pieces, **a**: raw at all four sides; **b**: one side with selvage, other sides raw.

a L. 32 cm   **b** L. 31 cm
   W. 66 cm   W. 40 cm

Technical analysis
Weave: loosely woven tabby with tapestry woven inscription.
Warp: bleached linen; S; count: ca. 25 ends per cm.
Weft: for plain ground, bleached linen; S; count: 15 picks per cm. Inscription in dark brown (originally red?) silk floss against bleached linen ground (S).

Inscription
The two fragments represent most of the original band which was approximately 115 cm long. The letters are executed in a thick and thin line, with bifurcated and foliated terminals. The low letters have rising tails. The final *mīm*s have rising tails which are almost isolated from the body of the letter. Delicate tendrils with blossoms consisting of three dots fill the background.

Text:

(و) وليه على (ابى الحس)ـن الامام

الظاهر لاعزاز دين الله امير المومنين بن

الامام الحاكم بامر الله امير المومنين

صلوات الله عـ(ـليهما وعلى)

a

(محمـ)ـد خاتم النبيين وسيد المرسلين

وعلى آله الطيبين الطاهرين الاحسن

(الاخيار) sic for وسلم عليهم تسليما

b

Ht. of letters 1.3 – 1.5 cm

Number 15.   ROM, 973.424.8, a.

Translation:
    a [and] his friend ᶜAlī [Abī'l-Ḥasa]n, the Imām al-Ẓāhir li-iᶜzāz-dīn-illāh, Commander of the Faithful, son of the Imām al-Ḥākim bi-amr-illāh, Commander of the Faithful. Allāh's benedictions upon [them both and upon]
    b [Muḥamma]d, Seal of the Prophets, Prince of the Apostles, and upon his family, the good, the pure, the virtuous, and grant them peace.

Acquired from Loewi-Robertson Inc., Los Angeles.

Number 15. ROM, 973.424.8, b.

16. **963.95.6**
Egypt
Fatimid Caliph al-Mustanṣir (A.D. 1036-1094)

Fragment. Selvage at right side, other sides raw.
L. 27.3 cm
W. 89 cm

Technical analysis
Weave: slightly loosely woven tabby with tapestry woven inscription.
Warp: bleached linen; S; count: 24 ends per cm.
Weft: for plain ground, bleached linen; S; count: 22 picks per cm. Inscription in red silk floss against bleached linen ground (S).

Inscription
The inscription band is damaged at the beginning and is incomplete at the end. The kufic script is executed in precise thick and thin lines, showing rising tails, with a tendency to coil the curving parts of letters (e.g., *wāw*, *ʿayn*). Medial *ʿayn* takes the form of a crown-like trefoil blossom. Terminals are bifurcated. Most unusual is the extensive use of the arc in base lines and within letters (initial *ʿayn*, rectangular letters), as well as for ligatures. The background of the inscription is treated as a series of small panels, demarcated by the vertical staffs. Each panel is decorated in a slightly different way (combinations of zigzags and dots in three registers or S-shaped motifs).

Text:

لا اله (بسم) الله الرحمن الرحيم

محمد وحده لاشريك له الا الله

صلى الله رسول الله على ولى الله

نصر من الله لعبد الله ووليه عليهما

معد (ابى تميم ٠٠)

Ht. of band 2.2. cm

Translation:
Bismillāh, the Merciful, the Compassionate, there is no God but Allāh alone, He has no partner, Muḥammad is the Prophet of Allāh, ʿAlī is the Friend of Allāh, may Allāh bless them both. Assistance from Allāh to the Servant of Allāh and His friends Maʿadd [Abī Tamīm]

The inscription refers to the Fatimid Caliph al-Mustanṣir Billāh.

Acquired from Michel E. Abemayor, New York.

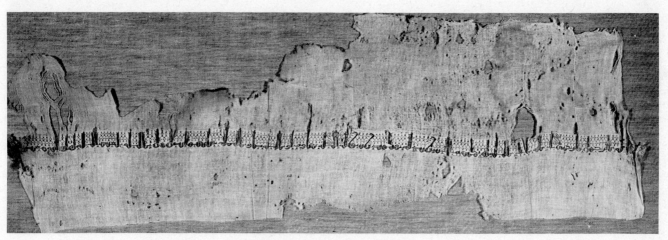

Number 16.   ROM, 963.95.6.

111

17. **970.364.17**
   Egypt
   Fatimid Caliph al-Mustanṣir (A.D. 1036-1094)

Fragment. Raw at all four sides.
L. 26 cm
W. 62.5 cm

Technical analysis
Weave: tabby with tapestry woven inscription.
Warp: bleached linen; S; count: ca. 24 ends per cm.
Weft: for plain ground, bleached linen; S; count: 16
   picks per cm. Inscription in dark blue silk floss
   (S?) against bleached linen ground (S).

Inscription
The initial is damaged and probably incomplete;
the end is missing. The reading of the inscription is
obscured by the delicate scrolling tendrils emanat-
ing from the letters and filling the background. Below the base line, repeated crescent motifs.

Text:

نصر من الله لمعد ابى التميم (...)

(؟) المستنصر بالله امير المومنين

صلوات الله عليه وعلى ابائه الائمة

الطاهرين مما امر بعمله (الوزير الاجل؟)

Ht. of letters 1 cm

Translation:
   . . . [Assistance from Allāh to Maʿadd Abī
   Tamīm?] al-Mustanṣir billāh, Commander of
   the Faithful. The benedictions of Allāh upon
   him and upon his ancestors, the pure Imāms.
   From that which was ordered to be made by
   [the *wazīr*, the most illustrious]

Acquired from Michel E. Abemayor, New York.

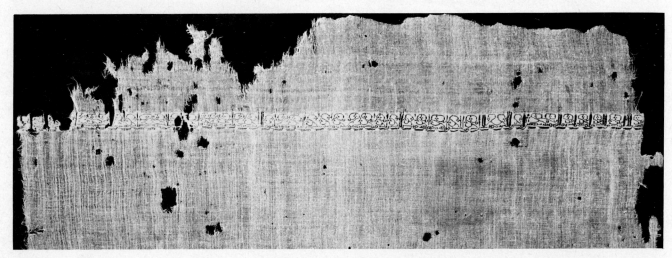

Number 17.   ROM, 970.364.17.

18. **970.117.3**
   Egypt
   11th century A.D.

Fragment. Left side with selvage, other sides raw.
L. 20 cm
W. 23.4 cm

Technical analysis
Weave: tabby with tapestry woven decoration and
inscriptions.
Warp: linen; Z; count: ca. 22 ends per cm.
Weft: for plain ground, linen; Z; count: 17 picks
   per cm. Decoration in coloured silk floss (red,
   yellow, blue, and some black) and bleached

linen (Z), originally probably outlined in black silk floss. Inscriptions in bleached linen (Z), probably with black silk outlines, against red silk floss ground, ornaments in yellow silk floss.

Description

The decorative band consists of three parts: a wide frieze (ht. 8 cm) of lozenges containing animals, bordered by two inscription bands (ht. 5 cm). The sole remaining hexagonal lozenge contains a striding winged goat or griffon.

Inscription

This kufesque decoration is probably derived from the word اليمن (Good fortune). Between the thick vertical staffs, formed by the merging of the rising tail of *nūn* and the article *alif-lām*, were large trilobial flowers, now barely visible.

Ht. of letters 3 cm

Commentary

The angularity in the body of the animal recalls a series of tapestry woven bands with similarly reductive renderings of animals,* some of which have been attributed to the eighth and ninth centuries.** The style of the kufesque, however, rules out an early date. It does not appear before the eleventh century.†

Acquired from the Galerie Heidi Vollmoeller, Zürich.

---

*The Cleveland Museum of Art, acc. nos. 29.934, 50.530, 50.531, 50.535, 50.536. The Metropolitan Museum of Art, New York, acc. nos. 27.168.1, 3-4, 7 (gifts of George D. Pratt), 27.-170.58-60, 67 (Rogers Fund).
**Britton (1938), 11,89 (figs. 15-16).
†Cf. Kühnel, Bellinger (1952), 15, 1303 (fig. 55).

Number 18.   ROM, 970.117.3.

19. **970.117.4**
   Egypt
   11th century A.D.

Fragment. Raw at all four sides.
L. 18.1 cm
W. 15.6 cm

Technical analysis
Weave: tabby with tapestry woven decoration and inscription.
Warp: bleached linen; S; count: 20 ends per cm.
Weft: for plain ground, bleached linen; S. Decoration in coloured silk floss (crimson, mustard yellow, blue, green, dark brown) and some bleached linen (S). Inscription in crimson silk floss against bleached linen (S) ground; ornaments in mustard yellow, green, blue, and black silk floss.

Description
This fragment represents an incomplete section of a decorative band. It consisted of at least one wide band of lozenges, a narrower band with zigzag meander, and a wide inscription band. The bands are separated by a series of narrow guards. None of the elements of the design are clearly formulated. Identifiable motifs are a trilobial leaf, a full palmette, and a curving Y-shaped ornament, perhaps a bird.

Inscription
The kufesque band features a series of paired vertical staffs with addorsed arcs at midpoints. Below the base line run crescent-shaped strokes, unrelated to the letters above. The kufesque is perhaps based on the word اليمن (Good fortune).*

Ht. of letters 4 cm

Acquired from the Galerie Heidi Vollmoeller, Zürich.

*Cf. Britton (1938), fig. 67, no. 15.376; second half 11th century A.D..

Number 19.   ROM, 970.117.4.

20. **963.95.13**
Egypt
12th century A.D.

Fragment. Right side with selvage, other three sides raw.
L. 15.5 cm
W. 33.8 cm

Technical analysis
Weave: tabby with tapestry woven decoration and inscriptions.
Warp: not fully bleached linen; S; count: ca. 27 ends per cm.
Weft: for plain ground, bleached linen; S; count: ca. 26 picks per cm. Decoration in coloured silk floss (yellow, crimson, blue, green, black) and some bleached linen (S). Outlines in black silk floss.

Description
The tapestry consists of a wide central band bor-dered by narrow inscription bands (ht. 8.7 cm). The central band contains three rows of lozenges. The middle row has larger lozenges with rabbits alternating with smaller ones containing birds, while the upper and lower rows have lozenges with kufesque ornament, palmettes, and birds. The background is filled with a linear scrolling design.

Inscription
The inscription bands are dominated by the rinceau ornament which almost occupies their full width. It contains a single large leaf or blossom. In minuscule letters, a kufic word, perhaps حليمة (Power), is repeated across the bands.*

Ht. of letters 1 cm

Acquired from Michel E. Abemayor, New York.

---

*This reading was given to a similar inscription: Britton (1938), 30,674, p. 67, fig. 80.

Number 20.   ROM, 963.95.13.

21. **970.117.5**
Egypt
12th century A.D.

Fragment. Raw at all four sides.
L. 23 cm
W. 22.3 cm

Technical analysis
Weave: tabby with tapestry woven decoration and inscriptions.
Warp: bleached linen; S; count: 35 ends per cm.
Weft: for plain ground, bleached linen; S; count: 30 picks per cm. Decoration in coloured silk floss (crimson, golden yellow, black, green-blue),

and some bleached linen (S). Inscriptions in bleached linen (S) with details in black silk floss against crimson silk ground; ornaments in golden yellow silk floss with black outlines.

Description

The tapestry consists of three wide bands. Those above and below the broader central band (ht. 9.4 cm) are identical (ht. 5 cm). They are filled with diamond-shaped lozenges, each containing a bird. These bands are framed by arcades sprouting a pair of bell-shaped blossoms in the spaces between the lozenges. The central band consists of nine horizontal sections: a black guard, a kufic inscription, a linear meander, a scroll band composed of intersecting circles containing a rabbit within six-pointed stars, and the repeat of the first three bands with the inscription band inverted.

Inscription

Along either side of the central band are kufesque borders whose forms are probably derived from the repetition of the word حليفة (Power). Between the regularly repeated vertical staffs are scrolls containing a single trilobial flower.

Ht. of letters 1.3 cm

Acquired from the Galerie Heidi Vollmoeller, Zürich.

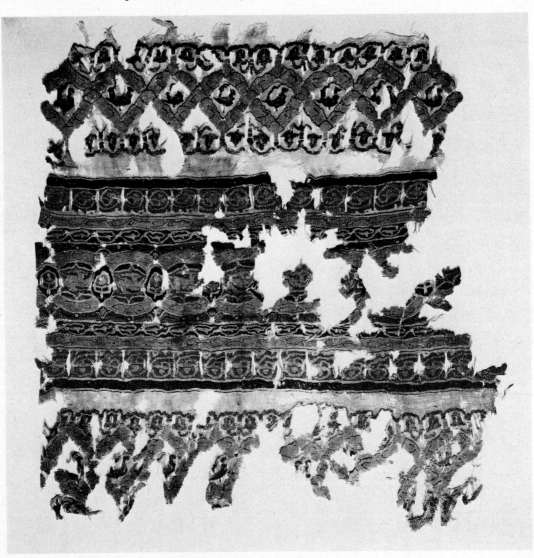

Number 21.   ROM, 970.117.5.

22. **963.95.2**
   Egypt
   early 12th century A.D.

Fragment. Raw at four sides. Fabric of background sewn together from three parts with bleached linen thread (A); a decorated piece (B) is sewn on top. Part of a garment?

A L. 21.6 cm **B** L. 14.6 cm
   W. 39 cm   W. 28 cm

Technical analysis

A
Weave: tabby.
Warp: bleached linen; Z; count: 26 ends per cm.
Weft: bleached linen; Z; count: 24 picks per cm.
B
Weave: tabby with tapestry woven decoration.

Warp: blue linen; S; count: 24 ends per cm.
Weft: for plain ground, blue linen; S; count: ca 25 picks per cm. Decoration in coloured silk floss (crimson, green, mustard yellow, brown) and some bleached linen (S). Outlines in brown silk floss.

Description
The patterned part consists of three bands. Framed by meander guards, the top and bottom bands are composed of tangent octagons containing roundels with striding rabbits and winged beasts. The backgrounds are marbled with spiralling lines. The central band is filled with a large rinceau pattern of pomegranates and grape clusters.

Acquired from Michel E. Abemayor, New York.

Number 22.   ROM, 963.95.2.

23. **961.107.3**
Egypt
mid-12th century A.D.

Fragment. Selvage at right side, other three sides raw.
L. 39.3 cm
W. 17.8 cm

Technical analysis
Weave: tabby (glazed) with tapestry woven decoration and inscriptions.
Warp: bleached linen; S; count: 20 ends per cm.
Weft: for plain ground, bleached linen; S; count: 17
    picks per cm. Decoration mainly in yellow and
    some red silk floss, small details in dark blue
    silk floss and bleached linen (S). Inscriptions in
    red silk floss against golden yellow silk ground.

Description
The fragment preserves part of a wide, solid band of tapestry, consisting of four narrow inscription bands alternating with three fields of decoration.* The top and bottom fields are similar and are composed of interlocking diamonds formed by stylized meanders. Each diamond contains a central arch-shaped medallion with rabbit, on top and bottom of which are pairs of birds. The central field, which is wider, consists of a diamond grid whose interstices are filled with rabbits and a U-shaped motif.

Inscription
In *naskhi* script, the inscriptions are repetitions of two words.
Text:

اليمن   والاقبال

Ht. of letters 1.6 cm

Translation:
    Good fortune and prosperity

Acquired from Michel E. Abemayor, New York.

---

*Britton (1938), 07.466 (fig. 87) has identical inscription and similar decorative bands.

Number 23.   ROM, 961.107.3.

24. 910.122.25
Egypt
14th century A.D.

Fragment. Bottom hemmed, sides and top raw. Sewn together from three pieces. Probably part of the hemline of a long, shirt-like garment.
L. 3.6 cm
W. 58.2 cm

Technical analysis
Weave: tabby.
Warp: not fully bleached linen; S; count: 17 ends per cm.
Weft: not fully bleached linen; S; count: 17 picks per cm.
Surface decoration: embroidered simulating inscription in black silk floss with back stitches, worked on counted thread ("Holbein stitch").*

Description
The band consists of a series of identical square-shaped motifs composed in outline stitches. None of these are complete.

Ht. 1.7 cm

The Walter Massey Collection. Acquired by Dr. C.T. Currelly in Egypt, 1907-1909.

*C.J. Lamm, "Some Mamluk embroideries", *Ars Islamica*, vol. 4 (1937), pp. 65-76, fig. 3. Victoria and Albert Museum, London, acc. nos. 792-1898, 804-1898, 1126-1900, 1136-1900, 1149-1900, 1157-1900, 1171-1900, 1172-1900, 1175-1900, 2174-1900, T.137-1928, T.252-1958; Metropolitan Museum of Art, New York, acc. nos. 27.168.8, 29.179.43. For embroidered Mamluk garments, see note 35.

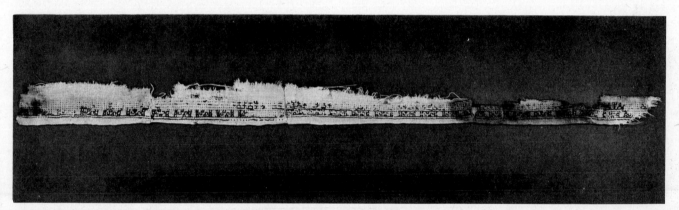

Number 24. ROM, 910.122.25.

Notes

This study was undertaken as a joint project of the Textile and West Asian departments of the Royal Ontario Museum. The inscriptions were read by Lisa Golombek, and the technical analysis undertaken by Veronika Gervers. Since the completion of this manuscript, Dr. Golombek has lectured on "Tiraz and patronage", Islamic Art Seminar, Hunter College, New York, N.Y., October 1975.

The authors are indebted to Miss Susan Boyd, Curator of the Byzantine Collections, Dumbarton Oaks, Washington, D.C.; Dr. Marilyn Jenkins, Associate Curator of Islamic Art, Metropolitan Museum of Art, New York; Mr. Donald King, Keeper of Textiles, Victoria and Albert Museum, London; Miss Louise

W. Mackie, Curator of Islamic Art, Textile Museum, Washington, D.C.; and Miss Dorothy G. Shepherd, Curator of Textiles, Cleveland Museum of Art, for the research facilities offered in their collections and for their helpful suggestions.

1. Eleven of the ROM's *tiraz* fragments are not included in this catalogue: 910.122.13 (linen tabby with embroidered inscription; Egypt, Abbasid), 963.95.1 (linen tabby with tapestry woven decoration; Egypt, Fatimid), 963.95.10 (linen tabby with tapestry woven decoration; Egypt, Fatimid), 963.95.12 (linen tabby with tapestry woven decoration; Egypt, Fatimid), 963.-95.14 (linen tabby with tapestry woven decoration; Egypt, Fa-

timid), 963.95.16 (linen tabby with tapestry woven decoration; Egypt, Abbasid/Fatimid), 970.117.2 (linen tabby with tapestry woven decoration; Egypt, Fatimid), 972.428.3 (linen tabby with embroidered inscription; Egypt, Abbasid), 975.403.1 (linen tabby with tapestry woven decoration and embroidered factory mark; Egypt, Fatimid); 975.403.3 (cotton tabby with painted inscription; probably Iraq, tenth century A.D.), 975.-403.4 (linen tabby with embroidered inscription; Egypt, Abbasid). See also ROM 970.364.10 (tapestry woven in wool and cotton; probably Iraq, eighth century A.D.), 975.403.5 (linen tabby with tapestry woven decoration and kufesque inscription in wool; Egypt, Fatimid).

2. See article on *tiraz* by A. Grohmann (*Encyclopaedia of Islam*, first ed., Leiden, Brill, 1913–1936). While still useful for textual sources, its presentation of actual examples is outdated. The most complete bibliographies are in E. Kühnel and L. Bellinger, *Catalogue of dated tiraz fabrics: Umayyad, Abbasid, Fatimid, The Textile Museum, Washington, D.C.*, Washington, D.C., 1952; N.P. Britton, *A study of some early Islamic textiles in the Museum of Fine Arts Boston*, Boston, 1938; R.B. Serjeant, *Islamic textiles: Material for a history up to the Mongol Conquest*, Beirut, Librairie du Liban, 1972 (collection or articles originally published serially in *Ars Islamica*, vols. 9–14, 1942–1951).

3. A fragment with the name of the Fatimid Caliph al-Ḥākim (A.D. 996–1021) used to belong to the treasury of Notre Dame, Paris. See G. Marçais and G. Wiet, "Le 'voile de Sainte Anne' d'Apt", *Monuments et mémoires*, vol. 34/1-2 (1934), p. 185, note 3. For further bibliography on the "veil of Saint Anne" see note 36 in this study. An early Muslim fabric served as cover for the "veil of our Lady", now in the Cathedral of Chartres. See X. Delaporte, *Le voile de Notre Dame*, Chartres, 1927, p. 13, pls. 6–7; R. Ettinghausen, "Islamic art and archaeology", in *Near Eastern culture and society*, ed. T.C. Young, Princeton, 1951. The "veil of Hisham II" (A.D. 976–1012) was formerly housed in the Church of San Estaban de Gormaz (110 x 40 cm; linen, with tapestry woven decoration and inscription in silk and gold filé, the ornaments show strong Fatimid influence, perhaps made in Egypt), now in the collection of the Academy of History, Madrid. See D.T. Rice, *Islamic art*, New York, Praeger, 1965, fig. 78; José Manuel Pita Andrade, *Les trésors de l'Espagne*, Geneva, Skira, 1967, p. 118 and colour pl.

4. " 'Cairo Geniza documents' refers to material dating from the tenth through the thirteenth centuries A.D., written mostly in Hebrew characters but in Arabic language, and originally preserved in a synagogue, and partly also in a cemetery of Fustat. The material comprises every conceivable type of writing, such as official, business, and private correspondence, detailed court records and other legal documents, contracts, accounts, checks, receipts and inventories, writs of marriage, divorce, and manumission, prescriptions, charms, and the like. These writings originated mostly in the middle and lower classes, and are therefore invaluable for the knowledge of social groups to which the historian, until now, has had little or no access." (S.D. Goi-

tein, "Cairo: An Islamic city in the light of the Geniza documents", in *Middle Eastern cities: A symposium*, University of California Press, 1969, p. 80.) A selection of the Geniza documents has been published by S.D. Goitein, *Letters of medieval Jewish traders*, Princeton, Princeton University Press, 1973.

5. Since the Toronto collection includes nothing which may be attributed to either Spain or Sicily, the problem of textiles from these countries will not be discussed here. Resist-printed fabrics of Indian origin, questions of Asiatic tapestries, and knitting are also excluded.

6. R. Pfister, "Matériaux pour servir au classement des textiles égyptiens postérieurs à la conquête arabe", *Revue des Arts Asiatiques*, vol. 10/3 (1936), pp. 1–16, 73–85; R. Pfister, "Toiles à inscriptions Abbasides et Fatimides", *Bulletin d'Etudes Orientales*, vol. 11 (1945–1946), pp. 46–90; C.J. Lamm, "Some woollen tapestry weavings from Egypt in Sweden", *Le Monde Oriental*, vol. 30 (1936), pp. 43–77; C.J. Lamm, *Cotton in medieval textiles of the Near East*, Paris, Geuthner, 1937; Kühnel and Bellinger, *Dated tiraz fabrics* (1952), pp. 101–109; L. Bellinger, "Textile analysis : Early techniques in Egypt and the Near East", *Textile Museum Workshop Notes*, nos. 2–3.

7. *Kitāb laṭā'if al-ma 'ārif*, ed. P. de Jong, Leyden, 1867, p. 97, cited by Lamm, *Cotton* (1937), p. 106.

8. Letter no. 20 in Goitein, *Letters of Jewish traders* (1973), p. 107.

9. On *mulham* see Britton, *Early Islamic textiles* (1938), p. 30; R.P.A. Dozy, *Dictionnaire détaillé des noms des vêtements chez les arabes*, Amsterdam, Jean Müller, 1845, p. 113; Kühnel and Bellinger, *Dated tiraz fabrics* (1952), pp. 101–109. Pfister suggests that there were difficulties in producing sufficiently strong cotton yarn, hence silk was used for the warp in these fabrics (*Bulletin d'Etudes Orientales*, vol. 11, 1945–1946, pp. 56–87). Other references indicate the use of double warp threads (Serjeant, *Islamic textiles*, 1972, chapter 2 and Appendix on costume, pp. 89, 92).

10. al-Washsha (d. ca. A.D. 936–937), cited by Lamm, *Cotton* (1937), p. 184.

11. Maqdisī (wr. A.D. 985–986), cited by Lamm, *Cotton* (1937), p. 194.

12. al-Washsha, cited by Lamm, *Cotton* (1937), p. 183.

13. Ibn Rusta (ca. A.D. 903), quoting Harūn b. Yaḥyā (A.D. 880–890), cited by Lamm, *Cotton* (1937), p. 198.

14. Various authorities, cited by Lamm, *Cotton* (1937), pp. 182–184, 194, 198, 199, 200, 210. See also Serjeant, *Islamic textiles* (1972).

15. Kühnel and Bellinger, *Dated tiraz fabrics* (1952), p. 106.

16. Kühnel and Bellinger, *Dated tiraz fabrics* (1952), p. 108. Some *mulham* fragments in museum collections are decorated with allover printed and gilded ornaments: Cleveland Museum of Art, 50.558, attributed to Iraq, tenth century *(Handbook of the Cleveland Museum of Art*, 1969, p. 214); another fragment of the same textile is in the Metropolitan Museum of Art, New York, 31.106-64 (gift of George D. Pratt), attributed to Iran, tenth to eleventh century. See also a fragment with floral ornaments in the collection of the Textile Museum, Washington, D.C., 73.-552. A Fatimid group of laid and couched embroidery, worked in coloured silk and silver/gold filé on *mulham* ground, has been associated with some of the eastern and western provinces of the Caliphate. Their relatively large ornaments, which often almost entirely cover the ground fabric, exhibit complicated floral meanders, highly stylized birds, and inscription bands. For examples see: Cleveland Museum of Art, 38.300, 50.533, 50.560–562, 52.257; Museum of Fine Arts, Boston, 31.447 (attributed to Mesopotamia or Egypt, twelfth to thirteenth century), 30.682 (attributed to Sicily or Spain, twelfth to thirteenth century), 30.684 (attributed to Egypt or Mesopotamia, twelfth to thirteenth century), illustrated in Britton, *Early Islamic textiles* (1938), figs. 88–90. For further examples see also Lamm, *Cotton* (1937), pp. 124–127; Gaston Wiet, "Tissus brodés mésopotamiens", *Ars Islamica*, vol. 4 (1938), pp. 54 f.; Dorothy G. Shepherd, "Two Islamic embroideries in gold on *mulham*", *The Bulletin of the Cleveland Museum of Art*, vol. 40 (1953), pp. 190–191.

17. Pfister, *Revue des Arts Asiatiques*, vol. 10 (1936), pp. 78–81; Lamm, *Cotton* (1937), pp. 144–156; Britton, *Early Islamic textiles* (1938), pp. 72–74; Pfister, *Bulletin d'Etudes Orientales*, vol. 11 (1945–1946), pp. 69–83; Kühnel and Bellinger, *Dated tiraz fabrics* (1952), pp. 87–91, 108; A. Bühler, *Ikat — Batik — Plangi : Reservemüsterungen auf Garn und Stoff aus Vorderasien, Zentralasien, Südosteuropa und Nordafrika*, Basel, Pharos Verlag Hansrudolf Schwabe AG., 1972, vol. 1, pp. 11–33, vol. 3, figs. 7–20.

18. Examples listed in Kühnel and Bellinger, *Dated tiraz fabrics* (1952), pp. 123–124. They date between H. 270–311/A.D. 883–924.

19. Fringed veils, presumably worn by women, are known with both embroidered and painted inscriptions. Examples with embroidered inscriptions: ROM no. 4; Textile Museum, Washington, D.C., 73.213, illustrated by Kühnel and Bellinger, *Dated tiraz fabrics* (1952), pl. 46; Metropolitan Museum of Art, New York, 29.179.17, 29.179.21. Examples with painted inscriptions: ROM, nos. 5(?) and 6 (?); Textile Museum, Washington, D.C., 73.65, 73.62, 73.63 (?), 73.61(?), 73.64(?), 73.570 (?), 73.567 (?), 73.377 (?), 73.481, 73.59; Metropolitan Museum of Art, New York, 29.179.9, 29.179.10; Cleveland Museum of Art, 50.353, 50.524; Dumbarton Oaks, Washington, D.C., 33.37. Other examples, however, bear no inscriptions at all; see for example: Ethnographical Museum Basel, 11957, illustrated by Bühler,

Ikat — Batik — Plangi (1972), vol. 3, fig. 1; Metropolitan Museum of Art, New York, 29.179.7, 29.179.34. One wonders whether these fragments of plain *ikat* are simpler variants within the group, or whether only one end of such veils used to be adorned with inscription(s).

20. Lamm, *Cotton* (1937), pp. 235–238.

21. Lamm, *Cotton* (1937), pp. 150–156, 182, 184, 210–212.

22. Cited by Lamm, *Cotton* (1937), p. 182.

23. Egyptian *ikat* fabrics (linen) from Fustat (eleventh to twelfth century) in the collection of the Metropolitan Museum of Art, New York : 27.170.4 and 27.170.28. See also A. C. Weibel, "Egypto-Islamic textiles", *Bulletin of the Detroit Institute of Arts*, vol. 12/7 (1931), p. 97, fig. 7. F. Day describes a linen (sic) cloth which fits the description of an *ikat* cotton, and whose inscription mentions the place of manufacture, the Yaman, and the date, H. 289/A.D. 901–902. She reports that the identification was made with the aid of microscopic inspection ("Dated tiraz in the collection of the University of Michigan", *Ars Islamica*, vol. 4, 1937, pp. 424–425). Decorated with tapestry woven bands and inscriptions in silk, striped (less frequently checkered) linens in different shades of blue (or to a lesser extent blue, green, and tan) might also be considered Egyptian imitations of Yamanite *ikat*s; for examples see: Cleveland Museum of Art, 19.27, 29.946, 50.528, 50.542; Museum of Fine Arts Boston, 30.691, illustrated by Britton, *Early Islamic textiles* (1938), fig. 75; Metropolitan Museum of Art, New York, 27.-170.44 (Fustat, tenth to eleventh century), 27.170.51, 27.170.72 (Fustat, twelfth century), 31.19.4; Victoria and Albert Museum, London, 1661–1888, 327–1889, 296–1891, 297–1891, 791–1898, T.109–1963; Detroit Institute of Art, an example illustrated by Weibel, *Bulletin of the Detroit Institute of Arts*, vol. 12(1931), p. 96, fig. 3. Simple striped Yamanite cotton fabrics are also known, for examples see: Metropolitan Museum of Art, New York, 29.179.16 (embroidered inscription, tenth century), 31.106.46 (embroidered inscription containing the date H. 250/A.D. 864–865, and a statement that the piece was made at Sanᶜā'); Dumbarton Oaks, Washington, D.C., 33.40 (painted inscription); Textile Museum, Washington, D.C., 73.60, illustrated by Kühnel and Bellinger, *Dated tiraz fabrics* (1952), pl. 48. Other examples from Basel (11873, 11874, 15492), Detroit (31.-18), and Lyon (28.929.19) are illustrated by Bühler, *Ikat — Batik — Plangi* (1972), vol. 3, figs. 12–15, 17, 20.

24. Lamm, *Cotton* (1937), pp. 155–156, 210.

25. Cited by Lamm, *Cotton* (1937), p. 212.

26. The fabric is generally bleached linen, but may in a few cases be dyed blue or green. For striped or checkered textiles see note 23.

27. Kühnel and Bellinger, *Dated tiraz fabrics* (1952), p. 102.

28. Probably influenced by tapestry woven Fatimid fabrics from Egypt, a group of Asiatic cotton textiles is decorated with bands of floral motifs and cartouches filled with birds and/or animals, accompanied by inscriptions. Instead of being executed in tapestry weave, the ornaments of these examples are painted and gilded, and outlined in black ink. For examples, see: Cleveland Museum of Art, 50.551; Metropolitan Museum of Art, New York, 31.106.16, 36.106.18–19, 36.106.65, 32.129.3, 35.141.4, 1972.120.4; Textile Museum, Washington, D.C., 73.-50, 73.525.

29. For other examples see M. Dimand, "Egypto-Arabic textiles, recent acquisitions", *The Metropolitan Museum of Art Bulletin*, vol. 22 (1927), p. 278, fig. 10; C.J. Lamm, "Some Mamluk embroideries", *Ars Islamica*, vol. 4 (1937), pp. 65–76.

30. Kühnel and Bellinger, *Dated tiraz fabrics* (1952), p. 106. Worked in pale yellow silk floss, a fine and almost unnoticeable inscription is embroidered underneath the colourful tapestry woven band of one of the ROM's Egyptian linens (975.403.1). Since a large proportion of this embroidery is worn out, it is hard to decipher the inscription, which may be a factory mark. In other cases, small, embroidered factory marks (?) in more distinct colours are placed in a corner of richly decorated Egyptian fabrics, quite apart from the tapestry woven ornaments (a piece with such a mark has been in the collection of Mrs. Loewi-Robertson, Los Angeles, 1975, no. 15663–4). The Textile Museum in Washington, D.C., has a group of embroidered "factory notes", all on cotton or *mulham* fabrics from Iraq, which date from the ninth to tenth century: 73.8, 73.29, 73.37, 73.671, illustrated by Kühnel and Bellinger, *Dated tiraz fabrics* (1952), pp. 40–41, 95–97, pls. 17, 39, 51. The Metropolitan Museum of Art in New York has both embroidered (29.179.37–38, 29.179.44, 31.106. 20–22, 53.124.5) and printed "factory notes" (32.129.2). Another group of such textiles has been in the collection of Mrs. M. Abemayor, New York (1976). These hastily embroidered "notes" are generally unassociated with other inscriptions, and can seldom be convincingly read.

31. For a stylistic analysis of these tapestry woven decorations see G. Wiet, "Les tissus et tapisseries de l'Egypte musulmane", *Revue de l'Art Ancien et Moderne*, vol. 68 (1935), pp. 3–14, 61–68.

32. While the use of gold filé appears only on a modest scale on the Toronto pieces, the tapestry woven bands of some richer examples contain a considerable amount of this precious thread. See for example : Cleveland Museum of Art, 50.549 (reign of al-Ḥākim, A.D. 946–1020), 50.556, 65.313 (reign of al-Mustaʿlī, A.D. 1094–1101), 50.555, 50.541 (late eleventh century), 50.526, 46.258, 50.550, some of these are illustrated in *Handbook* (1969), p. 213; Metropolitan Museum of Art, New York, 27.170.47 (Fustat, eleventh century), 31.106.66 (eleventh century). In the decorative and/or inscription bands of these textiles, gold filé is most characteristically employed to form the solid part of the background. In a few cases, gold is also employed for the lettering and for some of the ornamental details

of the script. The extensive use of yellow silk for the elaborate, plaited backgrounds of some highly decorative pieces may be imitations of fabrics woven with gold filé (ROM no. 23). Gold filé was also employed on some of the Asiatic embroidered "factory notes" (examples in the collection of the Metropolitan Museum of Art, New York, are mentioned in note 30). For the use and manufacture of gold filé, its possible qualities, and quality control, see C. Cahen, "Documents relatifs à quelques techniques iraqiennes au début du onzième siècle", *Ars Islamica*, vols. 15–16 (1951), pp. 23–28; C. Cahen, "Un texte inédit relatif au tiraz égyptien", *Arts Asiatiques*, vol. 11 (1964), pp. 165–168. It is, however, unclear from the written sources quoted by Cahen whether the gold filé with which they are concerned was used for tapestry woven or embroidered decoration in fabrics similar to the above mentioned examples, or whether it was rather employed for silks woven on the drawloom.

33. Kühnel and Bellinger, *Dated tiraz fabrics* (1952), p. 106.

34. See examples in the collection of the Cleveland Museum of Art : 32.27, 32.23 (reign of al-Rāḍī, A.D. 934–940), 65.313 (reign of al-Mustaʿlī, A.D. 1094–1101), 50.555.

35. L. Mayer, *Mamluk costume*, Geneva, Albert Kundig, 1952, pp. 56–64.

36. Numerous examples come from the Geniza, e.g., Goitein, *Letters of Jewish traders* (1973), p. 265.

37. E.g., Britton, *Early Islamic textiles* (1938), fig. 99.

38. The term *qaṣab* generally refers to the hollow reed or similarly hollow tube-like objects. Its specific textile meaning is dual. It can refer to metallic threads (which are composed of a silk core with metallic casing, i.e., filé), or to garments made with such threads. On the first meaning see Cahen, *Arts Asiatiques*, vol. 11 (1964) and note 32. *Qaṣab* as a type of cloth (Serjeant, *Islamic textiles*, 1972, numerous examples, see index) or set of clothes (Goitein, *Letters of Jewish traders*, 1973, p. 38) is more common, but it is not clear whether the garments referred to were of linen, silk, or some other material (Serjeant, 1972, p. 37), or whether only the border was of *qaṣab* (Serjeant, 1972, p. 49).

39. ROM 963.95.14 and 16 might be identified as *qaṣab*.

40. Marçais and Wiet, *Monuments et Mémoires*, vol. 34 (1934), pp. 177–194; H.A. Elsberg and R. Guest, "The veil of Saint Anne", *The Burlington Magazine*, vol. 48 (1936), pp. 140–145; *The arts of Islam*, an exhibition organized by the Arts Council of Great Britain in association with the World of Islam Festival Trust, London, Hayward Gallery, April to July 1976, Catalogue, London, The Arts Council of Great Britain, 1976, no. 8, pp. 76–77.

41. There are three Egyptian tapestry woven medallions

worked with silk and gold filé wefts and linen warps in the collection of the Cleveland Museum of Art (50.541, late eleventh century; 52.255, first half of the twelfth century; and 46.258; two of these are illustrated in *Handbook*, 1969, pp. 213–214). These fragments must have belonged to garments similar to the "veil of Saint Anne". Another roundel has been in the collection of Mrs. A. Abemayor, New York (1976). For related material see also notes 43 (Metropolitan Museum of Art, New York) and 44 (Victoria and Albert Museum, London). Innumerable tapestry woven roundels worked with coloured woollen wefts, imitating the patterns of compound silks and generally described as "Coptic" textiles, may also be connected to the *tiraz* problem.

42. Marçais and Wiet, *Monuments et Mémoires*, vol. 34 (1934), pp. 192–194, fig. 9.

43. (1) Acc. no. 29.136.44, *The Metropolitan Museum of Art Bulletin*, vol. 25 (1930), p. 129, fig. 5. Early twelfth century. Loosely woven green linen tabby with tapestry woven decoration in coloured silk, bleached linen and gold filé (natural silk core). One selvage is preserved (loom width over 53 cm).

(2) Acc. no. 32.96, *The Metropolitan Museum of Art Bulletin*, vol. 28 (1933), p. 37. From the reign of the Fatimid Caliph al-Musta'lī (A.D. 1094–1101). Blue linen tabby with tapestry woven decoration in coloured silk (loom width 74 cm).

(3) Acc. no. 1974.113.14a. Loosely woven bleached linen tabby with tapestry woven decoration in coloured silk and bleached linen (loom width ca. 59 cm).

(4) Acc. no. 1974.113.14b. Very loosely woven, coarse, not fully bleached linen tabby with tapestry woven decoration in coloured silk, and bleached and blue linen (loom width 66.2 cm).

Acc. no. 27.170.6 might have belonged to an *'abāya*-type mantle (fragment of linen tabby with a medallion depicting a horseman, and an inscription band, executed in tapestry weave of coloured silk wefts). We are greatly indebted to Dr. Marilyn Jenkins of the Metropolitan Museum of Art, who has been working on this important group of textiles, for showing us the pieces and any available information.

44. (1) Acc. no. 128-1869. Eleventh to twelfth century. Loosely woven medium blue linen tabby with tapestry woven ornaments in coloured silk. One selvage is preserved (loom width over 41.5 cm). Decoration : medallion filled with confronting stylized birds, framed by a "beaded" border; bands.

(2) Acc. no. 707-1898. Eleventh to twelfth century. Very fine, loosely woven, turquoise-blue linen tabby with warp stripes of bleached linen, decorated with tapestry woven bands of *nashki* inscriptions (?) in coloured silk and gold filé.

45. Middle Eastern *'abāyas* in the collection of the ROM show measurements similar to those of the "veil of Saint Anne" and to the examples in the Metropolitan Museum of Art, New York. See 911x32.5 (w. 295 cm, l. 142 cm, sewn together from two widths; heavy, black woollen fabric with tapestry woven ornaments in metallic filé), 920.41.7 (w. 255 cm, l. 124.5 cm, sewn together from two widths; heavy woollen fabric with brown and white stripes formed by coloured wefts), 943.4.5 (w. 263.5 cm, l. 139 cm loom width; fine pink silk with tapestry woven ornaments in metallic filé), 941.22.245 (w. 262 cm, l. 132 cm, sewn together from two widths; fine light blue silk with tapestry woven ornaments in metallic filé). For additional ethnographic material see also M. Tilke, *Oriental costumes, their designs and colors*, London, Kegan Paul Trench, Trubner, 1922?, pls. 9 (North Africa, Tunis), 29 (East Arabia), 31–32 (Syria), 33 (Syria or Palestine).

46. Pfister, *Revue des Arts Asiatiques*, vol. 10 (1936), pl. 47.

47. Although the so-called *tiraz* group provides little evidence for the reconstruction of complete tunics, woollen tunics might have been worn as much by the Arabs as by the Copts. Tunics decorated with applied bands (generally blue or red woollen tabby ground patterned with an extra weft of heavier linen thread in allover lozenges or zigzags) may represent another group of Islamic garments (see for example Victoria and Albert Museum, London, 409-1890, T232-1923; Whitworth Art Gallery, University of Manchester, T8360). The problems of the so-called Fayyūmī textiles are also connected to these suppositions, and are discussed in greater detail in the section on "Source of patronage".

48. While some late Coptic tunics are constructed from three narrow widths of fabric, the characteristic product of a horizontal loom, their "cut" still imitates those which were woven in a single piece on a vertical loom. The horizontal use of the selvages may stem from an old convention where it was a necessity. See for example ROM 910.1.9 (D. K. Burnham, *Cut my cote*, Toronto, ROM, 1973, p. 11); Victoria and Albert Museum, London, 2071-1900. There are three linen shirts in the ROM, all of them found in Egypt, which were not only made from narrow widths, but were constructed vertically from the fabrics in a fashion characteristic of the East and rare in the Mediterranean during the early centuries of the Middle Ages (910.1.9; 910.1.-13; 910.1.10, The Walter Massey Collection, acquired by Dr. C. T. Currelly in Egypt, 1907–1909). For the cut of these shirts see Burnham, *Cut my cote* (1973), p. 11. None of them can be securely dated. 910.1.13, made of a fabric with looped pile, thus having a "shaggy" appearance, is so similar to the shirts worn by Adam and Eve on some twelfth-century mosaics in Norman Sicily that one tends to believe that all three shirts in the ROM originate from the twelfth century, and represent not only an Islamic style, but a definite change in fashion. In Mamluk Egypt, shirts and tunics were constructed from narrow widths with vertical use of selvages (Victoria and Albert Museum,

London, 790–1898, Circ.357-1924, 1147-1900, T.66-1925, T.94-1924).

49. Day, *Ars Islamica,* vol. 4 (1937), p. 424, no. 4 (22504).

50. See for example : P. du Bourguet, *Musée National du Louvre: Catalogue des étoffes coptes,* vol. 1, Paris, Editions des Musées Nationaux, 1964, figs. H.103; I.23, 25–27, 29, 30, 32–34, 36–37, 39, 42, 45–49, 54, 92, 117. Many more examples could be quoted. Indeed, the entire question of dating and identification of the so-called "late Coptic" textiles should be carefully re-examined and re-interpreted.

51. Acc. no. 59.48 : *Handbook* (1969), p. 213; Dorothy G. Shepherd, "An early *tiraz* from Egypt", *Bulletin of the Cleveland Museum of Art,* vol. 47 (1960), pp. 7–14.

52. G. Wiet, *Soireries persanes,* Cairo, Institut Français d'Archéologie Orientale, 1948; *Survey of Persian art,* ed. A.U. Pope et al., Oxford University Press, 1931, vol. 3, pp. 2029–2042. See also the recent controversy over the Buyid silks with further bibliography in *Bulletin de liaison du Centre International d'Etude des Textiles Anciens* (CIETA), no. 37 (1973-I), studies by M. Lemberg, G. Vial, and J.H. Hofenk-de Graaf on the silks of the Abegg Foundation, Riggisberg, near Bern, and nos. 39–40 (1974-I,II), "Medieval Persian silks in fact and fancy: A refutation of the Riggisberg report", by Dorothy G. Shepherd. Besides these oriental examples, silks manufactured in Spain may also be linked to the problem. Woven silks were also used, if not produced, in Egypt. In addition to these complicated and costly drawloom fabrics, simple silks were produced with tapestry woven, personalized inscription bands; see for example Metropolitan Museum of Art, New York, 31.106.27 (green and yellow striped silk; inscription in red silk against yellow ground; Iran, [N]ishapur, Abbasid, dated A.D. 879–880).

53. See notes of ROM no. 18, in "Catalogue".

54. Britton, *Early Islamic textiles* (1938), figs. 15–16.

55. Certain Mamluk embroideries have been associated with the Coptic community : Lamm, *Ars Islamica,* vol. 4 (1937), p. 75.

56. An early exception is the procession of isolated bovine animals found on two *tiraz* fabrics of the Abbasid Caliph al-Muṭīᶜ (A.D. 946–974), one of which is in the Mallon Collection and the other in the Arab Museum, Cairo (10837); see E. Kühnel, "Four remarkable tiraz textiles", *Archaeologica Orientalia in memoriam Ernst Herzfeld,* New York, J.J. Augustin, 1952, pp. 144–145.

57. Oleg Grabar associates this with the dispersal of the Fatimid treasures in the mid-eleventh century ("Imperial and urban art in Islam : The subject matter of Fatimid art", *Colloque International sur l'Histoire du Caire,* Cairo, 1972, p. 186). Many of our fine tapestry woven textiles 'are, however, earlier (ROM no.

12), dating from the end of the tenth and the early eleventh century. They are, in fact, almost contemporary with a major classical revival in Byzantium, the so-called Macedonian Renaissance, which may have promoted an interest in classical subjects throughout the Mediterranean world.

58. Britton, *Early Islamic textiles* (1938), figs. 17–19; Kühnel and Bellinger, *Dated tiraz fabrics* (1952), pp. 84–85. For examples with historical inscriptions see Lamm, *Le Monde Oriental,* vol. 30 (1936), p. 76; G. Wiet, "Tissus et tapisseries du Musée Arabe du Caire", *Syria,* vol. 16 (1935), p. 286; E. Kühnel, "Tirazstoffe der Abbasiden", *Der Islam,* vol. 14 (1925), pp. 85–86.

59. In the Fayyūmī group, Coptic inscriptions occasionally appear alongside kufic/kufesque ones. While the Arabic script is generally executed in tapestry weave, the Coptic texts are usually embroidered.

60. Wiet, *Syria,* vol. 16 (1935), pl. 47 (no. 62).

61. Lamm, *Le Monde Oriental,* vol. 30 (1936), p. 76.

62. The relationship of the Fayyūmī group with Fatimid *tiraz* has been discussed by Deborah Thompson, "A Fatimid textile of Coptic tradition with Arabic inscription", *Journal of the American Research Center in Egypt,* vol. 4 (1965), pp. 145–149. Coarse linen with tapestry woven ornaments and kufesque inscriptions in coloured wool may also relate to the problem of the Fayyūmī textiles. See for example : ROM 975.403.5; Victoria and Albert Museum, London, T.97-1949; Dumbarton Oaks, Washington, D.C., 33.41. Some Egyptian linens with exquisite tapestry woven ornaments in silk show distinct similarities with these textiles (Victoria and Albert Museum, London, 121-1891).

63. S.D. Goitein, "Petitions to Fatimid Caliphs from the Cairo Geniza", *The Jewish Quarterly Review,* vol. 45 (1954), pp. 30–38.

64. Goitein, *Letters of Jewish traders* (1973), p. 16 : "In the Middle Ages, textiles were the number one item of commerce in both general and luxury goods."

65. Grabar, "Imperial and urban art in Islam" (1972), p. 186.

66. The *Ḥisba* manuals provided the *muḥtasib* (morality officer) with the practical and technical details for the supervision of the trades and the marketplace. His duties included exposure of fraudulent practices, improper weights and measures, and the control of the quality of workmanship. He also took responsibility for maintenance of streets, sanitation, and other public facilities. For further detail see article *ḥisba* in *Encyclopaedia of Islam,* 2d ed., Leiden, Brill, 1960-.

67. Cahen, *Arts Asiatiques,* vol. 11 (1964), pp. 165–168.

68. Goitein, *Letters of Jewish traders* (1973), no. 28, p. 141 (garment for Yom Kippur); no. 11, p. 77 (festive robe); no. 60, p. 265 (wedding).

69. Goitein, *Jewish Quarterly Review*, vol. 45 (1954), p. 35, n.8.

70. The following letters from the Geniza illustrate the control over the finished product exercised by the merchant ordering it : "After each roll is finished, the craftsman is to receive 3 quarter dinars. The embroidering [or tapestry, authors' suggestion] will require ¹⁄₆ dinar and ¹⁄₂ qīrāt and the bleaching and pounding, 5 qīrāts, the total (for a roll) being 1¹⁄₈ Nizāriyya dinars. The material is with the craftsman up to the present time. He will present it this week. I shall inform you how much of the yarn went into the weaving and how much remained. The bleaching will not be completed until after Passover. . ." (Goitein, *Letters of Jewish traders*, 1973, p. 108); and from another letter : "From the threads belonging to R. Yeshūᶜa I had two pieces of *maqtaᶜ* garments and one *baqyar* turban woven. I took them from the weaver and handed them over to the blancher. The rest of the (linen) thread is coarse, while the cotton is fine, so that it does not fit in with it." (p. 134)

71. The Spanish anthologist Ibn ᶜAbd Rabbihi recorded verses used in *tiraz* bands by girls and lovers (Serjeant, *Islamic textiles*, 1972, p. 173).

72. Two remarks should be made about the inscriptions of these silks. First, very few if any were made for members of the chief ruling families. The names and titles seem to indicate members of the landed or military aristocracy who are not known from textual sources. Secondly, the inscriptions contain poems or aphorisms suitable to mortuary furnishings, and indeed many of these are reputed to come from tombs. A few of the aphorisms are similar in tone to those of the contemporary Samanid epigraphic poetry from Khurasan (see note 79). These observations suggest that the silks in question were made specifically for the funereal occasion, but that similar textiles, which have not survived as a result of burial, could have been made for other purposes.

73. E.g., in the Vienna Galen frontispiece (R. Ettinghausen, *Arab painting*, Skira, 1962, p. 91); numerous examples on Seljuq ceramics (E. Atil, *Ceramics from the world of Islam*, Washington, D.C., Freer Gallery of Art, 1973, pls. 41–42, 46, 52–53).

74. Serjeant, *Islamic textiles* (1972), p. 172. On *ḥisba*, see note 66.

75. Goitein, *Jewish Quarterly Review*, vol. 45 (1954), p. 34, n. 7.

76. Goitein, *Letters of Jewish traders* (1973), no. 20, p. 108; no. 60, p. 265.

77. One exception may be found in Goitein, *Letters of Jewish traders* (1973), no. 63, p. 275.

78. Kühnel and Bellinger, *Dated tiraz fabrics* (1952), p. 90.

79. L. Volov (Golombek), "Plaited kufic on Samanid epigraphic pottery", *Ars Orientalis*, vol. 6 (1966), p. 122; G. Miles, "The development of ornament in 9th century Islamic tombstones in Egypt", unpublished MS, 1962, n.p.

80. See note 79.

81. Formerly in the Nahman Collection, Cairo, recorded in the *Répertoire Chronologique d'Epigraphie Arabe*, vol. 4, no. 1544. Lamm (*Cotton*, 1937, p. 146) gives the dates of the Imām, and Kühnel (Kühnel and Bellinger, *Dated tiraz fabrics*, 1952, p. 90) mentions another historical painted *ikat* in Dumbarton Oaks, Washington, D.C., which names a relative of the Imām (33.37).

82. Serjeant, *Ars Islamica*, vols. 11-12 (1946), p. 111.

83. Serjeant, *Ars Islamica* (1946), pp. 116, 118.

84. Serjeant, *Ars Islamica* (1946), p. 116.

Notes on Italian and Spanish Textiles of the Seventeenth Century

Ruth Grönwoldt

A contribution commemorating Harold Burnham should perhaps, strictly speaking, deal primarily with the technical aspects of our discipline, since Harold, being a weaver, considered them largely as the basis of his work. In addition, though, he was also aware of other research methods familiar to us, such as the analysis of garments and fabrics in paintings, a method used in this study.

Textile historians continue to be interested in the problem of defining the production of the different textile centres. With great reservations, this question can be resolved for some mediaeval centres. Through the centuries, however, the task becomes increasingly difficult, since the volume of production grew and better means of communication brought about the spread of technical innovations from one centre to another. We must face the fact that similar designs were undoubtedly being woven in different textile centres at that time. Yet only one of them can, in each case, be considered the place of origin for the creation and development of a given design, so that our approach to the problem is therefore quite justified. Because of the difficulties mentioned, certain technical terms have come into use, such as "Lucca" and "Venice" for fourteenth-century Italian fabrics. However, such terms are subject to verification. Since basic studies are, as yet, not available in many cases, each element of proof, no matter how minor, must be taken into consideration.

The long-lived pomegranate pattern still dominated the sixteenth and even the early seventeenth century. From the mid-sixteenth century on, the re-peats became larger; the design of the pattern and the tapered oval outline stiffened to a formal arrangement. The fabrics were woven in the most diversified fashion, sometimes in very precious materials, such as damask velvet with brocaded loop weft accentuating the design.[1] For these textiles, Italy[2] as well as Spain[3] have been regarded as production centres. At the same time the disintegration of the large patterns into smaller scrolls or arabesque designs and, eventually, into the so-called small patterns took place, a development usually regarded as being connected with the appearance of Spanish fashion. In contrast to the oversized pomegranate pattern, the design of the post-Renaissance period reached a peak in these small patterns and their almost endless variations, which were considerably influenced by sixteenth- and seventeenth-century Persian fabrics.[4] Current studies have shown that this style must have originated in the textile centres of northern Italy, such as Florence, Venice, Milan, Genoa, and Lucca.[5]

Further conclusions concerning this problem may be drawn from a comparison of two paintings dating to the first quarter of the seventeenth century.[6] The "Adoration of the Magi" by the Italian artist Matteo Rosselli in San Salvi in Florence[7] (fig. 1) is dominated by the large figure of the kneeling king. He wears an ermine-trimmed cope featuring a dark velvet pattern on a light background. This pattern consists of very loose, regular, highly stylized scrolls with flowers and buds. The same composition was used by Eugenio Caxés in his "Adoration of the Magi"[8] which is today in the Szépmüvészeti Múzeum in Budapest (fig. 2). Caxés, too, leaves much

Figure 1.   Matteo Rosselli, *Adoration of the Magi*.
Florence, San Salvi.

Figure 2.   Eugenio Caxés, *Adoration of the Magi*.
Budapest, Szépmüvészeti Múzeum.

128

space in his composition to the kneeling figure of the king who, as in Rosselli's depiction, faces to the right. This master too pictured the king's precious cope with the greatest care. In this case, however, the cope is made of a fabric with the large pomegranate pattern described above. Eugenio Caxés,[9] born in Madrid in 1577, was the son of an Italian who had immigrated to Spain from Tuscany, and Caxés was influenced all his life by the Florentine school of painting. The composition of the painting is clearly borrowed from the Florentine school,[10] but in the details of costume Caxés's painting follows the Spanish taste dominant at that time.[11] This marked departure from the Florentine "model" certainly allows us to conclude that Caxés was deliberately trying to emphasize a splendid local fabric.

Textiles of this type have been preserved in great numbers. A comparable example is a fragment in the Art Institute of Chicago with a pomegranate pattern in looped weave, surrounded by a very elongated frame[12] (fig. 3). According to the conclusions set out here, this fragment almost certainly originated in a Spanish production centre. Another example can be given to confirm this hypothesis.[13] The "Adoration of the Magi" in the Szépmüvészeti Múzeum in Budapest, painted in 1620 by the Spaniard Luis Tristán, is closely related to the representations by Rosselli and Caxés and contains many elements derived from the Florentine school.[14] Here again, the aged king is shown kneeling, facing to the right, and wearing a cope with the elongated pomegranate pattern, which, however, is rendered inconspicuous by the tight folds of the cope.

The fabric depicted by Matteo Rosselli is part of the scroll-arabesque pattern group[15] which did not become as popular as the small pattern fabrics. As mentioned earlier, the small pattern fabrics originated in northern Italy. Rosselli's fabric, which is closely related to this group, may well be of the same provenance and may even be a product of Florence. For a comparison with fabrics preserved to this day, we refer to a fragment in the textile collection of the Kunstgewerbemuseum in Berlin (fig. 4)[16] and to another fragment (fig. 5) in the Württembergisches Landesmuseum, Stuttgart.[17] The fabric on the painted Giovanni altar frontal in Santo Spirito in Florence (fig. 6), a seventeenth-century overpainting, also belongs to this group.[18] This work especially confirms the above hypothesis regarding the origin of the fabric painted by Rosselli.[19]

Figure 3.   Part of a chasuble.
Art Institute of Chicago.

Figure 4.   Velvet, fragment.
Berlin, Kunstgewerbemuseum.

130

Figure 5. Velvet, fragment.
Stuttgart, Württembergisches Landesmuseum.

Figure 6. Detail of painted altar frontal, Bardi Chapel.
Florence, Santo Spirito.

Notes

1. Cf. a cushion in the Cathedral of Uppsala. A. Geijer, *Textile treasures of Uppsala Cathedral from eight centuries*, Stockholm, Almqvist & Wiksell, 1964, pl. 55, no. 33.

2. Geijer, *Textile treasures* (1964), p. 41 ff.

3. H. Schmidt, *Alte Seidenstoffe*, Braunschweig, 1958, fig. 349; I. Errera, *Catalogue d'étoffes anciennes et modernes*, Brussels, 1927, no. 229 ff.

4. This type is well represented by numerous fragments in the textile collection of the Württembergisches Landesmuseum, Stuttgart, to which the textile collection of the Landesgewerbemuseum was added in 1968. On the subject of connections with Persia, see R. Grönwoldt, "Bemerkungen zu zwei Seidengeweben des Frühbarock", *Jahrbuch der staatlichen Kunstsammlungen in Baden-Württemberg*, vol. 5 (1968), p. 84; M. Taszycka, *Włoskie jedwabne tkaniny odzieżowe w Polsce w pierwszej połowie XVII wieku* [Italian silk fabrics used for clothing in Poland in the first half of the seventeenth century], Wrocław, Zakład Narodowy im. Ossolinskich, 1971, p. 91.

5. Taszycka, *Włoskie jedwabne* (1971), p. 5 ff.

6. Both examples are from a paper by S. Jacob, "Florentinische Elemente in der spanischen Malerei", *Mitteilungen des Kunsthistorischen Instituts in Florenz*, vol. 13 (1967-1968), p. 117 ff. We cordially thank Dr. Jacob for letting us use her illustrations.

7. Jacob, "Florentinische Elemente" (1967-1968), fig. 24.

8. Jacob, "Florentinische Elemente" (1967-1968), fig. 27.

9. A.L. Mayer, *Geschichte der spanischen Malerei*, Leipzig, Klinkhardt & Biermann, 1922, p. 211 and p. 388 ff.

10. Jacob, "Florentinische Elemente" (1967-1968), p. 139 ff. The author even assumes that Caxés was intimately acquainted with the development of the Florentine school of painting.

11. This phenomenon may be observed fairly frequently in times of a strong dependence on a certain tradition in painting. However, in mediaeval painting it was the style of the garments, rather than the pattern of the fabric, as in our examples, that was adapted to the taste of the times.

12. Ch. Ch. Mayer, *Masterpieces of western textiles from the Art Institute of Chicago,* Chicago, 1969, pl. 54.

13. Jacob, "Florentinische Elemente" (1967-1968), fig. 21.

14. Jacob, "Florentinische Elemente" (1967-1968), p. 136. Cf. also S. Jacob, "A drawing attributed to Luis Tristán", *Bulletin of Rhode Island School of Design Museum Notes* (Winter 1970), p. 3 ff.

15. Cf. note 7.

16. J. von Lessing, *Die Gewebesammlung des K. Kunstgewerbe-Museums,* Berlin, 1900, pl. 278 left, acc. no. 73,359.

17. Violet silk velvet from the Württembergisches Landesmuseum, Stuttgart, acc. no. 3690.

18. B. Markowsky, "Eine Gruppe bemalter Paliotti in Florenz und der Toskana und ihre textilen Vorbilder", *Mitteilungen des kunsthistorischen Instituts in Florenz,* vol. 17 (1973), p. 105 ff., fig. 22.

19. The fabric in Berlin, and the fabric of the altar frontal in Santo Spirito in Florence of a somewhat later date, can be compared with the style phase characterized by Peter Thornton under A III 1610-1630 (*Baroque and Rococo silks,* London, Faber, 1965, p. 86), while the fragment in Stuttgart appears to be considerably looser in construction and may possibly belong to a later phase (Thornton XIV, 1630-1645).

Icelandic Mediaeval Embroidery
Terms and Techniques

Elsa E. Gudjónsson

IN modern Icelandic the general term for embroidery is *útsaumur*, a word not known prior to the eighteenth century.[1] During the Middle Ages the word *saumur*, meaning sewing, designated both decorative and constructive needlework. No word for stitch is known from that time; the word *spor (nálspor)*, in use today, was first known with this meaning in the early eighteenth century.[2]

Sources of mediaeval embroidery stitches are of two kinds: surviving embroideries, most of which are in the National Museum of Iceland, Reykjavík (NMI), and the National Museum, Copenhagen (NMK); and documents, predominantly church inventories, published in the *Diplomatarium Islandicum*.[3] On the ca. twenty surviving Icelandic mediaeval embroideries occur a number of embroidery techniques: stem stitch, split stitch, long-legged cross stitch, appliqué, laid and couched work, pattern darning and straight darning, and perhaps also Holbein stitch and lacis, i.e., darned netting. Of

these, the laid and couched work, on eleven embroideries, and pattern darning, on three or perhaps five others, predominate. In the documents, at least nine terms, mentioned in connection with textiles, designate or can be assumed to designate mediaeval embroidery techniques: *sprang, skorningur, veandasaumur, varp, glitsaumur (glit), refilsaumur, krosssaumur, borusaumur,* and *pellsaumur*. In the following pages an attempt will be made to clarify the meaning of these terms through examination and comparison of the written sources and their possible connections with the extant mediaeval embroideries. Comparisons will also be made with existing Icelandic embroideries of more recent times as well as with embroidery terms and descriptions in post-mediaeval written sources, particularly the unpublished inventories of the seventeenth and eighteenth centuries in the National Archives of Iceland (NAI).

Sprang

In Icelandic mediaeval inventories, the noun *sprang* appears mainly in connection with ecclesiastical textiles. It occurs as a separate word, *[dukur] med sprang* (cloth with *sprang*), as well as a compound expression, *sprangdvkur* (*sprang* cloth); both forms are known from as early as 1394.[4] In the same sources the verb *spranga* is mentioned as early as 1318: *duk sprangadann*[5] (*sprang*ed cloth), and it is also found associated with women's crafts in the *Thomas saga erkibyskups hin yngri,* which is believed to date from the first half of the fourteenth century.[6] In more recent sources, compound words such as *ridsprang* (literally netted *sprang*), 1674,[7] *sprangsaumur* (sprang

This paper is a revised and rewritten version (25 September 1974) of an article by the author, published in Icelandic and Danish: "Íslenzk útsaumsheiti og útsaumsgerdir á midöldum", *Árbók hins íslenzka fornleifafélags 1972*, Reykjavík, 1973, pp. 131–150. By the same author and relevant to the material presented here are the following titles: "A study to determine the place of Icelandic mediaeval couched embroideries in European needlework", unpublished M.A. thesis, University of Washington, Seattle, 1961. "Traditional Icelandic embroidery", *The Bulletin of the Needle and Bobbin Club*, vol. 47 (1963), pp. 4–31. *Íslenzk sjónabók*, Reykjavík, 1964. "Martinus. Island", *Kulturhistorisk leksikon for nordisk middelalder*, 11, Reykjavík, 1966, col. 476-477. "Språngning. Island", *Kulturhistorisk leksikon for nordisk middelalder*, 16, Reykjavík, 1971, col. 538–539. "Íslenskur refilsaumur", MS, July 1974.

sewing), 1719,[8] and *litsprangssaumur* (coloured *sprangsaumur*), 1735,[9] occur.

The term *sprang* cannot with certainty be connected with existing mediaeval needlework. Mid-seventeenth-century sources, mentioning an altar frontal and a riddel, both of which are still in existence (NMI 7122 and 10951) and both decorated with insertions of lacis, show that *sprang* was then used to designate this type of work.[10] The compound term *ridsprang*, mentioned earlier, no doubt was used as well for such work. *Sprang* most likely also designated drawn work as shown in figure 1, which illustrates techniques on two embroideries from ca. 1700 (NMI 1924 and 11527), and possibly designated openwork in general. No mediaeval Icelandic embroidery worked in any of these techniques is known with certainty to exist. It is possible, however, that the above-mentioned *sprang* frontal (NMI 7122), first listed in a church inventory of 1641, is mediaeval; even if not, some of the scraps of darned netting which were used to repair the original lacis work might be remnants of the *lectaraduk . . . med glit oc sprang* (lectern cloth with *glit* and *sprang*) which is listed in an inventory of the same church in 1471.[11] A frontlet of white linen tabby (NMI 8901), worked partly in lacis, partly in Holbein stitch (fig. 2a), may possibly be dated prior to the Reformation, as may a fragment of lacis executed in polychrome silk (NMI 898), although the latter might be of foreign origin.[12] It should be pointed out that no remains or traditions of plait-work, now called *sprang* in other countries, are known in Iceland.

Skorningur

The word *skorningur* first appears in an inventory from 1394 as *[alltarisklædi] . . . med skorning* (altar frontal with *skorning*),[13] where it may have designated appliqué work. There is one Icelandic altar frontal (NMI 4797), dated to the close of the mediaeval period, which is predominantly executed in appliqué of wool, linen, silk, and gilt leather on a woollen tabby ground (fig. 9). In connection with textiles, the word *skorningur* is known only from the Middle Ages. Seventeenth-century inventories list textiles *med utskurde* (literally with carving, rather than cutting),[14] and *af út skornu klædj* (of cut-out

cloth),[15] indicating appliqué work. Related terms are found in eighteenth-century inventories.[16]

Veandasaumur

The term *veandasaumur* is known only from mediaeval times, occurring first in an inventory from 1470 as *merke . . . med veanda saum* (banner with *veanda* sewing).[17] It has been suggested that *veanda* was the same as *víginda* (gen. pl. of *vígindi*)[18] meaning texture in weaving. *Veandasaumur* might thus be interpreted as weave stitch, i.e., darning (cf. *glitsaumur*).

Varp

In connection with textiles the earliest occurrence of *varp*, used as a noun, dates from 1523/1525: *formadukur med sprang og varp* (lectern cloth with *sprang* and *varp*);[19] the verb *varpa*: *varpadur dukur* (*varp*ed cloth) appears at about the same time, 1525.[20] Compound words, indicating the pattern and use of such textiles, e.g., *bordhandklædi med varpraundum* (literally, tablehandtowel with *varp* stripes) and *varptialld* (*varp* hanging) occur in sources from the mid-sixteenth century (1548[21] and 1552–1554).[22] In these expressions, *varp* may at times indicate embroidery, most likely of the kind later known as *varpsaumur*. When first observed, in an inventory from 1675,[23] *varpsaumur* refers to an altar frontal from the first half of the sixteenth century (NMI 2028), which still exists and is executed entirely in stem stitch with polychrome wools on linen tabby (figs. 2b, 11).[24] Besides this piece there is a late mediaeval burse (NMI 11008), worked almost entirely in stem stitch with polychrome woollen and linen yarn upon linen.

Glitsaumur (glit)

Executed in polychrome wools on linen tabby, pattern darning of the kind shown in figure 3a is the dominating technique on three late mediaeval Icelandic altar frontals (NMK 15313, 1855; NMI 10885 [fig. 10] and NMI 2371 [fig. 13]). In addition, two altar frontals, undated but possibly mediaeval, are worked entirely in pattern darning (NMI 1997 and NMI 3552). On two of these frontals (NMK 15313, 1855; NMI 10885) some of the darning is worked in a manner similar to straight darning (fig. 3b), a technique which became common in Iceland during the seventeenth and eighteenth centuries. It is not unlikely that darning on all these frontals is *glitsaumur*, a term first recorded ca. 1540 as *alltaris bunijngur med glitsaum* (altar covering with *glit* sewing);[25] and that *glit* (noun), mentioned in 1394 as *iferdvkr halfur med sprang enn halfur med glit* (literally overcloth half with *sprang*, but half with *glit*),[26] and *glita* (verb), found as early as 1313: *altarisduk glitadann* (*glit*ed altar cloth),[27] at times also covered this technique. As mediaeval terms, these words have been considered rather to refer to glittering and colourful weavings or embroideries, and the previously mentioned term, *veandasaumur*, known from an earlier source than *glitsaumur*, does indicate that other words may have been used for darning during the Middle Ages. Besides this, such compound terms as *lausaglit* (loose *glit*), 1548,[28] and *knuta glit* (knot *glit*), 1569,[29] remain unexplained.

From post-mediaeval times, more precisely from as early as the last quarter of the seventeenth century, the more qualifying compound word *skakkaglit* (slanting *glit*) is known to have designated pattern darning (fig. 3a). In an inventory dating from 1692, *Saumad . . . Med skacha glit* (sewed with slanting *glit*)[30] is used to describe one of the mediaeval frontals (NMK 15313, 1855). In 1727 this frontal, however, is listed as executed in *glitsaumur*.[31] This, together with other early eighteenth-century sources, shows that *glitsaumur* was then used to designate both kinds of darning (fig. 3).

Refilsaumur

The term *refilsaumur* cannot be connected with an existing mediaeval embroidery until the year 1631, when an altar frontal (NMI 3924), dating most likely from the first half of the sixteenth century, and executed in laid and couched work, is listed as worked in *refilsaumur*.[32] There is no doubt, however, that the mediaeval word, first recorded in 1550 as *tiolld med refilsaum othelud, Alltarisklædi med theladan Refilsaum,* and *Refilsaumstialld* (i.e., hangings and altar frontal

with *refil* sewing),[33] refers to this embroidery technique. *Refilsaumur* was executed mainly in polychrome woollen yarn either on linen tabby or on *tvistur* (extended woollen tabby). Coarse yarn was used for laying the ground (fig. 4a), and finer yarn for tacking it down (fig. 4b, c). For outlines and occasionally to fill in small areas, secondary stitches such as stem stitch, couched outline stitch, split stitch, chain stitch, and surface satin stitch were used (fig. 2b-f). The outlines were usually worked first, and the inner areas filled in afterwards. Of the eleven extant mediaeval embroideries worked in *refilsaumur*, one is a *refill*, i.e., a long horizontal wall hanging, while ten are altar frontals. Eight of the frontals (NMI 3924; NMI 4380 b; NMI 10933; NMK CLV, 1819; NMK CXCVIII, 1820; NMK 15379, 1856; one in the Rijksmuseum Twenthe, Enschede; one in the Musée Cluny, Paris) are completely covered with stitchery, while on two (NMI 4279 and NMI 10866 [fig. 12]) only the design is covered, and on the *refill* (NMK CLII, 1819) only the ground is covered. This kind of difference in execution was indicated in the inventory listings given previously, where distinction was made between embroideries with filled in and voided ground: *thelad* and *othelad*. It should be noted that the term *refilsaumur* is known only from Icelandic sources.

Krosssaumur

The earliest connection found between the term *krosssaumur* and an existing embroidery, an altar frontal which carries the date 1617 (NMI 10940), is in an inventory from 1631.[34] The work on the frontal consists mainly of long-legged cross stitch, common to Icelandic needlework of the seventeenth and eighteenth centuries (fig. 5), with single stitches and, occasionally, single rows of ordinary cross stitch (fig. 6). The term, first mentioned in 1550 as *[Alltariklædi] . . . med krosssaum* (altar frontal with *kross* sewing),[35] has no doubt covered both types of cross stitch. As secondary stitches, these occur on the three mediaeval altar frontals executed primarily in darning stitch, previously discussed under *glitsaumur*. On these, however, long-legged cross stitch was used much more frequently than cross stitch. Examination of one of these frontals (NMI 2371; fig. 13)

135

showed that areas as well as single rows of stitches were usually worked as shown in figure 5c. In some instances, where single stitches made up slanting rows, these were worked as shown in figure 5d and e. Another of the three frontals (NMK 15313, 1855), listed in inventories from 1686 and 1748 as being cross stitched,[36] no doubt because of the fair amount of that work forming part of its decoration, is the only existing Icelandic example until the late eighteenth century, besides long-legged cross stitch, ordinary cross stitch used not only for single rows and stitches but for whole areas as well. In modern Icelandic, a distinction is made between the two techniques; long-legged cross stitch is termed either *gamli íslenski krosssaumurinn* (the old Icelandic cross stitch) or *fléttusaumur* (literally braid stitch), apparently a direct translation from Danish, while ordinary cross stitch is termed *krosssaumur*.

Borusaumur

The term *borusaumur*, first mentioned in 1550 as *borusaums tialld* and *[wænger] . . . med borusaum* (hanging and riddells with *boru* sewing),[37] cannot be linked with existing mediaeval embroideries, although it is possible to connect it indirectly with needlework of more recent times. By comparing inventories from the sixteenth and seventeenth centuries, it seems evident that the technique was synonymous with *gatasaumur* (hole sewing), first mentioned it would seem in 1657,[38] and *augnasaumur* (eye sewing), which occurs as early as 1659, even ca. 1654.[39] During the second half of the seventeenth century the term *borusaumur* seems to have disappeared from use, while *gatasaumur* is last known from the early eighteenth century. In an inventory of 1715,[40] where both *gatasaumur* and *augnasaumur* occur, the terms may have been used synonymously or to distinguish between variations. The term *augnasaumur* — in modern Icelandic *augnsaumur* — remained in use

and can be linked through nineteenth-century written sources with existing eighteenth-century embroideries executed entirely or partly in ordinary eye stitch, with each eye consisting of sixteen stitches as shown in figure 7a and b, or in the more rarely used diamond-shaped variations made up of twelve or sixteen stitches each (fig. 7c and d).[41] None of these stitches are found on existing Icelandic embroideries prior to the seventeenth century.

Pellsaumur

The term *pellsaumur* is first mentioned in an inventory from 1569 listing two beds with embroidered coverlets: *med fornum pellsaums aklædum* (literally with old coverlets with *pell* sewing).[42] The word cannot with certainty be linked with either mediaeval or later existing embroideries; the sources known, however, strongly indicate that during the seventeenth and eighteenth centuries, *pellsaumur* meant Florentine stitch (fig. 8a), worked from diamond-shaped patterns, four stitches to each diamond as shown in figure 8b. In modern Icelandic, *pellsaumur* has been used synonymously with *petit point*, a technique apparently unknown in Iceland prior to the nineteenth century.[43]

From the above it is evident that some techniques known from existing mediaeval embroideries do not seem to correspond with terms found in written sources of the period. Of these, split stitch (fig. 2d) merits special attention, since, besides being used as a secondary stitch on several of the mediaeval embroideries mentioned above, it was used as the primary technique on a burse (NKM, no inv. no.) of most likely Icelandic origin, dated ca. 1350,[44] and executed in polychrome silks and metallic filé on linen tabby.

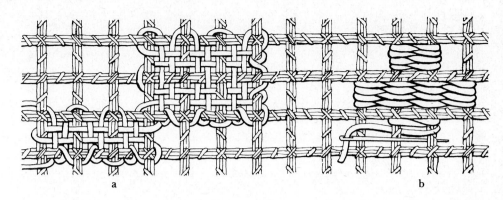

Figure 1. Drawn work: *a* cloth stitch or double darning; *b* weaving stitch or simple darning.

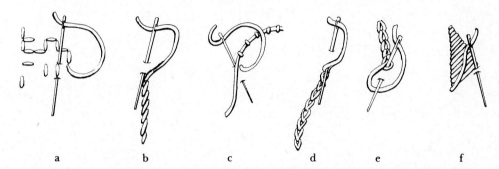

Figure 2. *a* Holbein stitch; *b* stem stitch; *c* couched outline; *d* split stitch; *e* chain stitch; *f* surface satin stitch.

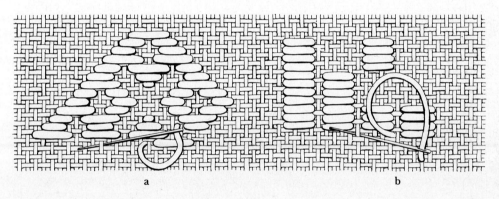

Figure 3. Darning: *a* pattern darning; *b* straight darning.

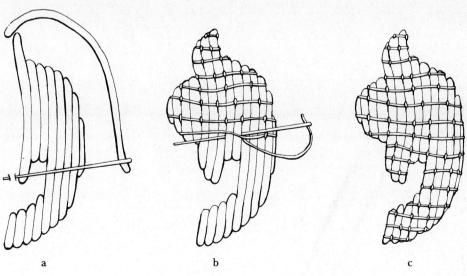

Figure 4. Laid and couched work: *a* laying ground threads; *b* couching; *c* finished work.

137

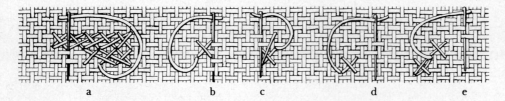

Figure 5. Long-legged cross stitch: *a* horizontal rows; *b* single stitch; *c* vertical row; *d* and *e* slanting row.

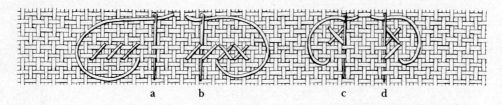

Figure 6. Cross stitch: *a* and *b* horizontal row; *c* and *d* single stitch and/or vertical row.

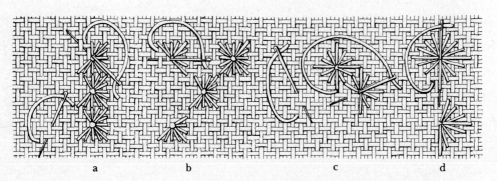

Figure 7. Eye stitch: *a* and *b* eye stitch on the square, sixteen stitches to the eye; *c* diagonal eye stitch, twelve stitches to the eye; *d* diagonal eye stitch, sixteen stitches to the eye.

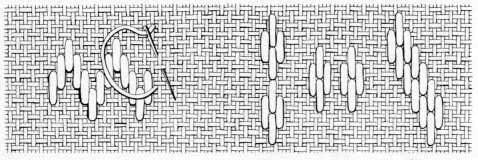

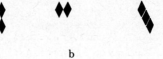

Figure 8. *a* Florentine stitch; *b* examples of Florentine stitch when worked from squared patterns.

Figure 9. Detail of an altar frontal. Appliqué. First half (?) of sixteenth century.
NMI 4797. Photo: Gísli Gestsson.

Figure 10. Detail of an altar frontal. Pattern darning predominantly. Ca. 1500.
NMI 10885. Photo: Gísli Gestsson.

Figure 11. Detail of an altar frontal. Stem stitch. First half of sixteenth century.
NMI 2028. Photo: Gísli Gestsson.

139

Figure 12. Detail of an altar frontal. Laid and couched work. First half of sixteenth century. NMI 10886. Photo: Gísli Gestsson.

Figure 13. Detail of an altar frontal. Pattern darning and long-legged cross stitch. Late mediaeval. NMI 2371. Photo: Gísli Gestsson.

Abbreviations

AM The Arnamagnæan Institute, Copenhagen (*Det Arnamagnæanske Institut*)
DI *Diplomatarium Islandicum* (cf. note 3)
NAI National Archives of Iceland, Reykjavík (*Thjódskjalasafn Íslands*)
NAI Bps. Bishops Archives, National Archives of Iceland, Reykjavík (*Biskupsskjalasafn, Thjódskjalasafn Íslands*)

NLI National Library of Iceland, Reykjavík (*Landsbókasafn Íslands*)
NMI National Museum of Iceland, Reykjavík (*Thjódminjasafn Íslands*)
NMK The National Museum, Copenhagen (*Nationalmuseet*)

Capital letters and numbers, following the abbreviated forms of institutions, are inventory numbers.

Notes

1. AM 433 fol., Dictionary of Jón Ólafsson.

2. NLI 360, 8vo, p. 90.

3. *Diplomatarium Islandicum*, I-XVI, Kaupmannahöfn, Reykjavík, 1857–1972. Christianity was adopted as the state religion in Iceland in the year 1000. The date marking the close of the Middle Ages in the country is 1550, when the state church became Lutheran.

4. DI III, pp. 520, 542.

5. DI II, p. 448.

6. C.R. Unger, ed., *Thomas saga erkibyskups*, Christiania, 1869, p. 301.

7. NAI Bps. A, VII, 1, pp. 123–126.

8. NAI Bps. B, III, 13, p. 91.

9. NAI Bps. B, III, 13, p. 172.

10. NAI Bps. A, II, 8, p. 64; 1641. Bps. B, VIII, 5, p. 3; 1657.

11. DI V, p. 631.

12. Both in design and execution NMI 898 appears to be rather closely related to an embroidery in the Nordiska Museet, Stockholm (inv. no. 9.970, 10.022), dated from the fifteenth century; cf. Anna-Maja Nylén, *Broderier från herremans- och borgarhem 1500–1800*, Stockholm, 1950, pp. 29–30 and fig. 12; Anna-Maja Nylén, *Hemslöjd*, Lund, 1970, p. 236, fig. 338. The most recent traditional examples of the term *sprang*, in the compound word *ridsprang*, date from 1831 and 1833: NAI Bps. C, I, 1, pp. 219, 289.

13. DI III, p. 515.

14. NAI Bps. A, II, 10, p. 75; 1642.

15. NAI Bps. B, III, 10, p. 44; 1693.

16. NAI Bps. B, VIII, 10, p. 7; 1741. Bps. B, III, 15, p. 123; 1742.

17. DI V, p. 583; the banner is listed in a similar way in 1523 in DI IX, p. 197. The term is not known from other sources.

18. DI V, p. 960. Cf. Hjalmar Falk, *Altwestnordische Kleiderkunde*, Kristiania, 1919, p. 25.

19. DI IX, p. 186.

20. DI IX, p. 298.

21. DI XI, p. 625.

22. DI XII, p. 499.

23. NAI Bps. A, II, 11, p. 49.

24. Another word for stem stitch, apparently not recorded prior to 1874 (1869), is *varpleggur*, cf. Sigurdur Gudmundsson, *Skýrsla um Forngripasafn í Reykjavík*, vol. 2, Kaupmannahöfn, 1874, p. 118.

25. DI X, p. 592.

26. DI III, p. 583.

27. DI II, p. 378.

28. DI XI, pp. 621, 625.

29. DI XV, p. 216.

30. NAI Bps. B, III, 10, p. 4. The term is apparently first mentioned in 1675 as *formadukur . . . med skackaglit* (lectern cloth with slanting *glit*) in Bps. A, II, 11, p. 42.

31. NAI Prófastsvísitasía 1725–1747, XVIII, 1, A, 1, n.p., 1727.

32. NAI Bps. B, III, 5, p. 31.

33. DI XI, pp. 852, 853.

34. NAI Bps. B, III, 5, p. 3. Owing to wear, the date can no longer be read.

35. DI XI, p. 852.

36. NAI Bps. B, III, 9, p. 78; Bps. B, III, 16, p. 64.

37. DI XI, p. 852.

38. NAI Bps. B, VIII, 5, p. 5.

39. NAI Bps. B, III, 6, n.p., 1659. Stefán Ólafsson, *Kvæði*, vol. 2, Kaupmannahöfn, 1886, pp. 198, 410; ca. 1654.

40. NMI without no. Copy, transcribed by Sigurdur Gudmundsson.

41. The variation of eye stitch mentioned last (fig. 7d) is known only through one Icelandic embroidery, a coverlet (NMK L. 763) worked predominantly in ordinary eye stitch (fig. 7a, b), dated to not later than the beginning of the eighteenth century. It is also found on remnants of a mediaeval Swedish frontlet, cf. Agnes Geijer, *Textile treasures of Uppsala cathedral*, Stockholm, 1964, p. 46 and pl. 49.

42. DI XV, p. 218.

43. Known also as *perluspor* in modern Icelandic. Florentine stitch, worked in the manner described, occurs as secondary stitches on three embroideries carrying the dates 1694, 1779, and 1811 (NMI 404, NMI 7177, and NMI 11055), while there exist three scraps covered with needlework of this kind, probably remains of a seventeenth– or eighteenth–century cushion cover or coverlet (NMI 3804 D I-III).

44. NMK. On exhibit in department 2, room 28, case 9F. Dating: cf. Tage E. Christiansen, ed., *Nationalmuseets vejledninger. Danmarks middelalder*, Copenhagen, 1972, p. 42.

Appendix

ICELANDIC MEDIAEVAL EMBROIDERIES

Embroideries executed in laid and couched work
NMI 3924. Altar frontal. Wool and linen on linen tabby.
NMI 4279. Altar frontal. Silk and metallic filé on linen tabby.
NMI 4380 b. Altar frontal. Wool, linen, and metallic filé on linen tabby.
NMI 10886. Altar frontal. Wool and linen on linen tabby (fig. 12).
NMI 10933. Altar frontal. Wool and linen on linen tabby.
NMK CLII, 1819. *Refill* (wall hanging). Wool on extended woollen tabby (*tvistur*).
NMK CLV, 1819. Altar frontal. Wool, linen, and silk on extended woollen tabby.
NMK CXCVIII, 1820. Altar frontal. Wool and linen on linen tabby.
NMK 15379, 1856. Altar frontal. Wool, linen, and metallic filé on linen tabby.
Rijksmuseum Twenthe, Enschede. Altar frontal. Wool and linen on linen tabby.

Musée Cluny, Paris. Altar frontal. Wool and linen on extended woollen tabby.

Embroideries worked predominantly in pattern darning
NMI 2371. Altar frontal. Wool on linen tabby (fig. 13).
NMI 10885. Altar frontal. Wool, silk, and metallic filé on linen tabby (fig. 10).
NMK 15313, 1855. Altar frontal. Wool and linen on linen tabby.

Embroideries worked in stem stitch
NMI 2028. Altar frontal. Wool on linen tabby (fig. 11).
NMI 11008. Burse. Linen and wool on linen tabby.

Embroidery worked in appliqué
NMI 4797. Altar frontal. Wool, linen, silk, and gilt leather on woollen tabby (fig. 9).

Embroidery worked in split stitch
NMK, no inv. no. (cf. note 44). Burse. Silk and metallic filé on linen tabby.

ICELANDIC EMBROIDERIES DATING POSSIBLY
FROM THE MIDDLE AGES

Embroideries worked in pattern darning
NMI 1997. Altar frontal. Wool on linen tabby.
NMI 3552. Altar frontal. Wool on linen tabby.

Darned netting (lacis)
NMI 898. Fragment. Cloth stitch. Silk on silk. Icelandic (?).
NMI 7122. Altar frontal. Linen tabby with lacis insertions, repaired with pieces of unmatching lacis work. Cloth stitch. Linen on linen.

Embroideries executed in several techniques
NMI 8901. Frontlet. Darned netting: cloth, weaving, and loop stitches, linen on linen; alternating with work in Holbein stitch, wool on linen tabby.
NMI 10951. Riddell. Apparently mediaeval, apart from renewed lacis insertions with the dates 1650 and 1651. Long-legged cross stitch, couched outline. Silk, linen, and metallic filé (?) on linen tabby and woollen tabby and twill.

Some Etruscan Textile Remains in the Royal Ontario Museum

John W. Hayes

T HE textiles of classical antiquity, represented in the Royal Ontario Museum by its large Coptic collection, were among Harold Burnham's lasting interests, and it seems appropriate to append here, by way of a footnote to those pieces which he was instrumental in making widely known, mention of some other woven remains which have recently come to light during the study of the old Greek and Roman collections in the Museum. Though more humble in appearance, and no longer preserved in their original state, they deserve mention as fresh evidence of the products of a poorly documented area and period, namely Etruscan Italy.[1]

The first of the ROM fragments is a piece of plain tabby weave of medium fineness, completely calcified (fig. 1), adhering to the bottom of a pottery jug (*oinochoe*) in late simplified Italo-corinthian style, to be dated around the first quarter of the sixth century B.C. (fig. 3).[2] The exact findspot of the jug is unknown, but it was purchased in Orvieto and most likely found thereabouts. Though not made for such a purpose, its final use was as the container for a cremation burial. The imprint on its bottom is presumably that of the cloth on which it was laid or in which it was wrapped in the tomb. The diameter of the foot of the vessel is 8.5 cm, the thread-count for the textile itself about 15–16 per cm for both warp and weft. The warp and the weft are singles with a slight Z-twist. The original material was probably linen. Though unremarkable in itself, it adds another scrap to the meagre list of early Etruscan textiles, so rarely preserved in any form.

More remarkable is the second fragment (fig. 2),

woven some four or five centuries later, but exhibiting a more primitive technique. It was discovered on the inside of a cylindrical clay burial urn, of a type peculiar to the region of Chiusi (ancient *Clusium*) in late Roman Republican times (second–first century B.C.).[3] The chief interest of these urns is that they bear some of the latest known inscriptions in the dying Etruscan language, signalling the final assimilation of the ancient Etruscan culture by that of Rome. The present one (figs. 4, 5) is uninscribed, so we are deprived of the knowledge of who was its "owner", though we may assume a half-Romanized local inhabitant. The original cremation burial has been removed, leaving behind only a few stains and the slight remains of the cloth in which it had been wrapped, preserved in several small fragments adhering to the vertical inner surface of the pot. Again the textile is completely calcified, so its original colour escapes us, but the details of the weave are quite clear. What we have is a simple twined weave of quite exceptional fineness which, at first glance, before the arrangement of the threads was closely observed, was mistaken for a gauze. The thread-counts are about 14 per cm for the warp and 14 pairs per cm for the weft. The warp is two-ply twisted Z, the weft is singles, a grouping of filaments with a slight Z-twist. One cannot be sure what the original material was: perhaps a very fine long-stapled wool or, in view of the filament-like appearance of the weft, more probably silk.

The appearance of so primitive a technique in Italy at so late a date is surprising. The origins of twined weaves in Mediterranean countries go back

144

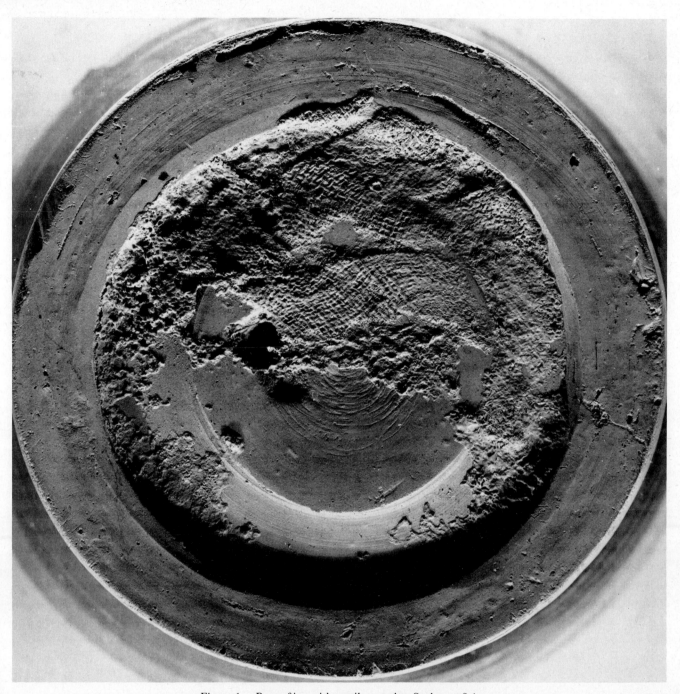

Figure 1.   Base of jug with textile remains. Scale: ca. 2:1.

several millennia,[4] and by the last centuries B.C. they had generally been supplanted by the products of the warp-weighted loom. On the other hand, the piece is of quite remarkable fineness. Moreover, there is no guarantee that the fabric was made locally in Etruria, for the period to which it belongs was one when Etruria and Italy at large were ready markets for the luxury products of the Hellenistic East. Though there can be no proof that it is not a local product, it is perhaps more reasonably seen as an import from Syria or one of the neighbouring regions, where the weaving of luxury products was well established and where a variety of techniques can be documented. The painstaking labour necessary to produce such a fabric is by no means exceptional in terms of the local traditions there. One may perhaps reflect that the art of wool-weaving—which required less labour—was regarded as the traditional virtue of the Roman matron, though there is plenty of evidence from later Roman times that linen and fine fabrics were produced also. Only further discoveries can show whether the fragment documented here is indeed a rarity.

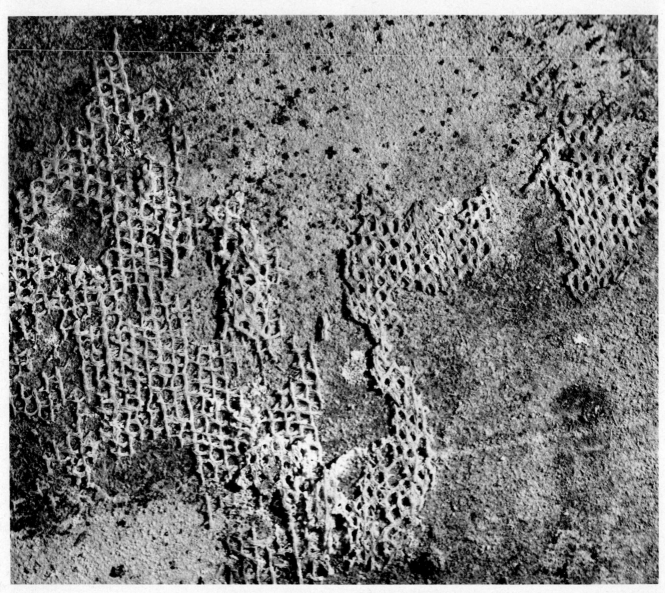

Figure 2.   Detail of inside of urn with textile remains. About five and a half times actual size.

146

Figure 3. Italo-corinthian jug bearing remains shown on figure 1.
ROM acc. no. 919.5.64.

Figures 4-5. Burial urn with lid bearing remains shown on figure 2.
ROM acc. no. 920x100.4.

Acknowledgments

This article could not have appeared in its present form but for the constant assistance in all technical matters of Dorothy K. Burnham, to whom I am deeply indebted for the lively interest she has shown in the scraps published here. The staff of the Textile Department of the Royal Ontario Museum, and in particular Mr. and Mrs. Mark Burnham, have also freely shared their knowledge with me, and I acknowledge my debt to all of them. I also take this opportunity to thank Mme Krishna Riboud (Paris) and M. Gabriel Vial (Lyon) for their helpful comments on photographs of the objects which were submitted to them.

Notes

1. For a recent brief discussion of Etruscan textiles, see D.L. Carroll, "An Etruscan textile in Newark", *American Journal of Archaeology*, vol. 77 (1973), pp. 334-336, pls. 61-62. The Newark fragment, like the present ones, survives only in an altered state.

2. Acc. no. 919.5.64. Ht. (max.) 23.7 cm. Published in Robinson, Harcum, and Iliffe, *Catalogue of Greek vases in Toronto*, Toronto, University of Toronto Press, 1930, no. 207.

3. Acc. no. 920x100.4 A–B. Ht. with lid ca. 35 cm, dia. of lid 21.2 cm. The lid has been cleaned; it bears a painted floral wreath.

4. The technique was documented by Harold Burnham at Çatal Hüyük: see H.B. Burnham, "Çatal Hüyük – The textiles and twined fabrics", *Anatolian Studies*, vol. 15 (1965), p. 171, fig. 2.

Manndalen Revisited:
Traditional Weaving in an Old Lappish Community in Transition

Marta Hoffmann

MANNDALEN is the name of a valley in Lyngen in Troms, northern Norway (fig. 1). Among people interested in old textile crafts it has become known for its characteristic striped, thick woollen blankets (fig. 2). The reputation of these blankets is due less to their looks than to the instrument they are woven on. This is known as the warp-weighted loom, and it has an ancient history, not only in Norway. Traces of it have been found in European and Near Eastern Neolithic sites as well as in later settlements. Loom-weights have come to light in abundance in all classical Greek sites, and the loom itself was depicted on vase paintings dating from as early as ca. 600 B.C. In Manndalen the loom is still in common use.

In about 1930 some museums, especially in Scandinavia, became interested in acquiring examples of this loom for their collections. Among these was the Norwegian Folk Museum in Oslo. The sudden interest was probably caused by an article about the Lappish loom and warping frame written by a Swedish scholar, Emelie v. Walterstorff, in 1928. She pointed out that the Lappish warp with its starting border was practically identical with an archaeological find of a complete warp, dated to about the third – fifth century A.D.[1]

Looms were bought from the Lappish-speaking population living in the fjords of the Lyngen area, and were subsequently exhibited in several museums, though without any comments. Somewhat later, about 1950, an interest in the warp-weighted loom arose again at the Norwegian Folk Museum. It was then realized that very little was known about the traditional use of the instrument. The

museum had in its collections several examples of such looms, most of them originating from the western coast and acquired around 1900. No descriptions of weaving had been noted at the time, and there were no photographs of women weaving. This has often been the case in the early collecting phase in museum history, when the objects themselves were regarded as sufficient, and were presumed to speak for themselves. New generations have different viewpoints. The technical operation of the loom in traditional use has become the centre of interest, and that can only be studied by watching experienced weavers at work.

Since the loom had once been of great importance in the Old World, it seemed worthwhile to try to find somebody who was familiar with the traditional use of the instrument. Archaeologists and textile historians had tried to make reconstructions, but it was felt that the living tradition was better as a firm starting point for understanding the instrument and its products.[2]

A study in northern Norway was planned in co-operation with the curator of the Lapp Department at the Folk Museum, A. Nesheim, who is also a professor of Lapp language, culture, and history at the University of Oslo. He first made a study of the Lappish terminology connected with the loom and the weaving, and the results were of great interest. He was able to show that the terms of the different parts of the loom were loan words in Lappish from primitive Norse, borrowed not later than about A.D. 600 from Norse-speaking neighbours.[3]

Manndalen[4] was chosen for the study of weaving from a technical point of view (fig. 3). It is a valley

149

Figure 1.   Map of Norway showing the location of Manndalen.

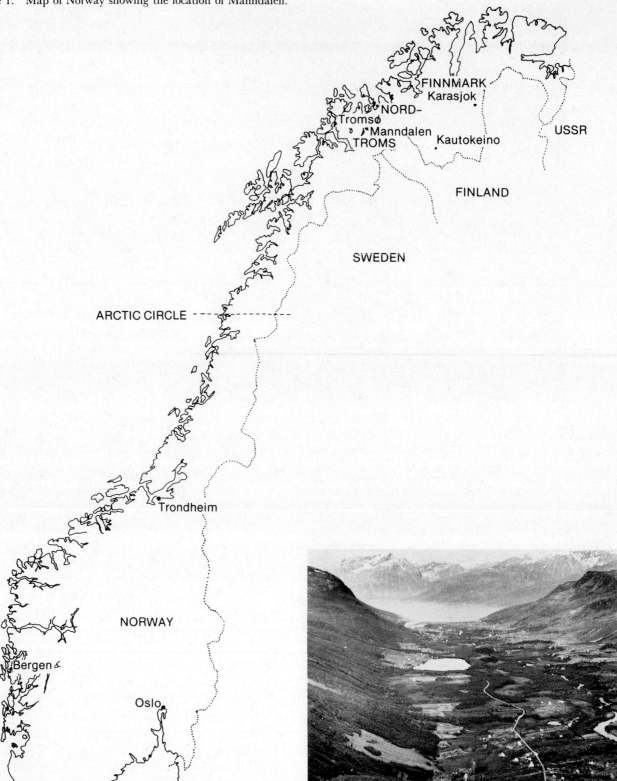

FINNMARK
Karasjok

NORD-
Tromsø
Manndalen   Kautokeino   USSR
TROMS

FINLAND

SWEDEN

ARCTIC CIRCLE - - - - - - -

Trondheim

NORWAY

Bergen

Oslo

Figure 2.   Manndalen.
Photo: T.B. Schjøtt, 1955.

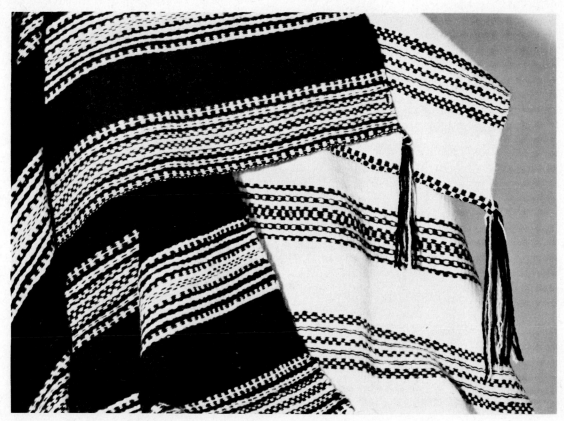

Figure 3. Modern black and white *grener*. Starting borders
with tassel.
Photo: N.F., 1974.

with a resident population of about one thousand, of mixed Lappish and Norwegian origin. The common language was Lappish, and weaving on the old loom was still carried on by several persons. Manndalen is situated just below the 70th degree of latitude, and the climate does not permit ordinary farming. Potatoes can be grown, and haymaking takes place everywhere grass can grow. Before the last war, the men used to work in the large fisheries on the coast of northern Norway, while the women took care of a few cows and sheep. There was no industry in the valley, and no roads connected it with the outer world. The only transportation was by boat or by foot across the mountains. The women used to spin their wool and weave *grener* (sing. *grene*), striped blankets, on their home-made warp-weighted looms for barter or for sale at local markets. Migrating Lapps and merchants from cities as far away as Bergen came two or three times a year to buy and sell. The majority of customers for *grener* were the migrating Lapps who needed them for cov-

erlets in their tents and for rugs in the sledges. When the *grener* became old, the nomads covered their tents with them (fig. 4).

Some of the women among the resident Lapps — called Sea-Lapps because they have always lived along the coast — used to prepare skins and sinew thread in order to make typical Lappish boots. But they no longer wore Lappish costume. They also knitted mittens and stockings, and a few of them possessed an ordinary horizontal loom for weaving cloth for the family. Textile work was very important in the economy of the people of Manndalen.

In 1955, when I first visited the valley to study the weaving on the old loom, the reconstruction following the total destruction of the area at the end of the war was still not completed. In 1944, when the Russians marched into Finnmark, the German occupying forces withdrew, using scorched earth strategy. The population of North Troms, together with the greater part of the Finnmark population, was evacuated at a moment's notice, and all that would

Figure 4.   Old Lappish nomad tent with worn *grener*.
Photo: N.F., 1974.

burn was destroyed. The reconstruction started as soon as the war was over. When people returned in 1945, they had to build huts from turf and thin local birch wood, as no other building material was available. These huts resembled the old traditional Lappish *gammer* (sing. *gamme*), whose construction was familiar to the people. As soon as possible they were replaced by wooden houses, most of them of a light, non-permanent type. In 1955 one could still see a few *gammer* for cattle and for people (fig. 5). Sheep and cows were again grazing in Manndalen, and better houses made of timber imported from southern parts had been built. New looms had been made to replace the ones destroyed during the war, and the weaving of *grener* went on as before. But the demand for them had declined and the prices were low. The old customers, the migrating Lapps, now bought cheap blankets manufactured in the cities for coverlets and canvas for their tents. Only a few people outside the district showed any interest in the *grene*, or *radno*, which is the Lappish term (its origin seems to be Norse, but its meaning is a matter of contention). Many old weavers had given up their craft.

An elderly widow, Anne Hansen, who had woven *grener* most of her life, for sale or in exchange for other necessities of life, wove a *grene* during my stay in her house in 1955. Her command of the Norwegian language was limited, but during the long days while I watched her work, she was able to give me a vivid impression of life in Manndalen (fig. 6).

The weaving itself was most interesting. The weaver did not sit during her work, but walked back and forth carrying the weft and beating it upwards towards the beam with her fingers. For arranging the warp she first wove a band using a rigid heddle mounted on a special warping frame. The weft of the band was drawn out on one side to form long loops which became the warp of the *grene* (fig. 7). This band was sewn to the beam and formed a third selvage on the finished blanket, one of the characteristic and distinctive features of the *grene*. A similar band or starting border has been found on many fragments of prehistoric textiles from different areas of the Old World. It makes a strong and even starting edge of the warp, which is subjected to a special strain, as it is stretched by means of two rows of weights. In Manndalen these weights are natural stones, picked up on the beach, while in other areas of the world they were made of fired clay with a hole for attaching the warp threads.

The weave in the *grene* is always a weft-faced tabby, and the different stripes are variations in the coloured picks.

The study of Anne Hansen's warping and weaving brought a solution to several technical problems connected with the use of the loom. By comparing her working procedure with details in textile finds from archaeological sites, it became clear that the tradition had been kept alive and principally unchanged through thousands of years and had spread over wide areas.

A natural wish to help the weavers sell their products led the Folk Museum to offer to act as an intermediary for them. Pictures of the weaving were exhibited in the Lapp department of the museum, together with *grener* and looms, and small leaflets were printed with information about the old craft and its classical counterparts. Lectures, interviews, and radio reports were given. More than a thousand *grener* have since been sold through the museum to visitors interested in the history of weaving and to

152

Figure 5.   Sea-Lappish house in Manndalen built just after the war and still used in 1956.
Photo: U. Fürst, 1956.

other museums (including the Royal Ontario Museum,[5] which also bought a loom). Most of the *grener* were in natural colours, white with brown stripes. Some weavers used chemical dyes and coloured stripes on a white or grey background, as they used to do for some of the migrating Lapps. Since the museum had to accept the *grener* unseen, the natural colours were preferred. A new colour type was introduced when a customer asked for a dark brown *grene* with white stripes, i.e., with the colours reversed (fig. 2). The weavers accepted the idea, and the type soon became very popular. The people in Manndalen consequently got themselves more black sheep, which had always been regarded as inferior. The "black" *grener* are now woven in great numbers.

The Folk Museum practised a certain quality control. The increased sale stimulated the weaving and more women took up the old craft again. In several cases *grener* were used by interior designers for decorating a ship, a public lounge, or the like. After some years a private sales organization in the north became interested and took over. The museum, which had sold *grener* on a non-profit basis and whose capacity was limited, now only occasionally obtained *grener* from old suppliers.

Not satisfied with the new sales organization, in 1966 the weavers in Manndalen organized a local handicraft society to control quality and prices, and to prevent the weavers from underselling each other. The sale now took place from the home of the very active and able chairman of the organization,

a mother of five children. The contact with the Folk Museum was never broken, however, and from time to time its advice was asked, as when a migrating Lapp village in Finnmark wanted to organize courses in *grene* weaving, so that they too could learn to weave on the old loom and sell blankets to the tourists who passed through the village. The women in Manndalen felt this initiative from Finnmark was unfair competition and warned their members, whose main source of income was from their weaving, not to teach *grene* weaving outside the valley. The migrating Lapps had only occasionally woven in the past; they did not keep sheep and had no wool; but they did have other traditional handicrafts such as working in bone, skin, and fur.

The controversy took place in connection with an attempt by the authorities to organize Lappish handicraft among the migrating Lapps of Finnmark to help them supplement their income. Very few families can now live from reindeer breeding alone, and as the *grener* were considered to be typically Lappish, and the migrating Lapps felt that they were the true Lapps, they had some difficulty in accepting the intervention of the weavers in Manndalen.

It must be added that although Lappish was their mother tongue, people in Manndalen did not call themselves Lapps. As was already mentioned, they did not dress in the characteristic Lapp costume, nor did they keep reindeer. A certain discrimination against the Lapps by the non-Lappish population in the north had made the resident Sea-Lapps reluctant to identify themselves as Lapps. They lived like other Norwegians from fishing and husbandry, and felt that they should be regarded as Norwegians. At one time I was asked point-blank by my friends in Manndalen if it was necessary for the museum to call the *grene* Lappish, since neither loom nor technique was Lappish in origin, but only a continuation of an old European tradition. "We do not feel that we are Lapps."[6] Outside the chairman's gate in Manndalen there is now a large printed poster, telling that Manndalen is the only place where the thousands of years old European weaving tradition has survived and where *grener* woven on the warp-weighted loom can be bought.

When I visited one of the two Lapp villages in Finnmark in 1974 the controversy seemed to be

more or less settled. After a weaving course had
been held (one of the Manndalen weavers did take
the job as a teacher despite the warning from the organization), very few people had taken up *grene*
weaving, and some of the leading handicraft people
said that this should be left to the weavers in
Manndalen. The *grener* in the handicraft shop had
in fact been woven in Manndalen, but by people
outside the new weavers' organization. As a result of
this new conflict an antagonism had arisen between
two groups of weavers in the valley.

Since my visit to Manndalen in 1955, I had
wanted to make a film of the whole work: carding,
spinning, warping, and weaving. It is the only way
of documenting the work, the rhythm of the experienced weaver and the trick of the implement which
alone can tell about its special qualities. It had so
far been impossible to raise money for a film from
ordinary sources, because it was argued that this
was not a dying craft, but that on the contrary, it
was flourishing. Other old crafts were in danger of
disappearing and should be given priority. But as
the years passed I feared that changes had taken
place, and in 1973 I appealed to the Folk Museum,
which granted money to produce a film by a small
team from its own staff. It is consequently not a professional film, but it is nevertheless a document of
the weaving in Manndalen in 1973.

An active, old, experienced weaver was chosen by
the chairman of the *grene* weavers' organization to
weave for the film. Like Anne Hansen in 1955, she
had been a widow for many years and had to support her children. She had learned the art from her
mother and had started weaving at the age of sixteen. She was now sixty-eight. She believed she had
woven more than a thousand *grener* during her life,
for sale and in exchange for services or other things.
Such exchange was and still is very common in
Manndalen, where cash has always been scarce.

By 1973 a great deal had changed in Manndalen.
A road now connected the valley with the main
route northwards, which meant that it was now possible to communicate daily with the outside world.
In 1974 another new road was completed which
connects the valley with the main road southwards.
People are expecting great changes: tourists driving
through the valley, cafés, perhaps a small hotel or
two, souvenir shops and the opportunity for daily

Figure 6.   Weaving on the warp-weighted loom. Anne Hansen
walks back and forth inserting the weft.
Photo: author, 1955.

Figure 7.   Anne Hansen warping on the warping frame.
Photo: author, 1955.

Figure 8. Helene Mikalsen's house in Manndalen where the weaving took place in 1973. The house was built in the 1950s. The iron gate is characteristic of modern Manndalen.
Photo: N.F., 1973.

Figure 9. The loom is placed in the living room. Helene Mikalsen is attaching loom weights to the warp. The woven starting border has been sewn to the beam at the top. This loom belonged to Helene's mother and is one of the very few objects which escaped destruction in 1944; it was hidden behind a boulder. The supports of the uprights, which enable the loom to stand without leaning against the wall, are new. Beam length ca. 190 cm, upright originally 165 cm.
Photo: N.F., 1973.

commuting to Tromsø, the nearest town, which is rapidly expanding.

There have been other changes. In 1955 the men had to leave Manndalen for seasonal work in the fisheries or in the forests of Sweden. The women and unmarried girls stayed home, as did most of the young boys. The parents did not want their children to go out in the dangerous world outside the valley. Many of them did not speak Norwegian fluently, as Lappish was their mother tongue. Most people belonged to a special Lutheran sect, the Læstadians, named after the Swedish pastor who founded it in the nineteenth century. They were very strict about worldly things, such as dancing, smoking, and vanity in dress. No girl or woman could dress in "man's clothing", i.e., slacks. The average income was very low, so there was not much need for finery. Apart from one truck, no car could be seen on the 10 km long road through the valley.

In 1973, on the other hand, many of the young boys and girls worked in Tromsø in building and construction, in shops, as hairdressers, etc. The married men came home for the weekend on Friday evening, many of them in their own cars. Modern bungalow-style houses had been built in the main part of the valley with modern plumbing, television, upholstered furniture, and all the gadgets common in the western culture of today. A new feature was the elegant iron gates leading into different properties (fig. 8). The children had bicycles, plastic toys, and modern clothes, and women in slacks and with permanent waves were a common sight. There was nothing to distinguish Manndalen from any other district in Norway.

In 1955 I did not see a single *grene* in any of the houses I visited; no one could afford to keep one in her own home. Several weavers now had a *grene* placed on a sofa or an upholstered chair. It was astonishing to learn that these *grener* were not of their own make. I was told that they were woven on ordinary horizontal looms and that the yarns for the warp and the coloured bands were not hand-spun. It was cheaper to let another person weave on a horizontal loom and pay for it in money or in exchange for something else. The weavers could get more for a *grene* woven on the warp-weighted loom from hand-spun yarn. Evidently, time now means money in this part of the world too.

In the families I visited another change was conspicuous: the parents did not speak Lappish to their children any more, and many children did not understand Lappish at all. I have no doubt that this was in order to make life easier in a Norwegian-speaking society.

How could the weaving on the warp-weighted loom survive in modern Manndalen? First of all, there still was no industry in the valley to compete with the home work. The weavers were married women who stayed home with the children and the elderly. The young people left to go to secondary schools and to work. Secondly, the *grene* had found a new market to replace the one it had lost: instead of the migrating Lapps, who are now settled in modern houses (with the exception of the reindeer shepherds), the customers were tourists.

Each family in Manndalen had some sheep and it was still common to spin all the wool on a wheel. But attempts had been made to streamline some of the processes. In the 1960s three brothers in the neighbouring community started a small workshop for machine wool carding. They came around to fetch the wool and brought back the carded slivers. This machine made the laborious hand carding unnecessary and did not cost much. There is no doubt that it stimulated the spinning and weaving. The older women helped with the spinning while their married daughters did the weaving. The ones who had not been taught in their homes went to old, experienced weavers to learn. They got their menfolk to make looms of the traditional type, and by weaving for sale were able to earn some cash, which they could not have done otherwise. One family with three children, where the man had also started weaving since he had become unable to do heavy work, had sold *grener* for 11,000 kroner in one year (about $2,200). This meant that the family could live on their small farm without having to go outside the community to supplement their income.

These weavers were not interested in using a horizontal loom for *grene* weaving, because the genuine *grene* demanded by the tourists had to be woven on the old vertical loom with the traditional starting border.

The looms themselves had changed somewhat because of the change in houses and because of the new tourist market. The old looms from before the

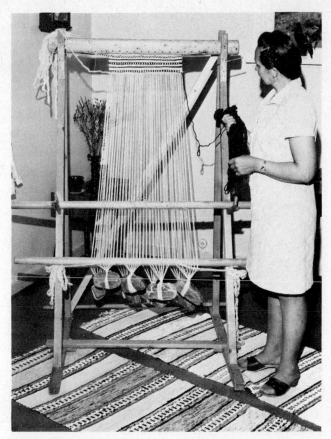

Figure 10.   A new, small loom for weaving streamers, placed in the living room. Manndalen.
Photo: N.F., 1973.

Figure 11.   Helene Mikalsen sitting on a stool and warping out-of-doors to demonstrate for the photographer.
Photo: A. Nesheim, 1952.

war were made of local slender birch wood. After the war all wood was imported in standard dimensions from the southern parts of the country, and the looms were made locally mostly from that material. A few years ago one weaver decided to weave *grener* in different dimensions. Nobody used them for blankets any more; the new customers hung them on the wall or used them as mats on the floor or on a davenport. The new sizes were smaller, so-called "half-size *grener*" for wall hangings, small table runners, or cushion covers, all in the same technique and pattern as the old blankets. Other weavers followed, as the new small *grener* were cheaper and easier to sell and to use in modern flats than the big, heavy coverlets.

The looms, originally about 190 cm wide (fig. 9), could now be made much narrower for the small weaves, and from very slender material. The uprights of the old loom, leaning at a slant, used to be nailed at the top to the wall. As people now had papered or painted walls, they did not like the big nail holes, and instead they made the loom into a permanent structure which could stand by itself without having to be supported by a wall. It was carried into the room all set up for use, and removed again when the weaving was finished (fig. 10). A parallel development had in fact taken place earlier in the century when the warping frame had become a fixed structure instead of three loose sticks to be put into holes in the floor.

Some people who had a shed or an attic avoided weaving in the living room, except in winter when they had to use a heated room. Others found space for the loom in the bedroom. I did not hear of people weaving in the kitchen, the room where people really lived and had their meals. The "living room" was not for everyday use.

The position of the weavers when warping had changed slightly since 1955. Instead of sitting on the floor with the legs stretched out between the sticks, an excellent working position (fig. 7), they now sat on a stool. This practice seemed to have been started by a respected old weaver who assisted in our film. She had acted as a teacher for many of the younger weavers. She told us that as a young girl she had started by using a stool because she was very small and it helped her reach farther. Now all the younger women used stools, and only the old

ones sat on the floor (fig. 11).

The weaving itself had changed as well. Since the *grene* was no longer an article for everyday use, the young weavers did not follow the old rules of strengthening the edges by taking the weft several times around the outer warp threads. They did not bother to make the ingenious weft skein with its hard head which is used instead of a shuttle and is admirably suited to the purpose. The old weavers complained about this carelessness. The traditional stern morality connected with all work was about to disappear, and the skill of uncounted generations was disintegrating little by little. The old thrift has disappeared together with poverty. The thrums from the weaving, which were spun together with new yarn in 1955, were now thrown away; nobody used unravelled yarn from old stockings for warp any more.

Several attempts at time-saving inventions were mentioned. One weaver was said to have tried a kind of flying shuttle and special shed-shifting devices, but she kept it to herself and was not willing to show her loom. Another had tried to combine the motor of a sewing machine with the spinning wheel, without much success (the motor was not strong enough). Some weavers in a neighbouring district tried to make *grener*, woven on ordinary horizontal looms, pass as "real" *grener*, faking a starting border. A customer without special knowledge would not notice the difference. But the handicraft association in Manndalen was very strict and did not recognize these as genuine *grener*. The latter were given a special guarantee label.

Since it was the loom and its history as much as the product that attracted the new customers, one would think that much change or improvement, either in the loom or in the weaving, might shake the whole basis for the new interest in *grener*. The history of the loom, however, and its appeal to the public, have already led to imitations on the part of professional weavers outside the Lappish area. Beautiful coloured *grener* are woven in Finnish arts and crafts weaving shops on horizontal looms with faked starting borders finished in tassels. They are sold with illustrated pamphlets telling the story of the Lappish *radno*. The starting border, which is the only feature that links a product with the warp-weighted loom, has become an important sales-promoting detail.

157

The weavers of Manndalen would have liked to claim exclusive rights to their loom and their technique. Their own organization is now building a small house for demonstration of the weaving and for exhibiting the *grener* for sale. It has been difficult for them to raise the money, and they were able to do so only with the aid of a public fund. The weavers hope to sell *grener* to tourists passing through the valley now that the new road has been finished. Economically the old handicraft is still of great importance in the valley.

The story of the *grene* weaving in Manndalen is probably more or less typical of other areas of the world. It illustrates the way in which traditional articles for everyday use that have lost their old function find a new role in the affluent society of today. *Grene* weaving would probably have died out little by little if the Folk Museum's work in spreading awareness of the history of the loom had not given it a special interest and attraction. For people working in museums, trying to make visitors see their own past in relation to the present, it is interesting to note that the knowledge of an old tradition which illustrates cultural influence through the ages and over long distances can so fascinate modern man. In this case the fascination is evident from the fact that the great majority of *grener* are sold directly by the weavers or their organization in Manndalen, or by the Folk Museum, to people who have heard about the loom. It is not a cheap souvenir; in 1974 it cost about $100 or more. The main handicraft shops in cities such as Oslo, which do not advertise the story of the loom and its origin, sell very few *grener*. The people who buy know what they want and why. That it is Lappish gives the blanket additional tourist value. There is a romantic feeling about Lapps as a primitive group of nomads in modern western society. All that is Lappish is related to this nomadic group. But the settled Sea-Lapps, whose way of life also goes back into prehistoric times, are little known as a special group. Without reindeer and colourful costumes, they are less striking, and they do not advertise their Lappish origin.

The future of the old weaving tradition is difficult to predict. At present it seems to be surviving. I was told in 1973 that about fifty weavers were active in Manndalen and eight to ten in the neighbouring community.

The loom may spread outside the Lappish districts, perhaps with some changes, as a hobby instrument. In an industrialized world with short working hours, the interest in making things by hand is growing. I already know of warp-weighted looms that are used by several young weavers out of weaving school, as well as by amateurs in England and Denmark. The spindle is becoming popular among young people in the Scandinavian countries today, and many old textile techniques which have only barely survived in certain districts are coming into use again. Among them are different types of band weaving, such as tablet weave. *Sprang* is another technique which has become fashionable, and so is *nålbinding*, a kind of single-needle knitting with a limited length of yarn which was re-introduced by the handicraft organization and has become very popular in Sweden during the last few years. Even the warp-weighted loom, which is easily made by any amateur, may become fashionable.

The starting border of the *grene* with its tassel on one side has become the symbol of the old tradition connected with the warp-weighted loom. It has already been taken over by professional hand-weavers and used in different types of weaves, isolated from the original technical background. It may perhaps outlive both the loom and the *grene*.

Notes

1. E.v. Walterstorff, "En vävstol och en varpa" [A loom and a warping frame], *Fataburen*, 1928, Annual, Stockholm, Nordiska museet och Skansen, 1929, pp. 147-159.

2. The result of the study was published by M. Hoffmann, *The warp-weighted loom: Studies in the history and technology of an ancient implement*, Oslo, Universitetsforlaget, 1964 (second printing 1974). Technical details about Lappish weaving, pp. 56-114.

3. A. Nesheim, "Den samiske grenevevingen og dens terminologi" [The Lappish *grene* weaving and its terminology], *Svenska Landsmål*, 1953-1955, vol. 78 (1956), pp. 321-341.

4. The same year a student of geography undertook a study in the area: T.B. Schjøtt, "Bosetning og erhverv i Manndalen" [Settlement and occupation in Manndalen], *Samiske Samlinger*, vol. 4-2, Oslo, Norsk Folkemuseum, 1956, pp. 1-100.

5. H.B. Burnham, "Four looms", *Art and Archaeology Division Annual*, Toronto, Royal Ontario Museum, 1963, pp. 77-79.

6. A. Nesheim, *Introducing the Lapps*, Oslo, Grundt Tanum, 1963. See also by the same author "Eastern and western elements in Lapp culture", in *Lapps and Norsemen in olden times*, Oslo, University Press, 1967, pp. 164 f.

How Many Apocalypse Tapestries?

Donald King

THE Apocalypse, a favoured theme of mediaeval painting and sculpture, also figured occasionally in wall hangings. Matthaeus, abbot of Saint-Florent at Saumur about 1133–1156, commissioned "dorsalia duo egregia quae praecipuis solemnitatibus extenduntur in choro, in quorum altero XXIV. seniores cum cytharis et phialis depinguntur; in reliquo Apocalypsis Johannis opere est descripta eleganti".[1] Adalbert II, abbot of Wessobrunn 1200–1220, commissioned for his church two "tapetia sive vela mirabilis picturae ac variae texturae", one of which depicted the visions of the Apocalypse of St. John; the record of the inscriptions on this hanging suggests that the subjects were arranged in two rows, with the first, third, fifth, etc. scene in the upper row and the second, fourth, sixth, etc., in the lower.[2] A posthumous inventory of the property of Isabella of France, Queen of England, who died in 1358, includes "unam aulam videlicet dorsorium cum duobus costeris longis, distinctis de istoria Apochalipsis".[3]

More important than these were the Apocalypse tapestries commissioned by Louis, Duke of Anjou, brother of Charles V of France. The project was presumably initiated some time after 1373, for in that year a manuscript of "L'Apocalipse, en françois, toute figurée et historiée, et en prose" was catalogued in the King's library, while a later note indicates, "Le Roy l'a baillée à mons. d'Anjou, pour faire son beau tappis".[4] This must have been one of the books consulted by the distinguished painter who appears in the Duke's accounts in January 1378 (1377 by mediaeval reckoning) as the designer of the tapestries:

A Hennequin de Bruges, paintre du Roy notre seigneur, sur ce qui lui puet ou pourra estre deu à cause des pourtraitures et patrons par lui faiz pour lesdiz tapiz à l'istoire de l'Appocalice par mandement dudit notre seigneur le lieutenant, donné le derrenier jour de janvier 1377, et quittance dud. Hennequin de Bruges donné le 28e jour dud. mois .... 50 franz.[5]

The text does not indicate clearly whether Hennequin supplied only small-scale designs, or the full-size cartoons as well, but in any case it is unlikely that the cartoons would have been executed single-handed by this artist, whose only certain autograph work is a miniature painting of Charles V, signed "Johannes de Brugis, pictor regis predicti, fecit hanc picturam propria sua manu".[6] Some of the designs and cartoons for the Apocalypse were presumably delivered before January 1378, for by April of that year Nicolas Bataille, the leading supplier of tapestries in Paris, received part payment for two Apocalypse tapestries which he had made:

A Nicolas Bataille, sur la façon de deux draps de tapisserie à l'istoire de l'Apocalice qu'il a faiz pour mons. le duc, par led. mandement rendu ci-dessus en la prouchaine partie et quictance dud. Nicolas, donnée le 7e jour d'avril 1377 .. 1000 frans.

A further payment later the same year may or may not be relevant:

A Nicolas Bataille, tappicier de Paris, sur la somme de 1500 fr., en laquelle mons. le duc lui estoit tenuz pour raison de certains tappis à ymages qui'il a faiz et livrez pour mond. seigneur par son mandement, donné le 8e jour d'octobre 1378, et quictance dud. Nicolas, donné le 6e jour de novembre l'an dessusdit .. 500 frans.

A further sum paid to the designer by instalments in

January 1379, July 1379, and March 1381 may relate to the Apocalypse tapestries, though this is not stated:

A Jehan de Burges, peintre et varlet de chambre du Roy nostre sire, pour don a lui fait, par monseigneur le duc, de la somme de VIˣˣ frans pour les bons services qu'il lui a faiz en faisant certaines pourtraictures pour mon dit seigneur, par un mandement adreçant aux gens des comptes de mondit seigneur donné le Ve jour de mars CCC IIIIˣˣ, et lettres closes, escriptes de la propre main de mondit seigneur, donné le Xe jour de janvier l'an M CCC LXXVIII dessus dit, avec III quittances dudit Jehan, la premiere de L frans donné le premier jour dudit mois de janvier CCC LXXVIII, et l'autre de L frans donné le IXe jour de juillet CCC LXXIX et la tierce le VIIe jour de mars CCC IIIIˣˣ contenant XX frans, pour tout .... VIˣˣ frans.[7]

In June 1379 there was a part payment for three tapestries which Bataille had contracted to make:

A Nicolas Bataille, tapissier de Paris, sur la somme de 3000 fr. qu'il doit avoir de mond. seigneur par marchié fait pour lui faire 3 tappis de l'istoire de l'Apocalice, renduz prises dedens Noel 1379, par mandement dudit mons. le duc donné le 9 juing l'an dessusdit et quictance dud. Nicolas, donnee le 16e jour dud. mois .... 300 fr.

Another payment at the same time may or may not be relevant:

Au dessusdit Nicolas Bataille .... 20 fr. que led. mons. le duc ordonna lui estre bailliez pour distribuer aux varlés de Robin Poinçon qui ont ouvré en la tapicerie de mond. seigneur, lesquelz il leur avoit donnez pour leur vin, par mandement donné le 20e jour de juing 1379 et quictance dud. Nicolas, donne le 16e jour dud. mois.

Bataille, a contractor on a very large scale, certainly subcontracted some of his work, and it is not improbable that Poinçon's workshop was concerned in weaving the Apocalypse tapestries.

The extant accounts of Louis I, Duke of Anjou, covering expenditure incurred from 1375 to 1379, leave the story incomplete. The Duke died in 1384, and no more is heard of his Apocalypse tapestries until 1400, when they may probably be identified with hangings which adorned the marriage at Arles of his son Louis II with Yolande of Aragon; these were described as "draps nobles et bels, en la qual draps eran estoriatz tota l'Apocalipse".[8] The will of Yolande, who died in 1442, bequeathed the tapestries to her son René: "Item nous donnons a nostre-

dit filz le Roy de Sicile la tapicerie de l'Apocalypse."[9] From 1458 onwards the accounts of King René include various sums for storage and maintenance of the Apocalypse tapestries at Angers and Baugé, and by his will of 1474 he bequeathed them to the cathedral of Angers: "Item donne et laisse à ycelle église la belle tapisserie sur laquelle sont contenues toutes les figures et visions de l'Apocalypse." After his death in 1480 the tapestries were conveyed from Baugé to the cathedral in two carts and the chapter-records reveal, for the first time, their number: "Six grandes pièces de l'Apocalypse." Thereafter they were hung in the cathedral at the great religious festivals each year, until 1782, when the chapter discarded all its tapestries. Gravely damaged, and cut into many pieces, the greater part of the Apocalypse set is now preserved in the castle at Angers. The extant pieces are woven entirely of wool, without silk or gold thread. Several bear the arms of Anjou and Brittany, and one the interlaced initials L and M, for Louis I d'Anjou and his wife Marie de Bretagne. Péan de la Tuillerie, who saw the tapestries hanging in the cathedral, estimated that "la plupart des pièces ont vingt aunes de long sur cinq aunes de hauteur" (about 23.76 m × 5.94 m).[10] Louis de Farcy, working from the surviving fragments, calculated that most of the hangings originally measured 22–24 m × 5.40–5.60 m.[11]

In 1386, the accounts of Philippe le Hardi, Duke of Burgundy, younger brother of Louis I d'Anjou, record the commissioning of another set of Apocalypse tapestries:

A Jehan Cosset, varlet de chambre de monseigneur, lesquels monseigneur mande que le receveur lui paie par lettre de mandement sur certains ouvrages d'une chambre que monseigneur lui avoit ordené a faire et pour achater C livres de fil d'or ou environ pour ent faire ledit drap de l'Appocalice dont Robert Pisson est chargié a faire, si comme par II mandemens de mondit seigneur appert, l'un donne le XVI d'aoust IIIIˣˣ et VI, l'autre le XIX de septembre ensuivant .... XIᶜLXXVI *l*.[12]

The projected use of gold thread was soon abandoned, for in December of the same year it appears that the six tapestries were to be woven of wool only:

A Robert Poinçon demourant a Paris sur la somme de Vm. frans d'or a quoy monseigneur a fait marchié a lui pour lui faire

161

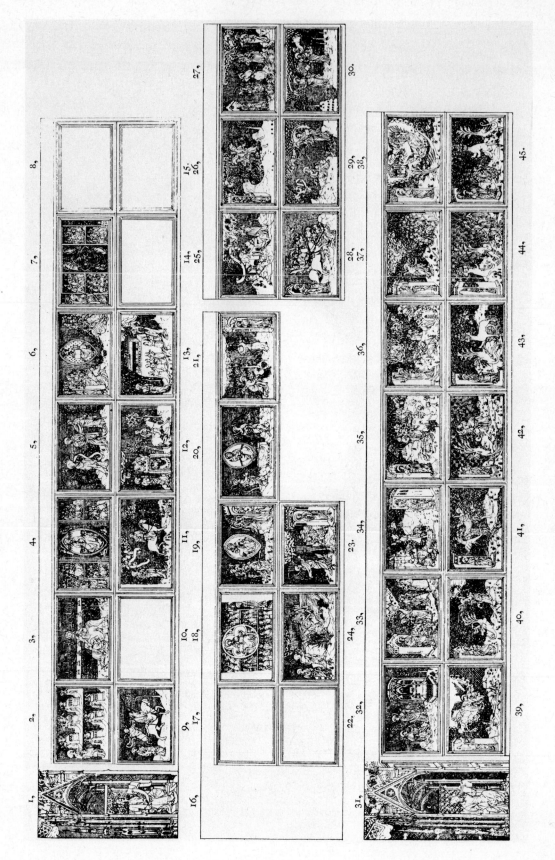

Figure 1. Louis de Farcy's reconstruction of the first three tapestries of the Angers Apocalypse, erroneously showing the second tapestry as two separate hangings, one of them of bizarre shape. These three tapestries were woven about 1378.

162

Figure 2. Louis de Farcy's reconstruction of the last three tap-estries of the Angers Apocalypse, woven from 1379 onwards.

163

et livrer six grans tappiz de haulteliche et de file d'Arras a l'istoire de l'Apocalipse, chascun tappiz contenant IIII^{xx}X aunes quarrées a l'aune de Paris, par mandement donné de XXIIIIe jour de décembre IIII^{xx} et VI .... XII^c frans.

This payment was actually made on 7 February 1387. There is no payment for designs, and it is reasonable to suppose that the Duke of Burgundy was content with those made for his brother by a very eminent painter only a few years before. It was normal practice for tapestry cartoons to be re-used, and no doubt those of the Anjou Apocalypse, one of the most ambitious pictorial enterprises of the Middle Ages, had been carefully preserved by the Dukes of Anjou, by Nicolas Bataille, or perhaps by Robert Poinçon, who is known to have been working on tapestries for Louis I d'Anjou at the time when his Apocalypse was woven (payment of June 1379, above). Indeed, since the Duke of Burgundy's set was to include the same number of tapestries, and of the same dimensions (each about 127 sq m), as the Anjou set, it is virtually certain that it was to be woven from the same cartoons. Poinçon received a further payment of 1,000 francs for these tapestries in January 1390 and again in January 1391, and it is clear that they were still unfinished at the latter date. In 1395, the Duke of Burgundy had his Apocalypse tapestries fitted with tapes for hanging, "tout de neuf".[13] But it does not appear that he ever received more than four of the six originally ordered. In 1403 these four, like other tapestries in the collection, were found to be too unwieldy for convenient use and were each divided into two.[14] The Apocalypse tapestries, now eight in number, recur in inventories of Philippe le Bon,[15] the Emperor Charles V ("chacune de huict aulnes de hault", or about 5.60 m, since these are ells of Brabant),[16] and King Philip II (mostly 7½ aulnes by about 16 aulnes, or 5.25 m × about 11.20 m).[17] Six of them survived the burning of the palace in Brussels in 1731.[18] Their ultimate fate is unknown.

Jean, Duke of Berry, brother of the Dukes of Anjou and Burgundy, possessed a single Apocalypse tapestry, recorded in his posthumous inventory of 1416 as "un autre tappis nommé le Tappis de l'Appocalice, contenant XIX aulnes de long et quatre aulnes et un quartier de large, lequel est de laynne de plusieurs couleurs, sanz or".[19] This tapestry, about 22.57 m × 5.05 m, almost the same size as those of the Anjou and Burgundy sets, was one of those delivered to his daughter Marie, Duchess of Bourbon, in December 1416.[20] It may have been identical with a single Apocalypse tapestry which a later Duchess of Bourbon — Anne de France, daughter of Louis XI and wife of Marie's grandson, Pierre de Beaujeu — gave to the chapter of Angers cathedral, accompanied by a letter:

Chers et grans amis, par la singuliere dévotion, que mon mary et moy avons à Dieu et à mons. Saint-René, qui est . . . en votre église, vous envoyons par Jean de la Barre, une pièce de tapisserie de l'Apocalypse, que avions en notre maison, pour aider à parer votre dite église, vous priant que vous veuilliez nous comprendre ès prières et bienfaits d'icelle . . . escript aux Chastelliers le 25 may 1490.[21]

The chapter naturally acceded to the request and included in the Calendar of the cathedral the names of the Duke and Duchess of Bourbon, noting that they had given "magnam peciam tapiceriae ex Apocalypsi Joannis Evangelistae figuris distinctam, quasique finistem [for similem?] ei quae de bonis regis Siciliae nobis advenit".[22] The cathedral inventory of 1505 lists the Anjou and Bourbon tapestries together:

Item septem petiae pulchrae magnificae tapiceriae sumptuosi operis elaboratae, vulgariter dictae et appellatae Apocalypsis quarum sex fuerunt datae per deffunctum Renatum regem Siciliae. Alia vero septima data fuit per dominam de Bourbonio.

The 1539 inventory speaks in similar terms.[23] But it does not appear that the Bourbon tapestry was ever hung in the cathedral as an integral part of the Anjou set. A document of 1533 speaks only of the Anjou Apocalypse covering the walls of the nave and transept:

Item les doyen et chapitre en la dite église ont belle grande et notable tapisserie entre les tapisseries de ce royaulme, historiée des hystoires de l'Apocalypse qui se tent aux festes solempnelles en la naif et chappelle qui couvre les longueurs de la nef et croisées d'icelle donnée par le feu roy de Sicile estimée valloir deux cens mils livres.

A text of 1623 indicates that four of the tapestries were hung in the nave:

Entrant dans la dite église, ils admirèrent la tapisserie, qui représente toute l'Apocalypse, dont les quatre pièces ou pantes suffisent pour tendre toute la nef.

"Deux pièces de l'Apocalypse" were hung in the arms of the transept until, in 1699, the demolition of the choir-screen opened up the view down the entire length of the cathedral and caused them to be transferred to the choir. The seventh tapestry had already been mutilated by 1643, when the inventory reads:

Sept pièces de tapisserie de l'Apocalypse, dont M. le fabriqueur en a fait couper une en deux, et dont la moitié se tend sur le reliquaire et l'autre au coing de la chapelle des Chevaliers, sur l'autel du Mas.

Nothing more is heard of the Bourbon tapestry, and Péan de la Tuillerie, in the eighteenth century, speaks only of the Anjou set.

The Anjou tapestries, according to the will of King René, included "toutes les figures et visions de l'Apocalypse". The Bourbon tapestry also depicted "figures from the Apocalypse", and its relationship to the Anjou set is described in the bungled phrase of the cathedral Calendar as "quasi similis(?)". This vague expression lends no support to the assertion, constantly repeated in the literature of the subject, that the Bourbon tapestry was an integral part of the Anjou set, which in some unexplained way had become temporarily separated from it. The evidence of the documents is that the Duke of Anjou's set and the set planned for the Duke of Burgundy, which was presumably based on the same cartoons, each comprised six tapestries, not seven. In these circumstances, the natural assumption is that the Bourbon tapestry was either a completely independent design, or else a repetition of one of the pieces in the Anjou and Burgundy sets, possibly part of a third set from the same cartoons, begun for the Duke of Berry and never completed. The gratuitous hypothesis that it formed an integral part of the Anjou set might be dismissed without further discussion, were it not for the fact that, for more than a century, it has been the basis of all attempts to reconstruct the Apocalypse tapestries from the surviving fragments.

In 1849, Abbé Joubert wrote of these fragments, "Lorsque les tapisseries me furent remises, elles étaient au nombre de 15, représentant 58 sujets réunis 4 par 4, sans ordre . . ."[24] This arrangement was soon dismantled, and in 1864 Joannis wrote, "Tous les tableaux sont aujourdhui separés, il n'en reste que quelques-uns qui se tiennent encore deux à deux."[25] Meantime, some additional pieces had been found and the total known today includes over seventy identifiable Apocalypse scenes, and five or six whole or fragmentary seated figures on a larger scale.[26] Xavier Barbier de Montault,[27] Louis de Farcy[28] and René Planchenault[29] have all assumed, contrary to the evidence of the documents, that the extant scenes are the remains of an Apocalypse sequence covering seven tapestries and they agree, with slight variations, on which of the extant scenes should be assigned to each of the seven:

I	10 extant scenes
II	6-7 extant scenes
III	5-6 extant scenes
IV	13-14 extant scenes
V	14 extant scenes
VI	12 extant scenes
VII	8-9 extant scenes

Farcy and Planchenault also agree that the first, fourth, fifth, sixth, and seventh tapestries, when complete, each comprised one large seated figure and fourteen Apocalypse scenes in two rows of seven each. But they disagree over the second and third tapestries, those with the smallest number of extant scenes. Farcy held that these two were always much smaller than the other five hangings, that the second originally comprised a large seated figure and eight scenes, while the third had no large figure and only six scenes. Planchenault rightly recognized that these assumptions were unjustified, and maintained that the second and third tapestries must have been similar to the other five in dimensions and design; but despite diligent search he confessed himself unable to suggest enough subjects for the twenty-eight scenes which the two tapestries would have depicted. There is only one satisfactory solution to this otherwise insoluble problem: to accept the documentary evidence that the Apocalypse sequence covered six, not seven, tapestries of equal size, and to recognize the fact that the extant scenes which have hitherto been assigned to the hypothetical second and third tapestries are really the remains of a single hanging. Evidently the seventh, or Bourbon, tapestry, which has not been recorded since 1643, is lost, along with many other mediaeval tapestries from the cathedral, and the pieces still preserved at Angers are the remains of the six tapestries of the Anjou set, which adorned the walls of the cathedral from 1480 to 1782. If the above table is now revised for a set of six tapestries instead of seven, it reads:

I	10 extant scenes
II	12-13 extant scenes
III	13-14 extant scenes
IV	14 extant scenes
V	12 extant scenes
VI	8-9 extant scenes

This reveals neatly graded states of preservation which may well reflect a clockwise (or counterclockwise) arrangement in the cathedral, with the two most damaged tapestries, I and VI, in the more exposed positions near the west door, and the two best preserved, III and IV, well protected in the transept or choir.

The conclusion that the extant pieces are the remains of six, not seven, tapestries also fits better with the documents concerning the weaving of the Anjou set. Of the extant Apocalypse scenes, twenty-three have plain backgrounds; with one doubtful exception, they are all from tapestries I and II, which are almost certainly the "deux draps de tapisserie à l'istoire de l'Apocalice" which Nicolas Bataille had made by April 1378. The remaining forty-eight scenes, with patterned backgrounds, are from tapestries III to VI. In III the backgrounds vary considerably, and this seems to have been an experimental piece; it was possibly one of the unspecified tapestries which Bataille had made and delivered by October 1378. The background patterns in IV, V, and VI are more uniform and it is likely that these were the "3 tappis de l'istoire de l'Apocalice" which Bataille had contracted to make, and for which he received a part-payment, in June 1379.

Thus all the evidence, both from the documents and from the extant pieces, confirms that the latter are the remains of the Anjou Apocalypse, which consisted not of seven tapestries, but of six. Incidentally, this conclusion eliminates speculation that the large seated figures were intended to represent bishops of the seven Churches of Asia, or any other group of seven.[30] There were only six of them.

Notes

1. E. Martène and U. Durand, *Veterum scriptorum et monumentorum, historicorum, dogmaticorum, moralium amplissima collectio*, Paris, 1729, vol. 5, col. 1130.

2. Georg Hager, "Die Bauthätigkeit und Kunstpflege im Kloster Wessobrunn", *Oberbayerisches Archiv*, vol. 48 (1894), pp. 223-228.

3. Sir Francis Palgrave, *Antient kalendars & inventories*, vol. 3, London, Record Commission, 1836, p. 246.

4. L. Delisle and P. Meyer, *L'Apocalypse en français au XIIIe siècle*, Bibl. Nat. Fr. 403, Delisle & Meyer, 1900-1901; L. Delisle, *Recherches sur la librairie de Charles V*, Paris, 1907, vol. 1, pp. 147f., vol. 2, p. 19.

5. This payment and those following, to Nicolas Bataille, were published and discussed by J.-J. Guiffrey, "Nicolas Bataille, tapissier parisien du XIVe siècle: Sa vie, son oeuvre, sa famille", *Mémoires de la Société de l'Histoire de Paris et de l'Ile-de-France*, vol. 10 (1883), 1884, pp. 275-281, 297-298. Guiffrey's transcription, reproduced here, modernizes the numerals, accents, and punctuation of the manuscript (Archives Nationales, Paris, KK. 242, fols. 66 r. and v., 92 r. and v., 93 r.), but is otherwise correct.

6. Further documents concerning this painter were published by Bernard Prost, "Un nouveau document sur Jean de Bruges, peintre du roi Charles V", *Gazette des Beaux-Arts*, 3e période, vol. 7 (1892), pp. 349-352.

7. This item (KK. 242, fol. 102 r.) was published by Chanoine Dehaisnes (*Documents et extraits divers concernant l'histoire de l'art dans la Flandre, l'Artois & le Hainaut avant le XVe siècle*, Lille, L. Danel, 1886, p. 560).

8. René Planchenault, "Transport en Provence de la tenture d'Angers", *Bulletin de la Société Nationale des Antiquaires de France* (1941), p. 137.

9. Lecoy de la Marche, *Le roi René*, Paris, 1875, vol. 2, p. 111. This and later texts concerning the tapestries are collected by Louis de Farcy, *Monographie de la cathédrale d'Angers*, vol. 3: *Le mobilier*, Paris, Desclée, de Brouwer et Cie., 1901, pp. 83-95.

10. Péan de la Tuillerie, *Description de la ville d'Angers*, Angers, Bibliothèque Angevine, 1869, p. 64 (first ed. 1778).

11. Farcy, *Monographie* (1901), pp. 95-96.

12. This and the following documents concerning Poinçon are quoted by Dehaisnes (*Documents*, 1886, pp. 639, 646, 666, 697). See also Bernard and Henri Prost, *Inventaires mobiliers et extraits des comptes des Ducs du Bourgogne*, Paris, Ernest Leroux, 1908-1913, vol. 2, 1449, 1641.

13. Henri David, *Philippe le Hardi, Duc de Bourgogne et co-régent de France de 1392 à 1404. Le train somptuaire d'un grand Valois*, Dijon, Bernigand et Privat, 1947, p. 91.

14. Alexander Pinchart, *Histoire de la tapisserie dans les Flandres*, Paris, Société Anonyme de Publications Périodiques, 1878-1885, p. 13.

15. Pinchart, *Histoire de la tapisserie* (1878-1885), p. 24.

16. H. Michelant, in *Compte-rendu des séances de la Commission Royale d'Histoire*, 3d series, vol. 13, Brussels, 1872, p. 245.

17. Michelant, *Compte-rendu*, vol. 14, 1872, pp. 199f.; A. Pinchart, "L'histoire de la tapisserie", *L'Art*, vol. 7 (1876), pp. 174, 210; P. Saintenoy, "Les tapisseries de la cour de Bruxelles sous Charles V", *Annales de la Société Royale d'Archéologie de Bruxelles*, vol. 30 (1921), p. 22.

18. L. P. Gachard, in *Bulletins de l'Académie Royale des Sciences, des Lettres et des Beaux-Arts de Belgique*, 2d series, vol. 35 (1873), Brussels, pp. 109-148; P. Saintenoy, "Les arts et les artistes à la cour de Bruxelles", *Mémoires de l'Académie Royale de Belgique,*

Classe des Beaux-Arts, 2d series, vol. 5 (1934), Brussels, p. 82.

19. Jules Guiffrey, *Inventaires de Jean Duc de Berry*, Paris, 1896, vol. 2, p. 207.

20. Guiffrey, *Inventaires* (1896), vol. 2, p. 294.

21. Farcy, *Monographie* (1901), p. 93.

22. Farcy, *Monographie* (1901), p. 318.

23. For these inventories and the following documents, see Farcy, *Monographie* (1901), pp. 93-95.

24. Farcy, *Monographie* (1901), p. 86.

25. Léon de Joannis, *Les tapisseries de l'Apocalypse de la cathédrale d'Angers*, Angers, 1864, p. 3.

26. On these larger figures, see René Planchenault, "L'Apocalypse d'Angers, elements pour un nouvel essai de restitution", *Bulletin Monumental*, vol. 111 (1953), pp. 227-235.

27. X. Barbier-Montault, *Les tapisseries du Sacre d'Angers*, Paris, Jules-Juteau et Fils, 1863.

28. Farcy, *Monographie* (1901), pp. 95-124.

29. Planchenault, "L'Apocalypse d'Angers" (1953), pp. 209-262; René Planchenault, *L'Apocalypse d'Angers*, Paris, Caisse Nationale des Monuments Historiques et des Sites, 1966.

30. Louis-Eugène Lefèvre, "Les sept églises d'Asie", *Gazette des Beaux-Arts*, 5e période, vol. 11 (1925), pp. 206-224.

Classical Tradition in Early Christian Art: A Textile Fragment in the Royal Ontario Museum

Neda Leipen

IN the rather extensive collection of late antique textiles from Egypt in the Royal Ontario Museum, comprising about 500 pieces, the fragment discussed here stands out for a number of reasons. It is, first of all, a very fine example of the Coptic art of weaving (fig. 1).[1] In addition, regarding both the style of its representation and its subject matter, our fragment is an excellent illustration of the tenacity of the classical Greek and Roman tradition in the declining centuries of the antique world.

The decorative scheme of the tapestry woven square, worked in the dark-silhouette style (dark purple wool against bleached linen ground), consists of a large central medallion surrounded by a border of medallions, a somewhat larger one in each corner and a pair of smaller ones along each side, together forming a square. All of these medallions are formed by an intertwining vegetable scroll with naturalistically shaped sprigs of leaves filling the interstices between the circles of the scroll. The three sets of pointed leaves, some of them veined, along the right vertical border, and the sprig of three leaves issuing from the medallion forming the lower left corner are particularly noteworthy. Though the tapestry woven part has suffered a fair amount of damage, all the essential details of the representation are preserved.

Each of the corner medallions contains a centaur riding to the right. All four centaurs are shown in an approximate three-quarter view in which the horse bodies appear properly foreshortened. While their hind legs are firmly on the ground, their front legs are in the air in front of them as if in spirited motion. This movement is further suggested by a turn of their human upper bodies, which appear almost frontal, and an even stronger turn of the heads with a sideways gaze from the large eyes. The upper and the lower centaurs at the left appear to have their outstretched left arms wound in a soft material (animal skin?), its end fluttering in the air by their side. The centaurs at the right, on the other hand, seem to be carrying a shield on their left arms. Each centaur raises his right arm: while in three of them the hand is free and open, the upper left centaur holds a round object, probably a stone, in his right hand. Their thick hair is indicated by the fine white outlines. Similar fine lines in front of their torsos probably represent their pectoral hair or perhaps long beards. Bits of vegetation fill the vacant areas within their medallions.

Each of the eight smaller medallions, formed by the intertwining double scroll along the sides of the square, encloses an animal. The animals face in a different direction from the rest of the figures: they stand, or run upward as it were, at a ninety-degree angle to the centaurs in the corners and the horsemen in the centre. This difference in planes occurs fairly commonly on late antique textiles and is to a certain degree due to the nature of the weaving process.[2] A variety of animals are represented. The medallions above the heads of the horsemen contain a lion with a great mane at the right and an ibex with two long, gently curving horns at the left. Below are a boar in the medallion at the right, and a long-eared hare at the left. Along the left side there

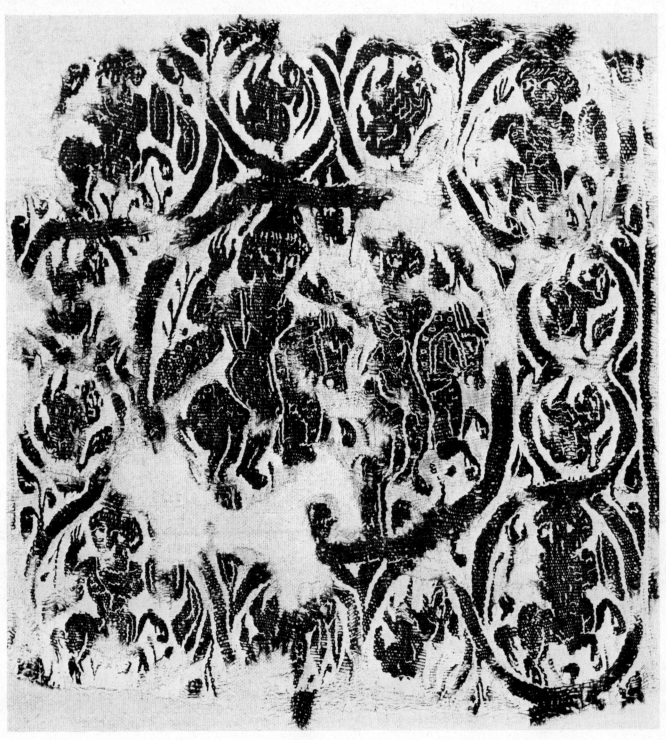

Figure 1.   Tapestry woven square from Egypt, about A.D. 500.
ROM acc. no. 910.131.8.

is a pair of lionesses, or possibly a lioness above and a leopard or cheetah below. A similar pair fills the medallions at the right.[3] As with the centaurs, the details of the animal anatomy are expressed by means of finely woven lines within the dark silhouettes of the figures, such as the mane of the lion, the separation and the outlines of the centaurs' and horses' legs, and the details of the human faces and the harnessed heads of the horses. Though the weaver tried, and definitely succeeded, in differentiating the animals, he limited his efforts to their heads and to some other details, but he conventionalized their bodies which are all similarly short and dumpy and in identical attitudes, with the hind legs under the body and the front ones outstretched.

The large central medallion is occupied by two horsemen riding to the right. Owing to the damage, neither horse and rider is fully preserved, the one at left having suffered in the bottom part where the legs of the horse are partly missing, while the one at right is mainly damaged at the top with the upper portion of his head and headdress missing. Fortunately, these losses complement each other, so to speak, so that the complete position of the left horse's legs can be deduced from the right horse, and the left rider's fully preserved head and headdress suggest the right rider's original appearance. Both horses are shown in the same attitude with their hind legs standing close together firmly on the ground, and with their front ones, as in the case of the centaurs, bent in the air in front of them. Like the centaurs, the two horsemen are represented in an animated attitude, each gesticulating in a lively manner with his right hand. The rider on the right adds an additional touch of animation to the scene: not only does he gesticulate with his right hand, he also turns his head and directs his gaze emphatically toward his companion. Both riders wear short tunics, boots, and flying short cloaks (seen here on the figure at left), a costume usually worn by huntsmen in ancient representations.[4] The better-preserved horseman at the left also wears a Phrygian cap over quite a lot of hair which is indicated by short vertical lines above the forehead and by a fullness at the side. Similar vertical lines, indicating the hair on his forehead, can be seen on the other rider, though his hat has disappeared together with the rest of the surrounding warps and wefts in that area.

The more completely preserved rider on the left was originally the more fully shown since he is in the front plane of the representation and closer to the viewer than his companion. Apart from his short cloak flying behind his right shoulder, which it was possible to include within the circular composition, we see that his tunic is adorned with short *clavi*, outlined in white. The *clavus* descending from the right shoulder is particularly visible. It has already been mentioned that he gesticulates with his right arm which, bent at the elbow, is raised high toward the side of his head. The solid straight line near, but not quite touching, his hand is most likely meant to depict a hunting spear (*venabulum* or *probolium*) he holds up: if the shaft had been completely joined with the fingers the result, in the dark-silhouette technique, might have been a blurred and incomprehensible representation. Whether or not in fact this is a spear, we shall see that the horseman may be identified as a hunter, and the whole scene as a hunting scene with two participants.

As in the smaller border medallions, the vacant areas in the field of the central medallion are filled with vegetable motifs of leaves and sprigs, e.g., below the horses' legs and to the right of the right-hand horseman. A handsome palm branch with long narrow leaves fills the space between the raised right arm of the rider at left and the plain frame of the medallion. As elsewhere in our fine and carefully woven textile, the details within the dark silhouettes of the men and the horses are rendered in thin white lines "drawn" by means of an extra weft. This is particularly obvious, for instance, in the horses' manes, which have a series of tiny circles intended to represent their elaborate dressing.[5] Equally, the circles and the lines on the flying mantle behind the horseman at the left suggest the decoration and the texture of this garment.

Keeping in mind the notorious uncertainty as to the absolute dating of the textiles which are commonly called "Coptic", it is generally agreed that those with naturalistically shaded, thus "modelled", figures or decorative motifs in polychrome wool belong, in terms of relative chronology, to the earlier, "Hellenistic" group of Graeco-Roman textiles from Egypt.[6] The dark-silhouette style seems to form a somewhat later phase though even within this group earlier and later stages have been distinguished.[7]

The latter technique was used in a large, if not the largest, group of textiles from late antique and Early Christian times in Egypt.

It is interesting to note that in classical antiquity the dark-silhouette or "black-figure" design had been used in other mediums and at other times before its appearance in textiles. In Greek vase painting the black-figure style of the archaic period with scratched-in lines to indicate detail (i.e., lines revealing the lighter colour of the clay) was practised more than a millennium earlier than our dark-silhouette tapestry woven textiles. Their chronologically much closer predecessors are the Roman black-silhouette floor mosaics, with inner lines represented in white. These monochrome mosaics reached their comparatively brief period of flowering in the second century A.D. Their development can be particularly well observed at Ostia where the style enjoyed a great popularity.[8] As with the dark-silhouette textiles, these mosaics are flat, two-dimensional, non-spatial, but very competent surface graphics. They lack the realism of a shaded polychrome representation but their compositions are no less lively, and their figures no less articulate and full-bodied. We shall see that in many aspects our textile reflects a long classical tradition: its dark-silhouette style is possibly one of these aspects.

Our square is one of a number of tapestry woven elements which were used to decorate a tunic, the characteristic costume worn during the late Roman Empire and the early Middle Ages. As attested by numerous monuments from the fourth century onward, the same fashion was widespread throughout the entire Roman Empire.[9] Most of the actually preserved textiles, however, come from Egypt. Designs, woven in multicoloured or purple wool with details in white linen, were either woven into the fabric of the linen garment or applied at the shoulders and above the hem at both front and back. Instead of squares, roundels (orbiculi) were also popular. Also common was a pair of ornamental stripes descending from the shoulders (clavi), as actually seen on our horseman on the left. The short cloak (Gr. chlamys), worn over the tunic and fastened on the shoulder, would most likely also have some decoration.[10]

Prominent in the decorative scheme of our piece is the so-called inhabited scroll motif surrounding the central medallion. Inhabited scrolls were one of the most popular decorative devices in the art of the Roman Empire. Originating in the Hellenistic period of the late fourth and third centuries B.C., the motif gained in popularity as time went on, and in late antiquity it was profusely used in pagan, Christian, and Jewish monuments alike. The dedicated and accurate observation in the Hellenistic period of birds, insects, and small animals, in their natural setting among the foliage and scrolls of trees and plants, resulted in a naturalistic rendering of both plant and animal in art. The well-observed details, however, soon became part of a fanciful and playfully incongruous composition as a whole, in which human figures, wild beasts, or fantastic mythological creatures were encircled by the tender, often very elaborate acanthus or vine scrolls.[11]

The surviving examples of peopled or inhabited scrolls in various techniques are countless. Among the earliest is an embossed gold diadem of the late fourth century B.C. in the Metropolitan Museum of Art in New York, on which ten small female figures playing musical instruments sit on the stems of a single running acanthus rinceau while Dionysus and Ariadne recline in the centre, their bodies supported by the arabesques of the scroll.[12] A somewhat later example is the handsome mosaic border from the royal palace of the Hellenistic Attalid kings of Pergamon where a rich polychrome rinceau on a black ground is peopled with delicate insects, minute putti, and other figures.[13] In the Royal Ontario Museum a fragment of a marble revetment from a gateway from Pompeii (acc. no. 930.157) exhibits an elegant, dainty scroll peopled with birds and chubby putti poised on or playfully hanging from the scrolls (fig. 2). Its stylistic features place it in the Augustan period and, though in a different medium, it compares very closely with the well-known silver crater from the Hildesheim Treasure.[14] In Roman architectural decoration friezes with peopled scrolls were particularly popular from the end of the second century A.D. and on, but the universal appeal of this decorative device in all parts of the Roman Empire is reflected in its continuous use in all the mediums, such as fine metalwork (of which the Hildesheim crater is a splendid example), mosaics,[15] ivory carvings,[16] and, of course, textiles.[17] The popularity of peopled scrolls continued unabated into the

171

Middle Ages, and they were a staple decorative device in Byzantine and Romanesque art.

Centaurs excited Greek imagination from very early times. Legend associated them with the deep mountain forests and the swift, rain-swollen, dangerous torrents of northern Greece, especially Thessaly, where these wild half-human and half-equine creatures dwelled, hunting, fighting, and revelling. While in earlier Greek art they are shown as completely human with only the hindquarters of a horse issuing from their backs, as for example on an Italo-corinthian amphora in the ROM (fig. 3), from the fifth century B.C. onward a classical type was established in which only a human torso was added to an otherwise fully equine, quadruped body.[18] Perhaps the most illustrious examples of the latter type are the centaurs raping the Greek women, from the west pediment of the temple of Zeus at Olympia of about 460 B.C., and the metopes with the combats of the Greeks and the centaurs from the Parthenon in Athens of some fifteen years later. A centauromachy was also represented on the frieze of the Hephaisteion, another fifth-century B.C. Athenian temple.[19]

On late antique or early mediaeval textiles found in Egypt centaurs occur fairly frequently, although they are by no means as commonplace as such other subjects from the classical repertoire as bacchic dancers, erotes or putti, and nereids. Almost without exception they are shown in the swift movements of pursuit or hunt, often brandishing a weapon, usually a rock or a broken-off branch.[20] Although many centuries separate the centaurs of these textiles, including the ones on our fragment, from those in classical Greek art, iconographically they conform fully to the ancient type, with their bushy hair, the long beard falling on the chest, and an animal skin wound around the left arm for protection. They are entirely in keeping with the characteristic action-laden classical representations, as demonstrated by the well-caught agitation, expressed in an almost rearing stance of the body, the momentary turn of the head with an intent sideways gaze, the expressive gestures of the hands, and the weapons they hold.[21]

We have seen that the smaller double-scroll medallions, two along the centre of each side of the square, are each inhabited by an animal. If the two horsemen of the central scene are hunters, and if the

Figure 2.   Fragment of marble revetment from Pompeii. Augustan.
ROM acc. no. 930.157.

172

Figure 3. Italo-corinthian amphora (detail with centaur).
End of seventh century B.C.
ROM acc. no. 969.224.1.

centaurs too are connected with hunts of wild animals, as seen on many Greek and Roman monuments, then it is quite logical that our weaver should have included such animals in his scene.

Hunts became one of the most popular genre themes during the Roman imperial period. In particular the large mosaic pavements in villas and palaces throughout the vast empire were prominently decorated with such scenes. Among the most splendid examples are the hunting representations at the luxurious Villa of Piazza Armerina of the fourth century in Sicily where preparations for, and various stages of, the hunt are most vividly represented, with the hunters pursuing their quarry both on foot and mounted.[22] In the rich Roman country estates in North Africa, hunting compositions are found at Zliten, Carthage, and El-Djem, to name only a few.[23] Spectacular also are the hunting pavements of the Roman province of Syria, particularly those from the city of Antioch.

Among the most remarkable hunting mosaics at Antioch are those in the Constantinian Villa, where four trapezoidal panels show hunters on horseback fighting a variety of wild animals, including a boar. The scene has in fact been identified as the Calydonian boar hunt of Greek mythology, in which the principal figure of the hero Meleager can be recognized attacking the charging animal with his spear,

together with the virgin-huntress Atalanta, shooting an arrow and standing next to him.[24] One of the earliest representations of the Calydonian boar hunt is on the famous Early Attic black-figure crater by Klitias and Ergotimos from the first half of the sixth century B.C. (the "François Vase", Florence). A boar hunt on one side of its neck shows the animal attacked by a number of legendary hunters on foot who are identified by their names neatly inscribed next to their figures. The leaders of the hunt, Meleager and Peleus, meeting the boar from the front, are closely followed by Atalanta and Melanion with others behind them.[25] Levi has suggested that, as time went on, such early representations of a specific mythological episode lost their original meaning and were understood, and reproduced, only as generic hunting scenes. Simultaneously, the ornamental qualities of the hunting motif became valued more and more for their own sake. Once the understanding of a mythological episode was lost, it was easy to excerpt or modify, and sometimes even add, individual scenes or single figures alien to the original story. As an example Levi quotes a mosaic *emblema* from the Leptis Magna with Meleager hunting the boar: a non-belonging addition is a lion shot at by Atalanta, and a figure at upper right, whose centaur-like torso alone can be seen, preparing to hurl a large stone with both hands at the wild beasts

173

below.[26] A similar rock-hurling personage is clearly a centaur on a lively second-century A.D. mosaic from Hadrian's Villa, now in Berlin, where centaurs have altogether replaced hunters after wild beasts. A similar scene is depicted on a Pompeian wall painting.[27]

Returning to our two horsemen, we note that they wear Phrygian caps over a mass of hair (the left-hand one very clearly wears it, and the right-hand one presumably also wore one). This fact suggests that the horsemen may be identified specifically as the Dioscuri, the Divine Twins, Castor and Pollux (Gr. *Polydeukes*). From very early on, the Greek legend visualized them as gods or heroes on horseback, fighting and helping in war, competing in games, or hunting.[28] According to a prevalent tradition they were the twin sons of Leda, born from an egg she laid, which had been fertilized by Zeus in the guise of a swan. In Alexandrian art and in most later representations the peaked close-fitting hats (*pilei*, from *pileus*, felt cap) they invariably wear are therefore interpreted as representing, appropriately, one half of an egg-shell from which they had sprung. Mythology involves them in a number of heroic episodes, among them the Calydonian boar hunt in which they helped their cousin Meleager, as depicted already on the François Vase. From Pausanias (VIII, 45, 4) we hear that Scopas sculpted Castor and Pollux in a hunting scene on the pediment of the temple of Athena Alea at Tegea; and in Ovid (*Metam.* VIII, 300) they figure as hunters *par excellence*. On a special class of Roman sarcophagi, the so-called Meleager sarcophagi, the Dioscuri are represented assisting the hero in the boar hunt.[29]

Via the Greek sanctuaries in South Italy the cult of the Dioscuri spread to Rome, where they were particularly revered by the wealthy and influential *equites* (knights): they thus assumed yet another aspect, that of patrons of merchants and financial affairs. That caused them, appropriately, to figure prominently on the Roman Republican coinage, in particular during the second and the first centuries B.C., where they were used as the main reverse type (fig. 4). Here they are most usually shown mounted, holding their spears horizontally and charging to the right. Their costume is a short tunic, with a flying cloak, and a *pileus* on their heads. Their galloping horses are shown with both hind legs on the

Figure 4. Roman Republican denarius. Reverse with Dioscuri. Ca. 133 – 126 B.C.
ROM acc. no. 969x134.95.

Figure 5. Silver coin of Bruttium, third century B.C. Obverse: busts of Dioscuri. Reverse: Dioscuri riding to right.
Drawing by Sylvia Hahn, ROM, after a coin in the Fitzwilliam Museum, Cambridge.

ground and both front ones in the air. An even earlier silver coin of Bruttium of the third century B.C.
seems in particular to foreshadow our representation (fig. 5). Here, in addition to their usual pranc-
ing horses and their flying cloaks, they both gesticulate with their raised right arms. Also, a victor's
palm branch, strikingly similar to the one behind
our front horseman, is shown behind each of the
Dioscuri. The obverse of the same coin bears their
two busts with a profusion of curly hair protruding
from under their laureate *pilei*, framing their faces
and covering their necks in a manner similar to that
on our textile.[30]

In some representations, both on coinage and
elsewhere, the *pileus* assumes a shape more closely
resembling a Phrygian cap in which the soft top of
the cap is tipped over to one side.[31] In the Hellenistic period the iconographical type of the Dioscuri
became definitely established: from then on they invariably wear a *pileus* or a *pileus*-like cap (as opposed
to the wide-brimmed *petasus* or no hat in earlier representations), and almost always a short cloak. In
sculpture their short tunics may be dispensed with
to show them in heroic nudity. The type of the head
is characterized by a profusion of hair under the
pileus or the Phrygian cap, a somewhat protruding
lower forehead, and large eyes. A good example is
the bronze statue from Paramythia in the British
Museum.[32]

Our suggested identification of the two hunters as
Dioscuri is consistent with the mythological tradition which associates them with hunts and hunting.
Iconographically, we have seen that in every detail
their representation here is consonant with some
others, such as on the Roman Republican coinage,
where their identity is indisputable.

Very interesting in our scene is the gesture of the
outstretched right arm in both hunters. The one on
the left may possibly be holding up a hunting spear,
as already mentioned, but the one on the right very
clearly makes the gesture with his hand open, turning his head, for emphasis, toward his companion.
The same gesture is frequently seen in representations of hunters on horseback not only on textiles
but in other mediums as well: it has been inter-

preted as a triumphal gesture of a successful hunter
who is showing his feat to his companions, and is
urging them on to further exploits.[33] Its origins are
believed to have been at least as early as the grand
Roman "battle sarcophagi" of the third century
A.D. The gesture of a victorious commander, often
seen on the scenes of battle depicted on these sarcophagi, was easily borrowed to show a successful
hunter at a later time and possibly also in a different medium. An excellent example of this iconographical detail, and its adaptation, is the splendid
Ludovisi sarcophagus in Rome, where, in the midst
of a tightly packed scene showing the Romans in
combat with barbarians, the Roman commander on
horseback triumphantly makes the gesture.[34] On a
later hunting sarcophagus, also in Rome, an identical gesture is made by the hunter on horseback in
the centre of the scene. Incidentally, he wears much
the same costume—a short tunic, boots, and flying
short cloak— as his earlier military counterpart and
as the hunters on our much later textile.[35]

Including the triumphant Dioscuri, the centaurs,
and the wild animals in his scene, our weaver obviously used all the proper iconographical ingredients
of a traditional hunting scene. Owing to the spatial
and technical limitations of his medium, however,
he did not depict a complex spectacle, such as
would be possible on a large mosaic floor for instance, but abstracted only some of its components,
a fairly common practice of his time. He proved his
skill as an artist and an artisan by correctly observ-
ing and rendering the figures, both human and animal, whose anatomy and articulated movement he
still fully understood, an ability typical of classical
times that was lost in the ensuing Middle Ages.

Our fragment is a comparatively modest product
of late antiquity, probably made about A.D. 500
when Christianity had already existed as recognized
state religion for about two centuries. Yet in all its
aspects—the theme of the Dioscuri as victorious heroes and hunters, the hunting centaurs, the use of
the inhabited scrolls motif, the very same centuries-
old dark-silhouette style—it illustrates how greatly
dependent the artist of this late period was on the
classical Greek and Roman traditions.

Notes

1. Acc. no. 910.131.8. The Walter Massey Collection. Provenance: said to have come from Akhmîm (C. T. Currelly, *I brought the ages home*, Toronto, Ryerson Press, 1956, reprinted by the Royal Ontario Museum, 1976, p. 286). Acquired by Dr. Currelly in Egypt, 1907-1909. Measurements: ht. 19.6 cm, w. 18.5 cm; mounted on natural linen tabby. Technical information (provided by Veronika Gervers, Textile Department, Royal Ontario Museum): tapestry woven. Warp: bleached linen, S (count: 11 groups of 2 or 3 warps per cm). Weft: bleached linen, S; and dark purple wool, S (count: ca. 46-50 per cm). Some details are freely outlined with an extra weft of bleached linen, S.

2. Deborah Thompson, *Coptic textiles in the Brooklyn Museum*, Wilbour Monographs 2, 1971, p. 14.

3. I am greatly indebted to C. S. Churcher of the Department of Zoology, University of Toronto, for his help in identifying the animals.

4. E.g., the hunter from the fox hunt episode in the "Piccola Caccia" pavement at Piazza Armerina, G. V. Gentili, *Mosaics of Piazza Armerina: The hunting scenes*, Milan, Ricordi, 1964, pl. 1 (The pursuit of the fox); or the hunter ("Teresias") in the Megalopsychia Hunt at Antioch, D. Levi, *Antioch mosaic pavements*, Princeton, Princeton University Press, 1947, pp. 324, 326, fig. 136.

5. Compare the corresponding detail on a similar square in the Cleveland Museum of Art, *CIBA Review*, vol. 12, no. 133 (August 1959), p. 9, fig. at right, where the manes of the horses are stylized in a "running dog" pattern.

6. E.g., the fragment with swimming fish from Antinoë, in the Louvre, acc. no. GU 1242, *L'Art Copte, Petit Palais* 1964 (catalogue of exhibition), no. 148, with colour illustration, dated second-third century A.D.; or the tapestry woven square in the Cleveland Museum of Art with a nereid, *Koptische Kunst–Christentum am Nil*, Exhibition catalogue, Villa Hügel, Essen, 3 May–15 Aug. 1963, no. 268, pl. 8 (colour), dated third—fourth century A.D.

7. For a discussion on dating and a stylistic analysis of Coptic textiles see A. F. Kendrick, *Catalogue of textiles from burying grounds in Egypt, Victoria and Albert Museum*, vol. 1, *Graeco-Roman period*, London, H.M.S.O., 1920; O. Wulff and W. F. Volbach, *Spätantike und koptische Stoffe aus ägyptischen Grabfunden in den Staatlichen Museen*, Berlin, Ernst Wasmuth, 1926; among the more recent works, P. du Bourguet, *Musée National du Louvre, Catalogue des étoffes coptes*, vol. 1, Paris, Editions des Musées Nationaux, 1964; G. Egger, *Koptische Textilien*, Vienna, Oesterreichisches Museum für angewandte Kunst, 1967.

8. Cf. the Triumph of Neptune, a large marine composition, on the pavement of the Baths of Neptune at Ostia, *Enciclopedia dell'arte antica*, vol. 5, Rome, Istituto della Enciclopedia Italiana, 1963, p. 217 f., fig. 307; also fig. 309 with scene of sacrifice; and colour pl. opposite p. 222, a square *emblema* with a black-silhouette bust of a bacchic figure, Rome, Museo Nazionale.

9. Cf. the "cup-bearer" on a fourth-century A.D. fresco from a house on the Caelian in Rome, now Museo Nazionale, Naples, R. Bianchi Bandinelli, *Rome, the late Empire–Roman art A.D. 200-400*, London, Thames and Hudson, 1971, fig. 86, and the fresco of the "candle-bearer" of about the same date from Roman Tripolitania, tomb of Aelia Arisuth at Gargaresh (*in situ*), ibid. fig. 87; the hunting and other figures on the mosaic pavements at Piazza Armerina, Sicily, of the fourth century A.D., G. V. Gentili, *The imperial villa of Piazza Armerina*, Rome, Istituto Poligrafico dello Stato, 1956, figs. 7, 8, 10, 11, 17-21, 27. Cf. also Constantius II (A.D. 337-361) on horseback, on a silver plate from Kertch, State Hermitage Museum, Leningrad, L. Matzulewitsch, *Byzantinische Antike*, Berlin and Leipzig, Walter de Gruyter, 1929, pp. 95-100, pl. 23.

10. For diagrams showing the decorative scheme of costume see K. Wessel, *Koptische Kunst–Die Spätantike in Aegyten*, Recklinghausen, Aurel Bongers, 1963, p. 254 f.

11. The subject is discussed exhaustively by J. M. C. Toynbee and J. B. Ward Perkins, "Peopled scrolls: A Hellenistic motif in Imperial art", *Papers of the British School of Archaeology at Rome*, 18, 1950, pp. 1-43, pls. 1-26.

12. G. M. A. Richter, *A handbook of Greek art*, 5th ed., London, The Phaidon Press, 1967, p. 259, fig. 381.

13. G. Kawerau and T. Wiegand, *Altertümer von Pergamon*, vol. 6, *Die Paläste der Hochburg*, Berlin and Leipzig, Walter de Gruyter, 1930, p. 63 f., pls. 29, 31, 37.

14. Ulrich Gehrig, *Hildesheimer Silberfund*, Bilderhefte der Staatlichen Museen Berlin, Stiftung Preussischer Kulturbestiz, Berlin, 1967, pls. 2-4.

15. I. Lavin, "The hunting mosaics of Antioch and their sources", *Dumbarton Oaks Papers*, no. 17, 1963, pp. 180-286, particularly p. 218, figs. 49-51 (from Piazza Armerina, Djemila, and Beisan, El-Hammam).

16. W. F. Volbach, *Elfenbeinarbeiten der Spätantike und des frühen Mittelalters*, Römisch-germanische Zentralmuseums, Mainz, 1952, nos. 73, 74, pl. 24 (ivory reliefs from the pulpit of the cathedral at Aachen, of the sixth century A.D., with Bacchus as the principal figure, and with animals, human figures, and putti "inhabiting" the scrolls).

17. Peopled scrolls on late Hellenistic and Coptic textiles are innumerable; see Thompson, *Coptic textiles* (1971), p. 14, no. 2 (with birds and rabbits within allover scroll issuing from a

vase); p. 34, no. 12 (individual gazelles, hares, and lions within a band of vine scrolls); du Bourguet, *Etoffes coptes* (1964), p. 90, Cl9 (tapestry woven square with a horseman in the centre, and individual animals, lions, hares, and others in the surrounding scrolls).

18. W. H. Roscher, ed., *Ausführliches Lexikon der griechischen und römischen Mythologie*, Leipzig, B. G. Teubner, 1884-1937, s. v. *Kentauren*; for a centaur of the archaic type strangling a fawn see a gold plaque from Camirus, Rhodes, of 700 to 600 B.C., in the British Museum, R. Higgins, *Greek and Roman jewellery*, London, Methuen, 1961, pp. xx, 113, pl. 18c; for the classical type, S. Reinach, *Répertoire de reliefs grecs et romains*, Paris, Ernest Leroux, 1912, vol. 2, p. 451, *1* (centaur hunting cheetah with a large branch in both hands on a relief from Athens); p. 68, *2* (*oscillum* from Pompeii, with a relief with a rearing centaur throwing rock with right hand, left wrapped in animal skin for protection); vol. 3, p. 517B (a sarcophagus in Leningrad with two centaurs fighting a lion and a lioness in a landscape setting).

19. R. Lullies and M. Hirmer, *Greek sculpture*, rev. ed., New York, Abrams, 1960, pl. 120 (centaurs attacking the bride of the Lapith king Peirithöos, from the west pediment of the temple of Zeus at Olympia); pls. 142-147 (duels of Greeks and centaurs from the metopes of the Parthenon); H. A. Thompson and R. F. Wycherley, *The Agora of Athens—Results of excavations*, vol. 14, Princeton, Princeton University Press, 1972, p. 147, pl. 74B (the centauromachy on the Hephaisteion).

20. du Bourguet, *Etoffes coptes* (1964), p. 95, C30; p. 169, D132; Kendrick, *Textiles from burying grounds* (1920), p. 67, no. 69, pl. 17; Wulff-Volbach, *Spätantike und koptische Stoffe* (1926), p. 57, no. 6998, pl. 66; p. 57, no. 11423, pl. 67; p. 43, no. 4630, pl. 75; p. 44, no. 9139, pl. 75.

21. See notes 18, 19.

22. Lavin, "Hunting mosaics" (1963), figs. 107-110; Gentili, *The Imperial Villa of Piazza Armerina* (1956), pls. 14, 17, 19, 20, 27; Gentili, *Mosaics of Piazza Armerina* (1964).

23. Lavin, "Hunting mosaics" (1963), p. 233, figs. 20, 21, 79, 80.

24. Levi, *Antioch mosaic pavements* (1947), pp. 236 f., pls. 56 f.

25. P. E. Arias and M. Hirmer, *A history of one thousand years of Greek vase painting*, New York, Abrams, 1961, pp. 286-288, pl. 42.

26. Levi, *Antioch mosaic pavements* (1947), p. 238, and S. Rein-

ach, *Répertoire de peintures grecques et romaines*, Paris, E. Leroux, 1922, p. 408, *3*.

27. Levi, *Antioch mosaic pavements* (1947), p. 238, and Reinach, *Répertoire de peintures* (1922), p. 246, *4*; p. 345, *1*, *2*. For the Hadrian's Villa mosaic, see also *Enciclopedia dell'arte antica* (1963), vol. 5, p. 217, fig. 304.

28. Roscher, *Lexikon* (1884-1937), s. v. *Dioskuren*; C. Daremberg and E. Saglio, *Dictionnaire des antiquités grecques et romaines*, vol. 2, Paris, 1892, s. v. *Dioscuri*; M. Albert, *Le culte de Castor et Pollux en Italie*, Paris, E. Thorin, 1883 (with a corpus of representations).

29. W. Helbig, *Führer durch die öffentlichen Sammlungen klassischer Altertümer in Rom*, 4th ed., Tübingen, Wasmuth, vol. 2, 1966, nos. 1402, 1526; H. Stuart Jones, *The sculptures of the Palazzo dei Conservatori*, Oxford, The Clarendon Press, 1926, (text) p. 33, no. 17; (plates) pl. 10 (Dioscuri wearing conical cap and a cloak over shoulder); (text) p. 99, no. 42; (plates) pl. 36 (Dioscuri mounted).

30. S. W. Grose, *Catalogue of the McLean collection of Greek coins, Fitzwilliam Museum, Cambridge*, Cambridge University Press, vol. 1, 1923, p. 181, no. 1493, pl. 47, *16* (where the gesture is described as salutation).

31. Grose, *McLean collection*, vol. 3 (1929), p. 416, no. 9751, pl. 362, *15* (kings of Bactria, second century B.C.).

32. H. B. Walters, *Catalogue of bronzes, Greek, Roman and Etruscan in the British Museum*, London, British Museum, 1899, p. 37, no. 277, pl. 6.

33. Levi, *Antioch mosaic pavements* (1947), p. 243, n. 113.

34. Helbig, *Sammlungen klassischer Altertümer in Rom*, 4th ed., vol. 3 (1969), no. 2354; for an excellent illustration see G. Becatti, *The art of ancient Greece and Rome*, New York, Abrams, 1967, p. 363, fig. 360; for a discussion on style and chronology, see G. Rodenwaldt, *Jahrbuch des k. deutschen archäologischen Instituts*, vol. 51 (1936), pp. 82-113, pls. 2-6, and *Mitteilungen des deutschen archäologischen Instituts, Römische Abteilung*, vol. 59 (1944), pp. 191-203, pls. 31-38, especially pp. 198-199, n. 3.

35. Helbig, *Sammlungen klassischer Altertümer in Rom*, 4th ed., vol. 2 (1966), no. 1701; Jones, *Sculptures of the Palazzo dei Conservatori* (1926), p. 73, no. 13, pl. 13 (*Fast. Mod.* I 13).

The Problem of Brown Wool
in Mediaeval Tapestries:
The Restoration of the Fourth Caesar Tapestry

Mechthild Lemberg

FOR almost nine years, from 1965 to 1974, the textile atelier of the Abegg-Stiftung has focused its efforts on the restoration of the fourth Caesar Tapestry of the Historical Museum of Bern (fig. 1).[1] In this laborious work, which called for a restorer with patience and flair, the usual method of restoring tapestries had to be abandoned and replaced by a new method, which is the subject of this report.

The tapestry in question belongs to a cycle of four wall hangings representing the story of Caesar according to the *Faits des Romains*, a work on Roman history written in the thirteenth century in French. Ordered by Charles the Bold, Duke of Burgundy, this unique series of tapestries was woven in Tournai around 1465-1470. The Duke of Burgundy probably gave these tapestries to Count William de la Beaume. The latter's coat-of-arms appears on all four of them. It is assumed that after Charles the Bold lost his own tapestries at the Battle of Grandson in 1474, he borrowed the Caesar Tapestries back for the engagement of his daughter, Maria, to Maximilian I, which took place in the Cathedral of Lausanne in 1476. Since the Burgundian army was defeated at Morat a few weeks later, the tapestries remained in the cathedral until 1537, when they came to Bern as a result of the conquest of Canton Vaud.[2]

In the late nineteenth century, before the tapestries entered the collections of the Historical Museum of Bern, they were thoroughly restored. It was then that part of the badly worn woollen weft was uniformly replaced with black wool.[3] Today the results of this work are unsatisfactory for two reasons.

First, the reweaving used a much thicker wool than that of the original, distorting the tapestries so that they no longer hang smoothly and uniformly. Secondly, the black wool of the nineteenth century has in the interim faded into an olive-green, which considerably mutes the total chromatic impact. The olive-green drowns out the colours that are still well preserved, and since it is the link between all the colours, the tapestries seem to be enveloped in a grey veil (fig. 2).

When we started restoring the fourth Caesar Tapestry, we did not consider the radical removal of the nineteenth-century restoration. Just as was done years ago with the Burgundian tapestries, after washing the piece, we started lining its holes and damaged parts with linen. The upper edge of the piece, where the selvage is almost completely destroyed, was strengthened with a 12-cm wide linen band in order to make the edge strong enough for suspension. Since the damage to the selvage could not have been repaired by reweaving, there was no other choice.[4]

After the most urgent repairs had been effected in this manner, the tapestry was clean and its holes were strengthened, but the overall chromatic impact was still unsatisfactory. The old repairs became even more evident than they had been before washing, and subdued the brilliance of the remaining colours. The distorted sections strained the tapestry. It became clear that the only way to eliminate the strain would be to remove the embroidered wool.

Up to that point, two obstacles had prevented the removal of later repairs to mediaeval tapestries. First, it was exceptionally difficult to find wool for

Figure 1.   Fourth Caesar Tapestry. Left: Caesar enters Rome
as a victorious general; Spurinna and his wife Calpurnia wel-
come him. Right: meeting of the Senate on the Ides of March.
Size: h. 432 cm; w. 750 cm.
Historical Museum of Bern, acc. no. 12-13.

reweaving of a quality that corresponded to that used in the original tapestry. Furthermore, wool dyes that were fast to light had not been sufficiently developed in the 1950s to be used in conservation. There was always a fear that the wool, woven in with great effort, would change colour within a short time, just as the nineteenth-century wool had faded. Thus the previous method of conservation for the other Burgundian tapestries of the Historical Museum had to sacrifice aesthetic aspects and concentrated on lining in order to strengthen the pieces. For the time being, the disturbing nineteenth-century weaving remained, but it was to be removed in due course.[5]

The moment for further conservation work came when by chance the proper quality of wool was found. In addition, since the development of wool dyes fast to light had also made considerable progress in the late 1950s and the early 1960s, we were

able to attempt a sweeping restoration of the fourth tapestry.

As work began, the thick olive-green wool from the previous restoration was removed. The results were surprising because the remaining colours became clearer and more luminous as soon as they were no longer next to the olive-green sections (fig. 4). Since the nineteenth century, the original colour of these parts had been assumed to be brown, a hypothesis based on the remainders of brown wool that are usually found where the weft has worn out. The assumption that it is always the brown or black wool of the weft that comes out in mediaeval tapestries is based on such observations and leads to repairs in either brown or black. At first, I myself followed this custom, and started to replace the olive-green wool of the Caesar Tapestry (among which remainders of old brown wool were found) with brown wool. The mistake, however, soon became

179

Figure 2. Fourth Caesar Tapestry, detail of Calpurnia's gown with restorations from the late nineteenth century. Size of section: 47 by 36 cm.

Figure 3. Fourth Caesar Tapestry, same detail as shown in figure 2 after recent restoration (1974).

Figure 4. Fourth Caesar Tapestry, detail, during the recent restoration. The olive-green wool has already been removed from the upper part and the warp ends are visible. Below, the olive-green parts from the previous restoration can be seen; they detract from the luminous power of the remaining original colours.
Size of section: 45 by 23 cm.

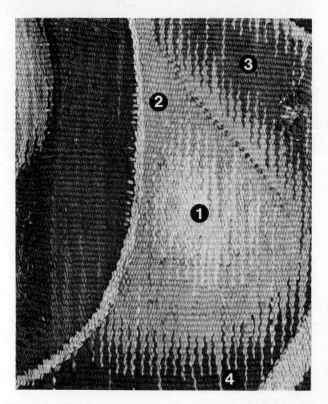

Figure 5. Third Caesar Tapestry, unrestored detail of armament showing four different degrees of brightness of the blue (no other colours are present).
Size of section: 17 by 13 cm.

180

Figure 6.   Fourth Caesar Tapestry, detail. The newly restored sections are shown in solid black. The restoration dealt with the shadows and patterns on the figures. The faces never had to be touched since they were executed in light colours which did not damage the wool.
Size of section: 223 by 249 cm.

evident. After a portion of the tapestry had been treated in this manner, it was obvious that the results would not be satisfactory. We had started with the patterned gowns of Calpurnia and her ladies-in-waiting. All the gowns in Calpurnia's suite were of different colours. The various patterns of the fabrics and the shadows of the pleats were carefully executed everywhere, and as mentioned above, they were at first rewoven at the Abegg-Stiftung in brown wool. Calpurnia's red gown overlaps the blue one of a lady in her suite. Here we realized at the last moment that continued restoration with brown wool would cover the tapestry with a dull brown net.

It was evident from the well-preserved figures and background details in all four Caesar Tapestries that, although the colours of separate motifs changed shades several times, a different dark colour never appeared completely isolated in contrast with the surrounding colours. This was, however, the impression that our uniform reweaving with brown wool had created. This net or screen effect, which is also recognizable in the Adoration of the Magi tapestry of the Historical Museum of Bern, uniformly restored with black wool in the late nineteenth century, completely distorted the original impact of the textile.

Speculation that the eroded brown wool which had fallen out was originally dyed in different colours was confirmed by a dye analysis of remainders of brown wool, taken from gowns of different colours. The analysis showed red and blue dyes. From Dr. E. Denninger's report[6] it can be concluded that when the wool was dyed with indigo, for example, the iron sulfate solution, used as a neutralizer and reducing agent, was probably often too concentrated. Sometimes it was not rinsed out carefully enough, and thus over the years residues of the oxidizing agent had an oxidizing effect on the dyed wool, not only turning the colours uniformly brown, but also destroying the fibres. The brown colour of the brittle woollen weft, which still covers some ends in our tapestry, is definitely not the original colour but is the last shade of colour in each case before final disintegration of the wool that was not carefully dyed.

The question arises as to what was the original colour. This can be answered only by comparing

the four tapestries of the set. It is clear that they were the products of a single workshop where work must have been done according to identical methods. If we compare the various figures and shapes with each other, it becomes apparent that the weavers generally used up to four hues of the same colour for a motif in different degrees of brightness, where the lightest shade can even be cream-coloured (fig. 5). They did this to accentuate the shadows and patterns, as can be gathered from the figures which are completely preserved; but where the weft wool came out, only light colours remained. The original colour of the worn-out wool must have corresponded to the undeteriorated wool on the rest of the figure, i.e., if wool has come out of a red gown, the original colour was probably red; or if it has come out from a blue gown, we can assume that the wool used to be blue. This rule makes it possible for us to determine the basic colour of the wool, and gives us a solid ground for restoring the tapestry.

Further observations made it possible to determine the brilliance of the colours. As was previously mentioned, three or four shades of the same colour were generally used to fashion the patterns within the figures on the Caesar Tapestries (fig. 5). We realized that the woollen weft was usually missing in places where, according to the design, dark shades could be expected (shadows, etc.), while the light shades were well preserved. Another key to the restoration was thus to replace the missing dark colours within the figures (figs. 2, 3).

The problem of ascertaining the original colour, or rather its exact shade, was solved neither by our observations, nor by dye analysis. Fortunately the solution was not too important for the restoration. Although the exact tones of the former colours interested us, we had to subordinate this interest to the colours that have emerged from the originals in the course of centuries. The new motifs we rewove had to be compatible with the present colouring. All the colours of the old tapestries have changed by exposure to light. Sometimes the colours simply became paler, but more often they have changed completely; it is extremely rare for colours to retain their original tone. For this reason, the present colour-scheme — a change in relation to the original — became the criterion for choosing the colours to restore the fourth Caesar Tapestry. Fortunately the restoration dealt only with the shadows and patterns on the figures. The faces did not have to be touched since they were executed in light colours which did not damage the wool (fig. 6).[7]

Notes

1. I am especially pleased to be able to report on the restoration of this particular tapestry in this memorial to our friend, Harold Burnham. For many years, it was the focal point of the atelier in Riggisberg, and Harold Burnham always observed the progress of its restoration with lively interest during his almost annual visits to the Abegg-Stiftung.

2. R.L. Wyss, "Die Caesarteppiche", *Jahrbuch des Bernischen Historischen Museums*, vols. 35 and 36 (1955 and 1956), pp. 104-232; M. Stettler and P. Nizon, *Bildteppiche und Antependien im Historischen Museums Bern*, Bern, 1959.

3. Material of the tapestry: *warp*, wool, count 6 ends per cm; *weft*, wool with silk highlights, count 24–26 picks per cm.

4. After cleaning and these first treatments had been completed in 1965 at the Historical Museum of Bern with the collaboration of Martha Widmer and Gisela Fuhrke-Cramer, the tapestry was transferred to the atelier of the newly opened Abegg-Stiftung at Riggisberg in 1967. Under the direction of the author, reweaving was entrusted to Eva Stähli-Burnham (1967–1971), Hannelore Herrmann (1969–1972), and Verena Huber (1972–1974). In addition, Marlene Erichson and volunteers of the Abegg-Stiftung worked temporarily on the tapestry.

5. M. Lemberg, "Beispiele der Textilkonservierung am Bernischen Historischen Museum", *Jahrbuch des Bernischen Historischen Museums*, vols. 37 and 38 (1957 and 1958), pp. 138–142.

6. We are indebted to Dr. E. Denninger for the colour analysis (Institut für Technologie der Malerei at the Staatlichen Akademie der Bildenden Künste, Stuttgart, laboratory report no. 331). The analysis was made possible by the kind offices of Professor R. E. Straub.

7. M. Lemberg, "Zur Restaurierung des vierten Caesarteppichs", *Jahrbuch des Bernischen Historischen Museums*, vols. 53 and 54 (1973 and 1974), in press.

Lace and Lace-Patterned Silks: Some Comparative Illustrations

Santina M. Levey

WRITERS on woven textiles have found the term "lace-patterned silks" a convenient one to use since it was coined by Otto von Falke in 1913.[1] The laciness of these silks seems obvious to all (fig. 3), yet the degree to which their designs were in fact influenced by contemporary or earlier laces has never been fully explored; although von Falke himself and some later writers, notably Dr. Vilhelm Slomann,[2] have remarked that not all of the lace-like ornament derives from lace.

What then are the main characteristics of these silks? Peter Thornton in his classic book on Baroque and Rococo silks describes them as consisting "of a central floral motif surrounded by a frame of some diaper-pattern which often resembles lace or net".[3] This large, formal pattern normally has a point repeat (figs. 3, 6) although there is a second, smaller group of asymmetrical lace patterns with comber repeats (fig. 2). Mr. Thornton himself has laid more emphasis on the formality of the large-scale, non-naturalistic patterns, particularly those of the first group, than on their lace-like features, and he included some silks that have no "lace" at all. Other writers have concentrated rather on the diaper grounds, on the lace-like fillings and the lace-filled bands which frequently form the ogival compartments around the central motifs (figs. 5, 6). The fact that these features are commonly brocaded in white silk has also served to underline their apparent debt to contemporary laces.

Before seeking to identify these laces, however, it is necessary to arrive at a fairly close dating for the silks. This has varied considerably[4] but Mr. Thornton's analysis of the chronological develop-

ment of eighteenth-century silk design, based as it is on surviving dated designs,[5] provides the best framework within which to work. Nonetheless, his initial conclusion that "this type of design was in particular favour during the 1690s and again in the 1720s"[6] has now been modified and he himself has reassessed some of the evidence on which it was based. The superb toilet set of lace-patterned silk at Ham House, for example, thought once to have been made for Lord Huntingtower on the occasion of his marriage in 1706, has now been ascribed to the fourth Earl of Dysart, who married in 1729.[7] That a once-fashionable style, having been overtaken by something as different as the bizarre, could reappear virtually unchanged after a gap of fifteen or more years seems unlikely, particularly as the early eighteenth century saw the development of yearly, if not seasonal, changes in silk designs.

The earliest known design which clearly heralds the arrival of the formal lace-patterned silk is one by James Leman dated 1711 (fig. 4). It is by no means a typical lace pattern but the basic elements are there in the large, diaper-filled cartouches, in the decorated edging that surrounds them, and in the overall formality of the composition. Designs for fully-fledged lace patterns followed later in the decade[8] and they survive in proportionately large numbers from the 1720s (fig. 5). There are no designs for asymmetrical lace-patterned silks from as early as 1711 but the silks themselves show clear links with the bizarre silks: figure 2, a copy of figure 589 in von Falke's book, shows a green and white silk from the Museum für Kunsthandwerk, Dresden, which is also illustrated by Dr. Slomann and

Mr. Thornton. Only the latter dates it precisely, to 1705–1710, which is perhaps slightly early since it would seem to link with the silks of the luxuriant bizarre period (1710–1720). Dr. Slomann shows the Dresden silk in conjunction with three other asymmetrical lace-patterned silks,[9] one of which is markedly more bizarre in character, looking back to the abstract bizarre phase of 1705–1710. It would seem likely, therefore, that the lace-patterned silks evolved during the bizarre period, with the asymmetrical patterns coming first, possibly by the end of the first decade of the eighteenth century, followed by the more formal point repeats which eventually replaced them. The whole group developed side-by-side with the bizarre silks, through the abstract, luxuriant, and increasingly naturalistic phases, until they were ousted by the fully naturalistic designs of the early 1730s (figs. 1–6).

It is, therefore, in the asymmetrical lace-patterned silks of ca. 1710–1720 that the first links between the silks and the contemporary laces should be found. Yet, if the term "lace-patterned" is temporarily disregarded in studying figures 1 to 6, it is not difficult to trace through the dated designs an alternative route by which the floriated diapers of the bizarre silks (fig. 1) could have been transformed into the formal meshes of the first lace patterns (fig. 4) to emerge as lace-like ornaments in the silks of the late 1720s (fig. 5). The origins of these diapers lie somewhere in the West's obsession with the Orient and in the two-way exchange of stylistic ideas which took place in the seventeenth and eighteenth centuries.[10] Although Dr. Slomann, in seeking an eastern origin for the bizarre silks, turned the evidence on its head, nonetheless he had some perceptive comments to make, in particular about the lace of the lace-patterned silks. He wrote, ". . . it can never have had anything to do with white linen lace. It was imported into Europe and imitated here, the little white figures overlaying the main design being rationalized according to European standards: patterns which at first were meaningless gradually assumed the appearance of lace, realistically or conventionally rendered."[11] Although wrong in believing that the silks originated outside Europe, Dr. Slomann was right in suggesting that their lace-like features were a rationalization of something totally un-lace-like. Part of this rationalization did take place in the eighteenth century but a further rationalization took place in the late nineteenth and early twentieth centuries, when writers looked back and fitted together the silks of the second and third decades with the laces of the third, fourth, and even fifth decades of the eighteenth century.

The independent development of the floriated diapers notwithstanding, it would be perverse to deny the lace-like features of the silks in figures 3 and 6; these must have been as obvious to the eyes of their eighteenth-century owners as they now are to us. It was presumably to silks such as these that Mrs. Delany referred when she wrote, "My clothes were grave, the ground a dark grass green, brocaded with a running pattern like lace, of white intermixed with festoons of flowers in faint colours. . . . my clothes were a French silk, I happened to meet with a great penny-worth — they cost me seventeen pounds."[12] Mrs. Delany was writing in March 1729, at the very end of what is now considered to be the era of the lace-patterned silks, yet her letter suggests not only that she had spent a great deal of money on a fashionable French silk but that the lace-like decoration of this silk was novel. To Mrs. Delany's eyes perhaps, the pretty diapers of the Dresden silk (fig. 2) or of the Leman design of 1711 (fig. 4) or even of his design of 1720 (fig. 5) would not have looked particularly lace-like. The silk of 1729 did look lace-like because the laces of 1729 also looked like that (figs. 7, 8); but the silks of 1720 — or even of 1725 — and earlier could not be matched to the laces in quite this way.

Figures 9 and 10 show typical fashion laces of the late seventeenth and early eighteenth centuries but between these and the full-blown lace-patterned laces of the late 1720s and 1730s (figs. 7, 8) is a gap which is not easily filled; there was no smooth transition from one style to the next comparable to that taking place in the field of contemporary silk design. The two sets of figures demonstrate not only a major stylistic change but also great technical innovations, particularly in the needle laces. This technical development is important because it underlines one of the difficulties of designing for lace: radical stylistic changes could result in radical changes of technique, since the surface pattern of a piece of lace also dictates its underlying structure, in a way not true of woven textiles once the basic problem of producing patterned fabrics had been overcome.

The period from approximately 1705 to 1715 saw a major change in fashionable dress which drastically affected the lace industry. The formal yet elaborate fashions of the late seventeenth century had relied extensively on lace for their effect; women had been clothed in lace from their petticoats to the tops of their towering head-dresses; men had been no less excessive in their use of this expensive fabric and even William III of England, a king not normally remembered for his personal extravagance, spent £2,459.19s on lace in a single year (1695–1696)[13] — most of it on the heavy needle laces of France and Italy. The new styles, however, which spread gradually through Europe during the early years of the new century, were less grand and the new, smaller head-dresses, softer ruffles, and more delicate scarves and aprons were commonly made of muslin and not of lace. Portraits of the first twenty years of the century show virtually every sitter wearing muslin accessories [14] and the few exceptions wear needle lace which could well have belonged to their parents or grandparents.

These new fashions had a shattering effect on the lace industry. Old styles and old techniques, which had survived virtually unchanged for half a century, were suddenly no longer acceptable. The lace producers were asked to create not just a new series of designs but a totally new fabric. Not all of the lace-making centres were able to meet this demand. References to Venetian needle lace, which had dominated the fashionable world during much of the seventeenth century, almost completely vanished from the account books, inventories, and conversations of fashionable society. It was an industry hampered by its non-professional organization, relying, for example, for many of its workers on the inmates of convents. It failed to adapt to the new styles and consequently entered a period of stagnation and then decline.[15] The nature of needle lace itself was, however, another disadvantage; it was in the late seventeenth century a relatively stiff and weighty textile and the dense rows of linked buttonhole stitches needed to produce an opaque area resulted in a fabric resembling a solidly woven linen rather than the airy muslins which early eighteenth-century fashions demanded.

All the needle lace industries were faced with the same problem, but that of France, the second major producer, was in a better position to tackle it. The French industry was more professionally organized. It had behind it nearly half a century of royal patronage and government backing and had close links with France's leading designers. Nonetheless, the period 1710 to 1720 saw even the French industry in a decline; it was no longer a government sponsored industry and was faced with technical problems which it could not overcome quickly enough to satisfy the needs of fashion.[16] What the French designers and lace workers eventually did was to concentrate on lightening and elaborating the mesh grounds so that, although the lace remained totally unlike muslin, having neither its softness nor its opacity, it could ultimately compete in terms of delicacy; and by the mid-1720s it was once more used for ruffles and other small accessories.

The large-scale, more grandiose French laces did continue to be made during the first quarter of the eighteenth century, but they were mainly for use as furnishing fabrics and remained closely linked to their seventeenth-century forerunners. They had formal, still faintly Bérainesque designs, set against grounds composed of irregular bars (fig. 9) which were sometimes decorated with little *picots* and which became more regular as the century progressed. They could not, however, have been the inspirational source for the bold, regular, and ornamented meshes of the bizarre and early asymmetrical lace-patterned silks (figs. 1, 2). Nor were they in any other way related stylistically to the silks.[17] The superb dress and furnishing flounces with silk-like patterns and elaborate mesh fillings belong to the late 1720s, 1730s, and 1740s (figs. 7, 8, 16). There are no French laces to fill the stylistic gap between the laces of the late seventeenth century and those of the late 1720s, the period during which the lace-patterned silks developed.[18]

There was one group of laces, however, that did evolve during this period and did have close links with the contemporary silks. These were the bobbin laces of Flanders, which were technically able to respond to the demands of fashion and which consequently became the dominant fashion laces of the first quarter of the eighteenth century.[19] Although, in the late seventeenth century, large-scale pieces of Flemish bobbin lace were clearly based on the more fashionable needle laces of France and were considered inferior to them, the smaller Flemish laces had already developed distinctive techniques and styles (fig. 10) and were already extensively used for nightwear and for smaller accessories. It was from these smaller laces that the highly fashionable bobbin laces of the eighteenth century were to develop. Bobbin lace was favoured technically because the two worker bobbins could be used to weave in and out of the other threads to produce a piece of woven cloth similar to, or finer than, woven muslin. This fabric could be made even finer by taking only one of the worker bobbins through the other threads;[20] the two different textures can be seen in figure 11, which shows a detail of an engageante of Brussels bobbin lace. The bobbin lace workers could, therefore, produce — at considerably greater expense — a fabric that equalled muslin in its softness and delicacy and was in addition luxuriously patterned.[21]

The laces in figures 11 and 12 are Brussels bobbin laces and date from between 1715 and 1725.[22] Although at first sight they seem to bear little resemblance to contemporary silks, this apparent dissimilarity is really a matter of scale since the design, instead of being spaced over the width of a piece of silk, is compressed into some three or four inches. Also, the silks with which they most closely compare are not the lace-patterned silks but the bizarre. Figure 13 shows a luxuriant bizarre silk from the collections of the Victoria and Albert Museum. If it is compared with the laces, particularly with the lappet in figure 12, many similarities can be seen: there is the same overall density of design,[23] the same restless movement from side to side, the same use of odd, fluted wedge shapes with leaves sprouting from their tops, the same rich overlay of floral sprays, and the same use of buds or flower heads as fillings for the larger forms. Both lace and silk are grounded with a fine mesh; in the silk it is a simple hatched diaper, in the lace it is a more complex but equally unobtrusive *point de neige* réseau. The little spray of trumpet-like flowers in the detail of an engageante

shown in figure 11 appears also in a bizarre silk in the Metropolitan Museum of Art,[24] and many other similar comparisons can be made between particular pieces of lace and silk. In more general terms it can be seen that the Flemish bobbin laces and the contemporary bizarre and asymmetrical lace-patterned silks made use of many of the same motifs: pomegranates and elongated gourds, luxuriant clusters of feathery leaves and fruit, floriated diapers which are used on a large scale in the silks to look like mesh grounds and on a small scale in the laces where they figure as fillings; even the secondary, damask pattern of some bizarre and asymmetrical lace patterns is reproduced in the laces by the complementary use of cloth and half stitches.[25]

A final illustration from the late 1720s may serve to underline the interrelation of lace and silk designs in this period; figures 14 and 15 show a Valenciennes bobbin lace lappet together with a French silk design,[26] which has been reduced to the same scale for purposes of comparison. Apart from the obvious similarity of the overall design, the lappet also illustrates links with the whole group of early eighteenth-century silks; besides the floriated diapers which have already been referred to, diapers of pointed ovals slanting first one way and then the other appear also in the lace-patterned silks, as do zigzag lines with geometric or floral fillings. In this case the line may even be compared to the decorated band in Leman's bizarre silk design of 1708 (fig. 1). The serpentine line is interesting not only because it reproduces in miniature one of the most basic features of the lace-patterned silks (figs. 5, 6) but because eighteenth-century narrow laces were not yet composed in this way with small floral motifs sparsely scattered on mesh grounds. They were to become so by the middle years of the century but the development was anticipated in the silks and in the surface patterns of the laces associated with them (fig. 16). Larger pieces of Flemish lace (fig. 8) followed a similar pattern; their resemblance to the silks is more obvious since they were on the same scale and were designed to be used in a similar way. Their decoration with elaborate fillings which were directly comparable to those of the silks was, however, a late development and did not mature until the 1730s and 1740s.

In conclusion, it would seem that the links between the lace and the silk industries of the first quarter of the eighteenth century were strong, but they were not the links that appear obvious to modern eyes. The French and English silk weavers and the Flemish lace makers served the same fashionable clientele and they produced complementary textiles which were linked stylistically but which were each based on the resources of their own techniques. On the other hand, the once-dominant French needle lace industry, having been temporarily defeated by its failure to adjust to the changes of early eighteenth-century fashion, turned to the French silks for inspiration and, on its reappearance in the 1720s, reproduced in lace both the overall designs and the decorative features of the contemporary silks. The resulting lace fillings, which became increasingly rich and elaborate, were in their turn borrowed back by the silk designers and formalized in the late lace-patterned silks. Thus, for a brief period the surface pattern of one textile and the mixture of technique and pattern of another were fused to produce a common style. Their ways soon parted again but, since the delicate diapers of the lace-patterned silks had by then become the hallmark of the mid-eighteenth-century needle laces, it is not surprising that, to later observers, it is the indebtedness of the silks to the laces which has seemed to be so apparent, rather than the even stronger impact of the silks on the laces.[27]

Figure 2. Asymmetrical lace-patterned silk. French, ca. 1710 – 1720.
Museum für Kunsthandwerk, Dresden, no. 16364.

Figure 1. Design for a bizarre silk. James Leman, 1708.
Courtesy of Vanners Silks Ltd.

189

Figure 3. Panel of lace-patterned silk. French, 1720s.
Victoria and Albert Museum, T.138-1912.

Figure 4.   Design for a lace-patterned silk. Signed and dated "James Leman: 1711".
Courtesy of Vanners Silks Ltd.

Figure 5.   Design for a lace-patterned silk. James Leman. Dated "December 21st 1720".
Victoria and Albert Museum, T.183-1963.

Figure 6.   Panel of lace-patterned silk. French, 1720s.
Victoria and Albert Museum, T.183-1963.

192

Figure 7. Flounce of needle lace (detail). French, Point d'Argentan, 1720 – 1730. The lace designer appears to have turned a silk design upside-down.
Victoria and Albert Museum, T.99-1922.

Figure 8.   Flounce of bobbin lace (detail). Flemish, Brabant,
1720 – 1730.
Victoria and Albert Museum, T.292-1907.

Figure 9. Cravat end of needle lace. Point de France, ca.
1700. Similar but more densely packed designs were used for
the large-scale funishing laces.
Victoria and Albert Museum, 796-1890.

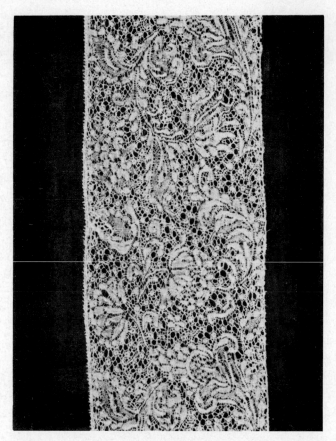

Figure 10. Border of bobbin lace. Flemish, Binche or Valenciennes, late seventeeth – early eighteenth century.
Victoria and Albert Museum, 786-1902.

Figure 11. Engageante of Brussels bobbin lace (detail).
1715 – 1725.
Victoria and Albert Museum, T.299-1965.

196

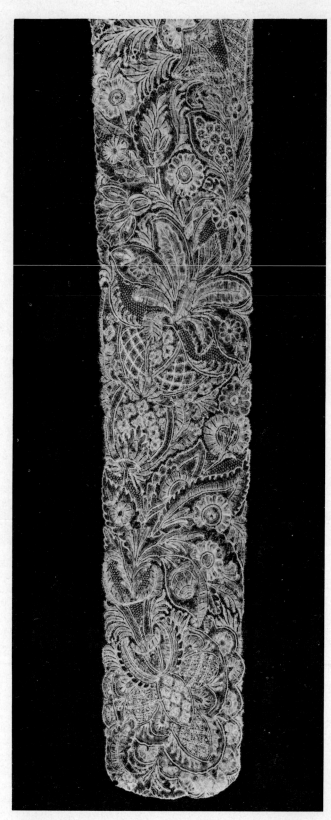

Figure 12. Lappet of Brussels bobbin lace. 1715 – 1725.
Victoria and Albert Museum, 165-1885.

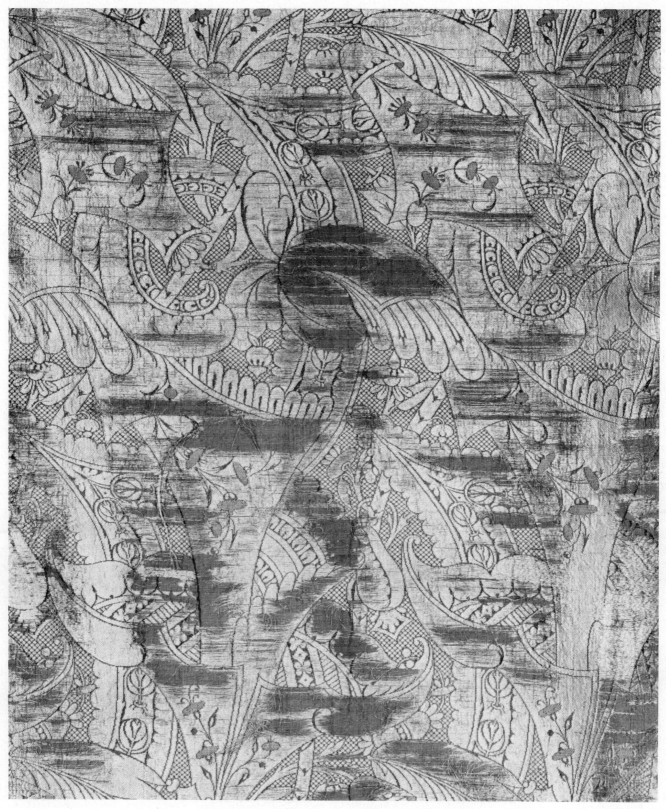

Figure 13.   Panel of bizarre silk. French, 1710 – 1720.
Victoria and Albert Museum, T.253-1921.

Figure 14. Silk design. French, 1720s.
Cabinet des Estampes, Lh.44a. Courtesy of Bibliothèque Nationale, Paris.

Figure 15. Lappet of Valenciennes bobbin lace. 1720s.
Victoria and Albert Museum, T.335-1913.

Figure 16. Flounce of needle lace (detail). French, Point
d'Argentan, 1730 – 1740.
Victoria and Albert Museum, T.744-1974.

SANTINA M. LEVEY

Notes

1. Otto von Falke, *Kunstgeschichte der Seidenweberei*, 2 vols., Berlin, Ernst Wasmuth, 1913.

2. Vilhelm Slomann, *Bizarre designs in silks,* trans. Eve M. Wendt, Copenhagen, Ejnar Munksgaard, 1953.

3. Peter Thornton, *Baroque and Rococo silks,* London, Faber and Faber, 1965, pp. 109–115.

4. Dr. Slomann usefully lists the dates given by earlier authors; they range from 1630 to 1750. *Bizarre designs in silks* (1953), pp. 127–128.

5. Thornton, *Baroque and Rococo silks* (1965), p. 19, n. 3, 4.

6. Thornton, *Baroque and Rococo silks* (1965), p. 109.

7. Victoria and Albert Museum, *Ham House*, 3d ed., London, H.M.S.O., 1973, p. 32. Mr. Thornton also illustrates a waistcoat from Rosenborg Castle, Sweden (pl. 26a) which is lined with a lace-patterned silk. The waistcoat was believed to have been worn by Frederick IV (1671–1730) at his marriage to Princess Louise of Mecklenburg in 1695. The cut of the coat and in particular the high placing of the pockets suggest, however, that it dates from later in the king's life, probably from the 1720s. I am indebted to my colleague Madeleine Ginsburg for her expert advice on this matter.

8. There is a dress of lace-patterned silk in the collections of the New York Historical Society (acc. no. 1949.115) which is by family tradition dated to the marriage of Cornelia de Peyster to Oliver Teller on 12 October 1712. If correct, this would seem to be the earliest dated example of a fully developed formal lace-patterned silk. The dress is published in Natalie Rothstein's article "Silks for the American market", pt. 1, *The Connoisseur*, vol. 166 (1967), pp. 70–94, pl. 6. I should like to record my thanks to Miss Rothstein for her advice and encouragement; it would not have been possible to write this article without having had access to her records and without all the information which she has generously given to me.

9. Slomann, *Bizarre designs in silks* (1953), fig. 86, pls. 46–48.

10. This two-way exchange of ideas has been most intensively studied by John Irwin and Betty Brett and is excellently summarized in their catalogue of the collections of Indo-European cotton paintings in the Victoria and Albert and Royal Ontario museums: J.C. Irwin and K.B. Brett, *Origins of chintz*, London, H.M.S.O., Victoria and Albert Museum, 1970. The relationship between Europe and China has recently been the subject of an exhibition in Germany. Much relevant information is contained in the catalogue: *China und Europa*, Berlin, Schloss Charlottenburg, Sept.–Nov. 1973.

11. Slomann, *Bizarre designs in silks* (1953), p. 134.

12. Mrs. Delany to Mrs. Anne Granville, "From my fireside. 14th March, 1728–29", The Rt. Hon. Lady Llanover, ed., *The autobiography and correspondence of Mary Granville, Mrs. Delany*, vol. 1, London, 1861, p. 198.

13. Great Wardrobe Accounts. William III, 1688–1702. Public Record Office, London. Quoted in Mrs. Bury Palliser, *A history of lace*, rev. ed., London, 1902, p. 343, n. 40.

14. See for example the portrait of Mademoiselle de Bethisy and her brother, painted by Alexis Simon Belle when they were children, about 1714. The little girl is wearing a superb bizarre silk dress with an apron, stomacher, and engageantes of soft muslin, slightly decorated with embroidery (Musée Nationale, Versailles). I am indebted to Miss Janet Arnold for drawing my attention to this portrait and for her advice on the changes in early eighteenth-century fashions.

15. Travellers to Venice continued to remark on the lace industry until the mid-eighteenth century but it is clear that the laces were still Baroque in style and technique and that their use was restricted to the church and to very formal occasions.

16. The French lace trade was also damaged by the War of Spanish Succession but the effect of fashion is recorded in the trade figures: according to *The history of trade*, London, 1702, "France is the wardrobe of the world . . . hardly a thing vends without a Gallic name." But by the time the *Atlas Maritime et Commercial* was published in 1727 the slump in the French lace trade was being blamed on the loss of the English market. Palliser, *A history of lace* (1902), p. 347 and n. 51, 52.

17. Some lace-patterned silks appear to copy the scallops and needle-point vandykes of early seventeenth-century laces but it is possible to trace these back through the bizarre silks to motifs based on linked flowers or vegetable stems, possibly introduced from the East. The early eighteenth-century laces were normally straight-edged.

18. It is interesting to note that no lace-patterned silks contain accurate copies of either the Point de France ground or the Alençon and Argentan meshes from which the more elaborate fillings developed.

19. Flanders was not the only bobbin lace centre; the Genoese and Milanese bobbin laces had been important during the seventeenth century and the latter were still fashionable in 1700. Neither centre, however, adapted its style or technique in accordance with eighteenth-century fashions, although Milanese lace remained important as an ecclesiastical furnishing fabric and also served as the basis for many of the eighteenth-century peasant laces of southern Europe.

20. The "stitch" based on two worker bobbins is called

200

"cloth" or "whole" stitch; that using only one worker bobbin is called "half" stitch.

21. Later in the century the whitework embroiderers, particularly in Germany, were to produce superb copies of bobbin lace, some of which are indistinguishable from lace except at very close quarters.

22. Brussels was only one of the Flemish laces; Mechlin, Binche, and Valenciennes were equally important. By the treaties of 1668 and 1678, Valenciennes was politically in France but stylistically and technically its laces remained part of the Flemish group.

23. The same density of design is found in some of the formal lace-patterned silks, for example in the designs drawn by Christopher Baudouin in the mid-1720s and by Anna Maria Garthwaite in 1727 and 1728 which are now in the collections of the Victoria and Albert Museum.

24. The Metropolitan Museum of Art, acc. no. 40.134.5.

Published in Slomann, *Bizarre designs in silks* (1953), pl. 44.

25. The largest number of bizarre and lace-patterned silks are illustrated in the following publications: Thornton, *Baroque and Rococo silks* (1965); Slomann, *Bizarre designs in silks* (1953); Emil Kumsch, *Kunstgewerbemuseum zu Dresden, Stoffmuster des XVI.–XVIII. Jahrhunderts,* vol. 3, Dresden, 1891. Illustrations of comparative material from the lace collection are in the companion volume, *Spitzen und Weiss-Stickereien des XVI.–XVIII. Jahrhunderts*, Dresden, 1889.

26. The design is in the Bibliothèque Nationale, Paris; vol. Lh. 44a. It is not dated but it is associated with other dated silks of the 1720s. I am grateful to Natalie Rothstein for permission to use her record photograph of this design.

27. Because of the need to restrict the number of illustrations, it has not always been possible to show the most apposite example to demonstrate a particular point.

Notes on Felt-Making and the Production of Other Textiles at Seh Gabi, a Kurdish Village

Louis D. Levine

THE village of Seh Gabi is located in the northeastern corner of the Kangavar valley in central western Iran. This valley, with others to the east and west, makes up part of the Great Khorassan Road, the major overland trade corridor connecting Mesopotamia to Iran and the Far East since prehistoric times. From 1965 to 1974, the Royal Ontario Museum conducted archaeological research and excavations in the valley which included work at an early prehistoric mound just outside the village of Seh Gabi in 1971 and 1973. During the latter season, Veronika and Michael Gervers visited the site, and suggested that I collect data on textile manufacture in the village, and more specifically that I commission the manufacture of a felt coat and observe the process of manufacture. Thus, the idea for this contribution stems from these colleagues, and I would like to express my appreciation to them for their encouragement. That an article on textiles written by a Near Eastern archaeologist should appear in this volume is most appropriate, for Harold Burnham was deeply interested in the textiles of the Near and Middle East, and contributed to the analysis of materials from archaeological sites.

The Felt-Maker

Seh Gabi has no resident felt-maker and no one living in the immediate vicinity practises this craft. There, as well as in the surrounding villages of Shahnabad, Munabad, and Kenjaran, all the felt is made by Mashd Heshmat Bakhtiari. He lives in the village of Serkan, 6 kilometres north of the town of Tuisserkan, some 32 kilometres east of Seh Gabi as the crow flies, but between 50 and 60 kilometres by road.

Mashd Heshmat, the oldest of three brothers, was forty-six years old in 1973. One of his brothers, Einullah, is a rug merchant who lives in the village of Sutlah on the slopes of Khan Gurmaz, the imposing mountain between Serkan and Seh Gabi. Azizullah, his half-brother by a different father, lives in Tehran where he owns a dry-cleaning establishment. Mashd Heshmat was born in Sutlah where his fa-ther was a villager, and moved to Serkan at the age of twenty-six when he was apprenticed to a felt-maker friend of his father. This master taught Heshmat how to card wool and cotton, how to make felt, and how to make mattresses. Since he has been working on his own, Heshmat has had two pupils, both of whom learned these same skills. He has two sons, one twenty-two years old, the other eight. Three sons and a daughter born in between have all died. His older son did not wish to take up his father's craft because he found the work too difficult. This son was educated in Serkan through grade six, and now lives and works in Tehran for a company whose name the father did not know.

Heshmat once owned a small plot of land but sold it. He possesses no flocks or other capital, and is thus entirely dependent upon felt-making and related activities for his income. Indeed, it is a bit of a mischaracterization to call him a felt-maker, for most of his time is spent in making mattresses, a job which he prefers as it is less strenuous than felt-making. He stuffs his mattresses with carded cotton, and covers them with a cotton or more recently a synthetic fabric. He also works with feathers in the manufacture of pillows. The coat which I commissioned was the first he had made that year, for mass-produced textiles and ready-to-wear clothing, both generally available, are rapidly replacing felt garments.

Mashd Heshmat has been coming to the Seh Gabi area for a long but unspecified time. Originally, he also worked in other villages between Tuisserkan and Seh Gabi, but he found that he got on well with the residents of Seh Gabi and the immediate vicinity and began to restrict his practice to that area. He now comes on a regular circuit, although it was unclear how often he made the trip. When he started working here, he would walk from Serkan to Seh Gabi. Today, he takes a bus from Serkan to Tuisserkan, then another from Tuisserkan to Kangavar, and a truck that shuttles back and forth from Kangavar to Seh Gabi. In the summer of 1973 the cost of his entire trip was 40 rials (ca. $0.60), which was equivalent to half a day's pay for a common labourer at the excavations. When he comes, he stays for a two- to three-week period in the village, and resides in the house of the family for which he is working, where he is received as a guest.

When asked, Mashd Heshmat identified himself as a Lur, and as a Shi'a Moslem. The people of Seh Gabi and Shahabad identify themselves as Kurds, and are members of a heretical sect called Ahlahaqis. When conversing with the villagers, he used local dialect as far as I was able to judge. He did not use standard or even Kangavar Persian.

Felt-making seems to be a dying craft in this part of Iran. Aside from Mashd Heshmat, there is only one other practitioner in Serkan, an old man who is the surviving brother of Heshmat's master. He was the only other felt-maker that Heshmat knew of. When he was asked how the needs of all the villages in the district were supplied by these two men, one of whom was very old while the other practised in a rather restricted area, no satisfactory answer was forthcoming.

Making Felt

In this part of Iran, felt (namad) is made only from lamb's wool (barageh) and never from sheep's wool (pashm). The lamb cannot be older than one year. When I asked why lamb's wool was used I was told, without further explanation, that it was not possible to felt sheep's wool.

For the manufacture of the coat which I commissioned, three kilograms of wool (two and a half kg of white and half a kg of black) had been bought for 600 rials (ca. $9.00) at Seh Gabi by Arab Ali, one of the workmen employed by us on the excavations. This wool had been washed by Arab Ali's wife, and it was in their house that the making of the coat took place. The manufacture of the garment took an entire day starting at about five o'clock in the morning and ending at five in the afternoon. The only break was for lunch which lasted a bit over an hour.

The first step was to card the washed wool (fig. 1). The pile of wool to be carded beside him, Mashd Heshmat knelt or sat on a small, stuffed cotton mat. The carding itself was done with a long bow whose cord was struck with a wooden mallet. The end of the bow was held above the edge of the pile with the cord just touching the wool. The vibrations served to separate the matted fibres and to remove any remaining impurities from the wool. The bow itself, called a kaman-i halaji (carding bow), was made from a hollow, round wooden beam and a flat wooden "sounding board" which had been drilled full of holes. The cord was made of sheep gut (zeh), and the entire structure was reinforced with string at the important stress points. A string guard covers the hand at the point on the shaft where the bow is held. The hollow shaft makes a lighter instrument for Mashd Heshmat to carry along with his other tools on his trip. The light weight also facilitates the work.

The mallet with which the cord was struck is shaped like a long-necked, pot-bellied bottle. It was

Figure 1.   Carding the wool.

Figure 2.   The black wool pattern completed and the beginning of the distribution of the white wool.

Figure 3.   Heshmat sprinkling the white wool on the canvas.

held in the right hand, the bow in the left. A slight ridge along the bottom rim of the mallet serves to catch the cord when it is hit. When a pile of carded wool had accumulated, a stick about one metre long was used to push it aside, making room for the next batch of carded wool. The carding was done twice. The entire process took about five hours, and was done in one of the store-rooms on the ground floor of the house which was specially cleared for the task.

Upon completion of the carding, the actual felt-making was begun in a room on the second storey of the house. This room was normally used as the women's room and kitchen during the day, and as a bedroom at night. It was chosen because it was the warmest room in the house and, particularly for the fulling, heat is a necessity. In the winter, the fulling is done in the *hamam*, the bath house.

Carpets were spread on the floor, and over them a large canvas, part of the equipment that Heshmat carries with him, was laid and carefully flattened. Having prepared the surface on which he would work, our master took some of the carded black wool and rolled it into a thick string along his thigh. To help the fibres adhere, he applied a small amount of cold water. The loose string was then gathered up into a ball and, while the canvas was sprinkled with cold water, was set aside ready to be laid out in a pattern. Generally the pattern can be chosen by the buyer, but in this case Mashd Heshmat was given free rein to produce what he wished. The only request was that it be traditional.

When the pattern had been laid out (fig. 2), the canvas was again sprinkled with water, and the fluffy white wool was gently distributed over the entire tarpaulin covering the pattern. To do this, Mashd Heshmat gathered a large batch of carded wool in his left arm, and using a large four-pronged wooden fork (*panjah*), he slowly spread the wool over the canvas. When it covered the tarpaulin to a height of about 20 centimetres, the wool was lightly padded down with the fork and shaped in the form of a large cross, whose arms would eventually become the arms of the coat. At this point, approximately half of the white wool had been used, and the process was continued with the rest (fig. 3). A small amount of black wool, which remained after the design string had been made, was finally spread

205

over the top, care being taken to keep it away from the edges, where it might show through to the outside of the finished coat. The inclusion of the black wool at this point was purely practical without any aesthetic consideration. Wool remained, so it was used. This second batch of wool was again flattened and shaped with the fork.

The pile of wool on the canvas now roughly resembled the shape of the garment that would eventually emerge, except that it was as if that garment had been slit down the seams under the arms and the sides, and opened out (fig. 4a). A stick was laid along one end of the canvas, then canvas and wool together were rolled up onto the stick. Mashd Heshmat took a long piece of rope and tied both of its ends around the ends of the roll. Then, holding the middle of the rope, he proceeded to wrap the rope around the canvas, moving the roll along the floor with his foot. When only a bit of rope remained, it was made fast in the middle of the roll.

Using the sole of his right foot to apply pressure, he spent the next ten minutes rolling the canvas-enveloped wool back and forth along the floor (fig. 5). Occasionally the right hand was placed on the thigh to provide extra pressure. From time to time, a small amount of water was sprinkled on the outside of the canvas. The work was rhythmical, with Heshmat stepping and rolling, stepping and rolling, and alternating with his foot along the length of the roll in order to apply equal pressure to all portions. Although the rolling was done with a back and forth motion, the roll always moved forward the length of the room, at which point he turned and worked in the opposite direction.

When this initial hardening had been completed, the roll was untied and the felt for the garment spread out. Then it was folded in half, the narrower front over the back (fig. 4b). The bottom edges of the coat were aligned, and any unevenness was folded under to make a more or less straight edge. A small hole was made at the neck by carefully parting the fibres and the neck was finished by folding them under. The wider back was then torn at an angle starting below the sleeve and ending at the point where the sleeve joined the garment. At this point, the flange from the back was folded over to meet the front, some tufts of white wool which had been set aside were added to the "seam", and the

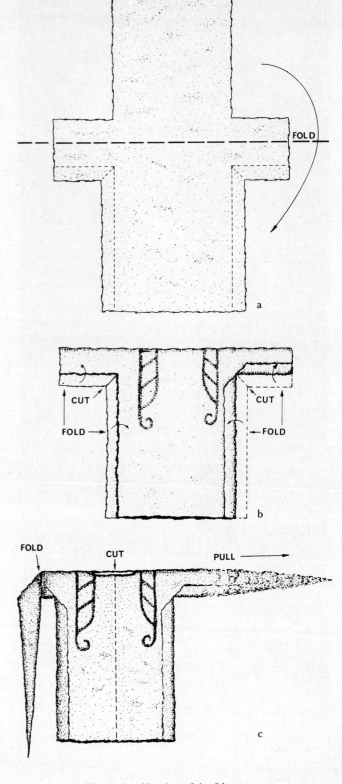

Figure 4. Shaping of the felt coat.

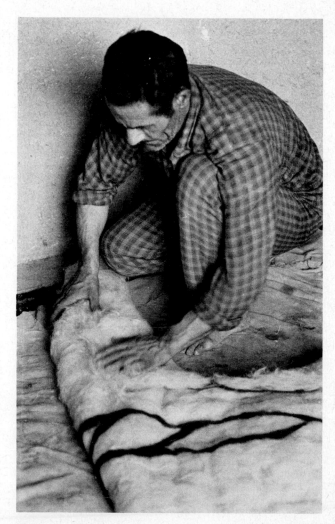

Figure 6. Heshmat making the seams and shaping the garment.

Figure 5. Heshmat rolling the bound wool on the floor.

207

edges felted together. The same process was re-peated for the sleeves which, still rather short and stubby (fig. 6), were then stretched until they be-came as long as the coat itself, whereupon they were folded down at a right angle (fig. 4c). A bit more of the white wool was added to the neck hole, and the ends of the sleeves, which now resembled long nar-row triangles, were tied in a knot. At this stage, the partially felted fabric had the definite shape of a garment (fig. 7). It was sprinkled once more with water, rolled back tightly into the canvas which was tied as before, and again stepped on and rolled as in the initial hardening. After no more than three or four minutes, however, Mashd Heshmat stopped for lunch.

During this break, we spoke of other places where felt was made, and I mentioned that in Turkey a reed mat rather than a canvass was used to do the rolling. Heshmat knew of this, and claimed, without further explanation, that the reed mat was superior to a canvas, but that his itinerant trade necessitated the use of the more portable cloth.

After lunch, the stepping and rolling continued for approximately thirty minutes, and at the end the canvas was unrolled. The front and back of the garment, which tended to felt together under the pressure of the rolling, were now separated, first from the bottom and afterwards from the neck opening. Thereupon hot water was sprinkled both inside the garment and over the outside. The sleeves were folded in, and the coat folded in half and rolled tightly. The canvas mat was now dispensed with, and the felt roll was placed on the rug which formerly lay under the canvas. Kneeling in front of the roll and applying pressure with his forearms, Mashd Heshmat began the final fulling by rocking it back and forth. Hot water was sprinkled onto the garment during the initial stages of this process. Soon afterwards, a bit of wool was dipped into a bowl of hot water and soaped. Using the wool as a sponge, he squeezed soapy water onto the felt (fig. 8). This soaping and rocking continued while the garment was periodically refolded in different direc-tions. With each folding, the coat was first rolled on itself in one direction and then in another, so that both front and back were exposed to the same type of pressure. Special care was taken to soap and full the design elements.

The fulling by rocking, rolling, and folding went on for hours. After the first hour, the garment was unfolded and stretched. This was done by standing on the bottom edge and pulling the neck opening, and by sitting on the neckline while holding the hem in one hand and kicking at the lower portion with the sole of the foot (fig. 9). Both the upper and lower parts of the coat were shaped in this fashion. This stretching was, however, but a brief interlude during the fulling, which was soon continued only to be interrupted again by further stretching. As the felt became firm, the stretching took on still other forms. By opening the bottom of the coat, and climbing inside, then pulling on the hem, he gave the garment its final flared form, with the bottom wider than the shoulders.

The fulling completed, the coat was laid out flat and its hemline trimmed straight with a pair of scis-sors. Then, starting from the neck opening, the front was slit to the hem with a knife. The coat was again folded, and rocked briefly with the forearms as well as by stepping. Thereupon it was unfolded and smoothed, and the sleeves tied together at the back. After drying overnight, the coat, called qaput, was ready to wear (figs. 10, 11). It is now part of the tex-tile collection of the Royal Ontario Museum (acc. no. 974.151).

In addition to coats, which are in little demand these days, Mashd Heshmat makes a number of other felt items. By far the most popular among these are the hats (kolar namadi), most often made from brown wool, and rugs which are simply called "felts" (namad). The manufacture of a rug is easier than that of a coat; before returning to his village, Heshmat made two of them in one day for members of the expedition (fig. 12). When there was still de-mand, he had made two other items of felt: a vest called jelezqah, and a horse blanket to be placed un-der the saddle. This "sweat collector" was called an araq qir. He had not made either item for some time.

A final note must be appended to this discussion. As mentioned previously, a labourer received 80 ri-als (ca. $1.15) for a day's work on the excavation. Mashd Heshmat was given 400 rials (ca. $7.80) for his one day of labour on the coat, and a similar amount for the manufacture of the two rugs which he made some days later. These were arbitrary figures, arrived at by guesswork and intuition, but

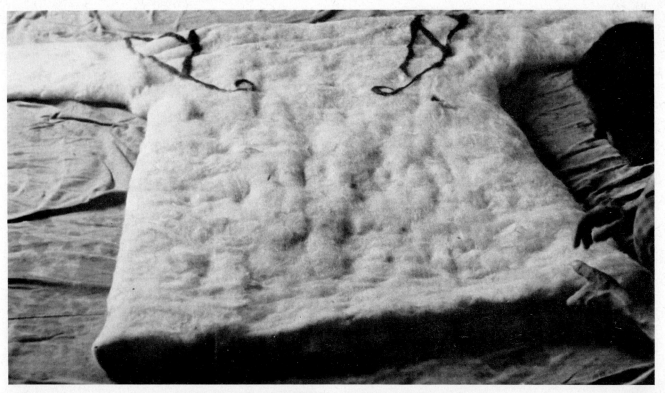

Figure 7.   The garment fully shaped and ready for rerolling.

Figure 8.   The felting process without the mat.

Figure 9.   Heshmat stretching the garment with his foot.

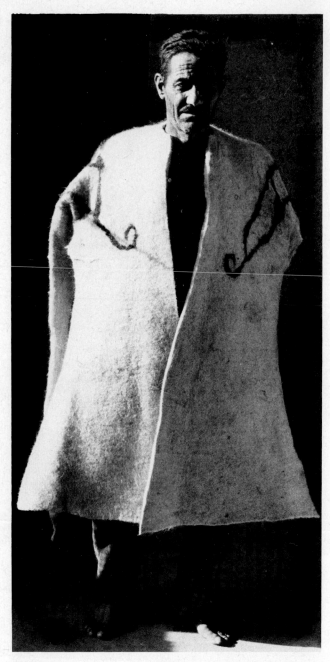 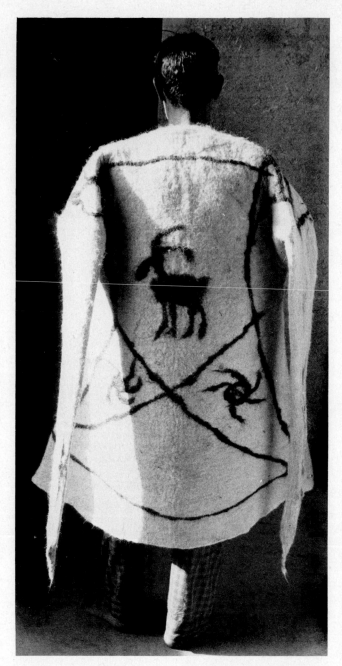

Figure 10. Heshmat modelling the garment, front view.   Figure 11. Heshmat modelling the garment, back view.

210

our felt-maker seemed satisfied.*

The manufacture of this coat, including raw materials and labour, cost 1,000 rials (ca. $14.30), an amount which represented ten days' wages for a simple worker and two to three days' wages for a specialized craftsman.

Other Textiles

While time limitations did not permit the collection of detailed notes on other textiles manufactured in the village, I was able to gather some general information which will be summarized on the following pages. My informants were Arab Ali and members of his family, especially his two daughters-in-law, Maryam Khanum and Khanum Gol.

A number of woven textiles are produced in the village. Some of these are wholly manufactured there, while others involve processes that are not available locally and must be done in the surrounding towns. With the exception of cotton string used in the manufacture of carpets and cloth shoes, all of the textiles are made from either sheep wool or goat hair. No other animals are available, and no vegetable fibres are raised in the vicinity, nor are they imported in unprocessed form.

All the animal hair produced in the village is initially processed there. The goats and sheep are shorn by the men in late spring; a mature animal produces about one kilogram of hair per annum. After shearing, the wool or hair is washed and spun by the women. If the wool is carded at all, it is not clear who does it before the spinning takes place. A hand-held spindle without a distaff is used for spinning. The whorl is made of wood, and is attached to a wooden shaft. The fibre is first spun into a single strand, plied (Z, 2S), and gathered in hanks. Provided that it is of acceptable quality, the wool is usually sent out to be dyed, while the goat hair remains in its natural colour. The latter produces a much coarser yarn and is used for the manufacture of lesser-quality textiles.

Wool for dyeing is sent to Tuisserkan rather than to the dyer in the town of Kangavar, even though the latter is much more convenient to Seh Gabi. My informants told me that in Tuisserkan, the wool remains in the dyeing vats for a week before the colour is fixed. Tuisserkan enjoys a good reputation in the village for fast dyes compared to those from Kangavar, which are said to run or fade since the yarn is only briefly dipped. Black wool is selected to make the deep blues, brown wool for the red, and white wool for the lighter and brighter colours. As far as I was able to determine, most if not all of the dyes now used are synthetic. Dyeing a kilogram of wool costs 135 rials (ca. $2.00). When the dyed hanks are returned to the village, they are washed twice, dried, and rolled into balls.

The undyed goat hair and the coarser grades of wool which are not sent for dyeing are used in the manufacture of two types of textiles: one is called a *qelim*, the other a *palas*. Both are very rough and crude flat-woven pieces, distinguished from each other by design, which are used as floor coverings. *Qelim*s are made by alternating rather uneven strips of different natural-coloured wools in the warp, while the *palas* is basically a single colour with perhaps some design at the border. None of the finer quality flat-woven pieces for which Iran is famous were in evidence in the village.

The dyed wools are employed for a number of different purposes. Their principal use is in the manufacture of pile carpets, which are made by women in virtually every home of the village. The weaving is done indoors, generally on the ground

---

Editor's note: This payment seems to be realistic and reasonable, particularly when one considers that the felt-maker himself came to the village to carry out the work. During the summer of 1973, I paid 4,700 rials (ca. $67.00) for two dark felt coats and a medium-sized felt rug to Abdol Ali Ougi, a professional felt-maker at Shiraz, Iran (ROM, acc. nos. 973.336.82, 83, 84). This price included the cost of the wool as well as the labour, and probably a slight surcharge for the foreign buyer. In addition, there is some question whether these items were entirely made of good quality wool, or whether some of lesser quality was added to their inner layers. Karim Afrasiyabi, a nomad from the Shiraz area, paid about 100 rials (ca. $1.40) per kg to have his own wool made into felt at the same workshop. According to my informants the price of one kg of black wool was then 170 rials (ca. $2.40), while one kg of white wool cost 250 rials (ca. $3.50), roughly the price of the wool at Seh Gabi.—V.G.

Figure 12.   Felt rug made by Heshmat for Mary McDonald.

ming with a pair of scissors (*qaichi*). This is done only after a weft thread has been inserted and beaten down with a heavy iron comb (*karkid*), and after the pile has been combed out with a small wooden or metal comb (*shuna*).

Normally, two women weave together. Maryam Khanum learned her patterns in her father's house from other relatives; her mother did not make rugs. Both she and Khanum Gol decide on the design before starting a new piece, often using the back of an older rug as their pattern. If a rug in some other house of the village strikes their fancy, they will borrow it so that they can copy the pattern.

Carpets are knotted in people's spare time, making it hard to estimate how long it takes to complete one. They are normally made in two sizes. The larger, approximately two by three metres, is called a *qali*, while the smaller (1.4 × 2.5 m) is a *qalicheh*. Carpets are made not only to meet the need for floor covering in the homes, but also as a capital investment. Arab Ali had a number of rugs stored at home as part of his "savings account".

There are other textiles which also use the finer quality wool. Among them are the *jajem*s, blanket-like cloths sewn together from strips measuring about 20 to 30 cm from selvage to selvage; the *moj*, a blanket used to wrap up bedding during the day; and the *hole*, a towel made usually of undyed wool, in which cloths are wrapped when going to the bath. The *moj* and the *hole* are woven in town by a professional weaver.

Little else is now manufactured in the village. From time to time, the women still knit sweaters (*jakat*), socks (*jurab*), neck scarves (*shal gardan*), or scarves that wrap around the midriff (*shal kamar*), but the availability of commercially made products has meant that these skills are not often called upon.

Shoes, called *giveh*, made of strong, highly flexible cotton thread, are crocheted by the women. These are attached to a sole made from the inner layers of old automobile tires. A finer quality *giveh* with a cloth sole is not made at Seh Gabi. As was the case with almost all of the other textiles, *giveh*s are also not as widely used as they once were because of the ever-increasing popularity and availability of plastic shoes.

floor of the house, on a vertical loom that is easily disassembled should the room be needed for other purposes. The loom is crudely made, with the upright beams set in holes in the floor (fig. 13). The beams are smoothed but not otherwise finished and are called *dar-i kul*. They are connected by a roughly squared warp beam (*bala dar*) set into notches in the uprights. The warp is weighted by a cloth beam on the lower end (*zir dar*). A heddle bar (*gord*) stretches across the two uprights, and the shed rod (*pusht gord*) sits above it, suspended from a string stretching between the uprights. The various colours are suspended from yet another string stretched between the uprights, and the weavers sit on a bench before the loom. The Ghiordes knot is used. The warp and the weft threads between the rows of pile are made of cotton. The pile of the rug is kept even by trim-

212

I have made no attempt to fit my observations into a larger picture of textile manufacture in Iran or Asia, nor have I attempted to deal with the numerous historical problems which are involved with these textiles. Both of these areas are beyond my competence, and to venture into them would be foolhardy. There are, however, a few general observations which should be made. Iran has long been a centre of textile manufacture, and while some of this has long been commercialized, much remains as "cottage industry", with home consumption a major objective. The opening of the countryside to trade, the improved communications, and the ready availability of many commercially manufactured goods are seriously affecting these folk traditions and "cottage industries". Iran is a country that is hurtling headlong into the twenty-first century, and in many parts of the country the traditional crafts are rapidly dying out. It is now that every effort must be made to collect data on these crafts and examples of their products, both as a record for the future and to better understand the poorly documented past. It is my hope that this study is a modest contribution in that direction.

Figure 13.   A typical carpet loom in the village of Seh Gabi.

John Holker's Mid-Eighteenth-Century
Livre d'Echantillons

Florence M. Montgomery

A SAMPLE book containing examples of printed chintz, silks, calendered wools, checks, plaids, and cotton velvets, with handwritten comments about their manufacture, provides rare documentation of eighteenth-century English textile terms. Within the pages of this folio manuscript in the Musée des Arts Décoratifs, Paris, are more than 115 swatches, some of them measuring up to about twelve inches (30 cm), which have been preserved in pristine condition except for slight damage by insects. The manuscript was prepared for the French by John Holker, a Lancashireman and ardent Jacobite who enthusiastically espoused the cause of Prince Charles Edward, the Young Pretender.[1] Captured at Carlisle and imprisoned in London, Holker made a dramatic escape, first to Holland and then to Paris, where in 1747 he joined other outlawed compatriots serving in Ogilvie's Scottish Regiment attached to the French army.[2]

Early in 1750 Holker met Marc Morel in Rouen. Morel, inspector for cotton manufactures in that area, was an enterprising man keenly interested in English textile production and especially in the benefits France might derive from English expertise. Seeking to learn progressive methods in textile technology, Morel had visited textile centres in England as early as 1738 and had established relations with manufacturers and inventors.[3] Acquainted with the English language, he could readily communicate with the English technicians who had been lured to France by the promise of exclusive privileges of manufacture, subsidies, and even pensions.

Realizing that he could never again live in England, Holker sought Morel's assistance to establish himself in the French textile industry. His previous training fitted him to work in Rouen, "the only progressive cotton manufacturing centre in France".[4] Holker, who from the age of twenty-one had worked in Manchester, a thriving centre of textile manufacture, particularly of cotton, had thoroughly acquainted himself between 1740 and 1745 with the processes and techniques employed by the English in the preparation, weaving, and finishing of cloth.

Although the exact contribution of each is not clear, Holker and Morel worked together to prepare the *Livre d'Echantillons* as a report to M. de Montigny. In the introduction signed by Morel he states clearly that the samples were collected by Holker. Presumably the information about them was also Holker's contribution. The report, as the title page tells us, gives the various kinds of textiles manufactured in the County of Lancashire (as well as several from Norwich and Spitalfields), made of linen thread, linen and cotton, silk and cotton, wool and cotton, and all cotton. Also detailed are their English names, their widths and lengths, and their value in English money reduced to the French equivalent. In translation Morel's introduction reads:

Almost all the samples contained in this work were obtained at Manchester, the principal town of Lancashire, a district of flourishing manufactures. The materials of which they are composed were obtained as follows: the cotton threads were spun near Manchester; the linen threads were from Scotland, Ireland, and Silesia; the silks brought by the ships of their companies, and in the town of Derby, capital of the County of Derbyshire, the throwing is done. They also receive silks from Spain,

214

Piedmont, and Italy, prepared in hanks. The samples were collected at the several places of manufacture by Mr. John Holker, a Captain in the Ogilvie Scottish regiment, and brought by him to France. One may observe that in England there are no official regulations imposed upon a manufacturer; that he is free to set in the loom whatever number of warp threads he chooses, he may weave pieces of any width, and the price depends upon the fineness of the cloth. The author, who, together with the public, appreciates the high degree of your enlightenment, will consider himself fortunate if he has attained the desired end. Presented to M. de Montigny, of the Royal Academy of Sciences, by his very humble and very obedient servant, Morel. [5]

The exact date of the report is not known to the writer, but 1750 seems reasonable—the year that Holker met Marc Morel and before 1751, the year in which he relinquished his commission in Ogilvie's regiment. During the latter part of 1751 Holker made a second visit to England where he recruited eight master workers in various branches of the textile industry and brought them to France. By 1752 Holker's first mill was established at Darnétal on the outskirts of Rouen. This operation was soon expanded and moved to Saint-Sever, another suburb of Rouen. There, on 19 September 1752, the title of "Manufacture royalle de velours et draps de coton" was conferred by the government on the factory then employing some 200 workmen.

Eighteen months later in a *Mémoire*, probably written by Holker, new proposals were set forth to increase the number of factories patterned after the model English colony at Rouen, which was then successfully producing cotton textiles claimed to be equal to those of England. [6] Holker proposed to go to England again to engage more workers and to purchase machines, models, and tools which he could arrange to have smuggled into Holland, since the export from England of any machinery for manufacturing purposes was strictly forbidden and ships' cargoes were subject to confiscation. To facilitate his efforts in obtaining English workmen, Holker requested that the title of inspector-general of foreign manufactures be conferred upon him. This was accorded him in 1755, and from that time he was responsible for manufactures based on foreign schemes and for the activities of foreign workmen already on French soil. [7]

Other collections of swatches also provide information about eighteenth-century European textile

trade and manufacture, but no other has such a wealth of detail concerning progressive English practices for fibre processing, weaving, and finishing, with current prices and trade arrangements. The Morel–Holker report is an unparalleled source for the mid-eighteenth-century English textile industry and its products.

The collection of documented textiles housed in the Bibliothèque Nationale, Paris, in eight volumes, known as the Richelieu collection, is much larger but includes only textiles woven in France or imported from European countries into France between 1720 and 1737. [8] These books are splendid sources of information about figured silks with details in precious metallic threads, woven for royal patrons, printed imitations of East Indian painted fabrics, and striped cottons called *siamoises*. The specialties of each French province are also shown.

A similar important archive of textiles imported into Sweden in the mid-eighteenth century was formed by Anders Berch (1711–1774), who held the first chair in economics at Uppsala University. That collection includes four pattern books of Norwich worsteds and over 150 loose pages bearing labelled swatches. [9]

Norwich worsteds also are known from two books of swatches in the Victoria and Albert Museum, London, prepared by John Kelly; from seven books in the Castle Museum, Norwich; and from six in the Henry Francis du Pont Winterthur Museum in Delaware. Swatch books of Manchester cottons dating from the 1780s and 1790s are found in the Cooper-Hewitt Museum, New York, and at Winterthur. Swatches of fashionable goods, especially for ladies' dresses, were tipped in Rudolph Ackermann's London *Repository of arts, literature, commerce, manufacture, fashions and politics* during the years 1809 to 1815. The *Journal für Fabrik, Manufaktur, Handlung und Mode*, published monthly in Leipzig in the 1790s, also contains swatches of the latest fashionable imports into Germany.

Beyond these extensive collections, and the merchants' records to be referred to below, an occasional scrapbook of beautiful pieces or a cherished quilt made of hundreds of patches from the cloth of a period is known. However cherished these be for their charm, they lack the fabric names and the period and country where they were woven, hence their documentary value is limited. This is also true of most eighteenth- and nineteenth-century merchants' sample books in which the tiny swatches, although neatly numbered for ease in ordering, are too small for identification, and titles are lacking.

With the invention in this century of synthetic fibres and an entirely new commercial nomenclature for man-made fabrics, the names of textiles woven from natural fibres—silk, wool, cotton, linen, and combinations thereof—are less and less well understood by economic and social historians. It seems appropriate therefore to bring together from the Holker manuscript definitions and visual documentation for a group of textiles which were once common but are no longer generally known.

In the study which follows, John Holker's comments for each textile are freely translated for the place of manufacture, the uses for which the cloth was intended, and the fibres employed. Those phrases or sentences set within quotation marks and without other identification are Holker's words in the author's translation. To his notations has been added a description of the swatch. Holker's statements are corroborated, when possible, by dictionary definitions. Textiles of the same name, known from other eighteenth-century manuscript sources, are mentioned. References are given from American inventories and newspaper advertisements to indicate the importation of each kind of textile into North America. Although some of the textiles shown in the manuscript have a long history of manufacture, their appearance may have changed over the years, and it seems advisable, for the most part, to limit the definition to the period of this manuscript. By and large Holker's arrangement of the textiles has been followed.

Checks (swatches 1 – 9)

The first nine swatches of the manuscript illustrate a variety of blue and white linen and cotton checks in plain weave with coloured warp and weft stripes intersecting at right angles to form squares. Except for one example with shaded wefts (no. 7), the arrangement of coloured warp threads is exactly repeated in the weft, and white predominates to give a neat, clean appearance in small-scale patterns.

Holker explains that these checks were made for home consumption and for export, especially to the colonies, and that they were used for sailors' blouses, children's clothing, and linings. Writing of Manchester textile manufactures, John Aikin remarked that about 1735 the manufacturers "took more to the making of coarse checks, striped hollands, and hooping".[10]

Checks were common to most countries, since cloth was easily ornamented in this way. However, these English checks with larger areas of white differ from French examples known from the Richelieu and Maurepas papers and from a group of checks, probably of German manufacture, found in the Pennsylvania-German country and now in the Henry Francis du Pont Winterthur Museum.[11]

Checks were advertised by James and Drinker in the *Pennsylvania Chronicle, and Universal Advertiser* (4–11 December 1769) by their breadths as "10 and 11 nail [2 ¼ inch] linen check, ¾, ⅞, and yard and ⅜ cotton ditto". James Beekman, merchant of New York, in orders to his Manchester agent generally requested "very small dark blue and white cotton checks", but occasionally asked that they be "broad" or "middling large checks".[12] From the same merchants, on 7 December 1770, he ordered fifty pieces of "yard wide Cotton Check, quantity 17 ells each at 13d" in eight different patterns. These he apparently selected from a book with numbered swatches. In the *Boston News-Letter* (18 December 1760), we find listed "¾, ⅞ & apron Manchester checks".[13] The related goods of "Wigan and Manchester checks" (towns in Lancashire) and "wiggon or housewife" cloth appeared in Philadelphia advertisements of the 1760s.[14]

Furniture checks (swatches 10 – 17). These bolder patterns, woven in a variety of colours with large white fields, were "made and sold in Manchester for curtains and chair coverings". For the most part coloured cotton threads formed the checks, although in number 11 (fig. 1) Holker identified a weft as scarlet wool. Number 12 has broad green checks in combination with red lines; number 13 scarlet banded by indigo; number 14 tan edged with red; and number 16 tan with red and blue. A typical material for slipcovers is the bold green check of number 17.

In 1768 Erasmus Williams of New York advertised in the *Gazette* "Saxon blue, green, yellow, scarlet, and crimson furniture checks".[15]

Handkerchief checks (swatches 77 – 79). Handkerchiefs, made entirely of linen in "Manchester and surrounding towns, were extensively sold at home, abroad, and in the colonies". A full piece, according to the manuscript, included five dozen handkerchiefs. One example has dark red and blue checks with wide borders of lighter blue; number 78 has the addition of red between the broader blue stripes. Characteristic is a greater predominance of blue and smaller white fields than in the household and furnishing checks.

Strong linen squares of this type, often with an owner's cross-stitched initials in one corner, are well known in America.

Hooping (swatches 18 – 20). These all-linen textiles (sometimes checked) are coarser and less expensive than the furniture checks (nos. 10 – 17). Number 18 has a *chiné*, or warp-printed, stripe in brown; the other two are pink checks. They were sold for "ladies' paniers".

Alice Morse Earle suggests that hooping, or hooping Holland, was made for petticoats into which reeds or bones could be run to stiffen them.[16]

Cotton Holland (swatches 21 – 30)

Cotton Holland, usually striped, was made for "dresses, petticoats, and furniture coverings". Holland, once the country of manufacture for a wide variety of linen goods, later became the generic name for linen cloth. Holker distinguishes numbers 21 to 30 as Cotton Holland, or Cotton Warps, and explains that cotton, in shades of blue, red and blue, tan, dark red, etc., formed the coloured warp stripes.

Compared with similar cloths with linen warp and cotton weft woven in Rouen, Holker judged the English examples to be superior in design, in wear, and in their suitability for calendering and lustering. Undoubtedly the comparable Rouen goods referred to were the brightly coloured weft-striped *siamoises*, extensively woven for the Levant trade from the 1730s and known from the Maurepas, Ri-

chelieu, and Moccasi papers.[17] The loss of "1 blew strip'd holland Waistcoat", belonging to a servant, was advertised in the *Boston Gazette* in 1731.[18]

Ticking (swatch 31)

To Holker's designation of the use of this linen twill "for distillers' and brewers' aprons", Savary des Bruslons adds (see *coutil*) that army tents were made of it, and it served to enclose feathers in mattresses, bolsters, and pillows.[19]

Superfine ticking (swatch 32). Herringbone twill used "to line garments, for women's stays, and for gaiters". It was bleached and of finer quality than the herringbone of number 41.

Herringbone (swatch 41). A coarse, sturdy herringbone patterned twill of linen warp and cotton weft used for "pockets in clothing".

Chereyderys (swatches 33 – 40)

Silk warp and cotton weft woven in stripes and checks for women's garments (fig. 2). Holker remarks that although similar "petites Etoffes" were made in Rouen, the English manufacture was superior owing to more even spinning of the cotton yarns. Number 40, made of finer cotton and with fancy silk stripes, cost more. Manchester and Spitalfields were centres for the manufacture of chereyderys and for kerchiefs of similar patterns.

Chereyderys were probably imitations of *charadaries* or *carridaries* from northeast India, defined by John Irwin as "striped or chequered woven cloth, probably of mixed silk-and-cotton. First mentioned in the late seventeenth century."[20] According to John Aikin they were being copied in Manchester by about 1735 when "the silk branch was attempted in cherry-derrys and thread satins".[21]

Cadrilles, façon de rose, à grain d'orge, écorces, mouches, étoiles, satin à plume et rayé are the titles given for comparable Rouen textiles in the Maurepas papers. Other floral half-silks in the same manuscript required the use of a drawloom for their fancier patterns.

Chereyderys were advertised in American newspapers from 1712 until the Revolution and were frequently specified as "narrow stript".[22] Kearny and Gilbert's advertisement in the *Pennsylvania Chronicle* (20 April 1767) included "India and English cherryderries". In Boston a runaway Indian woman "wore a narrow striped Cherrederry gown" in 1728.[23]

Fustians (swatches 42 – 53)

A general term covering a large category of linen and cotton, or all-cotton, textiles made in Lancashire. They formed an important part of England's textile export trade to the colonies and other European countries. Of the many varieties made, Holker includes pillow, barragon, jean, thickset, and silverret. The manufacture of these textiles in Manchester is corroborated by John Aikin, who says "the kinds of fustian then made were herring-bones, pillows for pockets and outside wear, strong cotton ribs and barragon, broad-raced lin[en?] thicksets and tufts, dyed, with white diapers, striped dimities, and lining jeans. Cotton thicksets were made sometimes, but as frequently dropped for want of proper finishing. Tufts were much in demand at that time [ca. 1735], and reached their full perfection in respect to the price."[24]

"Barragon", "Herinboun", "Pillows", and "Jeans" were ordered by John Banister of Newport in 1745.[25] Linen/cotton twilled fustian was commonly used for embroidery, and the *Boston Gazette* (19 December 1749) offered a reward for the return of "a Woman's Fustian Petticoat, with a large work'd Embroider'd Border, being Deer, Sheep, Houses, Forrest, &c., so worked".[26]

Pillow (swatches 42 – 44). Brown linen and cotton, or all-cotton, with a raised nap, the latter variety "with mechanically spun warp and weft yarns, had superior wearing qualities" and was suitable for the "clothing of workmen, domestic servants and hostlers". Pillow of finer quality and bleached (no. 44) encased feather beds, pillows, and bolsters.

"Twelve pieces plain dyed Pilloes" at prices ranging from 24 to 32 shillings a piece in "sorted midling browns and olives" were ordered by James Beekman from Manchester in 1767. Later he ordered "24 pieces Olive Coloured Pillows at 24/. 26/. 28/. 30/ and handsome browns".[27]

Barragon (swatches 45, 46). Napped cotton cloth used for men's clothing and dyed all colours (here two shades of brown). In the manufacture of these cloths, said to wear as well as wool, two warp yarns were spun together.

A definition of barragon as "a genteel corded stuff much in vogue for summer wear" was cited by Alice Morse Earle, who found listings for "barragons of various figures and colours" in the *Boston Evening Post* in 1761 and 1783.[28] John Banister's 1742 order included: "3 ps of fine Barragons, Vizt.

27½	yds a cloth collr.
21½	yds a deep blue
21	yds a deep blue
70	yds @ 4/ £14".[29]

Jeans (swatches 47 – 50). Linen and cotton twill dyed in shades of brown for men's clothing. Jeans of finer grade (no. 50) were used for "gentlemen's clothing and officers' greatcoats". The material had the advantage of being washable.

White jeans (swatches 73 – 76), differed in quality and price and were bleached. "Better grades were used for men's and women's clothing; coarser varieties for trouser and waistcoat linings. Some resemble those brought from India."

Thickset (swatches 51, 52). Brown linen/cotton velvet channeled (Fr. *cannelé*) to resemble fine corduroy (no. 51) ; all cotton dyed beige (no. 52).

In 1759 James Beekman ordered thicksets with shalloon (see nos. 113, 114), buttons, and mohair "to sute same" for lining and trimming. In 1766 he ordered sixteen pieces of 24 yards each in five different grades of "sorted Olives".[30] In New York and Boston in the 1760s a runaway servant and a Negro slave wore light-coloured thickset coats. The 1774 shop inventory of Samuel Neave of Philadelphia listed his thicksets as "long imported" and "not much worn now".[31]

Silverret (Fr. *sayette*; swatch 53). Light brown "silk and cotton twill used for men's clothing".

The Moccasi manuscript includes two twilled swatches of London manufacture, one with pink silk warp and blue wool weft, the other with pink silk warp and purple wool weft. Kearny and Gilbert's

Philadelphia advertisement of 1767 offered silver-rets for sale.

Cotton velvets, or *Manchester velvets* (swatches 54 – 60)

Here dyed in shades of brown and beige, "many patterns and qualities were manufactured in Manchester and its environs". At this time, according to Holker, they had begun to supplant Utrecht velvets made partly of wool. Dyed all colours, except scarlet which did not "take" on cotton, they were made of the finest yarns imported from Jamaica or the French Islands. Holker further tells us that the secret of their manufacture was jealously guarded, and only with infinite pains and almost insurmountable difficulties, even at peril of his life, was he able to bring to France the swatches included in this book.

Silk velvet (swatch 72). Holker says that in England this material (here black) is made entirely of cotton, but that in France they employ silk for the pile.

Flowered velvet (swatch 54). Cut and voided cotton velvet woven in a stylized foliate pattern. Holker states that these velvets improved in appearance with wear; his trousers made of similar cloth wore for three years and outlasted others two to one.

Thirty Rouen imitations of Manchester velvets dating from about 1760, and possibly from Holker's *Manufacture Royalle*, are seen in the Moccasi manuscript in superfine and channeled (corduroy) examples.

Grandurelle (swatch 61)

Warp of brown and white linen and cotton yarns spun together; weft of linen, or entirely of cotton. "Used for men's summer clothing and exported in considerable quantities to the colonies".

Two remnants of "Grand Durells, qt. 36 yds @ 3/" were appraised in the New York estate of Thomas Hysham in 1751.[32] "A complete assortment twilled and plain Grandurells, of every colour and kind" was offered for sale in *The Palladium*, Boston, 8 May, 1810.

Nankin, or *nankeen* (swatch 62)

Woven of the "best quality Island cotton, waistcoats and trousers made of it wear well". Defined in the *Oxford English Dictionary* as "cotton cloth originally made at Nankin, China, from a yellow variety of cotton and afterwards made at Manchester and elsewhere of ordinary cotton and dyed yellow". With the entry of American ships into the East India trade after the Revolution, the importation of nankeens increased to the point that "their price was almost a standard of exchange".[33] At this time the term nankeen was applied to a large variety of cotton goods sold in Canton. Rhode Island merchants gave directions to their supercargoes to purchase yellow, white, deep blue, and black nankeens.[34]

Dimity (Fr. *basin*; swatches 63 – 71)

Eight examples in this manuscript indicate that the term dimity in the mid-eighteenth century covered a wide variety of cotton cloth from fine birdseye (no. 63) to large flowered patterns (nos. 65 – 68), and simple stripes (nos. 69 – 71). All were sturdy and serviceable, as well as attractive, for furnishing and clothing. To these uses Savary des Bruslons adds counterpanes, summer bed hangings for the country, and window curtains.

Striped dimity (swatches 69 – 71). The three swatches of linen/cotton corded material differ only in quality and price.

Three striped and birdseye dimities manufactured in Nantes are found among the Richelieu papers (Lh45 I, p. 108)—one of them linen with coloured silk weft. At plate XII, "Miscellany", of his *Cyclopaedia*, Abraham Rees gives the "draught and cording of looms" for several kinds of dimity—striped, fancy, and spot diaper.[35] Willing and Shippen of Philadelphia imported "Clouting, Napkin & Tabling Diaper" in the 1730s.[36] The 1754 Boston broadside of Henrietta Maria Caine includes "Four ps. clouting Diaper ell wide, 73 Yds and ¼ each", "superfine stript corded Dimity", "flowered", "flowered and diamond", "small diamond", "one bundle Women's Dimothy Caps", and "one bundle fine Dimothy Stomagers [stomachers]".[37] From

London, Benjamin Franklin wrote his wife, Deborah, that he was sending her "Six coarse diaper Breakfast Cloths; they are to spread on the Tea Table, for no body breakfasts here on the naked Table, but on the Cloth set a large Tea Board with the Cups".[38] James Beekman's order to Manchester (1770) included "White corded" and "flowered" dimity.[39]

Cotton diaper (swatches 63, 64). A kind of dimity, linen/cotton woven on a harness loom. Used for "summer waistcoats, bodices and petticoats". In number 64 lozenges centre two dotted patterns in alternate weft rows.

Flowered cotton diaper (Fr. *basin à fleurs brochées*; swatches 65 – 68, fig. 3). Different patterns and qualities are used for "petticoats and for furnishing". The *Oxford English Dictionary* definition for diaper corresponds to Holker's swatches: "Since the fifteenth century a linen fabric (sometimes with cotton) woven with lines crossing diamond-wise with the spaces variously filled with lines, a dot or a leaf".

Handkerchiefs (swatches 80 – 83)

Pattern of white dots resist-printed in one or two shades of madder red (nos. 80 – 82, fig. 4); white dots resist-printed with indigo (no. 83). Of these samples Holker says that in London the English print fine linen cloth (Fr. *batiste*) from Cambray, Valenciennes, and St. Quentin for home consumption as well as for export to Europe and the colonies. A drawback of the import tax on white cloth is received when the printed handkerchiefs are exported.

To these prints can be added an untitled all-linen example with white floral sprigs reserved on an indigo ground which appears at the back of the manuscript.

Handkerchiefs described as "Paistwork", probably referring to the resist paste used in printing them, were advertised in the *Boston Gazette* on 26 May 1755.[40] In 1770 James Beekman ordered "10 dozen blue and white paste linnen Handkerchiefs at 11/" and "5 dozen red and white Handkerchiefs at 12/".[41]

Handkerchief (swatch 84). White linen with red cotton borders, made in Manchester.

Silk handkerchief (swatch 85). Twill weave, block-printed in red with dark blue borders on a mustard yellow ground. Holker says that foreigners buy these handkerchiefs believing them to have been printed in India, and that in Paris where they are called foulards (Fr. *foulas*), they are made into women's dresses.

Silk handkerchiefs (swatches 86, 87) made in "Spitalfields, one of the principal suburbs of London. A tax drawback is allowed on these goods when exported." Fine stripes surrounding broad fields, twill weave (no. 86); raspberry red, dark blue, and white, twill weave (no. 87).

Chintz cotton printed (swatches 88 – 100)

"To the French, a kind of calico of which the warp is linen thread and the weft cotton. They make them and print them in all the widths used for the calico fabrics from India. The sample adjoined [fig. 5] is taken from a bolt one yard in width and thirty yards long, which comes to the same as three-quarters of a French ell in width, and 22 ½ French ells in length. The price per yard is three shillings, or 4 livres 10 sous per French ell.

"This type of fabric is made in the Manchester district, especially at a small town called Blackburn. The output is so large that scarcely a week goes by without a thousand rolls being sold and sent to London unbleached. The merchants of that great city turn them over to bleachworks. The printing is done as soon as they are returned from the meadows. The king exacts a tax of 4 sols per yard on these fabrics, as well as on those previously described, but this tax is reimbursed if the goods are exported abroad. The volume of business done with foreign countries is infinitely greater than with the domestic market, although this is very extensive. They send large quantities to France, which are sold as Indian chintzes because of the special finish they are given and also because the purchasers of this type of English goods have but slight knowledge of them."[42]

Although from 1720 the printing of all-cotton cloth had been forbidden in England, the government regulation did not include linen and cotton fustian, and on this material London printers achieved surprisingly sophisticated patterns derived from fashionable Spitalfields silk dress goods. By means of the "special finish", or glaze, referred to by Holker, the prints were made to closely resemble costlier silk fabrics. Most of the patterns were printed in the "full" chintz style with as many as seven colours and shades. To red and purple (common madder-dyed colours) were added "penciled", or hand-painted, colours of indigo blue and weld yellow. The two were overpainted for green.

Godfrey Smith's description of calico printing in his *Laboratory: or, School of Arts* (2d ed., 1756) closely relates to the Holker patterns. The author says that they are generally "in imitation of the flowered silk-manufactory". "The fashion", he continues, "as with the brocaded silks, has run upon natural flowers, stalks and leaves; sometimes intermixt with ornaments, after the French taste, sometimes in groupes or festoons of flowers or fruit, or in sprigs and branches carelessly flung, in a natural and agreeable manner."

Descriptions of mid-eighteenth-century chintzes in American merchants' orders are meagre; many patterns were left to the discretion of the English agent, or were ordered by number from pattern cards, or were described in terms of the number of colours desired.

In Philadelphia the theft of a dress from Benjamin Franklin's house was reported: "a woman's gown of printed cotton, of the sort called brocade print, very remarkable, the ground dark, with large red roses, and other large red and yellow flowers, with blue in some of the flowers and smaller blue and white flowers, with many green leaves".[43]

Tobine messinets (swatches 101 – 103)

These were made for "women's clothes in Spitalfields and in Norwich, a flourishing centre for the manufacture of worsteds in Norfolk". White worsted weft with gold, brown, and white silk warp stripes (no. 101; fig. 6); white worsted weft with dots and floral stripe in pale green silk, fine stripes in pink silk (no. 102); white worsted weft with gold stripes and brocaded, polychrome floral sprigs in silk (no. 103).

Two *Missinits larghi* of London manufacture, included in the 1760 Moccasi manuscript, are plain weave with pink silk warp and blue wool weft; and pink silk warp and brown wool weft. "Dorsetteens, messinets, silverets", and "worsted damasks" are included in Kearny and Gilbert's advertisement in the *Pennsylvania Chronicle* (20 April 1767). Messinets are listed in James and Drinker's advertisement in the same newspaper (4 December 1769) with other worsted goods.

Messinet (swatch 104). Red-orange worsted weft with warp-float flowers in silk. This swatch resembles small-scale eighteenth-century French silk patterns known as *droguets*.

Irish stuffs (swatches 105, 106). Worsted weft and silk warp with coloured stripes in satin weave. They were "woven in Norwich and some in Spitalfields". Using less silk and without pattern, these goods were less expensive than messinets.

Harrateen (swatches 107, 108)

A "kind of woolen moiré [Fr. *moëre*] made in Norwich. The watered pattern is made by means of a hot press, the use of which is little understood in France. This material is used for furnishing." The colours shown are red and green.

Harrateen (swatches 109, 110). "The same material as numbers 107 and 108 but more common. The wavy pattern is here achieved by means of a hot copper cylinder." The colours shown are gold (fig. 7) and green.

Examples of large pieces of harrateen, with full repeats and widths, show that the meandering stamped pattern was intended to imitate silk damask furnishing fabrics with formal foliate patterns. In each the wavy lines are exactly repeated on either side of a central longitudinal axis. In calling them more common Holker may have meant that they were more popular and produced in greater quantity. In fabrics with weft yarns coarser than the warps, a watered effect was generally achieved by doubling the material lengthwise along the selvages and submitting it to great pressure (or by pressing two full widths superimposed on one another).

Thereby the yarns were forced and flattened against each other. On the other hand, the additional linear pattern in numbers 109 and 110 could only have been made with an engraved roller, as Holker states, which would have been costly to produce. A pattern achieved by this method, in the Essex Institute, Salem, Massachusetts, includes sprays of flowers and butterflies, in style not unlike the printed fabrics shown in this volume (fig. 5).

In both England and America at this period, harrateens in red, blue, yellow, and most frequently green were used for bed and window curtains and matching furniture coverings. Other stamped patterns, either in red or in blue, which more closely approximate formal foliate silk damasks, have survived in quilts, in bed hangings, and as the original coverings of easy chairs.

Fine wool damask (swatch 111)

"These are woven in all colours [here green; fig. 8]. Their luster is imparted by means of the hot press. Popular for men's dressing gowns, these damasks are of exceeding good wear."

Clearly these worsteds, finished to a high gloss, were a durable, warm fabric which resembled finer all-silk or silk/wool articles and were suitable for furnishing. The Moccasi manuscript contains swatches of green and red *damasco per mobili* from London. Two-coloured damasks, called "Flowered Sattins", are seen in John Kelly's pattern book dated 1763.[44] Colour combinations include red/yellow, green/gold, red or blue with white, and others. In the same manuscript coarser grades of worsted damask in solid colours are titled "Fine Bed Damasks".

In 1738 "Banjans made of Worsted Damask, Brocaded Stuffs, Scotch Plods and Calliminco" were advertised in the Boston *Weekly Rehearsal*.[45] On 9 November 1765, Jonathan Cobb wrote from London to a customer: "This day deliver'd to the Lyncoln Carrier, one long case, containing large green worsted damask Window Curtain all ready fix'd and strung to ye lath fit for putting up."[46]

Silk and wool damask (swatch 112). At Spitalfields, according to Holker, this kind of furnishing material was woven in all colours (here red; fig. 9). It cost twice the price of all-wool damask.

Four silk and wool damasks dating from about 1720 are preserved in the London Public Record Office.[47] In 1784 Richard Kip, New York upholsterer, advertised for sale in his shop "rich yellow silk and worsted damask" and "a sofa, twelve chairs, and three window curtains of sky-blue silk and worsted damask stuffs garnished and fringed".[48]

Shalloon (swatches 113, 114)

". . . or twilled serge, made in the West Riding of Yorkshire in several qualities for the lining of men's clothing" (here shown in red and blue). According to John Aikin, "the shalloon trade was introduced here [Manchester] about the beginning of this century [ca. 1700]." [49]

James Bischoff distinguishes shalloons from serge "by their clear quill [twill] and better quality".[50] David Booth describes shalloon as "a worsted article which, like Calamanco, may be either hotpressed or unglazed".[51]

Frequently mentioned as a lining material, it was ordered by John Banister of Newport (1739) in blue, black, green, "cloth colour'd", and "Mock scarlet".[52] In addition to these colours, James Beekman (1769) ordered "handsome cloth browns" and "Russett Colours".[53] In 1730 Col. Robert Carter's inventory listed yellow shalloon curtains, and in 1743 it was used for chair coverings in New Haven, Connecticut.[54] John Moore's New York inventory of 1757 and that of Anthony Rutgers in 1760 listed bedsteads hung with green shalloon curtains.[55]

Scotch plaid (swatch 115)

Red, blue, and green predominate in this twilled, checked fabric. According to Holker, this kind of cloth was used for clothing by the Scots, especially the highlanders, and for men's dressing gowns. He further states that this plaid was used for uniforms of the Scottish regiment serving in England.

Fine worsted plaids of this period can be seen in Edinburgh Castle where clothing of Bonnie Prince Charlie, the Young Pretender, is exhibited. In contrast to later, now traditional, clan tartans of heavy, fulled wool, the clothes are made of glazed worsteds patterned in small, bright checks. As seen in the Prince's trousers, and in Scottish prints known from copperplate printed textiles, narrow-legged, checked trousers were cut on the bias. Similar plaids are seen in long cloaks with standing collars preserved in American collections. "One Piece superfine Scotch Plaid red and green" was advertised in the *Boston Gazette* for 14 August 1758.[56]

Additional cotton and linen textiles, which may have been early trials made under Holker's direc-tion in Rouen, appear on the last pages of the manuscript. These include a stout corded cotton with shaded warp stripes which would have been suitable for furnishing; five cotton velvets in green and three shades of blue labelled "Ier assay de Velour fabriqué à Tours par les Srs. Salmon et Fromenteau" (one of these bears a handsome and intricate pattern stamped on brown cotton velvet, suitable either for furnishing or gentlemen's clothing); a striped dimity labelled as having been woven at Caux; below it two cottons in white and two in blue are woven with looped pile resembling "turkish" towelling; attached to another page are cotton cloths with blue and white warp printed velvet pile.

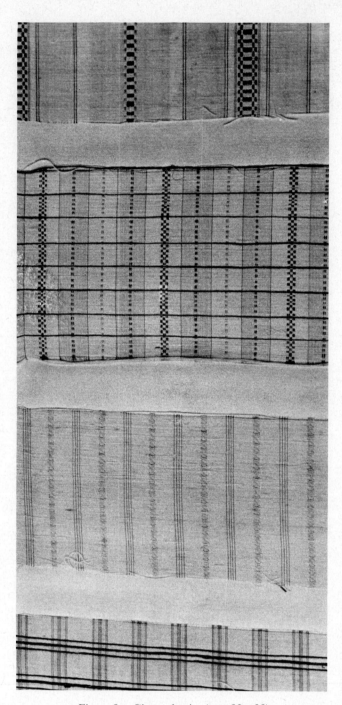

Figure 1.   Furniture checks (nos. 12 – 14). All of the textiles illustrated are of English manufacture and date from about 1750.

Figure 2.   Chereyderries (nos. 33 – 36).

Figure 3.   Flowered cotton diaper, a kind of dimity (no. 65).

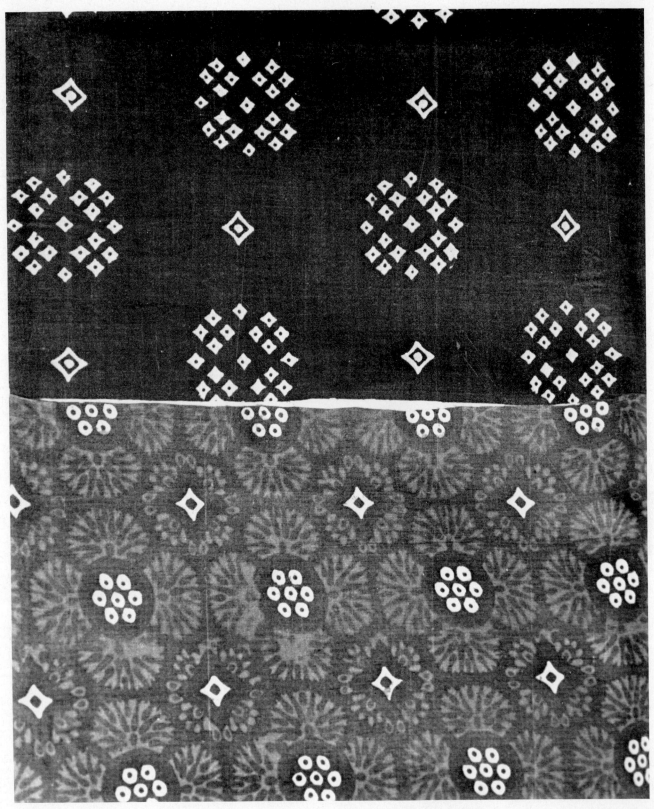

Figure 4.   Linen handkerchiefs resist-printed in red (nos. 80, 81).

Figure 5.   Two printed chintzes (nos. 88, 89).

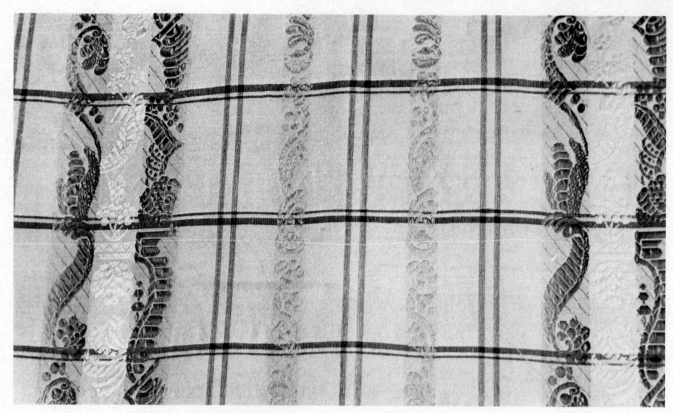

Figure 6. Tobine Messinet of worsted with silk warp-patterned stripes (no. 101).

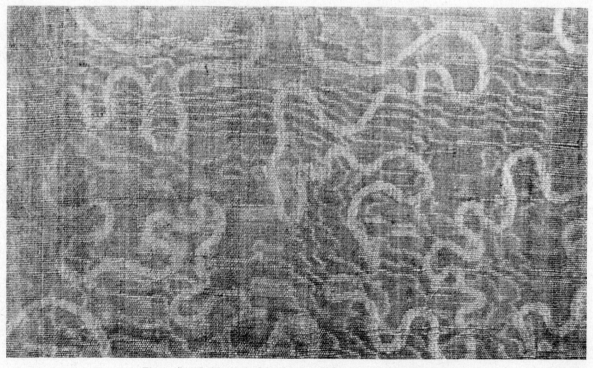

Figure 7. Gold worsted harrateen with a wavy pattern produced by stamping or embossing with a metal roller (no. 109).

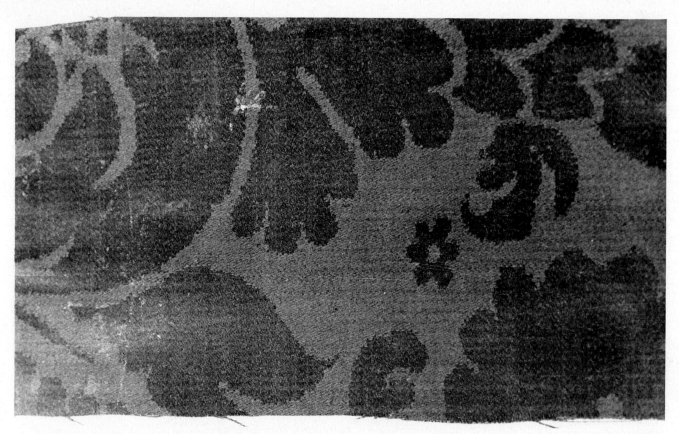

Figure 8.   Dark green worsted damask (no. 111).

Figure 9.   Red silk and wool damask (no. 112).

Notes

1. Musée des Arts Décoratifs, Paris. Folio manuscript, "Livre d'Echantillons contenant les diverses Etoffes qui se fabriquent dans l'Etendue de la province de Lankashire en Angleterre. . . présenté à Monsieur de Montigny, de l'Academie Royalle des Sciences", about 1750. Textiles gathered by John Holker. First published by the writer: "English textile swatches of the mid-eighteenth century", *The Burlington Magazine*, vol. 102 (June 1960), p. 240.

2. For biographical details about John Holker see the *Dictionary of National Biography*.

3. André Rémond, *John Holker, manufacturier et grand fonctionnaire en France au XVIIIme siècle, 1719-1786*, Bibliothèque d'Histoire Economique, Paris, Marcel Rivière et Cie., 1946, p. 24.

4. A. P. Wadsworth and J. De Lacy Mann, *The cotton trade and industrial Lancashire, 1600-1780*, reprint of 1931 edition, New York, Augustus M. Kelley, 1968, p. 193.

5. The Royal Academy encouraged technical invention, and de Montigny and other members toured French industrial sights at this time. He is not to be confused with Daniel-Charles Trudaine de Montigny, Director of Commerce and principal industrial official of France at this time.

6. P. Boissonade, "Trois mémoires relatifs à l'amelioration des manufactures en France; mémoire tendant à multiplier et perfectionner les fabriques de France. (Travail dû probablement à John Holker, inspecteur des manufactures étrangeres, redigé vers 1754)", *Revue d'Histoire Economique et Sociale*, 1914–18, p. 68.

7. Rémond, *John Holker* (1946), p. 81. Holker's and his son's later contributions to the diffusion of modern techniques and advanced methods in the carding, spinning, dyeing, and finishing of textiles are well described in Rémond's monograph. Holker's son served as French consul-general in Philadelphia during the Revolutionary War, and his activities are revealed in 39 volumes of letters and documents in the Library of Congress, Washington, D.C.

8. Samplings from these folio volumes were published by Roger-Armand Weigert in his magnificently illustrated book *Textiles en Europe sous Louis XV*, Fribourg, Office du Livre, 1964.

9. Publication of this collection is currently in progress at the Nordiska Museet, Stockholm, where it is housed.

10. John Aikin, *A description of the country . . . round Manchester*, London, John Stockdale, 1795, p. 158.

11. Richelieu papers: see note 8. Maurepas papers: eleven pages of French textile swatches and one page of English woolen textiles. The Henry Francis du Pont Winterthur Museum, Joseph Downs Manuscript and Microfilm Collection, Winterthur, Delaware (hereafter DMMC). The swatches are illustrated in colour and described in *Textiles et documents Maurepas*, Roland Lamontagne, ed., Ottawa, Lemeac, 1970, for which I wrote the introductory essay entitled "Les matières textiles au XVIIIe siècle".

12. Philip L. White, ed., *The Beekman mercantile papers, 1746-1799*, 3 vols., New York, New-York Historical Society, 1956. See especially orders to Robert and Nathan Hyde, vol. 2, pp. 833-842.

13. George Francis Dow, *The arts & crafts in New England, 1704-1775: Gleanings from Boston newspapers*, Topsfield, Mass., The Wayside Press, 1927, p. 169.

14. *Pennsylvania Chronicle, and Universal Advertiser*, 20 April 1767, advertisement of Kearny and Gilbert; same paper, 4-11 December 1769, advertisement of James and Drinker.

15. *New York Gazette*, 18 April 1768. Cited in R.T.H. Halsey and Charles O. Cornelius, *A handbook of the American wing*, 7th ed. rev. by Joseph Downs, New York, Metropolitan Museum of Art, 1942, p. 130.

16. Alice Morse Earle, *Costume of colonial times*, New York, Charles Scribner's Sons, 1894, p. 137.

17. Moccasi folio manuscript: "Manufacture de Francia, Inghilterra ed Olanda. Mostre racolte viaggiando dal Signor Moccasi, mercante di panni, e nel Suo ritorno verso il 1760 presentate al Conte Bogino", Paris, Bibliothèque Forney, 667,-004 moc. 39 pages of textile swatches.

18. Dow, *Arts & crafts* (1927), p. 173.

19. Jacques Savary des Bruslons, *Dictionnaire universel de commerce*, 6th ed., 4 vols., Geneva, Cramer & C. Philibert, 1750.

20. John Irwin and P.R. Schwartz, "A glossary of textile terms", *Studies in Indo-European textile history*, Ahmedabad, Calico Museum of Textiles, 1966, p. 61.

21. Aikin, *A description* (1795), p. 158.

22. Earle, *Costume* (1894), p. 83.

23. Dow, *Arts & crafts* (1927), p. 187.

24. Aikin, *A description* (1795), p. 158.

25. Order book of John Banister of Newport. Newport Historical Society, Newport, Rhode Island. DMMC, microfilm 191.

26. Dow, *Arts & crafts* (1927), p. 176.

27. *Beekman papers*, vol. 2 (1956), p. 837, p. 842.

28. Earle, *Costume* (1894), p. 53.

29. Order book of John Banister (see note 25).

30. *Beekman papers*, vol. 2 (1956), p. 662, p. 862.

31. "Inventory of the Goods and Chattels of Samuel Neave, late of the City of Philadelphia, Merchant deceas'd. Taken the 28th day of September 1774." Office of the Register of Wills, Philadelphia.

32. "Appraisements made by Christopher Bancker and Brandt Schuyler", New York, Appraisal Book 66, New York Estates. DMMC 53.190, p. 7 (hereafter "Appraisements").

33. Earle, *Costume* (1894), p. 166.

34. William B. Weeden, "Early Oriental commerce in Providence", Massachusetts Historical Society *Proceedings*, 3d series, vol. 1 (1908), p. 242, p. 271.

35. Abraham Rees, *The cyclopaedia, or, universal dictionary of arts, sciences and literature*, 39 vols. of text, 6 vols. of plates, London, Longman, Hurst, Rees, Orme and Brown, 1820, pl. 12, "Miscellany" in vol. 3 of plates.

36. Ledger A of Willing and Shippen, merchants of Philadelphia, 1730-1734. Yale University Library, Manuscript Collection.

37. Broadside. "Catalogue of Goods to be sold by Publick Vendue. . . 1754, at the House of Mrs. Henrietta Maria Caine. . . Marlborough Street, Boston", Massachusetts Historical Society, Boston, Mass.

38. Letter from Benjamin Franklin, dated 19 February 1758. In Leonard W. Labaree, ed., *The papers of Benjamin Franklin*, 1959—, New Haven and London, Yale University Press, vol. 7, 1963, p. 381.

39. *Beekman papers*, vol. 2 (1956), p. 842.

40. Dow, *Arts & crafts* (1927), p. 164.

41. *Beekman papers*, vol. 2 (1956), p. 930.

42. For illustrations of the thirteen chintz patterns see the author's *Printed textiles, English and American cottons and linens, 1700-1850*, New York, The Viking Press, 1970, pp. 24-30.

43. Hannah Benner Roach, "Benjamin Franklin slept here", *Pennsylvania Magazine*, vol. 84, no. 2 (April 1960), p. 156.

44. "Mr. John Kelly's Counterpart of patterns, from No. 1 to No. 239. Norwich, Febry. 15, 1763". Victoria and Albert Museum, Textile Department, London.

45. Earle, *Costume* (1894), p. 51.

46. Samuel Deland Papers (DE/34/3/1-84), Northumberland County Record Office. John Cornforth kindly gave the writer this reference.

47. "Samples submitted by the Weavers' Company to the Commissioners for Trades and Plantations, 1719–21". Public Record Office, London. CO 388/21, No. 209, f. 146.

48. *New-York Packet*, 13 December 1784. Cited by Rita Susswein Gottesman in *The arts and crafts in New York, 1777-1799*, New York, New York Historical Society, 1954, no. 472.

49. Aikin, *A description* (1795), p. 158.

50. James Bischoff, *A comprehensive history of the woollen and worsted manufactures and the natural and commercial history of sheep from the earliest records to the present period*, 2 vols., reprint of 1842 edition, London, Frank Cass & Co., 1968, vol, 1, p. 198.

51. David Booth, *An analytical dictionary of the English language*, London, Simpkin, Marshall and Co., 1836.

52. Account Book of John Banister, Invoice no. 6. Newport Historical Society, Newport, Rhode Island. DMMC, microfilm 191.

53. *Beekman papers*, vol. 2 (1956), p. 875.

54. Frances Little, *Early American textiles*, New York and London, The Century Co., 1931, p. 240, p. 236.

55. "Appraisements", DMMC 53.190, p. 42, p. 64.

56. Dow, *Arts & crafts* (1927), p. 167.

Examples of Mediaeval Tablet-Woven Bands

Sigrid Müller-Christensen

South German and Austrian churches and museums contain a large number of tablet-woven bands dating from the high Middle Ages which, due to the variety of pattern and execution, constitute fine examples of this technique. Some of these bands are still used as ornaments for old liturgical garments, such as those in the treasures of the cathedrals of Bamberg, Regensburg, Salzburg, and Brixen. In the vestry of the Cathedral of Bamberg, golden tablet-woven bands were carefully preserved for centuries to serve as replacement stock for alterations and repairs of garments and ecclesiastical furnishings, such as altar frontals.[1]

Bands found in tombs are hardly ever in so good a state of preservation, partly because they were exposed to many destructive influences, and also because they frequently formed parts of textiles that had been worn before being used as funerary garments. The following is a discussion of interesting examples from the cathedrals in Speyer and Bamberg.

When the emperors' and bishops' tombs were opened in the Royal Choir of the Cathedral of Speyer in the year 1900 a great number of silk bands were brought to light. These bands had been used as trim on garments or were worn as separate accessories such as belts, or, in the case of clergy, as insignia.[2] About twenty-four fragments with patterns are tablet-woven silk bands enriched by an extra weft of gold thread. Most of these bands date from the eleventh and twelfth centuries. Thanks to the almost pure gold used for them they still exhibit a wonderful lustre. The gold threads were formed

by flat-beaten gold strips, wound round a silk core.

Particularly remarkable among the early bands is the torn and well-worn fragment (fig. 1) of a very finely executed tablet-woven band (l. 4 cm, w. 3 cm). Because the selvages have broken away on either side, the original width of the band can only be estimated as approximately 4 cm.[3] The band was divided horizontally, the fields being filled with all-over braided designs of gold thread against a red silk warp ground. Forming a border for the horizontal division with its diamond pattern, two lines of slightly thicker gold thread were inserted by needle in *soumak* technique instead of shots of extra golden wefts. As wrapping wefts, using diagonal stitches in diverging directions, they completely cover the red silk warp. These stitches give the effect of braided stripes (fig. 2). They were very tightly sewn and were hammered flat on the surface, resulting in a contrast with the raised effect of the remaining parallel gold threads. On the reverse side of the band, the even structure of cords twisted in pairs becomes visible (fig. 3). The gold threads of the *soumak* stitches glitter between the individual warp threads.[4] I do not know of other examples of this "mixed technique" of partly weaving, partly *soumak* embroidery among other tablet-woven gold bands from the eleventh and twelfth centuries.[5]

Five fragments of another band from one of the tombs (complete l. 40 cm, w. 2.9 cm) also show horizontal divisions into fields of varying sizes.[6] This band (fig. 4), with an extra-weft of spun gold thread, shows finely differentiated allover braiding in red as background pattern in the fields in which stylized birds, probably ducks, are depicted. The de-

232

Figure 1. Fragment of a tablet-woven band, red silk warp, front brocaded with gold and with rows in *soumak* weft. Islamic, eleventh century.
Speyer, Diözesanmuseum. Photo: Bayerisches Nationalmuseum, Munich.

Figure 2. Detail of figure 1. Front, brocaded with gold, two rows in *soumak* weave.
Photo: Bayerische Staatsgemäldesammlungen, Munich.

Figure 3. Enlarged detail of figure 1. Reverse, the twists form chevrons, the *soumak* wefts show between the twists.
Photo: Bayerische Staatsgemäldesammlungen, Munich.

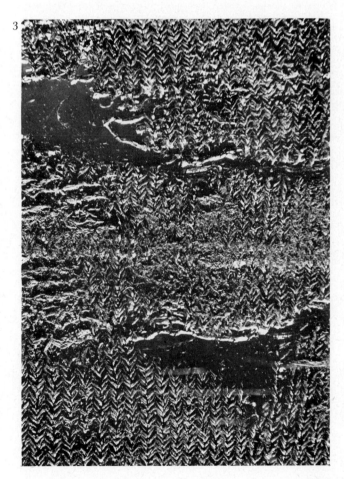

233

4

5

Figure 4. Fragment of a tablet-woven band, red silk warp, front brocaded with gold and white silk. Islamic, eleventh century.
Speyer, Diözesanmuseum. Photo: Bayerisches Nationalmuseum, Munich.

Figure 5. Reverse of figure 4. The twists form chevrons, the brocading silk weft is floating.
Photo: Bayerisches Nationalmuseum, Munich.

sign of the birds is brocaded with a white pattern weft of unspun silk, providing a rich contrast for the red warp threads in the ground pattern. The white brocading weft floats on the reverse side of the band (fig. 5). The design of the horizontal divisions is also brocaded in white. Two of them feature a pattern of heart-shaped leaves with small flowers.

The *soumak* band belongs to the finds discovered in a bishop's tomb, perhaps that of Bishop Sigisboth who died in 1314. This tomb revealed some Spanish silk textiles with gilt membrane strips from the twelfth century, and a pair of buskins with gold embroidery in *opus anglicanum* dating from about 1200, as well as several varieties of bands dating from the eleventh to thirteenth century. The bands are of German, Spanish, or Sicilian workmanship. The brocaded gold band with ducks came from the tomb of King Philip of Swabia who died in 1208. The textile accessories found in his tomb were of Byzantine, German, and western Islamic manufacture, and date from the eleventh and twelfth centuries. The disparate contents of the two tombs do not allow any conclusions to be drawn as to the age and origin of the tablet-woven bands. The stylized design of the ducks and the arrangement of the heart-shaped

leaves in rows indicate that the gold band is likely of Islamic workmanship, probably originating in Sicily or Apulia in the eleventh century. The same origin may be assumed for the *soumak* band.

Finally, I would like to discuss a tablet-woven band in the Cathedral treasury of Bamberg. The band (l. 13.5 cm, w. 2.8 cm) was attached to the cope of St. Kunigunde as a morse[7] and, with a pattern weft of gold threads, shows a typical design (figs. 6, 7). It is divided into fields by diagonal and horizontal stripes. The fields are filled with symmetrically arranged confronting large-eyed lions on either side of a stylized tree. The band, which is very finely executed, is enriched by brocading in green and blue unspun silk. This brocading serves to emphasize the rosette ornament on the flanks of the lions, the small trefoils on the trees, and the scroll and patterns of the stripes. A related gold band with silk brocading is in the Danish National Museum in Copenhagen and is a part of the Viking find discovered at Mammen.[8] It dates from about the year 1000. The design of these bands resembles the border frames of German illuminated manuscripts dating from the same period.

Figures 6, 7. Tablet-woven band, red silk warp, front brocaded with gold, small details in green and blue silk. Reverse showing the brocading silk. South German, eleventh century. Bamberg, Diözesanmuseum. Photo: Bayerisches Nationalmuseum, Munich.

Notes

1. In 1478, the beadwork embroiderer Jörg Spiess restored the choir cope of St. Kunigunde (Diözesanmuseum, Bamberg). He used old tablet-woven bands with gold thread to complete the gold embroidery. The embroidered altar frontal (about 1300) from the high altar in St. Peter's Choir of Bamberg Cathedral (Bavarian National Museum, Munich) was later enlarged by adding different kinds of gold bands, dating from the early eleventh to the thirteenth century (see M. Schuette and S. Müller-Christensen, *A pictorial history of embroidery*, New York, Praeger, 1964, p. 307, nos. 170, 171).

2. Sigrid Müller-Christensen, "Die Gräber in Königschor, mit Katalog der Textilfunde", in *Der Dom zu Speyer* by H.E. Kubach and W. Haas, Munich, Deutscher Kunstverlag, 1972, pp. 923-1024 (vol. 5 in the series *Die Kunstdenkmäler von Rheinland-Pfalz*).

3. Diözesanmuseum, Speyer, acc. no. 545; Müller-Christensen, "Die Gräber im Königschor" (1972), p. 988.

4. Tablet-woven band. Analysis: Ground weave in warp twill. Linen pattern weft in twill and *soumak*. Warp: light brown silk, 38 cords of 4 warp ends per cm. Binding weft: now brown, ca. 48 per cm. Pattern weft of gold filé: ca. 48 per cm. Gold lamella: w. 0.2 mm, Z-twisted around now light brown silk core, ca. 50 turns per cm. Regarding the hammered surface of gold bands, see A. Geijer, Birka 3, *Die Textilfunde*, Uppsala, 1938, p. 80; C.F. Battiscombe, ed., *The relics of Saint Cuthbert*, Oxford, printed for the Dean and Chapter of Durham Cathedral at the University Press, 1956, p. 378.

5. On the mitre from St. Peter's in Salzburg, in the Abegg Foundation at Riggisberg (M. Lemberg, *Abegg-Stiftung Bern in Riggisberg*, 2, *Die Textilien*, Bern, 1973, pl. 15), and among the textile relics of St. Cuthbert in Durham Cathedral (Grace Crowfoot, "The braids", p. 452, and J.F. Flanagan, "The design on the soumac braid", p. 464; both in Battiscombe, *St. Cuthbert*, 1956) are tablet-woven silk bands whose patterns depict stylized palmettes and heart-shaped figures executed in coloured silk using *soumak* technique.

6. Diözesanmuseum, Speyer, acc. no. 522b. Müller-Christensen, "Die Gräber im Königschor" (1972), p. 964, figs. 1518-1520. Tablet-woven band. Analysis: Ground weave in warp twill. Warp: brownish red, 42 cords of 4 warp ends per cm. Binding weft: red, 40 per cm. Pattern wefts: linen and gold filé. Gold lamella: S-twisted around silk core, 40 turns per cm. Brocading weft: white unspun silk.

7. Müller-Christensen, *Das Grab des Papstes Clemens II. im Dom zu Bamberg*, Munich, F. Bruckmann, 1960, p. 77, fn. 8. Tablet-woven band. Analysis: Ground weave in warp twill. Warp: red, 42 cords of 4 warp ends per cm. Binding weft: tomato red, 35 per cm. Pattern wefts: linen and gold filé. Gold lamella: S-twisted around light brown silk core. Brocading weft: green and blue unspun silk.

8. M. Hald, *Olddanske Textiler*, Copenhagen, Nordisk Forlag, 1950, p. 236.

Three Pieces of Unpatterned Linen from Ancient Egypt in the Royal Ontario Museum

Winifred Needler

EXCEPT for a few examples having border stripes in blue or rarely red and a remarkable piece in loop technique, probably no patterned textiles from ancient Egypt survive that may be dated before the New Kingdom, i.e., the sixteenth century B.C. [1] Patterns are occasionally seen on the dress of Old and Middle Kingdom statuary and on garments, hangings, sails, and other cloth-like objects represented in the wall pictures of the same periods; but among these only the brightly coloured strip designs on the costumes of the Asiatic bedouin band in the tomb of Khnumhotpe II at Beni Hasan (about 1900 B.C.) may be identified as woven patterns with reasonable certainty;[2] the rest have been variously interpreted as matting, painting on textile or leather, bead netting, feather work, appliqué work, or embroidery.

In contrast, the actual examples of patterned textiles surviving from the New Kingdom are numerous and complex. New techniques, including tapestry weaving, were doubtless brought to Egypt from southwest Asia in the sixteenth or fifteenth century B.C., when Thebes was rapidly becoming the cosmopolitan capital of a great empire. The vertical two-beam loom, on which the new patterns were probably woven, is first seen in wall pictures of the New Kingdom.[3] The patterned textiles, especially those from the tomb of Tutankhamun (fourteenth century B.C.) and from the still older tomb of Tuthmosis IV (fifteenth century B.C.), are famous not only for their virtuosity but also for their great age when compared with surviving textiles from other ancient lands.[4] The much older Egyptian unpatterned textiles, woven with surpassing skill on a ho-

rizontal ground-loom, are less well known although they have occasionally been the object of technical studies. Quantities of this simpler, less noticeable cloth are preserved in museum storerooms, unstudied and neglected.

The earliest known textile from any part of the world was formerly thought to be a single well-preserved fragment from the Neolithic settlement of the Egyptian Fayum ("Fayum A"), dated to about the middle of the fifth millennium B.C.[5] In 1961, however, textiles that probably belong to the first half of the sixth millennium were found at Çatal Hüyük in central Anatolia.[6] These are small fragments of wrappings from secondary burials in the settlement; they were accidentally preserved by fire which charred but could not consume them in a confined space. The brittle, carbonized fibres have been cautiously identified as sheep's wool. A coarse tabby weave with up to 12 by 15 threads per cm and a twined fabric of more primitive appearance were consistently associated. The exceptional survival of the woven fabrics in an adverse climate contrasts with the long, historically continuous record of textile finds in Egypt, which is explained, at least in part, by the preservative effects of hyperarid climate and extremely elaborate burial customs.

The fibre of the fragment from the Fayum Neolithic was identified as flax; that it is *Linum usitatissimum*, the cultivated species, was confirmed by examination of flax seed from the site.[7] The lightly spun yarn is two-ply in both warp and weft. The weave is a coarse, rather even tabby (warp 20 to 25, weft 25 to 30 threads per inch, or about 8 to 10 by 10 to 12 per cm). Almost all the woven fabrics which have been found in the burials of ancient Egypt, from Predynastic to Graeco-Roman times, are likewise linen.[8] All are in tabby weave, often varied with different combinations of multiple sheds and yarns of different character. Examination of pieces from Badarian and Predynastic graves in Upper Egypt (roughly 4000 to 3000 B.C.) suggests that the textile tradition was unbroken, with technical improvement over the centuries, until its extraordinary refinement in Dynasty I (about 3000 B.C.). We see progressively finer yarn, with more expert preparation of the fibre and firmer and more even spinning, always as in later times with S-twist, usually plyed Z; plying, particularly in the weft, became less frequent as the yarn became stronger. The evenness of the yarn invites speculation that the advanced spinning techniques with dropped spindle, known from wall pictures and models of the Middle Kingdom, were already developed before Dynasty I (the conical or barrel-shaped stone whorls which are frequently found in Predynastic settlements are similar to those employed in the later periods). The weaving became finer, and the warp threads, at first approximately equal in number to the weft, became relatively more numerous, a feature that is characteristic of ancient Egyptian textiles. A fragment from a grave of the Badari culture has 34 warp threads and 22 weft threads per inch (about 14 by 9 per cm); fragments from late Predynastic graves at Gerza and Badari have about 88 by 50 per inch (about 35 by 20 per cm), and one from the tomb of Djer, third king of Dynasty I, at Abydos, has 160 by 120 per inch (64 by 48 per cm).[9] There seems to be little doubt that a horizontal ground-loom is figured in the painted decoration of a dish of early Predynastic date (Naqada I) from a woman's grave. This type of loom is represented with greater precision in the scenes of textile manufacture of the Middle Kingdom. It is undoubtedly the loom on which all three of the pieces about to be discussed were woven.[10]

The three pieces in the Royal Ontario Museum are among thirty-one specimens of textiles selected for accessioning in 1944–1945, when the writer was carrying out an initial survey of the museum's Egyptian collection. At that time the collection included large quantities of undocumented "archaeological" material acquired by Dr. C.T.

Currelly in Egypt before 1911, when the museum was yet to be realized, and its accession records were virtually nonexistent. In 1945 it was debatable whether everything should be accessioned. Included among the thirty-one selected examples of textiles are six different types of fringe, a blue weft border, interwoven beads, and other features which appeared on superficial examination to be of interest. Few can as yet be shown to have an exact provenance, although it is probable that most were acquired at Deir el-Bahri, Thebes, between 1905 and 1907.[11] The number of warp and weft threads per inch (here converted to centimetres) was first determined in 1944–1945 by D.K. MacDonald (Mrs. H.B. Burnham), who also examined the twist of the yarn and the construction of the fringes. The present paper does not include a complete technical report; it is rather intended to suggest possibilities for future research among the textile fragments stored in the museum's Egyptian Department: others, as yet "undiscovered", may prove to be as interesting as these three examples.

Acc. no. 910.85.223

Fragment of fine, bleached linen cloth (figs. 1, 3).
Slightly stained and discoloured light brown. All edges raw and ragged.
Greatest length: 6 cm.
Late Dynasty III or early Dynasty IV (ca. 2650 B.C.).
From W.M.F. Petrie's excavations at Maidum, 1910.
Unlike the rest of the textiles in the museum's Egyptian Department, which were stored on cupboard shelves without covering or container, this fragment was found isolated in a small glass phial. On a piece of paper inside the phial was a note in an unidentified handwriting: "Meydum, M.W. of Ra-hetep. III Dyn." The accession book also states "Petrie's name on bottle", but neglects to say in what form. Currelly was in Egypt in the winter of 1910, when Petrie was working at Maidum, and it is possible that the gift was made on the spot, before samples were sent to W.W. Midgley, a textile specialist at the Bolton Museum (Lancashire). The tombs from which came the Maidum textiles of 1910 were situated close to the great mastabas of Re-hotpe and

Figure 1.   Linen cloth. Greatest length 6 cm. Late Dynasty III or early Dynasty IV (ca. 2650 B.C.).
ROM acc. no. 910.85.223.

Figure 2.   Linen cloth with herringbone pleating. Greatest length 30 cm. Dynasty XI (ca. 2000 B.C.) or earlier.
ROM acc. no. 907.18.20.

Nefermaat north of the pyramid. They were "minor mastabas and tombs down to the simplest hole in the ground". In the smaller, plundered tombs the textiles were unexpectedly well preserved because they escaped oxidation. Our fragment almost certainly came from this cemetery, but the tomb cannot be identified by name or number.[12]

There are about 55 warp and 26 weft threads per cm in this small piece of extremely fine fabric, enlarged fourteen times in the microphotograph (fig. 3). The yarn is very even and firmly twisted. We have no measurements for the diameter of the fibre, but it may reasonably be supposed that it is comparable to the finest of the Maidum specimens examined by Midgley, which has 120 by 42 threads per inch (48 by 16–17 per cm). Of the latter specimen ("Cloth D") Midgley wrote, "A white linen cloth, much cleaner than the others, and altogether finer texture: the mean diameter of the fibres in the weft indeed is finer than that of any present-day Irish linen I have measured."[13] When no selvages are preserved, warp cannot easily be distinguished from weft; thus they were sometimes mistaken for each other when only fragments were available for study. There are nearly always more warp threads to the centimetre in ancient Egyptian cloth; and since the weavers did not have a device for spacing these threads evenly, the warp tends to be denser towards the selvages of the fabric. Our fragment is too small for speculation upon its nearness to the middle of the cloth, but we may assume that the thicker, more variable yarn is the warp. Crowfoot published a microphotograph of a similar weave from Tarkhan, as an example of the great variety obtained by varying the size and quality of the yarn; she describes it as "a striped effect by thick soft warp used with almost invisible weft".[14] Across the middle of our fragment runs a conspicuous line of four or five weft threads in a single shed. Near each end there is a similar but lighter line of multiple weft threads, the three together suggesting another banded texturing at right angles to the first. There is no doubt that this cloth was woven with a continuously returning weft, as its quality alone would indicate; selvages on both sides survive on a piece dated to Naqada II and on at least one complete cloth of approximately the same date as ours.[15]

It is of course impossible to determine the dimensions of the cloth from which this fragment came, far less its function. But a few points may be considered, as an aid to inevitable speculation. The fragment is too fine, one might suppose, to have been manufactured expressly for the tomb, and there seems indeed to be evidence that in the Old Kingdom the dead were wrapped in garments of daily life and that used linen was sometimes placed in the coffin. A neat patch on one of three extra-large rectangular pieces of linen found with a burial of a slightly later period at Dishasha seems to prove that even these "winding sheets" had been used in the house or possibly as wrap-around garments.[16] Smaller rectangular pieces, more certainly designed as wrap-around garments, as well as simple tunics, were frequently found by Petrie at Dishasha and elsewhere. Describing the well-preserved burials in the Maidum cemetery from which our own piece probably came, MacKay wrote:

In the case of the men a short kilt was the article of clothing most generally found. The women were either wrapped or clothed in a garment which entirely covered the body and were then sometimes laid upon a pad or mattress of linen material, placed on the floor of the grave. The kilts of the men were coarse. Women's clothing usually of much finer texture.[17]

He also noted that, exceptionally, traces of a longer garment of fine linen were found over the coarser man's kilt. In view of its quality and the apparent predominance of clothing over other linen recovered in this excavation, our piece may in all probability be considered the vestige of a costume, either a woman's tunic or a wrap-around garment worn by a woman or perhaps by a man.

Acc. no. 907.18.20

Fragment of fine, bleached linen cloth, in fine herringbone pleating (fig. 2).

Stained and discoloured from light to dark brown. All edges raw. The pleating is unevenly preserved and can best be seen on the left half and middle bottom parts of the fragment.

Greatest length: 30 cm.

Probably from the tomb of King Nebhepetre Mentuhotpe, Dynasty XI (ca. 2000 B.C.).

Egypt Exploration Fund excavations at Deir el-Bahri, Thebes, 1906–1907.

Figure 3. Microphotograph of cloth shown in figure 1. Magnified fourteen times actual size. Late Dynasty III or early Dynasty IV (ca. 2650 B.C.).

Figure 4. Microphotograph of cloth shown in figure 5. Magnified fourteen times actual size. Dynasty XI (ca. 2000 B.C.).

Fragments of simple accordion pleating have frequently been reported from ancient Egypt, but I know of only one example of herringbone pleating, and that is without provenance. It is therefore particularly unfortunate that the piece in the Royal Ontario Museum lacks absolute documentation. Its antiquity cannot be doubted, nor can the fact that it came from Egypt through Dr. Currelly; and, considering the nature of the material, it is extremely likely that it came directly from an excavation rather than from a dealer. In the accession book is the notation " 'From the tomb of Mentu-hotpe III' (C.T.C., Feb./45)".[18] I have found no verification of this information, which was delivered orally, but it is quite possible that some pieces among the museum's large quantity of ancient Egyptian linen came from there. Currelly participated in the excavation of Nebhepetre's tomb at Deir el-Bahri in the winter of 1906–1907, if indeed he was not in charge before Naville's arrival. In spite of the existence in the same mortuary temple of another great tunnelled structure more plausibly identified as a cenotaph, Naville did not believe that this hypogeum reaching westward far beneath the cliff from its entrance in the colonnaded court was the actual tomb of the king. He called its shrine a sanctuary for the king's *ka* statue because it was too small to contain a stone sarcophagus, an argument no longer accepted. The plunderers had almost completely cleaned out this chamber, but Naville reported the finding of "heaps of mummy cloths. I believe they were the garments or the wrappings of the *ka*." Currelly, in his book of reminiscences, reported of the same chamber, "Pieces of the finest linen I have ever seen, except a piece of prehistoric linen Petrie found, were scattered everywhere." He also recounted finding there the remains of many smashed wooden models representing daily activities, as well as bows and arrows broken into small pieces; some of this material demonstrably found its way to Toronto.[19]

The stained condition of our piece of herringbone pleating suggests that it came not from a statue but from a burial, and because such pleating is not known from later periods, it could scarcely have belonged to an intrusive burial. It is strange that the piece is not mentioned in Naville's report, and it is equally strange that it is not mentioned in

Currelly's popular account, for the latter made a point of describing the linen from this tomb and he seldom missed an opportunity to present an object so rare and so technically interesting. If not from Deir el-Bahri, the piece most probably came from one of Petrie's excavations; through Currelly, the museum even received Petrie material from excavations which took place before 1902, the year when Currelly became associated with Petrie. The most likely site would then be Dishasha, where Petrie examined in 1895 a series of tombs dated to Dynasties V–VI. I do not know what became of the "mass of kilted stuff eight and a half inches deep", "another piece of kilted stuff on the body", and a "finely pleated kilt", which he found there and published without illustration or adequate description.[20] However tantalizing such speculations may be, Dr. Currelly's orally given provenance, the tomb of Nebhepetre, must be provisionally accepted for our piece, although representations in sculpture suggest that the vogue for fine herringbone pleating flourished in the Old Kingdom, not later.[21]

The cloth is finely woven, with about 47 warp and 15 weft threads per cm. The primary accordion pleats are repeated at intervals of about 16 mm of the straight cloth; the secondary pleats are spaced evenly at right angles, slightly farther apart than the primary pleats. In spite of the poor condition of the fabric and the flattening out of the pleating, the regularity and evenness of the pleats in both directions are visible on the photograph.

The only other existing specimen of actual herringbone pleating known to me is in the Cairo Museum.[22] It is covered with bands of plain accordion pleats alternating with bands formed by six herringbone pleats each. The piece is without provenance and, on obscure grounds, has been attributed variously to the Middle and to the New Kingdom. The way in which the herringbone pleating was produced is unknown, nor is there even agreement about the technique of the simpler but very fine and even accordion pleating. Although the production of the herringbone would have manifestly been much more difficult, an obvious hypothesis is that a second series of pleats was superimposed at right angles by the same method. The suggestion was once made that a corrugated wooden board of unknown provenance or date in the Flor-

ence Archaeological Museum may have served as a mechanical device in the production of accordion pleating, but this has not met with general acceptance. An equally enigmatic problem is whether a fixative, such as modern laundry starch, was used to preserve the pleats. Staehelin has cautiously suggested that a gelatin solution may have been used, which would account for the yellow colouring of the pleated overlap on many of the kilts represented, a detail elsewhere interpreted as gilding.[23] However complicated the unknown pleating techniques may have been, one consideration should not be overlooked: the ancient Egyptians had at their disposal labour so abundant and so skilled that constant washing and re-pleating would have been no problem. Modern analogy points to skilful fingerwork.[24]

It is highly probable that this rare piece of pleated linen was once part of a man's kilt. If indeed it was found in the tomb of Nebhepetre it must have come from the coffin of the king himself and doubtless was part of the fully pleated royal *shendyet* kilt. If, however, it came from Dishasha and not from Deir el-Bahri, it would have come from a private tomb, and probably from a nobleman's ceremonial half-pleated kilt. There is no doubt whatever that it was part of a garment, for it may safely be assumed that all pleated material found in ancient Egyptian tombs was designed for personal wear.

Acc. no. 906.18.41

Rectangular garment of fine, bleached linen cloth, with selvage fringe on one long side (figs. 4, 5).

Colour well preserved and free from stains. The piece is almost complete; worn very thin in places, with a few holes; a small section of the fringe is torn or cut off at one end.

Length of garment: 322 cm; width of garment without fringe: 117 cm; length of fringe: about 6 cm.

Dynasty XI (ca. 2000 B.C.).

From the tomb of Henhenet (No. 11) in the mortuary temple of King Nebhepetre Mentuhotpe.

Egypt Exploration Fund excavations at Deir el-Bahri, Thebes, 1904–1905.

The identification of this piece rests mainly on a modern mark, "Henhenet", faintly visible in pencil

Figure 5.   Rectangular linen garment. Dimensions of whole garment 22 by 123 cm. Dimensions of folded part visible 68 by 41 cm (including fringe). Dynasty XI (ca. 2000 B.C.). ROM acc. no. 906.18.41.

on the surface of the cloth. Henhenet was one of the six youthful members of Nebhepetre's *harim* buried in a row of six tombs along the eastern edge of the colonnaded court of his mortuary temple.[25] Describing Henhenet's burial, Ayrton stated: "Within the sarcophagus was the mummy of a woman, no doubt Henhenet herself, lying on the cloth wrappings," and he made no further mention of linen from her tomb. In *I brought the ages home*, Currelly wrote that Henhenet had been found "lying on a pile of her wrappings and two of her shawls. . . . In the ultimate division Henhenet's two shawls, one of them very expensive fine linen, were sent to Toronto."[26] One only of these "shawls", the piece described here, has been identified, and it must surely be the finer and more complete of the two. A few linen cloths of Dynasty XI date, including pieces from Henhenet's burial, bear ancient marks identifying the owner, the weaver, or the official in charge of royal linen supplies.[27] Examination has not revealed any such mark on this garment.

The weave has about 40 warp and 21 weft threads per cm. In the microphotograph (fig. 4) it is enlarged fourteen times, i.e., to the same degree as the first of the Royal Ontario Museum fragments (fig. 3). As we have seen, the latter has about 55 warp and 26 weft threads per cm. Comparison of the two microphotographs clearly illustrates the better quality of the Maidum piece, which is more than six hundred years older; but Henhenet's garment is made of cloth which is also very fine. In figure 5, this garment is folded to show an area of 68 (including the fringe) by 41 cm. The photograph may perhaps convey something of the quality that is still visibly impressive in spite of the delicate condition of the fabric. The selvage fringe was made during the weaving by continuously running through the selvage a group of extra threads which shortly turn back and emerge from the weave again; the depth of the 6 cm fringe thus formed was probably controlled by passing the threads around a rod or cord; the fringe was finished by twisting its threads in groups of about 100.[28] The opposite selvage is plain and even. One end of the piece has an unravelled edge bordered by four heavy multiple sheds, and the other end has a fine rolled hem.

The dimensions of the piece and the fine finish on all sides leave no doubt that it is a garment, and it

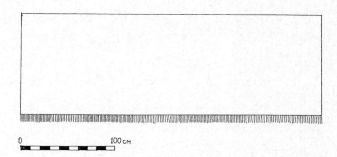

could only be of a wrap-around type.[29] It is too long to be a mantle falling from the shoulders, a costume not known to have been worn by women of the Middle Kingdom although frequently worn by men of that period. Experimenting with a modern piece of cloth of the same dimensions, the writer found that our garment would have gone more than three times around the hips of the lady Henhenet, and would have been about the right length for an "empire waistline" fitting beneath the breasts. Because it is of the finest quality, it was probably designed for life, and it was probably even worn in life. It is difficult, perhaps impossible, to distinguish marks of ancient wear in the present imperfect condition of the piece; but the garment has clearly been under greatest strain on either side of the median line through its length, where many small damages appear in thin areas; the corners at the fringe side show slight radial creases, as if gathered; and the fringe is tattered at the surviving end.

Long wrap-around garments, sometimes draped over the left shoulder, appear very frequently on sculptured representations of men of the Middle Kingdom, but this type of dress is seldom seen on representations of women of any period. A unique example is the limestone statue of Khamerernebty I, queen of Cheops,[30] who wears a pleated mantle wrapped around her body and carried diagonally over her right shoulder. I know of only one other representation of a feminine garment that can clearly be identified as the long rectangular type of wrap-around: the diorite statuette of the nurse Sat-Sneferu, Dynasty XII, in the Metropolitan Museum of Art.[31] Considering that the long rectangular fringed wrap-around for women has not been identified elsewhere in sculpture of the Middle Kingdom, we might be tempted to re-examine the simple form-fitting sheath dress of the Old Kingdom, which survived long afterwards in religious and funerary art and was probably still fashionable in the Middle Kingdom. Its high skirt often appears to be distinct from its shoulder straps or bodice and perhaps, in some cases at least, this dress was actually a wrap-around, as Riefstahl has recently suggested.[32]

In conclusion, I should like to summarize the points of interest which I believe these three examples of unpatterned fabric reveal.

The first piece (acc. no. 910.85.223) has a remarkably fine weave. Considering the number of its weft threads, it is unaccountably finer than any of the linen from the same excavations (Petrie, Maidum, 1910) submitted to microscopic examination. It is from an undistinguished group of private tombs, but for this very reason the quality of the fabric is the more remarkable. A piece of cloth from a private tomb at Dishasha, probably of Dynasty VI date, has a weave of 93 by 44 threads per inch (37 by 17–18 per cm). Writing of this piece as an exceptionally fine weave, Petrie commented: "None of these stuffs is as fine as the royal linen of the VIth Dynasty because they are only the common products used by ordinary people." [33] This line of reasoning dramatizes the superiority of our Maidum piece over the royal linen of Henhenet, shown graphically by comparison of the microphotographs (figs. 3, 4). I have found no reports of microscopic examination of royal linen of the Old Kingdom earlier than Dynasty VI, and these do not approach in quality the single piece of cloth from the tomb of King Djer, which Petrie stated had 160 by 120 threads per inch (64 by 48 threads per cm), as quoted above. For its weft the Djer piece is comparable to textiles from the tomb of Tutankhamun, which have about 280 by 80 threads per inch (about 112 by 32 threads per cm).[34] Our small fragment contributes to the general impression received from the textiles, as from other industrial products of the times, that the highly developed arts of the early Dynastic and early Old Kingdom periods, from which comparatively little has survived, equalled in virtuosity, if they did not excel, the skills inherited from them by later craftsmen. The linen lists of the Old Kingdom, which give names and numbers for many different types of cloth, suggest a great variety of quality,

width, and colour for the linen of the Old Kingdom.[35] The advanced spinning and weaving techniques pictured in tombs of the Middle Kingdom surprisingly do not appear on the walls of Old Kingdom tombs, although technical examination of actual pieces shows that these techniques must have already existed then. A possible explanation for the late appearance of such scenes may be that fine spinning and weaving began as an industry of the *harim*, to which artists had no access.[36] A comprehensive technical study of all dated specimens of Archaic and Old Kingdom cloth, wherever these may be found, should establish the pattern of ancient development where now we have little more than ground for speculation.

The second piece (acc. no. 907.18.20) is to my knowledge unique. The fragment in Cairo, perhaps the only other surviving piece of herringbone pleating, is in bands of herringbone alternating with plain accordion pleating, while our piece is clearly uniform in design. The Cairo fragment is without provenance; ours is probably from the tomb of Nebhepetre, with the possibility that it is from an earlier private tomb at Dishasha. Its publication may perhaps elicit news of other unpublished pieces of herringbone pleating in neglected collections.

The third piece (acc. no. 906.18.41) is of fine quality and is an excellent example of a fringed wrap-around garment. It deserves attention for its completeness and for its connection with a lady of King Nebhepetre's *harim*. Many garments of its type, with selvage fringe, are known from the Old and Middle Kingdoms, varying somewhat in dimensions, and worn by both men and women. The chief interest of the piece is the problem of how it relates to the feminine costume of its period, as known from the monuments, and I wonder whether wraparound garments may not have been worn more frequently by women of the Middle Kingdom than has been supposed.

All three cloths were undoubtedly designed as garments. In their lack of colour, they are typical of the great majority of ancient Egyptian garments known to us, both masculine and feminine.[37] Linen, the favourite if not the only dress material, cannot be satisfactorily dyed without a mordant, and the Egyptians probably had no knowledge of mordants until a relatively late period. There may have been a causal connection, possibly in both directions, between the ancient Egyptians' extraordinary love of brightly coloured jewellery and their use of natural linen as a dress material, for both these elements of costume enjoyed a long tradition in ancient Egypt and were ideally suited to each other.

Acknowledgments

My first thanks are due to Dr. N.B. Millet, Curator of the Egyptian Department in the Royal Ontario Museum, for permission to publish the three specimens discussed in this paper, and for his constant help and advice. Without the generous assistance of Mrs. Dorothy Burnham, to whom I have been indebted since I first "discovered" these textiles in 1944, Mr. Mark Burnham, and Mrs. K.B. Brett, all textile specialists in the Royal Ontario Museum, this paper could not have been written; for errors in statements relating to textile techniques I must take full responsibility, as unforeseen commitments and illness made it difficult to request, and to receive, as much assistance as we all should have wished. Mr. Leigh Warren, Head Photographer of the ROM, took the five excellent photographs. I am grateful to all members of the staff of the Egyptian Department for their attention to many small matters, and particularly to Mr. Alan Hollett for his assistance with the physical examination of the three pieces.

Notes

1. E. Riefstahl (*Patterned textiles in pharaonic Egypt*, Brooklyn, Brooklyn Museum, 1944, pp. 1, 6–19) summarizes the occasional patterning in textiles earlier than the New Kingdom.

2. P.E. Newberry, *Beni Hasan I*, Egypt Exploration Fund Archaeological Survey, vol. 1, London, 1893, pls. 30, 31; N.M. Davies and A.H. Gardiner, *Ancient Egyptian paintings*, vol. 1, Chicago, University of Chicago Press, 1936, pls. 10, 11. The polychrome patterns of the garments in this well-known scene are arranged in vertical strips, which appear to represent lengths of fabric woven on a narrow loom and sewn together. Very similar patterns are found today on traditional garments from Ghana and other parts of West Africa (e.g., ROM acc. no. 966.14.19). Their resemblance to the costume of the Beni Hasan bedouin has been pointed out to the writer by Harold and Dorothy Burnham.

3. The New Kingdom vertical loom is known from scenes in three private tombs at Thebes (nos. 50, 80, 133). It is different from the warp-weighted vertical loom of ancient Greece and northern Europe, for the weft is beaten downward to a breast beam. Representations of the horizontal ground-loom are unknown after Dynasty XII, although it must have continued in use. Both types of loom survived into the twentieth century of our era in Egypt, the horizontal with the bedouin and the vertical in the villages. Fragments of both types were found in houses of New Kingdom date at El-Lisht (W. C. Hayes, *The scepter of Egypt*, pt. 1, New York, Metropolitan Museum of Art, 1953, p. 218). For the vertical loom's probable use in the New Kingdom for unpatterned as well as for patterned cloth, see: C.H. Johl, *Altägyptische Webestühle und Brettchenweberei*, Untersuchungen zur Geschichte und Altertumskunde Aegyptens, vol. 8, Leipzig, Hinrichs, 1924, p. 54; L. Klebs, *Die Reliefs und Malereien des neuen Reiches*, Abhandlungen der Heidelberger Akademie der Wissenschaften, philologisch-historische Klasse, 9, Heidelberg, 1934, p. 187.

4. Riefstahl (*Patterned textiles*, 1944, pp. 20–48) discusses in detail the patterned textiles of Dynasty XVIII and later. A piece from the tomb of Tuthmosis IV, possibly an heirloom, shows the tapestry woven cartouche of his father, Amenophis II (ca. 1450–1423 B.C.), but the earliest known woven pattern is probably the warp-patterned braid of the saddle-cloth found in the tomb of Queen Hatshepsut's favorite, Senenmut (ca. 1500 B.C.), at Deir el-Bahri, Thebes (A. Lansing and W.C. Hayes, "The Museum's excavations at Thebes", *Bulletin of the Metropolitan Museum of Art*, vol. 32, January 1937, section 2, p. 14, fig. 15).

5. For recent radiocarbon dating of Fayum A Neolithic (four samples) from stratified deposits see: F. Wendorf, R. Said, and R. Schild, "Egyptian prehistory: Some new concepts", *Science*, vol. 169 (1970), pp. 1161–1171; R.M. Derricourt, "Radiocarbon chronology for Egypt and North Africa", *Journal of Near Eastern Studies*, vol. 30 (1971), pp. 271-292.

6. H.B. Burnham, "Çatal Hüyük — the textiles and twined fabrics", *Anatolian Studies*, vol. 15 (1965), pp. 169-174.

7. G. Caton-Thompson and E.W. Gardner, *The desert Fayum*, 2 vols., London, Royal Anthropological Institute, 1934, pp. 46, 49 and pl. 28, no. 3. Analytical summaries of what is known about the textile industry in ancient Egypt may be found in: G.M. Crowfoot, "Textiles, basketry and mats", in C. Singer, E.J. Holmyard, and A.R. Hall, eds., *A history of technology*, vol. 1, Oxford, Clarendon, 1958, pp. 413-447; A. Lucas and H.R. Harris, *Ancient Egyptian materials*, 4th ed. rev., London, Arnold, 1962, pp. 140-154.

8. A few early pieces have been identified as grass, hemp, or reed fibre (ramie has recently been ruled out; Lucas and Harris, *Ancient Egyptian materials*, 1962, pp. 149-150). The general absence of woollen fabrics and of scenes concerning wool production from Egyptian tombs of all periods until Christian times is perhaps explained, following Herodotus (2: 81), by religious proscription, which might have had its origin in the perishable nature of wool. Whether Egyptians of the high periods sometimes wore white woollen mantles over their linen garments in daily life is a matter of dispute. The inconclusive evidence for wool is presented by Lucas and Harris (*Ancient Egyptian materials*, 1962, pp. 146-147). I find it difficult to believe that woollen mantles were not occasionally worn on chilly evenings by the elite of the early periods, for example by the princess Nofret of early Dynasty IV in her famous painted limestone statue (Cairo CG 4, from Maidum), when the woollen garments of high-ranking Asiatics must have been known to the court, and superior Asiatic wool was produced in neighbouring sheep country with which the Egyptians were in close contact.

9. T. Midgley in G. Brunton and G. Caton-Thompson, *The Badarian civilisation and Predynastic remains near Badari*, Egyptian Research Account publications, 46, London, 1928, pp. 64–66 (Badari culture, ca. 4000 B.C. and Naqada II, ca. 3400 B.C.); W.W. Midgley in W.M.F. Petrie, G.A. Wainwright, and E. MacKay, *The Labyrinth, Gerzeh and Mazghuneh*, Egyptian Research Account publications, 21, London, 1912, p. 6 (Naqada II); I have not found the primary source for the excavation and examination of the Djer piece, probably found by Petrie in 1900–1901; it is mentioned, with warp and weft count, in: W.M.F. Petrie, *The arts and crafts of ancient Egypt*, Edinburgh and London, Foulis, 1909, p. 147; and W.B. Emery, *Archaic Egypt*, Harmondsworth, Pelican Books, 1961, p. 223.

10. For the dish, in University College London, see: Brunton and Caton-Thompson, *Badarian civilisation* (1928), pp. 51, 54 and pl. 38; Crowfoot, *History of technology* (1958), pp. 438-439. For the unconvincing interpretation of the scene as the erection of a palisade, see: J. Vandier, *Manuel d'archéologie égyptienne*, vol. 1, Paris, Picard, 1952, pp. 285-286. The dish indeed seems to show a loom with the warp stretched between two beams pegged to the ground, three rows of weft, a rod-heddle and shed rod for forming the shed and countershed, and perhaps a sword beater for beating in the weft. Above the loom two workers are perhaps hanging yarn over a horizontal pole in lengths of two sheds to produce a primitive selvage at one edge only, a hypoth-esis supported by the weft below. Tombs 3, 4, 15, and 17 at Beni Hasan, Tomb 2 at El-Bersha, and Tomb 103 at Thebes show scenes of weaving with similar looms in the Middle Kingdom, as well as roving, spinning, doubling, and warping; see: Crowfoot, *History of technology* (1958), pp. 438–439; and H. Ling Roth, *Ancient Egyptian and Greek looms*, Bankfield Museum Notes, 2d series, no. 2, Halifax, 1913, pp. 3–14. Wooden funerary models of the same date represent the same activities, notably one in Cairo from Tomb 280 at Thebes, and one of unknown provenance in the Metropolitan Museum of Art, New York (C.R. Clark, "Egyptian weaving in 2000 B.C.", *Bulletin of the Metropolitan Museum of Art*, vol. 3, 1944, pp. 24–29).

11. Currelly was attached to the expedition of Naville and Hall at the mortuary temple of Nebhepetre, Deir el-Bahri, for the two seasons of 1905–1906 and 1906–1907, sponsored by the Egypt Exploration Fund. He was also in Egypt during the winter of 1907–1908. During these three years, his collecting activities for the future Royal Ontario Museum reached a peak, while his association with Petrie had impressed upon him the importance of "common objects" (C.T. Currelly, *I brought the ages home*, Toronto, Ryerson Press, 1956, reprinted by the Royal Ontario Museum, 1976, pp. 125-156; W. Needler, "Sir Flinders Petrie and the Royal Ontario Museum", *Canadian Forum*, June 1953, pp. 61–62).

12. For the cemetery see: W.M.F. Petrie, E. MacKay, and G.A. Wainwright, *Meydum and Memphis III*, Egyptian Research Account publications, 18, London, 1910, pp. 6, 29, and pl. 1 (site plan); B. Porter and R. Moss, *Topographical bibliography of ancient Egyptian hieroglyphic texts, reliefs and paintings*, vol. 4, Oxford, Clarendon Press, 1934, p. 88 (key plan of Maidum, "North Cemetery of Petrie"). For further comments on the preservative action of sand, see: W.M.F. Petrie, *Deshasheh*, Egypt Exploration Fund memoirs, 15, London, 1898, p. 31. The examination of nine type specimens of cloth from this cemetery was reported separately (see note 13). For Currelly's presence in Egypt in 1910, see: Currelly, *I brought the ages home* (1956), pp. 184, 187 (he does not mention meeting Petrie then, but since he remained closely in touch with him it would be strange if he had not visited Maidum on this occasion, when he was still intent on acquiring Egyptian archaeological material).

13. W.W. Midgley, "Linen of the IIIrd Dynasty", in E.B. Knobel et al., *Historical studies*, British School of Archaeology in Egypt Studies, 2, London, 1911, p. 38 and pls. 2, 4. He found no trace of selvage on any of his pieces; his findings of consistent and marked preponderance of weft over warp threads per inch do not correspond with the general ratio pattern obtained by other and more recent investigators, and should be reversed for most, if not all, specimens. He also examined twenty specimens from Petrie's excavations at Tarkhan, mostly of Early Dynastic date (W.M.F. Petrie and E. MacKay, *Heliopolis, Kafr Ammar and Shurafa*, Egyptian Research Account publications, 24, London, 1915, pp. 48–51).

14. Crowfoot, *History of technology* (1958), p. 434 and pl. 11B. An irregular feature in our piece that helps to identify the warp is the isolated appearance of a pair of threads in one shed: cf. Petrie and MacKay, *Heliopolis, Kafr Ammar and Shurafa* (1915), p. 49 and pl. 58, fig. 9; and Brunton and Caton-Thompson, *Badarian civilization* (1928), pp. 64–65.

15. Crowfoot, *History of technology* (1958), pp. 431, 434, from Badari (Naqada II) and Tarkhan (Dynasty III).

16. Petrie, *Deshasheh* (1898), p. 32. The patched "sheet" measured 865 by 117.5 cm; it had a selvage fringe and a plain selvage on the sides, and a rolled hem at each end.

17. Petrie, MacKay, and Wainwright, *Meydum and Memphis III* (1910), p. 29.

18. The recorded quotation marks signify an oral reply to a question; it is not surprising, in view of the thousands of objects which he collected in Egypt, as well as the thirty-five or more intervening years, that Currelly's memory for specific objects required verification (this comment is not intended to belittle the valuable information that he was able to deliver informally).

19. E. Naville, *The XIth Dynasty temple at Deir el-Bahri* pt. 2, Egypt Exploration Fund memoirs, 30, London, 1910, pp. 3–5; Currelly, *I brought the ages home* (1956), pp. 143–145; for a more recent and authoritative description of the tomb see: I.E.S. Edwards, *The pyramids of Egypt*, 2d ed. rev., London, Parrish, 1961, p. 173. Currelly's anecdotal account should be taken seriously because in all probability he was the actual excavator of the tomb, as he affirms, without receiving due credit. The only hint in Naville's report that Currelly may have excavated the tomb is the statement: "During three weeks in December, 1906, before my arrival, Mr. Currelly, assisted by Mr. Dennis, was in charge of the excavations."

20. Petrie, *Deshasheh* (1898), p. 16.

21. I have found no representations of this kind of pleating that are dated later than the Old Kingdom; its disappearance may be due to changing fashions in art rather than in costume. It is represented frequently on statuary and relief sculpture of the Old Kingdom; on these it is mostly confined to the *shendyet* kilt, worn by kings, and to the ceremonial half-pleated kilt, worn by noblemen (Vandier, *Manuel*, vol. 1, 1952, pp. 106–110; E. Staehelin, *Untersuchungen zur ägyptischen Tracht im Alten Reich*, Münchner ägyptologische Studien, 8, Berlin, 1966, pp. 13–14). Staehelin notes two ways in which herringbone pleating is represented on the half-pleated kilt of the Old Kingdom: (1) in the great majority of examples, the primary pleats run across the width of the wrap-around garment and therefore appear vertical but radiating slightly at the curved end that is secured to the girdle; and (2) in a few sculptures of Dynasty III date, the primary pleats run parallel to the curved hemline of the garment. Both variations are meticulously represented in Hesy-

Re's series of sculptured wooden panels from Ṣaqqara (J.E. Quibell, *The tomb of Hesy*, Excavations at Saqqara, 1911-1912, Cairo, Service des Antiquités, 1913, pl. 29, nos. 1, 2; and pl. 30, nos. 3, 4). Herringbone pleating is also seen in at least two sculptures of the Old Kingdom representing women (Staehelin, *Tracht*, 1966, p. 13).

22. Cairo, JE 51513; W. Spiegelberg, "Altägyptische gefältete (plissierte) Leinwandstoffe", *Annales du Service des Antiquités de l'Egypte*, vol. 27 (1927), p. 156 and pl. 2, no. 3; K.H. Dittmann, "Eine Mantelstatue aus der Zeit der 4 Dynastie", *Mitteilungen des Deutschen Archäologischen Instituts Abteilung Kairo*, vol. 8 (1939), pl. 25b; Staehelin, *Tracht* (1966), fig. 20. Several fragments of simple accordion pleating have survived: e.g., H.E. Winlock, *Excavations at Deir el-Bahri, 1911–1931*, New York, Macmillan, 1942, p. 101 and pl. 36, no. 4 (from the tomb of Neferu, Dynasty XI); A.C. Mace and H.E. Winlock, *The tomb of Senebtisi at Lisht*, Metropolitan Museum of Art Egyptian Expedition publications, 1, New York, 1916, p. 42, fig. 25 (from Dahshur, Dynasty XII), and others of uncertain provenance, including one in the Royal Ontario Museum (acc. no. 907.18.19). In all of the above fragments the pleats probably ran vertically, but several complete tunics from different excavations, dated Dynasty VI to XI, are covered with horizontal pleating; they have been discussed by E. Riefstahl ("A note on ancient fashions; four early Egyptian dresses in the Museum of Fine Arts, Boston", *Bulletin of the Museum of Fine Arts*, vol. 68, 1970, pp. 244–249), who believes that they all probably came from female burials. H. Bonnet's suggestion that they may have been nightdresses (*Die ägyptische Tracht bis zum Ende des neuen Reiches*, Untersuchungen zur Geschichte und Altertumskunde Aegyptens, vol. 7, no. 2, Leipzig, Hinrichs, 1917, p. 61) seems plausible to the present writer in view of their warmth, and the unsuitability of sagging horizontal pleats for anything but a recumbent position. (Dr. Gervers, however, has recently shown me postcard photographs of voluminous horizontally pleated men's trousers and women's sleeves, from near Pisarovina in Croatia, Yugoslavia. See also V. Kirin, *Narodne nošnje Jugoslavije*, vol. 3, *Hrvatska*, Zagreb, Naklada Naša Djeca, n.d., pl. 10, man's costume from Donja Kupčina.)

23. The hypothesis of the pleating board, proposed by A. Erman in 1885, is mentioned briefly by Staehelin (*Tracht*, 1966, p. 14) and Riefstahl (*Bulletin of the Museum of Fine Arts*, 1970, p. 249). For the suggestion of gelatin see: Staehelin, *Tracht* (1966), pp. 14–15. Our piece of herringbone pleating was examined by Bernard Leech, former Curator of Conservation in the Royal Ontario Museum, for possible traces of a fixative; he reported negative but inconclusive results. It has been suggested that the yellow colouring of the kilt's overlap may represent "cloth of gold" (A. Erman and H. Ranke, *Aegypten und ägyptisches Leben im Altertum*, 2d ed. rev., Tübingen, Mohr, 1923, p. 235; E. Riefstahl, "An additional footnote on pleating in ancient Egypt", *American Research Center in Egypt Newsletter*, no. 92, Winter 1975, pp. 28–29); this is not convincing, for the colour appears only on the pleated part of the kilt.

24. I have found no mention of herringbone pleating from any other culture, ancient or modern. But fine accordion pleating was produced in secluded villages of Central Europe down to the beginning of the present century. In her paper for the annual meeting of the American Research Center in Egypt (*ARCE Newsletter*, no. 92, 1975, pp. 28–29) Mrs. Riefstahl quotes a letter from Harold B. Burnham reporting, on the basis of field information, that this accordion pleating was formed with the fingers and without the use of any fixative. Dr. Gervers has recently brought to my attention, in addition to the photographs mentioned in note 22, the description of an exhibit illustrating traditional pleated costume and its production in northern Croatia (M. Gušić, *Commentary on the exhibited material*, Zagreb Ethnographical Museum, 1955, p. 40): "Each fold (when wet) is smoothed and pleated with the fingers; it is then beaten with a small stone fold by fold, after which the pleats are pressed with a shallow wooden trough, weighted down with a large smooth clean stone." Miss Nora Scott of the Metropolitan Museum of Art, an Egyptologist well acquainted with ancient Egyptian pleating, told me that many years ago, for a college festival, she successfully pleated with her fingers a light material of approximately the same weight as the ancient Egyptian linen, keeping the cloth soaking wet, and rolling it with a twist to dry; the pleats stayed in without the aid of a fixative; the experiment was not extended to herringbone pleating.

25. For location and description of these tombs and their respective shrines above ground see: E.R. Ayrton in E. Naville and H.R. Hall, *The XIth Dynasty temple at Deir el-Bahari*, pt. 1, Egypt Exploration Fund memoirs, 28, London, 1907, pp. 50–51; Hayes, *Scepter*, pt. 1 (1953), pp. 160–162; Edwards, *The pyramids of Egypt* (1961), pp. 172–173. The six tombs were excavated the year before Currelly joined Naville's party. In their inscriptions each of the six ladies claims to be "Sole Favorite of the King"; Henhenet was also "Priestess of Hathor".

26. Naville and Hall, *XIth Dynasty temple*, pt. 2 (1907), p. 50; Currelly, *I brought the ages home* (1956), p. 146.

27. Winlock, *Excavations at Deir el Bahri* (1942), pp. 101-104; H.E. Winlock, *The slain soldiers of Neb-hepet-Rē' Mentu-hotpe*, Metropolitan Museum of Art Egyptian Expedition Publications, 16, New York, 1945, pp. 25–30 and pls. 13–20; Hayes, *Scepter*, pt. 1 (1953), p. 260; Dieter Arnold, "Sechster Vorbericht über die vom Deutschen Archäologischen Institut Kairo in Qurna unternommenen Arbeiten (8 Kampagne)", *Mitteilungen des Deutschen Archäologischen Instituts Abteilung Kairo*, vol. 27 (1971), p. 127.

28. Selvage fringes of this type were made from Dynasty III on (Crowfoot, *History of technology*, 1958, p. 434). Throughout pharaonic times, unpatterned linen showed a great variety of fringe design. In the initial survey of the Royal Ontario Museum's specimens, six distinct types of warp and weft fringes were found. See also: A. Braulik, *Altägyptische Gewebe*, Stuttgart, Bergsträsser, 1900, pp. 12–19; Winlock, *Slain soldiers* (1945), pls. 13–20.

29. Fringed, rectangular, wrap-around garments, found in both male and female burials dated from Dynasty III through Dynasty XII, have freqeuntly survived, e.g., Petrie, *Deshasheh* (1898), p. 32; Petrie and MacKay, *Heliopolis, Kafr Ammar and Shurafa* (1915), pp. 48–50; Hayes, *Scepter*, pt. 1 (1953), p. 304. A few cloths identified as "sheets" elsewhere may actually have been such garments.

30. Dittmann, *Mitteilungen des Deutschen Archäologischen Instituts Abteilung Kairo* (1939), pp. 165–170, from Giza, in Cairo (JE 48828); J. Vandier, *Manuel d'archéologie égyptienne*, vol. 3, Paris, Picard, 1958, pl. 9, no. 4. The wrap-around overgarment has simple accordion pleating; the tunic beneath it has herringbone pleating.

31. Metropolitan Museum of Art, New York, acc. no. 18.2.2. H.G. Evers, *Staat aus dem Stein*, vol. 1, Munich, Brückmann, 1929, p. 209, and pl. 62; Hayes, *Scepter*, pt. 1 (1953), p. 215; W.S. Smith, *Interconnections in the ancient Near East*, New Haven, Yale University Press, 1965, p. 14 and fig. 23. The statuette was found at Adana in southeastern Anatolia, but it is in Egyptian style and of Egyptian stone; it was undoubtedly made in ancient Egypt for an Egyptian. The ankle-length garment, which shows a selvage fringe on its upper edge, is wrapped around the body, under the breasts and right arm, across the back, and over the left shoulder. The conventionally represented fringe on this and other wrap-around garments of Middle Kingdom statuary has sometimes been called a braid (e.g., Vandier, *Manuel*, vol. 3, 1958, p. 253), an interpretation without external support.

32. Riefstahl, "A note on ancient fashions" (1970), p. 246: "The Old Kingdom sheath dress was a single-seam rectangle or perhaps simply a wrap-around."

33. Petrie, *Deshasheh* (1898), p. 32.

34. R. Pfister, "Les textiles du tombeau de Toutankhamen", *Revue des arts asiatiques*, vol. 11 (1937), pp. 207–218. Technical examination of the pieces in the Graf collection (Braulik, *Altägyptische Gewebe*, 1900) included specimens of royal linen from Dynasty VI to the Late Period. None of these appears to be as fine as the Djer piece.

35. W.S. Smith, "The Old Kingdom linen list", *Zeitschrift für ägyptische Sprache und Altertumskunde*, vol. 71 (1935), pp. 134–149.

36. L. Klebs, *Die Reliefs und Malereien des mittleren Reiches*, Abhandlungen der Heidelberger Akademie der Wissenschaften, philologisch-historische Klasse, 6, Heidelberg, 1922, p. 127. The early depiction of looms (?) with coloured cloth in the inventory painting of Hesy-Re's tomb (Quibell, *Tomb of Hesy*, 1913, pp. 23–25 and pls. 12, 16–18, Dynasty III) deserves the attention of textile specialists, as do the completely enigmatic objects which, by their position beside these looms (?), seem also to be connected with textile manufacture.

37. Garments were not always white. Wall pictures of the Old Kingdom occasionally show women in dresses of a plain colour. Cloths of different plain colours were certainly manufactured then and later, as is known especially from the ancient lists of offerings; and actual specimens of coloured cloth, from various periods beginning with the Late Predynastic, have been reported (Riefstahl, *Patterned textiles*, 1944, pp. 1–2; Staehelin, *Tracht*, 1966, pp. 169–170).

A Closer View of Early Chinese Silks

Krishna Riboud

AS recently as ten years ago, it seemed quite impossible to break new ground in the study of early Chinese silk production, especially of silks dating from the Han Dynasty (206 B.C.– A.D. 220).[1] Ever since Sir Aurel Stein's momentous discovery in 1913 of abundant Han textiles at Lou-lan in the Tarim Basin, and the articles on ancient figured silks by his adviser, F. H. Andrews,[2] a number of essays, observations, and evaluations have been published. In 1925, among a wealth of other fabrics, P.K. Kozlov[3] discovered a group of Chinese patterned silks at the Hunnish site of Noin-Ula in northern Mongolia, which supplied a fresh impetus for further studies and assessments. In the last twenty-five years, archaeological activity in China has revealed an impressive quantity of silk and other fabrics from various sites. Notable Chinese finds of Han silks were made in 1959 at Old Niya (Minfeng) in the Uighur Autonomous Republic (Sinkiang), and in 1972 at Mawangdui in Chang-sha, Hunan Province.[4] It has been obvious to scholars from the start that among Han fabrics, monochrome and polychrome figured silks constitute the most significant finds from a technical point of view. In skill and concept, in diversity of design and colour, in experimentation with fibre and dye, these outstanding silks are proof of advanced weaving technology and a distinctive art form.

Judging from the known textile specimens as well as from literary evidence, it is obvious that its *de facto* monopoly in the production of silk goods was an important factor in the pride and prestige of the Han Empire. Nothing in the finished silks suggests a fortuitous stroke of luck or mere skilful cottage industry. Rather, these silks represent extremely exacting standards of production and imply the existence of controlled workshops. In reviewing the bibliography of early Chinese silk production, however, one becomes aware that the chronology of these silks is still obscure. The Han Dynasty covered more than four full centuries, and thus an attribution to the "Han period" remains imprecise and indistinct. Despite the *air de famille* of these figured silks, when examined in depth they reveal nuances and variations which show diverse subtleties, in both concept and conditions of execution.

It is not within the scope of the present essay to attribute definitive dates to specific silk groups or to attempt more than limited assumptions regarding their chronology. The intention is rather to provide a brief and comprehensive report on certain recurring technical and iconographic characteristics of these silks and, whenever possible, to make tentative suggestions regarding conditions of manufacture. This study deals with a small but significant group of monochrome and polychrome patterned silks, predominantly those excavated by Sir Aurel Stein and P.K. Kozlov, which are preserved respectively in the collections of the National Museum in New Delhi and the State Hermitage Museum in Leningrad. Regarding their technical aspects, stylistic features, and archaeological associations, these fabrics have been grouped according to their affinities. Reference has been made to other textile finds, which may ultimately be of interest from an art historical point of view.

Literary references to the use of silk in China provide plausible evidence to trace its existence back to

252

periods pre-dating the Han Dynasty.[5] Xia Nai[6] traces knowledge of the silkworm in China back to an oracle bone inscription of the Shang Dynasty (ca. 1600–1027 B.C.).

Regarding technical assessments of early Chinese silks, the first investigations of ancient Chinese weaving as preserved in bronze patinas were made by Vivi Sylwan.[7] When the actual samples themselves have been destroyed or are unavailable, considerable research needs to be done to determine the type of fibres which were actually used for the weaving of fabrics. A very enterprising undertaking by John Vollmer of the Royal Ontario Museum may eventually supply more compelling evidence for the existence of woven silk on "pseudomorphs" left on bronzes.[8] Both authors positively identify silk fibres.[9] They assert that they can distinguish coarse from fine weaves, and that the fineness and uniformity of weave reflect, in many instances, great skill in reeling off the thread.[10] If this type of technical venture is to enhance our knowledge of silk structure on an extensive scale, however, some points still need further clarification.

That fibre identification and fibre analysis involve myriad complexities and intense study is apparent from the impressive research of Dr. Junro Nunome, the Japanese fibre expert. His statistical analysis of nearly five hundred fibre specimens emphasizes variations which, owing to the passage of time and processing methods, could affect the "circularity coefficient" of silk fibres. While he states that it is difficult to decide whether ancient silk fibres are of three- or four-moulters, he concludes that it is possible to distinguish the fibres of domesticated silkworms from those of wild ones, with the exception of the *kuwako* (*Bombyx mandarina* Moore). He adds that it is relatively easy to distinguish silk fibres from non-silk fibres (linen, cotton, wool, etc.) if the cross-sections of fibres are inspected with a high-powered microscope.[11]

The species *Bombyx mori* has been accepted by all Chinese and other authors as the silkworm cultivated by the Chinese from the earliest times in order to obtain silk yarns for woven silk. As stated by Nunome, the identification of wild or cultivated silkworms can become problematic in the case of variations within the same species.[12] Voskrensky and Tikhonov have used intensive chemico-technical re-

search on a group of figured fabrics from Noin-Ula with similar results.[13] While recent technical observations suggest that silk yarns were reeled off semi-cultivated silkworms belonging to the *Bombyx* species, a more complete picture may emerge when the research carried out by Nunome, Chinese specialists, and other teams is more fully studied and coordinated.

It is pertinent to devote some attention to the study and assessment of plain silks, for in doing so one begins to realize that even for such a simple weave, the problems remain slippery. Plain silk tabbies comprise well over half of all surviving early Chinese textiles. The Soviet archaeologist Rudenko mentions that among the oldest surviving specimens of Chinese silk are several examples of plain silks, including a silk pouch, found at Pazyryk in Barrows 3 and 5.[14] They are dated from the fifth to the third centuries B.C. Also found were two felt shabracks (saddle-cloths) covered with plain silk.[15] The silk is very fine in texture and feel. The thread count of the plain silk is 40 warps by 52 wefts per cm, and it has selvages with a loom width presumably between 44 and 49 cm.

Two other early examples, dating from the late Chou Dynasty (fifth to fourth century B.C.), are plain silks serving as ground for painting of calligraphy. One of them is a darkened silk with a lady, dragon, and bird, found in Chang-sha, Hunan Province, in 1949; the other is the silk ground of the Chu Manuscript, unearthed in Chang-sha in 1934, with painted texts and figures, and dated at ca. 450 B.C.[16] A considerable amount of technical research has been carried out on the latter by Noel Barnard and other specialists, in particular Dr. Nunome. Such technical investigation appears to be very detailed and exhaustive, though it is based on only one specimen. While the Han Dynasty abounds with silk fabrics, earlier textiles are rare, and consequently there are very few examples within the same group to fall back upon. It would certainly be appropriate to make a technical study of fibre and weave of all the known plain silks from a period contemporary to the Chu Manuscript; for example, of all the plain silks from Pazyryk, as well as of the finds from mainland China of the late Chou Dynasty.

My own work on Han monochrome and polychrome figured silks has so far consisted of direct observations and studies. My first principle has been to collect a select number of samples in a consistent manner. Out of a total of over fifty samples, twenty-four are from figured silks; others are of silk gauze, plain silks, wool, and such fibres as hemp and ramie. The work of analysis and observation is still in progress.[17]

When exactly monochrome figured silk (usually, and in our opinion, erroneously, referred to as "Han damask") first appeared is still a matter of some conjecture. Certain specialists believe that monochrome figured silks, because of their single colour and angular, rectilinear motifs, were necessarily the precursors of the more elaborate polychrome patterned examples. It might be argued, however, that the innumerable fragments of monochrome figured silks found among Tang Dynasty specimens signify a given aesthetic taste rather than any technical limitation. Lubo-Lesnichenko and I have identified two monochrome figured silks as belonging to the Six Dynasties period (A.D. 220–580).[18] Although among known Han specimens the polychrome patterned silks outnumber the monochrome ones, this is not proof that the monochromes are of earlier manufacture.

I am aware of the existence of almost thirty monochrome figured silks through either direct study or good descriptions and illustrations. These include monochrome figured silks from seven different fabrics found in Edsen-gol and Lop-nor, and fully described and illustrated by Vivi Sylwan;[19] several fragments from five different fabrics found by Stein in Lou-lan;[20] several fragments of seven different fabrics excavated by Kozlov in Noin-Ula, and one by Karesja from Kertch;[21] and fragments from nine monochrome figured fabrics found in the towers of Elahbel and Jamblique, Palmyra, fully described and illustrated by Pfister.[22] Three different specimens of monochrome figured silks, excavated in mainland China, are known from photographic reproductions and travelling exhibitions: one of them, found in 1959 in Dachamo (fig. 1), in the site of Old Niya, is a triangular fragment from a woman's skirt,[23] and the other two are fragments found in Tomb 1 at Mawangdui in Chang-sha in 1970.[24] It has also been indicated that other "Han damasks" were found at Mawangdui.

Denoting a fact of historical interest, there are finally several fragments of a monochrome figured silk fabric (fig. 5) found in the Kirgiz SSR of the Soviet Union. They were excavated from Tumulus 18 in Kara-Bulak, a small village in the mountains of the Ferghana Valley in the westernmost part of southern Kirgizya. The expedition was initiated by the Osh Regional Museum in Kara-Bulak and was led by Y.D. Baruzdin from 1956 to 1957. The textile discoveries of this site are considered of some importance by Soviet specialists, since the complex of finds indicated an origin which was essentially non-Chinese. Yet quite a number of textiles of Chinese origin have also been found at this site, thus proving a direct or indirect link between this region and the ancient Chinese Empire. The finds are dated to the third and fourth centuries A.D.[25] Out of well over twenty specimens from Kara-Bulak which I was able to examine with Lubo-Lesnichenko, we had no doubt that a good number of the silk specimens embodied technical and ornamental characteristics inspired by Han Dynasty design, but more characteristic of the Six Dynasties period. The monochrome figured silk in figure 5, a sample of which was given for technical and chemical analyses, is the same reddish-brown colour as two Lou-lan specimens. Its motif resembles the motifs of a specimen from Palmyra, which has been described by Pfister, and it also has some resemblance to the hexagonal motifs of the monochrome figured silk found in Lop-nor.[26] The count of the Kara-Bulak monochrome figured silk is 59 warps by 30 wefts; the one from Lop-nor is 60 warps by 28 wefts; and the one from Palmyra has 76 warps by 52 wefts per cm. The monochrome figured silks from Lou-lan have approximately 66 warps by 28-30 wefts per cm. They all have a ground of simple tabby, and a décor with three–span warp-floats.[27]

All the monochrome figured silks mentioned above may be subdivided into three technical groups:

A. Monochrome figured tabby, patterned with alternately aligned three-span warp-floats, also in tabby. This binding system involves only half of the total number of warp ends for the execution of the décor.

B. Monochrome figured tabby patterned with 3:1

twill. This binding system involves all the warp ends for the execution of the décor.

C. Monochrome figured tabby patterned with chevron (a derivation of 3:1 twill). As in the previous group, this binding system involves all the warp ends for the execution of the décor.

Of the seven fabrics found in Edsen-gol and Lop-nor, four pieces belong to type A, and two to type B. One fabric, the sea-green "damask" from Lop-nor, appears to be a variant of type A (see note 19). Among the five specimens found by Stein in Lou-lan, two belong to type A, two to type B, and one to type C. All seven specimens from Noin-Ula and the example from Kertch belong to type B. The monochrome figured silks found in Palmyra all belong to type A. The silk from the site of Old Niya is of type A, and the two fragments from Tomb 1 at Mawangdui belong to type B.[28] The fragment from Kara-Bulak is of type A. There is now no longer any doubt that all these monochrome figured silks are of Chinese manufacture and fall within the Han and even post-Han periods. From the excavations in China we are assured of two dates: the fragment from Old Niya is from the tomb of an Eastern Han couple (A.D. 25–220), and the one from Tomb 1 at Mawangdui dates from ca. 145 B.C.

From a technical point of view, the constructions of the monochrome figured silks reveal significant variations in the pattern binding system. These variations in turn indicate a differentiation to be made in *montage* and in the shedding mechanisms.[29] The monochrome figured silks show a greater range in the pattern binding system than the polychrome patterned silks, as the polychrome silks are invariably in the same binding system. They vary only in the number of warps used per series. Among the monochrome figured silk samples analyzed by Gabriel Vial, two from Noin-Ula (MR 1410 and MR 1068) appear to be particularly complex, because of the fineness of their weave and the high density of their warp threads.[30] MR 1410 (figs. 3, 4) has 118–120 warps by 32–34 wefts per cm, showing a warp density which is unusually high for monochrome figured silks. This density is, however, surpassed in MR 1068 where the thread count is 160 warps by 50–54 wefts per cm. These two specimens have a décor in 3:1 twill (type B) and Vial postu-

lates that they were woven on pattern-rod looms, necessitating 62 to 66 rods for MR 1410, and 72 to 80 rods for MR 1068. In these silks, all the warp ends are controlled, two by two, by pattern rods. Three other silks from Noin-Ula belonging to the same category (type B) have counts of 120 warps by 42 wefts, 120 warps by 55 wefts, and 130 warps by 55 wefts per cm.[31]

In its overall appearance and ornamentation, the monochrome figured silk from Noin-Ula (MR 1410) bears a striking similarity to the silk found in Tomb 1 at Mawangdui.[32] The specimen from Mawangdui has a thread count of 100 warps by 46 wefts per cm. In both instances the décor is in 3:1 twill; thus they have the same construction. The specimens L.C.vii.09 from Lou-lan (fig. 2) and S39 from Palmyra have a similar scheme of rhombuses, faulted angles, and confronting birds (phoenixes).[33] These, however, have a décor in three-span warp-floats and not in 3:1 twill. All the specimens mentioned are in perfect conformity with Han style, and yet there is an essential technical difference between the silks from Noin-Ula and Mawangdui, and those from other sites. All the other known monochrome figured silks with a décor in warp-floats or in twill (from Lou-lan, Palmyra, Kertch, Edsen-gol, Lop-nor, Dachamo) have a thread count which ranges between 40 and 66 warps per cm and never more.[34] In L.C.vii.09 and L.H.011, both from Lou-lan, the thread count is approximately 66 warps by 29–30 wefts per cm, a value which is close to that of S39 from Palmyra, with 60 warps by 38 wefts per cm (in these specimens only half of the total number of warp ends are controlled by pattern rods). L.C.vii.09 and S39, and other monochrome figured silks including the one from Dachamo, Old Niya, with a thread count of 66 warps by 32 wefts per cm, have certain characteristics which denote a similar value, and therefore they form a group of their own. The one from Old Niya is dated to Eastern Han, and therefore provides a hypothetical indication for dating the others belonging to the same group.

The only monochrome figured specimens with an unusually high density of warp ends (100 or more per cm, revealing an extraordinary fineness of weave) are the monochrome figured silks from Noin-Ula, and the silk with rhombuses and confronting birds from Tomb 1 at Mawangdui (see note 32). The ornamental spirit of this latter group is also quite consistent. In their balance of décor, execution, and texture, these monochrome figured silks are closely related. Mawangdui finds are dated to the Western Han Dynasty, around 145 B.C.[35] My own inference is that certain silks from Noin-Ula are of greater antiquity than they are generally believed to be. In other words, they could probably be dated before the first century A.D. (Western Han). Besides monochrome figured silks, other textiles also support this hypothesis. Gauzes and embroideries from both Noin-Ula and Mawangdui have a striking similarity, which is particular only to these two sites.

Because of the association of textiles with a lacquer cup found in Noin-Ula that bears an inscription with a date equivalent to 2 B.C. (fig. 16), all Noin-Ula finds are considered as belonging to the beginning of the first century A.D. and later.[36] The two characters *shang-lin,* written on the base of the cup, indicate that it was manufactured in an area reserved for service to the Imperial Court and known as the Shang-lin Park. It was a vast and beautiful park in a summer palace situated outside the western walls of Chang-an, today known as Sian. Precious materials were assembled there and transformed into objects of refinement and beauty. The height of Shang-lin's importance and reputation appears to have been around the second century B.C. Yetts states that the park was first laid out with lavish magnificence by the founder of the Chin Dynasty about 220 B.C. He also mentions the fact that Xiung-nu (Hunnish) raiders penetrated as far as the Shang-lin Park in 166 B.C. Lubo-Lesnichenko and I had earlier proposed that controlled workshops which supplied the Imperial Court were located in Chang-an, the capital of the Western Han.[37] It is certain that the silks excavated in Noin-Ula and found in the tombs of the *shan-yü* (nomadic heads or chiefs) were offered by the Chinese Court to the Xiung-nu. Emperor Wen-di (180 –157 B.C.) had to send out valuable consignments of silk to keep the enemy appeased.[38] Some Noin-Ula silks could, therefore, have been the products of a date prior to that of the lacquer cup, and it is also conceivable that they were manufactured in Chang-an.[39]

The earliest polychrome or bi-colour figured silk

comes from Pazyryk. It was found by Rudenko in Barrow 3, and dated to the Warring States period (fifth–third century B.C.) (fig. 6). It is woven in warp-faced compound tabby with two warps, one brown and the other brownish-green.[40] The cloth has an intricate geometric pattern consisting of four successive rows of rhomboids, formed by both open and complex rhombuses. The piece measures approximately 14 cm in length and 8 cm in width. The thread count, which includes the two warps, is 80–85 warps by 28 wefts per cm.[41] The width of the repeat is approximately 6 cm; the height is incomplete. I was extremely fortunate to get some fibres of this specimen from the State Hermitage Museum, and was able to have it analyzed for the first time. A microanalysis carried out by Mme Meyer showed that, like all Han samples so far tested, this too had been degummed, and that in all likelihood the degumming was done after the weaving process. The length of the sample fibres was too short, but the characteristics were unmistakably of grège silk.[42] In the microphotograph of figure 7, which shows a cross-section of the warp and a longitudinal section of the weft, the dark areas indicate the presence of a slight amount of sericin.

The other figured silks which have been attributed to the late Chou Dynasty are a pair of mittens and a bonnet from Chang-sha, now preserved at the Cooper-Hewitt Museum of Design, Smithsonian Institution, New York. After a sustained study of the Noin-Ula silks and observation of the Mawangdui finds, I now surmise that the Chang-sha mittens and bonnet are of polychrome figured silks which, stylistically and technically, are closely related to certain Noin-Ula fabrics. This suggests similar conditions of manufacture and probably the same dates, ranging from Western to Eastern Han.[43]

At present I am familiar with more than eighty Han polychrome patterned silks from various sites. Sir Aurel Stein had excavated in the Dunhuang Limes in 1906–1907 one bi-coloured (fig. 12) and two polychrome figured silks, and a shoe which he considered to be Han.[44] Through written documents which were found in this site, he had attributed the dates of 53 B.C.–A.D. 137 to a complex (T.XV.a) of the Dunhuang Limes watch towers, where two of the aforementioned fragments were excavated. Later, nearly thirty bi-coloured and polychrome silks (figs. 11, 13, 14, 15) were recovered at the Lou-lan site which, in my opinion, cover the entire span of the Han Dynasty. Eighteen patterned silks from Noin-Ula, the specimen from Pazyryk, a specimen from Ilvomaya Pad', and six different patterned silks from Oglakty are in the State Hermitage Museum, Leningrad. Two additional figured silks from Oglakty are in the collection of the Historical Museum, Moscow. Sven Hedin and Folkes Bergman had found some seven fragments of polychrome patterned silks in Edsen-gol and Lop-nor. Pfister discovered one figured silk in Palmyra.[45] We know of some ten polychrome patterned Han silks which were found in mainland China between 1959 and 1969 (for the most part in Old Niya [Minfeng], Sinkiang). Most of these fabrics have been published and are considered to date from the Eastern Han Dynasty (A.D. 25–220). This dating is consistent with archaeological evidence from scientifically conducted and well-documented excavations. Thus they help to provide clues for the identification of quite a few of the Stein finds, some of which are similar to these particular silks. Among these Chinese finds, three specimens carry inscriptional characters, and one of them a full inscription.[46] The most spectacular finds came to light in 1971–1972 in Mawangdui in Chang-sha, Hunan Province. The most probable date for Tomb 1 is the fifth year of the reign of Chung-yuan of Emperor Ching-di (145 B.C.).

Of the impressive quantity of textiles found in Mawangdui, relatively few are polychrome patterned silks. There are embroidered and plain silks, innumerable complex gauzes (painted, printed, and embroidered), and the monochrome figured silks already mentioned. The finest of the monochrome figured silks is considered to be a type of "pile brocade".[47] One is tempted to conjecture that this "pile brocade", or pattern executed in relief, has great technical and iconographic similarity to a warp-looped specimen, No. 14029 from Tumulus 15 in Noin-Ula (fig. 8).[48] This specimen, showing diagonal rows of different rhomboid patterns, is the only one of its kind among the Russian finds. It is described by Lubo-Lesnichenko as measuring 19.5 cm in length and 9.4 cm in width, having two warps and a weft, and woven in warp-faced compound tabby (140 warps by 40 wefts per cm). The colour

now appears to be brown, although in places a faded reddish-brown is preserved. It is certainly striking in its similarity to the Chinese specimens from Mawangdui and to their technique as shown in a Japanese catalogue (see note 47), where the diagram suggests that it is in exactly the same construction as the fragment found in Noin-Ula. If the hypothesis that the silks from Noin-Ula were manufactured at Chang-an is correct, the Mawangdui piece, firmly dated by archaeological content to the Western Han Dynasty, may also have been manufactured at Chang-an. There are no other sites where patterned silks of this type have been found or recorded.

While my own research has been based primarily on the technical aspects of early Chinese silks, I realize that it is not possible to isolate the technique from the symbolic background of the motifs. There are two schools of thought regarding the origin and significance of early Chinese décor. The first considers evolutions in certain motifs purely on aesthetic grounds: "a force . . . concerned with appearance or form alone, an aesthetic urge, fulfilled through artistic consciousness".[49] The second regards such motifs as being highly symbolic, especially the geometric and abstract motifs. In interpreting the ornamentation on the Noin-Ula figured silks, Lubo-Lesnichenko deals essentially with symbolic connotations which, according to his interpretation, have their origin in Shang and Chou bronze vessels, weapons, and mirrors.[50]

An important study of the development of the formal decorative motifs on lacquer and silk of the Han period was carried out by William Willetts.[51] A further attempt to deal with Han figured silks on the basis of stylistic features, and to suggest an ordered chronology, was made by John Lowry.[52] Although Lowry attributed most textiles from Stein's finds in Lou-lan, and Kozlov's finds in Noin-Ula, to the Han period in general, he nevertheless designated certain fabrics as belonging to either the Eastern Han or the early Six Dynasties period, or to a period which he refers to as "inter-Han–T'ang".[53]

Certain silks have a studied elegance, while others are more rigid in style. Some are rigorous in spirit, others again are "liberal" in ornamental interpretation. Lubo-Lesnichenko has postulated a hypothesis that some Lou-lan silks were perhaps created for expanding trade and establishing rapport with the West, which would account for the various types ranging from early to late Han.[54]

A detailed study of the inscriptions on silks (figs. 9, 10, 11, 17–19) may further contribute to the understanding of these textiles. In all the figured silks where characters in *li-shu* script (professional models of Han official writing) are present, the inscriptions, like those on bronze mirrors, denote wishes for felicity, longevity, and immortality (figs. 18, 19). Some inscriptions, however, remain enigmatic, as for example the one on the polychrome patterned silk MR 1405 from Noin-Ula (fig. 9).[55] Here the eight characters form a complete inscription (fig. 17). Yetts had translated this as "Kuang Ch'êng renews spiritually and extends longevity to a myriad years",[56] taking Kuang Ch'êng to be the personage of Taoist lore. Lubo-Lesnichenko, following Yetts' interpretation, suggested the following translation: "[May you be] a new holy Kuang Ch'êng and live ten thousand years".[57] Umehara, however, thinks that the first character *hsin* (new) refers to the "new dynasty", founded by Wang Mang (A.D. 9–23) and translates the inscription as "Long life, holy mighty, Hsin [Xin] Dynasty".[58] Maenchen-Helfen cites other possible interpretations, and declares that the problem has not yet been resolved.[59] Umehara's interpretation would obviously imply that this silk was a product of the Xin Interregnum (A.D. 9–23), while others could suggest a broader time range. I feel that such problems need to be resolved among competent sinologists before any attempt to narrow

down the time scale would be conclusive.

There are some twenty-six figured silks carrying either partial or full inscriptions (nine from Lou-lan, five from Noin-Ula, one from Ilmovaya Pad', four from Oglakty, one from Palmyra, at least three from Edsen-gol and Lop-nor, and at least another three from excavations on the Chinese mainland). So far a proper name (of the artisan or of the wearer) occurs on only one of Stein's finds from Lou-lan, together with an identical example from Lop-nor.[60] Thus, it would be of considerable interest to know whether *Kuang Ch'êng* represents a proper name or not, and whether its appearance is purely coincidental. Identification becomes all the more complicated by Chinese syntax, where one character might symbolize several meanings. Only the systematic study of related material can help to unravel the enigma.

In summarizing similarities and differences, in keeping the chronology unsophisticated, and in attempting to keep the occurrence of iconography and technique in order, I hope I have been able to point out a probable sequence of events concerning the manufacture of some of these remarkable silks. We must, however, recognize that new archaeological explorations in China, the USSR, and elsewhere will inevitably lead us towards more thorough and perhaps even revised assessments. The present inflow of information has only just begun. We have yet to grasp the full depths and dimensions of this important historical panorama.

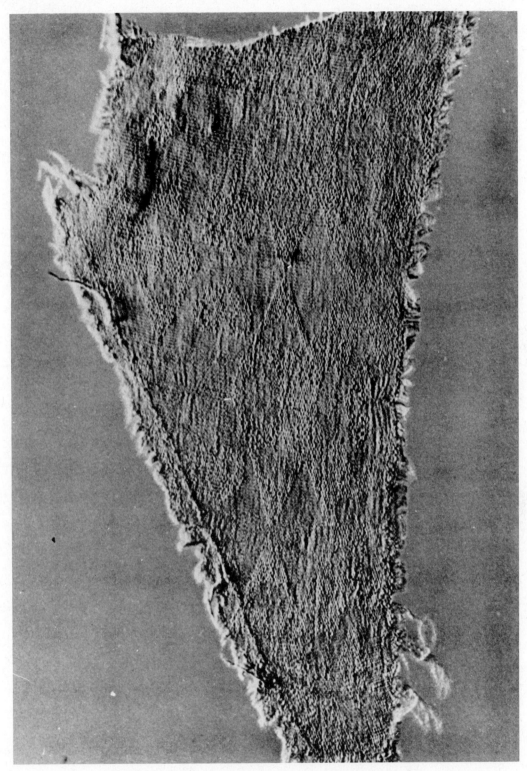

Figure 1. Monochrome figured silk with décor in three-span
warp-floats (warp direction ↑). Dachamo, Old Niya, Sinkiang.
Eastern Han.
Sinkiang Museum, Uighur Autonomous Republic, People's Republic of China.

259

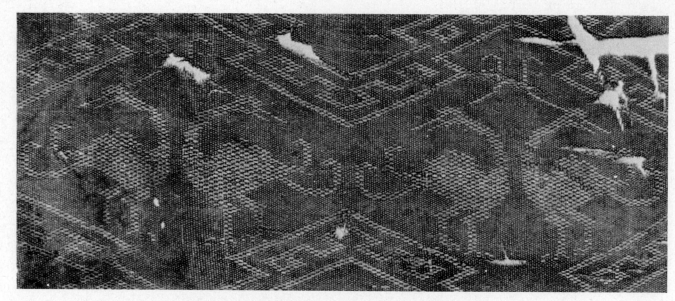

Figure 2. Monochrome figured silk with décor in three-span warp-floats (warp direction →). Lou-lan, Sinkiang, Uighur Autonomous Republic, People's Republic of China. Han Dynasty. National Museum, New Delhi, L.C.vii.09.

Figure 3. Monochrome figured silk with décor in 3/1 twill (warp direction →). Noin-Ula, Mongolia. Probably Western Han.
State Hermitage Museum, Leningrad, MR 1410.

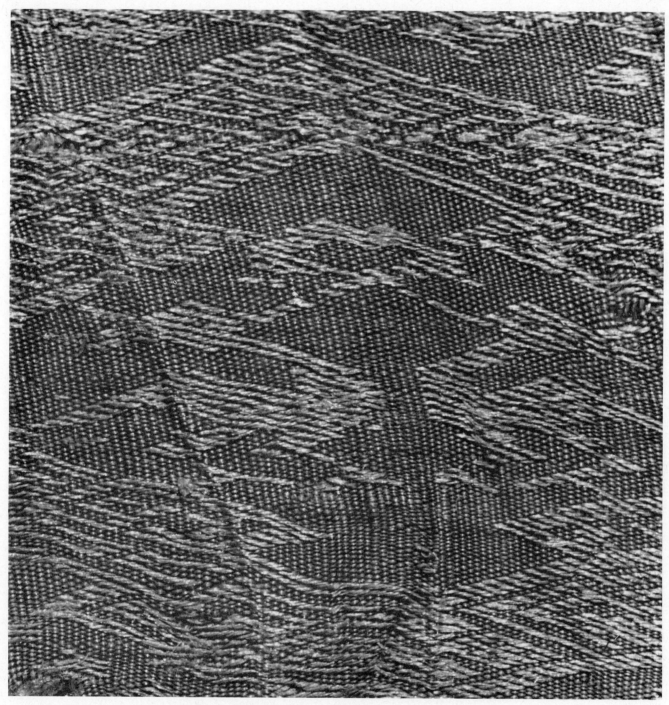

Figure 4. Detail of figure 3 showing paired and confronted birds within faulted angles and rhombuses.

Figure 5. Monochrome figured silk with décor in three-span warp-floats (warp direction ↑). Tumulus 18, Kara-Bulak, Kirgiz SSR, USSR. Perhaps Six Dynasties.
Institute of History of the Academy of Sciences of the Kirgiz SSR. Courtesy of Dr. Lubo-Lesnichenko.

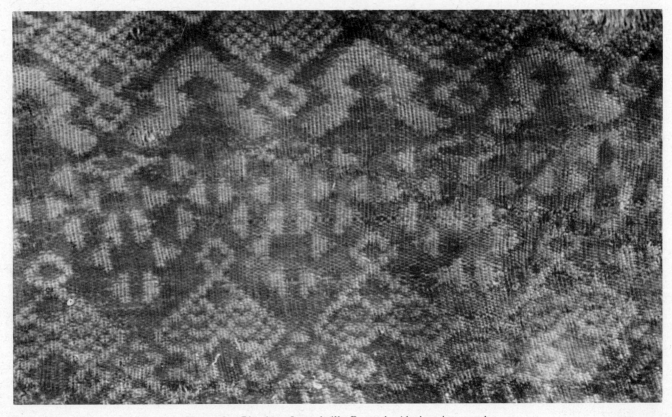

Figure 6. Bi-colour figured silk. Pazyryk, Altai region, southern Siberia, USSR. Warring States period, fifth – third century B.C. (warp direction →).
State Hermitage Museum, Leningrad.

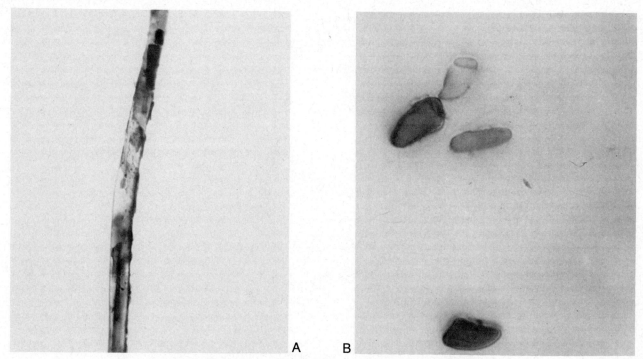

A   B

Figure 7.   Microphotograph of silk fibre from Pazyryk (fig. 6).
A: longitudinal weft, magnified 300 times. *B*: cross-section of
warp, magnified 650 times.
Photos: Mme H. Meyer, CRSIT Laboratory, Lyon.

Figure 8.   Silk in warp-faced compound tabby, in looped-warp
technique. Noin-Ula, Mongolia. Probably Western Han.
State Hermitage Museum, Leningrad, no. 14029.

Figure 9. Polychrome figured silk with eight-character inscription from Noin-Ula, Mongolia. Han Dynasty. State Hermitage Museum, Leningrad, MR 1405.

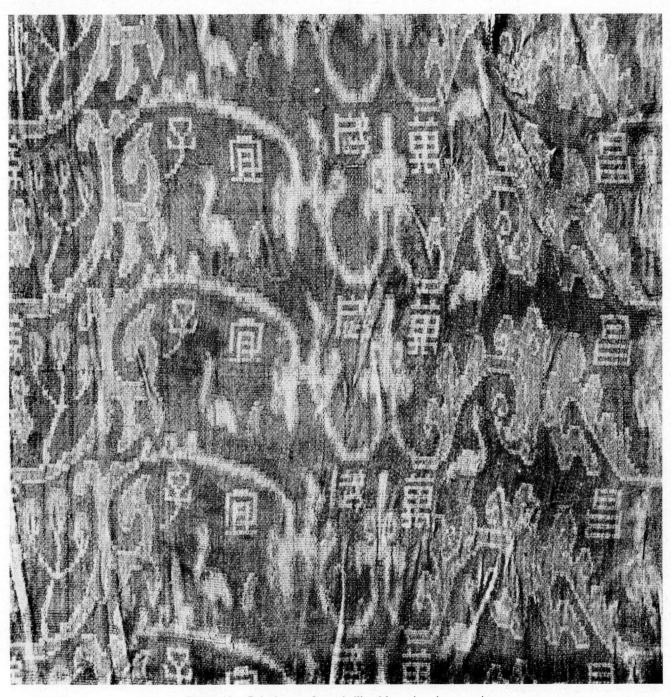

Figure 10. Polychrome figured silk with twelve-character inscription from Noin-Ula, Mongolia. Han Dynasty.
State Hermitage Museum, Leningrad, MR 1826.

Figure 11.   Bi-colour figured silk, complete width with six-character inscription from Lou-lan, Sinkiang. Han Dynasty. Present here are characters *chin* and *yi*.
National Museum, New Delhi, L.C.vii.02.

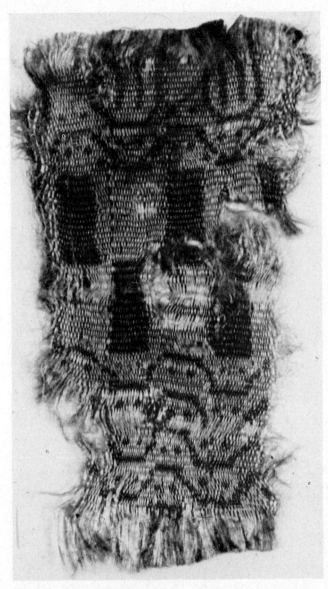

Figure 13. Bi-colour figured silk found by Sir Aurel Stein in 1913 – 1916 in Lou-lan, Sinkiang. Han Dynasty. National Museum, New Delhi.

Figure 12. Bi-colour figured silk found by Sir Aurel Stein in 1906 – 1908 in the Dun huang Limes. Han Dynasty. British Museum, London.

Figure 14.   Bi-colour figured silk found by Sir Aurel Stein in
1913 – 1916 in Lou-lan, Sinkiang. Han Dynasty.
National Museum, New Delhi.

Figure 15. Polychrome figured silk in four warps and five colours found in 1913 – 1916 by Sir Aurel Stein in Lou-lan, Sinkiang. Han Dynasty.
National Museum, New Delhi.

建平五年九月工王潭經

畫工獲壺天武省

Figure 16. Complete inscription on lacquer cup. Noin-Ula, Mongolia.[61]
State Hermitage Museum, Leningrad.

新神靈廣成壽萬年

Figure 17. Complete inscription on polychrome figured silk (see fig. 9). Noin-Ula, Mongolia.[62]
State Hermitage Museum, Leningrad, MR 1405.

續世 錦 宜 子 孫

Figure 18. Complete inscription from L.C.vii.02 (see fig. 11). Lou-lan, Sinkiang.[63]
National Museum, New Delhi.

長 樂 明 光

Figure 19. Complete inscription from L.C.iii.011. Lou-lan, Sinkiang.[64]
National Museum, New Delhi.

270

Notes

1. Although it might seem like an inflated claim to assert that during the last decade a more careful and systematic scrutiny of these silks has yielded startling new evidence, it must be pointed out that recent developments in the methods of textile studies, as well as the recent finds in mainland China and the Soviet Union, have served to raise questions which are more incisive and specific. The aim of rigorous technical analyses, on which I lay particular emphasis, has been to identify the basic materials and structures of these silks. Such analyses have helped to restore the balance between widely speculative theories regarding their external features on the one hand, and the structural precision of their construction on the other. Systematic examination of the specimens, coordinated with chemical and technical tests, shows hitherto unsuspected characteristics that indicate the need for a new appraisal of Han figured silks.

Note: Transliterations of inscriptions and Chinese words in general are given according to three systems: (A) Wade-Giles, (B) *Guoyupingyin*, (C) EFEO (Ecole Française d'Extrême-Orient), so marked by letters. Mr. Hou Ching-lang of the Musée Guimet has based his transliteration and interpretations on the EFEO system. Dr. Hsio-yen Shih, former curator of the Far Eastern Department, ROM, has transliterated most inscriptions into *Guoyupingyin*.

2. F.H. Andrews, "Ancient Chinese figured silks, excavated by Sir Aurel Stein at ruined sites of Central Asia", *Burlington Magazine*, vol. 37/1-3 (1920), pp. 3–10, 71–77, 147–152.

3. W. Percival Yetts, "Discoveries of the Kozlov Expedition", *Burlington Magazine,* vol. 48 (1926), pp. 168–185; Camilla Trever, *Excavations in Northern Mongolia, Memoirs of the Academy of History of Material Culture*, vol. 3, Leningrad, 1932; Sueji Umehara, *Moko Noin Ura hakken no ibutsu* [Studies of Noin-Ula finds in northern Mongolia], in Japanese, Tokyo Bunko, series A, no. 27, Tokyo, 1960; S.I. Rudenko, *Die Kultur der Hsiung-Nu und die Hügelgräber von Noin-Ula*, Antiquitas 3, vol. 7, Bonn, 1969.

4. A major exhibition of recent Chinese archaeological finds was shown at the Petit Palais, Paris, in 1973. Another major exhibition comprising finds from Mawangdui and other areas was shown in the same year in Tokyo, and, like the first exhibition, was circulated internationally. These two exhibitions gave me the opportunity to see some important early silks discovered by Chinese archaeologists in the last twenty years. Through studies which appeared in two Chinese archaeological journals (*Wenwu* and *Kaogu*), and actual silk fragments of these exhibitions, I became aware of about twenty monochrome and polychrome figured silks from mainland China. My present study has been necessarily confined only to those specimens which are known to me in a precise way. Among these are the fragments found at the site of Wuwei in Kansu (*Sichon Zhi lu Han Tang zhi wu* [The fabrics from the Han to Tang Dynasty], in Chinese, Museum of Sinkiang–Uighur Autonomous Republic, Peking, 1972, pl. 1), and the Han fabrics found in Djalainor in Inner Mongolia (*Wenwu*, 9, 1961, p. 18, and fig. 8). I have seen only the repro-

duction of a polychrome figured silk from Tomb 2 in Mawangdui (*Wenwu*, 7, 1974, pl. 14, fig. 2). The same publication mentions several other fragments of polychrome figured silk recovered in Tombs 2 and 3 at Mawangdui (p. 45). Hiong Chuan Sin's important article, "Silks from the Warring States period recently found in Chang-sha" (*Wenwu*, 2, 1975, pp. 49–52) has also been consulted together with two art books which illustrate early textiles: *Sichon zhi lu Han Tang zhi wu* (1972); and *Changsha Mawangdui yihao Hanmu* [Han Tomb 1 at Mawangdui, Changsha], in Chinese with English summary, 2 vols., Peking, Wenwu Press, 1973.

Regarding Han, post-Han, and Tang Dynasty silks, the bibliography by Japanese authors includes the following titles: Yoshito Harada, *Kan Rikucho no Fukushoku* [Chinese dress and personal ornaments in the Han and Six Dynasties], in Japanese with English summary, Tokyo Bunko Ronsho, series A, vol. 23, Tokyo, Tokyo Bunko, 1937 (a revised edition was published in 1967 as vol. 49). Five volumes in Japanese dealing with technical aspects of ancient textiles, published under the heading *Report of the Textile Institute at Kawashima, Kyoto* by Shinzaburo Sasaki: vol. 1, *Jingo-ji Kyo Chitsu Nishiki Aya Shiken* [My opinion on the complex figured fabrics of the Jingo-ji Temple], 1958; vol. 2, *Nippon Jodai Shokugi no Kenkyu* [Study on the manufacture of ancient Japanese textiles], 1950; vol. 3, *Jodai Aya ni Miru Nanako Giho* [The technique of *nanako* as seen on ancient figured fabrics in twill], 1958; vol. 4, *Ragi Shiko* [My opinion on the technique of the gauze], 1960; vol. 5, *Jodai nishiki Aya Tokui Giho Ko* [Study of the inhabitual techniques of *nishiki* and *aya* on ancient textiles], 1973. Shinzaburo Sasaki, *Shosoin no Ra* [Patterned *ra*-weave (gauze) fabrics in the Shoisoin], in Japanese with English summary, Tokyo, Nihon Keizai Shimbun-Sha, 1971. Heizo Tatsumura, *Nishiki to Boro no Hanashi* [The story of a torn fragment of silk], in Japanese, Tokyo, Gakuei sha, 1967. *Sekai Bijutsu Zenshu*, in Japanese, vol. 13, no. 2, *Shin-Han* [Han China], 1949, and vol. 14, no. 3, *The Six Dynasties*, 1968, in the series *Library of World Art*, Tokyo, Kadokawa. *Chuka Jinmin Kyowakoku Shutsudo Bunbutsuten* [Archaeological treasures excavated in the People's Republic of China], in Japanese, exhibition catalogue, Tokyo National Museum and Kyoto National Museum, 1973. Takashi Okazaki, *Tozai Kohno no Kokogaku* [Archaeology of the cultural intercourse between East and West], in Japanese, Tokyo, Heibonsha, 1973. Pp. 11–16 contain a chart with "sites where silk textiles of Han and Tang Dynasties have been found in Central Asia and in North China", listing site, period, placement, kind of textile, publication, and year of discovery. Lubo-Lesnichenko and I have consulted this list, but feel that more research is needed before we can pronounce on the technical and stylistic characteristics of these textile finds.

Kan-To no Senshoku — Shiruku Rodo no Shin Shutsudo-hin [Chinese textiles discovered along the Silk Road from Han to Tang dynasties], in Japanese, Tokyo, Shogakukan, 1973. This volume has the same plates as the Chinese *Sichon zhi lu Han Tang zhi wu* (1972); the text is considerably amplified and consists of the following chapters: Preface by Y. Harada; "The Silk Road: Textiles of the Han and Tang dynasties" by the Wen-wu Exhibition Working Team; "The foundation of the Silk Road and its historical framework" by Takashi Okazaki; "A list of sites where textiles of the Han and Tang dynasties have been found"; "Textile techniques during the Han and Tang dynasties in ancient Japan" by H. Nishimura. I wish to acknowledge the help of Miss Masami Kishimoto, Assistant at the Ochanomizu University at Tokyo, for transcribing the titles and helping with translation.

5. E. Lubo-Lesnichenko, *Drevniye Kitaiskiye shelkoviye tkani i vyshivki V v. do n.e.–III v. n.e. v. sobranii Gosudarstvennom Ermitazha* [Ancient Chinese silk textiles and embroideries, fifth century B.C. to third century A.D., in the collection of the State Hermitage Museum], in Russian, Leningrad, 1961. An English translation of this book by Nora Priverts of the Royal Ontario Museum, edited by H.B. Burnham, was made available to the CIETA (Centre International d'Etude des Textiles Anciens) library in Lyon. Throughout the present article the original publication in Russian has been referred to.

6. Xia Nai, "Woguo gudai can sang si chou de lishi" [The history of silk making, mulberry trees, and cocoons in ancient China], in Chinese, *Kaogu* (1972), pp. 12–27, n. 4. I wish to acknowledge Shih-Chen and Ruth Ellen Peng of Oakland University, Michigan, who translated this article for me.

7. Vivi Sylwan, "Siden i Kina under Yin-dynastien" [Silk fabric in China under the Yin Dynasty], in Swedish, *Malmo Museums Ersberattelse* (1935), pp. 19–21, figs. 1–10; V. Sylwan, "Silk from the Yin Dynasty", *Bulletin of the Museum of Far Eastern Art*, vol. 9 (1937), pp. 119–126; V. Sylwan, *Investigation of silk from Edsen-gol and Lop-nor*, Report of the Sino-Swedish Expedition, vol. 7 : 6, Stockholm, 1949, pp. 18–19, 107, fig. 55, pl. 4.

Sylwan analyzed a *ji* urn and a *yue* axe from the site of Anyang, Honan, attributed to the Yin Dynasty (terminal date eleventh century B.C.). By analyzing textile imprints on these bronze objects, she could clearly identify coarse and refined tabby, twill, and a mixture of tabby and twill. Although I have some doubts regarding her conclusion of a "pheasant-eyed pattern" on the silk damask of the axe (K. Riboud, "A reappraisal of Han Dynasty monochrome figured silks", *Bulletin de liaison du CIETA*, no. 38, 1973/II, pp. 122–138), in other words a complex twill bind, nevertheless if we accept that the objects were wrapped in silks during the period to which they belong, we find very early evidence of woven fabrics in China.

8. John Vollmer, "Textile pseudomorphs on Chinese bronzes", *Irene Emery Roundtable on Museum Textiles, 1974 Proceedings, Archaeological Textiles*, ed. Patricia L. Fiske, The Textile Museum, Washington, D.C., pp. 170–174. Vollmer defines pseudomorphs (false forms) as mineral formations assuming the shape of textile structures once in contact with bronze objects. From them, he claims, it is possible to recognize textile remains, and often to identify construction and fibres, as well as to collect related information concerning fibre preparation, patterning, or other surface treatments. Vollmer's study covers two types of

bronzes, vessels and weapons, and records seventy-four occurrences of textiles. Of the forty-seven which he concludes are silk, all but three employ a tabby bind. The exceptions include a figured damask(?) on a bowl from the Eastern Han period, a 2:1 twill on another bowl of the same date, and what may be gauze on a *ko* dagger axe, so effaced that a detailed examination was inconclusive.

9. By the length of the threads (fibres?) and the lack of twist, Sylwan ("Siden i Kina", 1935) concludes that the fibre is indubitably silk. Vollmer ("Textile pseudomorphs", 1974) identifies silk by pairs of filaments acting as a unit. That this is cultivated and not spun wild silk is evident from the parallel or nearly parallel arrangement of fibres in each thread produced by reeling.

Vollmer's identification on pseudomorphs of silk through "pairs of filaments acting as a unit" needs further clarification. The "pairs" that he refers to could either be a warp with two ends (*bouts*) or a pair of warps. Twin filaments (brins) constituting the bave in a cocoon become separated from each other when degummed. Usually the baves of more than one cocoon are reeled off for forming a single warp or weft thread. Supposing that the baves were reeled off simultaneously from ten cocoons for making a warp or weft, one should then find either 10×2 brins if the silk has not been degummed, or twenty independent brins if it has been entirely degummed. We have found that it is extremely difficult to discern the number of brins in a warp thread even through a microscope because of the brittleness of the samples, and consequently of the fibres. That a brin count can, nevertheless, be made is apparent from Noel Barnard's scientific examination of an ancient Chinese document as a prelude to decipherment, translation, and historical assessment: "The Chu Manuscript", paper presented at the 43rd Congress of Australian and New Zealand Association for Advancement of Science, May 1971, p. 41 of a photostat copy (see note 16). The brins can be made visible in cross-section through a microscope. In order to get a statistical mean, it would be necessary to take several thread counts from each specimen. I intend to use some plain Han silk samples which have been recently obtained for such tests. However, Dr. Nunome's find of approximately 36 brins in both warp and weft of the Chu Manuscript (Barnard, 1971, p. 41) is a fact to be kept in mind, since he believes that it is close to the values of the twenty-eight Chinese Han and Lo-lang fibre samples that he has already examined.

10. Sylwan, "Silk from the Yin Dynasty" (1937): "The A fragment, Fig. 1:A, Pl. A, is a plain, loose, medium fine, tabby weave. The number of threads to one cm differ somewhat. In the various places there are 37, 40 and 50 threads in one direction and 30, 30 and 35 in the other. The variation is probably and primarily due to the silk's having been torn and drawn here and there. There is no selvedge" (p. 121). "The urn's tabby weaves, a fine rep with 72 warp and 35 weft threads to 1 cm, and one somewhat coarser with 40 and 17 threads respectively" (p. 124). According to Vollmer ("Textile pseudomorphs", 1974, p. 172), the thread counts for the silk

pseudomorphs range from 75 by 50 to 8 by 7 per cm, with more than half occurring above the 30 by 20 range. The problems of statistics of thread counts per cm of plain silks are manifold. Of surviving Han silks, plain fabrics greatly outnumber figured silks. More than ninety per cent of the Han silks in the State Hermitage Museum, Leningrad, are monochrome tabbies.

In this connection it is interesting to compare the statistics given by Lubo-Lesnichenko (*Drevniye Kitaiskiye,* 1961, pp. 7–8). Of 217 plain monochrome textiles examined, he attributes 185 specimens to the group of *taffeta* or of warp-rep (warp-faced tabby). Of fourteen textiles with complete loom width, he points out a fluctuation in the thread count within the same fabric. He states that the lowest density of warp threads can be observed most often in the centre, the density gradually increasing towards the selvages. At the National Museum in New Delhi, more than half of the 220 Han fragments studied are plain single coloured silks. The thread counts are so varied, and occur in such diversely combined proportions of warp and weft, that it is difficult to decide which warp and weft proportion was the most typical of the time. It is amazing how the texture of the silks remains uniform, smooth, and fine, whether the count be 160 warps by 100 wefts (Leningrad), 124 warps by 68 wefts (New Delhi), or 70–40 warps by 50–28 wefts per cm (Leningrad and New Delhi). But in no known instance have I come across a silk tabby with a thread count of 8 warps by 7 wefts per cm as stated to have been found on a silk pseudomorph by Vollmer. Such counts are only found in coarse linen, hemp, or wool.

11. Since this article was written we have received several offprints from Dr. Junro Nunome, Kyoto. Among these, the most relevant to my study is "Sen-shin gidai no kinu-seni oyobi sonota seni ni tsuite" [Studies on silk fibres and other fibres of the pre-Ch'in period], in Japanese with English summary, *Study Report,* vol. 7, no. 1, University of Industrial Arts and Textile Fibres, Kyoto, 1973, pp. 74–95. See also "On the cocoon shell of Yang-shao age excavated at Hsi-yin-ts'un of Shan-si province", 1967, pp. 187–194; "Development of the Japanese civilization and silk", *Shasi-Gizutsu,* no. 87 (August, 1973). Dr. Nunome has analyzed several fibres, notable among which are fibres adhering to the bronzes, a *chih* urn and a *yue* axe from the Yin Dynasty (see notes 7 and 10) in the collection of the Museum of Far Eastern Antiquities, Stockholm (until now we had believed that these bronzes were pseudomorphs [see note 8], and were entirely unaware that there were actual fibre remains adhering to the patina [fig. 1]); fibres of the Chu Manuscript (fig. 10; see notes 14 and 16); fibres from the silk lining of a bonnet, a silk kerchief, and a silk bonnet tie from Chang-sha, the Cooper-Hewitt Museum of Design, Smithsonian Institution, New York (fig. 6; see note 43); fibres from a silk kerchief that adhered to the cover of a lacquer box, in the collection of Dr. Paul Singer. Upon the evidence of these examinations, Nunome has made the following observations: differences in climate and silkworm strains; pre-Ch'in materials show tendency of weft>warp, while post-Han materials show warp>weft; no sign of "lousiness" found among the Warring States period samples; the brin count in threads of the plain-weave silks (tabby) suggests that single reelings were generally made from seven to ten cocoons (see note 9); the density of threads per square cm of the plain-weave silks of the Warring States period is somewhat greater than those of the Yin Dynasty and the Han–Lo-lang period (English summary, pp. 94–95). Comparative fibre research carried out by similar methods on well-documented archaeological textiles can only help to reinforce such an important undertaking.

In noting the variations in physical and chemical properties of various silk fibres, Nunome has drawn certain conclusions regarding the differences in fibre characteristics. These include specimens from different historical periods. He examined fibres from the silk fabrics of the Wang Hsu's tomb in Lo-lang (first century A.D.) and found especially small the cross-section of silk fibres belonging to the Han period; he consequently suggests the use of three-moulters fibre in their case (Nunome, *Kinuseni Ibutsu no Kenkyu* [Studies on silk fibre remains from the viewpoint of sericultural technique], in Japanese, with English summary, Laboratory of Rearing and Physiology of Silkworms, Kyoto, Taishogun Sakata-cho, Kita-Ku, 1967, pp. 1–56). Regarding "lousiness" (*raujinesu* in Japanese), a term frequently used by Nunome for denoting a fibre characteristic, Barnard argues that it refers to the fine hair-like fibres branching from the main strands of fibre ("The Chu Manuscript", 1971, pp. 29–30; see also note 16). He also says that it does not appear to be extensively used as a textile technical term by either English or American authors. The term seems to suggest a subjective assessment of a visual aspect of the fibre. It is nevertheless interesting that no "lousiness" was found to occur in the twenty-eight Han and Lo-lang fibre samples examined by Nunome (Barnard, "The Chu Manuscript", 1971, chart on p. 31, column on China). I have also tried to obtain further clarification of terms such as "lousiness". A suggested interpretation is that it refers to the fibrils (minute fibres forming the main fibre), which become visible only after degumming. It is possible that the microscopic observation of varying degrees of "lousiness" could help to reveal some fundamental characteristics relating uniquely to ancient fibres from pre-Ch'in or Han times.

Opinions vary regarding the diameter of a silk thread. Félix Guicherd (*Cours de théorie de tissage,* Lyon, Editions Sève, 1946, pp. 14–15) has pointed out that in a silk thread which is reeled off the cocoon, attaining a length of 800-1000 m, it is extremely difficult to find a diameter which remains uniform throughout. According to him, the diameter of a bave varies according to the quality of the cocoon, and variations exist between one cocoon and another. In fact, variations of diameter exist even within the same cocoon; the maximum diameter is usually located in the central layers of a cocoon.

12. Nunome, *Kinuseni Ibutsu no Kenkyu* (1967), p. 56. See also Sylwan, *Edsen-gol and Lop-nor* (1949), p. 163, where R. Pfister states, "Examen des soies etc. trouvées par l'Expédition de Sven Hedin à Edsen-gol: quelquefois j'ai indiqué le diamètre de la soie. 15 reste le maximum pour soie de Chine, mais il est très difficile d'établir une moyenne." Pfister's assertion that it is difficult to establish a mean diameter is of particular significance. On the basis that the fibres and filaments produced by silkworms vary in shape, microscopic image, *mu* diameter and

"titre en deniers", Pfister established a chart showing the origin and provenance of the silkworm in his *Textiles de Palmyre*, Paris, Editions d'Art et d'Histoire vol. 1, 1934, pp. 39, 55–58. He differentiated between the different types of *Bombyx mori* silkworms, and listed those which were reared in Han China, modern China, Syria, or Japan. Other specialists, such as William Willetts and Louisa Bellinger, used this chart as established fact, and attributed geographic provenances to silkworms, and hence to the origin of the silk yarns used in extant specimens.

13. A.A. Voskresensky and N.P. Tikhonov, "Technical study of textiles from the burial mounds of Noin-Ula", *Bulletin of the Needle and Bobbin Club,* vol. 20, nos. 1 and 2 (1936). The original version of their work was published in Russian in the "Bulletin (*Izvestia*) of the State Academy for the History of Material Culture", vol. 11 (1932), of which only parts 7 to 9 have been translated into English by Eugenia Tolmachoff in the above article.

Other interesting remarks have been made by Voskresensky and Tikhonov regarding the silk fibre of polychrome figured textile no. 14112 (Lubo-Lesnichenko, *Drevniye Kitaiskiye*, 1961, pl. 7, 1). The two Russian specialists state: "Technical analysis of material in warp no. 2: A preliminary microscopic study of the fibre, enlarged 500 times showed many characteristics of silk. Other fibres than silk were also found in the threads. Thus, assuming that the thread is in silk, it is imperative to make a most complete and thorough analysis of the nature of the fibre in this yarn" (*Bulletin of the Needle and Bobbin Club,* 1936, p. 29). The same comment is made for warp no. 3 of the same specimen. We have been given two sample fragments of this fabric and will soon be in a position to give further chemical and technical details. Another fragment of this fabric (Philadelphia Museum, no. 34–2–4) has been analyzed by H.B. Burnham (*Bulletin de liaison du CIETA,* no. 22, 1965, pp. 41–42).

14. Sergei I. Rudenko, *Kultura Khunov i noinulinskie Kurgany* [The culture of the Xiung-nu and the barrows of Noin-Ula], in Russian, Moscow-Leningrad, Izdaltel'stvo Akademii Nauk, 1962; S.I. Rudenko, *Frozen tombs of Siberia*, London, Dent, 1970. (The silk pouch is reproduced in pl. 134B; its thread count, 30 warps by 50 wefts per cm, is given on p. 206.)

15. The embroidered shabrack is reproduced in several publications. The silk is in tabby weave, finely worked with multicoloured silks portraying birds (phoenix?) sitting on branches in different poses. The following works discuss the specimen: Rudenko, *Frozen tombs* (1970), pp. 173–178 and pl. 178; Lubo-Lesnichenko, *Drevniye Kitaiskiye* (1961), p. 50 and pls. 49–50; I. Rudenko, *Drevneishiye v mire houdozhestveniye kovriye i tkane* [The world's most ancient art work in carpets and textiles], in Russian, Moscow, Isskousstvo, 1968, pp. 81–82, pls. 74 and 76. This shabrack was shown in the exhibition entitled "From the Land of the Scythians", Metropolitan Museum of Art, New York, 1975 (Exhibition Catalogue, no. 117, pl. 23). The other shabrack is of plain silk with a thread count of 40 warps by 52 wefts per cm. Selvages suggest a loom width of 44 to 49 cm. Rudenko (*Frozen tombs*, 1970, p. 206) gives the width as 44 cm.

Lubo-Lesnichenko (*Drevniye Kitaiskiye,* 1961, p. 50) gives the size of the embroidery extending from one selvage to another as 48 cm.

16. Of the two, only the Chu Manuscript has both selvages (loom width 47 cm, count ca. 57 warps and 27 wefts per cm). Photostat copies of papers presented by Noel Barnard, Minao Hiyashi, and Jean Mailey at the Symposium of Early Chinese Art and its Possible Influence in the Pacific Basin, Columbia University, N.Y.C., August 1967. All three papers were concerned with different aspects of the Chu Manuscript. For technical information regarding the weave, structure, and identification of the ground silk in plain tabby, see "Suggestions concerning the ground of the Chu Manuscript in relation to silk-weaving in pre-Han and Han China" by Mailey (no. 4). In addition to the loom width and thread count, this paper gives the information that the fabric is woven of untwisted and apparently undyed cultivated silk (*Bombyx mori*). Mailey made comparisons with the widths of other early Chinese silk fabrics, most of them from the Han period. She has also explored the Chinese terminology for silk and has supposed the silk fabric of the Chu Manuscript to be the *po* or *pi* type referred to in late Eastern Chou literature. On ancient Chinese technical terms for silk, see E. Lubo-Lesnichenko, "Nekotoriye terminiye dlya shelkovyh tkanii v drevnem Kitaye" [Some terms for silk textiles in ancient China], in Russian, *Trudii Gosudarestnnovo Ermitazha*, vol. 5 (1961), pp. 251–256.

In his report on the Chu Manuscript (1971), in which the different groups of results are summarized, Barnard analyzed the emplacement of the written characters, but more particularly emphasized and interpreted Nunome's report on the examination of the silk fibres. A fuller publication consisting of two volumes is announced. Barnard has taken considerable trouble to clarify Nunome's terminology, and to interpret the means employed by Nunome for his singular type of research (with particular reference to his *Kinuseni Ibutsu no Kenkyu*, 1967). Barnard affirms that results which have been mathematically processed and interpreted in terms of social-historical connections and of sericultural data, and which take into account factors such as geographical provenance, modes of cultivation, or methods of processing, "appear not only to confirm the importance of the type of research but also to illustrate how essential it is that more relevant materials be sampled and examined in the laboratory in order to establish a really comprehensive fund of data" (p. 34). We fully agree with this conclusion, and feel due regard for the type of work which Nunome has undertaken. A difficulty, however, regarding the correct understanding of points of approach and terminology has been raised by a number of colleagues and specialists in our team. It is to be hoped that in the future this difficulty will be overcome with clearer understanding and appraisal of Nunome's work.

17. For some years, I have established a close collaboration with M. Gabriel Vial, Technical Secretary of the CIETA, Lyon, who is responsible for analyses of weave; with Mme H. Meyer, analyst at the Centre de Recherches de la Soierie et des Industries Textiles (CRSIT), Lyon, who is responsible for microanalysis

and microphotography of fibres; and with Mrs. J. Hofenk de Graaf, textile analyst at the Central Research Laboratory for Objects of Art and Science, Amsterdam, who is responsible for analysis of dyestuff. For studies of ancient manuscripts, Chinese art history, and iconography, I have received constant help and advice from Dr. E. Lubo-Lesnichenko, Curator of the Far Eastern Department at the State Hermitage Museum, Leningrad, and from Mr. Hou Ching-lang, Sinologist at the Musée Guimet, Paris. The help of the junior technical assistants at the National Museum, New Delhi, is also to be acknowledged for making inventory and physical verification of objects in the Aurel Stein Collection. A project is under way to assemble a techno-historical report on all the silk samples from the Han and Tang dynasties which have been provided by the National Museum in New Delhi and the State Hermitage Museum in Leningrad. At present we possess nearly sixty samples for technical and chemical analyses. The publication will be undertaken by the team mentioned above.

For Han polychrome silks, see the exhaustive studies of H.B. Burnham: "Technical aspects of the warp-faced compound tabbies of the Han Dynasty", *Bulletin de liaison du* CIETA, no. 22 (1965), pp. 25–45; "Han polychrome silks", *Oriental Art* (1967), pp. 245–249; and "Some additional notes on the warp-faced compound tabby silks of the Han Dynasty", *Bulletin de liaison du* CIETA, no. 34 (1971/2), pp. 16–17. These articles treat every significant aspect of structure, concept, and execution in a most coherent and elucidating manner. In meticulously underlining the various subtleties of this intricate weave (warp-faced compound tabby), and in defining its structure, Burnham has rendered a true service for the study of Han silks. In studying the samples of figured silks from Noin-Ula and from Lou-lan, I have followed Burnham's guidelines and feel indebted to him. A study by Donald King ("Some notes on warp-faced compound weaves", *Bulletin de liaison du* CIETA, no. 28, 1968, pp. 9–18) provided us with further insight into the construction of the Lou-lan silks. Both Burnham and King have supplied persuasive proofs regarding the use of the pattern-rod loom for the weaving of these fabrics.

Through Vial's technical analyses of well over thirty Han samples, the use of the pattern-rod loom has been further examined. All samples were taken from specimens on which we have carried out technical studies in the last ten years. Our study has indicated that the technical characteristics of bi-colour and polychrome patterned silks, all in warp-faced compound tabby weave, show little variation except in the number of warps per series. We have detected up to four warps and five colours in certain specimens. I am intentionally curtailing all detailed information concerning warp and weft proportion at present, for such elements will be exhaustively dealt with when all textile samples have been examined.

18. After a study by Lubo-Lesnichenko and myself of monochrome and polychrome figured silks, which we attributed to the period of the Six Dynasties, we concluded that the monochrome figured silk S9 in Pfister's *Textiles de Palmyre*, vol. 1 (1934, p. 44, fig. 10 and pl. 11), is not from the Han period but from the early Six Dynasties. S9 has all the iconographic

elements warranting this attribution. In weave it is similar to several Han monochrome figured silks which are "monochrome figured tabby, patterned with alternately aligned three-span warp-floats" (type A). Another monochrome figured silk specimen which we attribute to the Six Dynasties period is from Kara-Bulak (for archaeological details see note 25). It has the same construction as the preceding example, and has firmly dated archaeological evidence from the post-Han period, presumably from the Six Dynasties period.

19. According to Sylwan (*Edsen-gol and Lop-nor*, 1949), four "warp rep damasks" (monochrome figured silk with ground in tabby and décor in three-span warp-floats) were found from mass grave 34 by Sven Hedin in the Qum-darya delta (p. 104, pls. 13A, B, C and figs. 51, 52). These fabrics belong to type A. Sylwan also refers to two "silk twill damasks" (monochrome figured tabby with ground in tabby and décor in twill), one from the dress of a young Chinese woman in grave 35 (p. 109, pls. 2C, 14B), and another from Edsen-gol, found by Folkes Bergman (p. 110, pl. 14A). These latter specimens belong to type B. A sea-green Han "damask", discovered by Sven Hedin in the site of the ancient Lou-lan station "on his first hazardous exploration expedition to the Lop Desert 1899-1901" (p. 106, fig. 53, pl. 11C), appears to be a variant of type A.

20. Sir Marc Aurel Stein, *Innermost Asia*, 4 vols., Oxford, 1928 (see Descriptive List, vol. 1, pp. 246–259). Of these five monochrome figured silks, four have been dealt with in my article, "Han Dynasty monochrome figured silks" (1973), pp. 122–138 (L.C.vii.09, pp. 126–129; and L.C.vi.01, pp. 130–131, of which there are two fragments from two different fabrics; L.C.ii. 05b and L.C.09b, p. 131, of which there are several fragments with the same ornamentation and thread count). L.H. O11, which is described here for the first time, is a monochrome figured silk in reddish-brown, very frayed, with classical Han ornamentation in the form of elongated lozenges or rhombuses. The height of repeat is probably 6 cm, the width is incomplete. Its thread count is 68–70 warps by 26–28 wefts per cm. Its ground is in tabby with décor in three-span warp-floats.

21. Lubo-Lesnichenko, *Drevniye Kitaiskiye* (1961), pp. 9–10, 29–35, pls. 8, 9, 10/1–2, 14/1–2, 18. The fragment from Kertch, found by Karesja in 1842, was the first Han fragment ever found (pl. 9), and is now definitely attributed to the second century A.D.

22. Pfister, *Textiles de Palmyre*, vol. 1 (1934). The monochrome figured silks, referred to as "soie damassée" are S4 (p. 40), S5 (p. 41), S6 (p. 42), S9, S10 (p. 44), and S11 (p. 45), pls. 9, 10b, 11, 13. Although S6 has been referred to as "soie damassée", it appears to be bi-coloured. For further observations on S6, see vol. 2 (1937), p. 36, fig. 17. Gabriel Vial says that he and Félix Guicherd were unable to follow the diagram of the weave in fig. 17b clearly. Pfister calls the weave twill, but Sylwan's diagram seems to indicate satin. S39 was a spectacular find: see vol. 3 (1940), pp. 39–40, 43–62, pls. 11 and 12. This fragment is a

close counterpart of L.C.vii.09 (Riboud, "Han Dynasty mono-chrome figured silks", 1973, pp. 126–129).

23. This fragment was exhibited at the major exhibition of archaeological finds from China in the Petit Palais, Paris, in 1973 (French exhibition catalogue no. 242). See also Riboud, "Han Dynasty monochrome figured silks" (1973), p. 127; Xia Nai, "Xinjiang xinfaxian de gudai sizhipin qi jing he cixiu" [New finds of ancient silk fabrics recently found in Sinkiang], in Chinese, *Kaoguxuebao*, no. 1 (1963), pp. 45–76 (an English summary in manuscript form, offered by H.B. Burnham, is in the CIETA library, Lyon); and *Sichou zhi lu Han Tang zhi wu* (1972), pl. 9.

24. *Changsha Mawangdui yihao Hanmu* (1973), vol. 1, pp. 48–49, and vol. 2, pl. 120; *Archaeological treasures excavated in the People's Republic of China*, exhibition catalogue, no. 32, Tokyo, 1973. These reports indicate that there are 100 warps by 46 wefts per sq cm. It is mentioned that while the outer décor is drawn vertically, the inside motifs are placed horizontally. The decoration consists of confronting birds with heads turned back, and two variants of floral ornaments. Each pattern unit measures 6.2 cm in length and 4.8 cm in width. Among the rest of the finds, a perfume bag (ref. no. 6511), a pillow cover (ref. no. 446), and a cover for a musical instrument have a similar type of silk. This fabric is a monochrome figured tabby patterned with 3:1 twill. Another monochrome figured silk patterned with 3:1 twill was discovered in Tomb 1 at Mawangdui (*Changsha Mawangdui yihao Hanmu*, 1973, pl. 140). It was exhibited at one of the major exhibitions of archaeological finds from China (Brussels Catalogue, 1975, no. 63; Japanese catalogue of archaeological treasures, 1973, no. 34). The weave diagram shows a ground in tabby with décor in 3:1 twill.

25. Together with other objects, the textiles in Kara-Bulak were discovered in a tomb belonging to a cemetery stretching almost two and a half kilometres from north to south, and 150 to 250 metres from east to west. Barouzdine had excavated 136 of the 900 tumuli. Soviet archaeologists believe that the cemetery was located on a vital point of the Silk Road. The finds indicate relations with Eastern Turkestan, Sogdia, and Iran. Finds of Chinese origin were mirrors of the *jingbai* (B) type (*ching-pai* [A]) with spirals. The textiles covered almost every category: fragments of garments, votive bands, embroidered mortuary eye- and face-covers, and a great amount of plain silk. Among the silks of Chinese origin are a fragment of monochrome figured silk (see note 18) and some very small textile fragments with quatrefoil motifs. There are also some small and frayed fragments of polychrome figured silk, and embroideries showing simple outlines of human figures and floral motifs. On one of these embroideries, the personages appear to wear pointed caps resembling Phrygian bonnets. In a series of lectures given at the Collège de France, Paris, in May 1975, Lubo-Lesnichenko traced the ornamentation of the Kara-Bulak silks to the Six Dynasties period. Through his kindness I was able to see these specimens, housed in the Institute of History of the Academy of Science of the Kirghiz Republic. I have had fruitful discussions with him on these textiles when in Leningrad in 1974, then again in Paris in 1975.

Other objects from Kara-Bulak show different influences. An Indian bronze statuette, now in the collection of the State Hermitage Museum, Leningrad, is illustrated by A. Belenitsky (*Central Asia,* in the series *Archaeologia Mundi*, Geneva, Nagel, 1971, pl. 65). Medallions with representations of the sun and the moon show Sassanian and Sogdian influence, while woven baskets might be connected with products of eastern Turkestan.

26. Specimen S11 from Palmyra with hexagonal motifs is illustrated by Pfister (*Textiles de Palmyre*, vol. 1, 1934, fig. 12). The monochrome figured silk with hexagons, found in Lop-nor, is reproduced by Sylwan (*Edsen-gol and Lop-nor*, 1949, figs. 51 and 52, pl. 13A and C). Although the fragment from Kara-Bulak is dated to the third to fourth century A.D., it is difficult to decide whether the two others could be of an earlier manufacture.

27. It would appear that there are some additional fragments of monochrome figured silks from other sites: one, excavated by Radlov in Shibe (collection of the Historical Museum, Moscow?); and another, excavated by Toll in 1936 in Haleby-Zenobia in Syria, see N.P. Toll, "The necropolis of Haleby-Zenobia: Preliminary exploration", *Annales de l'Institut Kondakov* (Seminarium Kondakovianum), vol. 9, Prague, Institute Kondakov, 1937, pp. 11–12. Toll's publication states that several fragments of Chinese silk were excavated at Haleby-Zenobia. Regarding T.11.2, one may assume that it was a bi-coloured silk. Toll mentions that "it is similar to, but not identical with the silk textile found in Palmyra, S4" (Pfister, *Textiles de Palmyre*, vol. 1, 1934, p. 40, fig. 7), yet Pfister clearly shows the weave diagram of a monochrome figured silk, on the obverse and reverse. These silks have been dated to the second to third century A.D. We are unaware of their present whereabouts, and feel unqualified to comment on them.

28. The diagram of the weave given in no. 32 of the Japanese catalogue (*Archaeological treasures*, 1973) proves that it is of the type of ground in tabby with décor in 3:1 twill.

29. Riboud, "Han Dynasty monochrone figured silks" (1973), p. 132.

30. Lubo-Lesnichenko, *Drevnije Kitaiskiye* (1961), p. 32 and pl. 14/2. MR 1403 (reproduced by Lubo-Lesnichenko) and MR 1410 (samples analyzed by Vial) are from the same fabric. For MR 1068, see p. 34 and pl. 18. See also note 31.

31. The scale of pattern repeat in MR 1403 and in the monochrome figured silk from Mawangdui (*Changsha Mawangdui yihao Hanmu*, 1973, pl. 120) correspond to each other. While the scale of pattern repeat in other silks of this group is much smaller, the iconography is the same. The decoration consists of classical variants of rhomboids (MR 1804, 1984, and 2111), or complex rhombuses and greatly stylized parts of birds (the pattern repeat of MR 1068 has an intermediary scale).

Monochrome figured silks, belonging to type B and possessing an unusually high density of warp ends, include : MR 1068 (160 warps by 50 wefts per cm, the scale of pattern repeat is ht. 5.8 cm, w. 5.8 cm); MR 1403 (118–120 warps by 32–34 wefts per cm, the scale of pattern repeat is ht. 8–8.2 cm, w. 3.8–3.9 cm); MR 1804 (120 warps by 55 wefts per cm, the scale of pattern repeat is ht. 1.7 cm, w. 1.7 cm); MR 1984 (120 warps by 42 wefts per cm, the scale of pattern repeat is ht. 2.1 cm, w. 0.9 cm); and MR 2111 (130 warps by 55 wefts per cm, the scale of pattern repeat is ht. 1 cm, w. 1.9 cm). In this group, only the découpure of MR 1068 and MR 1403 is known. Vial has calculated that while seventy-two pattern rods were used for the execution of MR 1068, sixty-two to sixty-six pattern rods were employed for the manufacture of MR 1403.

MR1410 and MR 1403 belonged to the same fabric. Since there exist several fragments from this silk, we were offered two samples for examination (10×7 cm; 7.5×5.8 cm; one with a selvage). The sample of MR 1068 given to us for analysis measures approximately 6.8×1.5 cm, and also has a selvage. For a diagram of these specimens see Lubo-Lesnichenko, *Drevniye Kitaiskiye* (1961), pls. 14/2 and 18. The other monochrome figured silks from Noin-Ula (State Hermitage Museum) belong to the same group as MR 2111 and MR 1984 (Lubo-Lesnichenko, 1961, pl. 10/1, 2), and MR 1804 (pl. 14/1). According to Lubo-Lesnichenko, these silks were found in tumulus 6. MR 1410 and 1403, however, came from tumulus 12. All five monochromes of this group, incredibly fine both in design and texture, are woven in the same technique, and reach a warp density between 120 and 160 ends per cm.

32. *Changsha Mawangdui yihao Hanmu* (1973), vol. 1, pp. 48–49, vol. 2, pl. 120.

33. Pfister, *Textiles de Palmyre*, vol. 3 (1940), pls. 11, 12.

34. Pfister (*Textiles de Palmyre*, vol. 1, 1934, p. 45) mentions only one exception, S11. The thread count of this fragment is 76 warps by 52 wefts per cm, which is still well below a count of 100 warps per cm.

35. *Changsha Mawangdui yihao Hanmu* (1973), see text in vol. 1, and English abstract (separate folio), p. 8.

36. For this lacquer cup and its inscription (fig. 16), and similar cups and associated finds, see Yetts, "Discoveries of the Kozlov expedition" (1926), pp. 168–185 and pl. 4L (mainly visible here is the base of the cup with the characters *shang-lin* written on it); Trever, *Excavations in Northern Mongolia* (1932), pls. 29/2, 30/1 (the inscription has been reproduced upside down); Umehara, *Moko Noin Ura* (1960), p. 30, pls. 59 centre (the inscription has been reproduced in the correct manner), 60, 61; Otto Maenchen-Helfen, book review of Umehara, *Moko Noin Ura* (1960), *Artibus Asiae*, vol. 27, no. 4 (1965), pp. 365–369; Rudenko, *Die Kultur der Hsiung-Nu* (1969), pp. 108–112 (tumulus 6). The lacquer cup, and several figured silks, mentioned in Lubo-Lesnichenko, *Drevniye Kitaiskiye* (1961), were found in tumulus 6, Noin-Ula.

37. K. Riboud and E. Lubo-Lesnichenko, "Nouvelles découvertes soviétiques à Oglakty et leur analogie avec les soies façonnées polychromes de Leou-lan, Dynastie Han", *Revue des Arts Asiatiques*, vol. 28 (1973), pp. 139–164.

38. Michael Loewe, *Crisis and conflict in Han China*, London, George Allen and Unwin, 1974, pp. 24–27; Hou Ching-lang, *Monnaies de l'offrande et la notion de trésorerie dans la religion chinoise*, vol. 1, Collège de France, Institut des Hautes Etudes Chinoises, Mémoires de l'Institut des Hautes Etudes Chinoises, Paris, 1975, p. 114.

39. Dr. A.G. Bulling mentioned in a letter to me that she had come across a great number of inscribed bronze vessels dated from 51 to ca. 19 B.C., which were found in Gao-yaocun, Sian, Shensi, in 1961, a little north of the place where in the Han period the A-fang palace had stood (*Kaogu*, no. 2, 1963, pp. 62 f.). According to Dr. Bulling, the Chinese publication indicates that together with the name of the artisan and other details, the name Shang-lin occurs as the place of manufacture on many of the vessels. We should, however, like to point out that inscriptions of this kind seem to indicate a "list" or "inventory", whereas the inscriptional characters found on polychrome figured silks are of a different nature relating to felicity, prosperity, and longevity. A typical instance of an "inventory"-type inscription appears in Umehara, *Moko Noin Ura* (1960), p. 30, pl. 59. It shows a lacquer cup from Noin-Ula (tumulus 5), which has a long inscription of sixty-nine characters on its base, giving the names of artisans who participated in the execution of the cup. Presumably this object is preserved in a museum in the People's Republic of Mongolia (Ulan-Bator?).

40. While all bi-colour figured silks known to us share the same technical characteristics as the ones in polychrome (warp-faced compound tabby), Lubo-Lesnichenko and I believe that there is a group of bi-colour silks in indigo blue and yellow whose ornamental features might warrant an earlier dating than that given to most of the polychrome figured silks (finds from Lou-lan and Oglakty).

41. In 1974, Lubo-Lesnichenko had the Pazyryk bi-colour figured silk taken out of the glass frame for a close study. It struck me that all photographic reproductions of this specimen show the ground in dark, and the motifs in light colour. On closer examination it seemed that the reverse could be the case. Through a continuing study of Han bi-colour silks, one begins to notice subtle differences in texture between the surface and the reverse side. Figure 6 shows the silk as it has usually been represented.

42. Mme Meyer reports: "Pazryk Travaux exécutés: Schirlastain sur fils. Chaine: soie décreusée en parfait état de conservation. Microphoto sur fil: coupes des fibres. Trame: traces de grès; il apparait à certains endroits du fil une mince pellicule qui se teint en rouge très foncé, légèrement craquelée. En raison des fibres trop courtes en trame il n'a pas été possible de faire une coupe." (See note 17.)

43. Jean Mailey and Calvin S. Hathaway, "A bonnet and a pair of mitts from Chang-sha", *Chronicle of the Cooper Union Museum*, vol. 2, no. 10 (December 1958), pp. 315–372. According to Mailey and Hathaway, it is possible that the Chang-sha mittens and bonnet date from the late Eastern Chou. They would then, with the Pazyryk fabric, be the only figured specimens known from this period. It seems more logical, however, to compare the Chang-sha specimens with some Noin-Ula fabrics. In both instances the same technical features, the same type of ornamentation, and even the same colour scheme occur. Regarding the authors' contention that a "felicitous balanced asymmetry of all over aspect" seems to prevail in the Chang-sha specimens (p. 337), while it is absent in the Noin-Ula silks (and therefore the Chang-sha silks are earlier), I may point out that certain finds in Tomb 1 at Mawangdui (*Changsha Mawangdui yihao Hanmu*, 1973, pls. 123 and 124) share the same ornamental and balanced asymmetry. The Mawangdui finds certainly belong to the Western Han period. Whatever the case may be, technically speaking, many Noin-Ula silks have only a single repeat from one width to another, and therefore have asymmetrical patterning in the width.

In a recent article in *Wenwu* (no. 2, 1975, pl. 1, figs. 17, 18, p. 56) fragments of polychrome figured silk, similar to the bonnet and mitts in the collection of the Cooper-Hewitt Museum of Design, Smithsonian Institution, are reproduced. Careful note has been taken of all the technical descriptions of the textiles, including the inscription on the selvage of one of the fragments (pp. 51–52). The inscription is presumed to be in an archaic *chuan* style; it denotes the name of the workshop and that of the weaver. The dating to the Warring States period (475 B.C. –A.D. 221) was based on the finds and the forms of the tomb. The attribution of the textiles to the Warring States period was made on the basis of stylistic features. It has also been mentioned that the tombs had been pillaged. It seems difficult to conclude from the publication whether or not these tombs and their contents can be scientifically dated to a pre-Han period.

44. Three specimens found in the Dunhuang Limes are preserved at the British Museum, London (T.XV.a.002a, T.XV.a.iii.0010a, and T.xxii.c.0010a. See Stein, *Serindia*, vol. 4, 1921, pl. 55). A woven string shoe with scraps of polychrome figured silk (T.XV.a.1.006, ibid., pl. 55) is preserved at the Victoria and Albert Museum, London. For all technical details of these silks, see King, "Some notes on warp-faced compound weaves" (1968), pp. 9–18. The ornamental features of T.xxii.c.0010a (in two separate fragments; I refer here to the larger piece) bear little resemblance to any other specimen in the entire repertoire of Han ornamentation in figured silks. It seems to correspond rather to the stylistic trends of the Six Dynasties period.

45. Since the publication of my article entitled "Some remarks on strikingly similar Han figured silks found in recent years in diverse sites" (*Archives of Asian Art*, vol. 26, 1972–1973, pp. 12–25), I now feel confident that this patterned silk from Palmyra (Pfister, *Textiles de Palmyre*, vol. 3, 1940, pl. 16a) can be grouped together with L.C. 08 and with two Oglakty fragments from the border of the arrow-sheath. The two inscriptional characters (*wan* and *ming*) are the same as two of the six characters in L.C. 08 and the Oglakty finds.

46. For the piece with complete inscription, see *Sichon zhi lu Han Tang zhi wu* (1970), pls. 4, 5. Two other polychrome patterned silks are mentioned at the nomadic site of Djalai-nor in Inner Mongolia (*Wenwu*, 1961, no. 9). In the diagram given in figure 18, one can read two inscriptional characters (*ru* and *yi*), which are the same as those on a polychrome silk from Minfeng (Xia Nai, *Kaoguxuebao*, 1963, no. 1, colour pl. 1). The characters in the latter specimen are *wan, si, ru,* and *yi* meaning "ten thousand generations, desires be fulfilled". A brief report on the textile finds in Tomb 2 at Mawangdui states that these are polychrome figured silks and that they are more complex in design than those found in Tomb 1 (*Wenwu*, 1974, no. 7, p. 45). They have motifs which are geometrical, with quadrupeds and confronting birds. A full published report is eagerly awaited.

47. Several examples of silk in "pile brocade" are presented in *Changsha Mawangdui yihao Hanmu* (1973), vol. 1, colour pls. 123, 124, 137; and vol. 2, pp. 49–51, figs, 42, 43. A "pile brocade" was also reproduced in the Japanese catalogue (*Archaeological treasures*, 1973, nos. 27–28). Although the diagram of the weave seems to imply that it is essentially in warp-faced compound tabby (no. 28), the Chinese description of the construction is not very clear to us: "The 'pile brocade', a new variety of Han Dynasty 'brocades' . . . is woven with four sets of warps, with each square cm containing 176–224 warps and 41–50 wefts. Its manufacture required a combined use of the fancy weave mechanism and the pile mechanism. This indicates that a rather elaborate loom was already in use in the Chinese silk industry over some 2,100 years ago."

48. The fragment from Noin-Ula (Lubo-Lesnichenko, *Drevniye Kitaiskiye*, 1961, pl. 13) is described in the following way: "Cloth 14029 from tumulus 15, while completely resembling the interlacings of other polychrome silks of the Han period, has one essential difference. This difference consists in the pattern being executed in relief. Probably the weaver achieved it by loosening at certain intervals the second pattern-forming warp, and after fastening it with the weft threads, tightened it again. As a result, the threads formed shallow loops, but remained fastened by the weft. Thanks to this process, the ornament on the textile showed up not only in colour, but also in relief. Using this manner of weaving where the ornament appears also in relief was particularly important for a design of small dimensions, because a supplementary clarity could be achieved, and the pattern resembled an embroidery. This manner of weaving is evidenced only by the above described sample." (Mrs. Priverts' translation, p. 16.) Specimen 14029 was also published by Voskresensky and Tikhonov as no. 13930 in *Izvestia,* vol. 9 (1932).

49. Max Loehr, *Ritual vessels of Bronze Age China*, New York,

Asia House Gallery, 1968, pp. 11–12, on Han decoration. See also William Watson, *Style in the arts of China*, Penguin Books, 1974, pp. 95–98. His technical concept regarding the execution of Han silks, however, is not very clear.

50. Lubo-Lesnichenko, *Drevniye Kitaiskiye* (1961).

51. William Willetts, *Chinese art*, 2 vols., London, Penguin Books, 1958 ("Lacquers and silk", vol. 1, part 4, pp. 174–187); W. Willetts, *Foundations of Chinese art*, London, Thames and Hudson, 1965.

52. John Lowry, "Han textiles excavated by Sir Aurel Stein and others", *Oriental Art* (N.S.), vol. 6, no. 2 (1960), pp. 3–7; J. Lowry, "Early Chinese silks", *CIBA Review*, 1963/2, pp. 10–12. He attributes L.C.07a from Lou-lan and MR 1405 from Noin-Ula (Lubo-Lesnichenko, *Drevniye Kitaiskiye*, 1961, pl. 40b) to the Eastern Han or early Six Dynasties period.

53. Lowry ("Early Chinese silks", 1963, p. 13) states that a textile from the National Museum, New Delhi, "presumably dates from the inter-Han-T'ang period" (L.C.02; see Stein, *Innermost Asia*, 1928, pl. 36). On p. 16 he refers to another fragment of the National Museum as "probably Six Dynasties period". While Lubo-Lesnichenko and I believe that some of these textiles could belong to Eastern Han, none in our opinion belongs to the Six Dynasties. Regarding the dating of the fragment reproduced by Lowry ("Early Chinese silks", p. 16: L.C.01; see also Stein, *Innermost Asia*, 1928, pl. 35), see Riboud and Lubo-Lesnichenko, "Nouvelles découvertes soviétiques" (1973), p. 143, pls. 12a–b.

54. Riboud and Lubo-Lesnichenko, "Nouvelles découverts soviétiques" (1973), p. 145.

55. For the best photographic reproduction of MR 1405 from Noin-Ula, see Umehara, *Moko Noin Ura* (1960), pls. 35, 57.

56. Yetts, "Discoveries of the Kozlov expedition" (1926), p. 181.

57. E. Lubo-Lesnichenko, "Nadpisi na kitaiskih shelkovyh tkanah perioda Han v gosudarstvennom Ermitazha" [The inscription on a Chinese silk fabric of the Han period at the Hermitage Museum], in Russian, *Epigrafika Vostoka*, vol. 13 (1960), Moscow, Institute of Archaeology, Academy of Sciences of the USSR, pp. 95–99, pl. 7. In this article, the author deals with the inscriptions of five of the seventeen polychrome figured silks from Noin-Ula. Kuang-Ch'êng is identified as a mythical philosopher and sage of antiquity, mentioned in the book *Kuan-tzu* in the third century B.C. (Lubo-Lesnichenko, *Drevniye Kitaiskyie*, 1961, pp. 47–49; Mrs. Priverts' translation, pp. 78–81). He adds that this writing indicates the popularity of Kuang-Ch'êng as a mythical heavenly inhabitant among the dominant classes of the Han period.

58. Umehara, *Moko Noin Ura* (1960).

59. Maenchen-Helfen, *Artibus Asiae* (1965), p. 367. In this article Professor Shih-hsiang Chen proposes that Kuang Ch'êng was an ancestor of Wang Mang. Hou Ching-lang, however, claims that one does not find any evidence of Kuang Ch'êng having been sanctified or made a divinity during the Han Dynasty. He makes a tentative suggestion that Kuang Ch'êng be interpreted as a new spirit, a new cycle or the apogée of an evolution ("Que cet esprit nouveau possède sa puissance et rassure une grande récolte et longévité pendant dix mille ans"), (fig. 17).

60. L.C.07a (Stein, *Innermost Asia*, 1928, pl. 34). See also Riboud, "Han Dynasty monochrome figured silks" (1973), pp. 17–23, 24, note 23 (fragment found in Lop-nor).

61. Transliterations : (A) *Chien-p'ing wu nien chiu yüeh kung Wang T'an-ching hua kong Huo hu T'ien-wu shĕng*; (B) *Jianping wu nian jiu yue, gong Wang Tanjing hua gong Huo Hu, Tianwu sheng*; (C) *Kien-ping wou nien kieou yue, kong Wang T'an-king, houa kong Houo Hou, Tien-wou cheng*. One of the first translations of this inscription is in Trever, *Excavations in northern Mongolia* (1932), pp. 14–15 : "September of the 5th year of the *Chien-p'ing* (2 B.C.). The manufacturer — *W'ang-t'an-ching*. Painter of the decoration — '*Huo*', [another] manufacturer '*T*', superintended by '*Pien wu*'." The second decipherement is given by Umehara, *Moko Noin Ura* (1960), p. 60 (A). Umehara does not give a translation, but Hou Ching-lang translates his transliteration (C) the following way : "The era *Chien-p'ing* fifth year ninth month / the artisan *Wang T'an-ching* / the painter-artisan *Hou-Hu* [*huo-hu*] / [made at] *T'ien-wu shêng*". Dr. Michael Loewe, Head of the Faculty of Oriental Studies, University of Cambridge, has suggested the following "as a very tentative rendering" (personal communication, 1975) : "Fashioned by *Wang T'an*, the artisan, and inspected by *T'ien wu*, the painter and *huo-hu* in the ninth month of the fifth year of *Chien-p'ing*". According to Dr. Loewe, "*Huo-hu* is . . . a technical term for one of the craftsmen involved in the process; it appears on another inscription (also on a lacquer vessel) as *hu-huo*."

62. Transliterations :(A) *hsin shên ling kuang ch'êng shou wan nien*; (B) *xin shen ling guang cheng shou wan nian*; (C) *sin chen ling kouang tch'êng cheou wan nien*. For a suggested translation of this inscription by Hou Ching-lang, see note 59.

63. Transliterations : (A) *Hsü shih chin yi tzŭ sun;* (B) *su shi jing i zhi sun;* (C) *siu che kin yi tseu souen*. The translation given by Dr. Lionel Giles (Stein, *Innermost Asia*, 1928, vol. 2, p. 1046) is the following : "May your posterity continue to adorn each succeeding generation." While this is the first instance where a horizontal inscription reads from left to right, Stein and Giles had read it from right to left, as is customary with all other silks with inscriptional characters. The six characters from left to right are : *hsü* (prolonged), *shih* (generations), *chin* (brocade), *yi* (may), *tzu* (sons), *sun* (grandsons). Hou Ching-lang (C) tran-

scribes it from left to right : *siu (prolonger)*, *che (générations)*, *kin (brocart)*, *yi (convenir)*, *tseu (fils)*, *souen (petit fils)*. Dr. Hsio-yen Shih (B) gives the following translation : "Brocade of continuing generations. May it bring luck to your descendants."

64. Transliterations : (A) *ch'ang lê ming kuang;* (B) *chang le ming guang;* (C) *tch'ang lö ming kouang.* Translation : *ch'ang* (eternal) *lê* (joy) *ming* (clear, bright) *kuang* (brilliant light). An interpretation of this inscription is given by Dr. Lionel Giles (Stein, *Innermost Asia*, 1928, vol. 2, p. 1046, under L.C.ii.07a) : "May your joy be [constant] and your faculties bright." Through a study of technical, ornamental, and inscriptional features, I have been able to establish that L.C.11.07a and L.C.iii.011 are fragments of the same fabric. See also Stein, *Innermost Asia* (1928), vol. 1, p. 237.

The Introduction of the Jacquard Loom to Great Britain

Natalie Rothstein

ROBERT Graham, a Spitalfields manufacturer, told the House of Commons Select Committee investigating the silk trade in 1832 that "the Jacquard engine was probably the greatest invention that ever was introduced into the silk trade".[1] Yet in 1835 Claude Guillotte, a manufacturer of jacquard looms, told the Select Committee on Arts and Manufactures that he did not sell any for use in the cotton industry and that in his opinion it was much too expensive to use in the Scotch shawl trade.[2] This statement was made thirty-four years after Jacquard had shown his loom in the Paris Exhibition of 1801. Why did it take so long for an apparently useful invention to be accepted in the country regarded as the home of the industrial revolution? When did it reach that country; when and where did it come into general use?

In order to get a free pattern upon a woven textile (as opposed to simple patterns of squares and chevrons all over the cloth) the warp threads of the textile must be controlled individually, or at least in very small groups. For two or three thousand years such control was obtained by the drawloom, an ingenious device of cord, wood, and lead weights.[3] The warp is entered through the figure harness, through the eyes of the mails on each cord, and then through the heddles on the shafts to produce the weave of the textile. The cords of the figure harness go through the comber board above the loom and are tied at the neck and carried to the side of the weaver's shop. The strings attached to them which

hang at the side of the loom constitute the simple. The whole was referred to as a "mounture".[4] The pattern was set up by selecting the correct cords on the simple and tying them with lashes, one bundle of lashes for each line of the design. The drawloom was slow to set up and changing the pattern took a long time. To operate the loom required not only a weaver to open the shed with treadles but also a drawboy to pull the lashes for each line of the design. Because it was made of wood and string it was impossible to work each warp thread individually. They had to be grouped in mails of three to ten threads to avoid friction. The outline of a drawloom woven pattern was thus necessarily jagged. Much skill was needed both to design for it and to weave on it successfully. The materials it made were, therefore, expensive, but since silk, gold and silver thread, and even fine worsted were all intrinsically expensive anyway, the labour costs were, relatively, acceptable. It was on this loom that the grand silks of the eighteenth century were woven and as long as large patterns were fashionable[5] it did its work excellently.

From about 1770 there was a profound change in the patterns of dress materials, and drawloom woven furnishings hardly come into the picture. Patterns became smaller and materials softer, and the silhouette was more romantic, rounded to the form. Silks faced competition from printed cottons, muslins, and even embroideries, in France as well as in England. In such conditions the expensive drawloom was becoming irrelevant.

Jacquard's invention was the result of a series of improvements designed by others in the course of the eighteenth century but it was he who brought

The first draft of this paper was prepared for a History of Science discussion group at the Royal Institution, London, on 20 February 1974.

them together. The cords of the figure harness were replaced with hooks and needles, and the simple and lashes with cards punched with holes. One card represented one colour in one line of the design, and a hole was punched when the warp thread had to be raised. When the card was in position on the top of the loom the weaver depressed his treadle, the needles pressed against the card, and only where there were holes could the needle pass through, carrying upwards the appropriate warp thread. The machine turned on automatically after each card.

The great advantage of the jacquard lay in its total elimination of the drawboy. Secondly, it enabled each warp thread to be controlled separately, theoretically at any rate, making the designer's task much easier: he had no need to worry about curved lines. Thirdly, the pattern could be changed in a few minutes, provided the cards were cut and laced together (which begs several questions). Fourthly, the jacquard could imitate any weave, make any figure, and introduce a range of effects hitherto unknown. Finally, since the motive power was reduced to the treadling action of one man it could be operated by power. Logically, then, the jacquard should have come into immediate use, so many were its advantages, but in fact it took at least ten years before the loom was accepted commercially in Lyon. According to Claude Guillotte, the jacquard was used commercially in 1810, improved in 1814, and established by 1815.[6] The delay is less surprising if we turn from technical considerations to the fashions of the time. At no time in the century before or the nearly two hundred years since have the materials for fashionable dress been so plain as in the decade from 1800 to 1810. Such patterns that did appear were virtually unchanged from those of the 1790s — quite unlike the situation in the first seventy years of the eighteenth century, when patterns changed with the season. Hence dress accessories, shawls and ribbons, became extremely important. If there was a demand for a loom which could make patterns better and more cheaply it was in the shawl and ribbon industries, but since they were making fashionable accessories no one expected their products to be cheap and for expensive goods the drawloom was perfectly efficient.

The next chapter in the story contains the one dramatic interlude. Every witness to the early nine-

teenth-century Parliamentary Committees agreed that Mr. Stephen Wilson, of Lea, Wilson, & Co., was the first to introduce the jacquard loom into the British Isles. In 1818 he was the first to mention it, though not by name, and his evidence does not suggest that he was familiar with it.[7] William Hale told the Select Committee which sat in 1821 that Spitalfields was superior to Lyon in every way, "but there was one piece of machinery which far exceeds ours . . . a method of weaving very fine figured works with one treadle", and he estimated the saving of time and labour as twenty per cent in the cost of the piece.[8] Even two years later an operative weaver who was questioned on the subject simply refused to believe in the jacquard.[9] Stephen Wilson also gave evidence to the Committee.[10] He had been a prisoner of war in France and thus spoke French. He too described the "superior machinery for the finer figured works which greatly surpass our's . . . it enables them to change their pattern in a few minutes." He spoke about the abolition of the drawboy but did not think that the jacquard would come into general use very quickly, "as it requires a great height, eleven or twelve feet and the rooms in most weavers' houses are only from eight to nine feet" (a valid point, and it led to the use of a slightly differently arranged jacquard in Spitalfields). He did not tell the Committee that he had sent an industrial spy to Paris who wrote back to him a most enthusiastic letter.[11] The spy had "seen the beginning, the middle and the end of the process — the reeding in — the stamping of the paste-boards — the tacking of them together". He had "seen them at work" for he had "mounted a platform and looked into the very bowels of the machine", and, indeed, was bringing back a hook as Wilson had requested, "and also a small bit of the Pasteboard to show its texture". Again Wilson failed to tell the Committee that he was already experimenting with the construction of the loom.

Two years later we learn rather more. This time William Hale said that he and his family had seen the jacquard when touring Switzerland and Italy in 1816 and that he had told his fellow manufacturers about it, "and Mr Stephen Wilson after a time went over and saw the loom and got a patent for it".[12] Wilson repudiated any debt to Hale and gave the Committee a long list of mechanical inventions impossible to introduce into London because of the Spitalfields Acts which regulated wages. It may be added that he started a myth about the effects of Protection which has continued to this day. Not one of the mechanisms he described[13] came into use after the abolition of the Spitalfields Acts because they were irrelevant to the kinds of textile woven in London. Wilson then discussed in detail the new French loom for which he had a patent. He had first heard of it in 1810 from a literary publication. It was not generally used in France and he said that he was the only one to have built a machine in England and had been operating it for nearly two years. Since he said that he was ready to make them for the trade if the Spitalfields Acts were repealed, and since the weavers' houses had not grown a couple of feet, one can only deduce that he had in mind the creation of a factory system in London. The abolition of the fixed list of prices — the piece rates to be paid for different silks — in Macclesfield in 1818 had enabled the masters to build up their factories using semi-skilled labour at the expense of their outworkers.

The Select Committee was given some idea of the technical innovations which were possible. Wilson showed them two shawls which could only be made on the jacquard because of the "immense weight and quantity of lash" which would have been needed on a drawloom. On the latter "they would never work clear", that is, the cords would have rubbed against one another and either broken or become entangled, lifting more than the required threads and thus spoiling the pattern. Figure 1 shows a pattern for a shawl or handkerchief dated 1823. It has long technical instructions for drafting it and a very unusual admonition that "it must be read in very correct not a lash wrong when read as far as here must have further direction". On the back of the pattern is the reason for this caution (fig. 2). The pattern was "to be shot 50 to the inch which will make it longer. Should it still not be long enough a few duplicate pasteboards may be introduced." This is one of the first tentative British attempts at a jacquard woven fabric. The pattern is part of the large collection from the Warner archive, and there are grounds for thinking that Stephen Wilson's firm passed ultimately into the hands of Warner's.[14] Wilson emphasized the speed at

which a material could be woven; three or four yards a day and 7,000 lashes were possible in the length of a pattern, which would make a fairly large design. This is especially interesting in the light of the surviving patterns. There is virtually no difference between those of, for instance, 1793, 1809, or 1818, and those of 1826 which specify "the jacquart machine" (figs. 4, 5, 6, 7). It is much later that we begin to see really long patterns. Stephen Wilson's relative, Samuel Wilson, also tried out a jacquard woven fabric in 1826. "The work must be made with a Jacquart machine on account of the ground being 2 thread, were the tabby is it is cut by single threads, all the art and mystery is in putting on the rule paper, there must be separate papers or each lash must be drawn separately, when prepared for reading in the paper will have no appearance of a pattern."[15]

We now come to an uncomfortable hiatus, for Stephen Wilson's efforts were by no means the end of the story. The witnesses who touched on this subject when giving evidence to the Parliamentary Committees of 1832 and 1835 and those giving evidence to the Handloom Weavers Commissions are unanimous on one point — the decline in the use of the jacquard. Stephen Wilson made shawls with it, yet Claude Guillotte said it was too expensive to use for shawls. In any case, it seems that both "tissued" and gauze shawls went out of fashion by about 1821 and 1824 respectively.[16] It is worth considering what kinds of patterned fabrics were being produced in the late 1820s: carpets at Wilton, Kilmarnock, and Edinburgh; shawls in Spitalfields, Norwich, Edinburgh, and Paisley. Paisley was also making fancy gauzes and figured cottons. Ribbons were being woven in Coventry, Nuneaton, and the countryside about. Fancy quiltings and worsteds were produced especially for waistcoats in the West Riding in and around Halifax and Huddersfield, with an increasing tendency to weave all cotton goods as one moves up the Colne Valley towards Lancashire. In Bolton cotton goods were woven — on the drawloom — while linen damasks were produced chiefly in Scotland, also on the drawloom.[17] Despite Wilson's claim and despite the occasional well-publicized royal order it is difficult to find any place in England or Scotland which was producing much patterned upholstery at the time.

According to Guillotte, in Norwich the expense "has prevented its being much used in the silk manufacture", and he had only sold a few jacquards to London firms.[18] Among the Warner point-papers there is little evidence of its application. There is one from the firm of Stephen Wilson after 1826 but it was probably not intended for a jacquard (fig. 3),[19] and most of the point-papers have too small a number of cords and lashes to suggest that they were used for jacquard weaving. Unfortunately, the vocabulary of the technical instructions on both the point-papers in the Warner archive and the designs for shawls in Paisley tended to be conservative. It is sometimes evident that drawloom terms such as "cord" and "lash" were used for the jacquard. It is only the use of terms such as "pasteboards" or "hooks" that is a certain indication, since these terms have no counterpart in drawloom weaving.

The period after the opening of the English market to foreign silks in 1826 was one of catastrophic slump. The causes were complex; although foreign competition brought a loss of confidence this was not the only reason, since the French industry also had some lean years at this time. Far from making use of new inventions, witnesses explained why they had had to give up their jacquards. Thomas Stone of Stone and Brooks said that since the introduction of French goods a third of the weavers were unemployed and the industry had been concentrated in the hands of a few firms.[20] He had taken over a firm in 1825 from a weaver who had given up the weaving of fancy goods because of the lack of demand. The use of the jacquard had declined, for "the profit was the same as the common engine . . . when you take into account the expenses of the jacquard".[21] William Bridges claimed he had examples woven in 1822 of the first jacquard materials. He had had 140 jacquards in 1824, the greatest number he had ever had, but said that there was hardly any fancy trade left in Spitalfields.

Coventry faced the same desperate situation as Spitalfields when French ribbons were permitted into the country in 1826. According to several accounts a Mrs. Dresser introduced the jacquard loom to Coventry in 1822.[22] There were said to have been five jacquards in Coventry in 1823, 219 in 1826, and by 1831, although there were 700, most of them were idle.[23] A number of the point-papers in the

Warner archive are for ribbons and were imported from France. They bear the Customs stamp for George IV (1821–1830) which gives a terminal date. Several are sufficiently elaborate to be for jacquard woven fabrics,[24] while others contain revealing instructions mentioning, for example, "258 hooks", "224 cartroni", or the "méchanique" instead of the "métier" or "remisse".[25] They bear out a point made by a Coventry manufacturer that they were able to keep in touch with French taste not by importing ribbons but by seeing and importing designs.[26] William Merry of Brown and Merry of Cheapside and Coventry said that they had first used the jacquard in 1825: "It made the figures much larger and in fact cut to a thread which was very superior work to that made before by the old description of looms."[27] A handloom weaver made one significant point that fewer fancy ribbons had been made in the countryside since the introduction of the jacquard because "the machine is so expensive it is therefore applied more to the engine looms than the single hand-looms used in the country".[28] In 1832 a ribbon manufacturer of Nuneaton had bought jacquards being sold off for £18, which had cost £40-50 when they were built in 1827.[29] Cleophas Ratcliff summed up the "regret" of those who had put up jacquards.

The textile industries of Paisley were in a sense an offshoot of those in London. Several London gauze manufacturers had set up there in the late eighteenth century and the link between the two remained, although the industry was diversified to include muslins, cottons, and shawls. The latter were a "different fabric" from those woven in London,[30] and there are two pattern books in Paisley dating from 1811 and 1808–1815 which contain a few samples of shawl fabric very different from the silk shawls of Spitalfields.[31] Several of the earliest jacquard patterns are connected with Paisley. A pattern in the Warner archive dated 1824, Paisley, bears the instructions: "Read 20 lashes on one simple. Stamp 1 dozen lashes and they must tried before the others are stamped. Read the green and the red as one colour every two lines one lash"[32] (a pleasant mixture of vocabulary, but only on a jacquard would the "lashes" be *stamped*). Another on a paper watermarked 1819 tells the workman to read the white on one card and the yellow on a second card.[33] There are also several designs which may be and others which must be for jacquard woven fabrics from the thirties onwards. It would, however, be wrong to assume from this evidence alone that the jacquard made the greatest progress in Scotland. In his *Art of weaving*, published in 1827 and based on the linen industry, John Murphy speaks of the "New French Drawloom" and misses several technical points when describing it. The Paisley Museum and Art Gallery is the only institution in the British Isles which owns a full-size drawloom and it is certainly no older than the 1840s. In the 1820s and 1830s shawls were still articles of high fashion. James Forbes, a Paisley shawl manufacturer, told the Handloom Weavers Commission of 1834 that he used very few power looms though they were used for a "cheap kind of shawl" made of cotton cloth with some bordering but he had never made any of them. Forbes explained that the two markets for shawls were Glasgow and London. Moreover, the Weavers Association remained quite powerful in Paisley and succeeded in keeping up the wages for making the best quality figured shawls. They owned jointly their own card-cutting matrix in the 1860s.[34]

Claude Guillotte mentioned one other area to which he had sold jacquards. While he received orders in London for six to ten at a time, from Yorkshire he had orders for sixty to eighty. He told the Select Committee on Arts and Manufactures that they were used for merinos and damasks and similar goods in Bolton and Manchester, where he had agents. He described a trip he had made, accompanied by an interpreter, to Halifax, Huddersfield, and the surrounding countryside, which had resulted in an order from Mr. Gill followed by a further order for a hundred jacquards. "These were to replace the old mechanism which was employed in producing small patterns, those [which] are principally used for waistcoats."[35] According to James' *History of the worsted manufacture in England*, published in 1857, the jacquard was introduced into the damask trade in Halifax in 1827 by James Ackroyd of Old Lane, supplied by a Mr. Sago of Manchester.[36] This became a traditional story but proof one way or the other is lacking. Another later account tells of a Frenchman who came to Huddersfield in 1830–1831 and invited inspection of the jacquard at the George Inn.[37] Most of the manufacturers were not impressed, preferring their own drum witch with a capacity of 40 shafts and the engine witch with 24-160 shafts (fig. 14). One manufacturer, Gill and Sugden of Woodsome Lees, decided to use the jacquard. The patterns on their fancy vestings were limited to 160 threads while the jacquard could make a pattern on 400. This story is so close to Guillotte's evidence that it can surely be accepted.

Even this is far from being the end of the story. The witch loom was perfectly adequate for small patterns (fig. 8), and the wages were extremely low. Consequently it remained in use, just like the drawloom in Paisley. Several examples of the witch loom have survived, some dismantled and some in working order.[38] In the pattern book of Robert Roebuck of Honley, near Huddersfield, dated 1830, there is a series of typical waistcoat materials (fig. 9), some of which have technical notes such as "21 bars" or "30 bars", terms without any meaning in jacquard technology. Devoge (see below) supplied several customers in 1844 and even 1845 with what appear to be accessories for witch looms. William Whyte's *History and directory of Huddersfield* of 1837 listed the goods made there including "fancy goods to a great extent in an endless variety embracing shawls, waistcoatings of the most elegant patterns, in worsted, silk and cotton".

Since the mechanization of the textile industries occurred first and went furthest in Lancashire, the jacquard loom should have made rapid progress there. In 1834 Thomas Myerscough of Bolton gave an account of his life in the cotton quilt industry to the Handloom Weavers Commission.[39] He had gone to Bolton in 1811 when the wage for weaving a quilt using two simples and two drawboys was 11s. He spoke of the reduction in wages since and he thought that the "jacquard will lower the rate of wages" without affecting the weaver. John Scott of Manchester gave evidence the next year.[40] He had been offered a jacquard a few months previously which he had declined as it would have cost £5 to get it going and the difference in wages did not make it worthwhile.[41] Henry Tootal of Manchester had made silk handkerchiefs and mixed goods since 1822.[42] He thought that about thirty jacquards were in use in 1828 and by 1835, the date when he was giving evidence, they were getting into "pretty general use" for both pure silk and mixed goods, though he qualified that statement a little later by saying that only about sixty were used for pure silk out of the six to seven hundred in or around Manchester. It cost £15–20 to put the jacquard to work. He was, moreover, using the domestic system and mentioned the weaver coming to his warehouse, discussing which were the weaver's expenses. Eight years later, in the most vivid of the Handloom Weavers reports, we hear of a visit of the Commissioners to Messrs. Tootal's factory in which there were "power looms employed on figured silks with jacquard machines one man attending to two looms".[43] Whether all of Tootal's work force was employed in this way is another matter. Nevertheless, this evidence from 1840 is the first we have of the jacquard being used as one might expect it to be and as Stephen Wilson must have anticipated. Why had it taken so long?

Although the first initiative came from the silk industry the fact that it coincided with the triumph of the free traders could not have been more disastrous. At a time when the demand for figured materials was only just beginning to revive, the silk industry faced fierce competition from France. Though obviously ahead of Great Britain in adopting the jacquard, French industry was favoured not on the whole so much by its technological lead but, as far as one can judge, by the low wages of the *canut* whose cost of living was lower than that of the London artisan. There was reality in the demand for the repeal of the Corn Laws. The organization of the London silk industry, which had been extremely efficient and productive in its time, could not change overnight. In London a host of small independent firms had been grouped in technical divisions or branches with a strongly paternal feeling towards their labour force, all outworkers. Some journeymen families had worked for three generations for the same master weavers, as we can see from the inscriptions in the Warner pattern books.[44] The initial cost of the jacquard would have necessitated a factory system which did not exist. The only major difference between the broad silk industry, still centred in London in the early nineteenth century,[45] and the ribbon industry of the Midlands was that the social organization had broken down much further in the Midlands than in London. There are only too many harrowing stories to prove

that labour had become extremely cheap. Capitalism, as such, had advanced much faster.

There is then a basic question of technology. Who was able to supply jacquards in the 1830s? Claude Guillotte said that he was one of two manufacturers of jacquards in the country and that he employed about thirty-eight to forty men in his London workshops, as well as teaching others, which does not seem very much. We know nothing about the establishment of Mr. Sago of Manchester. Writing in 1835, Andrew Ure thought that silk manufacturers will "ere long apply the power loom to the weaving of fancy as well as plain goods", and he thought that Sharp and Roberts would supply the machinery.[46] We have no evidence that they supplied jacquards — though power looms as such is another matter. The two Manchester firms we can trace are J. Jacquier and Devoge. Jacquier was essentially a Spitalfields manufacturer of jacquards and point-paper. Many of the papers in the Warner archive were printed by or for him and on the earlier ones he gives two addresses, 26 Wood Street, Spitalfields, and 36 Back Mosely Street, Manchester.[47] According to Clinton C. Gilroy, writing in 1845, a friend, William Webb, who worked for the firm of Jacquier, had shown him a particular kind of jacquard in 1836[48] and a little later he describes a loom that Jacquier had invented for weaving velvet face to face. Jacquier must have produced several types of loom since Devoge repaired "one 400 (Jacquier No757)" in 1844 for 21/6d.[49] We have some grounds for thinking that the Jacquier connection with Manchester began in the 1840s.[50] In the early 1830s, as Jacomb of Nuneaton explained, there was simply no inducement to invest in machinery.[51]

Devoge & Co. became one of the leading suppliers of jacquards in the country, though they by no means monopolized the trade. Although they supplied Tootals, they sold the firm comber boards[52] and cards, not the jacquards that the Handloom Weavers Commissioners so admired. The Devoge account book for the years 1836–1847 has been carefully preserved by the firm and it is most relevant to this study. They supplied firms in Manchester, Huddersfield, and in the districts around each town, Macclesfield, Leek, Coventry (a large number of orders), Worcester, Kidderminster, Dublin, and elsewhere. From 1840 they also supplied firms in

Nottingham, a particularly interesting point since Felkin told a Parliamentary Committee enquiring into the export of machinery in 1841 that the application of the jacquard principle to bobbin net machinery had not yet been successful.[53] The account book starts in 1836 but there is reference to a previous one. Devoge supplied everything a weaver needed, not just jacquards: velvet wires, plush rods, lingoes, glass rods, ribbon battens, "1 gross of weavers quills", harnesses, shuttles, French bar looms, several crimping machines, brass comber boards, an occasional warping frame, japanned shafts, etc. Some customers only bought accessories such as lingoes. They also sold to a customer in Huddersfield "one old comber board, mounture" in 1838,[54] and to Andrew Hall of Brown Street (presumably in Manchester) in September 1839, "2 mountures" for £1.10.6d, much cheaper than the jacquards,[55] though he also bought jacquards and their accessories. Some customers were, therefore, still retaining the drawloom, for which "mounture" was the traditional term, as late as 1839. They sold dobbies and such items as a "wood drum 1/6d, turning, do. 3/=, and 2½ gross pegs [at] 3/=".[56] There are orders for pegs, an accessory of the witch loom, not the jacquard, up to 1845.

The sizes of the jacquards bought were 100, 200, 300, 400, 600, 900, and 1200, with a very occasional 500. The most popular seem to have been the 400, 600, and 300, but as one might expect, more of the smaller counts appear in the earlier orders than in the later ones. Some types were apparently suited to particular industries. A firm in Worcester bought a number of 200 machines, in Nottingham nearly all the firms bought "double griffe" or double machines, and in October 1844 and again in 1845 Ingoldby, Tabor and Clarke bought two machines "Lever motion" for £7.10s and two double machines for £8.[57]

The textile industries, like most others, were based upon a wood technology. Wood is a most versatile material and a measure of its usefulness is that in the eighteenth century (and presumably earlier) it is difficult to find more than the occasional loom maker in the records of the textile districts. Specialists making reeds or weights are another matter but every local joiner, to say nothing of the weaver himself, was able to make a loom, keep it in repair,

adapt it, and eventually nail a jacquard on top of it. The dismantled looms in the Bankfield Museum are a bewildering array. The Devoge firm was the forerunner of a new industry, that of the machine maker. In the first years of its account book it is evident that the looms and parts it was selling were for the most part made of wood, for there are specific mentions of an "iron griffe". A certain George Lee of Stone Chair near Halifax bought both wood and iron machines in 1838.[58] There was little difference in price. Many of the earlier bills in the Devoge account book are for repairs to machines, which is understandable if most of them were made of wood with the minimum of iron parts.[59] Certainly Devoge bought a lot of wood from local timber merchants, chiefly oak and birch and rather less iron and steel; though brass was used in some quantity, and, of course, lead for the lingoes. Gradually any mention of wood is dropped, presumably because everything except the basic frame of the loom was being made in metal (except for the harness, made from linen thread, and the mails, which were sometimes of glass). There is one very interesting item in a bill towards the end of the accounts: "October 3rd 1845 16lbs 10oz anti-friction metal . . . 14/—", and on the next day, 7 lb. 4 oz. of "patent metal" costing 6/0½d. Both items were supplied by Fenton and Ball of Lower Mosely Street, Manchester.[60] There is an enormous variation in the number of machines supplied at any one time. Quite early in the accounts we find a group of weavers in Failsworth, outside Manchester, buying one machine each in 1836–1837, which suggests that they were local handweavers;[61] while in 1844, taking one firm at random, we find that they had been supplied with eighty-two machines between January and June.[62] The other ingredients which went into the making of the jacquards were large quantities of thread for the harness, and coal, of which Devoge bought large amounts very cheaply. ("Best coal" cost 8d per cwt, "engine coal" 5d.) The large orders in the mid-1840s and the anti-friction metal both suggest the use of power looms.

The cost of the jacquards supplied declined while the capacity increased. Thus the most frequently supplied machine up to ca. 1842 was the 400, and after that the 600. The table below gives the price for the 400 machine:[63]

Year	Price
1836	£2 "iron", £3, £3 "improved", £3.2s (an order from Macclesfield)
1837	£3
1838	£3.3s
1839	£2.17s
1840	£2.15s
1841	£2.10s and £2.12s
1842	£2.10s
1843	£2.5s (£3, with patent hooks for a Nottingham lace manufacturer)
1844	£2.8s
1845	£2.2s–£2.5s
1846	£2.5s (£13.3.6d, 400 machine and mounting, an order from Leek; £4.15s, 400 double griffe ordered by John Croppers of Nottingham)
1847	—

Devoge supplied every part together or separately: plates, presses, cards (ready punched or blank), "design paper" of different counts,[64] hooks, needles, springs, comber boards, comber frames and the slips for them, "jack ladder with iron frame" and just jack ladders(?), machines "made to order", a "600 machine octagon cylinder" in 1845, hand punches, punch boxes, lacing frames and, even in the earliest accounts, an occasional "repeating machine" (£9) and, even more expensive, a 400 reading machine for £40 (a 600 cost £55). Both these machines were surely intended for factories — a handweaver did not need to duplicate his patterns, nor could he afford such an outlay. Such items become increasingly evident. The impression formed on reading the accounts is that production was continually increasing and becoming more sophisticated. The occasional sale of a second-hand machine or an old "mounture" stands out. Sales of parts increased while the number of repairs seems to have stayed stationary or even to have declined.[65]

It would not be difficult to trace all the customers of Devoge who are mentioned in this account book since there are ample trade directories for the period, but many are in any case familiar names: J.T. Clay of Rastrick, whose records are now in the Halifax record office; Barlow and sons of Bolton;[66] James Tolson of Huddersfield, founder of the Tolson Memorial Museum; J.T. Brocklehurst of Mac-

clesfield, whose factory still survives; Jonathan Schofield of Rastrick, from whose firm there is a pattern book in the Tolson Memorial Museum. They bought jacquards from Devoge from 1840 and showed waistcoatings in the 1851 exhibition. Louis Schwabe of Manchester gave evidence to the 1832 Select Committee on the silk trade.[67] The firm remained important customers of Devoge after Schwabe's death. Only two London firms appear but they include Stone and Kemp, an important Spitalfields firm that showed in the 1851 exhibition.

If the jacquard with all its necessary accessories was initially expensive for a group of industries that had been unaccustomed to heavy capital outlays on equipment (materials were different: silk, good worsted, and even fine linen had never been cheap), it was also not easy to design for or prepare the drafts. It is notable how often Devoge apparently cut the cards for the customer — for they were specialists, even in the 1840s. Claude Guillotte had given as one of the chief reasons why the jacquard cost so much, the high cost of cards,[68] for a high duty had to be paid on entry to England. Complaints about this were still being made in 1849 in the *Journal of Design*.[69] The lashes for the drawloom were only bits of string. Moreover, the cards had to be punched and the tools for this developed from a single hand punch using a matrix to various forms of stamp, all quite cumbersome and expensive. An ordinary worker might cut 100–150 cards a day, while the French card-cutting machine current in 1845 could punch 2,500–3,000.[70] A package deal offered a machine with copier and simples (?) to cut cards for a manufactory containing 300 looms. Even so, while a machine operator on a modern machine can touch-type the pattern from the point-paper, it needed two operatives according to the illustrations of the mid-nineteenth century (figs. 11, 12); moreover, two adults, not a drawboy. The cards then had to be laced together, which could take as long as two days, a ruinous loss of time for the handweaver. Changing the pattern was, therefore, hardly any cheaper than it had been on the drawloom, if for different reasons. According to James,[71] a Mr. Dracup of Horton made the first card-cutting machine in 1833 and a repeating machine in 1834, which would both speed up production in a factory. It is self-evident that no one would build such factories until there was a demand for their products.

The long hiatus in the demand for patterned materials had left the British without major textile designers in this field (everyone admitted there were plenty for printed cottons). A jacquard woven fabric is not drafted in the same way as a drawloom woven one. As Samuel Wilson said, the whole art and mystery is in the ruled paper. Two colours cannot be shown in one line, for example; they each need a separate card, whereas a century earlier James Leman had told his draftsmen to do precisely the opposite to save time by painting several brocaded colours in one line. Guillotte thought that the problem of drafting was so important that he subsequently wrote a letter to the Committee on this point.[72]

The final acceptance of the jacquard seems to have come in a fairly short period, bearing in mind that weavers retained their existing looms for all kinds of materials. The crucial years were about 1837 to 1845 — oddly enough a period of general slump. This may seem illogical, just as it may seem illogical that the Coventry ribbon manufacturers were not able to sell their ribbons in a period when ribbons were generally worn. While it is very difficult to pick out certainly jacquard woven textiles made before the 1840s, or the point-papers for them, we have a mass of textiles in the 1840s, culminating in the extraordinarily important objects shown in the Great Exhibition. Once more taste had changed and patterned materials were primarily for a market governed by changes in taste. The sample books of J.T. Clay & Sons illustrate the point.[73] In February 1837 they received an order for "6ps Jacquards at 8/6" from Kesteven and Sons of London, who wrote again in April, "We are much in want of a few more of your large machine patterns to our two styles."[74] While in the years 1834–1836 there are lots of checks and silk flecked squares, which are very pretty but hardly significant as patterns, from 1839–1840 there is little doubt that all the patterned samples are jacquard woven (fig. 10). In April 1842 Clay's received an order for "1 ps each colour jacquard sprig send large patterns."[75] In a splendid book labelled "Customers Ideas" from the same firm there is a note of 1844: "The permanency of the colours is not always material provided a better and more varied effect can be produced." How well we know the result of a thousand manufacturers taking this advice. J.M. Gabriel, on 6 May 1846, "wishes his large rich shawl patterns to be made as the original or larger if possible".[76] It was now worthwhile for the manufacturer to buy Devoge looms in quantity and set up factories to house them (fig. 13). It is certainly clear from museum collections that the manufacturers responded to the demand. The dated shawl designs in Paisley get larger and larger and for the first time large patterned upholstery fabrics and cheaper cloths were made. The problem of making a cotton warp for mixed worsteds and cottons was overcome in 1837,[77] so that cheaper patterned waistcoatings could be produced. The larger patterns meant either a revival of the drawloom or the opportunity for the jacquard, since none of the substitutes, not even the witch loom, could do the same job. The first universal interest in the jacquard was accompanied by a flurry of patents and improvements. Many were needed and it was at last worthwhile for the manufacturer to bother with them. In 1839, for instance, there was a patent for raising the knobs on "marseilles" quilts made by the jacquard, a device important to Bolton. Of wider application were those applying to ribbons or for improvements in the manufacture of figured pile fabrics, woven carpeting, and such purely technical innovations as the double lift jacquard. Not only was the machine refined, it was applied to steam-power. Of all the writers, nineteenth-century or modern, only Clinton C. Gilroy was honest about the story of the jacquard. Writing in 1845, he said, "Like many other great inventions the progress of this machine was not near so rapid as its merits might have led us to suppose."[78] As explanation, he gave the opposition of the weavers, which is not true — it was power looms which were smashed by Luddites, not jacquards;[79] the latter were admired by both masters and men. But Gilroy also added a second consideration: the imperfection of some of the movements of the machine itself.

Not only had taste changed, there were other factors. The repeal of the Corn Laws in 1845 may not have actually lowered wages — they could hardly have been lower — but repeal did help to increase purchasing power in a wider section of the community and thus, at last, we have the beginning of the mass demand in which an expensive machine like the jacquard could be put to best use. Other studies have revealed the 1840s as the decade crucial in the decline of the handloom weaver.[80] They did not go joyfully into the factories, which they justifiably hated; but went or died of starvation or disease. But it was in factories that the jacquards could be best used. Perhaps illogically, the handweavers left in Spitalfields benefited, in that the jacquards became cheaper, as we have seen from the Devoge account book, and more efficient. The goods shown in the 1851 exhibition are not an accidental selection. They were new and startlingly elaborate textiles, whether the cotton and worsted furnishings from Halifax (figs. 16, 17) or the shawls from Paisley, which aroused astonishment and admiration in the visitors. Very bright colours and very large patterns met the demand. It was not until the time of William Morris and even later that the aesthetic possibilities of a large woven pattern were, briefly, grasped.

This is a tangled story with many loose ends. The first histories of the industrial revolution were written by master manufacturers or their relatives to justify the horrors of early nineteenth-century Free Trade, and to do so they had to decry the past. It was really part of their propaganda to say that new patterns were not introduced under the protective system, to argue that everything British was best, and that industrially the nation was a wonderful innovator in all things mechanical. The distortion of the picture grew worse with the years.[81] The present writer has learned in this as in so many other fields not to believe a word of any of the secondary accounts, unless supported by a first-hand study of the textiles, the words of the people alive at the time, and, in this instance, the surviving machinery, what little there is of it.

Figure 1. Point-paper for a handkerchief, English, dated 1823. Intended for the jacquard loom.
Victoria and Albert Museum, T.507ᴬ-1972.

290

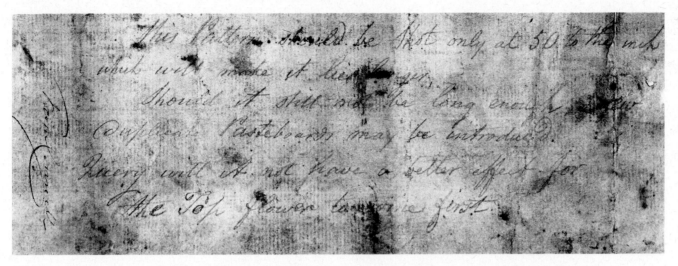

Figure 2.   Detail of inscription on back of figure 1.

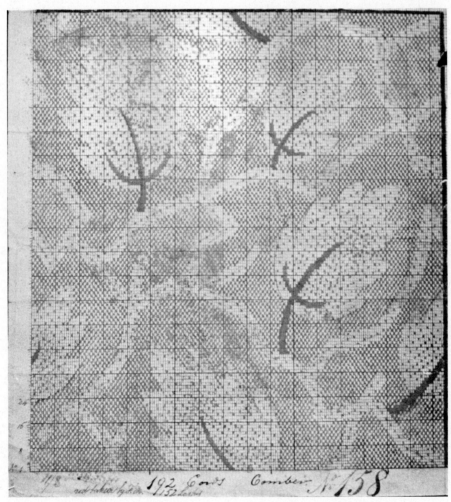

Figure 3.   Point-paper for a woven silk, English (Stephen Wilson & Co.), ca. 1826 – 1838.
Victoria and Albert Museum, T.453-1972.

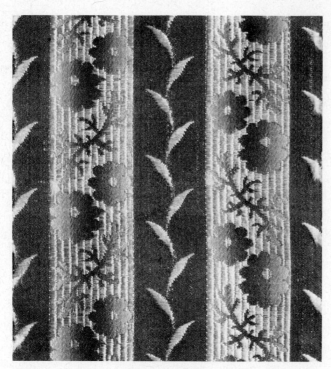

Figure 4. Sample on page of pattern book of English silks from the Warner archive, Winter 1793.
Victoria and Albert Museum, T.378-1972, p. 360.

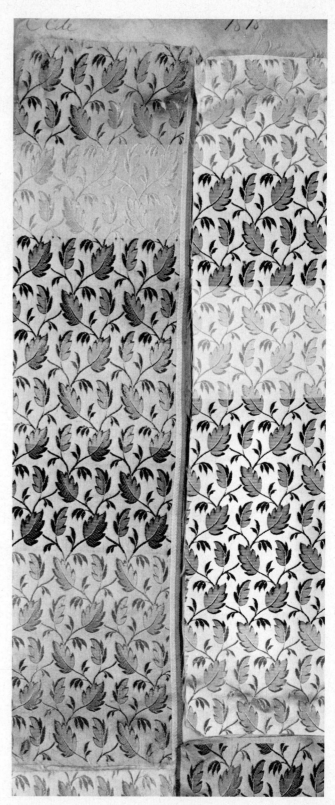

Figure 6. Detail of jacquard woven sample from pattern book in the Warner archive, dated 1825.
Victoria and Albert Museum, T.385-1972, p. 277.

Figure 5. Detail of a sample of English silk from pattern book in the Warner archive, dated 1818.
Victoria and Albert Museum, T.385-1972, p. 55.

Figure 7.   Page dated 1809 from the Album of Barbara Johnson.
Victoria and Albert Museum, T.219-1973.

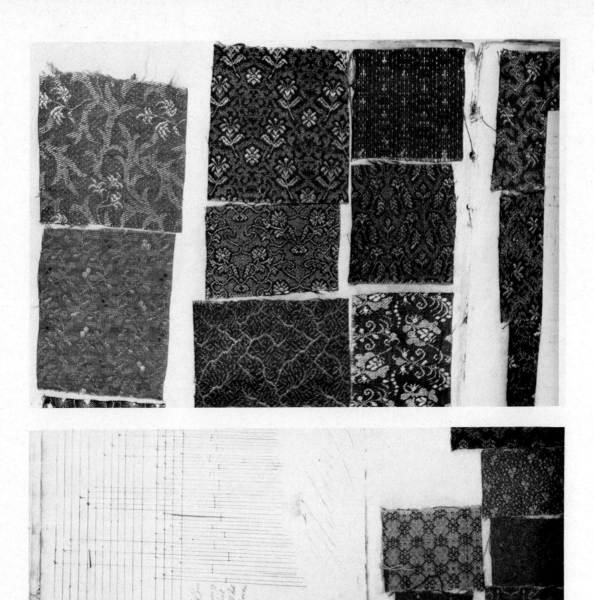

Figures 8-9.   Two pages from the pattern book of Robert Roebuck of Honley, near Huddersfield, 1830. Samples woven on witch loom.
Tolson Memorial Museum, Huddersfield.

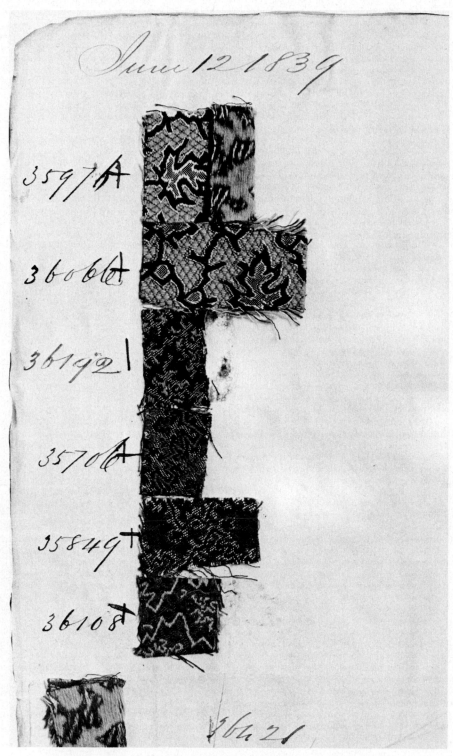

Figure 10.   Page dated 1839 from correspondence of J.T. Clay
& Co. Worsted Manufactures, Rastrick, near Halifax. Jac-
quard woven samples.
Halifax Central Libray, Archives Department. Courtesy of the
Metropolitan Borough of Calderdale.

515.—Jacquard-card making.

Figure 11. Charles Knight, *Pictorial gallery of the arts*, vol. 1,
Useful arts, 1847, p. 120. Left: stamping. Right: lacing.

4.—PIERCING THE CARDS FOR THE PATTERN.

Figure 12. *Ladies treasury*, 1857, p. 85.

513.—Jacquard Power-looms: Stuff-manufacture.

Figure 13. Charles Knight, *Pictorial gallery of the arts*, vol. 1, 1847, p. 120, pl. 9.

Figure 14. Detail of witch loom.
Tolson Memorial Museum, Huddersfield. Courtesy of Kirklees
Metropolitan Borough Council.

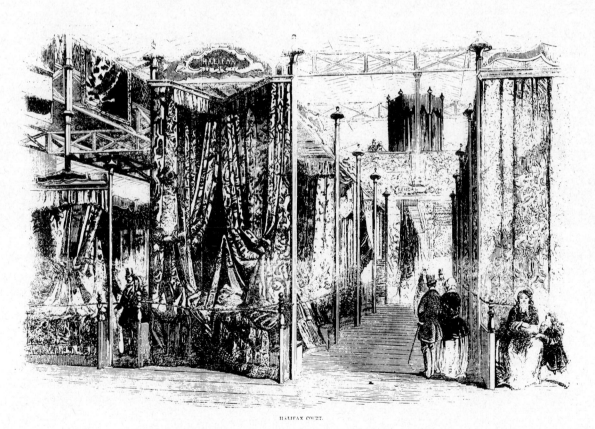

HALIFAX COURT.

Figure 15. View of the Halifax Court in the 1851 Exhibition,
from the Official Descriptive illustrated catalogue cl. XIX.
From the watercolour sketch by Philip Henry Delamotte, working 1851-1889, now in the Victoria and Albert Museum.

Figure 16.   Cotton warp, worsted weft. Presented to the South Kensington Museum by Messrs. Ackroyds of Halifax (close to textiles shown in the Great Exhibition by H.C. McCrea & Co., Halifax).
Victoria and Albert Museum, T.27-1959 (formerly AP 173/9).

Figure 17.   Damask by H.C. McCrea & Co., Halifax, from London Great Exhibition 1851 Illustrations, vol. 11, p. 38.

Notes

1. *House of Commons Papers.* Minutes taken before the Select Committee on the Silk Trade, 1832, p. 912, para. 12740.

2. *House of Commons Papers.* Reports from committees, Arts and Manufactures, vol. 9(3), Feb.-Aug. 1835, p. 61, para. 813.

3. The best albeit abridged account of the drawloom is by Paulet, *Art du fabricant d'étoffes de soie*, Paris, Académie des Sciences, Descriptions des arts et métiers, T.IX, 7e partie II (copies in Lyon, Ecole de Tissage; London, Victoria and Albert Museum; and Boston, Museum of Fine Arts).

4. "Half ell flush mantuas on mountures" are listed, for example, by the journeymen in the 1769 List of Prices in the Foot Figured and Flowered Branches of the London Silk Industry.

5. See the plates in Peter Thornton, *Baroque and Rococo silks*, London, Faber and Faber, 1965.

6. 1835 Reports, p. 62, para. 828.

7. *House of Commons Papers.* Reports from committees, Ribbon Weavers, vol. 9, Jan.-June 1818, p. 193.

8. *House of Lords Sessional Papers.* Minutes of evidence relative to foreign trade (silk and wine trade), May 1821, p. 18.

9. *House of Lords Sessional Papers.* Committee enquiring into operation of the Spitalfields Acts, vol. 13, 1823, p. 70, evidence of James Baker, operative weaver in figure work.

10. 1821 Committee, p. 39.

11. The original letter dated 3 August 1820 belongs to Warner & Sons Ltd. Sir Ernest Goodale published it in the *Journal of the Royal Society of Arts*, April 1960, p. 375. I am indebted to Mr. L. St. John Tibbets for kindly showing me the original.

12. 1823 Committee, p. 12.

13. 1823 Committee, p. 173.

14. My colleague, Miss Wendy Hefford, is making a detailed study of the point-papers from the Warner archive. The succession appears to be Lea, Wilson & Co., Wilson & Keith, Keith & Shoebridge.

15. Pattern book of Samuel Wilson, 1811-1826. Property of Vanners Silks Ltd., p. dated January 1826. Bearing this in mind I have made a careful examination both of the textile collections in the Victoria and Albert Museum and of the point-papers acquired from the Warner archive.

16. 1823 Committee, evidence of Edward Jones, journeyman silk weaver: "Shawls have very much gone out of use" (p. 47). He explained that scarves had taken their place but were also going out of use (pp. 51-52). Shawls were being made from other materials, not silk. Thomas Gibson, master weaver, said that tissued scarves *had been* much in request. Tissued shawls were an "article not made any more" (p. 132). 1832 Minutes, George Stephen's evidence on gauzes, that shawls from Spitalfields had been unsaleable since 1826 (p. 710). William Bridges showed the Committee a gauze shawl made in 1822-1823 and said that the Paisley fabric was quite different (p. 701). 1835 Reports, evidence of Samuel Smith of Pall Mall that the spun silk shawl made in Stockport was "no longer in use, and has not been for the last ten or fifteen years", i.e., 1820-1825.

17. John Murphy (of Scotland), *A treatise on the art of weaving*, 2d ed., rev. and enl., Glasgow, Blackie, Fullarton & Co., 1827, gives only a few slightly inaccurate pages to "the new French drawloom" (pp. 325-328). John Ballance, in the 1832 Minutes, did not know of jacquards being used for large damask table cloths (para. 8553). Claude Guillotte, 1835 Reports, said that they used "a drawboy instead of a jacquard to make the figure" on shawls in Scotland (p. 61, para. 813). Had he had Scottish customers from the damask industry one feels he would have mentioned them.

18. 1835 Reports, paras. 812, 813.

19. Victoria and Albert Museum, T.453-1972. It was drawn by J. Soilleux, a pattern drawer of Brick Lane, Spitalfields, and is inscribed "192 cords 152 lashes". The speckled effect, however, suggests a jacquard. It is also inscribed "Stephen Wilson Son & Co." and dates from 1826-1838.

20. 1832 Minutes, p. 337. This is not quite a move towards capitalism in the modern sense, for the firms were not owners of factories but entrepreneurs.

21. 1832 Minutes, para. 6019, evidence of Thomas Stone. He thought the number of jacquards in Spitalfields was less than formerly (para. 6017).

22. There is a point-paper for a ribbon in the Warner archive (Victoria and Albert Museum, T.445-1972) inscribed "sent to Mr Dresser". The design is dated 21 April 1824 and inscribed "384 cords 150 lashes". There is nothing to suggest that it was to be jacquard woven. Mr. Thomas Pittifor, giving evidence to the 1832 Committee (p. 846), spoke at length about Mrs. Dresser, who he said employed over 200 weavers on jacquard looms. The obituary of a certain Thomas Brown said that together with the late Mrs. Dresser he had introduced the jacquard loom into Coventry "about the year 1827" (*Coventry Times*, 21 May 1871, Coventry Reference Library).

23. 1832 Minutes, evidence of David Smith, p. 71, and James Perkins, para. 1558.

24. Victoria and Albert Museum, T.652-1972, handkerchief, 600 cords, 634 lashes; T.445-1972, see note 22; T.479-1972(?) dated 1824; T.491-1972, etc.

25. Victoria and Albert Museum, T.438-1972, "258 hooks" mentioned in inscription; T.434-1972, French inscription but mentioning "cartroni"; T.441-1972 dated 11 August 1824, "200 cords . . . 112 lashes . . . the white stamped"; T.529-1972 before 1830, ". . . laisserez 15 cordes de chaque côté de la méchanique".

26. 1832 Minutes, para. 2623, evidence of William Merry of Merry & Brown, 26 Wood Street, Cheapside and "a manufactory" at Coventry, fourteen years in fancy branch of the ribbon trade.

27. 1832 Minutes, para. 2469.

28. Reports on Handloom Weavers, vol. 13, 1835(9), Feb.-Sept. 1835. Evidence of Edward Good, p. 245 (267 in ink), para. 3706.

29. 1832 Minutes, evidence of William Jacombs, para. 1592.

30. 1832 Minutes, evidence of William Bridges. See note 16.

31. Pattern book of James Whyte, after 1811 and probably before 1814. The book contains muslins, nets, gauze, silk, and wools as well as shawl materials. Manufacturers' account book, 1808-1815. I am much indebted to Mr. James Hunter, Keeper of Textiles at the Paisley Museum and Art Gallery, for showing me these and other early pattern books and the very large collection of designs, and for his help and advice.

32. Victoria and Albert Museum, T.484-B-1972, the paper watermarked A. Blaikie 1819.

33. Victoria and Albert Museum, T.672-1972.

34. "Proof plate . . . the property of the United Weavers of the Causeyside District May 1863". I am very much indebted to Mr. James Hunter for showing me this and subsequently sending me a photograph, and for showing me the articles of the Handloom Weavers of Paisley, instituted in 1849, remodelled in 1853, altered and amended in August 1857 and again in 1871. They did not drop the description "handloom weaver".

35. 1835 Reports, p. 61, para. 812.

36. John James, History of the worsted manufacture in England, from the earliest times, London, Longman, Brown, Green, Longmans, and Roberts, 1857, p. 440.

37. John Beaumont, "The jacquard machine and its introduction into Huddersfield", Textile Recorder, 15 April 1886, partly quoted in W.B. Crump and G. Ghorbal, History of the Huddersfield woollen industry, Huddersfield, Tolson Memorial Museum, 1935. I am very grateful to Miss Attwood and Mr. R.J. Millen of the Holborn Branch of the Science Reference Library for tracing this article. Beaumont adds enough circumstantial detail to suggest that his information is independent of the 1835 Reports, though this cannot be proved.

38. I am very grateful to Mr. J.C.S. Magson of the Bankfield Museum and to Mr. Robert McMillan of the Tolson Memorial Museum for showing me the looms in their collection, and to Mrs. Green of the Colne Valley Museum at Golcar, not only for opening the museum especially for me but also for demonstrating to me the working of the witch loom.

39. Handloom Weavers Reports, vol. 10, 1834, p. 356 (ink 362).

40. Handloom Weavers Reports, vol. 13, 1835, p. 171 (ink 193).

41. Andrew Ure (The philosophie of manufacturers; or, An exposition of the scientific, moral, and commercial economy of the factory system of Great Britain, London, C. Knight, 1835, p. 276) said that the most skilful weavers of fancy goods in Manchester were natives of Paisley.

42. 1835 Reports, p. 614, paras. 9523, 9536, et seq. George Stephens told the 1832 Committee that mixed Manchester goods were made on the jacquard.

43. Handloom Weavers Reports, vol. 24 9 pt. 4, 1840, p. 21.

44. The inscriptions in T.376-1972 and T.379-1972 (Victoria and Albert Museum) which cover the years 1774-1795 and 1795-1821 include the following: Agombar, 1781-1821; Dixon, 1774-1820 (Dixon 1774, Dixon's boy 1789, Dixon junior 1801, Dixon senior 1820); Jones, 1774-1806 (Jones 1774-1795, Jones junior 1795, Jones senior from 1793, Jones' boy 1804); James Pulley, 1774; Pulley, 1805; and many other families for slightly shorter periods.

45. This statement is discussed in detail in my forthcoming book The English silk industry 1700-1825.

46. Ure, Manufactures (1835), p. 275.

47. E.g., on T.547-1972 (Victoria and Albert Museum), part of "Gothic" pattern. Paper watermarked 1848.

48. Clinton G. Gilroy, The art of weaving by hand and by power, London, 1845, p. 208 (first publ. New York, G.D. Baldwin, 1844; 2d ed. Manchester, J. & J. Thomson, 1847).

49. Devoge customers' order book, 1836-1847, p. 380. Property of Devoge & Co. Ltd. I am deeply indebted to Mr. A.B. Fielding for permission to use and quote from this order book.

50. See notes 14 and 47.

51. 1832 Minutes, pp. 83-84, para. 1601.

52. Devoge order book, p. 384. Each of the orders for three comber boards has a name in brackets after it, which suggests that they were intended for individual handweavers and not for factories. The orders were placed in 1844, four years after the Commissioners had visited Tootal's factory. E.g., "1844 March 16 8000 10/–, 1 comber Bd 6/– (P. Pollitt) £4.6.0d", that is, 8,000 cards at 10/– per thousand.

53. *House of Commons Papers and Reports*. Acts connected with trade, 1841 (201)7, exportation of machinery (400), 2d report. Minutes of evidence, p. 135 et seq., para. 2354.

54. Devoge order book, pp. 98-99. It cost £1.5s.

55. Devoge order book, p. 141. By 1844 he was buying only accessories for the jacquard.

56. Devoge order book, p. 106. William Walker, Cannon Street, 3 May 1844. The whole cost of 12/– was much cheaper than any jacquard.

57. Devoge order book, pp. 224, 406.

58. Devoge order book, pp. 11-12.

59. It may not seem easy now to visualize the appearance of a wooden jacquard. I am much indebted to Mr. Cyril Scott of the Coventry Museum and Art Gallery for his help and advice, for devoting a whole Saturday to giving it, for lending me a slide of a wooden jacquard in the Deutsches Museum, Munich (published in the guide to the museum), for showing me relevant material in both the Coventry Museum and Art Gallery and in the Reference Library, and for suggesting that I write to Devoge & Co.

60. Devoge order book, p. 502.

61. Devoge order book, pp. 54-55.

62. Devoge order book, p. 368. The orders were made by William Kaye & Sons of Clayton West, near Huddersfield.

63. This table has been made not from an analysis of every purchase in these years but from a survey of the highest and lowest prices paid by a representative number of firms.

64. Every textile industry in every country tends to invent its own vocabulary. In eighteenth-century London the term used was "rule paper". The "ruled paper" was divided into large squares called "dezines" onto which the design was transferred from the first sketch or fair copy. The paper was marked off in different counts, 8 and 10, etc., according to the cloth which was to be woven. Once the design had been painted onto the paper it could be transferred to the loom (whether drawloom or jacquard). The term used by Warner & Sons, founded in 1870, was "point-paper", and we have adopted this in the Victoria and Albert Museum. It is much less likely that the patterns were drawn straight onto the "design paper" than that they were drawn, as in earlier times, on plain paper and then transferred. "Design" paper could therefore be a corruption of "dezine" (itself, of course, a corruption of "dessin").

65. Again, this is an impression and not a strict analysis. The orders are arranged by firms, in neither alphabetical nor chronological order.

66. Alfred Barlow patented a double action jacquard in 1849. In his *History and principles of weaving*, 1879, Barlow does not say whether the invention was his. Perhaps it was well known to his contemporaries. There is a series of woven cotton pictures in the Victoria and Albert Museum (880-883-1900) woven by Barlow and Jones of Manchester in 1881.

67. 1832 Minutes, p. 638. He was very proud of his damasks and even paid Devoge on one occasion with a piece of damask valued at £10. Andrew Ure admired him and thought it would be Louis Schwabe and other enterprising Manchester manufacturers who would first use the power loom for figured materials. Schwabe bought jacquards from Devoge from 1836 to 1845 and after his death the firm continued to do so under the name of Jo. Houldsworth, Portland Street, Manchester.

68. 1835 Reports, p. 62, para. 821. The production of a handloom jacquard was not very startling: "a loom can only produce two or three or four pieces in a week" according to Thomas Pittifor (1832 Minutes, p. 850, para. 12042).

69. In *Journal of Design*, 1849, p. 167, a detailed account of the excise duty and its effect was set out. I am indebted to Miss Wendy Hefford for this reference.

70. Gilroy, *Art of weaving* (1845), p. 209.

71. James, *Worsted manufacture* (1857), p. 440.

72. 1835 Reports, p. 64.

73. I am indebted to Mr. A. Betteridge, archivist of the Metropolitan Borough of Calderdale, for giving me every possible facility on two visits to Halifax to use the Clay correspondence.

74. Halifax, Clay papers 23(109).

75. Halifax, Clay papers 27(9).

76. Halifax, Clay papers 70(30).

77. James, *Worsted manufacture* (1857), p. 471.

78. Gilroy, *Art of weaving* (1845), p. 192.

79. During November 1831 Joseph Beck's machinery was destroyed in Coventry but it was essentially the power looms which were smashed. Valerie E. Chancellor, ed. and with an introduction by, *Master and artisan in Victorian England: The diary of William Andrews and the autobiography of Joseph Gutteridge*, New York, A. M. Kelley, 1969. There are contemporary newspaper reports of the incidents. A clear account is given in John Prest, *The Industrial Revolution in Coventry*, London, Oxford University Press, 1960, pp. 47-49.

80. G.A. Feather, "A Pennine worsted community in the mid 19th century", *Textile History*, vol. 3 (Dec. 1972), pp. 64-91, for example.

81. Stephen Wilson and other advocates of the repeal of the Spitalfields Acts set the tone in their evidence to the 1823 Select Committee. An enlightened writer like Sir Edward Baines (*History of the cotton manufacture in Great Britain; with a notice of its early history in the East, and in all the quarters of the globe*, London, H. Fisher, R. Fisher, and P. Jackson, 1835, pp. 450 et seq.) 1835, ridiculed the suggestion that factory workers did excessive and injurious work. The manufacturer witnesses to the 1832 Committee deplored attempts to regulate industry. Barlow, in his *History of weaving* (1879) repeated the free traders' myth that the silk industry moved out of London once French silks were prohibited (pp. 165-166). Fred Bradbury, in *Jacquard mechanism and harness mounting*, 1912, said that the jacquard loom reached Halifax in 1827 "after which machines were rapidly distributed into every manufacturing centre and in the course of a few years the Jacquard almost entirely replaced every other method of figure weaving" (pp. 66 et seq.). Luther Hooper, in a lecture of which there is a draft in the Victoria and Albert Museum, said that in 1820 "a few jacquard machines were smuggled into England. In spite of much opposition they soon came into general use, first for handlooms and silk weaving but afterwards for power looms." The most distorted account is that in *The Victoria history of the counties of England* article on Coventry (*The Victoria history of the county of Warwick*, 1965– , London, published for the University of London Institute of Historical Research, reprinted by Dawsons of Pall Mall, vol. 8, 1969, p. 169). The earlier account in the *VCH* was much more factual. The 1969 article repeats all the nineteenth-century Free Trade arguments: "complacent belief in the rightness of their methods . . . as long as prohibition remained there was no incentive to developments in design or the improvement of machinery", etc. The factory system "increased efficiency" and supervision in a factory would have prevented "the leisurely attitude to work which was inherent in the domestic system". Even Professor Walter English in what is fundamentally a very useful book, *The textile industry: An account of the early inventions of spinning, weaving, and knitting machines*, Harlow, Longmans, 1969, saw the jacquard loom in its early days as "mainly used in the silk industry" (p. 112) and later, after refinements, used for the weaving of fine qualities of cotton, linen, and worsted, without realizing that the first application of the jacquard proved abortive and that it was a very long time before it was used widely in any industry.

Textile Finds
in the People's Republic of China

Hsio-Yen Shih

IT may seem presumptuous for a student of Chinese archaeology and art history to venture into such a specialized field as textile studies. The only possible excuse is that this contribution is offered in honour of Harold B. Burnham, who pioneered in many aspects of the field and was one of the few western specialists to have given unusual attention to ancient Chinese textiles.

The great increase of archaeological activity during the first twenty-five years of the People's Republic of China has encouraged improvement in conservation and analyses of textile finds. The quantity of archaeologically authenticated textiles has multiplied many-fold but, as excavation reports and specialized studies are published in Chinese (very seldom accompanied by abstracts in either English or Russian), these data have remained generally inaccessible to textile specialists in the West. It may, therefore, be useful to offer a survey of these finds.

This survey is arranged in order of chronology as is the bibliography accompanying it. The bibliography is numbered consecutively and references to it in the text are by such numbers. Readers of the original sources will notice that techniques of reporting and analyzing textile finds gradually improve, especially in the post-1972 publications. The most recent studies are the most detailed and sophisticated in approach. *No critical commentary, addition, or alteration has been made to summaries of Chinese findings,* except in the decision to use the most recent published information for each site or specimen.

Transliteration of Chinese is in the *Guoyupinyin* system, as it transcends orthographical differences in various western languages. Textile terminology follows the vocabulary submitted by Harold B. Burnham to the Centre International d'Etude des Textiles Anciens in Lyon.

Yin-Shang Dynasty
(1523–1028 B.C.)

Indirect evidence for the existence of sericulture from the thirteenth century B.C. on may be seen in small jade or other hard-stone sculptures of silkworms placed in tombs (Bib. **42**). These have been excavated at Dasikongcun in Anyang, Henan province, and Sufudun in Yidu, Shandong province.[1] Silkworms also appear as a decorative motif on some black pottery sherds from a site at Meiyan, Jiangsu province, belonging to the "Liangzhu Culture" which is considered contemporary to the late Shang Dynasty in the central Yellow River valley to the north.[2]

More direct evidence appears on the surface corrosion of some excavated bronzes, either in the form of "pseudomorphs" or as actual remains of textiles impressed or adhering to surface encrustations, although Chinese reports do not specify which occurs. A tomb at Wuguancun in Anyang yielded three

305

bronze *ge* (dagger-axes), one of which is reported to bear traces of fine silk tabby, another to show feather adhesions, and a third to retain "cloth" patterning.[3] A bronze *pen* (basin) excavated at Zhengzhou, Henan province, in 1955 is also mentioned as having vestiges of textiles on its surface (Bib. **42**).

The site of Qianshanyang in Wuxing, Zhejiang province, produced the only preserved textile finds. These were discovered in a bamboo basket in Trench 22 excavated in 1958 (Bib. **19**). A carbon-14 dating equivalent to 2750 ± 100 B.C., based upon rice husk samples, has been published for this site.[4] The textiles have been listed and described as follows:

Ramie tabby. Three fragments: 60 warps by 60 wefts per inch, yarn with slight Z-twist, warp roughly twice the weft thickness; 40 warps by 40 wefts per inch, yarn with Z-twist, warp and weft about the same thickness; 78 warps by 50 wefts per inch, yarn with S-twist, warp and weft about the same thickness.

Tabby of silk from the domesticated silkworm (2.4 × 1 cm), 120 warps by 120 wefts per inch, warp and weft of equal diameter.[5]

In addition, ramie cords, a braided silk sash, and a mass of reeled silk showing a slight S-twist are noted (Bib. **19**, pl. 10:3–8).

The eminent archaeologist Xia Nai has proposed that three basic weaving techniques already existed in the Yin-Shang period (Bib. **34**, p. 14 and p. 19, fig. 5A): first, the tabby weave with 30–50 warps and wefts per cm, both of approximately the same diameter; second, the warp-faced compound tabby with 40–72 warps by 17–35 wefts per cm; and third, monochrome patterned silk with tabby binding and warp-float patterning in 3:1.[6] Though the last shows only a relatively simple lozenge motif, he suggests that it required over ten sheds and, therefore, over ten heddle rods. Thus, he proposes that a simple type of shaft loom was in use. Xia Nai also notes that the use of grège was particularly suited to embroidery, as a slight loosening of the silk thread would give the pattern a denser effect. Poil with a slight twist seems to have been used only for edging of embroidered patterns, which were restricted to rhombs or zigzags.

Western Zhou Dynasty
(1028–722 B.C.)

So far only one site of this period has yielded an identifiable textile. A burial, identified as early Zhou, produced a bast-fibre fragment wrapped around the wood haft of an unusually shaped bronze weapon (Bib. **40**, p. 6). This is described as a hemp tabby with 13 warps by 12 wefts per cm.

Late Eastern Zhou or Warring States Period
(481–256 B.C.)

The ancient state of Chu has been the focus of extensive archaeological activity. Textile finds from the fifth and fourth centuries B.C. now form a respectable body of data.

Excavation of Chu tombs at Xinyang, Henan province, in 1957 provided a monochrome rhomb-patterned silk and a mock leno (Bib. **34**, p. 15).

Two Chu tombs at Wangshan in Jiangling County, Hubei province, produced a greater variety of textile finds (Bib. **31**, pp. 36, 38, 39, fig. 11 and p. 54, fig. 26):
— Monochrome patterned silk square wrapped around a square bronze mirror in Tomb 1.
— Five bands of silk tabby wrapped around the blade and wood handle of a bronze engraving knife,

placed in the tool-box found in Tomb 1's front chamber.

— Silk tabby clothing and silk artificial hair on wood figurines in Tomb 2.

— Silk tabby (18.5 × 15 cm) with embroidery in Tomb 2.

— Bast-fibre and another fine silk textile are also mentioned but not illustrated.

Textiles were discovered in five of the Changsha tombs excavated between 1951 and 1971. Xia Nai considers these to be of the fifth century B.C., or the early Warring States period (Bib. 34, p. 15).

Tomb 406 at Wulipai (Bib. 1, pp. 63–65, pls. 31–33)[7] contained silk tabbies, one piece hemmed and another with embroidery in satin or plain line stitch found under the corpse's head; two mono-chrome patterned silks, one with rhombs, the other with rhombs and dogtooth pattern; two mock lenos, the finer example having been found by the corpse's head; a silk tabby silk-padded quilt on the body; bast-fibre tabby fragments with 28 warps by 24 wefts per cm.

Tomb 15 at Zuojiakongshan (Bib. 2, p. 96, pl. 2:7) contained a painted silk textile beneath armour of small leather squares sewn together. The silk was found folded, and was damaged in an attempt to open it.

Tomb 5 at Guangjiqiao (Bib. 4, pp. 59, 62, 63)

contained two bast-fibre pouches with leather edging around the mouths (dia. of mouth 20 cm). One pouch has silk on one side and bast-fibre on the other but is without an opening and is, therefore, of unknown function; the other is made of a single silk strip (l. 24 cm, dia. 55 cm).[8] Two silk sashes with openwork patterns (fragmentary lengths 15 and 22 cm, w. 5 cm) and a monochrome patterned tabby sewn on one side (19 × 10 cm) were also unearthed from this tomb.

Tomb 3 at Lieshigongyuan (Bib. 18, pp. 67–69, figs. 11, 14–17) contained a silk tabby coverlet fragment, embroidered and painted (36 × 27 cm); and two silks pasted on the interior of the outer coffin-casing, embroidered in chain stitch.

A tomb at Liuchengqiao (Bib. 34, p. 15) contained a silk textile with 42 warps by 32 wefts per cm.

In addition, bast-fibre shoe soles have been excavated from several of these tombs, and another silk tabby banner painted in gold and silver pigments was salvaged from a previously plundered tomb at Zitanku in Changsha.[9]

Xia Nai posits that the development from a vertical to a horizontal or slanted loom occurred during this period (Bib. 34, p. 16).

Western or Former Han Dynasty
(206 B.C. – A.D. 8)

While four sites have provided textile finds from the second and first centuries B.C., the greatest quantity and best studied have emerged from one burial at Mawangdui in Changsha. Its description will be reserved for the later part of this section though it may be chronologically the earliest.

The Tomb of Dou Wan (d. late second century B.C.) at Mancheng, Hebei province (Bib. 33, p. 14, fig. 1) contained fragments of a warp-faced compound tabby in two-series, a fine silk tabby of 200

warps by 90 wefts per cm, an embroidered silk, and a mock leno.

A tomb at Djaranor in Inner Mongolia (Bib. 23, p. 18, fig. 8) contained a polychrome patterned silk with the graphs "ru" 如 and "yi" 意 worked in two vertical rows.

Tomb 48 at Mojuzi in Wuwei County, Gansu province (Bib. 44, pp. 11, 19–21) contained bast-fibre cloth pasted on the coffin, lacquered black on the interior and red on the exterior, and for a jacket on the female body; silk tabbies for the silk-padded robes of both female and male tomb occupants, their under-robes, trousers, skirt, and face coverings; three silk tabbies with resist-dyed stencilled decoration covering three reed boxes on the female occupant's coffin (sample no. 20, warp. dia. 0.25 mm, weft dia. 0.11 mm, 44 warps by 18 wefts per cm); and a mock leno (sample no. 19 measuring 37 × 18 cm, warp and weft dia. both 0.05 mm, 31 warps by 29 wefts per cm).

Tomb 1 at Mawangdui, of the Lady of Dai (d. ca. 160 B.C.), in Changsha, Hunan province (Bib. **48**, pp. 46–75, pls. 78–153) provided large quantities of textiles as follows:

— W side-case, bamboo boxes nos. 329 and 357 contained eleven robes, three under-robes, two pairs of socks, and a robe-border; in bamboo boxes nos. 340 and 354 were forty-six rolls of uncut lengths; in bamboo boxes nos. 337 and 346 were two fragments; also a *se* (zither) bag and a *yu* (pan-pipes) bag.

— N side-case, centre, and W sections contained a lined robe, an embroidered pillow, a tablecloth, an incense-pouch, two pillow-cloths, two pairs of shoes, two cloths for wrapping a lacquer *lian* (cylindrical covered box), inside of which were a pair of mittens, a cloth for wrapping a bronze mirror, a needle-case, sashes, etc.

— E side-case held another *yu* (pan-pipes) bag with embroidered patterns, a bamboo box no. 65 containing two incense-pouches and a pair of shoes, other bamboo boxes with herbs or medicines and food in ramie or silk tabby bags, clothed wood figurines, and a bamboo fan with silk tabby binding.

A painted silk tabby banner was laid over the inner coffin, itself covered with polychrome patterned silk, embroidery, and feathers. The body's clothing was very decayed, but its binding in many layers of coverlets or shrouds was much better preserved.

The tomb is especially important for having yielded twenty-seven items of intact clothing, including twelve robes (one with only silk tabby lining, the rest with silk padding; Bib. **44**, figs 54–56 show cutting diagrams), two skirts (each of four gores and with a waistband), three pairs of mittens, two pairs of socks, and four pairs of slippers or shoes.

Technical analyses of the textile finds at Mawangdui were undertaken by the Shanghai Textile Technology Research Institute and the Shanghai Silk Industry Corporation. Most of these textiles were woven of domesticated silk, but some hemp and ramie bast-fibre also appeared. The latter were poorly preserved, except for pieces contained in the coffin.

Brin diameter ranged from 6.15 to 9.25 microns in the Mawangdui silks, as compared to 6 to 18 microns for modern silk. Their cross-sections varied between 77.46 and 120 sq mm, as compared to the average 168 sq mm for modern silks. Study of the silk yarn preparation was based upon light and thin gauze samples. These natural-coloured gauzes showed weft with 2,500-3,000 twists per m, quite close to modern machine-prepared poil of 3,500 twists per m. Two dyed (Find nos. 354–4 and 354–8) and one plain gauze (Find no. 329–6) revealed warp brin of 10.2–11.3 dernier. In the case of one pile warp weave (Find no. N6–2)[10] the main warp and weft are variously composed of 10, 13, or 17 baves reeled for each grège, the pile warp itself being of 4 or more grèges.

Silks

Various types of silk textiles were distinguished from the forty-six lengths found in bamboo baskets of the W side-case in Tomb 1 at Mawangdui. These were rolled from both ends towards the middle, wrapped around two, three, or five reed stems, and tied in three places with silk thread; miniature imitations of rolls of silk. These may be divided as follows.

Monochrome silk tabbies (twenty-two samples, of which four bore embroidery): eight samples have 55–75 warps per cm, ten have 80–100, and four have 120 or more. Of these, eleven samples have half the number of wefts as warps, six have less than half, three have about two-thirds, and two have more than two-thirds. The average thickness of these tabbies is about 0.1 mm, but four samples measure 0.06 mm and two others 0.15 mm. Seven samples, including one with embroidery, seem to be compound weaves. Of these, two (Find nos. 340–26 and 340–30, Bib. **48**, pl. 134) show the introduction of a thicker warp (dia. ca. 0.13 mm) after each 20–30 warps, thereby giving a striped effect. The densest example, with 164 warps per cm, is on the border of an incense-pouch (Find no. 442). A robe border (Find no. 329–7) and the palms of a pair of mittens (Find nos. 443–2 and 443–3) show about 140 warps per cm. Tabby of soft silk with about 100 warps per cm was used for padded or lined robes, a tablecloth, a pillow-cloth, the border of a wrapping-cloth, mittens, and incense-pouches. It is suggested that degumming was done after weaving. Tabby of 60–100 warps per cm was used for padded robes, wrapping-cloths, a tablecloth, the lining of a pillow-cloth, skirts, and socks. Tabby of less than 60 warps per cm sometimes appears as the lining for garments but more often as bags for herbs, medicines, and food. The coarsest tabby with 34 warps per cm (Find no. 441) was used for the lining of a wrapping-cloth.

Mock lenos (seven samples, of which three were printed or printed and painted; for the last, see Bib. **48,** pl. 118, Find no. N5): Warp and weft are both of poil; the former with relatively slight S- or Z-twist irregularly thrown, the latter with a strong Z-twist and more even. The weave varies, 58–64 warps by 40–58 wefts per cm, 0.05–0.08 mm in thickness. The lightest examples weigh slightly more than 12 g per sq m. The selvage is of doubled warps with a single weft. It is suggested that these fabrics are evidence for the use of both the spinning wheel and heddle bars. Monochrome mock lenos were used for two under-robes (Find nos. 329–5, Bib. **48,** pl. 78; and 329–6), while printed and painted mock lenos appear on three silk-padded robes (Find nos. 329–12 to 14, Bib. **48,** pls. 93, 79, 80).

Monochrome patterned silks (three samples; Bib. **46,** col. figs. 34, 35): These are also called "Han damasks" or "armura Han"; but are in fact warp-faced compound tabbies of the two-series type. Find nos. 340–1 (Bib. **48,** fig. 39 and pl. 140) and 354–19 both bear a pattern of compound rhombs with partial rhombs at two corners, their straight repeat being of fourteen units alternated with thirteen units (the former with each unit 3 × 3 cm, the latter 2.5 × 2.5 cm). Their repeat equals 116 warps by 92 wefts. The ground weave is 40 warps by 30 wefts per cm. As the warp varies in thickness, the pattern appears irregular and quite loose. It is suggested that

two heddle rods were used for the main warp and sixty for patterning. Find no. 340–25 (Bib. **48,** fig. 40 and pl. 120) has 100 warps by 46 wefts per cm. It is patterned with stepped-edged rhombs in straight and inverted repeats, each row of rhombs enclosing either of two floral motifs or a pair of birds confronted on a weft axis. Each rhomb measures 6.2 × 4.8 cm.[11] An incense-pouch with embroidered surface (Find no. 65–1, Bib. **48,** pl. 85 left), a pillow-cover (Find no. 446), and the embroidered outer layer of the body's covering (Find no. N3) are in similarly patterned warp-faced compound tabby, while a *yu* (pan-pipes) bag shows 78 warps by 78 wefts per cm.

Patterned gauzes (ten samples, of which two were embroidered; Bib. **46,** col. fig. 32): These are true gauze weaves of great complexity. The usual proportion is 100 warps by 35 wefts per cm. A looser sample (Find nos. 340–20 and 340–21, for the latter see Bib. **48,** pl. 122) shows 64 warps by 40 wefts per cm. Selvages are of tripled warps. The pattern is of two types of rhombs overlapped at two corners by a partial rhomb, differentiated in alternate rows of straight repeat by use of a darker tone or maintenance of the ground colour, and by different internal details. Straight repeats have eleven to fourteen of the darker pattern units, or eleven to thirteen of the ground colour ones. Each pattern unit measures 5 × 2 cm, but is slightly larger near the selvages. The gauze unit is of four picks, while the pattern decoupure is of two. Using Find no. 340–18 (Bib. **48,** pl. 139) as an example,[12] a pattern unit requires 332 warps by 204 wefts. Half of the ends function as fixed ends, while half function as doup ends twisted with the use of a stick. Of the 116 main warp ends, 81 are balanced for the darker pattern and require only forty-one rising sheds, while the remaining 85 need asymmetrical movements using 126 rising sheds. Half of the picks were used for the warp twist which could be controlled by use of a treadle. The other half involved fifty-two different passes. It is suggested that at least two artisans worked on this weaving; one to control the treadle, twisting stick and shuttle, while the other controlled a figure harness. Find nos. 354–1 (Bib. **48,** pl. 121) and 354–2 are said to be more complex than the sample described above. Similarly patterned gauzes were used for twelve items of made objects (of which six are embroidered with the "xinqi" 信期 pattern), including silk-padded robes, lined robes, incense-pouches, mittens, and curtains. The finest gauze, 100–120 warps by 35–40 wefts per cm, appears in clothing. Two incense-pouches (Find nos. 65–2 and 65–4, for the latter see Bib. **48**, pl. 85 right) show a coarser weave of 88 warps by 30 wefts per cm.

Polychrome patterned silks (four samples): These are warp-faced compound tabbies in multiple-series and, at least in this find, seem not to have been used for clothing.[13] All four samples are badly faded, but Find no. 354–9 (Bib. **48**, fig. 42 and pl. 124) is distinguishable with a pattern composed of five different geometric motifs. The others had either floral or wave motifs.

Polychrome pile warp silks (fifteen samples, of which twelve served as the borders of garments; see Bib. **46**, col. fig. 28): The excavation report analysis was based upon Find no. N6–2 (Bib. **48**, fig. 43 bottom), a fragment from the body's wrappings. This showed a four-series warp with 44–56 ends per cm, including the main warp in two-series, a binding warp, and a pile warp of thicker diameter; thus a total of 176–224 ends for the series. If the original width was 50 cm (approximately one Han Dynasty foot), a grand total of 8,800–11,200 ends would have been used. The binding warp, one quarter of the total ends, was woven in 1:3 twill and controlled by a single set of shafts. The other three warps, about 150 ends per cm (the largest pattern unit of 13.7 cm requiring 2,055 ends), must have been controlled by heddle rods and at least two shed sticks. As the main and binding warps are organized in 1:3 or 3:1 weaves, they could use one set of shafts, but since the pile warp had to be raised in loops, at least one other set must have been needed. Ground and pattern wefts have a ratio of 2:1, 41–50 per cm; the pattern weft, removed after the finished weaving, served only to raise or loop the pile warp. This textile should be described as a warp-faced compound twill with velvet pile.[14]

Ribbons of two types[15]

The "qianjin" 千金 type, as named by graphs wo-ven into the ribbon in seal script, is woven in three strips with alternating bands of dark patterns on light ground or vice-versa (Bib. **48**, fig. 45 centre and right). The patterning is composed of T-edging, with graphs on criss-crossed dark and light strips in the centre. The palm borders of three pairs of mittens (Find nos. 443–2 and 443–3, Bib. **44**, pls. 104 and 106) show a width of 0.9 cm. Their light and dark alternation occurs each 5.8, 6.2, or 6.5 cm. An example on a grey bast-fibre shroud (Find no. N26) has a width of 2.7 cm, with a repeat each 4.5 cm (Bib. **48**, fig. 45 right). The "xushou" 繡緞 type is similarly woven in three strips with a slightly different arrangement of patterns in light and dark tones, horizontal light or dark bars rather than graphs. Its width is 1.6 cm, and the repeat each 5.25 cm (Bib. **48**, fig. 45 left, pl. 87, Find no. 443–1 a border on a "xinqi" embroidered silk tabby wrapping-cloth; pl. 146, Find no. N7 a border on a "xinqi" embroidered gauze silk-padded robe).

Bast-fibre tabbies

Hemp: three fragments (Find no. N29) show 18 warps by 19 wefts per cm (w. 45 cm, longest fragment 1. 1.36 cm).

Ramie: seventeen grey fragments (Find no. N26) have a width of 20.5 cm, and a length of 36–150 cm, with 32–38 warps by 36–54 wefts per cm. Sixteen white fragments (Find no. N27) have a width of either about 20 or 51 cm, with 34–36 warps by 30 wefts per cm. Some samples reveal evidence of starching and roll-pressing (Find nos. N30:5, N29:2, and N27:10, Bib. **48**, pl. 153).

Dyeing and printing

Over twenty colours have been distinguished, including those for dyeing embroidery threads. Of these, the cinnabar-red is mercuric sulphide, a dark red of alizarine from the plant *Rubia cordifolia*, var. *mungista*, a blue of indigotin, a grey of lead sulphide, and a powdery-white of $KAl_2(Si_2Al)0_{10}(OH.F)_2$.

Two separate pieces of gold and silver-paste printed mock leno gauze (Find nos. 340–11 and 340–24, Bib. **48**, fig. 47 left and pl. 117) show patterns of linear feather-like or cloud-scroll motifs in silver-grey and white interspersed with dots in gold or cinnabar-red, which are arranged in roughly rhomboid forms. Each piece has a total of thirteen pattern units, each unit being 6.1 × 3.7 cm. The pattern is extremely dense, with less than one mm between each motif element. The printing was probably done with three relatively small relief-blocks (of 2.8 sq cm, 4.3 × 3.6 cm, and 3.5 × 2.8 cm) which could not be properly keyed and, therefore, produced some areas of overlapping or irregular distribution. As the width is 48 cm, each metre would have 430 pattern units requiring a total of 1,200 block impressions.

For printed and painted mock lenos at least five colours were used, though they are not clearly identifiable in their present state of preservation (Bib. 48, pl. 141, Find no. 340–32 a separate piece; pls. 93, 79 and 80, Find nos. 329–12 to 14 silk-padded robes; fig. 47 and pl. 118, Find no. N5 a fragment of a silk-padded quilt, as is Find no. N2, not illustrated). The pattern suggests a creeper-like plant with tendrils, buds, pendant flowers, and leaves, also arranged in roughly rhomboid form. Each pattern unit is small, 4 × 2.4 cm, and is linked continuously and densely. The width shows twenty repeats. Breaks in lines may indicate the use of stencils, though relief-blocks could also produce such faults. If stencils were used, four would have been combined to form each large rhomb, 8 × 4.4 cm, thus accelerating the printing process. Nevertheless, a width of 48 cm would require 800 pattern units for each metre and, thus, 200 repetitions. Many details were clearly applied with a brush as, for example, cinnabar-red on the buds, black dots on the flowers, and silver-grey for the leaves.

Embroideries

Of forty embroidered items in seven patterns, except for one example worked in satin or plain line stitch, all are executed in variations of chain stitch (Bib. 46, col. figs. 29 and 30).

"Xinqi" 信期 (Bib. 48, fig. 48, pls. 81, 83, 85, 87, 92, 95, 111, 128–130, 144–147) is seen on patterned gauze silk-padded robes (Find. nos. 329–10 and 329–11); incense-pouches (Find nos. 65–2 and 65–4) and separate pieces (Find nos. 354–18, N7:1,

N9:1, N14:12); on tabby mittens (Find no. 443–4), a silk-padded wrapping-cloth (Find no. 443–1), an incense-pouch (Find no. 442) and a separate fragment (Find no. 354–20); on a monochrome patterned silk incense-pouch (Find no. 65–11); and on a lined mock leno fragment (Find no. 337–2).

"Changshou" 長壽 (Bib. 48, figs. 49 and 50, pls. 84, 94, 109, 110, 126, and 127) appears only on silk tabby; a pillow-cover (Find no. 440), a tablecloth (Find no. 439), a wrapping-cloth (Find no. 441–1), a silk-padded robe (Find no. 357–3), and two separate fragments (Find nos. N1–1 and N4–1).

"Chengyun" 乘雲 (Bib. 48, fig. 51, pls. 86, 131, 148, and 204) was used on silk tabby, including a pillow-cloth (Find no. 446), a tablecloth (Find no. 444) and fragments of garments in the coffin (Find no. N8); and on monochrome silks patterned with the confronted bird motif, including a *yu* (pan-pipes) bag (Find no. 78–1) and two coverlet fragments (Find no. N3). A dogwood pattern is identified on the fragment of a silk tabby robe from the coffin (Find no. N10–1, Bib. 44, fig. 48:4, pl. 125).

Lozenge patterns executed in unconnected chain stitch also appear on two silk tabby garment fragments from the coffin (Find nos. N12 and N18, Bib. 48, fig. 52, pls. 132 and 150).

Loose cloud-scrolls embellish three silk tabby pieces (Find nos. 354–6 and 340–3, Bib. 48, fig. 53, pl. 152). These are coarsely executed and may have been expressly made as mortuary offerings. The other embroideries are all more densely stitched, though their base designs in fine thread plain line stitch sometimes show through as the artisans interpreted them freely.

Among the embroideries the most unusual is at the exterior of the coffin lid. A border of zigzag-edged rhombs enclosing tree-like motifs in cinnabar-red, black, and grey against a grey ground is worked in allover satin stitch (Bib. 48, fig. 28, pl. 115). The centre field shows small and large, complete and partial rhombs in greenish-black against an orangey-red ground; all executed in feathers pasted on the wood, though with silk tabby strips separating motif elements (Bib. 48, pl. 116).

Tombs 2 and 3 at Mawangdui, of the Lord of Dai and one of his two sons (d. 168 B.C.), have only been reported in brief, but include the same categories of silk weaves as Tomb 1 at the site, as well as three more painted silk banners and many manuscripts written on silk (Bib. **56**). Most intriguing is mention of a polychrome weave patterned in leopard spots.

Eastern or Later Han Dynasty
(A.D. 25–220)

Finds from this period are generally less well described in the excavation reports but appear to have been better studied by specialists. They have been better preserved and are, therefore, better suited for technical analyses. With one exception, the sites are in desert regions where climatic conditions have been favourable for textile conservation.

Salvage of four brick chamber tombs at Jiayuguan in Gansu province revealed two textiles in Tomb 2. Equally important are two bone rulers, demonstrating that 23.8 cm equalled one foot. Two monochrome patterned silks also emerged; one in grey with differently sized rhombs, irregularly and loosely woven, with different diameters of warp and weft, the other in a bright red jacket and skirt, with the collar in white print or dye on pink, a three-coloured waistband on the skirt (ht. 2 cm), and pale yellow silk tabby lining (Bib. **45).**

Tomb 62 at Mojuzi in Wuwei County, Gansu province, contained a lacquer *erbei* (double flange-handled ovoid cup) inscribed with an 8 B.C. manufacture date. The burial is considered to be of the first century A.D.[16] A male body, covered in a bast-fibre shroud, was found wearing a hat of mock leno pasted on a bamboo frame, a red tabby robe and sash with a belt-hook of bronze, two layers of silk-padded jackets, and leather boots (Bib. **44,** pp. 11, 12, 18, 19). The following silks have been analyzed:

Mock leno on the visor of the hat's inner cap (Find no. 26) in four layers fixed with red lacquer, 30 × 3.2 cm, 78 warps by 66 wefts per cm, warp and weft dia. 0.05 mm, 42 warps by 30 wefts per cm, warp and weft dia. 0.08 mm, 30 warps by 24 wefts per cm, warp and weft dia. 0.09 mm, with V-shaped pattern on the surface and wave pattern in cross-section; on the inner cap's crown (Find no. 27), 66 warps by 40 wefts per cm, warp and weft dia. 0.033 mm, of thrown silk; on the hat itself (Find no. 29), 7 warps by 7 wefts per cm, warp and weft dia. 0.2 mm, of thrown silk stiffened with a layer of blackish-purple lacquer, then coated with red lacquer. A grain-pouch (Find no. 30) found on the coffin lid was also of mock leno, 33 × 17 cm, 16 warps by 13 wefts per cm, warp and weft dia. 0.066 mm.

Warp-faced compound tabby for a mirror-bag (Find no. 31), 20 × 18 cm, 78 warps by 48 wefts per cm, warp dia. 0.2 mm and weft dia. 0.13 mm; for hatties (Find no. 32), 66 warps by 48 wefts per cm, warp dia. 0.18 mm and weft dia. 0.16 mm; and for the visor of the cap (Find no. 33), 30 × 3 cm, 104 warps by 54 wefts per cm, warp dia. 0.11 mm and weft dia. 0.15 mm.

Patterned gauze with rhombs on a grain-pouch (Find no. 13) found under the corpse's head, 48 × 17 cm, the warp twisted in a complex manner,[17] 144 warps by 30 wefts per cm, warp dia. 0.03 mm (the grège of 6 baves) and weft dia. 0.05 mm (the grège of 10 baves); another identical example (Find no. 20) placed on a glazed earthenware *hu* (storage jar) but with slightly different rhombs, 20 × 13 cm.

Monochrome pile warp weave with rhombs (Find no. 22) pasted on a wood cane, 14.5 × 2.2 cm, 50 warps by 47 wefts per cm. This is a three-series compound weave, with grège of different diameters for each series. Main warp dia. 0.2 mm, binding warp dia. 0.15 mm, pile warp dia. 0.4 mm. Each cm has 44 warps of each series, thus a total of 132 warps per cm. The weft dia. measures 0.2 mm, main and pattern wefts totalling 46 per cm. For a width of 50 cm, there would be 2,200 warps for each series, or a total of 6,600 ends. The pile is 0.7–0.8 mm high, and the pattern unit, of a compound rhomb with two small partial rhombs at opposed corners, measures 1 × 0.5 cm.[18]

In addition, silk ribbon and embroidery on silk tabby were discovered in this tomb.

Tomb 49 at Mojuzi is reported as of second-century A.D. date. It also contained a hat made of mock leno, with rhomboid openings and lacquered on both sides (Find no. 16), 11 × 5 cm for the crown, 14 warps by 14 wefts per cm, warp and weft dia. 0.15 mm.

Tomb 22 at this site was excavated in 1959 and produced a woven reed box covered with a polychrome patterned compound tabby border surrounding a chain stitch embroidered tabby centre (Bib. **32**, pl. 1).

Another major cache of textiles was uncovered in a double burial at Niya in northern Minfeng County, Xinjiang province (Bib. **20**, pp. 5, 6, and 11). Pre-World War II salvage work in this area had revealed a bamboo slip inscribed with a date of A.D. 269, and Han dynastic histories indicate that the site was abandoned in the late third century. These finds may be grouped as follows:

Cotton cloth for a coarse yellow handkerchief, 26 sq cm; man's coarse white trousers (Bib. **20**, p. 6, fig. 8); and two resist-dyed border fragments patterned in white on blue (Bib. **20**, p. 5, figs. 5, 6), one 80 × 50 cm with geometric patterns of triangles, asterisks, circles, and dots, the other 89 × 48 cm with the half-figure of a bodhisattva on the corner square, lozenges and other less distinguishable motifs in bands within; the latter laid over a wooden bowl containing sheep bones and an iron knife.

Monochrome silk tabbies were used for the woman's shroud, camisole, embroidered inner jacket, robe, outer jacket, embroidered sock-ties (Bib. **32**, pl. 8), embroidered mirror-pouch, embroidered powder-pouch, rouge-pouch, and wood comb-case (Bib. **20**, p. 5, fig. 4 right, p. 6, figs. 9–12). Other fragments were also found (Bib. **32**, pls. 10, 11).

Monochrome patterned silk, partly embroidered, was used for the woman's skirt (Bib. **32**, pl. 9). Now yellowed, this was originally natural-coloured, and patterned with large rhombs alternated with heart-shaped leaves. The weave is a warp-faced compound tabby, 66 warps by 18–19 wefts per cm.[19] Its pattern unit measures 3.9 × 8.2 cm (Bib. **27**, fig. 6 and pl. 1). Another fragment, also natural-coloured and with a pattern of birds and animals emerging through grapevines, is recorded, 66 warps by 26 wefts per cm (Bib. **25**, p. 75, not illustrated).

Polychrome patterned silk in warp-faced compound tabby weave was used for the woman's socks (Bib. 20, p. 5, fig. 4 right), the man's robe, socks, and mittens (Bib. **20**, p. 5, figs. 1–4, p. 6, figs. 7, 8), and two pillows' ends (Bib. **20**, p. 11, fig. 10). These tabbies are distinguished by graphs worked into their patterns:

"Yang" 陽 on the woman's socks (Bib. **32**, pl. 6) woven between the lozenge-patterned field and the selvage of 0.75 cm width. Brownish-red, purple, and natural-coloured warp threads are paired, while the yellowish-brown wefts remain single. As a three-series weave, there should be 150–180 warps by 34–36 wefts per cm. Its lozenge pattern unit measures 1.5–1.8 × 2.3–2.4 cm; the repeat about 90 ends to 84 picks. Thus, the pattern could be controlled by about twenty-one heddle rods and two sets of shafts (Bib. **27**, p. 62 and pl. 3 upper).

"Wanshi ruyi" 萬事如意 appears on the man's robe (Bib. **20**, p. 5, figs. 1, 2, p. 6, fig. 7). The warp is in five colours (brownish-red, purple, pale blue, dark green, and white), used three at a time in each pattern area with a total of twelve areas for this example. The brownish-red and white warps appear in all areas. As 56 ends are visible on the surface, and the weave is in three-series, there should be 168 warps by 25–26 wefts per cm. The pattern unit has a height of 3.9 cm and, therefore, a repeat of 100 picks. It may be that the pattern of complex S-scrolls, spirals, dogwood flowers, and the four graphs spaced from right to left required about fifty pattern rods and two sets of shafts (Bib. **27**, pp. 57–59, col. pl. 1).

"Yannian yishou dayi zisun" 延年益壽大宜子孫 appears on the man's socks and mittens, as well as on the ends of two pillows (Bib. **20**, p. 5, fig. 4, p. 11, fig. 10). A piece with these graphs was also used for the man's robe border. These examples too show five colours (brownish-red, sapphire-blue, greyish-buff, pale orange, and white) used three in each pattern area, but with many faults. Its selvage width is 1.05 cm. As 40–44 ends per cm show on the surface and this is a three-series weave, there should be 120–132 warps by 26–28 wefts per cm, a looser weave than the previous examples (Bib. **27**, pp. 59 and 60, pl. 2; Bib. **32**, pls. 4 and 5; Bib. **39**, pl. 9).

Monochrome patterned gauze is sewn on the quatrefoil mouth of the woman's powder-pouch (Bib. **32**, pl. 7). Patterned in a rhomb with two smaller partial

HSIO-YEN SHIH

rhombs at opposed corners, it has 120–128 warps by 35 wefts per cm (Bib. 25, p. 69, figs. 7, 8).

About 3 km southeast of the tomb, another fragment of polychrome patterned silk was found in a dwelling-site (Bib. 32, pl. 14). It is patterned with realistically represented grapevines (including bunches of grapes and leaves) and large-nosed figures. This example is described as weft-patterned and may be of non-Chinese origin. Also in this area was a fragment of a wool blanket (Bib. 32, pl. 15) showing quatrefoils in red enclosed in hexagons defined in white on a blue ground.[20] This is suggested to be of local manufacture.

Xia Nai, now Director of the Archaeological Research Institute of the Chinese Academy of Sciences, has published several studies of Han textiles based upon finds summarized above (Bib. 27 and 34). In the earlier study, he paid particular attention to warp-faced compound weaves, while these as well as gauzes are studied in the later article.

Han Dynasty monochrome patterned silk has the main warp in a 1:1 tabby weave and the flushing warp in a three-tread float to one binding pick. Usually there are double or triple the number of ends as picks. Thus, as most such intact examples measure 2.2 Han feet (50.38 cm), 2,970–3,300 ends would have been required and at least two sets of shafts, with as many as thirty-eight to sixty pattern rods as well as two treadles. The Eastern Han shuttle was knife-shaped and used for both passing and beating the weft.

Han Dynasty polychrome patterned silk is warp-faced on both sides. If more than two colours are used, a three-series division is observed by varying colours in different areas. However, four-series does also exist. In general, the weft is of a single colour but divided in function between main and pattern wefts which alternate. This permits warp floats to form the pattern without losing firmness of weave. Usually, the underlying warp and weft will not be entirely concealed but this looseness becomes disturbing only in four or more series. Again, the pattern unit is relatively short, no more than several cm in height, though it continues across the entire width. A unit 3.9 cm in height would require 100 picks. These polychrome weaves seem to be narrower than the monochromes, measuring 35–38 cm. Thus, 5,000 or more ends were necessary, using at least two sets of shafts controlled by treadles and about fifty heddle bars for patterning. Xia Nai suggests that draw cords may already have been used, requiring a second artisan to serve as the drawboy.

Han Dynasty patterned gauzes are woven either on a simple ground with warp threads twisted with the aid of a stick (the twisted warp to the main warp's right or left) in a variant of a tabby weave, and with two pattern rods; or on a more complex ground with paired warps, alternate pairs functioning as doup or fixed ends which are reversed after each throw. Three sets of shafts were used for the gauze ground and a number of pattern rods for its rhomboid design. The first type of gauze has finer openings and is also used without patterning. The second type has larger openings and patterning in bigger scale. Xia Nai also notes a mock leno in poil warp and weft, very tightly twisted with the weft paired in opposed twists, which is often mistaken for true gauze.

Finally, he comments on Han dyes, stating that alizarine plus iron salts produced green, or brown when oxidized; while alizarine plus aluminium salts (alum) produced red.

Six Dynasties
or Northern and Southern Dynasties Period
(A.D. 221–589)

From the later fourth century on, a number of dated or datable tombs offer textile evidence. Almost all were excavated in the Turfan area, either at Astana (tombs labelled TAM) or at Kharakhojo (tombs labelled TKM). The importance of what is now the Uighur Autonomous Region in Xinjiang province on the old Silk Road is too well known to require further comment. The region's isolation in the first

314

half of the twentieth century, and its dry desert air, have both helped to preserve perishable materials from destruction at the hands of man or by natural inclemencies.

TKM 3, dated to A.D. 348 by a coffin inscription, had fragments of a red silk tabby embroidered in green and yellow chain stitch with irregular floral scrolls. These were cut-pieces pasted on a silk tabby banner (Bib. **52**).

TAM 39, containing documents dated to A.D. 367 and 370, yielded a fragment from a silk-padded waistcoat lined in natural silk tabby, the surface in red silk tabby with a silver-grey silk tabby border, and embroidered in black, green, and yellow with irregular floral scrolls and dots (the latter in coiled chain stitch which is considered a special feature of Han Dynasty embroidery) about a central tulip-like flower (Bib. **52**, fig. 51); also a pair of slippers with soles of braided bast-fibre, a woven reed lining, and sides of a "Fuqiechang yihouwang tianyanming-chang" 富且昌宜候王天延命長, poly-chrome patterned silk specially woven for this use (Bib. **32**, pls. 22 and 23; **35**, pl. 5:2; **39**; **52**), eight colours (brownish-red, white, black, blue, yellow, buff, gold, and green) in tapestry weave, the toes patterned with the graphs above, a dragon and their reverse repeat, alternated with bands at the toes and sides patterned in small rhombs and scrolls.

TAM 305, with a document of A.D. 384, held a double burial with both woman and man dressed in Chinese-style garments (Bib. **21**).

In front of Caves 125 and 126 at Mogaoku in Dunhuang, Gansu province, fragments of an embroidery were excavated from crevices (Bib. **37**, pp. 54–60, pls. 11 and 12). Chain stitch following pattern motif outlines completely covers a yellowish-brown silk tabby (Bib. **32**, pls. 2 and 3, p. 3 notes that the ground is of two layers of silk tabby with a layer of bast-fibre cloth between). Geometric, floral, and figural elements are shown in shaded tones. A dedicatory inscription mentions the name of the Prince of Guangyang and the reign date (*Taihe*? 11th year or A.D. 487). The fragment, 75 × 51 cm, preserves the lower portion of a Buddha in

dharma-āsana with a bodhisattva standing on the right, and in a band below a row of monks and male donors to the right balanced by a row of nuns and female donors to the left. The thread is coarser in the border embroidery with about eight stitches per cm for honeysuckle motifs enclosed in roundels, while its interior field has nine stitches per cm vertically and eleven stitches per cm horizontally. The chain stitch is occasionally worked from the back, varying the surface effect.

TAM 306, with a document of A.D. 541, contained a bast-fibre jacket and trousers (Bib. **21**, p. 4, figs. 21 and 22); a miniature bed with green patterned silk stretched over a wood frame, two curtains of silk tabby in yellow with purple borders, and two pillows of white silk tabby over waste silk (Bib. **21**, p. 19, figs. 28, 29, and 31); and a polychrome patterned silk of two joined pieces, 21 × 9 cm, woven in warp-faced compound tabby, a technique transmitted from Han times but with new decorative motifs. Its five bands show first trees, then winged creatures (seraphim-like) alternated with scorpions beneath flying birds, confronted long-necked birds alternating with potted plants (?), confronted deer with reversed heads alternating with floral sprays, and finally, confronted birds alternating with plant and rosette motifs (Bib. **21**, p. 4, fig. 23; **27**, pl. 6:1).

TAM 303, dated by epitaph to A.D. 551, contained six painted silk tabby banners (all fragmentary); the female occupant's face covering in silk-padded silk tabby, purple with a silver border, two bone beads sewn on over the eyes and an agate bead at the nose tip (Bib. **21**, p. 3, fig. 11); silk tabby garments including two jackets, trousers, and an undergarment; a fragment of purplish-red patterned silk, 40 × 9 cm, with paired confronted birds or unicorns (?) within ovoids, quatrefoils between and spiral rosettes overlapping the ovals' conjunction (Bib. **21**, p. 3, fig. 8; **25**, p. 8, fig. 7; **27**, pl. 7:1); and three polychrome patterned silks also in the traditional warp-faced compound tabby but with new patterns. One in blue on a yellow ground shows confronted cattle, horses, and birds, all enclosed in beaded ovals, with rosettes overlapping the centres of their long sides (Bib. **21** cover; **27**, pl. 6:2). Two others have bands of trees containing and alternated with dotted lozenges, and connected by small squares and triangles in reverse repeat. One with a higher pattern band is in five colours: brownish-red, sapphire-blue, green, yellow, and white (Bib. **21**, p. 3, fig. 9; **27**, pl. 7:2; **32**, pl. 24). The other is divided into seven bands in three colours: blue, green, and white (Bib. **21**, p. 3, fig. 12; **27**, pl. 8).

TAM 88, dated by epitaph to A.D. 567, yielded another polychrome patterned silk in the same weave and with what appears to be a pattern evolved from Han motifs (Bib. **32**, pl. 25; **35**, pl. 6:2). A *kui*-dragon has a cloud-scroll tail covering a lion and a rhomb composed of four small diamonds. The warp is in three-series but five colours: red, blue, green, white, and yellow. This fragment, 30 × 16.5 cm, retains one selvage.

TAM 323 contained a document of A.D. 587 and a textile fragment sewn from five pieces (Bib. **25**, p. 9, fig. 14). Its outer border and an inner band are of a striped polychrome silk, a rosette enclosed by a beaded roundel, and two pieces with *kui*-dragon and rosette, all warp-faced compound tabbies. Its central part seems to be of an embroidered silk tabby.

TAM 323 contained a document of A.D. 588 and a polychrome silk fragment patterned in alternately dark and light squares (Bib. **25**, p. 9, fig. 15).

TAM 18, dated by epitaph to A.D. 589, offered yet another new pattern in the warp-faced compound tabby weave (Bib. **52**, p. 16, fig. 17, col. pl. 1:2). Red, green, and yellow in three-series show a cameleer and camel with the graphs "Huwang" 胡王 (barbarian prince) between, in inverted repeat; thus, the pattern is formed of this paired group within a beaded oval interrupted by a rosette form at its narrow ends. The fragment, 19.5 × 15 cm, retains a selvage and has 48 warps by 32 wefts per cm on its surface (being in three-series, actually 144 ends per cm), the warp diameter is 0.3 mm and the weft 0.2 mm.

Other finds from undated or later dated tombs are also considered to have sixth-century characteristics; that is, polychrome or monochrome silks in warp-faced compound tabby weave, with colours used in usually no more than three-series. TAM 307 contained a polychrome silk patterned with rosettes enclosed in beaded lozenges (Bib. **25**, p. 10, fig. 19). TAM 331, with a document of A.D. 619, included three polychrome silks; two with dotted rosettes alternating with geometricized quatrefoils (Bib. **25**, p. 9, fig. 11), and one with animal heads enclosed in beaded roundels. TKM 48, which had clothing lists of A.D. 596, 604, and 617, revealed a monochrome silk in pale violet, 32.5 × 24.5 cm, patterned in two bands. The wider band shows overlapping ovals defined in lines and continuous C-spirals, enclosing a floral motif and the graph "gui" 貴, and may actually be considered as two bands in itself. The narrower band is defined with parallel as well as inverted-V lines, alternating within a floral medallion and a vertical element composed of two larger rhombs connected by smaller rhombs (Bib. **32**, pl. 46; **25**, pl. 10:3). Its weave has 44 ends by 38 picks per cm on the surface. A polychrome silk from the same tomb is in three-series of red, blue, and white. This fragment, 18.5 × 8.7 cm, has double warps and shows 25 ends by 18 picks per cm on its surface.[21] Its pattern, in reverse and inverted repeat, shows the graph "gui" 貴 flanked by addorsed running animals and floral motifs, under a beaded roundel enclosing confronted peacocks which stand on a meander bar, floral motifs above and below (Bib. **32**, pl. 28; **35**, pl. 7:1; **36**, pp. 24 and 25, figs. 52 and 59). TAM 50, with documents of A.D. 541, 620, and 622, revealed a monochrome silk patterned with overlapping ovals (similar to the example from TAM 48 described above) enclosing geometricized floral motifs in inverted repeat (Bib. **32**, pl. 47), and a polychrome silk patterned in bands and with the graphs "Tianwang" 天王 (Bib. **32**, pl. 26). TAM 99, with a document of A.D. 631, had a polychrome silk fragment with an intact selvage, 18 × 13.5 cm, the selvage width 3 cm, in five colours (red, green, blue, yellow, and white) of three-series, patterned with an elephant and mahout, a playful lion, and a buffalo, each enclosed in squares of barred lines (Bib. **32**, pl. 27; **35**, pl. 9:2). The pattern unit is 4.1 cm wide, with 132 warps by 30 wefts per cm.

Wool textiles were discovered at TKM 3, its coffin inscribed to A.D. 348; at Bachu in the southwest of the province, the site of the ancient town of Tokuzilai (Chinese transliteration of a Turkic name), and at Yudian (Keriya), the site of another ancient town, Wuyulaike. The first is camel-hair-coloured, 1.5 × 6 cm, in tabby weave of 11 warps by 8 wefts per cm, the warp finer than the weft (Bib. **52**, pp. 19 and 26, fig. 49). The second produced a patterned wool carpet fragment said to be in tapestry weave (Bib. **39**, pl. 10). The third yielded three wool fragments: one with dotted rosettes resist-dyed in white on blue, one plain in purplish-red, and the third woven in bands and stripes of beige and grey said to be of camel-hair (Bib. **32**, pls. 18–20; **39**). With

these wools were found a tie-dyed red silk tabby and a wax-resist white on blue cotton fragment (Bib. **32**, pls. 17 and 21). The earliest example of tie-dyed fabric from a dated tomb emerged out of TAM 1 with an epitaph of A.D. 418, showing dotted lozenges on a brownish-red silk tabby with 52 warps by 45 wefts per cm (Bib. **52**, pp. 18 and 26, fig. 50). TAM 85 also contained two pieces of tie-dyed silk tabby, red and brownish-red, and a resist-dyed white dotted rosette and lozenge pattern on blue silk tabby (Bib. **32**, pls. 48–50).

Tang Dynasty
(A.D. 618–907)

Recent textile finds have been particularly revealing for the seventh and eighth centuries. Not only were many new motifs and patterns introduced from West Asia, then produced by Chinese for export to suit foreign tastes, but at the same time a new weaving technique with the weft-patterned compound twill rapidly gained popularity, though it replaced the traditional warp-faced compound tabby by gradual stages only. Remarkable advances may also be seen in the dyeing and printing of textiles. The importance of excavated examples can be recognized in the number of finds which have emerged from dated or datable contexts. Again, almost all of these were located in the Astana area of Turfan in Xinjiang province.

TAM 31, with a clothing list of A.D. 620, had a warp-faced compound tabby in three-series with four colours (pale and dark blue, green, and white), patterned with a pair of addorsed birds beneath another pair flanking a tree, in reverse and inverted repeat, thus appearing to form a rhomb shape (Bib. **52**, pp. 16 and 26, fig. 48). Its weave shows 52 ends by 34 picks per cm on the surface, the warp diameter being 0.4 mm and the weft 0.25 mm. Other pieces sewn on to this fragment are also patterned, but are indecipherable in their present state.

TAM 301, with a legal document of A.D. 643, had a painted silk tabby banner nailed to its tomb-chamber ceiling (Bib. **21**, p. 2, fig. 4), a bast-fibre fragment 110 × 50 cm, and two polychrome patterned

silks (Bib. **21**, pp. 16 and 17). One is patterned in red on a pale yellow ground with rhombs, 11 × 6 cm, and the other in two tones of red with wellhead motifs either in roundels or without surround, 22.5 × 15 cm (Bib. **21**, inside cover figs. 7 and 8; **27**, pl. 10).

TAM 42, dated by epitaph to A.D. 651, had a bast-fibre sheet of tabby weave sewn from three pieces of 45.5 cm width, the whole 138 × 246 cm, 10–11 warps by 8 wefts per cm tabby. Its selvages show no reinforcement of binding (Bib. **52**, pp. 18 and 17, fig. 21).

TAM 302, dated by epitaph to A.D. 653, contained three painted silk tabby banners,[22] and four fragments of polychrome patterned silks. Two of warp-faced compound tabby, each measuring 10.5 × 3 cm, are patterned in rosette-medallions and palmette quatrefoils in three-series of five colours, orangey-red, blue, green, yellow, and white (Bib. **21**, col. pl. and p. 2, fig. 6; **27**, pl. 9). These were found around a waisted stick near the female occupant's body. The other two pieces were placed on the body's breast and back. One in warp-faced compound tabby shows a pattern symmetrical to its weft axis, in inverted repeat, with two motif variations in alternate strips. Turned at a 90° angle, one band has confronted horses, beribboned and winged, right and left forelegs raised, a "wang" 王 graph in seal script above each head, and a symmetrical honeysuckle scroll below their feet; all enclosed by a beaded roundel. The second band is similar, except that the horses have no ribbons, their heads are lowered, and they flank a tree which rests on a floral-patterned ground. Rosettes overlap the conjunction of roundels and trefoils appear in their interstices (Bib. **27**, col. pl. 3). The second example is similar in having the same pattern as described for the first band above, but is woven in warp-faced compound twill (Bib. **21**, p. 2, fig. 1; **27**, pl. 11). Both are in three-series of four colours (orangey-yellow, dark blue, yellowish-green, and white with a pink tinge), used in uneven stripes between 0.9 and 5.4 cm wide. Their pattern unit is 7.5 × 9 cm, with 54 ends per cm visible on the surface; therefore, a total of 162 warps × 32–34 wefts per cm. The twill weave is 2:1, and the picks are equally divided between main and pattern wefts. It is thought that two sets of shafts and about sixty pattern rods would have been necessary for these silk weaves.

TAM 44, dated by epitaph to A.D. 655, included an example of warp-faced compound tabby patterned with hexagons and the "wang" 王 graph, in reverse repeat to either side of a blue stripe (Bib. **32**, pl. 32).[23]

TAM 337, dated by epitaph to A.D. 657, had three polychrome patterned silks, all in three-series with four colours, and warp-faced compound tabbies. One, 12 × 18.5 cm, is in bright red, pure yellow, blue, and white, patterned with confronted mandarin ducks enclosed in beaded roundels and alternated with rosettes, 26 warps by 26 wefts per cm visible on its surface, the picks being equally divided between main and pattern wefts (Bib. **25**, p. 10, fig. 16,[24] p. 74). Another, measuring 15 × 12 cm, shows a large stag enclosed by a beaded roundel with jade-green, brown-green, yellow, and white, 23 warps by 32 equally divided wefts visible per cm (Bib. **25**, p. 10, fig. 17).[25] Finally, a fragment with part of a horse and rider, 9 × 24 cm, is in blue, green, yellow, and white, 20 warps by 28 equally divided wefts visible per cm (Bib. **25**, p. 6, fig. 4).[26]

TAM 325, dated by epitaph to A.D. 661, had three examples of warp-faced compound tabbies in three-series and four colours. Two of these show beaded roundels and quatrefoils, one measuring 13.4 × 23

cm, in jade-green, brown-green, yellow, and white, 40 warps by 38 equally divided wefts visible per cm (Bib. **25**, p. 9, fig. 10, p. 74).[27] The second has a boar's head with gaping mouth in a beaded roundel, 17.5 × 23.5 cm, in blue, green, yellow, and white, 36 warps by 38 equally divided wefts visible per cm (Bib. **25**, p. 7, fig. 6; **27**, pl. 12:2).[28]

TAM 317, dated by epitaph to A.D. 662, contained a two-series warp-faced compound tabby patterned with hexagons enclosing furled leaves in pale yellow and gold on a pure yellow ground, 12 × 19 cm, with 28 warps by 30 wefts per cm visible on its surface (Bib. **25**, p. 9, fig. 13).

TAM 322, dated by epitaph to A.D. 663, contained a silk tabby banner (Bib. **25**, p. 10, fig. 20) and three polychrome patterned silks. One, with a pattern of horse and rider, may be compared to a find in TAM 337 dated to A.D. 657 (Bib. **25**, p. 10, fig. 18). Another is in three-series and four colours (blue, green, yellow, and white) patterned with a large stag in a beaded roundel (Bib. **25**, p. 6, fig. 3), the fragment 20 × 14 cm, with 24 warps by 24 wefts per cm visible on its surface. The third shows confronted birds in a beaded roundel, of three-series in bright red, sapphire-blue, and white. This fragment measures 14 × 16 cm, with 29 warps by 28 wefts per cm visible on its surface (Bib. **25**, p. 74, not reproduced).

TAM 134, with a document of A.D. 665, had what appears to be a warp-faced compound tabby showing confronted cocks standing on square stands and enclosed in plain roundels, alternated with a vertical element composed of two triangles above and below connected by a thin line flanked by two squares (Bib. **36**, pp. 20 and 27, fig. 55). It is described as three-series in red, yellow, and white, 26 × 17 cm.[29]

TAM 332, also with a document of A.D. 665, contained two more examples of warp-faced compound tabbies, both in three-series of four colours. One with a large stag in a beaded roundel is in the same colours as the example described for TAM 322 of A.D. 663, 7.5 × 20.5 cm, 26 warps by 26 wefts per cm visible on its surface (Bib. **25**, p. 74). The other shows a large phoenix within a beaded roundel (Bib. **25**, p. 7, fig. 5; **27**, pl. 12:1),[30] in blue, green, yellow, and white. This fragment measures 14.5 × 23.5 cm, and the pattern is 22 cm high.

TAM 92 had epitaphs of A.D. 639 and 668, and contained two fragments of polychrome patterned silk. One in warp-faced compound tabby, measuring 13 × 8.8 cm, is typically in bands of reverse repeat, showing a wider band with confronted birds flanking a boxed tree above landscape elements, these enclosed in a beaded roundel, the graph "tong" 同 in interstices between the roundels; alternated with a very narrow band of confronted lions with right and left forepaws raised, backed by a rectangle containing a geometricized motif (Bib. **32**, pl. 29). The other shows confronted ducks in a beaded roundel, 19.8 × 19.4 cm, and is described as with doubled warps and wefts in two- or three-series of four colours (brown, blue, yellow, and white); therefore, a weft-faced compound twill with 22 warps by 56–76 wefts per cm (Bib. **32**, pl. 30; **35**, p. 29, pl. 8:2).

TKM 48, with clothing inventories of A.D. 596, 604, and 617, already noted under the Six Dynasties entries, also contained an example of a well-developed Tang weave. A fragment with confronted peacocks in a beaded roundel is of weft-faced compound twill permitting many more variations of internal patterning detail (Bib. **32**, pl. 63; **36**, pp. 20 and 27, fig. 52). It seems to be in two-series of three colours (blue, yellow, and white), 21 × 15 cm.

TAM 330, dated by epitaph to A.D. 672, had two polychrome patterned silks. One fragment, 14.5 × 10 cm, is a warp-faced compound tabby in blue, green, yellow, and white, with 26 warps by 30 wefts per cm visible on its surface, and with a pattern of confronted deer in a beaded roundel (not reproduced, Bib. **25**, p. 74). The other shows an allover pattern of rosettes enclosed by quatrefoils, also a warp-faced compound tabby, but in two-series of pale green and blue (Bib. **25**, p. 9, fig. 12). This fragment, 30 × 20 cm, has 28 warps by 28 wefts per cm visible on its surface.

TAM 117, dated by epitaph to A.D. 683, contained a silk tabby silk-padded quilt with polychrome patterned silk borders (Bib. **32**, pl. 40; **36**, p. 18, fig. 25, pp. 20 and 28, fig. 56). These strips, 34 or 107 × 3.5 cm, are in weft-faced compound twill patterned with a rosette surrounded by four trefoils to form a quatrefoil, or with quatrefoils around a squared centre, or with naturalistically rendered rose blooms, or with plain and beaded stripes. Dark and bright green, red, yellow, brown, and white are sometimes used with shaded effects. Also found in the tomb were silk tabbies dyed after being folded and sewn (*tritik*), their patterns showing as white irregularly dotted rhombs on brownish-red (Bib. **32**, pl. 51; **35**, p. 30 notes one piece as 16 × 5 cm, 36 warps by 36 wefts per cm, pl. 8:1; **36**, p. 29, fig. 60).

TAM 29, which contained a document of A.D. 685, also yielded a monochrome patterned silk in pale yellow (not reproduced) and a resist-dyed silk tabby with a printed pattern of floral motifs, white on buff (Bib. **32**, pl. 54; **52**, p. 17).

TAM 304, dated by epitaph to A.D. 688, offered a pair of straw sandals soled with bast-fibres tied by silk thread (Bib. **21**, p. 3, fig. 13).

TAM 20, containing a document of A.D. 706, also offered a fragment of a weft-faced compound twill in four-series of red, green, reddish-brown, and yellow, patterned in floral medallions (Bib. **52**, p. 16, fig. 18, p. 19 and col. pl. 1:1).[31] Measuring 8 × 24.6 cm, its main warp is single and its pattern warp doubled, 44 ends by 40 picks per cm, the warp diameter being 0.2 mm and the weft 0.25 mm. Its colours are selectively shaded, and its selvage shows two additional bast-fibre ends of 1.5 mm each. Another extraordinary find from this tomb is a deep red silk tabby piece with a painted border of floral medallions (Bib. **32**, pl. 57; **52**, p. 18), 22.6 × 4 cm, the painting in colours of blue, green, yellow, reddish-brown, purple, black, and white.

TAM 363, with a famous manuscript of the Confucian Analects copied in A.D. 710, also yielded two bast-fibre sheets and three fragments of a warp-faced compound twill. One sheet, 240 × 136 cm, was sewn of three strips each 47 cm wide, in tabby weave with 10 warps by 8 wefts per cm (Bib. **38**, p.

10, fig. 1). The second is fragmentary, but shows its centre strip to be of 42.8 cm width, in tabby weave of 52 warps by 33 wefts per cm. The polychrome silk is patterned with confronted ducks in a beaded roundel.[32] It was found sewn on a bast-fibre sheet and served as the body's breast ornament. Its larger fragment measures 17 × 14.5 cm (Bib. **38**, p. 10, fig. 2), while two smaller fragments were 7.6 × 8 cm. Its selvage in white and green was intact, 0.5 cm wide. The weave is in two-series of five colours (orangey-yellow, pale yellow, blue, green, and white), with 63 warps by 20 wefts per cm.

TAM 108, datable by a legal document of A.D. 721 written on bast-fibre tabby (Bib. **32**, pl. 62), yielded two fragments of polychrome patterned silk striped with a small herringbone pattern and said to be a warp-faced compound twill (Bib. **32**, pl. 41; **39**),[33] as well as at least three fragments of resist-dyed stencilled or printed mock leno (Bib. **36**, p. 18, fig. 27, pp. 21 and 29, figs. 61, 64, and 65). One, 139 × 16 cm, has rosettes in white on a brownish-red ground.[34] A second, 57 × 31 cm, shows confronted mandarin ducks flanking a potted plant and alternated with floral sprays, in white on yellow (Bib. **32**, pl. 60; **35**, p. 30, pl. 6:1 where it is described as a tabby of 40 warps by 26 wefts per cm, the warp being either single or tripled, each being thrown twice before changing the shed). The third, 50 × 48 cm, is decorated with cotton blossoms in white on yellow.[35]

TAM 37, containing a document of A.D. 768, produced a cotton sheet, 118 × 224 cm, sewn from two pieces each 60.5 cm wide, and woven in tabby of 12 warps by 12 wefts per cm, therefore a total of 676 ends for the whole (Bib. **52**, p. 17, fig. 20, and p. 18).

TAM 381, found with a document of A.D. 778, also contributed a pair of "cloud-toed" slippers and a pair of socks in polychrome patterned silks. The slippers' exterior sides are of warp-faced compound tabby patterned in floral medallions with blue, green, brownish-green, and yellow (Bib. **32**, pl. 43, pl. 44 showing an example with identical pattern in different colours; **39**, pl. 11). Its side lining is also of warp-faced compound tabby patterned with birds and cloud-scrolls in a typically banded order, of

blue, green, brown, pink, and white. Finally, the slippers' toes and the socks are in weft-faced compound twill, with an overall *millefiore* design scattered with birds, of bright red, dark green, yellowish-green, yellow, sapphire-blue, dark purple, pink, and white (Bib. **32**, pl. 45; **35**, pl. 5:1, **36**, pl. 10). In addition, the slippers' interior soles are covered with a monochrome patterned silk of meanders on yellow.

At Bachu in Xinjiang province, silk cocoons and a fragment of a patterned wool blanket said to be in tapestry weave, 26 × 12 cm, emerged (Bib. **32**, pls. 64 and 65). Six Dynasties finds from the same area have been mentioned previously.

Gansu province also provided a great cache of Tang textiles, discovered in the course of restoration work on the Mogaoku caves. A hole, revealed in the south wall of Cave 130, was filled with the fragments of forty-odd silk tabby banners. Excavation in front of Caves 122 and 123 (adjacent to the area where the 487 embroidery was uncovered) yielded fragments of twelve more silk tabby banners, as well as other textiles.

Most of the silk tabby pieces were dyed. Floral sprays, rosettes, and medallions predominate in their patterning, either stencilled or printed[36] with resist, then dyed (Bib. **43**, p. 60, fig. 3, p. 66, figs. 5–7, p. 67, fig. 15, and back-cover figs. 1 and 2). However, tie-dyeing of the *tritik* type may also be seen (Bib. **43**, back-cover fig. 3). The tabby is described as having either single or tripled wefts, usually thrown twice before changing the shed, but with the tripled wefts sometimes thrown eight times consecutively.

Monochrome patterned silks were found on five silk tabby banners, a sash, and four other fragments. A herringbone pattern of relatively wide dimension is seen on one strip of a banner, executed in warp-faced compound tabby (Bib. **43**, p. 56, fig. 1, and back-cover fig. 4). Another banner has its top triangle and third body strip in a small rhomb-patterned silk, its first and fourth body strips in medallion-patterned silk (Bib. **43**, p. 67, fig. 13) and its second body strip in quatrefoil-patterned silk.

A warp-faced compound twill appears on another banner (Bib. **43**, p. 57, fig. 2, and p. 67, fig. 14). The fragment measures 15 × 4 cm, with 55 warps by 24 wefts (or 48 paired wefts) per cm. Its warp threads are in blue, green, brown, yellow, and white used in three-series, and forming shaded stripes. An area between the stripes and selvage is in extended tabby weave with doubled warp ends, as is the selvage itself.

Appliqué of eight-pointed stars decorates another silk tabby banner (Bib. **43**, p. 57, fig. 16).

A natural-coloured mock leno forms the top of a plain-dyed silk tabby banner. Its tabby weave uses single or doubled wefts, each thrown twice before changing over. The mock leno top is bordered in a brown silk patterned in meanders.

With these also appeared the fragment (ht. 29 cm) of a veiled hat in pieces of silk tabby.

As documents of A.D. 725 and 748 are associated with these finds, and as it is known from historical sources that Cave 130 was executed in the first half of the eighth century, it seems likely that the textiles were destroyed or concealed in the great suppression of Buddhism between A.D. 842 and 845.

Cotton fabrics from Xinjiang have received special attention (Bib. **49**). Though this plant fibre became quite widespread in China from the Northern Song Dynasty (eleventh century) on, its earlier appearance seems to have been confined to border areas. Excavated examples are listed as follows:
— three fragments from an Eastern Han Dynasty double burial at Minfeng;
— a cloth figurine wearing cotton garments from TAM 13, probably of the fourth century;
— a warp-faced compound tabby with geometric motifs in a mixture of silk and cotton from TAM 309 dated by epitaph to A.D. 586;
— a record of debts dated to A.D. 551 written on cotton and also from Astana;
— a saddle-bag, 21.5 × 14.5 cm, from Yudian (Keriya);
— a printed cloth, 11 × 7 cm, also probably of the sixth century and from Yudian;
— cotton tuft wicks for oil lamps at Astana and Kharakhojo;
— a purse, 48 × 24 cm, from TAM 20 dated by epitaph to A.D. 640;
— fragments sewn into paper slippers from TAM 44 dated by epitaph to A.D. 655;

— plain and dyed cotton, 26 × 12 cm, white on blue, as well as cotton seeds from a ninth-century site at Bachu. The fabrics are considered to be of local manufacture, woven on a vertical loom, and the seeds identified as *Gossypium herbaceum* Linnaeus. This variety of "African cotton" has also been found in Gansu province and has the advantage of requiring only 130 days for its growing period, thus making it suitable for desert regions.

Dyeing and printing of textiles are a special feature of Tang technological development. Analysis of dye pigments was undertaken by the Xinjiang Cotton Weaving and Dyeing Factory No. 71 (Bib. **51**). Alizarine from *Rubia cordifolia*, var. *mungista*, reported to have been cultivated already in the Han Dynasty, produced an orangey, brownish, or purplish-red. Indigotin from a deciduous magnolia, cultivated in China from early Eastern Chou times (sixth century B.C.), produced either clear or dark tones of blue when combined with an alkali and exposed to air for oxidization, the darker shades requiring nine or more dyeings. A dull yellow, often seen in monochrome patterned silks, came from steeping the fruit of the *Gardenia florida* or the root of *Coptis teeta*, Wall., the liquid being effective either cold or warm. A glossy yellow was produced by *Ligusticum acutilobum*, S. & Z., a buff-yellow by *Thalictrum omeiense*, W.T. Wang & S.H. Wang, and a greenish-yellow by *Saphora japonica*. These variations of primary colours could, of course, be combined to form other hues. Gum sericin could be removed from hard silk by a strong alkali of wood-ash and lime, but this was necessary for stencilled or printed patterns only. Bleaching before dyeing was also unnecessary, though use of sulphur is reported in some pharmaceutical texts. An acidic mordant seems to have been frequently used. Apart from tie-dyeing, and dyeing after stitching of pattern areas, stencilled or printed resist-dyed silks seem to have gained in sophistication and popularity during the seventh and eighth centuries.[37] Originally described as wax-resist dyed silks, at least ten specimens have now been analyzed to reveal far more complicated processes. Printed gauzes of hard silk in plain weave were first printed in an alkaline solution (possibly soybean milk and lime), then washed in water or a mild acidic solution, then dyed. The silk was, therefore, degummed in the pattern areas and shows even threads, 1–1.5 mm in diameter, under magnification. Silk tabbies, on the other hand, more frequently show the use of stencils (probably of paper) and more colours, sometimes requiring three or four phases of dyeing. Their ground colour was brushed on many times to achieve uniformity of tone, then fixed by steaming and washing. The resist consisted of a paste containing about five per cent zinc dust, or sodium sulphates ($NA_2SO_3 \cdot 7H_2O$ or $Na_2S_2O_4 \cdot 2H_2O$). One example of a stencilled patterned true gauze from TAM 38 may have used two different coloured pastes for its over-dyes.

Southern Song Dynasty
(A.D. 1127–1280)

The Qingshou Si temple was removed during the widening of Peking's main east-west thoroughfare in 1955. Its twin pagodas contained the ashes of a monk and his disciple, as well as a number of textile finds. These included an embroidered bag, 60 cm square, of reddish-yellow silk tabby decorated with lotus, peonies, moonflowers, and chrysanthemum, four graphs "xianghua gongyang" 香花供養 printed in gold, one at each corner; a piece of *kesi* *(k'o-ssu)* tapestry, 68 × 56 cm, with yellowish-green lotus and geese above waves on a blue ground (Bib. **11**, fig. 1); a cotton cap with embroidered ear-flaps (Bib. **11**, fig. 2); a fragment of monochrome silk tabby, 50 × 9 cm; a fragment of a polychrome patterned silk, 33 × 22 cm; and four fragments of a gold thread weave, 70 × 8 cm or 23 × 8 cm.

The burial of a warrior with his horse was accidentally discovered by herders in a remote area of Alar in the Uighur Autonomous Region, northeast Xinjiang province, as early as 1951, but archaeological workers were able to reach the site only five years later. The pastoral nomads had, however, forwarded a description of the interment and its burial goods to the authorities, and the textile finds are now in the Gugong Museum of Peking. A robe, lined in pale camel-coloured silk tabby, has three examples of weft-patterned compound twill. Its main body shows addorsed birds flanking a floral motif enclosed by roundels patterned in geometric configurations of rhombs and hexagons, the roundels with smaller rosettes overlapping their conjunctions and in their interstices (Bib. **17**, pls. 1 and 3). Its sleeve borders have confronted birds against a zigzag band (Bib. **17**, pl. 2), and its collar has finely worked mandarin ducks. These are all of four-series weft, in pale yellow, green or pale blue, black or beige, and white; the warp is in pale yellow. Another lined robe is also of four-series weft-faced compound twill, patterned with confronted sheep and *garudas* (Bib. **17**, pls. 4 and 6), in sapphire-blue, snuff, beige, and orangey-yellow weft; the warp is of pale yellow. A third robe is of monochrome white three-series weft-faced compound twill, showing alternate bands of ailanthus blooms and *ruyi* scrolls (Bib. **17**, pl. 5); its sleeve borders again of confronted birds against a zigzag band. A fourth robe is of plain white silk tabby. A five-series weft-faced compound twill appears in ten fragments, one of which shows a border in white wool and may have been a saddle-blanket. It is patterned with overall floral medallions and a *millefiore* ground; the weft in sapphire-blue, green, two different reds, pale yellow, and white, the warp in red or yellow (Bib. **17**, pl. 7). A similar weave is seen on nine other fragments with overall floral medallions; its weft in pale green, yellowish-green, dark blue, two different reds, and white, the warp in dark blue (Bib. **17**, pl. 8). A larger fragment is similar to the face of the first robe described, and in shades ranging from pale yellow to beige and snuff (Bib. **17**, pl. 9). A cowrie-shell motif appears on a two-series weft-faced compound twill; its weft in red and yellow, the warp in red (Bib. **17**, pls. 10 and 11). One end is embroidered with couched gold leaf. Finally, a piece of fine sapphire-blue silk tabby, 53 × 55.5 cm, is embroidered with red, brownish-red, orange, beige, green, blue, yellow, black, and gold thread; its centre with a quatrefoil containing floral motifs, a pair of confronted birds at one side and of confronted deer at the other. Its border of weft-faced compound twill is edged with a white cord and patterned with confronted birds against a zigzag band (Bib. **17**, pl. 12).

Yuan Dynasty
(A.D. 1281–1368)

Two similar burials were found in the foothills of Tianshan near Urumchi in Xinjiang province; Tomb 2 also containing a horse. Tomb 1 yielded a jacket of yellow glossy silk tabby bordered with two polychrome patterned silks and lined in coarse white cotton (Bib. **50**, p. 29, fig. 1). One silk has silk warps either single (dia. 0.15 mm) or doubled (dia. 0.4 mm). Its main weft is also of silk, while the pattern weft is divided into picks of gold lamella (dia. 0.5 mm) and dyed cotton (dia. 0.6–0.75 mm). This weft-faced compound tabby has its single ends binding with the pattern weft, and its doubled ends with the main weft, 52 warps by 48 wefts per cm (Bib. **50**, p. 29, fig. 2). The fragment retains one petal of a quatrefoil with internal floral-vine elements surrounded by lotus flowers on vines (Bib. **50**, p. 29, fig. 3 and p. 35, fig. 17). The other fragment is in double weave. Its single ends of silk bind with the pattern weft of gold filé in a 1:3 twill, while its doubled silk ends bind with the main cotton weft in tabby, 65 warps by 40 wefts per cm (Bib. **50**, p. 29, fig. 4). The pattern shows the right half of a bodhisattva's half-figure, with floral-vines above (Bib. **50**, p. 29, fig. 5 and p. 35, fig. 14). Cotton, found not only in the jacket lining, but also for an undergarment (Bib. **50**, p. 30, fig. 6) and trousers, is in widths of 32, 42, or 46 cm, woven in rather loose and uneven tabby, 12 warps by 10 wefts per cm, the thread diameter of 0.5–1.0 mm. Another important find was a pair of cowhide boots covered in *kesi (k'o-ssu)* tapestry (Bib. **32**, pl. 66; **50**, p. 35, fig. 15). The silk pieces are sewn together, presumably salvaged from other use, variously showing pink and green flowers on a purple ground, or simply pink on green, and including motifs of willow leaves, prunus blossoms, and crabapple blossoms. Their warp is of two grège threads strongly twisted, dia. 0.02 mm, while the weft is in single grège thread, 13 warps by 38 wefts per cm. Tomb 2 contained twenty-three silk fragments and a fragment of a wool saddle-rug. Most are silk tabbies, including one tie-dyed strip, but two polychrome weft-faced compound twills and a monochrome weft-faced compound twill also appeared. One is in four-series of a greyish-red, blue, yellow, and white, patterned in complex floral medallions and quatrefoils (Bib. **50**, p. 32, fig. 10 and p. 35, fig.

16). Its main warp is single while the threads of its pattern warp are doubled, 60 ends by 36 picks per cm (Bib. **50**, p. 32, fig. 11). Some fragments of a grey silk patterned in peonies (Bib. **50**, p. 32, fig. 12) are lined with plain silk tabby. Woven in 2:1 twill, they show 52 warps by 52 wefts per cm (Bib. **50**, p. 33, fig. 13). It is known that silks woven with metal threads were produced by Yuan official establishments in Xinjiang, while wool twills were the specialty of Kaifeng in Henan province.

The tomb of the parents of the Prince of Wu, Zhang Shi-cheng, has been excavated to reveal only the garments of his mother (d. 1365) preserved. These include two robes lined with silk tabby; one of a three-series weft-faced compound twill, with an overall design of rhombs enclosing reversed swastikas, each four of these units covered by the eight auspicious Buddhist symbols (Bib. **30**, p. 293, fig. 8:1). Weft-faced compound twill, velvet, and satin appear on four silk-padded jackets. The first is lined with yellow silk tabby and bound with silk gauze (Bib. **30**, p. 293, fig. 7:6). Its warp and weft are both in three-series; the design being of prunus, bamboo, and chrysanthemum, a magpie resting on a branch, and various auspicious symbols. The velvet is also lined in plain yellow silk tabby, its pile in patterns of cash and silver ingots for the ground with reversed swastikas on quatrefoils in higher relief (Bib. **30**, pl. 11:8). The five-end satin is similar on two other jackets, patterned in the swastika fret, and with *ruyi*-scrolls, coral, the jade ring, silver ingot, etc. between (Bib. **30**, pl. 11:9). Similar silks were used for six skirts (Bib. **30**, p. 293, figs. 1, 4, and 5, pl. 11:6). Other significant finds were four rolls of silk tabby found folded in fourteen to sixteen layers, a pair of slippers with polychrome patterned silk sides (Bib. **30**, p. 293, fig. 8:2), five silk-padded quilts covered in polychrome patterned silks (Bib. **30**, p. 293, fig. 7:2), a sash painted with a dragon, a pouch with its lower part of silk net and its upper part in polychrome silk patterned with dragons and phoenix on a geometric ground (Bib. **30**, pl. 11:10), two other fragments of painted silk tabby, and four embroidered tabbies with dragon motifs (Bib. **30**, p. 293, fig. 7:7).

Ming Dynasty
(A.D. 1369–1644)

Also excavated in Jiangxi province was the tomb of a Ming official, Zheng Yun-mei (1552–1614). It yielded thirteen garments and two pairs of boots (Bib. 28, p. 317, fig. 1:2). Of six official robes, two are in satin, two in light damask, and two in heavier damask. One satin is patterned with small peony sprays. This robe retains its square badges of rank at front and back, woven in gold and silver filé, then embroidered with confronted white *rukh*s amidst auspicious cloud-scrolls, peony sprays, and mountain symbols (Bib. 28, pl. 12:1). The other satin has overall auspicious cloud-scrolls. The damasks, used also for lining in one example rather than the more usual silk tabby, are variously patterned with overall large peony flowers, large peony sprays, auspicious cloud-scrolls, or meanders; all in yellow. Of five informal robes, two are in light damask, one in heavier damask, one in satin, and one in plain yellow silk tabby. An example of coffee-coloured thin damask patterned with reversed swastikas is lined with coarse white cotton, its collar and ties of yellow silk tabby. Another in yellow shows reversed swastikas, auspicious cloud-scrolls, and mountain symbols (Bib. 28, pl. 12:2), and is unlined. The heavier yellow damask has a meander pattern, and the yellow satin small peony sprays. An overcoat is made of dark green satin with yellow silk tabby lining and collar, and looks to be of a straight-cut (Bib. 28, p. 317, fig. 1:1). A travel garment is made of dark green silk gauze, its collar, waistband, and sashes edged with yellow silk tabby (Bib. 28, pl. 12:3; pl. 12:4–6 show details of peony spray, auspicious cloud-scroll, and meander patterns).

A third tomb excavated in the same province contained a body pickled in mercury and a bronze mirror inscribed with a date equivalent to 1589. Since four of the six garments discovered in this burial are dragon robes, it is suggested that the tomb's occupant belonged to the local prince's clan. A yellow satin patterned with auspicious cloud-scrolls has four medallions of rank woven in gold and silver filé, then embroidered in silk thread (Bib. 29, pl. 12:7 and 8). Another robe with four medallions is of heavy yellow damask patterned also in auspicious cloud-scrolls. A fragmentary yellow light damask is

embroidered with gold filé in a pattern of dragons amidst clouds. Two cotton undershirts are made with a centre-front opening and embellished with yellow silk tabby frogs, as well as borders of woven hemp fibre in blue and black floral patterns (Bib. 29, pl. 12:11).

Official weaving factories of the period were located in the areas of Nanjing, Suzhou, Hangzhou, Sichuan, Shandong, Fuzhou, and Quanzhou. A village, Shengzhe in Wujiang County, about 70 Chinese *li* from Suzhou, had over 1,000 families engaged in the silk industry, growing mulberry trees, raising silkworms, weaving, and embroidering. Each household had at least one loom, with thirty to forty looms constituting a marketing unit. In the eastern district of Suzhou itself, there were more than 10,000 weavers and dyers during the Wan-li reign (1573–1620). The city artisans had less freedom than weavers engaged in a cottage industry which depended only on the provision of capital by investors to maintain itself and did not undertake direct marketing. Suzhou textile workers were, by contrast, registered officially and organized by specialties. Thus, each thousand ordinary satin or gauze weavers, as well as silk-reelers or spinners, formed a unit to receive payment by production volume, with meals as part of their recompense. After the eunuch Sun Long was appointed to supervise the textile industry in 1601, each loom was taxed $3/10$ of a tael of silver with the result that a strike occurred, as far as is known for the first time in Chinese textile history (Bib. 54).

The Gugong Museum in Peking has examples of both Nanjing and Suzhou silk weaves. A specimen of the type used for hats, edging of garments, cushion-covers, and bed-curtains came from the first centre and is patterned overall with floral sprays shown in gold lamella; its red main and pattern warps alternately tie the gold lamella main and pattern wefts (Bib. 53, p. 75, fig. 2). A specimen from the second centre, identified as a type used for garments, quilt-covers, and also bed-covers, shows an overall pattern of overlapping floral medallions in complex weave (Bib. 53, p. 75, fig. 3). Again, its ends are divided into main and binding warps, while its wefts are more complicated: the first being a ground weft, the second for a geometric ground, the third for gold lamella outlining of floral elements, and the next three for brocading, changing colours every 3 or 4 cm and thus requiring twenty-one brocading shuttles.

Ming embroidery in the "Gu style" has been given special attention (Bib. 7). Various members of the family of Gu Ming-shih, housed at the Garden of the Dew's Fragrance ("Luxiangyuan" 露香園) in Shanghai, created this distinctive type of needle-work in the Jia-jing reign (1522–1567). They used hair, feathers, gold lamella, etc., as well as silk threads, to enhance textural effects. Their stitches follow the brush-lines of the under-painting, this pictorial intention being further heightened by shading of colours as in brush-painting and by areas of actual painting; a technique which greatly influenced Suzhou embroidery of the Qing Dynasty as well as that of present times (Bib. 8). A famous female literary figure, Ni Ren-ji (1607–1685), is as famous for her embroidery in the "Gu style" as for her calligraphy, painting, and poetry (Bib. 10).

The Gugong Museum has also collected an example of Ming *petit-point* mounted on a handscroll (Bib. 6). It is executed on a white gauze base, showing a deer outlined and with interior division into hexagons of snuff-coloured silk shading to white in some areas, with clouds in red, green, blue, and white above, a mountain rising from waves below, all against red. An inscription states that this work was repaired during the Qian-long reign (1736–1796), but is dated to 1799 when it was apparently considered to be of Song date.

Qing Dynasty
(A.D. 1644–1912)

Official weaving establishments were maintained at Nanjing, Suzhou, and Hangzhou. The first two were famous for their polychrome patterned silks, Suzhou's in the Song style and Nanjing's in the brocaded weave often executed with metal threads. They were also responsible for dyeing, as well as for rug, garment, and fur manufacture (Bib. 53). Investigations at Suzhou have produced some information about the textile industry there, partly based upon oral reports offered by old weavers who still remember the last days of the Qing dynasty, and partly derived from dedicatory inscriptions on stone steles at a number of former factory locations or temples. Each dyeing and weaving factory had 350 looms, employing 1,500 weavers and drawboys, as well as 120 embroiderers, foremen, and other administrators. The main factory had 450 looms, with 1,250 weavers and drawboys but the same number of workers in other capacities as the ordinary establishment. Initially, at least, payment was made in food grains. In 1647, Chen Yu-ming, an official responsible for the textile industry in both Suzhou and Hangzhou, changed certain practices. From that point, his office was responsible for the purchase of raw materials and their resale to the looms at cost during the early spring of each year. Furthermore, quality control was introduced, with each specialized branch being responsible for supply of fine thread, clarity of dyed colours, and evenness and accuracy of weave. Specific rewards and punishments were indicated, as were the numbers and ranks of supervisors to be appointed. At first, this transference of responsibility to individual factories prevailed only in Suzhou, Shanghai, and Changzhou, but by 1651, it was widespread and firmly established as the official policy. The pay scale gave $^{15}/_{100}$ of a tael of silver per day, plus food, to weavers of polychrome patterned silks and gauzes and two taels of silver each month to drawboys, but weavers of tabby or mock leno were recompensed by piece-work with $^{1}/_{100}$ of a silver tael for certain fixed lengths. By the early twentieth century, the industry had dwindled to the point that Suzhou had only six factories, each with about forty looms, but they still produced silk tabby, damask, polychrome patterned silks, gauze, and crepe, as well as tapestry and embroidery (Bib. 14).

The Gugong Museum has a number of important early Qing textiles in its collection. An example of Suzhou silk in Song style shows an overall pattern of fruit sprays on a geometricized rhomboid ground (Bib. 53, p. 74, fig. 1). This is a complex weave with its ground pattern in polychrome weft-faced compound twill and its fruit sprays in twisted doubled gold filé of brocade weave. Also from Suzhou, another double weave with brocading is patterned in rosettes and quatrefoils over a scaled ground (Bib. 53, p. 76, fig. 4). Its weft is in four shades of pale blue and green, with gold filé being used for outlining. This example is thought to be of the Kang-xi reign (1662–1723), while the former is considered Qian-long (1736–1796). A most spectacular pictorial silk of a Buddhist paradise scene is described but not reproduced. It includes 332 figures, as well as birds and animals, in a setting of buildings as well as landscape. The weft threads are in twenty-six different colours, with details added in both yellow and purple gold twisted filé. At least five artisans are considered to have been needed for this weave. Although the Gugong has several tens of thousands of Qing court robes, most are of the Qian-long reign or later. However, an unusual group was discovered during reorganization of the museum in 1955–1956. A yellow damask patterned in the eight precious things amidst auspicious cloud-scrolls appears on a court robe for the second Qing emperor (reigned 1637–1642). Three lengths for dragon robes in *kesi* (*k'o-ssu*) tapestry are thought to be slightly earlier in date, probably of the early seventeenth century. Two lengths for dragon robes of red tabby embroidered in gold lamella may be of 1654. Eight lengths of yellow satin with embroidered medallioned shoulder-surrounds must date from before 1638, as

this Ming ornament was forbidden to Manchus in that year. Finally, a length of pale yellow satin embroidered with four medallions at breast, back, and shoulders is of a pre-Qian-long type (Bib. 5; 15).

Qing embroidery from Suzhou, Guangdong, Hunan, Fujian, Sichuan, Wenzhou in Zhejiang, and Peking was exhibited at the Jiangsu Provincial Museum in the spring of 1958. It is reported that over 200,000 embroiderers are now working in Jiangsu province, with over 50,000 in the city of Suzhou alone (Bib. 7).

As the textile industry develops in the People's Republic of China, we may expect great advances in techniques of research on ancient textiles. This survey may, therefore, require revision within a very short space of time.

Acknowledgments

The English textile vocabulary of the Centre International d'Etude des Textiles Anciens, produced in 1964 (Harold B. Burnham, ed.), has been of inestimable help in translating Chinese terms which have not been standardized. Dorothy Burnham's current work on the reorganization and enlargement of that vocabulary, and her patience in dealing with many questions, have also been indispensable. All errors, and I fear that there may be many, are of course my own responsibility.

Notes

1. Chong-guo kexueyuan, Kaogu yenjiusuo, *Changsha fajue baogao* [Report on the excavations at Changsha, Hunan province], "Chong-guo tianye kaogu baogaoji kaoguxue zhuankan Series B No. 2." Peking, 1957.

2. Jiangsu sheng wenwu gongzuodui, "Jiangsu Wujiang Meiyan xinshiqi shidai yiji" [A Neolithic site at Meiyan, Wujiang County, Jiangsu province], *Kaogu*, 1963:6, p. 313, fig. 5:12. A carbon-14 dating equivalent to 1880 ± 95 B.C. has been published for a "Liangzhu" site in Jiaxing County, Zhejiang province; cf. Chong-guo kexueyuan, Kaoguyenjiuso shiyanshi, "Fangshexin tansu ceding niandai baogao" [Report on radioactive carbon datings], *Kaogu*, 1974:5, p. 335, sample no. ZK–242, a wood plank.

3. Bao-jun Guo, "1950 nianchun Yinxu fajue baogao" [Report on the 1950 spring excavation in the wastes of Yin], *Kaoguxuebao*, vol. 5 (Dec. 1951), pp. 17, 19.

4. Noel Barnard, *The first radiocarbon dates from China*, Monographs on Far Eastern History 8, Canberra, The Australian National University, 1972, p. 24, sample no. ZK–49.

5. Bib. **34**, p. 13 describes this silk tabby as 48 warps by 48 wefts per cm.

6. This type of monochrome patterned silk is sometimes called "damask" or *qi* in Chinese, and is the "armura Han" described by Pfister.

7. Over 162 tombs were cleared at Changsha between 18 Oct. 1951 and 7 Feb. 1952, but only the textiles of Tomb 406 were analyzed (or perhaps adequately conserved). Apart from the woven textiles, braided silk ribbons also emerged from the coffin. Tomb 345 is also reported to have contained monochrome patterned silk fragments.

8. Bib. **34**, p. 15 describes this as a silk tabby.

9. For bast-fibre shoe sole fragments, cf. Bib. **2**, p. 7, Tomb 6 at Yangjiawan; Bib. **18**, p. 67; Bib. **26**, p. 468, Tomb 25 at Deshan in Changde County, Hunan province, said to be of the mid-Warring States period, i.e., early fourth century B.C. The silk banner painting is said to be from the same tomb as a well-known and similar work removed in 1942 and now in an American collection. Bib. **47** notes that bast-fibre and silk textile fragments were also found in the tomb.

10. The Chinese reports have termed such a weave as a "pile-loop brocade".

11. Bib. **41** describes the pattern unit as 6.2 × 5.18 cm, with 518 warps requiring the use of twenty-six heddle rods. It is suggested that, if 224–1,682 warps had to rise and fall independently, heddle rods would have been too cumbersome and, therefore, the use of some type of figure harness may already have been introduced. However, it has already been noted that modern Thai weavers use a horizontal loom with two shafts for tabby ground plus a supplementary patterning mechanism of forty to sixty heddle rods which are raised as required; cf. Harold B. Burnham, "Some additional notes on the warp-faced compound tabby silks of the Han dynasty", CIETA Bulletin, 34 (1971), pp. 16–21.

12. Bib. **41** gives the thread-count of this sample as 104 warps by 34 wefts per cm, and the pattern unit as 6 × 4.3 cm. Each pattern unit includes 112 gauze repeats or 448 ends, of which alternate ones are twisted. Zhang Hong-yuan of the Gugong bowuyuan (Palace Museum, Peking), in commenting on the excavators' preliminary report, notes that pattern units vary from 6.5 × 2.26 cm to 9 × 3 cm, though all are rhomb variations. He describes the gauze openings as hexagonal in shape, with two main warps and two twisted warps for each four of the gauze repeats. He further suggests that a loom with at least seven shafts was used; one each for the main warp, doup, and fixed ends, and four for the pattern. Wei Gong-qing, also of the Gugong, singles out an under-robe with a false patterned gauze appearance, but actually of mock leno with a twisted thread. This is described as of 160 cm length, with sleeves of 190 cm length, decorated with silk tabby borders at the neck and sleeve-ends. The silk is of about 13 denier, the garment weighing about 48 g, with 62 warps by 62 wefts per cm.

13. Two other types of polychrome patterned silks were, however, found in the tomb. Bags for a *se* (zither) and *yu* (pan-pipes) (Find nos. 334–1 and 334–2, Bib. **44**, fig. 44 left and pl. 136)

show a red pattern on chestnut-brown ground, in two-series, with main, binding, and flushing warps, 46 warps by 42 wefts per cm. The two sides of an embroidered pillow-cover show red dogwood flowers on a snuff-coloured ground (Find no. 440, Bib. **44**, fig. 44 right and pl. 135), also two-series with three functions of warp, 52 warps by 40 wefts per cm. A third type is not fully described. Find no. N6–3, also a fragment from the body's wrappings, is said to have a relief pattern resembling the pile warp but not woven in the same technique.

14. This is suggested by Mrs. Dorothy Burnham. From the published evidence, this can be technically considered a velvet weave. The pile is raised over a thread, which is later removed, rather than over a regular velvet rod. This is an excellent example of the flexibility possible with a simple loom and a skilled weaver.

Bib. **44**, fig. 43, top left, Find no. N15; top right, Find no. 437; centre, Find no. 357–5; pl. 123, Find no. 329–10, the border of a "xinqi" embroidered patterned gauze robe; pl. 137, Find no. 65–2, the bottom of a "xinqi" embroidered patterned gauze incense-pouch; pl. 138, Find no. 439, the border of a "changshou" embroidered silk tabby tablecloth, represent other examples of this weave; all with geometric patterns. Bib. **41** adds Find no. 357–5, the border of a silk-padded robe of violet meander-patterned silk, the pile warp in red rhombs, with 232 warps by 44 wefts per cm, each pattern unit 6 × 14.5 cm, thus requiring 3,364 warp ends (half of which are controlled by the main shaft, the rest separately raised). Bib. **55** offers the fullest analysis of this weave, recognizing it as the precursor of velvet. The English abstract should be read with some caution, as its terminology is dubious; as for example the following quotation: " . . . it requires a jacquard heddle [sic, but the jacquard heddle was perfected in France only in the early nineteenth century] assembly besides two additional harness shafts to bring about lift action. In order to form the pile-loops, another warp beam must be provided to assure a steady supply of warp threads for the pile warp. Also it is necessary to insert some temporary filling yarns into the pile loop as additional supports which can be pulled out later when the product is finished." Analysis of the silk is shown in fig. 1 as follows: main warp first series of 13 baves, each 123.32 sq microns or 0.81 denier, the warp denier 10.53; binding warp of 10 baves, each 137.06 sq microns or 0.90 denier, the warp denier 9; pile warp of 54 baves, each 118.96 sq microns or 0.78 denier, the warp denier 42.12; main warp second series of 17 baves, each 129.2 sq microns or 0.85 denier, the warp denier 14.45; main weft of 17 baves, each 146.38 sq microns or 0.96 denier, the weft denier 16.32.

Find no. N6–2 showed differently coloured warp for the four-series, while the weft is monochrome. The soft silk yarns were, therefore, dyed before weaving.

Find no. N6–1 apparently showed a separate patterned warp. Among all finds of this weave, eleven geometric motifs were noticed, generally wider than high. It is suggested that the pattern weft may have been of ramie or bamboo fibres. This weave was also found on sashes, a mirror bag, and the borders of a pillow-cover.

15. Distinction of different types of ribbons, embroidery patterns, etc. depends on inscriptional identification either given on the textiles themselves or as written on bamboo slips with burial goods inventory.

16. Tomb 48 at the same site is considered to be of earlier date, and is reported under the Western or Former Han dynasty entries.

17. These have been analyzed in Bib. **34** and will be reported later in this section.

18. The fuller description of this weave in Bib. **44**, pp. 18 and 19, differs slightly from the sample, Find no. 22, described in the diagram of silks analyzed.

19. Bib. **25**, p. 75 gives the count as 66 warps by 36 wefts per cm.

20. Bib. **22**, pp. 121 and 122, pl. 2:2 and 4, show wool fragments excavated in a hearth (MN010) at the same area. One has red quatrefoils within white roundels on a blue ground, the other dark and light yellow quatrefoils in green roundels on a yellow ground.

21. There seems to be some confusion about this weave. Bib. **32** includes the fragment within the pre-Tang Dynasty textile types, but Bib. **35**, p. 29 describes it as a weft-patterned compound twill with a doubled warp and weft in three-series; thus, 25 warps by 18 wefts per cm showing on its surface, but 50 warps by 54 wefts per cm in fact. However, Xia Nai does not cite it for what he considers a technique imported from West Asia (Bib. **27**) and the reproductions display a tabby appearance.

22. Though all such banners were found in a fragmentary state, they could provide some measurements. Examples from TAM 303, dated to A.D. 551, are 250 × 60–37 cm, with the silk width of 47 cm. These specimens, of approximately a century later, measure 178 × 82–120 cm, the silk 55 cm wide. Painted silk tabby banners were also found in the undated tombs TAM 77 and 138 (Bib. **36**, p. 23, figs. 34 and 35 where TAM 138 is listed as TAM 43).

23. Compare with a fragment from TAM 317 dated to A.D. 662.

24. Compare with a fragment from TAM 134 associated with a document of A.D. 665.

25. Compare with fragments from TAM 322 dated to A.D. 663, TAM 332 with a document of A.D. 665, and three undated tombs, TAM 334, 84, and 50 (Bib. **32**, pls. 33 and 35).

26. Compare with fragments from TAM 322 dated to A.D. 663,

and an undated tomb, TAM 77 (Bib. **32**, pl. 34; **36**, p. 20, p. 27, fig. 51). The last, 13.5 × 8.1 cm, has been described both as a warp-faced compound twill and as a weft-patterned compound twill. Its reproductions seem to indicate the second to be more likely. It is, thus, in three-series of blue, green, and white, with tripled warps, 60 warps by 78 wefts per cm (Bib. **35**, p. 29, pl. 9:1).

27. Compare with fragments from TAM 323 with a document of A.D. 587, TAM 331 with a document of A.D. 619, TAM 302 dated to A.D. 653, and TAM 317 with a document of A.D. 662.

28. Compare with a fragment from an undated tomb, TAM 138 (Bib. **32**, pl. 38; **35**, p. 29, pl. 8:3), described as a weft-patterned compound twill, 16 × 14 cm, the weft in three-series of red, black, and white, 20 warps by 96 wefts per cm.

29. Bib. **32**, pl. 36 reproduces a similar but slightly different specimen for TAM 134, which it states is dated to A.D. 662 rather than 665. This may well be a case of mistaken identification, as its example shows the confronted cocks enclosed in a beaded roundel, with dotted squares marking the conjunction of the roundels.

30. A similar motif appears on a fragment from the undated tomb TAM 138 (Bib. **32**, pl. 37). It is described as a weft-patterned compound twill, 17.8 × 15.5 cm, with an intact selvage. The weft is in two-series of red and white, 21 warps by 42 wefts per cm (Bib. **36**, p. 30, pl. 10:1).

31. Compare with the more conventional or traditional treatment of an overall rosette-medallion and quatrefoil pattern on an example from the undated tomb TAM 76 (Bib. **32**, pl. 39), or with the geometricized motifs in Chinese taste on another warp-faced compound tabby in the undated tomb TAM 139 (Bib. **32**, pl. 31).

32. This example differs from other confronted duck motifs in TAM 337 dated to A.D. 657, or TAM 134 associated with a document of A.D. 665. Here, the ducks share a single foot and their roundels are alternated with bands of quatrefoils.

33. An undated tomb, TAM 105, offered a comparable example of this pattern in warp-faced compound twill (Bib. **32**, pl. 42; **36**, p. 18, fig. 26 and p. 29, fig. 62). The fragment from a woman's skirt, 89.8 × 22 cm, has 48 ends per cm (in red, tan, green, yellow, and white, with a shaded effect), the weft doubled (in yellowish-brown) with 24 picks per cm (Bib. **35**, p. 30, pl. 10:4).

34. Comparable specimens were found in this area from an unidentified site (Bib. **32**, pls. 52 and 53).

35. This may be compared to two pieces of silk tabby from the undated tomb, TAM 105; one printed in at least two stages and dyed twice (Bib. **32**, pl. 55; **36**, p. 29, fig. 63), the other hav-

ing as many as four colours (Bib. **32**, pl. 56). The most spectacular example of printing and dyeing from this tomb is on a mock leno with a truly pictorial scene created in dark on light green of six motifs: a mounted huntsman, a fleeing deer and hare, a bird in flight, floral sprays, and a landscape element with three trees behind a rocky foreground indication (Bib. **32**, pl. 61; **35**, pl. 7:2).

36. Printing by a rubbing technique is noted for some examples and these are considered to be of local manufacture.

37. Tie-dyeing was probably not commercially produced but was a matter of individual creation. Certain types were, however, prohibited to commoners in the Northern Song Dynasty. A variety called "lutai" 鹿胎 (deerskin), from Sichuan province, usually of a purplish-red, seems to have been reserved for military garments. Stencilled or printed silks were also exclusive to army use from ca. 1078 and an edict of 1329 definitely forbade their use by the populace. Further development of such dyeing techniques began again during the Ming Dynasty and especially for the cotton products of the Sungjiang area, now Shanghai (Bib. **12**).

Bibliography

1. Chong-guo kexueyuan, Kaogu yenjiusuo, *Changsha fajue baogao* [Report on the excavations at Changsha, Hunan province], "Chong-guo tianye kaogu baogaoji kaoguxue zhuankan Series B No. 2." Peking, 1957.

2. Hunan sheng wenwuguanliweiyuanhui, "Changsha chutu de sanzuo daxing muguomu" [Three large wood cased-coffin tombs uncovered at Changsha], *Kaoguxuebao*, 1957:1.

3. "Ala-er faxian munaiyi" [A mummy discovered at Alar, Uighur Autonomous Region, Xinjiang province], *Wenwu*, 1957:2.

4. Hunan sheng wenwuguanliweiyuanhui, "Changsha Guangjiqiao diwuhao Zhanguo muguomu qingli jianbao" [A short report on the clearing of a Warring States wood cased-coffin Tomb No. 5 at the Guangji Bridge in Changsha], *Wenwu*, 1957:2.

5. Wei, Gong-qing, "Qing Xunzhi shiyinian zhizao de kesi longpao" [A *k'o-ssu* dragon robe of 1654], *Gugong bowuyuan yuankan*, 1 (1958), p. 67.

6. Chen, Juan-juan, "Ji *Tianlu jin*" [A note on a divine deer worked in *petit-point*], *Wenwu*, 1958:9.

7. Chen, Yu-yin, "Jiangsu sheng bowuguan de cixiu zhanlan" [An exhibition of embroidery at the Jiangsu Provincial Museum], *Wenwu*, 1958:9.

8. Gu, Gong-shi, "Gu xiu yu Su xiu" [The embroidery of Gu and Suzhou], *Wenwu*, 1958:9.

9. "Handai Wulu Chong mu chutu de cixiu canpian" [Embroidered fragments from the Han Dynasty tomb of Wulu Chong], *Wenwu*, 1958:9.

10. Hung, Liang, "Ming nüshiren Ni Ren-ji de cixiu" [Embroidery by the Ming poetess Ni Ren-ji], *Wenwu*, 1958:9.

11. Peking wenwuguanliweiyuanhui, Wenwudiaochayenjiuzu, "Beijingshi shuangta Qingshou Si chutu de simianzhipin ji xiuhua" [Cotton and silk textiles, as well as embroidery, uncovered in the Twin Pagodas of the Qingshou Temple in Peking], *Wenwu*, 1958:9.

12. Shen, Cong-wen, "Tan ranxie: landibaiyinhuabu de lishifazhan" [On dyed silks: The historical development of cloth with white patterns on blue ground], *Wenwu*, 1958:9.

13. Shi, Shu-qing, "Mantan Xinjiang faxian de Handai sichou" [Remarks on the Han silks discovered in Xinjiang province], *Wenwu*, 1958:9.

14. Sung, Bo-yin, "Suzhou Qingdai zhishu diaocha jianbao" [A brief report on an investigation of Qing Dynasty textile administration in Suzhou, Jiangsu province], *Wenwu*, 1958:9.

15. Wei, Gong-qing, "Jieshao jijian chaopao yiliao" [Introducing some lengths of material for court robes], *Wenwu*, 1958:9.

16. Idem, "Luetan Chong-guo kesi di qiyuan" [Comments on the beginnings of *k'o-ssu* in China], *Wenwu*, 1958:9.

17. Idem, "Kao Ala-er munaiyi mu chutu de zhixiupin" [A study of the textiles and embroideries in the mummy tomb at Alar, Uighur Autonomous Region, Xinjiang province], *Gugong bowuyuan yuankan*, 2 (1959), pp. 153–164.

18. Gao, Zhi-xi, "Changsha Lieshigongyuan sanhao muguomu qingli jianbao" [A brief report on the clearing of a wood cased-coffin Tomb No. 3 at the Public Garden of Heroes in Changsha], *Wenwu*, 1959:10.

19. Zhejiang sheng wenwuguanliweiyuanhui, "Wuxing Qianshanyang yiji diyierzi fajue baogao" [Report on the first and second excavations of the Qianshanyang remains at Wuxing, Zhejiang province], *Kaoguxuebao*, 1960:2.

20. Xinjiang Weiwuer zizhiqu bowuguan, "Xinjiang Minfeng xian Beidashamochong guyiji muzangqu Tong Han hezangmu qingli jianbao" [A brief report on the clearing of an Eastern

Han double-burial tomb in the necropolis of an ancient site in the northern Great Desert of Minfeng County, Uighur Autonomous Region, Xinjiang province], *Wenwu*, 1960:6.

21. Idem, "Xinjiang Tulufan Asitana beiqu muzang fajue jianbao" [A brief report on the excavations of burials in the northern area of Astana, Turfan, Xinjiang province], *Wenwu*, 1960:6.

22. Idem, "Xinjiang Minfeng dashamochong de gudai yiji" [Ancient remains in the Great Desert of Minfeng County], *Kaogu*, 1961:3.

23. Cheng, Long, "Nei Meng-gu Janoer gumuqun diaocha ji" [A record of investigations of ancient burials at Djaranor in Inner Mongolia], *Wenwu*, 1961:9.

24. Li, Yu-chun, "Xinjiang Weiwuer zizhiqu wenwu kaogu gongzuo gaikuang" [A survey of archaeological and cultural properties work in the Uighur Autonomous Region, Xinjiang province], *Wenwu*, 1962:7 and 8.

25. Wu, Min, "Xinjiang chutu Han — Tang sizhipin chutan" [Preliminary investigations of Han through Tang silk textiles uncovered in Xinjiang province], *Wenwu*, 1962:7 and 8.

26. Hunan sheng bowuguan, "Hunan Changde Deshan Chumu fajue baogao" [Report on the excavation of a Chu state tomb at Mount De in Changde County, Hunan province], *Kaogu*, 1963:9.

27. Xia, Nai, "Xinjiang xinfaxian de gudai sizhipin — qi jing he cixiu" [Ancient silk textiles newly discovered in Xinjiang province—"damasks", polychrome patterned silks, and embroideries], *Kaoguxuebao*, 1963:1.

28. "Jiangxi Guangfeng fajue Ming Zheng Yun-mei mu" [The tomb of Zheng Yun-mei, 1552–1614, excavated at Guangfeng in Jiangxi province], *Kaogu*, 1965:6.

29. "Jiangxi Nancheng Mingmu chutu wenwu" [Objects uncovered in a Ming tomb at Nancheng in Jiangxi province], *Kaogu*, 1965:6.

30. Suzhou wenwuguanliweiyuanhui, "Suzhou Wu Zhang Shicheng mu Caoshi mu qingli jianbao" [A brief report on the clearing of the tomb of the Prince of Wu Zhang Shi-cheng's mother, formerly of the Cao clan, in Suzhou, Jiangsu province], *Kaogu*, 1965:6.

31. Hubei sheng wenwuguanliweiyuanhui, "Hubei Jiangling sanzuo Chumu chutu dapi zhongyao wenwu" [Many important objects uncovered in three Chu state tombs at Jiangling in Hubei province], *Wenwu*, 1966:5.

32. Xinjiang Weiwuer zizhiqu bowuguan, *Sichou zhi lu* [The Silk Road]. Peking, Wenwu, 1972.

33. Chong-guo kexueyuan, Kaoguyenjiusuo, "Mancheng Hanmu fajue jiyao" [Notes on the excavation of Han tombs at Mancheng, Hebei province], *Kaogu*, 1972:1.

34. Xia, Nai, "Woguo gudai can shang si chou de lishi" [The history of sericulture, mulberry cultivation, and silks in ancient China], *Kaogu*, 1972:2.

35. Zhu, Min, "Tulufan xinfaxian de gudai sichou" [Ancient silks newly discovered at Turfan County, Xinjiang province], *Kaogu*, 1972:2.

36. Xinjiang Weiwuer zizhiqu bowuguan, "Tulufan xian Asitana — Helahezhuo gumuqun qingli jianbao" [A brief report on the clearing of the ancient necropolis at Astana and Kharakhojo in Turfan County], *Wenwu*, 1972:1.

37. Dunhuang wenwuyenjiusuo, "Xinfaxian de Bei Wei cixiu" [A newly discovered Northern Wei Dynasty embroidery], *Wenwu*, 1972:2.

38. Xinjiang Weiwuer zizhiqu bowuguan, "Tulufan Asitana 363 hao mu fajue jianbao" [A brief report on the excavation of Tomb 363 at Astana in Turfan County], *Wenwu*, 1972:2.

39. Idem, "Sichou zhi lu shang faxian de Han Tang zhiwu" [Han through Tang textiles discovered on the Silk Road], *Wenwu*, 1972:3.

40. Ge, Jin, "Jingyang Gaojiabao zao Zhoumuzang fajue ji" [A record of the excavation of an early Zhou Dynasty burial at Gaojiabao in Jingyang County, Shensi province], *Wenwu*, 1972:7.

41. Zhang, Hong-yuan, "Changsha Mawangdui Hanmu de sizhipin" [Silk textiles from the Han tomb at Mawangdui in Changsha], *Wenwu*, 1972:9.

42. Hu, Hou-xuan, "Yindai de can shang he sizhi" [Sericulture, mulberry cultivation, and silk weaving in the Shang Dynasty], *Wenwu*, 1972:11.

43. Dunhuang wenwuyenjiusuo kaoguzu, "Mogaoku faxian de Tangdai sizhiwu ji qita" [Tang silk textiles and other finds from the Mogao Caves at Dunhuang, Gansu province], *Wenwu*, 1972:12.

44. Gansu sheng bowuguan, "Wuwei Mojuzi sanzuo Hanmu fajue jianbao" [A brief report on the excavation of three Han tombs at Mojuzi in Wuwei County, Gansu province], *Wenwu*, 1972:12.

45. Jiayuguanshi wenwuqinglixiaozu, "Jiayuguan Han huaxiangzhuanmu" [A Han tomb with pictorial relief tiles at Jiayuguan in Gansu province], *Wenwu*, 1972:12.

46. *Archaeological treasures excavated in the People's Republic of China*,

catalogue of the exhibition shown at the Kyoto and Tokyo National Museums. Tokyo, Asahi Shimbun, 1973.

47. Hunan sheng bowuguan, *Changsha Chumu bohua* [The silk banner painting from a Chu state tomb at Changsha]. Peking, Wenwu, 1973.

48. Idem, *Changsha Mawangdui yihao Hanmu* [The Han Tomb 1 at Mawangdui in Changsha]. Peking, Wenwu, 1973.

49. Sha, Bi-ti, "Cong kaogufajueziliao kan Xinjiang gudai de mianhua zhongzhi he fangzhi" [A glance at cotton cultivation and weaving in ancient Xinjiang based upon archaeological evidence], *Wenwu*, 1973:10.

50. Wang, Bing-hua, "Yenhu gumu" [Ancient tombs at the Salt Lake in Urumchi, Xinjiang province], *Wenwu*, 1973:10.

51. Wu, Min, "Tulufan chutu sizhiwu chong de Tangdai yinran" [Tang Dynasty printing and dyeing in the textiles found at Turfan County, Xinjiang province], *Wenwu*, 1973:10.

52. Xinjiang Weiwuer zizhiqu bowuguan, "Tulufan xian Asi-tana — Helahezhuo gumuqun fajue jianbao" [A brief report on excavation of the ancient necropolis at Astana and Kharakhojo in Turfan County], *Wenwu*, 1973:10.

53. Chen, Juan-juan, "Jieshao jijian youxiu de Ming Qing zhijing" [An introduction to some exceptional brocades of the Ming and Qing dynasties], *Wenwu*, 1973:11.

54. Wu, Fa, "Mingdai sizhiye chong zibenzhuyi de mengya" [The budding of capitalism in the textile industry of the Ming Dynasty], *Dagongbao*, 22 and 23 October 1974.

55. Study Group for Archaeological Finds, Shanghai Textile Research Institute and Shanghai Silk Industry Corporation, "The pile-loop brocade unearthed from the Han Tomb No. 1 at Mawangdui in Changsha" (in Chinese with an English abstract), *Kaoguxuebao*, 1974:1.

56. Hunan sheng bowuguan and Chong-guo kexueyuan kaoguyenjiusuo, "Changsha Mawangdui ersanhao Hanmu fajue jianbao" [A brief report on the excavation of the Han Tombs 2 and 3 at Mawangdui in Changsha], *Wenwu*, 1974:9.

Three Ladies in Tapestry

Edith Standen

WHEN Peter the Great visited the Gobelins manufactory in 1717, he was, of course, received by a very high official, the king's *Surintendant des Bâtiments, Arts et Manufactures,* then the Duc d'Antin. The visit was recorded by Louis François Dubois de Saint-Gelais in his *Histoire journalière de Paris 1716-1717*: "M. le Duc d'Antin aiant remarqué que le Czar avoit regardé avec beaucoup d'atention et de plaisir toutes les Tapisseries, reçut l'ordre du roi [Louis XV, then aged seven] d'ofrir à ce Prince celles qui lui plaisoient." A set of four large hangings with scenes from the New Testament and another of eight from the series known as the *Indies* were chosen by "Sa Majesté Czarienne", and to these were added "deux tableaux de tapisserie de Haute lisse, que le Czar avait paru désirer".[1] One was a head of Christ after Charles Le Brun; the other an *Espagnolette* after Jean Baptiste Santerre, woven by Jean Jans; this weaver was then head of an *haute-lisse*, or vertical loom, workshop. Jans was paid for this panel in 1720; the entry in the *Comtes des Bâtiments*, the register of the king's expenditures for these establishments, shows that he received 1,500 livres, a fairly substantial sum, for the tapestry picture and its gilded frame, which had been his personal property, "devant lui appartenant".[2]

It is not often that small tapestries like these are documented in official records, but they were frequently made by the Gobelins weavers for their own use, primarily to be given or sold to their superiors or to visitors to the manufactory. They were sometimes exhibited at Versailles, so that the king could see them, and to "encourager les jeunes gens", as the Duc de Luynes wrote in his memoirs. He listed the pieces shown in January, 1751, and gave the ages of the weavers.[3] There are three in the Metropolitan Museum of Art and two of these can provide some idea of what the Czar's *Espagnolette* looked like; one (fig. 1) is after Santerre and the other (fig. 4) represents an *Espagnolette*, though after another artist.

The lady holding a mask (fig. 1) has the name of the weaver, Jans, and the date, 1725, in the lower right corner. This is not the Jean Jans who made the *Espagnolette* for the Czar, but his son, Jean Jacques (1671-1731), who took over his father's workshop in 1723. A comparison with prints after Santerre, such as the *Lady with a Mask* (fig. 2) by Nicolas Chasteau, shows clearly the kind of model that was the basis for the weaver's cartoon.

Can the lady be given a name? When the tapestry was published on its arrival in the Metropolitan Museum, it was said to be "traditionally" a portrait of the actress Charlotte Desmares (1682-1753) as Thalia.[4] But we know what Charlotte really looked like from a portrait by Charles Coypel in the museum of the Comédie Française[5] and a print after it by Bernard Lepicié, dated 1733 (fig. 3). Santerre painted and Chasteau engraved at least three other pictures of young women, all with exactly the same bland and regular features, two of them holding masks.[6] According to d'Argenville, Santerre, though active as a portrait-painter, specialized in "têtes de fantaisie et des demi-figures, sous l'allégorie de la fable, des arts ou de quelque action naturelle".[7] The *demi-figure* in the Metropolitan Museum is certainly in fancy dress, but she is not necessarily an actress.

332

Another kind of fancy dress is worn by the girl shown in a tapestry panel in the Metropolitan Museum (fig. 4), a painting in the Staatliche Kunsthalle, Karlsruhe (fig. 5), and an engraving by Lepicié (fig. 6). The title of the print, *L'Espagnolette,* refers to the costume, not the nationality of the sitter. The slanting flat cap with a plume, the ruff, the roll of material at the shoulder, and the full, slashed or "paned" sleeve—all vaguely derived from sixteenth- or seventeenth-century fashions—made up what was called the "Espagnolette" or "à l'Espagnole" dress in France in the eighteenth century. The style might be compared to the well-known "Vandyke" costume in England, but it has been much less discussed.[8] The resemblance between the two was noticed in France. A portrait by Louis Michel Van Loo exhibited at the Salon in 1767 was described in the catalogue as "Petit jeune homme en pied, habillé à l'ancienne mode d'Angleterre", but in the Van Loo sale of December, 1772, it appeared as "Le portrait d'un jeune Mylord en pied, vêtu à l'espagnole, et ayant une fraise autour du col. . . .peint dans le gout de Van-Dick".[9] An early use of the word, curiously enough, is English; it appears in John Evelyn's *Mundus Muliebris* of 1690:

> . . .provision have for due undress,
> Nor demy sultane, *spagnolet,*
> Nor fringe to sweep the Mall forget. . .

"Spagnolet" is glossed by the author as "a kind of narrow-sleeved gown, à l'espagnole"; this might mean a sleeve full at the top, but tight around the lower part of the arm, as the "Spanish sleeve" of the late eighteenth century in England is puffed and melon-shaped, reaching halfway to the elbow, with ribbon panes.[10] The ruff round the neck and the melon sleeve are seen in a Boucher drawing of a girl with a fan in the Louvre, dated 1750; it was described in the sale catalogue of M. de Sireul, 3 December 1781, as "une jeune femme vêtue à l'Espagnole".[11] Ruffs and paned sleeves are worn by both men and women in Carle Van Loo's *Concert à l'Espagnole* in the Hermitage Museum, Leningrad.[12] The men also wear short cloaks, but, as the most important figure has the chain of the Golden Fleece, the concert is presumably supposed to be taking place in Spain, and, perhaps, in a bygone age, since

the gentry in Spain in the mid-eighteenth century dressed in much the same style as their French counterparts. The dancers, both men and women, but not the spectators, wear costumes of this type in a print by Martinet after M. A. Slodtz; this shows a maypole dance at Versailles during the carnival season of 1763.[13] Many other examples could be cited, but it seems likely that costumes of this type were worn only on the stage, at fancy-dress balls, or in the artist's studio.

The girl in the Karlsruhe painting has been described as "habillée en Espagnole" since the eighteenth century. The painting was one of a pair sold in Paris on 16 May, 1763; the *Catalogue raisonné des tableaux* du Cabinet de feu M. Peilhon, Secrétaire du Roi et Fermier Général (no. 68) describes it as "une Femme vue de profil habillée en Espagnolette". Both paintings are signed by Alexis Grimou (1678-1733) and the companion piece is dated 1731. There are other versions in the art museums of Avignon and Prague;[14] a particularly attractive, very free sketch is in the Dulwich College Gallery.[15] The engraving of 1740 (fig. 6) may record yet another variation. A painting by Grimou sold at Sotheby's, 30 June 1965 (no. 3), is described as representing a girl in a fur-trimmed red dress, so it may be closer to the tapestry than the others. Grimou was influenced by Rembrandt; the notice of his death in the *Mercure* for June, 1733, says, "Il peignait bien une tête dans le gout de Rimbrandt." Lacombe's *Dictionnaire portatif des beaux-arts* (first edition 1751) says, "Sa coutume était de coëffer ses figures d'un bonnet posé d'une façon assez singulière et de les habiller de fantaisie."[16] Many of his figures, including his self-portrait, and even a David with the head of Goliath, wear soft ruffs.

The tapestry version of the *Espagnolette* (fig. 4) has the inscriptions "Grimou f. 1729" and "Cozette. ex. 173—"; the last figure of the second date is illegible. Perhaps the weaver used the Karlsruhe painting as the basis of his design; the date of 1731 on the companion piece does not preclude the possibility that the *Espagnolette* was painted two years earlier. In this case, the design has been drastically simplified, very probably by the weaver himself, to make his task easier. Most of the passages that would mean long, slow work, such as the plume in the hat and the delicate intricacies of the ruff, have been omitted. The

Figure 1. *Young Woman Holding a Mask*. Tapestry, Gobelins
Manufactory, 1725.
Metropolitan Museum of Art, Joseph Pulitzer Bequest, 1929.

334

Figure 2. *Young Woman Holding a Mask.* Engraving by Chasteau after Santerre, 1708.
Bibliothèque Nationale, Paris.

Figure 3. *Charlotte Desmares.* Engraving by Lepicié after Charles Coypel, 1733.
Metropolitan Museum of Art, Dick Fund, 1917.

paned sleeve and the hand have gone and, by enlarging the eyes and adding an earring, the designer has concentrated attention upon the face, where, indeed, the weaver has put forward all his skill.

The same weaver's name, Cozette, appears on a third small tapestry panel in the Metropolitan Museum (fig. 7). There is little doubt about the sitter for this portrait; she is almost certainly Boucher's daughter, Jeanne Elizabeth Victoire, who married the painter (and tapestry designer) Jean Baptiste Henri Deshays in 1758. Boucher's pastel portraits of his daughters, Jeanne and Marie-Emilie, wife of the artist Pierre Antoine Baudouin, were copied in colour-engravings by Louis Marin Bonnet. The tapestry corresponds almost exactly to the colour-print of Jeanne, which is exceedingly rare.[17] The print of Marie, called *Flora*, has an inscription stating that the pastel original was made in 1757, but there is a version in the Louvre, signed by Boucher and dated 1756;[18] Jeanne was probably portrayed by her father at the same time, when she was twenty-one or twenty-two. There are later versions of the apparently very popular pastels. One pair was in the A. Danlos sale, Hôtel Drouot, Paris, 6 June 1928 (nos. 48, 49); *Mme Deshays* is signed and dated 1766. A previous owner of these pictures is recorded as saying that a pupil of Boucher had identified the sitters.[19] The tapestry was also repeated several times. An example with a similar inscription was in the Lowengard sale, Galerie Georges Petit, Paris, 10 June 1910 (no. 36), and another in the Félix Doistau sale at the same auction house, 18 and 19 June 1928. The latter is signed "Cozette fils" and is not dated.

Is the Cozette who signed the tapestry in the Metropolitan Museum (fig. 7) *père* or *fils*? The inscription, "Boucher Pixt [pinxit] Cozette Ex/it [excudit] 1769" is not woven into the background, like those on the two earlier works discussed in this article, but is written in ink. There is no reason, however, to doubt its authenticity; the inscription on two tapestry copies of Drouais' *Boy with a portfolio* are handwritten on the finished fabric. One, in the Tours museum, has "Cozette ex/it 1763", the other, in the Louvre, "Cozette fils ex/dit en 1764 âge de 10 ans". Cozette *père* was Pierre François (1714-1801); Cozette *fils* was his son, Michel Henri (1754-1822).[20]

As compared to Jean Jans and Jean Jacques Jans,

335

of whom little is known beyond the dates at which they took over the management of a Gobelins workshop and the tapestries they signed, the Cozettes have left a fairly full record of themselves. Cozettes, in fact, abounded at the Gobelins in the eighteenth century. Edouard Anne Cozette, who died in 1739, was the *concierge*; his duties included keeping the records of tapestries in storage. He had seven children and one of his sons was probably his successor in this position. "M. Cozette, concierge des Gobelins" is mentioned several times from 1758 to 1766 in the correspondence between Jean Germain Soufflot, director of the royal manufactories, and the *Surintendant des Bâtiments*, the Marquis de Marigny, his official superior and brother of Mme de Pompadour. Another Cozette, a dyer at the Gobelins, also appears in these letters.[21] But two of Edouard Anne's sons can be positively identified: Pierre François, the weaver, and his much younger brother, Charles Marie (1730-1797), a painter. In 1752, the weaver wrote to Marigny asking if Charles might be allowed to paint two *dessus de porte* for Choisy, a royal château. Marigny wrote "Je verray" in the margin, but there is no record that Cozette did any work at Choisy.[22] Four years later, however, he was taken on at the Ministry of War as a painter of battles and remained in this employment until the Revolution.[23] Some of his works still belong to the Ministry of National Defence,[24] and a portrait of Louis XV on horseback at Versailles is signed "C. Cozette 1763".[25]

Pierre François Cozette became the head of a workshop at the very early age of twenty-two or twenty-three. Though his father was only a *concierge*, he probably came from a family of weavers, as Charles Marie made a wild claim in 1776 that for more than two hundred years his ancestors had been "directeurs" of the Gobelins.[26] The last figure of the date after his name on the *Espagnolette* is illegible, but it seems likely that the piece was made before Cozette took over the management of a *basse-lisse*, or horizontal loom, workshop in 1735. In 1749 he became head of an *haute-lisse* workshop and remained in charge of it until 1801. His son, Michel Henri, who succeeded him, supervised the single *basse-lisse* workshop from 1792 to 1801.[27] There were only three workshops from 1751 until the end of the century, so Cozette's signature appears with those of

the other heads, Michel or Jean Audran and Jacques Neilson, on most of the petitions, complaints, stories of misery, and fast-approaching bankruptcy that poured out of the manufactory throughout the period. The king was always in arrears in his payments. Neilson, who was of Scottish descent, supported himself and his workmen by making tapestries for British customers; Cozette increased his income by producing many little panels, for which he found a variety of uses. Thus, when it was announced in 1768 that the king of Denmark would visit the manufactory, Cozette was ordered, two months ahead, to make a portrait of him from a medal. The weaving was to be done in a small workshop that would be closed to all, so that the portrait would be a surprise. Apparently it was not made, but Cozette did give the king a little head of a woman, woven by his son; the father proudly described it in a letter to Marigny as "bien tout ce que l'on a pû faire de mieux en ce genre jusqu'à ce jour".[28]

This son, Michel Henri, had indeed become useful to his father from a very early age, weaving the Louvre panel already mentioned when he was only ten. Marigny owned the painting by Drouais from which the tapestry was copied.[29] Cozette reminded the marquis in May 1764 that he had given him "le second petit polisson fait par mon fils" and that Marigny had then said that Cozette would be paid for a *Holy Family* that he had given to Marie Antoinette at Cozette's suggestion. The writer ended, "La grâce que je vous demande, Monsieur, est de vouloir bien me faire payer le plus tôt qu'il sera possible, indépendamment de l'à compte que nous espérons, MM. Audran et Neilson." The *Holy Family* had been woven nine years earlier and it is satisfactory to know that Cozette was finally paid 2,400 livres for it, though not until 1767.[30] The king's debt to the three heads of the Gobelins workshops and to the director of the Savonnerie carpet manufactory in August, 1764 was over 186,375 livres; by 1770 it was 303,139. The manufactories were then in "la misère la plus grande qu'elles aient jamais éprouvée".[31]

At least eighteen royal portraits were woven by the Cozettes between 1765 and 1782, with five and probably more by the son.[32] Several were shown at the Salons; two panels in the 1765 exhibition were said by a critic to have aroused "l'admiration et l'étonnement de tous les spectateurs". Diderot wrote that the king by Pierre François and the queen by his son, shown in 1769, would have been taken for paintings, and added, "Cela est si merveilleux, que le Pline moderne qui en parlera sera traité de menteur par ceux qui nous succéderont dans quelques trentaines de siècles."[33] Before Cozette *père* asked permission from Marigny to exhibit his son's portrait of the queen, he took pains to show it to several artists, including Boucher (then *surinspecteur*, or artistic adviser, at the manufactory), Lemoine, Van Loo, Cochin, and Chardin, all of whom approved the idea. The only known examples of the king and queen in tapestry dated 1769 are both signed "Cozette ex/it",[34] indicating that the omission of the word "fils" does not necessarily mean that the father was the weaver.

When Cozette was asked to make a portrait of a later queen, Marie Antoinette, he found that the paintings he was supposed to copy were not considered good likenesses. So he went to Versailles and was able to profit from "certaines observations, que j'ai faites plusieurs fois, en examinant la Reine, à son dîner". This was in 1774 and again it was his son who wove the panel.[35] On one occasion, the son's craftsmanship was criticized; Marigny, called in to look at his portrait of the king in 1770, found that "la figure du roi avait un air de dureté qui faisait un fort mauvais effet." Cozette wrote explaining the reasons for this and promising to correct it; Marigny answered politely, saying that he would look at the portrait again, and "si elle est bien je la présenterai à Sa Majesté." Michel Henri also made a portrait of the Austrian emperor in the same year, which Soufflot hoped that the King would give to the Dauphine (Marie Antoinette, the emperor's sister), but, in this case, he wrote to Marigny, Cozette, being in a "triste situation", would like to be paid

promptly and not through the regular channels: "si ce portrait est payé par les Bâtiments il ne le sera pas longtemps." By 1773, Michel Henri, though only nineteen, was in a position to weave merely the head of a full-length portrait, leaving the rest to two other men of less skill;[36] the two tapestry portraits in the Salon of that year were made "sous la conduite du Sr. Cozette par son fils".[37]

All this time, of course, Cozette's workshop was turning out its quota of huge tapestries for the king, and Cozette was responsible for paying the workmen whether or not he received anything from the Bâtiments. At least once, we find him making furniture upholstery for a private purchaser: "C'est un moyen d'occuper ses ouvriers sans que se soit aux frais du Roi," wrote Marigny to Soufflot in 1766.[38] He was not, however, as successful in this kind of enterprise as his colleague, Neilson.

Though the Bonnet engraving of Boucher's portrait of Mme Deshays has an inscription saying that the original pastel belonged to Soufflot, when Marigny's collections were sold in 1782 after his death, they included a version of the pastel (called a "tête de femme charmante") and the same head, "exécutée en tapisserie à la Manufacture royale des Gobelins, par M. Cozette"; the pastel brought 52 livres, the tapestry, 120.[39] It would be pleasant to think that this tapestry is the one now in the Metropolitan Museum, but there is no way to prove this. We would not today value such a tapestry at more than twice the price of a Boucher original and we do not consider the exact reproduction of a painting in tapestry to be such an admirable feat as Diderot thought. But the little panels woven with such skill at the Gobelins still have some of the charm of their epoch, a faint echo of Talleyrand's *douceur de vivre*. And at least they made a little extra money for their creators.

Figure 4. *L'espagnolette*. Tapestry, Gobelins Manufactory,
1733 (?).
Metropolitan Museum of Art, Bequest of Julie Heidelbach,
1932.

338

Figure 5. *L'espagnolette*. Painting by Alexis Grimou.
Staatliche Kunsthalle, Karlsruhe.

Figure 6. *L'espagnolette*. Engraving by Lepicié after Grimou.
New York Public Library, Prints Division.

Figure 7. *Boucher's Daughter, Mme Deshays.* Tapestry, Gobelins
Manufactory, 1769.
Metropolitan Museum of Art, Bequest of Julie Heidelbach,
1932.

Notes

1. Quoted in Maurice Fenaille, *Etat général des tapisseries de la manufacture des Gobelins*, vol. 3, Paris, Imprimerie National, Hachette, 1904, p. 14.

2. Fenaille, *Etat général*, vol. 4 (1907), p. 338.

3. L. Dussieux and E. Soulié, eds., *Mémoires du duc de Luynes sur la Cour de Louis XV*, vol. 11, Paris, 1863, p. 8.

4. Joseph Breck, "A tapestry portrait", *Metropolitan Museum of Art Bulletin*, vol. 24 (1929), p. 381, illus. p. 313.

5. Emile Dacier, *Le Musée de la Comédie-Française*, Paris, 1905, p. 133. Lillian Arvilla Hall (*Catalogue of the dramatic portraits in the theatre collection of the Harvard College Library*, vol. 1, Cambridge, Mass., 1930-1934, p. 361) accepts this as the only authentic portrait of Charlotte Desmares.

6. Gunnar W. Lundberg, "Jean Baptiste Santerre, 1651-1717", *Tidskrift för Konstvetenskap*, vol. 17 (1933), p. 45, fig. 8. This author accepts a Santerre painting of a lady holding a letter and Chasteau's 1708 print after it as portraits of Charlotte Desmares. There are several versions of this painting, including one in the Museum of Fine Arts, Boston (acc.no.47-245), and two tapestries after it or the print, one in the Palazzo Reale, Naples, and another that belonged to the dealer Jacques Seligmann in 1933. The sitter might possibly be the same person in 1708 that Coypel painted in 1733. Several paintings by or attributed to Santerre show women holding masks; there is one in the Musée Carnavalet, Paris, and examples have appeared in the Princesse Mathilde sale, Galerie Georges Petit, Paris, 17-21 May 1904, no. 45; and in Paris sales of 4 December 1941, 5 February 1947, and 4 December 1950. The mask is not necessarily an attribute of Thalia or an indication that the woman holding one is an actress.

7. A. J. Dezallier d'Argenville, *Abrégé de la vie des plus fameux peintres*, vol. 4, Paris, 1762, p. 259.

8. French dictionaries give only "jeune fille espagnole" for "espagnolette" in this sense. Women's "Vandyke" costumes are discussed by John Steegman, "A drapery painter of the eighteenth century", *Connoisseur*, vol. 97 (1936), pp. 309-335; those worn by men (with some still existing examples) by J. L. Nevinson, "Vandyke dress", *Connoisseur*, vol. 157 (1964), pp. 166-171.

9. Jean Seznec and Jean Adhémar, eds., *Diderot, Salons*, vol. 3, Oxford, Clarendon Press, 1957-1967, pp. 17, 18, pl. 14 (reproduction of sale catalogue entry). The picture has not been identified.

10. This information was kindly given by Mr. J. L. Nevinson.

11. Alexandre Ananoff, *L'oeuvre dessiné de François Boucher*, vol. 1, Paris, F. de Nobele, 1966, p. 72, no. 205, fig. 35.

12. A.-P de Mirimonde, "La musique orientale dans les oeuvres de l'école française du XVIIIe siècle", *Revue du Louvre*, vol. 19 (1969), p. 246, fig. 26.

13. Armand Dayot, *De la Régence à la Révolution*, Paris, 1906, p. 168.

14. Karlsruhe, Staatliche Kunsthalle, *Französische Meister*, exhibition catalogue, 1963, no. 22.

15. *Catalogue of the pictures in the gallery of Alleyn's College of God's Gift at Dulwich*, London, 1892, p. 19, no. 74. This painting has recently been attributed to Fragonard (Pierre Rosenberg and Isabelle Compin, "Quatre nouveaux Fragonard au Louvre", *Revue du Louvre*, 1974, p. 191, fig. 9).

16. C. Gabillot, "Alexis Grimou, peintre français (1678-1733)", *Gazette des Beaux-Arts*, 4th series, vol. 5 (1911), pp. 426-157, 158, illus. pp. 159, 321.

17. Jacques Hérold, *Louis-Marin Bonnet (1735-1793), Catalogue de l'oeuvre gravé*, Paris, Société pour l'Etude de la Gravure Française, 1935, p. 88, no. 59, pl. 12.

18. Geneviève Monnier, *Pastels, xviième et xviiième siècles*, Musée du Louvre — Cabinet des Dessins, Inventaire des Collections Publiques Françaises, Paris, 1972, no. 26. The pastel of 1757 is said to be in a private collection in Paris.

19. The identifications were not used for another pair of similar pastels sold at the Palais Galliera, Paris, 19 June 1970, nos. 11, 12.

20. Michel Henri Cozette's date of birth is given as 1744 in works of reference, but the inscription on the Louvre tapestry clearly says he was ten in 1764.

21. Jean Mondain-Monval, *Correspondance de Soufflot avec les Directeurs des Bâtiments concernant la manufacture des Gobelins*, Paris, A. Lemerre, 1918, pp. 66, 96, 188, 205.

22. Fenaille, *État général*, vol. 3 (1904), p. 321; B. Chamchine, *Le Château de Choisy*, Paris, 1910.

23. Marguerite Jallut, "Les peintres de batailles des xviie et xviiie siècles", *Archives de l'Art Français*, vol. 22 (1959), pp. 121-123.

24. *Deux siècles de l'histoire de France (1589-1789)*, exhibition catalogue, Versailles, 1937, nos. 240-242.

25. Eud. Soulié, *Notice du Musée Imperial de Versailles*, vol. 3, Paris, 1859-1861, p. 218, no. 3752.

26. Jallut, "Les peintres de batailles" (1959), p. 123. Tapes-

tries were not woven at the Gobelins before the early seventeenth century. There were no *directeurs* before the establishment of the Manufacture Royale in 1662; they were always distinguished painters or architects. Pierre François Cozette's official title was *entrepreneur*, which can be translated as "contractor"; he was responsible for paying the weavers under him as well as directing their work.

27. Another son, Pierre Louis (1749-1798), is also sometimes mentioned as succeeding his father, but his name does not appear on the list of *entrepreneurs* at the Gobelins (Jules Guiffrey, article on Michel Henri Cozette in Thieme-Becker, *Allgemeines Lexicon der Bildenden Künstler*, Leipzig, vol. 8, 1913, p. 34). Perhaps he was the Cozette *fils* who, with the sons of the other two *entrepreneurs*, Audran and Neilson, was accorded the right to become a student of the "Ecole du dessein" at the Academy in 1764 (Anatole de Montaiglon, *Procès-verbaux de l'Académie royale de Peinture et de Sculpture*, vol. 7 Paris, 1886, p. 273). Pierre François, the father, exhibited a painted self-portrait in the 1798 salon, listed as "Cozette, chef d'atelier à la manufacture des Gobelins: Le portrait de l'auteur peint par lui-même, à l'âge de 85 ans." On the strength of this entry, an attempt has been made to attribute other portraits signed "Cozette" to the weaver, but it seems far more probable that they are the work of his brother, Charles Marie (G. Leroy, "Le tapissier Cozette, peintre portraitiste au xviiie siècle", *Réunion des Sociétés des Départements*, vol. 23, 1899, pp. 137-144; this author states that Cozette seems to have relinquished his workshop to his son in 1788).

28. Mondain-Monval, *Correspondance* (1918), pp. 227, 233, 237; Fenaille, *État général*, vol. 4 (1904), p. 313.

29. *Diderot, Salons*, vol. 1 (1957-1967), pl. 54.

30. Fenaille, *État général*, vol. 4 (1907), pp. 339-343. In considering the value of the livre, an official report of 1776 is enlightening. It states, "Un gain par semaine de 12 livres est, semble-t-il, le medium d'un bon et d'un faible ouvrier" (Mondain-Monval, *Correspondance*, 1918, p. 287, note 1). There were also fringe benefits, such as free quarters for some weavers and tips from visitors.

31. Mondain-Monval, *Correspondance* (1918), pp. 160, 247, 251.

32. Fenaille, *État général*, vol. 4 (1907), pp. 326, 347-348.

33. *Diderot, Salons*, vol. 2 (1957-1967), p. 56; vol. 4, pp. 62, 117.

34. Fenaille, *État général*, vol. 4 (1907), p. 314.

35. Fenaille, *État général*, vol. 4 (1907), p. 319.

36. Mondain-Monval, *Correspondance* (1918), pp. 252, 253, 268, 269.

37. Fenaille, *État général*, vol. 4 (1907), p. 323.

38. Mondain-Monval, *Correspondance* (1918), p. 186.

39. From the priced copy of the sale catalogue in the Frick Art Reference Library, New York City.

Archaeological and Ethnological Considerations of the Foot-Braced Body-Tension Loom

John E. Vollmer

Archaeological Evidence

THE earliest archaeological evidence of a loom in eastern Asia is a specialized variant of the body-tension loom,[1] which utilizes the weaver's feet to brace the warp beam. Parts of such a loom were found at Shizhaishan[2] during a series of excavations conducted by the Yunnan Provincial branch of the Chinese Academy of Sciences through its Institute of Archaeological Research. Forty-three tombs were uncovered at the site revealing an impressive Bronze–Iron Age culture which had flourished on the southwestern frontier of the Western Han empire (206 B.C.–A.D. 8).[3] Both archaeologically and stylistically, the rich tomb furnishings from Shizhaishan remain quite apart from what is known from finds in other parts of southwestern China. This site's relationship with other areas of Asia is still debated.[4] In contrast to the civilization of nuclear China, Shizhaishan has many affinities with the Dongson culture of Indochina.[5] Although certain of the decorative motifs on some Shizhaishan bronzes are comparable with Chinese Huai style motifs,[6] the vigorous animal style with its emphasis on realism and action is totally non-Chinese in feeling.[7]

Tomb 17 yielded four parts of a loom:[8] a cloth beam with pronged ends and removable centre section to clamp woven cloth in place, a warp beam, a sword beater, and a tubular shed stick with a bow-shaped bar (fig. 1). The loom appears to be functional although it is made of bronze. Precise measurements are not available, but calculations from

the scale indicated in the excavation report give beam measurements of 45 cm. Such measurements are within the range for full-sized looms, but it is impossible to determine if this loom was ever intended for weaving. Shizhaishan is a princely cemetery. The presence of many highly ornamented utilitarian objects among the grave-goods suggests they may have been specially created for ceremonial or ritualistic purposes rather than for use in daily life.

Clues for identifying these objects as pieces of weaving equipment come from the site itself. A three-dimensional scene on the lid of a drum-shaped cowrie container from Tomb 1 depicts an enthroned woman surrounded by standing and kneeling figures who bear various offerings (fig. 2).[9] Facing the central figure are six women weaving on foot-braced looms. Despite surface corrosion and the small scale of the representations, loom mechanics are clearly visible. The weavers sit on the ground with legs outstretched, using their feet to brace a flattened warp beam in order to maintain tension on a circular warp. Cloth beam and backstrap are obscured by their costumes. Each weaver manipulates a large sword beater. Four figures grasp the sword in both hands as they pull it toward themselves beating the weft in place (fig. 2). One holds her sword on edge to facilitate opening a shed (fig. 3). Apparently interest in realistic effect outweighed considerations of accuracy, as the sword is actually shown inside the warp rather than positioned between layers of warp. Another woman is either inserting or withdrawing the sword with her right hand, while in her left hand she holds a pointed instrument poised over her weaving (fig. 4). This may depict a pin beater used to straighten single tangled threads. The shedding mechanism (shed stick and heddle rod) and lease rod have been eliminated, more a result of artistic license than an indication that such features were missing, since an actual shed stick has been recovered from the site.

In 1972 further archaeological evidence was uncovered at the cemetery site of Lizhaishan 40 kilo-metres southeast of Shizhaishan.[10] Socketed bronze end pieces for warp and cloth beams were found in four tombs. In each case the pair for the cloth beam have pronged ends. Those in Tomb 17 have traces of wood preserved in the hollow sockets and their placement indicates that the warp beam measured 44.4 cm and the cloth beam 48.4 cm. Tomb 17 also yielded a bronze sword beater. In addition, three shed sticks with bow-shaped bars were recovered from the site.

Ethnological Material

The identification of the Shizhaishan shed stick (fig. 6A) or those from Lizhaishan is reinforced by comparison with an Atayal loom in the Royal Ontario Museum, acquired in the last third of the nineteenth century in northern Taiwan by George Leslie Mackay (figs. 5, 6C).[11] This loom has a two-part cloth beam; each is semicircular in cross-section and terminates in a pair of prongs to hold the backstrap, which is now missing. The warp beam is cylindrical and is incised with geometric designs at either end. A continuous circular warp of Z-spun ramie is stretched between these members. Each complete circuit of warp is wound around a lease rod, forming the circular cross which maintains thread order. A cylindrical shed stick with bow-shaped bar encloses the warp of one shed, and two small rods with continuous thread heddles looped under the warp threads control the other two sheds required for the 2/1 chevron twill of the fabric. The lease rod and one heddle rod have squared finials at one end incised with geometric designs. Separate parts of the loom include a sword beater with carved decoration on one side of the butt consisting of two anthropomorphic figures against dentated stripes, and a stick shuttle made of a small stick around which unspun ramie is wound diagonally. Two illustrations of the MacKay loom[12] show an additional piece which is now missing. It was a pointed rod with square finial like one of the heddle rods. In one photograph it is shown inserted into a shed between the shed stick and the first heddle rod; in the other, it occupies a shed between the heddles. It is probably a pick-up stick employed in this particular three-shaft twill tie up to help form sheds. Presumably it was inserted at the back of the last shed opened to facilitate opening the next. In this way any shed would be raised first from one-third of the warp, then from the remaining third, rather than being raised from the total warp in one movement.

The warp beam of the MacKay loom appears to be different from the warp beam of the Shizhaishan loom. In figure 1 the ridges aligning with the thickened ends of the cloth beam cast rounded shadows, suggesting that the beam itself is flat. Cloth beams, swords, and shed sticks are similar. Both looms have two-part rounded cloth beams which are slightly thickened at the ends and terminate in prongs. Each part of the Atayal beam is an identical half with two prongs at either end resulting in double pairs, as compared to the Shizhaishan loom in which only half of the central section is separate. With tapered end and square butt, sword beaters retain similar profiles. Both shed sticks feature a bow-shaped bar. The bamboo Atayal shed stick bar, wedged into depressions at either end of the stick, although now dry and rigid, was originally flexible and removable. From its resemblance to the Atayal shed stick, it seems likely that the Shizhaishan bar was also removable.

Foot-braced body-tension looms are used by several other aboriginal groups in Taiwan.[13] In principle the looms are the same, but individual parts exhibit a wide range of variability with many overlapping similarities from tribe to tribe. Lengths of bamboo without a bow-shaped bar serve as shed sticks on examples of looms used by the Bunun (fig.

6G)[14] and Rukai tribes (fig. 6D).[15] An Ami loom (fig. 6B)[16] has a barred shed stick which closely resembles the shed stick of the Atayal loom described above. The same Ami loom has a distinctive heddle rod shaped like a slotted board. Heddles attached to the warp ends making the countershed are suspended from the lower part, while the upper part functions as a handle. Similar objects function as shed sticks on some Atayal looms (fig. 6F).[17] Five such objects are among the parts of an Atayal loom now in the ROM acquired by Richard J. Pearson (fig. 6E).[18] One is carved with a long narrow prong attached at one end of the stick; another has a slot which has been slit open at one end; a third is also slit at one end but is made of different wood and does not exhibit the same amount of wear as the other parts of the loom. Such sticks with similar, but less flexible, bar elements than those of the MacKay and Shizhaishan looms are slipped over the required warp ends to secure the shed. In most examples of Atayal looms having heavy slotted shed sticks, a simple heddle rod controls the countershed;[19] however, the other two slotted parts of the Pearson loom are closed at both ends and were identified as heddle rods when the loom was accessioned.[20] They resemble the heddle rod identified in the Ami loom.

The cloth beam of the Pearson Atayal loom is flattened, roughly oval in cross-section, with a narrow wedge-shaped channel in the larger piece into which a blade-like second member is fitted to hold the cloth. Such cloth beams noted on other Atayal looms are present on looms of the Bunun, and of the Thao tribes (fig. 6H).[21] When engaged, these form a single pair of prongs as in the Shizhaishan beam. The Rukai and Ami looms employ a pair of pronged sticks, as does the MacKay loom. Only the MacKay Atayal loom and the Ami loom have a single pointed sword like the one found at Shizhaishan. All other Taiwanese looms feature a double-pointed, handleless sword. Warp beams vary even more in size and shape. Those of the MacKay and Ami looms are cylindrical. Solid, square-sectioned beams are featured on the Thao and Rukai looms. The warp beam of the Bunun loom is square in cross-section, but hollow with an opening at the top. Most Atayal looms employ an even larger drum-like warp beam which is roughly triangular in cross-section.

Although foot-braced body-tension looms are by no means common, they appear ethnologically in several parts of southern Asia. A similar loom is used, although not exclusively, by the Angami Naga tribe of the Assam highlands.[22] The Mnong Nong[23] and the Maa' tribes[24] living in southern Vietnam weave on this type of loom, as do the Li tribe of Hainan Island off the south coast of the China mainland.[25] Other examples are found among Melanesians on the north coast of West Irian (formerly New Guinea) at Sarmi and some of the small offshore islands,[26] and in the St. Mathias Islands in the Bismarck Archipelago.[27] A single sculptural representation of a nursing woman weaving at such a loom might also be mentioned in this context.[28] Although no definite provenance or interpretation has been offered, the piece is prized as an heirloom by a family in Flores, thus suggesting a possibility that the loom might have been known in eastern Indonesia in the past. Compared to Taiwanese looms, the foot-braced body-tension looms used in other parts of Asia are generalized in their characteristics.

Features and Limitations

Foot-braced body-tension looms are completely self-contained. A fully set up loom can be rolled into a compact bundle, easily transported from place to place, and quickly made operative without the assistance of another person or supplementary equipment. When reduced to its basic components, the loom consists of seven parts: warp beam, cloth beam, lease rod, shed stick, heddle rod, sword beat-er, and backstrap. Although the shapes of individual parts differ from region to region, their functions remain constant. This is clearly demonstrated in the movable warp beam, the loom's most definitive characteristic, which exhibits more variation in size and shape than any other part.

All foot-braced looms employ a circular warp which is simply stretched around the beams and which can be moved freely to any position desired by the weaver. To counteract the tendency of the warp to slide over the cloth beam when the weft is beaten into place, these looms are consistently provided with a means of clamping the warp to the cloth beam. Various devices are used: simple sticks either placed on top of the warp and lashed to the beam, or given a half turn to wedge them under the beam as on some of the Maa' or St. Mathias looms; two-part beams which sandwich the cloth between them as in some of the Taiwanese looms; and specialized clamps as observed on the Shizhaishan, Bunun, Thao, and some Atayal looms. The fact that the cloth is clamped to the cloth beam is not peculiar to foot-braced looms, but is necessitated by the circular warp which is also employed on other types of body-tension looms.[29] It is unnecessary on looms which use a non-circular warp where the fabric is rolled up on the cloth beam as it is woven, thus providing the required firmness. Foot-braced looms seem to have neither reed nor temple to help maintain uniform fabric width. Controlling the width is largely a matter of the weaver's skill.

Foot-braced looms rely mainly on the friction of the warp to hold the various movable parts in position. The shed stick occupies a critical and particularly vulnerable position, subject to any torsion the weaver may cause by failing to keep uniform tension. The bow-shaped bars on the Shizhaishan, MacKay Atayal, and Ami looms essentially lock the shed stick in place and were probably developed to prevent mishap. The absence of the bow-shaped bar on other foot-braced looms may indicate that this is only a regional development.

Dimensions of the cloth produced on foot-braced looms are dependent on several physical limitations of the loom. The length of the warp, being circular, is twice the distance between the beams. For foot-braced looms this distance is determined by the length of the weaver's leg, and establishes the maximum length of cloth which can be woven. Minimum lengths can be determined by the weaver, but the warp will always remain the same length. Similarly, the maximum width of fabric is dependent on the distance the weaver can comfortably spread her feet and still maintain tension on the warp. A modification can be seen on one of the Maa' looms in which there is a double warp beam. A wide circular warp is stretched over one beam which is lashed to a second braced by the weaver's feet inside the lashings.[30] When more fabric is required than can be warped on the loom, as in the long Atayal coats which require two lengths, the loom must be warped and tied up a second or possibly third time.

These restrictions do not affect the kinds of cloth which can be woven. In addition to tabby, the Atayal weave fancy twills as well as weft-figured cloth with elaborate pick-up patterns. Pick-up patterns are common among other ethnological groups using the loom. Although no actual fabrics survive from Shizhaishan, depictions of stripes and patterns on the costumes of some of the bronze figures suggest that patterned cloths were produced on foot-braced looms in antiquity as well.

Conclusions

The gap of some 2,000 years separating the antique and modern examples of this specialized loom poses many questions. It is impossible to isolate the origins of this loom. Its survival among some of the more isolated peoples of southern Asia whose cultures remain relatively uninfluenced by the major political and cultural forces which have shaped the continent, gives credence to theories supporting Pacific Basin diffusion. The chronological priority of the loom at Shizhaishan points to Yunnan as a source for later manifestations in southern Asia. Parallels have been drawn between Shizhaishan and the Dongson culture of Indochina. The late Bronze–Iron Age cultures apparently penetrated into many areas of southern Asia either through trade or possibly by migrations of peoples.[31] Stylistic affinities of the Shizhaishan bronzes with the so-called "animal style" of southern Siberia or the even more far-reaching sources suggested for South Asian cultures by Robert von Heine-Geldern[32] raise the possibility of Central Asian or even more westerly sources for aspects of Shizhaishan culture. These could conceivably include the loom.

A second question raised by this paper concerns the development of weaving technology in eastern Asia. Although body-tension looms are characteristic in this part of the world, individual types exhibit wide ranges of modification, refinement, and flexibility. Tadao Kano divides body-tension looms into two groups. He considers movable warp beam looms (foot-braced) a continental form, while he identifies fixed warp beam looms with Indonesia and the islands of southern Asia.[33] H. Ling Roth's study of similar looms favours an evolutionary development based on criteria of shedding mechanisms.[34] Chinese scholars, using ethnological material in the study of ancient Chinese looms, emphasize developments based on concerns for increased efficiency. At one end of the scale are looms in which all weaving operations are controlled by hand, following one after another in laborious succession; at the other are looms capable of increased productivity, having shafts and treadles which utilize both hands and feet. One group of Chinese

scholars, among them Son Boyin and Li Zhongyi, favours using the vertical loom to explain the Chinese Han Dynasty loom which has a warp supported at an oblique angle on a frame with shafts operated by treadles.[35] Song Chaolin and others claim that the Han loom evolved from horizontal body-tension looms, citing the evidence at Shizhaishan and the prevalence of other types of horizontal looms among minority groups in present-day China.[36]

If warping is considered a factor bearing on the efficiency of cloth production, foot-braced looms are extremely primitive pieces of equipment. Fixing the warp beam to a frame or point of support beyond the weaver's feet increases the length of warp considerably, reducing the frequency of setting up the loom. On the other hand, if the circular warp is dispensed with, and a non-continuous warp is rolled from the warp beam to the cloth beam, then the length of the finished cloth can be further increased. Although all types of warping are utilized on body-tension looms in Asia, one cannot determine if the foot-braced loom is any more ancient than any other type.[37]

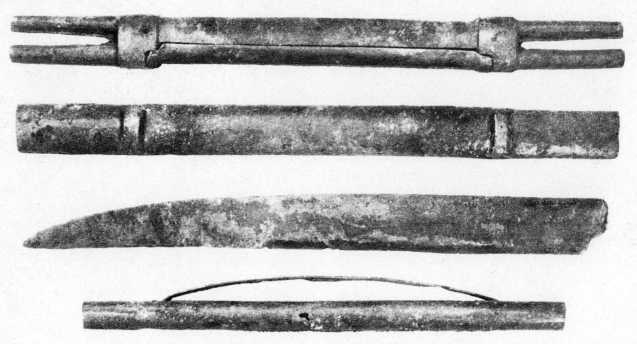

Figure 1. Four parts of a bronze foot-braced body-tension loom, Shizhaishan, Tomb 17, late second – early first century B.C.
Yunnan Provincial Museum (?), People's Republic of China.

Figure 2. Bronze cowrie shell container lid, Shizhaishan, Tomb 1, late second – early first century B.C.
Yunnan Provincial Museum (?), People's Republic of China.
Photo: William B. Robertson, ROM.

Figure 3.   Detail of figure 2.
Photo: William B. Robertson, ROM.

Figure 4.   Detail of figure 2.
Photo: William B. Robertson, ROM.

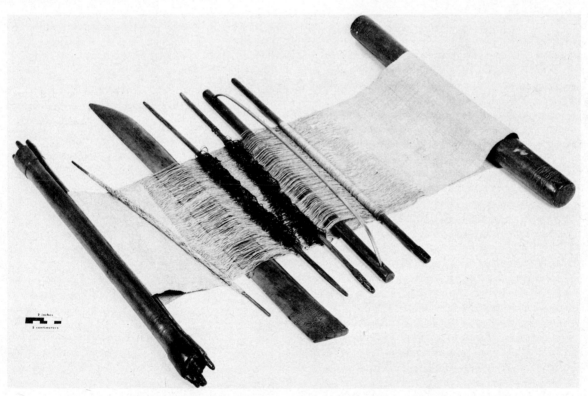

Figure 5.   Foot-braced body-tension loom, Taiwan, Atayal
tribe, late nineteenth century.
ROM acc. no. 915.3.258.

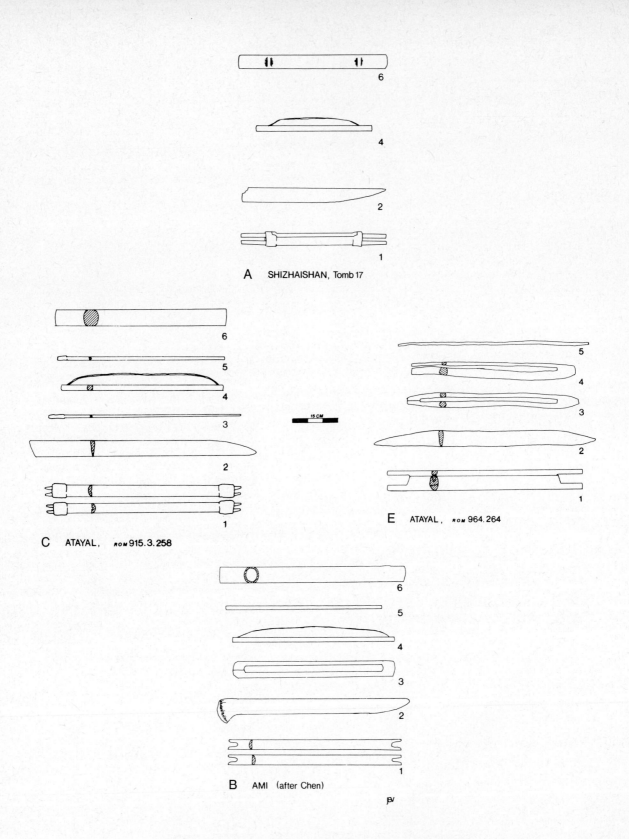

A   SHIZHAISHAN, Tomb 17

C   ATAYAL,   rom 915.3.258

E   ATAYAL,   rom 964.264

B   AMI   (after Chen)

Figure 6.   Ethnographical examples from China and Taiwan of the foot-braced body-tension loom. *1*, cloth beam; *2*, sword; *3*, heddle rod; *4*, shed stick; *5*, lease rod; *6*, warp beam.

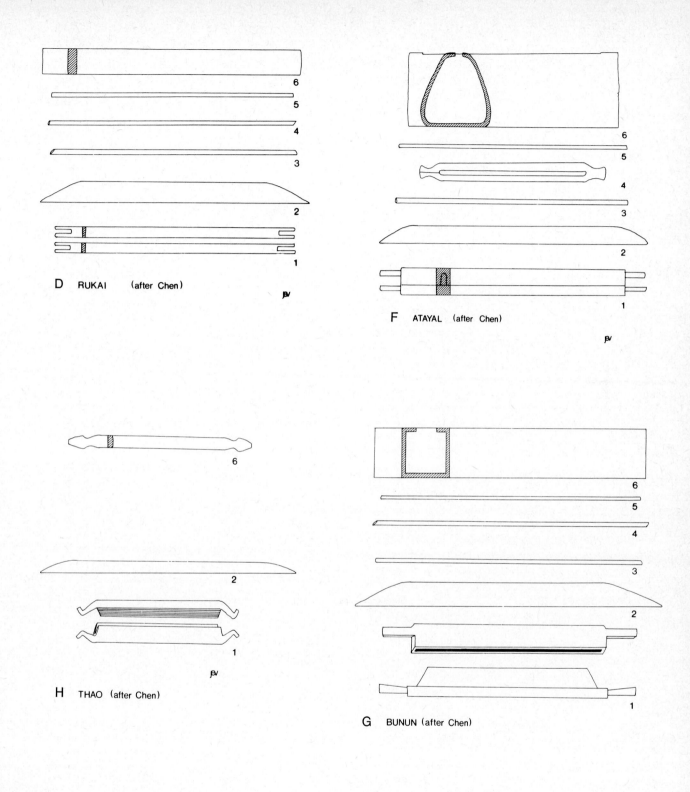

D RUKAI   (after Chen)

βⁿ

F ATAYAL (after Chen)

βⁿ

H THAO (after Chen)

βⁿ

G BUNUN (after Chen)

15 CM

351

JOHN E. VOLLMER

Notes

I wish to acknowledge the advice of Dorothy K. Burnham of the Textile Department, ROM, whose suggestions have clarified many points in this paper. Chinese terms have been romanized according to the *Guoyupinyin* system and I appreciate the time spent by Hsio-yen Shih of the Far Eastern Department, ROM, for checking the Chinese references. Both Rita Bolland of the Royal Tropical Institute, Amsterdam, and M.J. Adams of the Textile Museum, Washington, D.C., have given valuable assistance in tracing references to ethnological occurrences of similar looms.

1. Wherever possible I have utilized terminology approved by the Centre International d'Etude des Textiles Anciens (CIETA); see H.B. Burnham, ed., *Vocabulary of technical terms*, Lyon, CIETA, 1964 (presently being revised and expanded under the editorial direction of D. K. Burnham). Where names for loom parts are missing, I have attempted to use simple terms to avoid confusion. The term "foot-braced" points to the most outstanding characteristic of this class of Asian body-tension loom.

2. The site of Shizhaishan, located on the shores of Lake Dian roughly 30 miles (19 km) south of the capital of Yunnan province, Kunming, was excavated between 1954 and 1957. Bibliography: "Yunnan Jinning Shizhaishan guyizhi ji muzang" [Excavations of early dwelling sites and tombs at Shizhaishan, Jinning, Yunnan], *Kaogu Xuebao*, 1956.1, pp. 43-63; *Yunnan Jinning Shizhaishan gumuqun faque baogao* [Excavation report of the ancient cemetery at Shizhaishan, Jinning, Yunnan], Peking, 1959, 2 vols. (final excavation report, hereafter referred to as *Report*); "Yunnan Jinning Shizhaishan gumu disici faque jianbao" [Fourth preliminary report of the ancient cemetery at Shizhaishan, Jinning, Yunnan], *Kaogu*, 1963.9, pp. 480-485; "Yunnan Jinning Shizhaishan gumuqun chutongtieqi buyi" [Appendix of bronze and iron objects recovered from the ancient necropolis at Shizhaishan, Jinning, Yunnan], *Wenwu*, 1964.12, pp. 41-49; all in Chinese, for English summaries see: Wang Zhunming, "The bronze culture of ancient Yunnan", *Peking Review*, 1960.2, pp. 18–19; Richard Rudolph, "An important Dong-son site in Yun-nan", *Asian Perspectives*, vol. 4, 1960, pp. 41-49; John F. Haskins, "Translation of plate captions and brief resumé of Chapter IV from Report", dittographed, New York, Columbia University, 1960, and "Cache at Stone-Fortress Hill", *Natural History*, vol. 72, no. 2 (Feb. 1963), pp. 30-39; Magdalene von Dewall, "The Tien culture of southwest China", *Antiquity*, vol. 41 (1967), pp. 8-21; Emma C. Bunker, "The Tien culture", in *Early Chinese art and its possible influence in the Pacific Basin*, ed. Noel Barnard, vol. 2, *Asia*, New York, Columbia University, 1972, pp. 291-328.

3. Identification of Shizhaishan as the royal cemetery of the Kingdom of Dian is substantiated by the discovery of a gold seal in Tomb 6 bearing a Chinese inscription stating "Seal of the King of Dian" (*Report*, 1959, vol. 2, pl. 107, fig. 3). It is believed to be the actual seal given by the Han emperor to the Dian chieftain after his submission to Chinese control in 109 B.C. recorded in the *Shiji* of Sima Qian, chapter 116 (see Burton

Watson's translation, *Records of the Grand Historian of China*, New York and London, Columbia University, 1961, vol. 2., pp. 290-296).

Further information concerning the Dian people recorded in the *Shiji* relates that the chief of the Dian was the most important ruler of the Mimo tribes (Southwest Barbarians). Like the Yelang tribes, they wore their hair in mallet-shaped fashion (buns), worked the fields, and lived in settlements (in contrast to the Shu people further to the west who had braided hair and a nomadic existence). Dian chieftains traced their lineage to the royal house of Chu. One of their chieftains detained a group of ambassadors sent on a secret expedition by the Han emperor, Wudi, to find a southwestern route to Shendu (India) after the year 122 B.C. Partly because of this friendly encounter and the status of the leader of the Dian, the king was restored to his position and granted the seal mentioned above. The Dian are not mentioned again after the conquest of 109 B.C. and drop completely from later histories.

Shizhaishan has been dated to the Western Han Dynasty (206 B.C.–A.D. 8) on the basis of imported Chinese coins, seals, and mirrors. Three *banliang* coins of a type not minted before 175 B.C. establish a top limit for Tomb 13 (*Report*, 1959, vol. 1, p. 103, fig. 25 and vol. 2, pl. 98, fig. 3). The gold seal (see above, *Report*, 1959, vol. 2, pl. 107, fig. 3) establishes an upper limit of 109 B.C. for Tomb 6. Tombs 5 and 8 contain a large number of *wushu* coins which were first minted in 118 B.C., but several examples were not minted until after 32 B.C. (*Report*, 1959, vol. 1, p. 103, fig. 25). Most of the mirrors date from the latter part of the Western Han Dynasty with the exception of a third-century B.C. mirror of a Chu type from Tomb 3 (*Report*, 1959, vol. 1, p. 71, fig. 1) and a late Eastern Zhou mirror in Tomb 10 (*Report*, 1959, vol. 1, p. 71, fig. 2). Tomb 13 contains a mirror type Karlgren dates to the early first century B.C. (*Report*, 1959, vol. 1, p. 72, fig. 3); Tomb 20 has a mirror of a type dated from 80 B.C. onward (*Report*, 1959, vol. 1, p. 72, fig. 4). The excavators consider Tombs 14, 15, 16 and 17 to be the earliest and suggest dates of 220-175 B.C. for them, but both Bunker ("The Tien culture", 1972) and von Dewall ("The Tien culture of southwest China", 1967) think these dates are much too early. Bunker suggests that Tombs 12 and 13 (with *banliang* coins not dating before 175 B.C.), which are both rich in drums and have a mixture of styles, are probably the earliest and are related to Tombs 14, 15, 16 and 17.

4. For a summary of views as to how Shizhaishan fits into the cultural totality of China, see Cheng Te-k'un, *Archaeology in China*, vol. 3, *Chou*, Cambridge, Heffer and Sons, 1963. For opinions favouring an independent explanation, see Chang Kwang-chih, *The archaeology of ancient China*, rev. and enl. ed., New Haven and London, Yale University, 1968, particularly chapter 9, "Early civilization in South China", pp. 376-440.

5. For a bibliography concerning the Dong-son culture see: O.R.T. Janse, *Archaeological research in Indo-China*, vols. 1 and 2, Cambridge, Mass., Harvard University, 1947 and 1952; vol. 3,

352

Bruges, St. Catherine's Press, 1958; H.R. van Heekeren, *The Bronze-Iron Age of Indonesia*, The Hague, Martinus Nijhoff, 1958; John Loewenstein, "The origin of the Malayan metal age", *Journal of the Malayan Branch of the Royal Asiatic Society*, vol. 29, pt. 2 (May 1956), pp. 5-78. For an excellent summary of the problem, see Richard Pearson, "Dong-So'n and its origins", *Academia Sinica Bulletin of the Institute of Ethnology*, no. 13 (Spring 1962), pp. 27-50.

6. Bernard Kaelgren, "Huai and Han", *Bulletin of the Museum of Far Eastern Antiquities*, vol. 13 (1941), pp. 1-125.

7. For summary and bibliography see Emma C. Bunker, C. Bruce Chatwin, and Ann R. Farkas, *'Animal style' art from East to West*, New York, Asia Society, 1970.

8. *Report*, 1959, vol. 2, pl. 98, fig. 1 identifying these as four parts of a *dao* (knife)-shaped bronze utensil found in one case. J.F. Haskins was the first to suggest they might be parts of a loom ("Translation of plate captions", 1960, p. 25).

9. Ht. 27.5 cm, dia. at base 30.9 cm, exhibited in "The Exhibition of Archaeological Finds of the People's Republic of China" shown in Paris, London, Toronto, and elsewhere (William Watson, *The genius of China*, London, Times Newspapers, 1973, entry 176, p. 114 and figs.). For Chinese bibliography see: *Kaogu Xuebao*, 1956.1, p. 54, fig. 12.4.

10. Within the cemetery site of Lizhaishan twenty-seven tombs were excavated. These were divided into three groups by the excavation team from the Yunnan Provincial Museum. The twenty-one tombs assigned to group one are highly characteristic of the Dian culture and the report suggests that the Lizhaishan inhabitants may have been kinsmen or vassals of the Dian kings. Group one tombs are considered contemporaneous with those at Shizhaishan. Weaving equipment in Tombs 11, 17, 18, 22, and 23 led to the supposition that these were women's graves, in contrast to the weapon finds in graves 21 and 24 which are supposed to be male burials. "Yunnan Jiangchuan Lizhaishan gumuqun faque xiago" [Excavation of an ancient cemetery at Lizhaishan, Jiangchuan County, Yunnan], *Kaogu Xuebao*, 1975.2, pp. 97-156, particularly figs. 4 and 36.

11. ROM 915.3.258. This loom is part of a large collection of Atayal material transferred to the Royal Ontario Museum from Knox College (now part of the University of Toronto). It was collected between 1872 and 1895 by George Leslie MacKay, missionary for the Presbyterian Church in Canada, while working in northern Taiwan.

12. See George Leslie MacKay, *From far Formosa: The island, its people and missions*, ed. Rev. J.A. MacDonald, New York, Chicago and Toronto, Fleming H. Revell, 1895, pl. facing p. 306. The loom was set up for display in 1944 and photographed without the warp beam (ROMA negative 2915).

13. Tadao Kano, *Tōnan Ajia Minzokugaku Senshigaku Kenkyū* [Studies in ethnology and prehistory of Southeast Asia], vol. 2, Tokyo, Yajima Shobo, 1952; Chen Qilu, *Material culture of the Formosan aborigines*, Taipei, Taiwan Museum, 1968, pp. 100-110; Martin A. Nettleship, "A unique South-east Asian loom", *Man, Journal of the Royal Anthropological Institute*, vol. 5, no. 4 (Dec. 1970), pp. 686-698.

14. Chen, *Material culture* (1968), p. 103, fig. 29.

15. Chen, *Material culture* (1968), p. 104, fig. 30 (upper) .

16. Chen, *Material culture* (1968), p. 105, fig. 31 (upper) .

17. Chen, *Material culture* (1968), p. 102, fig. 28; Kano, *Studies in ethnology* (1952), pl. 3, fig. 2; Nettleship, "A unique loom" (1970), fig. 1 (based on Chen's fig. 28); and Wu Yanhe, "Becoming a Seqoleq – socialization processes of the Nan-ao Atayal", *Academia Sinica Bulletin of the Institute of Ethnology*, no. 16 (Autumn 1963), pl. 8:2.

18. ROM 964.264, parts of an Atayal loom collected by Richard J. Pearson near Shakiyo in the central Taiwanese mountain range.

19. See note 17.

20. Catalogued by H.B. Burnham, Textile Department, ROM, presumably on information supplied with loom. No additional documentation has been found.

21. Chen, *Material culture* (1968), p. 104, fig. 30 (lower).

22. H.E. Kauffman, "Das Weben in den Naga-Bergen (Assam)", *Zeitschrift für Ethnologie*, vol. 69 (1937), pp. 113-135, fig. 112; Chen, *Material culture* (1968), p. 109.

23. Paul Huard and A. Maurice, "Les Mnong du plateau central indochinois", *Institut indochinois pour l'étude de l'homme, travaux et mémoires*, vol. 2, pt. 1 (1939), pp. 27-148; other illustrations in Howard Sochurek, "Viet Nam's Montagnards", *National Geographic*, vol. 133 (1968), pp. 443-487.

24. Jean Boulbet, "Modes et techniques du pays Maa' ", *Bulletin de l'Ecole Française d'Extrême-Orient*, vol. 52, no. 2 (1965), pp. 359-415, particularly pls. 21–24, 32; Kano, *Studies in ethnology* (1952), pl. 1, fig. 1.

25. Hans Stübel, *Die Li-Stamme der Insel Hainan*, Berlin, 1937, pl. 42, p. 154; Chen, *Material culture* (1968), p. 109; Kano, *Studies in ethnology* (1952), pl. 2, fig. 2.

26. B.M. Goslings, "Het primitefste der primitieve Indonesische weefgetouwen" [The most simple of all simple looms in Indonesia], *Nederlansche Indië Oude-en-Nieuwe*, no. 13 (1928-1929), pp. 119-121, fig. 13; G.J. Held, *De papoea cultuur improvisator*, Den Haag, Wivan Hoene, 1951, p. 12.

27. Goslings, "Het primitefste" (1928-1929), p. 121; Alfred Bühler, "The development of weaving among primitive peoples", *CIBA Review*, no. 3 (1940), fig. on p. 1078; Christian Kaufmann, *Papua Ningini*, Basel, Museum für Völkerkunde, 1975, fig. 21.

28. Marie Jeanne Adams, "A 'forgotten' bronze ship and a recently discovered bronze weaver from eastern Indonesia", paper read at a Problem Seminar at University Seminars on Primitive and Pre-Columbian Art, Columbia University, 11 February 1972; to be published in *Asian Perspectives*.

29. H. Ling Roth, *Studies in primitive looms*, 3d ed., Halifax, Bankfield Museum, 1950, p. 65, fig. 122 and p. 90, fig. 151.

30. Boulbet, "Modes et techniques" (1965), pl. 21a.

31. Chang Kwang-chih, "A working hypothesis for the early cultural history of South China", *Academia Sinica Bulletin of the Institute of Ethnology*, no. 7 (Spring 1959), pp. 75-103; Pearson, "Dong So' n" (1962).

32. Robert von Heine-Geldern, "L'art pre-boudhique de la Chine et de l'Asie du Sud-est et son influence en Oceanie", *Revue des Arts Asiatiques*, vol. 11 (1937), pp. 177-206.

33. Kano, *Studies in ethnology* (1952).

34. Roth, *Studies in primitive looms* (1950).

35. Song Boyin and Li Zhongyi, "Cong Han Huaxiang Shicaisuo Hantaizhiji Kozau" [Attempt to discover the construction of Han looms from Han relief stones], *Wenwu*, 1962.3, pp. 25-30.

36. Song Chaolin, "Yunnan Xishuang Banna Daizudi fangzhi jishu jiantan gudai fangzhi dijige wenti" [Spinning and weaving technology of the Dai people of Xishuang, Banna, Yunnan Province with discussion of ancient spinning and weaving], *Wenwu*, 1965.4, pp. 6-13.

37. Laying aside considerations of efficiency, circular warping appears in scattered instances across a wide area of southern Asia, extending from the Himalayas to the islands of Melanesia and Micronesia. See Hans Nevermann, *Die indo-ozeanische Weberei*, in the series *Mitteilungen aus dem Museum für Völkerkunde in Hamburg*, vol. 20, Hamburg, 1938, particularly p. 335, fig. 67.
In her study of Lombok body-tension looms (none of which is foot-braced) used for weaving sacred cloths, Rita Bolland ("A comparison between the looms used in Bali and Lombok for weaving sacred cloths", *Tropical Man*, vol. 4, 1971, pp. 171-182) identifies two kinds of loom: type A uses a non-circular warp with laze rods; type B has a circular warp and a lease rod. Although the cutting of the warp, resulting in fringes at either end of the cloth, is an important factor in the use of such tubular cloths, Bolland cannot determine which type of loom is older or more primitive.

The Rise and Spread of Old World Cotton

Andrew M. Watson

WHAT is known about the origin, enno-blement, and early use of the two cotton plants of the Old World, *Gossypium arboreum* L. and *Gossypium herbaceum* L.?[1] To survey the state of our knowledge may seem premature, since uncertainty reigns in several areas and on a few crucial points little or nothing is yet known. But there seem to be several reasons to attempt the task. In the first place, we hope to show that much of the story *can* now be pieced together. Botanists, archae-ologists, historians, and textile specialists—often working in isolation—have all carried out research bearing on this subject; when their findings are as-sembled, and combined with our own research on Islamic sources, large parts of the tale can be told. Where uncertainty still prevails, we shall sometimes be able, by examining what *is* known, to frame hy-potheses to be tested by later investigations. In other cases, we shall at least be able to identify the gaps most urgently needing research and at times to sug-gest the kind of research most likely to bear fruit.

Clouded Origins and Early Development

Botanical investigations have not yet yielded any certain or nearly certain answers about the origin of the Old World cotton plants and their early devel-opment. Until recently most botanists thought that the study of supposedly wild cottons in Asia and Af-rica would locate the primitive forms of *G. arboreum* and *G. herbaceum* and possibly throw light on the places and stages of their ennoblement. Thus in the second half of the nineteenth century, de Candolle, basing his conclusions on the work of a number of researchers, claimed that *G. herbaceum* was developed from certain wild cottons found in present-day Pak-istan, notably *G. stocksii,* and that the ancestors of the domesticated *G. arboreum* were to be found grow-ing wild in Upper Guinea and along the valley of the Upper Nile.[2] Other investigators have put for-ward other theories. A good many have maintained that both plants descend from the wild cottons of India, Pakistan, and Baluchistan.[3] Some have sug-gested different origins: Arabia, the Sudan, or other parts of the Sahara and the savannah lands sur-rounding this desert.[4] More recently, Hutchinson and others have claimed that the primitive ancestor of the Old World cottons is *G. herbaceum* var. *africanum* Watt, which grows wild in Southwest Af-rica and Angola.[5] As the seeds of this plant have no usable lint, and as the cultivation and use of cotton are not known to be ancient in this part of Africa, Hutchinson had further to postulate that this plant reached southern Arabia and the Persian Gulf in prehistoric times—perhaps as a weed or perhaps as a plant cultivated for the oil from its seed—and was developed there as a fibre plant.

Serious doubt, however, has been cast on the value of this kind of deduction by Stephens, who ar-gues, convincingly, that the lint-bearing cottons which appear to grow wild in India, Pakistan, and several parts of Africa are in fact escapes from culti-

XYLON SIVE GOSSIPIVM HERBACEVM: Geim.Baum-vvul: Belg.Blomvvul: Gall. Cotton: It. Cotone, Bombace.

Xylon aliud *Arboreum*, de quo mox, aliud *Herbaceum*: & fert vtrumq; Nucem, quapropter hunc locum tibi vendicant. Hoc ce veteribus plerisque Græcis fuit incognitū, vt illud Theophrasto. Dicitur etiam Latinis *Bambax, Bombyx, Bombax, Bombacium, Bābacium, Cotto,nis*: Cottonum, ni: Cottum,ti: & Cotum,ti. Sed Lanugo ipsa propriè dicitur *Bombax.*

Calidis autem gaudet locis, & Martio atq; Aprili seritur: Septembri & Octobri colligitur. Olim plantabatur solùm in Ægypto, nunc ferè per totam Europam habetur. Vsum quod attinet, nullum Lini genus est quod huic lanugini candore & mollitie præferatur.

XYLON, siue GOSSIPIVM ARBOREVM

Hujus arboris laniferæ, vt annotat Bellonius, primus mentionem fecit Herodotus, quem postea secuti sūt Theophrastus & Plinius, ac plures alij, estque è numero semper virentium.

Dissimile est ab Herbaceo proceritate caudicis, & glabritie foliorum, quæ in Herbaceo hirsuta sunt: Eandem autem quam Herbaceum fert lanuginem.

Nascitur in Ægypto & Arabia, authoribus Alpino & Bellonio: atque ex eo sericeis ipsis tenuiores & subtiliores texunt Arabes telas.

Montbelgardi in S.Principis hōrto vtrūmque Gossypium coluimus. *Plura in Appendice.*

Figure 1.   One of the earliest European botanists to distinguish clearly between *Gossypium arboreum* and *Gossypium herbaceum* was Dominique Chabré (1610 – 1667) in his *Stirpium icones et sciagraphia* (Geneva, 1677).
Courtesy of the Thomas Fisher Rare Book Library, University of Toronto.

vation, incapable of surviving as truly wild plants.[6] Even *G. herbaceum* var. *africanum,* which does grow wild, is not seen by Stephens as the original ancestor of the cultivated cottons but rather as a partially ennobled plant which has escaped and established itself as a wild plant. The true ancestor or ancestors (for there may be more than one) of the cultivated cottons are probably now extinct, having disappeared perhaps because of climatic changes or with the spread of sedentary agriculture. Stephens maintains that the primitive cotton plants must have differed in three fundamental ways from the fibre-bearing plants used by man from prehistoric times onwards: their bolls were often closed and always non-flaring; their fibres were very short, undifferentiated into lint and fuzz, and adhered strongly to the seed coat; and the mature fibres were inelastic, unconvoluted, and narrow in perimeter. In short, the primitive cotton plants could not be used as a source of textile fibre. They may have been used by man initially for the oil pressed from the seeds. How and where a fibre-bearing plant was developed is not clear, nor even whether both *G. arboreum* and *G. herbaceum* spring from a common ancestor. Though further botanical research on wild, semi-primitive forms of Old World cottons and on hybrids of these and more ennobled forms may eventually throw light on the evolutionary path followed by the cultivated plant, for the moment these questions remain unanswered.

Some clues about the origin of the Old World cottons and their early ennoblement are, however, offered by the archaeological and literary evidence. This suggests that the northwestern part of the Indian subcontinent was probably the cradle of cotton cultivation, from which an ennobled plant was diffused to other parts of Asia, the Middle East, Africa, and Europe. Furthermore, the great antiquity of cotton culture in this region makes it unlikely that the plant originated or was ennobled in a very distant part of the world. The earliest clearly identified cotton is found in a fragment of cloth from Mohenjo-Daro in the Indus Valley and may be dated 1760 B.C. ± 115. Microscopic examination suggests that the fibres came from a close relative of *G. arboreum*. Archaeological finds also have yielded bits of cotton fluff spun into silk and flax threads at Nevasa and Chandoli, which lie farther to the south; these may be dated between 1000 and 1500 B.C.[8] Although, rather surprisingly, no certain word for cotton can be found in the earlier Vedic literature, which probably dates from about the same period, there are many references to cotton garments—and a few references to the plant—from the fifth century B.C. onwards.[9] Herodotus (fl. fifth century B.C.) states that in India "wild trees bear wool more beautiful and excellent than the wool of sheep" and that the Indians made clothing from this "wool". Elsewhere he relates that the Indian contingent of the army of Xerxes wore clothes of cotton.[10] The *Kauṭilīya Arthaśāstra*, which perhaps dates from the late fourth century B.C., suggests that the cotton industry was already highly organized and an object of concern to governments: one learns in these texts of a Superintendent of Yarns who was to have thread spun by widows and crippled women, of "mills" for the weaving of cloth, and of a Director of Agriculture responsible for the collection and sowing of cotton seeds.[11] Other texts describe the different stages in the manufacture of yarn and cloth, and the ginning of cotton is depicted in a wall-painting at Ajanta which dates from about the sixth century A.D.[12] By about that time the *Bṛhatsaṃhitā* implies that cotton was an important crop and the chief fibre for garments.[13]

Quite early, however, the cultivation of cotton seems to have spread outward from India, though there is much room for doubt as to the extent of this diffusion. Cotton cultivation probably reached the island of Tylos, or Bahrain, and possibly other parts of the Persian Gulf in ancient times; for accounts of the "wool-bearing tree" of the island were carried back by Alexander's naval expedition to the eastern seas in 323 B.C.[14] From the Persian Gulf, or perhaps directly from India, it may have spread to Arabia Felix. Theophrastus and Pliny, who are perhaps not reliable on this point, repeat reports that tree cotton grew there, and the shrouds found in some Himyari-

tic graves were made of cotton that may have been locally grown.[15] The growing of cotton may also have spread into Ethiopia, Nubia, and Upper Egypt. Julius Pollux and Pliny speak of the cotton "trees", "bushes", or "shrubs" which grew in Ethiopia and Upper Egypt, and an Axumite inscription of A.D. 350 claims the destruction of Nubian cotton supplies.[16] Fragments of cotton cloth dating from the first seven centuries of the Christian era have been found at the Nubian sites of Karanog, Meroë, ᶜAdda, and Ibrīm, while other cloths dating from the fourth to seventh centuries have been found in the Upper Egyptian monastery of Phoebamon.[17] Whether the fibres from which these cloths were woven, or the stocks of cotton destroyed by the Axumites, were locally grown is difficult to know; but microscopic examination of some of the cloths from Karanog suggests that the fibres may have come from a plant similar to a Sudanese variety of *G. arboreum*. Cotton does not seem to have been grown in Lower Egypt or in the Mediterranean in pre-Islamic times.[18] Interestingly enough, however, it probably was cultivated by post-Biblical times in the area of Lake Tiberias and in the Jordan valley; for it is mentioned in both the Mishna and the Palestinian Talmud, and in the sixth century Gregory of Tours, writing of the area around Jericho, speaks of "arbores quae lanas gignunt" and of the whiteness and fineness of the cloths made from their fibres.[19]

While cotton cultivation was spreading westward from India, it also seems to have been diffused to the East. From a work composed from Han materials between A.D. 318 and 445, we learn that the Ai-Lao "barbarians" grew cotton along the banks of the Irrawaddy River. Another Han work, written in either the first or second century A.D., speaks of the cotton tree grown in Indochina and in Kuangtung; and writings of the third to sixth centuries A.D. show that cotton—sometimes described as the cotton tree—was cultivated in the southerly provinces of Kuangtung and Yünnan.[20] Elsewhere in China cotton does not seem to have been grown before the seventh century, or even much later, and the Chinese seem to have been only slightly familiar with the exotic cloth woven from its fibres.[21] Although the diffusion of the plant into Southeast Asia is not well documented, it appears to have occurred there

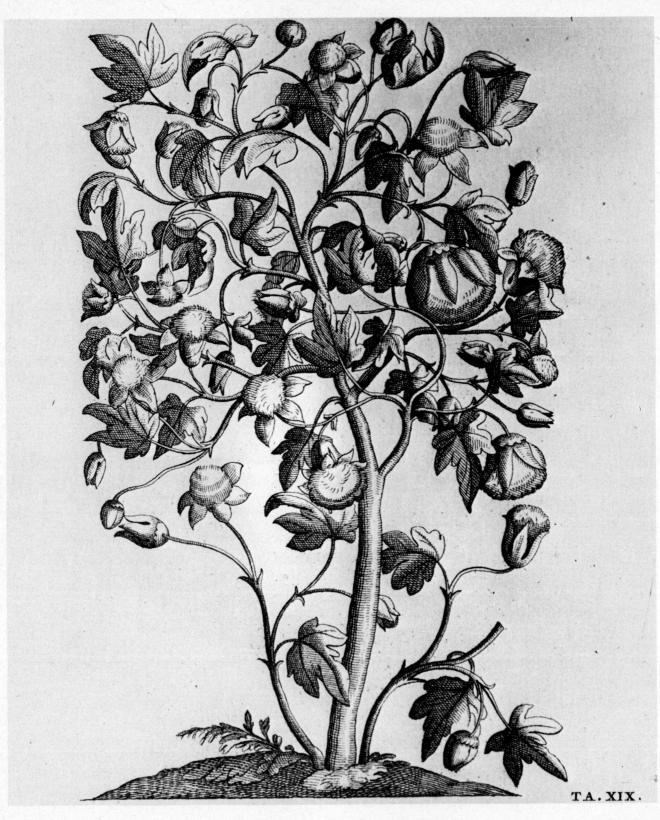

Figure 2.   *Gossypium arboreum* illustrated in Prosper Alpino's *De plantis Aegypti liber* (Leyden, 1735).

T.A. XIX.

at about the same time as in China. In A.D. 430 a gift of cotton was sent from Java or Sumatra to the Chinese court, while in A.D. 523 a mission arrived in Nanking bearing cotton goods from either Sumatra or Malaya.[22] According to one legend, a Hindu from Indonesia or Malaya, shipwrecked in Japan, was responsible for introducing the cotton plant to that country in A.D. 799 or 800; but as there is no further mention of cotton growing in Japan for many centuries this introduction seems to have failed.[23]

Diffusion in Islamic Times till A.D. 1500

One of the curious facts of the diffusion of cotton cultivation in pre-Islamic times is that it seems to have been strictly confined to regions with very warm climates where heavy watering was available from rainfall or artificial irrigation. In fact, the region of this early diffusion corresponds very closely to the present-day distribution of *G. arboreum,* which Harland gives as India, Malaya, and South China, with some diffusion into Abyssinia and the Sudan.[24]

Was *G. arboreum* then the only cotton plant known in pre-Islamic times? This hypothesis receives some slight confirmation from the microscopic examination of archaeological finds: the fibres of the very early piece of cotton cloth from Mohenjo-Daro and some early Christian fragments from Nubia appeared to those who have examined them to be *G. arboreum.*[25] The literary evidence might also confirm this suggestion, since all the descriptions of the plants speak of trees, shrubs, or bushes. Even the ninth-century Persian scholar, Abū Ḥanīfa al-Dīnawarī, seems to have heard only of an arborescent cotton: "The cotton trees [in the lands of Kalb tribe] grow high until they look like apricot trees, and last twenty years."[26] But since there are perennial forms of *G. herbaceum* which, after a number of years, take the form of a bush, we cannot be certain that *G. herbaceum* was unknown. Both species may have been cultivated over greater or smaller areas in their perennial forms.

What does seem clear, however, is that a fundamental obstacle to the northward diffusion of the cotton plant in pre-Islamic times was the absence of annual varieties which could mature in a shorter, colder season towards the end of which the days were markedly shorter. If *G. herbaceum* was known at all—and there is no clear evidence of it—it must have existed only in the perennial form. The annual varieties of both species, capable of a more northerly diffusion, had yet to be developed. This fact no doubt explains the apparent lack of success of an Assyrian king, Sennacherib, in introducing the cotton plant into Mesopotamia in the seventh century B.C.,[27] as well as the probable failure to establish it in Japan at the end of the eighth century A.D.[28]

Where and when the new plant was developed is not certain, but there is now some evidence that it made an early appearance, if not its first, in the eastern part of Central Asia. A Chinese work of the late sixth and early seventh centuries A.D. stated that in the region of Turfan in Sinkiang "there grows in great abundance a plant, the fruit of which resembles a silk cocoon; the natives weave [the fibre] into a cloth which is soft and white, and send it to the markets of China."[29] By the eighth century other texts related that cotton was sent as tribute from the Turfan region to the Chinese court.[30] In the western part of Sinkiang, near Khotan, archaeologists have discovered a small pile of cotton seeds dating from about the eighth century, which they take as clear evidence of cotton cultivation in the region.[31] Cotton seeds and fragments of cotton cloth have also been found at a ninth-century site near Kashgar in western Sinkiang; the seeds have been identified by the Chinese Academy of Sciences as *G. herbaceum.*[32] Archaeologists have also discovered in the region of Lop-nor in Sinkiang a good many fragments of cotton cloth which appear to date from roughly the same period, and which may have been made from locally grown fibre.[33] By Tang times (A.D. 618–907) cotton seems also to have been grown in the province of Lung-yu (corresponding approximately to the modern Kansu), from which it was exacted as official tribute.[34] Though the archaeological reports on the finds of seeds and fragments of cloth do not specify the variety of cotton plant, it must in every case have been an annual variety of either *G.*

arboreum or, more probably, *G. herbaceum,* which could survive in the region's harsh, continental climate.

The new plant, however, seems to have encountered obstacles to its outward diffusion, for it did not make much progress for several centuries. Perhaps these difficulties were simply those which any new crop might meet where communications were poor and peasants conservative, compounded no doubt by the challenge of growing this particular crop in a hostile environment—especially in early times when the varieties available may not have been very resistant to drought or cold. But the factor most important in slowing down the crop's diffusion may have had to do rather with industrial technology: workers may have learned only with difficulty the techniques of ginning, spinning, or weaving this new fibre. Several modern writers have suggested that the widespread diffusion of cotton into China had to await improvements in the technology of ginning, while a Chinese source tells of a woman who, in the thirteenth century, brought to the lower Yangtze region superior spinning and weaving techniques which greatly improved the industry.[35] The evidence concerning the cotton or partly cotton cloths from the early Islamic world, and even from pre-Islamic times, may also be revealing. As early as the second century B.C., Julius Pollux wrote that cotton (perhaps grown in Upper Egypt or Nubia) was used only for the weft thread, linen being used for the warp. Similarly, in the early Islamic world the earliest cloths in which cotton or partly cotton threads were used usually, though not always, had warps of linen, silk, or wool.[36] The all-cotton cloths produced in the Yaman in the ninth and tenth centuries A.D. had warp threads which were very coarse and close together, while the weft threads were fine and widely spaced.[37] Whether this evidence of the textiles is in fact proof of technological difficulties in using cotton for the warp, and whether these difficulties attached only to the new annual varieties or to all varieties of one or both species of Old World cotton, are questions that deserve investigation but cannot at present be answered.

But if any obstacles did slow the progress of *G. herbaceum* through more temperate climates, they were eventually overcome. For after a delay of several centuries following its apparent development the new plant was widely diffused through Asia, the Middle East, and Africa; it also had a limited diffusion into parts of Mediterranean Europe. Several scholars have suggested that it reached the central part of China by two routes: from Sinkiang in the west and from Indochina in the south. An introduction from Indochina seems unlikely, however, since there is no evidence that an annual, herbaceous cotton plant was known there before it appeared in central China or even long afterwards. The western route seems the more probable, though there is still no evidence to support this route either. All we know from the sources is that by the thirteenth century cotton was sent as tribute by the eastern provinces of Hunan, Hupeh, Fukien, Chekiang, and Kiangsu, and by the central provinces of Szechwan, Shansi, and Shensi, where it was presumably grown.[38] A fifteenth-century source stated that "by our times [cotton] has spread throughout the Empire; it is used a hundred times more than silk or hemp."[39] Various texts on the cultivation of the plant describe what are clearly varieties of an annual, herbaceous cotton.[40] The stages in the processing of the fibre in China are outlined by several authors.[41]

Moving westward, the new cotton plant was diffused through the whole of the mediaeval Islamic world up to the frontiers of Christian Europe and pagan Black Africa. Although almost nothing is known of the process of diffusion, by the tenth century cotton was found growing in almost every region of the Islamic world. Cotton industries sprang up around centres of cultivation, many producing specialty cloths or garments for export. A network of intermediaries arose to channel raw cotton to the workshop, the semi-finished product through the various stages of manufacture, and the finished good to its ultimate, often distant destination.[42]

In the eastern part of the Islamic world, cotton was grown on a very wide scale. A number of authors tell of its cultivation at many places in both Upper and Lower Mesopotamia; in the early tenth century, the technique of growing the plant there was described in detail by the agricultural writer, Ibn Waḥshīya.[43] In Iran cotton is mentioned at scores of places and in almost every region.[44] Still farther to the east, it was found in various parts of Transoxania, and in the thirteenth century Marco

A   B

C

Figure 3.   Stages in the manufacture of cotton cloth illustrated in a Persian manuscript. *A*: ginning the raw cotton with a roller. *B* and *C*: carding the raw cotton with a bow. *D*: preparing the warp (?). *Muftāḥ al-Fuẓala* by Muḥammad b. Dāʾūd b. Muḥammad Shādiyābādī, probably late fifteenth century. British Library, Oriental Manuscripts OR 3299. Courtesy of the British Library, London.

D

Polo saw it growing abundantly in Kashgar.[45] The sources speak often of the great variety of cotton goods made in Iraq, Persia, and Turkestan; they relate that Baghdad had a special wharf for the cotton merchants and a house for trading cotton.[46] In the Arabian peninsula, cotton was grown at Bahrain, in the Yaman, and in the Hejaz; there were several famous centres of cotton manufacture in the Yaman and on the island of Sokotra.[47] Many travellers saw cotton growing in different parts of Palestine, Syria, and Asia Minor; probably from here the plant was taken to Greece, the Aegean Islands, and Cyprus.[48] By the twelfth century, cotton from the Levant and Cyprus was exported to Italy.[49]

Many places in the western part of Dār al-Islām —Egypt, the Maghrib, Spain, and Sicily—also came to grow cotton and make cotton goods. There is much evidence that cotton was traded in Egypt in the early centuries of Islam;[50] one papyrus of the eighth or ninth century suggests that cotton was an article of common use in households.[51] By the end of the tenth century, the geographer, Ibn Ḥauqal, states that cotton was grown in Egypt.[52] But it may not have become an important crop until later: even in the eleventh century, al-Thaʿālibī remarked that "people know that cotton belongs to Khurāsān [in the region of Merv] and linen to Egypt."[53] By the thirteenth century, however, there is clear evidence that cotton had become a major crop in Egypt; the sources from this time onwards speak of it growing in Nubia, Upper Egypt, the Delta, and the Fayyūm.[54] Although some cotton cloth was still imported into Egypt even in the fifteenth century, Egyptian cotton was also sent from Alexandria to Europe.[55] Farther to the west, Ibn Ḥauqal and later travellers noted cotton growing in Tripolitania, around Tunis and Carthage, on the island of Pantellaria, and near several towns in present-day Algeria; cottons from Djerba, Tunis, and other parts of

Ifrīqiya were exported to Spain and Italy.[56] Cotton cultivation was probably taken from Tunis to Sicily, where it was noted in Islamic times or after the Norman conquest near Catania, Agrigento, Mazara, and Giattini.[57] In Morocco, the sources speak of the growing of cotton in many places.[58] In Spain, cotton cultivation is first mentioned in sources of the ninth and tenth centuries, and the manner of growing it is later described by the agronomists Abū al-Khair, Ibn Baṣṣāl, and Ibn al-ʿAwwām.[59] Although the early sources speak of its cultivation only in the south, notably in the Algarve and in the hinterland of Seville and Elvira, later sources state that it was also grown at Guadix and, more surprisingly, in Valencia and Majorca. Andalusian cottons were exported to other parts of Spain and to the cities of the North African coast.[60]

Cotton was diffused by Muslims not only to Mediterranean Europe but also to parts of Black Africa, both along the east coast and in the west. This diffusion was closely connected with the penetration of Islam into Africa, since Islam taught—in practice if not in doctrine—that the faithful should be clothed, preferably from the neck to the ankles, with only the head, hands, and feet showing. Wherever Muslims settled in Africa, or wherever converts were made, clothes appeared: the rich had expensive cotton garments made from imported cloth, while the poor, though they might have a fine robe for feast days, usually went about in simple cotton shirts or something which offered less cover. The greater part of the demand for cotton seems to have been supplied locally, for we learn of many places in which cotton was grown and many places where it was spun. Thus an entirely new demand came hand in hand with a radically new religion. And not long after, over the same routes, came an altogether new industry to satisfy that demand.[61]

Pinnacle—and Decline

By the end of the European Middle Ages, cotton cultivation had spread across nearly the whole of the Eurasian continent below the 40th parallel, from the Atlantic to the Pacific, and in some places had reached still farther north. Cotton was also grown widely in Africa north of the Sahara and in many other parts of that continent. Over nearly all of this vast area and beyond, cotton had become the chief fibre from which clothes were made, and had revolutionized the textile industry. The cotton plant was also used in a variety of other ways: the fibres were used to stuff the quilts, mattresses, and pillows with which houses in the cotton-growing world abounded, and the seeds yielded an oil which had culinary, industrial, and medical uses. By 1500 the cotton plants of the Old World were at their zenith. In the centuries following the Voyages of Discovery they were in large measure eclipsed by new, long-fibred cotton plants from the New World. But the ease with which these new plants could displace the old may be explained by the tastes, agricultural skills, and industrial techniques which had been acquired in the Old World with *G. arboreum* and *G. herbaceum* over a period of more than three millennia.

Notes

I should like to acknowledge generous help received from Dr. Miquel Barceló, Miss Elisabeth Crowfoot, Dr. Veronika Gervers, the Reverend William Hayes, Professor Karl Helleiner, Mr. John Irwin, Professor Maureen Mazzaoui, Professors Thomas and Evelyn Rawski, Professor Roger Savory, Dr. Hsio-yen Shih, Dr. S.G. Stephens, Professor G.M. Wickens, and Professor A.K. Warder.

1. *G. arboreum* L. and *G. herbaceum* L. are sometimes erroneously referred to as tree cotton and herbaceous cotton. In fact, both species have perennial forms which develop into bushes or shrubs, and both have "herbaceous" annual forms; these latter were almost certainly late developments. The term "Old World cotton" is used to distinguish *G. arboreum* L. and *G. herbaceum* L., and their ancestors and relatives (which appear to have originated in Asia or Africa), from the possibly more ancient "New World cotton", *G. barbadense* L. and *G. hirsutum* L., and their ancestors and relatives (which appear to have originated in some part of the Pacific or in the Americas). Researches of botanists in Russia, America, and England during the 1920s showed that these two families are botanically distinct: the Old World species are diploids with thirteen chromosomes ($2n = 26$), while the New World species are amphidiploids with twenty-six chromosomes ($2n = 52$). They can be crossed only with great difficulty. See S.C. Harland, *The genetics of cotton*, London, Jonathan Cape, 1939, p. 42f.; and G.S. Zaitzev, "Un hybride entre les cotonniers asiatiques et américains: *Gossypium herbaceum* L. et *G. hirsutum* L.", *Revue de Botanique Appliquée*, vol. 5 (1925), pp. 628–629.

2. A. de Candolle, *Origin of cultivated plants*, New York, Appleton, 1886, pp. 402–408.

3. Sir G. Watt, *The wild and cultivated cotton plants of the world*, London, Longman, 1907; N.I. Vavilov, *The origin, variation, immunity and breeding of cultivated plants*, Waltham, Mass., 1951, p. 28; Sir J. Hutchinson, et al., *The evolution of* Gossypium, London, Oxford University Press, 1947 (though as will be seen in note 5 the authors appear to have abandoned the view put forward in this book); and P.M. Žukovskij, *Cultivated plants and their wild relatives*, trans. P.S. Hudson, Farnham Royal, Commonwealth Agricultural Bureaux, 1962, pp. 74-81.

4. A. Chevalier, "La systématique des cotonniers cultivés ou ayant été cultivés anciennement en Afrique tropicale", *Revue Internationale de Botanique Appliquée et d'Agriculture Tropicale*, vol. 28 (1948), pp. 228–241, and "Le Sahara, centre d'origine des plantes cultivées", *Mémoires de la Société de Biogéographie*, vol. 6 (1938), pp. 318–319; Sir J. Hutchinson, "The dissemination of cotton in Africa", *Empire Cotton Growing Review*, vol. 26 (1949), pp. 256–270; G. Roberty, "Hypothèses sur l'origine et les migrations des cotonniers cultivés et notes sur les cotonniers sauvages", *Candollea*, vol. 7 (1938), pp. 297–360; G.P. Murdock, *Africa: Its people and their culture history*, New York, McGraw-Hill, 1959, p. 64 f. With regard to Murdock's views, however, see H.G. Baker, "Comments on the thesis that there was a major centre of plant domestication near the headwaters of the River Niger", *Journal of African History*, vol. 3 (1962), pp. 229–233.

5. Sir J. Hutchinson, "New evidence on the origin of the Old World cottons", *Heredity*, vol. 8 (1954), pp. 225–241, and *The application of genetics to cotton improvement*, Cambridge, 1959, p. 11 f.

6. S.G. Stephens, *Factors affecting seed dispersal in* Gossypium *and their possible evolutionary significance*, North Carolina Agricultural Experiment Station Technical Bulletin No. 131, Raleigh, N.C., 1958. In a personal communication to this author, Professor Stephens has pointed out that *G. herbaceum* var. *africanum* is found along old caravan routes, a fact which suggests that it is feral rather than truly wild. On the other hand, he states that the fibre pigments more closely resemble those of a wild plant than those of a cultivated plant. One African cotton plant, *G. anomalum* Wawr. and Peyr., is truly wild; but although it will produce a weak, fertile hybrid with the Old World cottons, it seems to be only a distant relative of the ancestor of these.

7. Sir J. Marshall, *Mohenjo-Daro and the Indus civilization*, London, A. Probsthain, 1931, vol. 1, pp. 33, 194, and vol. 2, pp. 585–586; A.N. Gulati and A.J. Turner, *A note on the early history of cotton*, Indian Central Cotton Committee Technological Laboratory Bulletin No. 17, Bombay, 1928; this article also appeared in *Journal of the Textile Institute*, vol. 20 (1929), Transactions, pp. 1-9. These authors date this material at about 3000 B.C. However, recent revisions in the chronology of Harappan culture, based partly on carbon-14 datings, suggest that the

late-level material from Mohenjo-Daro should be dated about 1760 B.C. ± 115. See B.B. Lal, "A picture emerges: An assessment of the carbon-14 datings of the protohistoric cultures of the Indo-Pakistan sub-continent", *Ancient India,* vol. 18–19 (1962–1963), pp. 213–214; and B. and R. Allchin, *The birth of Indian civilization,* Harmondsworth, Penguin, 1968, p. 337.

8. Allchin, *Indian civilization* (1968), p. 264; J. Clutton-Brock, V. Mittre, and A.N. Gulati, *Technical reports on archeological remains,* Poona, Deccan College Post-Graduate and Research Institute, 1961, pp. 56–58.

9. These are summarized in L. Gopal, "Textiles in ancient India", *Journal of the Economic and Social History of the Orient,* vol. 4 (1961), pp. 60–61.

10. A.D. Godley, ed. and trans., *Herodotus,* London/New York, Heinemann, 1921–1924, vol. 2, pp. 123–135 (Book 3, 106); vol. 3, pp. 178–179 (Book 7, 65). The fact that Herodotus describes the trees as "wild" is interesting but, in view of his unreliability, may not be significant.

11. Kauṭalya, *The Kauṭilīya Arthraśāstra,* ed. and trans. R.P. Kangle, Bombay, University of Bombay, 1960–1965, vol. 2, pp. 168–171.

12. D. Schlingloff, "Cotton manufacture in ancient India", *Journal of the Economic and Social History of the Orient,* vol. 17 (1974), pp. 81–90.

13. *Bṛhatsaṁhitā,* Book 94, 15, as cited in Gopal, "Textiles" (1961), p. 61, n. 3.

14. H. Bretzl, *Botanische Forschungen des Alexanderzuges,* Leipzig, 1903, p. 136 f. The information gleaned on this voyage was used by Theophrastus (370–ca. 285 B.C.) and Pliny the Elder (A.D. 23–79). See Theophrastus, *Enquiry into plants,* ed. and trans. Sir A. Hort, London/New York, Heinemann, 1916, vol. 1, pp. 342–345 (Book 4, 7); Pliny, *Historia naturalis,* ed. and trans. H. Rockham, London/Cambridge, Mass., Heinemann and Harvard, 1942–1962, vol. 4, p. 29 (Book 12, 21–22).

15. For references in Theophrastus and Pliny, see above. The information about the Himyaritic graves is given in A. Grohmann, *Südarabien als Wirtschaftsgebiet,* Schriften der Philosophischen Fakultät der Deutschen Universität in Prag, vol. 7, p. 260 f. and vol. 13, p. 40 f.

16. Julius Pollux (fl. 2d c. B.C.), in *Onomasticon,* ed. W. Dindorf, Leipzig, Kühn, 1824, vol. 2, p. 79 (Book 7, 75), says only that "Egyptians" make clothes from mixed linen and cotton fabrics, and describes the "tree" from which cotton is obtained; Pliny, *Historia,* vol. 4, pp. 152–153 (Book 13, 28) and vol. 5, pp. 428–429 (Book 19, 2). The text of the Axumite inscription is given in E. von Littmann, *Deutsche Aksum-Expedition,* Berlin, Staatliche Museen, 1913, vol. 4, p. 33. See also G.E. Nicholson, "The production, history, uses and relationships of cotton (*Gossypium* spp.) in Ethiopia", *Economic Botany,* vol. 14 (1960), pp. 3–36.

17. A.M. Greiss, "Les plus anciens spécimens de tissus et de fibres de coton découverts en Egypte", *Chronique d'Egypte,* vol. 27 (1952), pp. 321–323; and *Anatomical identification of some ancient Egyptian plant materials,* Mémoires de l'Institut d'Egypte, vol. 55, Cairo, 1957, pp. 104–105, 122; F.L. Griffith and G.M. Crowfoot, "On the early use of cotton in the Nile Valley", *Journal of Egyptian Archaeology,* vol. 20 (1934), pp. 5–12; R. Pfister, "Toiles à inscriptions abbasides et fatimides", *Bulletin d'Études Orientales,* vol. 11 (1945–1946), p. 10; R.E. Massey, "A note on the early history of cotton", *Sudan Notes and Records,* vol. 6 (1923), p. 231. Miss Elisabeth Crowfoot has kindly sent me two samples (T.214 and T. 237) of threads from Ibrīm in Egyptian Nubia, dating from the late Meroitic and X-group periods (up to A.D. 600); these have been identified by Veronika Gervers as cotton. The expedition of the Royal Ontario Museum to ᶜAdda, under the direction of Dr. N. Millet, has discovered many fragments of cloth dating from late Meroitic, X-group, and Early Christian times; some of these, coming from Cemetery III (tombs 26, 645, 778, 807, and 821), have been identified by Veronika Gervers as cotton.

18. This point is discussed in Pfister, "Toiles" (1945–1946), p. 10.

19. Cotton does not seem to have been grown in the Near East in biblical times. See H. Moldenke, "The economic plants of the Bible", *Economic Botany,* vol. 8 (1954), p. 162; and I. Löw, *Die Flora der Juden,* Vienna/Leipzig, R. Löwit, 1926–1934, vol. 2, pp. 235–243. However, identical passages referring to its cultivation appear in later Jewish literature, which may be dated roughly from the third to the fifth centuries A.D. See *The Mishnah,* trans. H. Danby, London, Oxford University Press, 1933, p. 36 (Kil. 7, 2); and *Le Talmud de Jérusalem,* trans. M. Schwab, Paris, Maisonneuve, 1878–1890, vol. 2, p. 291 (Kil. 7, 1). See also Gregory of Tours, "Liber in gloria martyrum", in *Monumenta Germaniae Historica: Scriptorum rerum Merovingicarum,* Hanover, Hahn, 1855, vol. 1, p. 499. It has also been shown that cotton was known to the seventh-century writer Jacob of Edessa, but it is not clear from the text whether this is a plant which Jacob had seen in the Near East. See A. Hjelt, "Pflanzennamen aus dem Hexaëmeron Jacob's von Edessa", in *Orientalische Studien Theodor Nöldeke,* ed. C. Bezold, Giessen, A. Töpelmann, 1906, vol. 1, p. 579. At Palmyra, which was abandoned in A.D. 273, small amounts of cotton or partly cotton cloth have been found, but these are thought to have been imports from India. See R. Pfister, *Textiles de Palmyre,* Paris, Editions d'art et d'histoire, 1934–1940, vol. 1, pp. 13, 22; vol. 2, p. 16; vol. 3, pp. 11, 18; and *Nouveaux textiles de Palmyre,* Paris, Editions d'art et d'histoire, 1937, pp. 16, 20–21. Similarly, the few pieces of cotton cloth found at the sixth-century site of Zenobia are considered to be Indian. R. Pfister, *Les textiles de Halabiyeh (Zenobia),* Paris, Geuthner, 1951, pp. 9, 32. However, in C.J. Lamm, *Cotton in medieval textiles of the Near East,* Paris, Geuthner, 1937, pp. 8–10, it is suggested that some partly cotton cloths

were made in "Syria" in the two centuries before the Arab conquests, as must indeed have been the case if cotton was grown in the region at this time. A passage in the writings of Pausanias (fl. 5th c. B.C.), in which the author speaks of *byssos* growing in the island of Elis in the Aegean, has sometimes been cited as proof of cotton cultivation in ancient Greece. See Pausanias, *Description of Greece,* ed. and trans. W.H. Jones, London, Heinemann, 1918, vol. 2, p. 400 (Book 5, 5). However, this interpretation is almost certainly wrong. The word *byssos,* which also appears on the Rosetta Stone, is normally used for flax and linen. Where cotton is intended (as in the text of Julius Pollux referred to above in note 16), this special meaning is clearly indicated.

20. *Hou Han Shu, I Wu Chih,* and other works cited in K. Wittfogel and Fêng Chia-Shêng, *History of Chinese society: Liao (907–1125),* Transactions of the American Philosophical Society, n.s., vol. 36 (1949), pp. 155–156, n. 74; P. Pelliot, *Notes on Marco Polo,* Paris, A. Maisonneuve, 1959–1963, vol. 1, pp. 444, 463, 473, 489–491; C. Dietrich, "Cotton culture and manufacture in early Ch'ing China", in *Economic organization in Chinese society,* ed. W.E. Wilmott, Stanford, Stanford University Press, 1972, p. 111. Evidence of a large cotton industry in Kwangtung is given in E.H. Schafer, *The vermilion bird: T'ang images of the south,* Berkeley/Los Angeles, University of California Press, 1967, pp. 180–181.

21. B. Laufer, *Sino-Iranica,* Chicago, Field Museum, 1919, pp. 491–492; Dietrich, "Cotton" (1972), pp. 110–111; Wittfogel and Fêng, *History* (1949), pp. 157–158; n. 74; L.C. Goodrich, "Cotton in China", *Isis,* vol. 34 (1942–1943), p. 408; Pelliot, *Notes* (1959–1963), p. 491; Motonosuke Amano, *Chūgoku nōgyō-shi kenkyū* [Studies in Chinese agricultural history], Tokyo, 1962, pp. 482–498. Professor Evelyn Rawski kindly translated the relevant passages of this book for me.

22. Chau Ju-Kua, *Chu-fan-chi,* ed. and trans. F . Hirth and W.W. Rockhill, Amsterdam, Oriental Press, 1966, p. 218; Goodrich, "Cotton" (1942–1943), p. 408.

23. Pelliot, *Notes* (1959–1963), p. 456.

24. Harland, *Genetics* (1939), p. 31; and H.R. Mauersberger, ed., *Mathews' textile fibres: Their physical, microscopic and chemical properties,* 6th ed., New York/London, Wiley, 1954, p. 120. It is interesting to note that the present-day distribution of *G. herbaceum* is quite different: on p. 32, Harland gives this as most of India (especially the northwest), Turkey, Persia, Iraq, Turkestan, southeastern Europe, and some areas of Africa.

25. Gulati and Turner, *A note* (1928); Griffith and Crowfoot, "Cotton in the Nile Valley" (1934).

26. Abū Ḥanīfa al-Dīnawarī, *Le dictionnaire botanique d'Abū Ḥanīfa ad-Dīnawarī,* ed. M. Hamidullah, Cairo, Institut Français d'Archéologie Orientale du Caire, 1973, p. 217.

27. G. Goossens, "Le coton en Assyrie", *Annuaire de l'Institut de Philosophie et d'Histoire Orientales et Slaves,* vol. 12 (1952), pp. 167–176.

28. See note 23 above. The fact that cotton was grown in pre-Islamic times in the Jordan Valley, a region which is much more northerly than the other areas where cotton was grown in early times, is explained by the exceedingly hot climate of the Jordan Valley, much of which lies below sea level.

29. Yao Ssu-lien (d. A.D. 637), *Liang-shu,* cited in Chau Ju-Kua, *Chu-fan-chi* (1966), p. 218.

30. Pelliot, *Notes* (1959–1963), p. 491.

31. Sir A. Stein, *Serindia,* Oxford, Oxford University Press, 1921, vol. 1, p. 160.

32. Bi-ti Sha, "Cong kaogufajueziliao kan Xinjiang qudai de mianhua zhongzhi he fangzhi" [A glance at cotton culture and weaving in ancient Sinkiang based upon archeological evidence], *Wenwu* (1973), pp. 48–51. I am grateful to Dr. Hsio-yen Shih for drawing my attention to this report and for translating the relevant parts.

33. F. Bergman, *Archeological researches in Sinkiang. Reports from the scientific expedition to the north-western provinces of China under the leadership of Sven Hedin,* vol. 7, Stockholm, Thule, 1939, pp. 56–57, 103–105, 111, 114–117; and Stein, *Serindia* (1921), vol. 1, pp. 339, 423, 435. Not all of this material can be easily dated. Bergman suggests ca. A.D. 600–1000 for the piece given on pp. 56–57. The pieces mentioned by Stein in vol. 1, p. 435, were found at a site which was abandoned in the fourth century A.D. See also the study by Dr. Hsio-yen Shih in this volume.

34. E.H. Schafer, *The golden peaches of Samarkand: A study of T'ang exotics,* Berkeley and Los Angeles, University of California Press, 1963, p. 106.

35. E.g., Dietrich, "Cotton" (1972), p. 110. It is difficult to see, however, why the simple techniques of ginning which allowed the industry to be established on a wide scale in India were not adequate for China. For the introduction of new ginning techniques into China, see Pelliot, *Notes* (1959–1963), pp. 457, 484–485; J. Needham, *Science and civilisation in China,* Cambridge, Cambridge University Press, 1965-, vol. 4, pt. 2, pp. 122–124. On the story of the woman who introduced new spinning and weaving techniques, see Goodrich, "Cotton" (1942–1943), pp. 408–409; Amano, *Chūgoku* (1962), p. 495; Pelliot, *Notes* (1959–1963), pp. 484–485.

36. Lamm, *Cotton* (1937), passim; Pfister, "Toiles" (1945–1946), p. 84 f.; N.P. Britton, *A study of some early Islamic textiles in the Museum of Fine Arts, Boston,* Boston, Museum of Fine Arts, 1938, pp. 29–39; E. Kühnel and L. Bellinger, *Washington D.C. Textile Museum: Catalogue of dated tiraz fabrics,* Washington,

Textile Museum, 1952, pp. 10, 14, 19. Two early Islamic textile fragments with silk warp and cotton weft are in the collection of the Royal Ontario Museum: 963.95.8 (Iraq, late tenth century) and 963.95.3 (Persia, tenth century?). See also the study on the Toronto *tiraz* collection by L. Golombek and V. Gervers in this volume. In Europe, too, cotton threads were used almost exclusively in the weft throughout the Middle Ages. See F. Borlandi, " 'Futaniers' et futaines dans l'Italie du moyen âge", in *Hommage à Lucien Febvre*, 2 vols., Paris, Colin, 1953, vol. 2, pp. 133–140; M. Gual Camarena, *Vocabulario del comercio medieval*, Taragona, Diputación Provincial, 1968, pp. 284–285, 324–326; H. Wescher, "Cotton and cotton trade in the Middle Ages", *CIBA Review*, vol. 44 (1948), p. 2339 f.

37. Pfister, "Toiles" (1945–1946), pp. 69 f., 84 f.; Britton, *Early Islamic textiles* (1938), pp. 74–75; Lamm, *Cotton* (1937), p. 144 f.; A. Bühler, *Ikat, Batik, Plangi: Reservemusterungen auf Garn und Stoff aus Vorderasien, Zentralasien, Südosteuropa und Nordafrika*, Basel, Pharos-Schwabe, 1972, vol. 1, pp. 11–27; Kühnel and Bellinger, *Catalogue* (1952), pp. 87–90. Three *ikat*s from the Yaman, dating probably from the tenth century, are in the collection of the Royal Ontario Museum: 963.95.9, 970.364.19, and 970.364.20. See also the study on the Toronto *tiraz* collection by L. Golombek and V. Gervers in this volume.

38. Pelliot, *Notes* (1959–1963), p. 501–504; Amano, *Chūgoku* (1962), pp. 491–493.

39. Ch'u Hua, *Mu mien p'u* [A treatise on cotton] as cited by Dietrich, "Cotton" (1972), p. 110. On the basis of the study of many county and prefectural gazetteers, Dietrich (p. 111) has concluded that by late Ming and early Ch'ing times between 3/5 and 4/5 of all *hsien* manufactured some cotton cloth.

40. Pelliot, *Notes* (1959–1963), pp. 425–531 passim; Amano, *Chūgoku* (1962), pp. 482–498 passim.

41. Pelliot, *Notes* (1959–1963), p. 501–502; Amano, *Chūgoku* (1962), p. 491; Schlingloff, "Cotton manufacture" (1974), p. 85.

42. The spread of cotton cultivation through the Islamic world will be treated in greater detail in my forthcoming book, *New crops in the early Islamic world: A study in diffusion*. For a discussion of the agricultural changes which accompanied the introduction of cotton and other new crops into the Islamic world, see A.M. Watson, "The Arab agricultural revolution and its diffusion", *Journal of Economic History*, vol. 34 (1974), pp. 9–35.

43. Al-Iṣṭakhrī (fl. 10th c. A.D.), *Das Buch der Länder*, trans. A.D. Mordtmann, Hamburg, Akademie von Hamburg, 1845, p. 46; Ibn Ḥauqal (wr. A.D. 988), *Configuration de la terre*, trans. J.H. Kramers and G. Wiet, Paris, G.-P. Maisonneuve, 1964, pp. 207, 216, 238; A.A. al-Dūrī, *Ta'rīkh al-ʿIrāq al-iqtiṣādī* [Economic History of Iraq], Baghdad, Muʿārif, 1948, p. 32; Lamm, *Cotton* (1937), p. 218 f.; Ibn Waḥshīya, *Al-filāḥa al-nabaṭīya* [The "Nabatean" book of agriculture], Dār al-Kutub, Cairo, Agric. MS. 490, vol. 2, pp. 213–214.

44. Anon (wr. A.D. 982), *Hudūd al-ʿālam* [The earth's boundaries], trans. V. Minorsky, London, Luzac, 1970, pp. 102, 105, 132, 143; Ibn Ḥauqal, *Configuration* (1964), pp. 296, 330, 354, 358, 369; al-Qazwīnī (ca. A.D. 1203–1282), *Kitāb ʿajā'ib al-makhlūqāt wa gharā'ib al-maujūdāt* [Cosmography], ed. F. Wüstenfeld, Göttingen, Dietrich, 1847–1848, vol. 2, p. 163; Lamm, *Cotton* (1937), p. 197 f.

45. Ibn Ḥauqal, *Configuration* (1964), pp. 447, 470, 490; V.V. Bartol'd, *Historiia orosheniia Turkestana* [History of irrigation in Turkestan], St. Petersburg, 1914, p. 193. Marco Polo (A.D. 1254?–1324?), *The travels of Marco Polo*, trans. R.E. Latham, London, Harmondsworth, Penguin, 1958, p. 31; Lamm, *Cotton* (1937), p. 193 f.

46. Ibn Ḥauqal, *Configuration* (1964), pp. 293, 354, 369, 371, 422, 436, 437, 447, 463, 469, 470, 497; Abū al-Fidā (A.D. 1273–1331), *Géographie d'Aboulféda*, trans. M. Reinaud, Paris, 1840–1848, vol. 2, pt. 2, pp. 169, 197; Anon., *Hudūd* (1970), pp. 102, 103, 104, 110, 121, 125, 131, 132, 134, 138, 139; al-Yaʿqūbī (wr. A.D. 889), *Les pays*, trans. G. Wiet, Cairo, Institut Français d'Archéologie Orientale, 1937, p. 85; B. Spuler, *Iran in früh-islamischer Zeit*, Wiesbaden, Franz Steiner, 1952, p. 405; G. le Strange, *Baghdad during the Abbasid Caliphate*, Oxford, Oxford University Press, 1924, pp. 84, 181, 265; R.B. Serjeant, "Material for a history of Islamic textiles up to the Mongol conquest", *Ars Islamica*, vol. 9 (1942), p. 80 f., vol. 11–12 (1946), pp. 129–130, 131 f.; Lamm, *Cotton* (1937), p. 193 f.; Kühnel and Bellinger, *Catalogue* (1952), list all-cotton cloths made in Iraq or Persia from 866–869 onwards. Pelliot, *Notes* (1959–1963), p. 495, cites a Chinese source which mentions the manufacture of cotton goods in Merv by A.D. 817.

47. Al-Qazwīnī, *ʿAjā'ib* (1847–1848), vol. 2, p. 186; al-Hamdānī (A.D. 892?–945?), *Südarabien nach al-Hamdānī's "Beschreibung der arabischen Halbinsel"*, trans. L. Forrer, Leipzig, F.A. Brockhaus, 1942, p. 131; Ibn Ḥauqal, *Configuration* (1964), pp. 371–372; Ibn al-ʿAwwām (fl. 12th c. A.D.), *Libro de agricultura*, ed. and trans. J.A. Banquieri, Madrid, Impr. real, 1802, vol. 2, p. 104; Ibn Baṭṭūta (b. A.D. 1304), *Voyages d'Ibn Batoutah*, ed. and trans. C. Defrémery and B.R. Sanguinetti, Paris, 1853–1858, vol. 2, p. 199; M. Meyerhof, "Sur un traité d'agriculture composé par un sultan yéménite du XIVe siècle", *Bulletin de l'Institut d'Egypt*, vol. 26 (1943–1944), p. 62; Polo, *Travels* (1958), p. 271; Serjeant, "Islamic textiles", *Ars Islamica*, vol. 13–14 (1948), p. 86; Lamm, *Cotton* (1937), p. 234 f.

48. Al-Muqaddasī (ca. A.D. 942–ca. 991), *Aḥsan at-taqāsīm fi maʿrifat al-aqālīm* [The best categorization for knowing the provinces], trans. A. Miquel, Damascus, Institut Français de Damas, 1963, pp. 176–177, 218–219; Yāqūt (A.D. 1179–1229), *Jacut's Geographisches Wörterbuch*, ed. F. Wüstenfeld, Leipzig, F.A. Brockhaus, 1866–1870, vol. 2, pp. 21, 308; al-Qazwīnī, *ʿAjā'ib* (1847–1848), vol. 1, pp. 122, 179; Ibn al-ʿAwwām, *Libro* (1802), vol. 2, 195; Ibn ʿAsākir (A.D. 1105–1176), *La description de Damas d'Ibn ʿAsākir*, trans. N. Elisséeff, Damascus, Institut Français de Damas, 1959, p. 117; M. Benvenisti, *The Crusaders in the Holy*

Land, Jerusalem, Israel Universities Press, 1970, p. 386; Lamm, *Cotton* (1937), pp. 223–234.

49. W. Heyd, *Histoire du commerce du Levant au Moyen-Age,* Leipzig, Harrassowitz, 1885–1886, vol. 2, pp. 661 f., 684 f.; A. Schaube, *Handelsgeschichte der romanischen Völker des Mittelmeergebiets bis zum Ende der Kreuzzüge,* Munich/Berlin, R. Oldenbourg, 1906, pp. 161, 162, 197, 214; F. Balducci Pegolotti (fl. A.D. 1310–1347), *La pratica della mercatura,* ed. A. Evans, Cambridge, Mass., Medieval Academy, 1936, passim; M.F. Mazzaoui, "The cotton industry of northern Italy in the late Middle Ages", *Journal of Economic History,* vol. 32 (1972), p. 266.

50. *Papyrus Erzherzog Rainer. Führer durch die Ausstellung,* ed. J. Karabaček, Vienna, 1894, pp. 9, 193, 227; *Arabic papyri in the Egyptian Library,* ed. A. Grohmann, Cairo, Dār al-Kutub, 1934–1962, vol. 5, pp. 86–95; R. Pfister, "L'introduction du coton en Egypte musulmane", *Revue des Arts Asiatiques,* vol. 11 (1937), p. 170; S.D. Goitein, *A Mediterranean society,* Berkeley, University of California Press, 1967– , vol. 1, p. 105; Lamm, *Cotton* (1937) ; pp. 218, 245; Ibn Ḥauqal, *Configuration* (1964), vol. 1, p. 135.

51. "Texte zur Wirtschaftsgeschichte Ägyptens in arabischer Zeit", ed. A. Grohmann, *Archiv Orientální,* vol. 7 (1935), p. 463.

52. Ibn Ḥauqal, *Configuration* (1964), vol. 1, p. 135.

53. Cited in Lamm, *Cotton* (1937), p. 198.

54. Ibn Mammātī (d. A.D. 1209), *Kitāb qawānīn al-dawāwīn,* ed. A.S. ᶜAṭīya, Cairo, Agricultural Society, 1943, pp. 240, 241, 244, 248, 250, 252, 265–266; al-Maqrīzī (A.D. 1364–1442), *Kitāb al-Khiṭaṭ,* al-Shīya (Lebanon), 1959, vol. 1, pp. 182, 337, vol. 2, pp. 13, 15, 18, 19; C. Cahen, "Le régime des impôts dans le Fayyūm ayyūbide", *Arabica,* vol. 3, pp. 14–15; Lamm, *Cotton* (1937), p. 240 f.; B. Müller-Wodarg, "Die Landwirtschaft Ägyptens in der frühen ᶜAbbāsidenzeit", *Der Islam,* vol. 32 (1956), pp. 38–39.

55. Schaube, *Handelsgeschichte* (1906), p. 164; al-Maqrīzī, *Khiṭaṭ* (1959), vol. 1, p. 136; C. Dufourcq, *L'Espagne catalane et le Maghrib aux XIIIe et XIVe siècles,* Paris, Presses Universitaires Françaises, 1966, p. 543; S.Y. Labib, *Handelsgeschichte Ägyptens im Spätmittelalter (1171–1517),* Wiesbaden, F. Steiner, 1965, pp. 101, 311–312.

56. Ibn Ḥauqal, *Configuration* (1964), pp. 70, 76, 82; al-Idrīsī (fl. 12th c. A.D.), *Description de l'Afrique et de l'Espagne,* ed. and trans. R. Dozy and M.J. de Goeje, Leyden, Brill, 1866, pp. 109, 122, 130, 156; al-Bakrī (d. A.D. 1094), *Description de l'Afrique septentrionale,* ed. and trans. Macguckin de Slane, Algiers, A. Jourdan, 1913, p. 124; al-ᶜUmarī (A.D. 1301–1349), *Masālik al absār fi mamālik al-amṣār,* trans. L.J.M. Gaudefroy Demombynes, Paris, Geuthner, 1928, p. 111; *Biblioteca arabo-sicula,* ed. M. Amari, Leipzig, F.A. Brockhaus, 1857, vol. 1, pp. 134, 137, 148; S.D. Goitein, "La Tunisie du XIe siècle à la lumière des documents de la *Geniza* du Caire", in *Etudes d'orientalisme dédiées à la mémoire de Lévi-Provençal,* Paris, G.-P. Maisonneuve, 1962, vol. 2, p. 571; C. Vanacker, "Géographie économique de l'Afrique du Nord selon les auteurs arabes, du XIe siècle au milieu du XIIe siècle", *Annales; économies, sociétés, civilisations,* vol. 28 (1973), p. 677, map 13; Dufourcq, *L'Espagne* (1966), pp. 264, 546; L. de Mas Latrie, ed.; *Traités de paix et de commerce et documents divers concernant les relations des chrétiens avec les arabes au Moyen Age,* Paris, H. Plon, 1866, vol. 1, p. 221.

57. Ibn Ḥauqal, *Configuration* (1964), vol. 1, p. 118, speaks of a part of the market in Palermo set aside for cotton merchants and carders, but it is not clear that in his time cotton was grown locally; Abū al-Khair (fl. 11th c. A.D.) *Kitāb al-Filāḥ'a ou le Livre de la Culture,* trans. A. Charbonneau, Algiers, 1946, pp. 26–27; Yāqūt, *Wörterbuch,* vol. 2 (1866–1870), p. 84; Balducci Pegolotti, *Pratica* (1936), pp. 111, 367; *Biblioteca,* ed. M. Amari, vol. 1, pp. 43, 110, 137, 159; M. Amari, *Storia dei Musulmani di Sicilia,* Florence, 1854–1872, vol. 2, p. 444, vol. 3, p. 807; Schaube, *Handelsgeschichte* (1906), p. 284.

58. Ibn Ḥauqal, *Configuration* (1964), pp. 76, 77; al-Idrīsī, *Description* (1886), pp. 70, 81, 84, 85; al-Bakrī, *Description* (1913), pp. 143, 295; al-ᶜUmarī, *Masālik* (1928), p. 80; al-Wazzān [= Leo Africanus, fl. early 16th c.], *Description de l'Afrique,* ed. and trans. A. Epaulard, Paris, Adrien-Maisonneuve, 1956, pp. 170, 252; Vanacker, "Géographie" (1973), p. 667, map 13.

59. Probably the earliest mention of cotton cultivation in Spain is found in a text of Abū Bakr Aḥmad b. Ishaq b. Ibrahīm al-Hamadhānī, written around A.D. 903. See J. Alemany Bolufer, "La geografia de la península Ibérica en los escritores árabes", *Revista del Centro de Estudios Históricos de Granada y su Reino,* vol. 9 (1919), pp. 119-127. I am indebted to Dr. Miquel Barceló for drawing my attention to this source. Other early references are found in al-Rāzī (A.D. 888?–955), "La 'Description de l'Espagne' d'Ahmad al Rāzī", trans. E. Lévi-Provencal, Al-Ándalus, vol. 17 (1953), p. 93; and Ibn al-Faqīh (wr. ca. A.D. 903), *Description du Maghreb et de l'Europe au IIIe-IXe siècle,* ed. and trans. M. Hadj-Sadok, Algiers, 1949, p. 53; and *Le Calendrier de Cordoue* (wr. A.D. 961), ed. and trans. C. Pellat, Leyden, 1961, p. 62. For the early agronomists, see Abū al-Khair, *Filāh'a* (1946), p. 267; Ibn al-ᶜAwwām, *Agricultura* (1802), p. 103 f; Ibn Baṣṣāl (d. A.D. 1105), *Kitāb al-filaḥa* [Book of agriculture], ed. and trans. J.M. Millás Vallicrosa and M. Aziman, Tetuan, 1955, pp. 151–153.

60. Al-ᶜUdhrī (A.D. 1002/3–1085/6), *Nuṣūṣ ᶜan al-Andalus* [Texts on Moorish Spain], ed. ᶜAbd al-ᶜAzīz al-Ahwānī, Madrid, Instituto de Estudios Islamicos, 1965, p. 96; Yāqūt, *Wörterbuch* (1866–1870), vol. 1, pp. 275, 474; J.M. Millás Vallicrosa, *Nuevos estudios sobre historia de la cienca española,* Barcelona, CSIC, 1960, pp. 173–182; Lautensach, *Maurische Züge im geographischen Bild der Iberischen Halbinsel,* Bonn, F. Dümmler, 1960, pp. 61–62; C.E. Dubler, *Uber das Wirtschaftsleben auf der Iberischen Halbinsel vom XI. zum XIII. Jahrhundert,* Geneva, Droz, 1943, pp. 49, 60–61, 95; al-Himyarī (fl. 15th c. A.D.?), *La péninsule ibérique*

au Moyen-âge, ed. and trans. E. Lévi-Provençal, Leyden, Brill, 1938, p. 233, mentions cotton growing at Guadix; see also p. 27. The reference for Valencia is in Francisco Ximénez (1340?–1409?), *Regiment de la cosa publica,* ed. D. de Molins de Rei, Barcelona, 1927, p. 26. That for Majorca is in al-Zuhrī, ᶜAbd Allāh Muḥammad b. Abī Bakr (fl. 12th c. A.D.), *Kitāb al-jughrāfiya,* ed. M. Hadj-Sadok, Damascus, 1968, p. 178. I am indebted to Dr. Barceló for drawing my attention to this last reference.

61. Al-Bakrī, *Description* (1913), pp. 325–326; al-Idrīsī, *Description* (1886), p. 3; al-ᶜUmarī, *Masālik* (1928), p. 66; Ibn Baṭṭūṭa, *Voyages* (1853–1858), vol. 4, pp. 422, 437; V. Monteil, "Le Coton chez les noirs", *Bulletin du Comité d'Etudes Historiques et Scientifiques de l'A.O.F.,* vol. 9 (1926), pp. 585-684; R. Mauny, "Notes historiques autour des principales plantes cultivées d'Afrique Occidentale", *Bulletin de l'Institut Français d'Afrique Noire,* vol. 15 (1953), p. 698 f.; R. Mauny, *Tableau géographique de l'ouest africain au Moyen Age,* Dakar, IFAN, 1961, pp. 231–232, 245. A. Ca da Mosto (d. A.D. 1483), *The voyages of Cadamosto,* trans. G.R. Crone, Hakluyt Society, Works, 2d series, vol. 80 (1937), pp. 31-32. For cotton in Christian Abyssinia, see al-Qazwīnī, *ᶜAjā'ib* (1847–1848), vol. 2, p. 12; R. Pankhurst, *An introduction to the economic history of Ethiopia,* London, Lalibela House, 1961, p. 211 f. It is interesting to note that even as late as the fifteenth and sixteenth centuries, many of the Portuguese explorers describe the clothing of the Muslim communities in West Africa, contrasting this to the nakedness of the pagans. See V. Fernandes (wr. A.D. 1506–1507), *Descripçam de Cepta por sua costa de Mauritania e Ethiopia,* ed. and trans. T. Monod et al., Bissau, Centro do Estudos da Guiné Portuguesa, 1951, p. 13; D. Pacheco Pereira (wr. ca. A.D. 1506–1508), *Esmeraldo de situ orbis,* ed. R. Mauny, Bissau, 1956, pp. 69, 73, 125. The accounts of cotton in mediaeval West Africa do not make clear the kind of plant which was grown. However, one Portuguese voyager in the fifteenth century speaks of tree cotton growing abundantly in one place on the West African coast and on the island of Gomera in the Canaries. See Gomes Eanes de Zurara (ca. A.D. 1405–ca. 1474), *Chronique de Guinée,* Mémoires de l'Institut Français d'Afrique Noire, vol. 60, Dakar, 1960, pp. 168, 246.

Notes on Contributors

Bolland, Rita
Curator of Textiles, Koninklijk Instituut voor de Tropen (Royal Tropical Institute), Amsterdam.
Interests: simple looms, weaving techniques.

Brett, Katharine B.
Curator Emeritus, Textile Department, Royal Ontario Museum, Toronto.
Interests: Indian painted and dyed cottons made for the European market (seventeenth and eighteenth centuries), European printed cottons (eighteenth and nineteenth centuries), English embroidery, fashionable costume.

Burnham, Dorothy K.
Research Associate; former Curator, Textile Department, Royal Ontario Museum, Toronto.
Interests: early handweaving in Canada, North American Indian costume, straight-cut garments, textile techniques and terminology.

Crowfoot, Elisabeth Grace
Consultant on archaeological textiles to the Ancient Monuments Laboratory, Department of the Environment, London; to the Archaeological Department, Ashmolean Museum, Oxford; and to the Department of Mediaeval and Later Antiquities in The British Museum, London.
Interests: archaeological textiles from England (Anglo-Saxon and mediaeval) and Nubia (Meroitic to mediaeval).

Geijer, Agnes
Former Curator of Textiles, Riksantikvarieämbetet och Historiska Museet (Museum of Swedish National Antiquities), Stockholm; Vice President of the Centre International des Etudes des Textiles Anciens (Lyon).
Interests: mediaeval textiles, archaeological and oriental textiles in Sweden.

Gervers, Michael
Assistant Professor, Department of History, Erindale College, University of Toronto; Research Associate, Pontifical Institute of Mediaeval Studies, Toronto.
Interests: mediaeval social and economic history, military orders, mediaeval rock-cut churches.

Gervers, Veronika
Associate Curator, Textile Department, Royal Ontario Museum, Toronto; Associate Professor, Department of Fine Art, Scarborough College, University of Toronto.
Interests: archaeological textiles of the Middle Ages from Egypt and the Near East, East European and West Asian regional costume, felt making, Turkish ceramics, mediaeval central churches.

Golombek, Lisa
Associate Curator, West Asian Department, Royal Ontario Museum, Toronto; Associate Professor, Islamic Studies Department, University of Toronto.
Interests: Arabic epigraphy, Timurid architecture, the Islamic city.

Grönwoldt, Ruth
Curator of Textiles, Württembergisches Landesmuseum, Stuttgart.

Interests: European mediaeval embroidery, woven textiles of the Renaissance.

Gudjónsson, Elsa E.
Curator of Textiles, National Museum of Iceland, Reykjavik.
Interests: European mediaeval and regional embroidery.

Hayes, John W.
Associate Curator, Greek and Roman Department, Royal Ontario Museum, Toronto.
Interests: Greek, Roman, and Byzantine pottery; Roman glass.

Hoffmann, Marta
Curator, Department of Crafts and Rural Culture, Norwegian Folk Museum, Bygdöy, Oslo; Member of the Norwegian Academy of Sciences and Letters.
Interests: textile tools, techniques, and traditional working methods.

King, Donald
Keeper, Department of Textiles, Victoria and Albert Museum, London.
Interests: European and oriental textiles, European tapestry.

Leipen, Neda
Curator, Greek and Roman Department, Royal Ontario Museum, Toronto; Associate Professor, Department of Fine Art, University of Toronto.
Interests: Greek and Roman sculpture, ancient minor arts.

Lemberg, Mechthild
Keeper of Textiles, Abegg-Stiftung, Riggisberg, Bern.
Interest: textile conservation.

Levey, Santina M.
Research Assistant, Department of Textiles, Victoria and Albert Museum, London.
Interests: lace, mediaeval and later embroidery in western Europe.

Levine, Louis D.
Associate Curator, West Asian Department, Royal Ontario Museum, Toronto; Associate Professor, Department of Near Eastern Studies, University of To-

ronto; Secretary of the American Institute of Iranian Studies, Tehran.
Interest: Iron Age Iran.

Montgomery, Florence M.
Assistant Curator in charge of textiles, Henry Francis du Pont Winterthur Museum, Winterthur, Delaware.
Interests: Seventeenth- to nineteenth-century furnishing fabrics and textile terminology in America, English and American printed textiles, American needlework.

Müller-Christensen, Sigrid
Curator Emeritus, Textile Department, Bavarian National Museum, Munich.
Interests: European and Near Eastern mediaeval textiles.

Needler, Winifred
Curator Emeritus, Egyptian Department, Royal Ontario Museum, Toronto; former Associate Professor, Department of Near Eastern Studies, University of Toronto.
Interest: Egyptology (Pre-Dynastic to Old Kingdom periods).

Riboud, Krishna
Chargée de Mission, Musée Guimet, Paris.
Interest: early Chinese silks.

Rothstein, Natalie
Deputy Keeper, Department of Textiles, Victoria and Albert Museum, London.
Interests: English silk industry, European silks and woven textiles from the seventeenth to the nineteenth century.

Shih, Hsio-Yen
Director, National Gallery of Canada, Ottawa; former Curator, Far Eastern Department, Royal Ontario Museum, Toronto.
Interests: Chinese Neolithic archaeology, Chinese painting, Chinese aesthetic theory.

Standen, Edith
Associate Curator in charge of the Textile Study Room, Metropolitan Museum of Art, New York.
Interest: European post-mediaeval tapestry.

Vollmer, John E.
Assistant Curator in charge, Textile Department, Royal Ontario Museum, Toronto.
Interests: Chinese court costume from the seventeenth to the nineteenth century, regional costume from Southeast Asia, oriental export fabrics from the sixteenth to the seventeenth century, weaving technology in Bronze Age China.

Watson, Andrew M.
Professor, Department of Political Economy, University of Toronto.
Interest: economic history of the mediaeval Islamic world.